BOMBING, STATES AND PEOPLES IN WESTERN EUROPE 1940–1945

Bombing, States and Peoples in Western Europe 1940–1945

Edited by Claudia Baldoli, Andrew Knapp and Richard Overy

continuum

Published by the Continuum International Publishing Group

The Tower Building
11 York Road
London
SE1 7NX

80 Maiden Lane
Suite 704
New York
NY 10038

www.continuumbooks.com

First published 2011

British Library Cataloguing-in-Publication Data
A catalogue record for this book is available from the British Library.

ISBN: HB: 978–1–4411–9254–7
ISBN: PB: 978–1–4411–8568–6

Typeset by Fakenham Prepress Solutions, Fakenham, Norfolk NR21 8NN
Printed and bound in India

Contents

Preface and Acknowledgements

The conference that gave rise to the present volume was part of a three-year AHRC-funded project of the same title, which ran from 2007–2010. The editors gratefully acknowledge the financial support of the AHRC which made the project possible. They would also like to acknowledge the assistance granted by the Universities of Exeter, Reading and Newcastle in running the project and the help of the conference staff at Exeter, where the conference was hosted in September 2009. We would particularly like to thank Claire Keyte, the project administrator, who has provided invaluable assistance over the whole three years and was the principal administrator of the conference. We would also like to acknowledge the valuable contribution to the success of the project of the Advisory Board members – Gabriella Gribaudi, MacGregor Knox, Phil Reed, Nick Stargardt – and of Neil Gregor, who also participated in the project conference. Finally, thanks are also due to the editor at Continuum, Ben Hayes, who has throughout been an enthusiastic supporter of the book.

Claudia Baldoli
Andrew Knapp
Richard Overy

September 2010

List of Illustrations

Introduction

Richard Overy

The story of bombing in Western Europe has never been told as a single, integrated history. It has been divided up into accounts of the 'Blitz' on Britain, or the Combined Bomber Offensive against Germany. By contrast, the bombing of France, Italy and the Low Countries has been largely ignored in the popular narrative of the Second World War. Yet over the six years of war most of urban Europe from the French Atlantic ports to the major cites of central Germany, from the Dutch and Belgian cities to the ports and towns of Sicily, were subject to bomb attack, much of it heavy and prolonged. Throughout the whole region perhaps as many as 700,000 were killed; 410,000 of them were Germans and around 60,000 each from Britain, Italy and France. The overwhelming majority of victims were civilians.[1] The purpose of this collection of essays is to explore the immediate effects and the short-term consequences of that wartime disaster, both for the urban communities that suffered it and for the surrounding society and political order that had to cope with evacuation, higher levels of crime or non-compliance and changing attitudes towards authority. As the essays in this volume will make clear, bombing had ripple effects far beyond the areas immediately targeted by the bombers.

The perspective on bombing 'from below' has until recently not generated the academic interest it deserves. There exists a rich mine of local studies in all four of the bombed states considered here, usually based on the experience of a single city, and often of high scholarly standard.[2] Many of these appear in the bibliography and footnotes of the essays. There is a substantial body of literature on the experience of the Blitz in Britain, much of it popular or anecdotal, designed to sustain the myths of social solidarity and the 'we can take it' culture, though some of it is also scholarly and critical.[3] But as yet there is still no serious academic history of the German bombing of Britain in 1940–41. Perhaps more surprisingly, there is still no single study on the impact of bombing in Germany throughout the war period, despite the fact that this was a major element of the social experience of war for almost all of German society. Much of the academic literature on bombing in the Second World War has focused instead on three distinct approaches: bombing as a strategic component, where the emphasis is on estimating the damage to the enemy economy and capacity for war; bombing as a moral issue, in which the emphasis is on seeing bombing in the context of other forms of extreme violence in wartime; and finally, bombing as a geographical fact, inviting comparison with natural disasters and dictating patterns of urban development and renewal.

The first of these approaches was begun even before the end of the war with the establishment of the United States Strategic Bombing Survey and the British Bombing Survey Unit.[4] Their brief was to assess just how effective bombing had been in relation to the set of planning objectives under which the bombing forces had been operating. The conclusion of the principal reports was ambiguous, since it could not be denied that German war production had increased by at least a factor of three over the period of intense bombardment. This ambiguity has fuelled ever since a historical debate about the strategic achievement of the bomber forces. It has proved possible to argue from the same data that bombing did not achieve its strategic objective or that bombing decisively inhibited German capacity to wage war. Similar analysis was attempted of the bombing of Japan but that, too, was not free of controversy because despite the extensive destruction of Japan's cities, many Japanese officials and businessmen attributed the crisis of production to the sea blockade and war-weariness, as well as the bombing.[5] No attempt was made to estimate the aggregate strategic economic and military consequences of bombing Italy and it has proved difficult since to do more than speculate about the statistical results.[6] The bombing of other areas of Western Europe was part of the general plan to reduce Germany's access to strategic materials or production, and has also not been subjected to any systematic statistical analysis.

The second approach to bombing is related to the argument that its strategic effectiveness was ambiguous at best, negligible at worst. Recent studies of the morality or otherwise of bombing in the Second World War have emphasised that its relative strategic failure means that any arguments for strategic utility or necessity as a moral justification also fail. The implication, as the philosopher Anthony Grayling has argued, is that bombing of cities where neither the strategic advantages nor the military necessity are evident constitutes a war crime not only in contemporary terms (it would now violate the Geneva Protocols of 1977) but at the time these operations were conducted during the war.[7] The German historian Jörg Friedrich has similarly concluded from his controversial study of the bombing of German cities that the campaign was strategically flawed and morally indefensible. His indictment has suggested that British area bombing in particular was tantamount to genocide, and much of the language he uses suggests a direct comparison between bombing holocaust and racial holocaust. Friedrich's book *Der Brand* prompted a searching debate in Germany when it was published in 2002 about how the bombing should now be evaluated in moral terms.[8] A similar approach had been taken in 1995 when Erik Markusen and David Kopf published a comparison of genocide and bombing, but the thesis then was subjected to harsh criticism.[9] The reception of Friedrich's and Grayling has been more positive, not least because in the last twenty years there has been a growing discourse on the nature of excessive violence against civilians in twentieth-century warfare. Allied bombing has come to be seen very much as part of that narrative of excessive violence, with the explicit assumption that bombing cities and killing civilians *en masse* was a violation of international law and of the practice of *jus in bello* (justice in the conduct of war). This could be the case even where the principle of *jus ad bellum* (just war) could still be demonstrated by the states doing the bombing.

Michael Bess has recently argued that city-bombing constituted 'the single greatest moral failure of the Anglo-American war effort'.[10] It is, of course, important to recall that German bombing of Britain also displayed some of the same legal lapses once Hitler decided to shift in the autumn of 1940 to the bombing of British urban targets in the hope of producing a moral collapse.

The wider discussion by international lawyers, human rights campaigners, political scientists and philosophers of the place of bombing in the history of twentieth-century atrocity does not always have a very clear historical base. But the issues this discussion has raised – what can be regarded as legitimate targets, what degree of proportionality can be accepted to be within the rules of engagement, what protection can be given to the civilian in war – were issues also addressed at the time as part of a current debate on how to define the legitimate limits of wartime violence. These origins are explored here by Jay Winter in the concluding chapter on the evolution of the human rights regime in the war and immediate post-war years, which took place at a time when disregard for civilian casualties had become routine for both sides. Most writers today who relate International Humanitarian Law back to the violence of the war period take the view that bombing conducted against urban targets, where the degree of death and destruction imposed on civilians was disproportionate and when attacks were undertaken with the clear objective of undermining civilian morale, violated existing rules of warfare laid down in the pre-1914 Hague Conventions. But precise instruments for outlawing the use of force in this way were only finally codified in the 1949 Geneva Convention and strengthened in the 1977 Additional Protocols.[11] The central issue of defining the circumstances under which force, even excessive force, is justified remains a key problem for the twenty-first century as well.[12]

The third approach to bombing has been to locate its effects in wider discussion of the impact of disaster (usually natural disaster) and the ways in which societies adapt to the problems of recovery and reconstruction. Bombing did constitute an exceptional disaster, distinguished from earthquake or volcanic eruption or tidal wave by the fact that it continued in many cases for years as an ever-present threat, and was capable of exceptional levels of physical destruction. In Germany, more than 50 per cent of the urban area of major cities was destroyed, not simply damaged. In Japan the urban area of 115 of the 250 cities subjected to attack was more or less obliterated.[13] The pattern of destruction reflected to some extent the understanding by those doing the bombing of what a city was in terms of social structure, economic geography and destructibility.[14] The area bombing of Germany and Japan was not, in that sense, random but fitted with pre-conceptions about city damage. In the case of the bombing of Italy, for example, detailed studies were made of the architectural patterns of all Italian cities to determine whether or to what extent they would be vulnerable to incendiary attack.[15] In this case it was recommended that Italian cities were difficult to burn down; the pattern of high-rise building round enclosed courtyards led to the conclusion that it was better to use high-explosive bombs because in the confined space of the courtyard the blast effect would be magnified and the level of destruction much higher. For economic geographers, however, the experience of bombing itself has not been the primary concern. Bombing has been used as a particular example of temporary disaster in order to measure how communities react to shock in the longer term. It is striking that none of the cities apparently obliterated during the war failed to be rebuilt, or even to expand, within a short period of time. A recent study of the impact of bombing on city growth in West and East Germany after 1945 concluded that in West Germany at least the evidence suggests that 'large, temporary shocks will have at most a temporary impact.'[16] The rebuilding of Japan's cities suggests a similar conclusion, though it is evidently important to recall that the rebuilt city is not the same as the city that was destroyed. The social patterns, physical environment and economic structure will demonstrate continuities but also sharp divergences from the ruined predecessor.

None of these three major perspectives on bombing has engaged seriously with the communities that actually experienced the bombing. There exists a historical gap in much of the writing on bombing as a strategic factor, moral outrage or geographical exception. This is also evident in other narratives of the victims of mass violence, where less attention is often paid to the social history of those victimized than to understanding the context and motivation of the perpetrators. Like all victim communities, the urban populations subject to bombing were not passive witnesses to their own victimhood, but living communities. They responded to the shock of being bombed in a wide variety of ways, some of them generic, some of them the product of particular or local circumstances, but that response has its own narrative, independent of the operations that caused the crisis in the first place. The restoration of historical meaning to those who were bombed is an urgent task because many of the assumptions that underlay the large bombing offensives in the Second World War, or later in Vietnam or Iraq, have not been laid to rest. Indeed the idea of a 'political dividend' as a result of bombing is still widely held to be one of the strategic advantages of this form of warfare.

The assumption that bombing must be capable of exerting direct psychological and material pressure on populations to abandon a conflict can only be validated or challenged by a proper historical understanding of how bombing actually affected the social life, political outlook and individual perceptions of those being bombed. The strategic concept of 'shock and awe', originated at the American National Defense University in 1996, was designed precisely to paralyse the 'will to carry on' in an enemy population and armed forces, a view that would not have been out of context in the discussions of air doctrine in the 1920s.[17] Yet these arguments remain speculations, reflecting as they did in the Second World War an uncritical acceptance that bombing ought to have certain effects, without ever testing its credibility. It is a paradox of British war-making in 1941 that morale was finally chosen as a worthwhile target in Germany only after nine months in which the Blitz had demonstrated that morale in Britain was in fact capable of coping with unprecedented levels of civilian casualty without collapsing. British policy was justified largely in terms of crude racial stereotyping of the Germans, who were expected to crumble when someone hit them back. Very few of the perceptions held by those doing the bombing, from the Second World War to Iraq, have been based on any hard evidence of what bombing can do and one of the principal purposes of this volume is to try to show more exactly what responses heavy bombing actually provoked.

The history of the social, cultural and political reactions to being bombed form the core of the essays presented here. The fact that they deal with the bombing experience in four different countries raises important considerations about the nature and limits of comparative history. The geographical area has an obvious unity; bombers could fly around 1,000 to 1,500 miles fully loaded during the war, which defined the frontiers of what could or could not be bombed. The pattern of urban growth in the four countries was not identical but there were many shared characteristics. The research analysis produced for the RAF on the common factors in the geography of German cities could have been applied to many non-German cities too: a tightly congested central residential and commercial centre; a less congested outer ring of residential housing; an industrial belt often forming an outer ring of industrial parks and suburbs; and a zone far from the city centre where the wealthy and professional classes lived.[18] The bombing of Hamburg in July 1943 took account of this pattern, destroying the mainly working-class areas in the city centre and leaving the merchant villas on the outskirts undamaged. The level of industrial development differed between the four states, but the pattern of rural hinterland and industrial city was the same: in each country the response to bombing was to move as much of the vulnerable population as possible to small towns and villages, leaving a smaller productive rump which had to rely on purpose-built shelter or improvised refuge. Expectations about levels of food supply and welfare were also common throughout the area, forcing governments and local authorities to find ways of meeting the sudden demand for emergency provisions, clothing or furnishings for the bombed-out population.

What was different comes out clearly in many of the essays. The contrasts are partly to do with different social conditions, levels of policing and administrative capability. Where this was generally similar, for example the experience of Britain and Germany, it is possible to draw some effective comparisons. The chapters by Dietmar Süss and by Marc Wiggam show some evident convergence of experience despite the marked differences in political system. High levels of social discipline could be enforced in both cases as a result of the nature of the state apparatus and inherited respect for authority. This was more difficult in the case of Italy, where the state was less centralised and respect for authority undermined by the circumstances of bombing, but also in France where the Vichy authorities were not universally regarded as legitimate, and much initiative devolved to the regions. Claudia Baldoli in her study of religion in Italy shows the extent to which the failing legitimacy of the Mussolinian state was replaced by growing respect for the Catholic Church and reliance on religious convention. The most obvious difference between the four states lies in their different experience of the war itself. Germany and Britain remained at war with each other over the whole period from 1939 to 1945, and each regarded the other as a principal enemy. France was defeated in 1940, divided into occupied and unoccupied zones, both ruled by an authoritarian nationalist regime based at Vichy. In November 1942 the whole country was occupied by Germany. The Allies ostensibly bombed France in order to 'liberate' Frenchmen from foreign rule.[19] The Italian case was even more complicated, since Italy entered the war at Germany's side in June 1940, surrendered to the Allies in September 1943, became an Allied co-belligerent, but was occupied thereafter by a hostile German army which forced the central and northern areas of the country to work for the German war effort. Bombing Italy up to the autumn of 1943 was to bomb an enemy; bombing Italy thereafter, when most of the bombing occurred, was to liberate Italians from the German grip.[20] In these terms bombing France and Italy after 1943 was not to force surrender but to accelerate the defeat of Germany.

The studies of the effects of bombing presented here reflect many of these contrasts and ambiguities but also highlight some of the similarities in the way in which states, local government or the people themselves reacted to, coped with or were affected by the immediate experience of bombing. The volume has been divided into four sections which focus in turn on one particular element of the story, though they are not intended to be mutually exclusive. The first section deals with the relationship between states and peoples as it was affected by the experience of bombing. This was not a unitary experience since the relationship depended on the nature of the regime, and the structures and institutions at national, regional and municipal level which were responsible for coping with bombing. The structures of government, at least in terms of the formal links between the central state apparatus, the regions (counties, provinces, departments etc.) and the municipalities, had much in common in the four countries. However, the nature of the regimes differed a great deal, and this in turn affected the way in which the state prepared for bombing and coped with its consequences. It also affected the way in which the populations reacted to authority. As Wiggam shows in his study of the blackout in Germany and Britain, the room for dissent, even if it existed, was much narrower in Germany than it was in Britain. In Italy, by contrast, the capacity of the state to enforce air-defence measures even on its own institutions was called into question. Mussolini himself complained to the Air Minister in November 1940 that Littorio air base was a blaze of light, while the same month the Ministry of War sent out warning letters to all ministerial offices in Rome about the fact that many of their windows remained illuminated at night.[21]

The problems raised by the relationship between state and people was at its most acute when it came to the question of offering adequate protection. It is seldom sufficiently appreciated what a problem this posed for modern, heavily urbanized societies when it became evident that bombing of civilian centres might well be a major feature of any future war. No European state had been required in the modern age to devise, approve and pay for effective means of protection from acts of war for their entire urban civilian population. When proposals were put forward in the late 1930s for a series of deep shelters under London capable of housing all the threatened population, the cost and scale of the project appeared simply fantastic.[22] None of the four states featured here provided fully adequate protection by the time bombing started in 1940, either through shelter for the bombed population or through evacuation. The provision of gas masks was also incomplete, except in Britain where masks were available for all the urban population by 1940. Even that was no guarantee of quality. In York a 'gas chamber' was set up and the local community invited to come and test their masks under simulated conditions. Few did so, but of those tested 13 per cent were found to be defective.[23]

The nature of state provision for protection from bombing is the subject matter of the first four chapters. Süss discusses the different strategies pursued in Germany and Britain for placing the population underground in shelters, cellars and tunnels. In both cases shelter communities represented what he calls 'the mobilization of everyday urban life'. Shelters were sites of reassurance, but simultaneously sites of vulnerability. They were also contested sites, where arguments existed over who was or was not entitled to enter, and where the authorities had to confront acute social problems and voices of dissent. Exclusion from shelter in the German case had strong links with the ideology of 'People's Community' (*Volksgemeinschaft*) – Jews and foreign workers, for example, were left to fend for themselves. It is interesting to note that in Britain too there were forms of exclusion. In London 'vagrants' were barred from public shelters, but unlike the response in Germany, where vagrants had largely disappeared to the camps as 'asocials', Christian pacifists set up a communal shelter just for vagrants in the heart of London.[24] This contrast in cultures, one excessively punitive, one limited by the rule of law, is made clear in Wiggam's analysis of the operation of the blackout in Britain and Germany. Like shelter policy, the blackout reflected a special form of mass mobilization, helping in the German case to embed the idea of 'People's Community' and in Britain's case to overcome liberal hostility to regimentation and popular conscription. What Wiggam calls 'the militarization of society' was important in both contexts, and the blackout with its absolute forms of obedience and compliance, and the supervision of local Air Raid Precautions (ARP) or 'block' wardens, acted as a daily reminder of national duty and social obligation. Indeed the blackout appears to have been one way in which the experience of being bombed transcended the differences between dictatorship and democracy.

The third way beyond blackout and shelter to protect the civil population was evacuation. This, too, was a large and complex phenomenon. It required a high level of organization and voluntary participation by those registering and embarking the evacuees and those at the receiving end who had to find adequate housing and cope with problems of welfare, food supply and education for the displaced population. Elena Cortesi, in her study of Italian evacuation, highlights the many problems associated with a policy that promised large-scale disruption, but which the state wanted to be able to control on its own behalf. The failure to plan evacuation before it became, in 1942, an urgent necessity resulted in what Cortesi describes as a 'retroactive mobilization'. For many Italians the problem was solved quite simply by absenting themselves from the threatened cities, with or without authorization. When this flow swamped the surrounding countryside, the Italian authorities tried to persuade Italians to return to the bombed cities to heighten their sense of self-sacrifice for the community, a message that seems to have had little effect. This was almost certainly because of the regime's manifest failure in a great many other areas. Cortesi shows that the evacuation of children, as part of a programme sponsored by the youth organization of the Fascist Party, was developed very late, in the winter of 1942/3, by which time bombing had already been widely experienced. The official figures show 2.3 million evacuees by May 1944, but the actual number must have been considerably in excess of this. Unauthorized evacuation was widespread in both Britain and Germany, even though the formal programme of evacuation was better organized and on a large scale.[25]

What all four states also had to cope with was providing satisfactory emergency aid, housing and longer-term welfare for the bombed-out population. This was a vexed question, and in cities where bombing was long-term and heavy (in London during the Blitz, or the main German cities of the Ruhr-Rhineland, Hamburg and Berlin) providing effective welfare and replacement accommodation was difficult. In Britain the assistance was often grudgingly given and many houses remained unrepaired or uninhabitable, while families were expected to double up in dwellings already cramped for the existing residents. Bombed-out victims depended a great deal on voluntary assistance. This tension between state assistance and private welfare is the subject of Lindsey Dodd's study of aid for the bombed-out (*sinistrés*) in France. Here, too she shows that state-based welfare was underdeveloped before the war and had to evolve in reaction to the consequences of bombing. What emerged was a mixture of state assistance and the mobilization of national aid agencies, the most important being the Secours National, which provided immediate assistance, financial help and welfare. The state had a priority in controlling social unrest and getting workers back to work, so temporary repairs were effected to damaged housing. For the very poor or for 'bomb' widows, regular welfare payments were worked out. Dodd shows how much of this aid came with ideological strings attached, reflecting the different political constituencies that made up the Vichy regime. Whether the state's problem was shelter policy, evacuation or welfare, none of the policies was entirely free of the ideological imperatives and social concerns of the state. In turn, these imperatives were either internalized and accepted by the population, or became the site of potential dissent or non-compliance.

The second section examines cultural responses to bombing. Of course, bombing itself was the antithesis of culture, respecting neither age, nor magnificence nor uniqueness in the destruction of Europe's cultural heritage. The damage done to Germany's medieval cities was in most cases irreparable. In Münster 91 per cent of the old town was destroyed, in Mainz 80 per cent, in Ulm 80 per cent, and so on.[26] So extensive was the destruction that two-thirds of the urban built environment in Germany stems from the period after 1948.[27] In the bombing of Italy, the Allies respected only those sites clearly part of the world's artistic heritage – the centres of Venice, Florence and Rome. Even then Rome and Florence were eventually bombed by specially trained crews, as were the mainland areas of Venice Mestre. The threat to cultural treasures was very real and great efforts went into ensuring that the most important collections were removed from threat and that monuments could be protected by improvised blast walls and sandbag fortifications. In Britain an elaborate exodus of art treasures was organized for the last week of August 1939, in anticipation of an immediate bombing onslaught if war broke out. Museum directors asked for permission to arm their staff as they guarded the trains and trucks bearing the artwork away from the capital, but the police refused.[28] In Italy millions of sandbags were ordered to help protect Europe's richest concentration of historic monuments and ancient cities.[29]

The effectiveness of the Italian plans to protect monuments and works of art is the theme of Marta Nezzo's chapter. The regime began planning in case of war in the early 1930s, but a definite programme was only ordered shortly before Italy entered the war, on 6 June 1940. Nezzo shows that efforts to protect historic buildings were little defence against heavy bombing. But in the case of Veneto, which forms the core of her chapter, the transfer of movable art was more successful until the later stages of the war, when the dual threats of bombing and German looting forced Italian officials to keep moving the artwork from place to place. The problem in this case was not an absence of planning or goodwill but the unpredictable shifts in the war situation which made most of Italy a war zone from 1943 onwards. The end result was that much was preserved but a great deal also lost, both to the bombs and to the retreating Germans. Sometimes survival was a matter of luck. At a villa outside Florence two British journalists arrived in July 1944 to interview Indian army troops under the shadow of German tanks, only to see Botticelli's *Primavera* unboxed on the floor among soldiers brewing tea.[30]

The cultural response to bombing also has two other important senses. First, bombing itself generated a reactive culture in works of art, literature and poetry which derived directly from observing (and sometimes experiencing) the effects of aerial bombardment. Some has had a lasting value: images of the crowds in the London underground stations by Henry Moore or Edward Ardizzone are instantly recognisable; Helga Schneider's *The Bonfire of Berlin*, based on her childhood recollections of life under the bombs, has become an international best-seller. Some of the reaction deplored the destruction and highlighted its pathos. But some welcomed the bombing as a kind of release, a necessary apocalypse for an enervated, corrupt Europe. Hans Nossack in *Der Untergang* [The End], one of the finest evocations of the bombing, written shortly after he had witnessed the firestorm of Hamburg in July 1943, did not blame either Allies or the Hitler regime:

> This was what everyone had been waiting for, what had hung like a shadow over every-
> thing we did, making us weary. It was the end … Everything utterly silent, unmoving,
> unchanging. Denuded of time, [the city] had become eternal.[31]

The sense of the apocalyptic permeates much of the literary and poetic response to bombing, as Lara Feigel shows in her account of British and German wartime writing, which opens with a Stephen Spender poem recalling the 'black final horror' of a bombing raid. Feigel uses Nossack too as a point of reference, for like Spender and other British writers, his imagery evokes the modern world of the photograph or the film still, caught in time but also timeless. For those writers who survived their direct experience of bombing, the acute moment of drama – a collapsing wall, the flash of an exploding bomb – are caught as a single image, like a photograph. There is here an ironic echo in the fact that the destruction really *was* viewed as a series of photographs. Air Marshal Harris kept a large book of aerial photographs of the obliteration bombing carried out by Bomber Command which he would show to visitors to his headquarters as gloating evidence of what bombing could do to an enemy city.

The cultural history of bombing has a third dimension which is concerned more with the ways in which local culture, in the broader anthropological sense, was mobilized as a coping mechanism for the otherwise insupportable experience of being bombed. Claudia Baldoli and Vanessa Chambers both explore the role of religion and superstition as ways of mediating the psycho-logical damage done by bombing or fear of it. Baldoli shows that this reaction in Italy was based on long traditions of popular religiosity. For example, the response to bombing involved visions of the Madonna or a belief that priests could levitate. The cultural roots of these phenomena lie in medieval or early-modern Italian history. Priests and bishops played an important part in helping their local congregations to cope with the state's apparent failure to offer protection. As Baldoli shows, some of that help was in the form of injunctions to behave morally or to be better Catholics, on the assumption that bombing was either a punishment for former moral lapses, or that bombing itself encouraged moral laxity. Ordinary people, however, wanted practical help rather than sermons. They ordered special services, or left *ex voto* images in churches in the belief that this might save their house or family from destruction. It was a manifestation of fear, but it also represented, as Baldoli argues, a 'lack of faith in the regime'. If Fascism can be seen as a form of 'political religion', the impact of bombing undermined whatever legitimacy the moral universe of the dictatorship enjoyed, and replaced it with one which for Italians had a familiar resonance and apparently greater efficacy.

It is important to recall that popular religiosity and superstition were not confined to Italy. In other bombed environments it was tempting to invoke the supernatural or to explain in irrational terms the survivability of a region or a city or simply oneself. Nossack, who had left Hamburg just days before the firestorm, to go to his country cottage outside the city, had always thought that Fate was preserving him:

> For three years I said: I won't get hit. And the one standing next to me won't get hit either. Let the buildings fall right and left; there is nothing to fear; I didn't say it often; I especially didn't say it out loud. For as soon as it is spoken it becomes false and worthless ...'[32]

Nossack did, indeed, survive and attributed his survival to this not altogether lucky instinct. Fate, he thought, had saved him for something worse. Chambers explores how the anxieties generated by bombing in Britain also showed a surprising reliance on the supernatural. Some of this was linked to formal systems of belief. Churches, as in Italy, played an important part. During the Blitz clergymen opened up churches and church halls as welfare centres but also as centres of spiritual succour, though it is difficult, as Chambers acknowledges, to decide how genuinely spiritual a sudden recourse to prayer might be. There are, however, some features common to both the British and Italian experience. The sight of a surviving crucifix or an image of Christ in a bombed church seems to have had a restorative effect on those who beheld it in both countries, though the reality was that churches were little more immune from destruction than any other building.

In the British case there was also a tradition of spiritualism, which had been evoked a great deal during the First World War. In some cases the world beyond the here-and-now was mobilized as popular propaganda when accounts or diaries by airmen, some of whom had been killed, were published as if a voice from beyond the grave.[33] But Chambers shows that the government was generally worried by the public's attention given to horoscopes and fortune-telling. Astrology, it was feared, might encourage people to act against their own or the state's best interests. Nevertheless good luck charms, lucky colours, fears of the number thirteen and other popular superstitions were mobilized to support coping mechanisms in the face of the bombing. This public and private manifestation of 'bomb culture' was one of the most important aspects of the immediate reaction to being bombed; it was spontaneous, difficult for the state to monitor or control, but it also played an important part in sustaining the popular capacity to master the fear and horror.

The third section of the book deals with this question of the capacity of societies to withstand or adapt to the impact of bombing. At the time and since there has been a tendency to reduce this to the single question of 'morale' and how it was sustained during the war. The standard image of Britain is still the one that 'Britain can take it'; much of the discussion of German society has focused on the argument that morale was actually strengthened rather than undermined by being bombed, the opposite of what the two air forces bombing Germany actually wanted. This has proved something of a red herring. 'Morale' was never properly defined as a target for bombing, nor by the authorities which were responsible for monitoring and sustaining it. In general it was taken to be a manifestation of the popular will to continue working and supporting the war effort. In Britain, the Air Ministry saw one of the few ways of measuring 'morale' to be absenteeism from work, and ordered Bomber Command to destroy as much working-class housing as possible, because, as Churchill's scientific adviser Lord Cherwell impassively put it: 'Investigation seems to show that having one's house demolished is most damaging to morale.'[34] But the subsequent intelligence supplied from Germany in 1943 and 1944 gave no grounds for assuming, as some British politicians and air commanders did, that morale bombing might lead to the overthrow of the regime. Only in Italy was it possible to draw a clear link between the problems faced by Italian urban society as a result of bombing and a major crisis of legitimacy for the regime. A secret report to the American Office of Strategic Services on 16 July 1943 indicated that 'heavy air bombardment might possibly bring about a leftist revolution.'[35] Nine days after this report Mussolini fell from power, thanks to the army and the king.

As a social concept 'morale' is not particularly useful. As the chapters by Juliet Gardiner and Stephan Glienke demonstrate, the social impact of bombing produced a fractured response, determined partly by the scale, intensity and length of time in which bombing was experienced, and partly by the social characteristics of the areas being bombed. For most people the experience of being bombed was demoralizing, but the state of their 'morale' was not the way in which they viewed their social situation. Issues of simple daily survival, resurrecting the 'normal' as a series of social reference points, hunting for family or friends, hoping for food and shelter were much more important issues.[36] Even for those whose instinct might have been to say 'I can't go on', this was difficult to articulate and in the German case almost certainly dangerous. What comes out clearly from Gardiner and Glienke is the simple fact that a society of many millions of people is far too amorphous, socially heterogeneous and geographically diverse to suggest that anything like a single state of 'morale' could be historically reconstructed. Instead the social impact of bombing needs to be treated as a social history narrative. In the case of reaction to what came to be called the 'Blitz' (a strange misuse of the term *Blitzkrieg* or lightning war), Gardiner shows that social anxieties were generated by many things other than the bombing, but also that towns subject to the same intense bombing could react in very different ways according to how effective local authorities were in coping with the aftermath, or how economically buoyant a city had been before the attack. It also seems to have been the case that people

used the official propaganda of social solidarity and stoical resistance as a
language they could adopt and identify with, so that social pressure to display
the proverbial British 'stiff upper lip' did produce that very effect. Nor perhaps
should the British propensity for 'taking it' be dismissed entirely as myth. One
correspondent from Peckham in south-east London, following two narrow
escapes from bombs and eight dead neighbours, concluded by writing: 'it quite
unnerved us, but we have since had a week's rest in the country and feel very
much better for it.'[37]

The experience in Germany differed chiefly because bombing lasted for
five years and was a social reality which almost all German communities had
to come to terms with. Few areas of social life were not touched by bombing
and its direct and indirect consequences. Glienke highlights two different
approaches in the social history of bombing in Germany. One has concentrated
on the cities actually bombed (many, like Cologne or Essen, were bombed up to
250 times); the other has recognized that as a social fact bombing affected very
much wider circles of the population, either through the need to provide assistance and welfare, or as centres for emergency evacuation or more permanent
transfer, or because of the endless hours spent in air-raid shelters and cellars
because Allied bombers were flying overhead to some more distant target. He
shows that these are not exclusive narratives, since both represent a particular
social reality. For those who were forced to shelter repeatedly without being
bombed, there was sustained fear to cope with. Indeed, in other countries too,
anticipation of bombing seems to have generated as much nervous anxiety
as the actual experience, if not more. Even for those villages and small towns
where people huddled as bombers flew overhead, there was the prospect of
accidental destruction when bombers mistook their target centre and dropped
bombs in rural areas. Glienke argues that it is essential to 'define the different
forms of effect and to categorize the different regions accordingly', something
which much of the social history of bombing in Germany has failed to do effectively.[38] The experience of sitting in a heavily bombed town month after month
was self-evidently distinct from life in a small rural township which had to
cope with a sudden influx of urban mothers and children whose demands and
behaviour many rural Germans were unhappy to put up with. Jill Stephenson
has shown for the province of Württemberg how this meeting of different social
worlds was very far removed from the idea of 'People's Community' which the
regime mobilized in order to paper over the many cracks in German social
reality.[39]

The second two chapters in this section deal with aspects of the social history of
bombing in France and Italy. Here the context in which societies had to cope with
bombing was different. In France society had to cope with bombing which was
directed at an occupying power; the war was fought over French territory against
French urban targets, but was a war between Britain and the United States on the
one hand, and Germany on the other. There was thus little in any military sense
that the French population could expect in their defence, though the German

authorities supplied anti-aircraft guns and fighter aircraft to protect the installations that mattered to them. Social responses to bombing were as a result more
like the social response to a natural disaster, over which the victims can have
little or no control. Michael Schmiedel explores here a variation on the theme of
'morale' which this experience provoked. In order to cope with the bombing the
regime encouraged what Schmiedel has called 'orchestrated solidarity', the attempt
to create a language of national community which emphasized shared sacrifices
and a common fate in order to underpin the legitimacy of the Vichy regime. This
was done chiefly by town-twinning, an unbombed urban area adopting a bombed
one. The first experiment involved Brest (heavily bombed because it was a German
submarine centre) and Lyon, in the southern zone, and thus unoccupied until
1942. Although the experiment did not go entirely as planned, the Vichy regime
soon saw the policy of adoption of '*communes sinistrées*' as a means to underpin
the rhetoric of national solidarity, and further twinning took place in 1942 and
1943. Much of the work involved collections of money, clothes and food in the
unbombed cities to donate directly to those that had been adopted. This supplied
what Schmiedel calls a form of 'moral reassurance' for the damaged populations
which was supplied, despite the intervention of the regime, by voluntary social
action.

The issue of moral solidarity and moral collapse is the theme of Gabriella
Gribaudi's discussion of Naples and its hinterland during the bombing. She
highlights the extent to which the Allies had greater confidence in the vulnerability of Italian society to the threat of bombing than they did in the German
case. She shows, like Glienke, that bombing was experienced differently in city
and countryside, and between different social classes. Her description of the
social experience of bombing in Naples highlights the incapacity of the regime
or local authorities to cope with basic social provision, and as a result the failure
of 'orchestrated solidarity' in the Italian case. She observes active expressions
of dissent from as early as 1941, but by 1943 the situation had moved, in her
words, from 'authoritarianism to anarchy'. It is worth asking why in the Italian
case, alone of the four states, the potential for dissent and de-legitimization was
so much stronger. Gribaudi argues that this was not just the result of bombing.
As in Britain or in Germany, 'demoralization', when it occurred, could be
caused by a variety of pressures other than the consequences of air raids. In
the Italian case, however, bombing exposed the deficiencies of the regime more
directly and immediately than any other problem. After the Italian surrender in
September 1943, the bombing in northern and central Italy worsened but did
not produce the overthrow of the German occupying force, any more than it did
in France. This was almost certainly a result of the utterly ruthless way in which
the German army, security forces and administration ran the areas under their
control.

The final section of the book deals with an aspect of the reaction to bombing
which has perhaps attracted the least attention in the existing literature: the
popular perception by the bombed populations of those doing the bombing.

This was a complex issue because the battle lines of the war were complex. It was never the case that everyone in the bombed population wanted revenge against the enemy, nor that everyone being bombed regarded the airmen doing the bombing as an enemy. Perception could also shift with the changing fortunes of war, and in paradoxical ways. Allied bombing of targets in Belgium, the Netherlands and northern France in 1942 was less resented than later bombing, even though victory over Germany looked by no means certain and liberation a long way off; bombing in 1944 was often more damaging, and prompted, as Simon Kitson shows, stronger resentment at the slow pace of Allied advance. Even in Britain, where the situation was never so ambiguous, there was uncertainty over the legitimacy of revenge attacks and opposition to the policy of indiscriminate night-bombing organized by the Committee for the Abolition of Night-Bombing (later the Bombing Restrictions Committee) set up in London in April 1941.[40] In Germany, too, as Glienke shows, the attitude of different social and political constituencies was not likely to be consensual, a point appreciated by some on the Allied side who advocated bombing German villages and small towns because that was where they thought most National Socialist voters were to be found.[41]

Some of these ambiguities are explored in Marco Fincardi's study of the revival of Italian public opinion in the later stages of the Mussolini regime and the months surrounding the armistice on 8 September 1943. By 1942 the priority for many Italians was to find a way to end the war, and as a result their attitude to Allied bombing was not unrelieved hostility but a hope that the Allies would win quickly by destroying Italy's war-making potential. This was not a view that all Italians took, as Fincardi makes clear, but it coloured much of the popular attitude to bombing before the fall of Mussolini, during the brief period of army rule up to September, and in the two years of German occupation. British and American leaflets, dropped intermittently between the bombs, also tried to exploit this ambiguity by telling Italians to stop working for the Germans and to leave the cities, or face the consequences. A leaflet dropped in March 1943, for example, claimed 'We do not have the sadistic German desire to impose atrocities on the civil population, and we aim at war-related objectives; but inevitably nearby zones are in danger and could be hit'.[42] These leaflets differed from the ones dropped on German cities, which simply told urban workers that they would go on being killed until Germany surrendered unconditionally.[43] By contrast, the propaganda of the Italian Social Republic (the so-called Salò Republic) presented the Allies as barbarians, wrecking Italy's cultural heritage and destroying its social cohesion. Fincardi shows that many Italians simply detached themselves from any of those involved and waited until the war was over, unable to resolve the ambiguities presented by dictatorship, patriotism, hopes for liberation and hatred of war.

The same difficulty faced the French population as it confronted the longing for liberation and the reality of ever more destructive and deadly air attacks on French cities. Kitson argues that the popular attitude to the bombing was the reverse of the Italian case – a general approval in the early years of bombing, and then a growing chorus of disquiet or hostility in the year or so before liberation. Up until 1943 it was widely understood that the Allies only wanted to attack elements of the German war effort on French soil, and this was a legitimate act of war, even in the case of the bombing of the Renault factory at Boulogne-Billancourt in Paris in March 1942, which killed more civilians in one night than had yet been killed in any raid on Germany. The attitude changed in 1943 as the severity and number of raids increased, and the notorious inaccuracy of high-level bombing left widespread destruction of housing and civilian casualties. But it also changed because of the long lead-up time to the Normandy invasion. Those being bombed assumed that air raids were a prelude to ground action and real liberation; hostility to bombing reflected these frustrations as well. Conditional approval of bombing could still co-exist with more negative evaluations, producing what Kitson calls 'variables of acceptance'. It is striking that in both the French and the Italian case, more blame was put on American daylight bombing, which was supposed to be more accurate, than on night-bombing by the RAF, which was governed by special rules of engagement for attacks on French soil.

Kitson argues that among the least sympathetic French constituencies to Allied bombing was the body of French prisoners of war in Germany. They were more hostile to the British, partly because of their memories of the defeat in 1940, partly because they were subjected more easily to *vichyiste* propaganda. The perception of prisoners in an enemy country is the theme of Neville Wylie's study of British POWs in German camps, who experienced the bombing campaign at first hand. Of course here too was a community hoping that bombing would be a prelude to their liberation, and unlike French POWs there was an easy identification with those overhead. But at the same time the prisoners were also victims, with an estimated 1,000 British POWs killed by air action. As the air war intensified and prisoners were marched from camp to camp, the dangers became more acute. Wylie shows that prisoners were also capable of demonstrating the same terror of bombing as the German civilians around them, and experienced the same level of disruption. One work group was made to go to the shelters 170 times in March 1945, though it seems remarkable at that stage of the war that German guards cared that much what happened to their Allied charges. But he also highlights the extent to which British POWs sympathized with the plight of German civilians caught in the final months of truly apocalyptic destruction. In this, as in other forms of perception, there was no entirely straightforward way of relating to either friend or foe.

The final chapter in this section, by Olivier Dumoulin, explores the way in which these perceptions were represented in newsreel coverage on the bombings in German, French and British newsreels. He argues that the pre-war bombing fear in Europe helped to create a shared imaginative view of an air raid, which was almost certainly justified by the reality in wartime.

Nevertheless, the purpose of newsreel footage of the bombing in each country was not identical. In France it was presented in a way designed to encourage solidarity with the regime in the face of a perfidious former ally; in Germany the difficulty was to show the bombing in such a way that it did not highlight the evident weakness of German air defences in the face of Allied attacks; in Britain newsreels brought home to the non-bombed population the reality of war. Dumoulin shows, however, that the most potent images proved in each case to be the destruction of churches and cathedrals. Ecclesiastical buildings had the advantage of presenting a particular wartime aesthetic (the iconic image of St. Paul's rising majestically above the shrouds of smoke on 29 December 1940 is only the most famous); but the destruction of churches was also an instantly recognizable sacrilege even in countries where Christianity's hold was less substantial. This form of representation encouraged perception of the enemy as an enemy of Christian civilization.

It is now between sixty-five and seventy years since the bombing of much of urban Western Europe. Most of the states subjected to bombing joined forces in the European Economic Community only a dozen years after the war's end. The rebuilding work after the war involved not simply the reconstruction of apartment blocks, commercial centres and communications but the recon-struction of the communities and networks that were rudely torn apart by the bombing experience. The apparent collapse of civilization was followed by a new rhetoric of revival and progress. Bombing provided a starting point for elaborate programmes of town planning and urban renewal; it also became a reference point for a variety of cultural representations of the experience of total war.[44] There is now serious historical interest in the many forms of memoriali-zation of the bombing, although this has in general been much less marked than other forms of post-war memorialization.[45] For example, there are now three major monuments to the 544 pilots who died in the Battle of Britain but as yet no collective monument to the 27,450 civilians who died from the bombing between July and December 1940.[46] The pattern of post-war memory of the bombing reflects the differing perceptions held by the bombed populations during the wartime period and the often confused pattern of victory or defeat. It is striking that in Italy early memorials apportioned no blame but deplored the fact of war itself. In other cases there has also remained an evident ambiguity. The bombing of Dresden was exploited by the Communist authorities as an example of ruthless capitalist imperialism, while at the same time it was used as a beacon of reconciliation between the local communities in Dresden and Coventry.

The essays collected in this volume have tried to recapture the wartime experience of the victim populations with narratives on the social, cultural and political impact of bombing as a lived experience, rather than as a preparation for recovery and memory. What is more difficult to recapture in the narrative is the exceptional violence of bomb attack; civilians often found themselves caught in a situation worse than the soldiers trapped in the trenches of the

Western Front between 1914 and 1918, and with less prospect of shelter. The estimated 700,000 dead (and as many again seriously wounded or more lightly injured) were killed indiscriminately and in hideous ways by fire, blast or shrapnel. However dispassionate the analysis of the different narratives of that experience must be, and whatever contrasts it is possible to elucidate, the harsh reality for all bombed communities was mass death and mutilation. This is a comparison that needs no qualification and it is a reality that permeates implicitly the contents of the book.

Notes

1   There is no generally accepted set of statistics on the deaths and injuries caused by bombing during the war. Accurate figures are available for Britain, where the number of dead were 60,595 (excluding service personnel). See B. Collier, *The Defence of the United Kingdom* (London: HMSO, 1957), 528. On German estimates see O. Groehler, *Bombenkrieg gegen Deutschland* (Berlin: Akademie Verlag, 1990), 316–20. Estimates for deaths in Italy and France vary widely, though a figure between 60,000 and 70,000 is now generally given in both cases. The statistical problems will be explored in greater depth in the forthcoming volume by A. F. Knapp and C. Baldoli, *Forgotten Blitzes: France and Italy under Allied Air Attack, 1940–1945* (London: Continuum, 2011).

2   A number of good examples are D. Busch, *Der Luftkrieg im Raum Mainz während des Zweiten Weltkrieges* (Mainz: Hase & Koehler, 1988); M. P. Hiller (ed.), *Stuttgart im Zweiten Weltkrieg* (Gerlingen: Bleicher Verlag, 1989); A. Rastelli, *Bombe sulla città: Gli attachi aerei alleati: Le vittime civili a Milano* (Milan: Mursia, 2000); I. Permooser, *Der Luftkrieg über München 1942–1945: Bomben auf die Hauptstadt der Bewegung* (Oberhachung: Aviatic Verlag, 1997); G. Gribaudi, *Guerra totale: tra bombe alleate e violenze naziste. Napoli e il fronte meridionale, 1940–1944* (Turin: Bollati Boringhieri, 2005); B. Garnier and M. Pigenet, *Les victimes civiles des bombardements en Normandie* (Caen: La Mandragore, 1997).

3   On the nature of the myth see M. Connelly, *We Can Take It! Britain and the Memory of the Second World War* (Harlow: Longman, 2004), 128–53; M. Smith, *Britain and 1940: History, Myth and Popular Memory* (London: Francis & Taylor, 2000); A. Calder, *The Myth of the Blitz* (London: Jonathan Cape, 1991). Two academic studies on British attitudes during the war are J. R. Freedman, *Whistling in the Dark: Memory and Culture in Wartime London* (Lexington: Kentucky University Press, 1999) and A. H. Bell, *London Was Ours: Diaries and Memoirs of the London Blitz* (London: I. B. Tauris, 2008). The best historical account remains J. Ray, *The Night Blitz 1940–1941* (London: Arms & Armour, 1996).

4   S. Cox (ed.), *The Strategic Air War Against Germany 1939–1945: The Official Report of the Bombing Survey Unit* (London: Frank Cass, 1998), xvii–xxi; G. Daniels (ed.), *A Guide to the Reports of the United States Strategic Bombing Survey* (London: Royal Historical Society, 1981), xvi–xxvi.

5   See the recent analysis in J. Brauer and H. van Tuyll, *Castles, Battles and Bombs: How Economics Explains Military History* (Chicago: Chicago University Press, 2008), ch. 6. They argue that bombing was economically worthwhile until a point was reached of diminishing returns in continuing to bomb already damaged or destroyed areas.

6   S. Harvey, 'The Italian War Effort and the Strategic Bombing of Italy' *History*, 70 (1985) 32–45; P. Ferrari, 'Un'arma versatile. I bombardamenti strategici anglo-americani e l'industria italiana' in Ferrari (ed.), *L'Aeronautica Italiana: Una storia del Novecento* (Milan: FrancoAngeli, 2004), 391–432.

7   A. C. Grayling, *Among the Dead Cities: Was the Allied Bombing of Civilians in World War II a Necessity or a Crime?* (London: Bloomsbury, 2006).

8   J. Friedrich, *Der Brand: Deutschland im Bombenkrieg 1940–1945* (Munich: Propyläen Verlag,

2002); L. Kettenacker (ed.), *Ein Volk von Opfern? Die neue Debatte um den Bombenkrieg, 1940–45* (Berlin: Rowohlt, 2003).

9   E. Markusen and D. Kopf, *The Holocaust and Strategic Bombing: Genocide and Total War in the Twentieth Century* (Boulder, Col.: Westview Press, 1995).

10 M. Bess, *Choices Under Fire: Moral Dimensions of World War II* (New York: Alfred Knopf, 2006), 110. This is also the central message of N. Baker, *Human Smoke: The Beginning of World War II, the End of Civilization* (New York: Simon & Schuster, 2008).

11 T. McCormack and H. Durham 'Aerial Bombardment of Civilians: The Current International Legal Framework' in Y. Tanaka and M. B. Young (eds), *Bombing Civilians: A Twentieth-Century History* (New York: The New Press, 2009), 215–30; C. A. J. Coady, 'Bombing and the Morality of War' in Tanaka and Young, *Bombing Civilians*, 191–214. There is much of interest in the collection of essays edited by W. Wette and G. Ueberschär, *Kriegsverbrechen im 20. Jahrhundert* (Darmstadt: Wissenschaftliche Buchgesellschaft, 2001).

12 See G. P. Fletcher and J. D. Ohlin, *Defending Humanity: When Force is Justified and Why* (New York: Oxford University Press, 2008), esp. ch 1.

13 I. Yorifusa, 'Japanese Cities and Planning in the Reconstruction Period: 1945–55' in C. Hein, J. M. Diefendorf and I. Yorifusa (eds), *Rebuilding Urban Japan After 1945* (London: Palgrave, 2003), 18.

14 J. Konvitz, 'Représentations urbaines et bombardements stratégiques 1914–1945' *Annales*, 1989, 823–47; D. Voldman, 'Les populations civiles, enjeux du bombardement des villes (1914–1945), in H. Rousso et al (eds), *La violence de guerre 1914–1945* (Paris: Éditions Complexe, 2002), 151–174; R. J. Overy, 'Allied Bombing and the Destruction of German Cities' in R. Chickering, S. Förster and B. Greiner (eds), *A World at Total War: Global Conflict and the Politics of Destruction 1937–1945* (Cambridge: Cambridge University Press, 2005), 277–95.

15 Library of Congress, Washington DC, General Carl Spaatz papers, Box I/184, Ministry of Home Security, Dept RE8 report, 30 December 1942, 'Note on Italian construction and its vulnerability to I.B. and H.E. bombs'.

16 S. Brackman, H. Garretsen and M. Schramm, 'The strategic bombing of German cities during World War II and its impact on city growth', *Journal of Economic Geography*, 4 (2004), 216.

17 H. Ullman and J. Wade, *Rapid Dominance – A Force for All Seasons* (RUSI, London, 1998); idem, *Shock and Awe: Achieving Rapid Dominance* (Washington D.C.: National Defense University, 1996).

18 Churchill College, Cambridge, papers of Air Vice-Marshal Sidney Bufton, 3/27, memorandum 'The Employment of H.E. Bombs in Incendiary Attack', 1-2.

19 See for example A. F. Knapp, 'The Destruction and Liberation of Le Havre in Modern Memory', *War in History*, 14 (2007), 476–98; A. F. Knapp and L. A. Dodd, ' "How Many Frenchmen Did You Kill?" British Bombing Policy towards France (1940–1945)', *French History*, 22 (2008), 469–92.

20 On these paradoxical issues see C. Baldoli and M. Fincardi, 'Italian Society under Anglo-American Bombs: Propaganda, Experience and Legend, 1940–1945', *The Historical Journal*, 52 (2009), 1017–1038.

21 Archivio Centrale dello Stato, Rome (ACS), Ministero dell'Aeronautica, b. 82, Duce's secretariat to Air Ministry, 16 November 1940; Ministry of War to all ministers, 19 November 1940.

22 J. B. S. Haldane, *A.R.P.* (London, 1938), 200–1.

23 York City Archives, Acc. 89/1, minutes of York ARP emergency committee, 9 April 1940.

24 London School of Economics Archive (LSE), Fellowship of Reconciliation papers, Box 4 (2), F. of R. bulletin, 16 December 1940.

25 German figures from Groehler, *Bombenkrieg gegen Deutschland*, 282. By January 1945 there were 7,174 million planned evacuees, and 1,769 million self-evacuees. On British figures see R. Titmuss, *Problems of Social Policy* (London: HMSO, 1950), 543–5. On British evacuation of children see J. Welshman, *Churchill's Children: The Evacuee Experience in Wartime Britain* (Oxford: Oxford University Press, 2010).

26 N. Lambourne, *War Damage in Western Europe: The Destruction of Historic Monuments during the Second World War* (Edinburgh: Edinburgh University Press, 2001), 147.

27   H. Beseler and N. Gutschow (eds), *Kriegsschicksale Deutscher Architektur: Verluste-Schäden-Wiederaufbau* (Neumünster: 2 vols, Karl Wachholtz, 1988), vol I, xxxvii.

28   The National Archives, Kew, London (TNA), HO 45/18128, report from M. Bennett to R. Wells (Home Office), 31 August 1939.

29   ACS, Ministero dell'Aeronautica, b. 82, 3/V/5, Ministry of War to all prefects, 7 June 1940. Rome was promised 1,900,000 sandbags, Florence 300,000, Milan 450,000, and so on.

30   L. Nicholas, *The Rape of Europa: The Fate of Europe's Treasures in the Third Reich and the Second World War* (London: Macmillan, 1994), 260.

31   H. Nossack, *The End* (Chicago: University of Chicago Press, 2004), 8, 40. The original was published in 1948. The title *Der Untergang* translates as 'downfall' or 'decline', echoing Oswald Spengler's *Decline of the West [Der Untergang des Abendslandes]*.

32   Nossack, *The End*, 58.

33   Ministry of Information, *We Speak from the Air* (London: HMSO, 1942).

34   Nuffield College, Oxford, Cherwell papers, F254, 'Estimates of Bombing Effect', War Cabinet paper, 9 April 1942, 1.

35   Franklin D. Roosevelt Library, Map Room files, box 72, OSS Bulletin, 16 July 1943 (report from OSS station Bern).

36   See, for example, S. Barakat (ed.), *After the Conflict: Reconstruction and Development in the Aftermath of War* (London: I. B. Tauris, 2005).

37   LSE, Fellowship of Reconciliation papers, Box 4 (2), letter from Sybil Hughes (Peckham branch) to Doris Steynor, 27 October 1940.

38   See Groehler, *Bombenkrieg gegen Deutschland* and E. Beck, *Under the Bombs: The German Home Front 1942-1945* (Lexington: Kentucky University Press, 1986).

39   J. Stephenson, *Hitler's Home Front: Württemberg under the Nazis* (London: Continuum, 2006).

40   Friends House, London, T. C. Foley papers, Mss 488 2/2, 'The Bombing Restrictions Committee: Its origins, Purpose and Publications', November 1944, 1.

41   TNA, AIR 40/1271, 76th meeting of German Bombing Target Information Committee, 6 November 1942, 2: 'it having been suggested in some quarters that there was greater support for Hitler and the Fascist regime in the countryside than in the cities.'

42   ACS, Ministero dell'Interno, A5G, b. 22, prefect of Catanzaro to the Ministry of Interior, 28 March 1943, encl. leaflet 'Le bombe e la verità'.

43   RAF Museum, Hendon, papers of Air Marshal Arthur Harris, H51, draft leaflet 'Why We Bomb You', July 1942, 5: 'we are going to flatten Germany end to end'.

44   On this see W. Wilms and W. Rasch (eds), *'Bombs Away.' Representing the Air War over Europe and Japan* (Amsterdam: Rohop, 2006); J. M. Diefendorf, *In the Wake of War: The Reconstruction of German Cities after World War II* (New York: Oxford University Press, 1993); N. Gregor, *Haunted City: Nuremberg and the Nazi Past* (New Haven: Yale University Press, 2008).

45   On this see particularly J. Arnold, D. Süss and M. Thiessen (eds), *Luftkrieg: Erinnerungen in Deutschland und Europa* (Göttingen: Wallstein Verlag, 2009); W. Niven, 'The GDR and the Memory of the Bombing of Dresden' in Niven (ed.), *Germans as Victims* (London: Palgrave, 2006), 109-29.

46   The three monuments are on the Victoria Embankment in London (2005), next to Croydon airport in Surrey (1991) and at Capel-le-Ferne in Kent, site of the principal Battle of Britain National Memorial (1993).

PART I

States and Peoples

1

Wartime Societies and Shelter Politics in National Socialist Germany and Britain*

Dietmar Süss

The art of war changed fundamentally from the beginning of the twentieth century with the introduction of aircraft, which brought new possibilities for destruction and new forms of death. Air power thus belongs to the specific form of power exercised by modern societies in the twentieth century. This contribution, like much recent military history, deals with 'war as a condition of society'[1] and thus also with the cultural and existential ways in which bombing was managed in Germany and Great Britain. At the centre stand two very differently constructed political systems, British democracy and National Socialist dictatorship, and the question of the specific and common features they employed in overcoming and appropriating the experience of bombing. In the First World War, both Germany and Great Britain, two highly industrialized nations, had already exploited the new military possibilities then available by dropping bombs on enemy cities. For a long time systematic conceptual comparisons in the tradition of historical-comparative method were out of favour, standing in the shadow of the theoretical battles during the Cold War over the weight to be attached to the concept of totalitarianism. If it was done at all, it was fascism and communism that served as foils for the comparative analysis of totalitarian power, but not democracies like Britain, Sweden or the United States. Only since the late 1970s have attempts been made to compare National Socialism with liberal democracies as elements of the broader crisis of modernity – not in order to relativize them but in order to examine precisely the convergences, differences and the potential for contradiction within and between modern societies.[2] The bulk of the comparison here consists of establishing exact observations on the internal structure of dictatorship and democracy under a permanent state of emergency. In the first place, such a perspective allows the air war to be analysed as a European phenomenon and as a part of the age of total war, without having to follow the German-British controversies over the political-moral blame for the bombing war which have dominated debates from the war down to the present. Second, the comparison makes possible answers to the question about what the core of the 'people's community' in war represented; with an eye on the British experience, it shows the specific mix of factors made up of National Socialist integration and power,

*Translated from German by Nick Terry and Richard Overy

of mobilization and terror; and finally, it becomes possible, according to both the system-specific and system-independent answers to the threat from the air, to ask: was the organization of air defence and bunker life something specifically 'National Socialist'? Were the strategies and interpretative models, rituals and myths of community solidarity demonstrated in other industrial societies in a similar way and were there parallel answers to the threat from the air? Was there a conception independent of any political system to protect the civilian population in war and to destroy the morale of the enemy?

My central thesis can be expressed thus: the 'emergency' of the air war inspired equally in both Great Britain and Germany the mythical 'supercharging' of the wartime experience as a national community of fate and as the normative form of civilian behaviour. The study and observation of 'war morale' were part of the power to define who did or did not belong to the people or the nation and was thus a central field of social conflict. These considerations are dealt with in this contribution through the example of the organization of shelter life in Germany and Great Britain. The temporary dispersal of wartime society under the earth signified a massively dynamic mobilization of urban daily life. In the bunkers and galleries the war showed itself to be 'war as a condition of society' in a deeper way. Bunkers were spaces in which dictatorship and democracy exercised control and disciplined behaviour. They were an object of propaganda, sites for the promise of protection and the establishment of normative gender roles. Even though the instruments of state repression were less clearly marked in Great Britain than in Germany, there is much to indicate that the contemporary strategies of crisis management were evidently not system-specific but were to a certain extent an expression of the dynamic involvement of society in the conduct of industrialized warfare.

These issues are examined here in three steps. First, the differing interpretations of what the building of bunkers and air defences signified for both wartime societies are addressed, while at the same time discussing the differing expectations and conceptions of war as 'a condition of society'. In the second section questions are posed about power, dominance and security in the social practice of wartime societies dispersed underground. How was access to the bunkers regulated? What role did power and the social regimentation of behaviour play in the organization of the 'home front'? The third section looks at the relationship in shelter life between normative behaviour, health provision and controls. In both wartime societies bunkers were also regarded as places which posed a threat to public order and which constituted a danger-point for outbreaks of disease. How did both states react to this very similar alleged danger and what was the significance of gender-specific stereotypes about 'female' behaviour in wartime?

IMPENDING APOCALYPSE

Air-raid shelters were the internal bulwark against an external threat. They were meant to offer protection against the weapons of modern war, both gas and bombs. Yet their significance in propaganda terms extended far beyond deep bunkers and sturdy cellars. From the start of the war the social structure of the shelter held a special interest for Germany and Great Britain; overcoming individual fears and maintaining collective order was a basic precondition for the protection of 'war morale' and thus for the nation's fight for survival.[3] Indeed, in Germany well before the start of the war there was much public discussion about air-raid protection,[4] though in practice construction measures remained far behind the expectations of planners. The reason lay first of all in the logic of contemporary warfare, in which everything had been anticipated except a lengthy bombing campaign. The first British air attacks in 1940 caused consternation, and in Berlin it came to be recognized that the loyalty of the national comrades (*Volksgenossen*) could only be maintained in the long term if people were given permanent protection from attacks. A few months after the adoption of the 'Immediate Führer Programme' for the construction of bomb-safe air-raid shelters on 10 October 1940, the chief of air-raid protection in the Reich Air Ministry, Kurt Knipfer, outlined his vision of future bunker policy.[5] The construction programme was from the outset bound up with grand ambitions: women and children were to be protected, and at the same time arrangements made to safeguard armaments workers. Night-time security was designed to buy day-time productivity.

In the winter of 1941/2 it was already clear that such an ambitious programme would be a fiasco. This outcome was all the more dangerous because in several respects bunkers performed a central function for the morale of the population and thus for the self-understanding of the 'people's community' (*Volksgemeinschaft*) at war. In the end both the internal and external form of the bunkers was supposed to reflect the military strength and the martial outlook of the nation: they were spaces in which the ordered structure of National Socialist society maintained its wartime complexion – as a struggle for membership of 'the community', as a pledge of protection by the Third Reich and as a blueprint for the future of a new National Socialist society.[6]

'Fortresses and castles in times past,' maintained Germany's Plenipotentiary General for Construction in 1942,

have in many cases served not only the purely material purpose of defence but have given their designers opportunity to find for defensive use a corresponding form which in many cases has remained a cultural monument to an era, far beyond the original material purpose.[7]

The design of the bunkers, too, was not merely functional. Far more was intended to be displayed: the past and present of the *Volksgemeinschaft*, whose architectural showpieces were symbols of the unrestrained will to survive. At the end of the war the tall, undamaged tower shelters would not only be proof of success, but would also stand for the future as an expression of the creative ingenuity of the *Volksgemeinschaft*, and would thus be part of a new, well-fortified National Socialist city.

As early as 1941, town planners in Hamm in Westphalia began to integrate the projects for the construction of shelters into a master concept of urban development, as they did in other cities built on medieval models.[8] Nine tower shelters along the old ring wall enclosing the town centre would turn the town into an impregnable fortress and transform the inhabitants into fighting citizens defending themselves against the robber barons of the air. But by the autumn of 1943, it was clear that the grandiose plans had foundered because of a lack of resources and because of the force of Allied air attacks on Europe's largest marshalling yard, and that shelter spaces were available for only a fraction of the population. Instead of tower shelters, the city went over to constructing tunnels and private air-raid shelters and to the creation of as many underground shelter spaces as possible.

In Hanover town planners considered moving substantial parts of the urban infrastructure underground; a 'bunkered' city would emerge, combining the vision of a well-fortified medieval town with the extensive conversions of modern National Socialist architecture, one that entirely breathed the architectural spirit of Albert Speer.[9] In the first two years of building work, shelters and their large construction sites developed into central locations of self-assurance regarding the protective function of the National Socialist state.[10] Nothing unfortunate could happen, it was argued, if at the initiative of the *Führer*, the threatened security of the population was rapidly and decisively safeguarded and shelter space actively created. Nevertheless this staged security was a double-edged sword, since on the one hand such public rituals documented the ability of the *Volksgemeinschaft* to put up a fight, while on the other hand they were also, as a direct result of the duration of the war, the mirror image of internal vulnerability. Thus it was no surprise that from 1942 onwards, images of the first ground-breaking ceremonies for the planned bunkers disappeared once again from public view.

In Great Britain, however, a comparable shelter programme never existed, neither before the war nor during it; the mass production of individual shelters was preferred over larger tunnels or bunkers above ground. This choice was not without risk, for the situation dramatically intensified with the first heavy bombings of London in September 1940; the feared losses did not in fact arise, but it was soon clear that the existing capacities in the shelters themselves were insufficient even if a majority of Londoners did not use them and only a minority actually sought mass accommodation. Life in the shelters was not regarded, as it was in Germany, as a national fate. At the start of the attacks many sought shelter in public buildings, in churches and schools, but not in the London Underground, which at the outbreak of war was not at first intended as a place of refuge. On the contrary: the ministries were convinced that under no circumstances could the tube be occupied or blocked by masses of people.[11] It was a pivotal means of transport at the heart of public infrastructure and therefore particularly vulnerable. This attitude changed as the scale of the damage and the discontent of the population grew ever greater with the expansion of the attacks. The government was accused of being unable to provide sufficient protection. The tube tunnels were opened under considerable public pressure.[12] The construction of shelters, hygienic conditions in mass accommodation, safety precautions and escape routes, supplies of food and water, the announcement of opening times and the effectiveness of the air-raid warning systems, all became by at least the late summer of 1940 a flashpoint for internal political conflict, with the state's capacity for crisis management at the centre.

'London sleeps'. Cartoon by David Low, *Evening Standard*, 24 September 1940. Courtesy of Associated Newspapers Ltd.

Thus it was not in the end decisive how many people actually sought out the shelters: the important thing was that shelter spaces lay at the intersection of various conflicts, whose origins reached back into the pre-war era, but which experienced a noticeable radicalization during and because of the war. These issues included the state's fear of the political unreliability of the working class as well as the social conflicts discernible during evacuation, which resulted from the class character of British society. The squalor of workers' housing in the major cities had been the subject of fierce polemics for some time. Journalists and writers had again and again complained about such conditions. After the conflicts over evacuation, shelters too became a further site where the social tinderbox threatened to ignite.

Life underground, the conditions of protection and supply, of welfare and state assistance were part of an ever more intense debate from 1940 over the state of the nation, over the meaning of the conflict with fascist Germany and the hope for a 'New Jerusalem'[13] that would bring the material freedom that had eluded the working class for so long. In this respect, conditions in air-raid shelters afforded not only the external manifestation of the necessity for reform but also the material basis for social conflict. The response to such conditions thus became an acid test of the authorities' readiness to implement serious social improvements – an impulse that had nothing to correspond to it in the Third Reich, for in the end German bunkers were sites to secure dominance and not really zones in which a just post-war order could be publicly discussed.

POWER, DOMINANCE, SECURITY: SHELTERS AS NEW SITES OF THE WAR ON THE GERMAN HOME FRONT

Order and dominance were thus the central categories in which, especially in Germany, the future of air defence was debated. Although the necessity for building shelters was very different in the Third Reich and in Great Britain, not least because of the different intensity of the air war, nevertheless the bunkers and tube tunnels in both wartime societies were treated as an important test case for the capacity of both political systems to produce security for the population and therefore to legitimate their rule. There was also something else, which belonged to the core problem of the wartime mobilization of the nation and showed the extent to which the character of the air war experience embraced the whole system. In the bunkers and air-raid shelters, 'war morale' was to pass its field test.[14] For the urban population, shelters were central spaces for creating a sense of wartime community.[15] They were the spatial expression of a new architecture of war society and at the same time social areas where power, dominance and control were constantly struggled over and recreated anew.[16] Behaviour in the air-raid shelters and the 'war morality' of the population stood at the interface of different sets of problems: for the local officials of the National Socialist regime, the decision over access to the bunkers offered a central checkpoint for the community's capacity for integration. Admission was linked with conformist behaviour and a racially 'normal' biographical profile: from the start access was regulated by shelter cards, which determined the degree of risk involved in admitting their bearer. Those who were permitted entrance to one of the air-raid shelters with sleeping berths were allowed to visit the shelter every night if they chose, but were duty-bound to be in their bunks during every air-raid alarm. Anyone who failed to abide by this regulation could lose their place. For passers-by taken by surprise by an attack, only the common shelter areas without beds were available. The shelter populations represented an attempt to relocate social and neighbourhood connections 'underground', and thereby to maintain and stabilize social relationships in a state of emergency, but they also contained a fraction of society experiencing a forced mobility as a result of the air war, for whom bunkers were more like 'transit spaces'[17] in which people of different backgrounds and experience were of necessity thrown together in order to survive the night.

Local police nominated a district air-raid warden from the circle of regular shelter users in the immediate neighbourhood, who had the challenging task of maintaining order and the National Socialist system of domination at one and the same time: it was the warden's responsibility to appoint stewards, mostly from among the air-raid officials responsible for individual apartment blocks, who also controlled night-time life in the shelters; the warden decreed who would serve in lookout groups to stand at the entrance gates to regulate access to the blockhouse bunker. Insufficient foresight and ever more rapid destruction led to a change in the winter of 1942–3 in the criteria for admittance. With growing emphasis, the regime urged that scarce shelter resources should be limited to a few population groups: no space was allowed any longer for men between 16 and 60 years of age. In mid-June 1943, Göring confirmed this practice, already enforced in regions especially threatened by the air war: in view of the scarce number of bunker places, 'male *Volksgenossen*' were prohibited entry to the shelters. It was however their task to fight against the bombing in the 'air-raid protection communities'.[18]

Meanwhile such regulations gave rise to considerable resentment, because the few newly constructed tunnels were not used exclusively for the civilian population, but were also occupied by the NSDAP's local officials (*Kreisleitung*). Did the Party bosses thus secure their privileges at the expense of the 'little man'? Similar stories circulated in a great many places, and the germ of truth is confirmed from official records. The police president of Hanover reported in mid-November 1944 on the results of an investigation of the city shelters which showed that numerous officials and employees of public authorities from the immediate vicinity were among those who fled to the air-raid shelters even before the air-raid alarm had sounded. This behaviour provoked great indignation among the working population, who were given no opportunity to leave their workplace ahead of time. The police president hoped in the future to call to account all those who persisted with this shoddy practice.[19]

The 'Jewish question' also created problems for the regime. On 7 October 1940 the Reich Air Ministry had indicated in a decree that Jews could not be denied entry to public air-raid shelters entirely, because it was feared that this would provoke 'detrimental effects' and that these 'could also disadvantageously affect the population of German blood'. What was meant by 'detrimental effects' Göring left open, but it was less likely to be an expression of solidarity with Jewish fellow-citizens than a product of the anti-Semitic anxiety of being robbed by Jews while people sat in the shelters and could not guard their property. Göring campaigned for the accommodation of Jews in separate areas and if necessary the division of available air-raid shelter space in such a way that Germans and Jews did not have to sit in the same room.[20] The driving force behind this pattern of anti-Semitic demarcation were first of all the NSDAP-*Ortsgruppen* (local groups), who were scandalized by the appearance of 'non-Aryans' and played a part in refusing them entry; they did so not because they were ordered to, but through obedience in anticipation.[21] The Dresden scholar, Viktor Klemperer, reported just such an experience of the self-mobilization of the *Volksgemeinschaft* in his wartime diary: quietly and surreptitiously he had sought refuge during an attack on Dresden on 20 January 1945 in the 'Aryan' air-raid shelter of the house and squeezed into a corner, whereupon a woman yelled at him 'You are not allowed to stay here!', while a second resident asked emphatically, 'What are you doing here?' He told them he had only entered the cellar in order to fetch coal and just wanted to rest a brief moment, but the 'house community' did not grant him admission, and so he trudged back upstairs to his apartment, while below the *Volksgemeinschaft* remained safely seated.[22]

Another problem also acquired increasing importance as the war went on: how should the growing army of millions of foreign workers be treated? Prisoners of war and Eastern workers (*Ostarbeiter*), according to the air-raid shelter ordinance of 18 September 1942, were categorically prohibited entry into air-raid shelters.[23] For other foreigners, for example Italians, or even the French, the shelters were only to be made available when there was enough space for them. In any case, they had to take second place behind the needs of the *Volksgemeinschaft*. Instead of safe shelters, it was planned to give them protective trenches, which were of dubious value but also inexpensive, and which they would have to dig for themselves.[24] Occasionally, the factory shelters or large bunkers[25] remained open for western forced labourers. Indeed, shelter wardens had a certain leeway that could be used in favour of foreign workers who wanted help – but which also allowed them to decide, for example in the case of hospital shelters, whether those deemed to be racially of 'lesser value' should be admitted to the safer protective rooms or not. Here, too, practice was far from uniform.[26] This was probably the reason why at the beginning of January 1944, for example, the shelter wardens of the city of Bremen were reminded by the security police that prisoners of war and forced labourers were in general forbidden to enter public air-raid shelters unless there happened to be any vacant spaces left by the native population.[27] But for the most part nothing else remained for them but to seek shelter in the protective trenches or other insecure installations often with the result that a disproportionately large number of those killed in the air attacks were East European forced labourers, who as a result became a kind of double victim, first of German exploitation, second of the air war. However, policies of racist exclusion and economic exploitation collided directly over this question. The Reich Air Ministry thought it necessary in mid-August 1943, evidently as a result of the radical exclusionary practices at local level governing access to shelters, to point out to the municipalities that there was no Reich-wide prohibition about foreign workers using air-raid shelters.[28] Even in January 1945 the Ministry indicated that foreign workers used in the German economy were to be protected insofar as it was possible to do so.[29]

Shelters could thereby change their character from an instrument of crisis management to become the site of social unrest and of new forms of potential conflict. From the beginning of 1944, the Security Service (SD) reported intensified complaints from the population against the fact that women with children still received preferential places in the shelters. According to one report, the opinion was heard more and more among those in work that

> unemployed women, children and older, frail persons have no place in the zones affected by the terror. In particular, in the heavily overcrowded transport system one can hear ever more frequently – so the reporter noted – that women with infants ought no longer to have the right to preferential treatment, since they only took away seats from the working population. However, in the shelters it was above all employed women who were the ones to come out in opposition to the privileging of mother and child.[30]

Not only was security coupled with a need for protection, but it was part of popular (*völkisch*) self-mobilization to demand that willingness to work should also be a guarantee that the individual should face less risk. It is obvious that official conceptions of protection and the self-empowerment of the *Volksgemeinschaft* came into conflict here. The radicalization of the policy of exclusion was therefore not simply a consequence of state or party regulations, but could sometimes manifest itself as an 'act from below' in defiance of the official will. Such acts went too far for the apparatus of wartime authority and caused a loss of certainty among SD reporters. The spontaneous behaviour of the population represented a completely distinctive 'morality' – a *Volksgemeinschaft* that had manifestly brutalized itself.

SHELTER IN GREAT BRITAIN

Were these conflicts hallmarks of the National Socialist *Volksgemeinschaft* alone? Did other nations, such as Great Britain, solve these questions in a similar way? Admittedly, in Britain the heavy destruction and human losses feared in September 1940 had at first failed to materialize, but it was soon clear that the available capacity of the shelters for the minority of Londoners who needed them was inadequate, as it was elsewhere.[31] Since most Britons did not use the public shelters from the start of the war onwards, there was no public discourse on the solidarity of life in them. It was the political left in particular who accused the government of being unable to provide sufficient protection for the working population and who exposed the reality of conditions for those who, by choice or necessity, sought to use public shelters. In the end the authorities had to cave in to massive public pressure[32] and open the Underground tunnels, despite the worry of a potentially damaging 'deep shelter mentality'.

From the end of 1940 the readers of the *Daily Herald* and *New Statesman* could follow the reports of Richard Calder about the forms taken by life underground.[33] His accounts talked about poor creatures who under the pressure of the bombs had sought a new place for survival. The shock over the conditions, the concern over the influence of the 'other', and the state of morale – all this was only a part of what distinguished Calder's coverage. For what he saw in the shelters was a world contrary to the one needed by a nation in order to be able to defeat fascism. What he believed he recognized was a hitherto unknown form of self-organization, a new form of democratic community that made a virtue out of hardship and invented the nation anew. The people had, as it were, created their own rules for themselves, elected democratic committees, and created an entertainment programme for the nights of bombing – the 'people's war' was born in this underworld of the Empire and now looked outwards with wit, charm and irony for the elimination of class society. In fact, new urban spaces had emerged in the shelters, at first from pure necessity and against the will of the government. Indignant local residents had themselves fought to get the Underground opened for shelter. This was a 'victory for the working class', in the celebratory rhetoric of the communist *Daily Worker*, a paper that had for some time made the Communist Party of Great Britain into the voice of a 'class-conscious' civilian defence policy and had resonantly criticized the lack of care in the handling of air-raid protection for workers.[34]

In September 1940, following the forced opening of the Underground, the police and Ministry of Health monitored with some concern the way people began to arrange themselves in the shelter; one anxious supervisor reported that they even took along their own bedding.[35] This was not a reassuring spectacle. The authorities laboriously debated how to compel people to find smaller, private shelters in their immediate neighbourhood, rather than use the Underground tunnels, which were regarded as morally dubious and a danger to health. The smaller shelters carried less acute danger of contagious diseases and generally fewer risks than the unsupervised mass gatherings in the tube tunnels. But according to what formal or informal rules was someone to obtain entry to the underground sites? Who would decide this, and who would resolve disputes? Actual social practice may have been at first far less decisive than Calder was aware of in his reports. In the first few weeks, it was unclear in many cases who was responsible and for what tasks, and also how communal life should be organized. The police were indeed responsible for preventing breaches of the peace as well as for safety. However, they transferred the bulk of their duties to self-appointed 'shelter wardens', who in emergencies organized entry into the large-scale shelters and the care of those inside them.[36] Only after some weeks, at least according to the reporters of Mass Observation, did distinctive rules develop, unwritten laws that had to be observed in order to avoid conflict: passageways were to be kept clear, and no one was allowed to stay or settle down to sleep in them; an offence was committed if someone stepped on another's blanket or settled down in a new berth.[37] The reserved spot was sacrosanct – and that also counted for the area surrounding it, since in a situation where there was no longer any privacy, it was important at the very least to retain a small buffer zone that no-one was permitted to invade.[38]

Society began – literally – to observe itself, an experience that was anything but pleasant.[39] Where people of different social backgrounds were brought into contact with one another, boundaries of social distinction still remained, as the police and Mass Observation unanimously reported.[40] Of course people lived together, remained polite, and endeavoured to show their best side, yet 'ordinary' people separated themselves spatially from their 'betters'. Clothing remained an important criterion for differentiation, and although this distinction was not openly expressed, it was nonetheless one that everyone was aware of.

What kinds of projections and conflicts were bound up with life inside the shelters is revealed by the disaster at Bethnal Green, which caused a stir outside London as well. In March 1943, 173 people died in a mass panic at the entrance to Bethnal Green tube station. Bethnal Green was among the largest air-raid shelters in London, used chiefly by workers from the surrounding neighbourhood. As with many other shelters, Bethnal Green was not planned as a mass refuge and was at first only a stopgap. It is no surprise, therefore, that the safety precautions were inadequate: only one entrance, uneven, narrow steps, no railings on the walls, poor ventilation.[41] This was a disaster that many had feared would come much sooner. A commission of inquiry was set up to clarify the background and circumstances of the catastrophe. Questions were asked by the public: could the government not have made better provision, or have raised more money for the protection of the people, or have improved the safety precautions?[42] The waves of indignation rose steeply, and the Home Office was flooded with letters of protest, not least because the Home Secretary, Herbert Morrison, had decided not to publish the report of the planned inquiry.[43] Only a few days after the accident, rumours were rife. In addition to the administrative chaos, it was asked, were there not in fact other causes for the accident and the subsequent distress suffered? Numerous petitions to the Home Secretary were distinctly anti-Semitic in tone: it was alleged that Bethnal Green was a 'Jewish' shelter, and it was the Jews, above all the 'foreign' Jews, who had, quite unlike the British, lost their heads in a difficult situation and now had the victims on their conscience because of their lack of discipline; others claimed that it was the 'false' air-raid officials (because Jewish) who had failed to supervise things properly, a view that conveniently fitted the conspiracy theory that the Jewish air-raid officials were all communists.[44] Xenophobia and anti-Semitic recriminations were by no means a marginal phenomenon and were in fact a part of the discursive self-affirmation of national belonging. The chairman of the commission of inquiry in the end felt compelled to eliminate all doubt regarding the alleged misbehaviour of the Jews by denying that it had any foundation.[45] This step, clearly designed as an act of official duty to call a halt to the wild rumours, highlighted the limits to anti-Semitic discourse in British society.[46]

THE PATHOLOGY OF SHELTER LIFE

The practice of power thus indicated one of the principal differences in the politics of crisis management, even though the perception of the problem was in some respects very much the same. Among these similarities can be numbered the attempt to understand behaviour in the shelters scientifically, so as to eliminate possible sources of danger to public security. The spread of diseases featured alongside panic reactions or a lack of discipline as an expression of 'poor morale', and therefore as a pathological state which came under the purview of doctors and psychologists.

The search for the clinical effects of disorder was a reason why from 1940 scientists from different disciplines cooperated at very diverse levels to acquire the most 'objective' picture possible of the situation in air-raid shelters. One of the leading experts was P. E. Vernon, head of the Department of Psychology at Glasgow University, who at the end of July 1940 had already published the first lessons learned regarding conduct in the air-raid shelters. In his paper, he conceptualized for the Ministry of Information a comprehensive code of conduct that would prevent the widely-feared effects of 'shellshock' and at the same time help air-raid wardens and those seeking shelter to deal appropriately with the novel problems and symptoms of illness.[47] Vernon wrote that no-one should be ashamed of their fear or their feelings in the shelter since air attacks were, after all, existential threats. Nevertheless, he recognized that exaggerated fear or even cowardice could result in a loss of control over one's feelings – a danger that threatened not only the individual but also the community and therefore had to be avoided. In his analysis, Vernon pointed out that fear could manifest itself in different forms of behaviour and therefore had to be closely watched. Apathy or nervous restlessness could be the result of fear, but so too could physical illness.

Vernon advised people to dress warmly and to make themselves as comfortable in the shelter as was humanly possible and thereby to create an atmosphere in which people could overcome fear together. Distraction from the threat seemed to him to be the most important means: cards, darts, knitting, reading, looking after children, keeping busy, drinking tea together, listening to music or singing with others. This would foster community spirit and allow people to forget for a few moments just what a life-threatening situation they were in. Should people nonetheless succumb to panic, then Vernon also had the right recipe for that: people who had conspicuously given way to panic were first of all to be separated from others and then calmed down; they were to be assured that they were well-protected and that the enemy aircraft were still far away. If that did not help, then more drastic steps such as a slap in the face were justified. If fear turned to anger and the person became uncontrollable and a danger to others, then only isolation from the group would help – a reaction that in Vernon's estimation would not be necessary very often, because he found that the majority of people calmed themselves down after a short time. In any event, he maintained that the good example set by wardens and caretakers in the air-raid shelters would be far more helpful than any form of coercion or force.

Even before the heavy air attacks began on London from September 1940, Vernon predicted that humans would swiftly get used to the exceptional situation. That also seemed to be the learning experience from the First World War, when soldiers soon became accustomed to being bombarded day after day. In Vernon's interpretation, citizens in the shelters became 'civilians in the frontline', but adaptable and dogged civilians endowed with the same ability to suffer as soldiers. This reinterpretation of civilian life makes comprehensible what was actually a genuine surprise: namely that, contrary to expectations, the majority of the medical and psychological profession hardly ever diagnosed serious nervous disorder and panic attacks among shelter occupants. Yet how was this phenomenon to be explained? Numerous researchers, including Vernon, attempted to get to the bottom of this question during the period of the Blitz itself. [48]

Unlike the pre-war fears, shelter experiences resulted in no new forms of neurotic illness, in contrast to the psychiatric conditions first defined in the First World War. Though very cautious about drawing sweeping conclusions, Vernon nevertheless suggested an entire series of reasons why in his view the war-neurotic state of shock failed to materialize. The first was the particularly steadfast attitude of the population; this was a pattern of social behaviour that could hardly be rated more highly and arose entirely, he thought, from the spirit that 'Britain can take it'. [49] As a result, every town wanted to follow London's example by matching the great capital's readiness to defend and to suffer. At the same time, Vernon believed he could discern a 'social tradition' of the Empire, as he put it, in which the nation could show its true complexion when faced with a tough situation. What Vernon and others saw as an explanation for the courageous 'shelter mentality' was in fact a self-fulfilling prophecy. The formula of 'Britain can take it' was both cause and consequence in equal measure of a cross-class communal solidarity and the reason why people did not fall ill. Forms of deviant behaviour did not fit into this interpretative field of vision at all. As a result, psychologists began to search for ways to substantiate empirically this phenomenon of 'standing alone' which they had conjured up in their discourse. They concluded that an amalgamation of 'civil mentality' and of group-dynamic solidarity prevented a psychic collapse. The experience also directed the attention of the medical profession to the apparent connection between the decline in the number of female psychiatric patients and the effect of the 'Blitz'.

The German medical profession and German psychologists were also particularly interested in the behaviour of women in the shelter, because they classified their emotional character as a potential security risk. The monitoring of the shelters therefore served a social-sanitary purpose: to do everything in order to avoid 'female' ailments such as 'bunker rage' or 'hysteria' or any other form of uncontrollable emotion. The National Socialist regime spared no effort to regulate the individual's emotional space and to identify a pathology of shelter experience.

Psychologists, the medical profession and health policy makers had from the start of 1941 already identified the shelter as the danger spot for the 'racial body' (*Volkskörper*). With the expansion of the air war from 1942/3, reports accumulated from air-raid protection medical staff and doctors regarding the increasing dangers of the spread of epidemics, the lack of hygienic provision and the progressive neglect of some shelters.[50] The bunker not only offered greater security; on the contrary, over the course of the war it increasingly became a focal point for bacteria and the site of infection, a source of danger of the first magnitude, which was more and more difficult to control through strict health regulation.

From at least 1942 onwards, public health experts anxiously debated the pressing question of the monitoring of the large shelters by the health police. They drafted a wide range of disciplinary regulations to cope with the problem: strict entrance checks, the spatial separation of sick men and women, hospital shelters with double door systems and special hygienic standards, epidemic control regulations to combat contagious diseases and new methods to eliminate swarms of insects. Above all else there was grave concern over the further spread of tuberculosis, for which the air-raid shelters offered ideal conditions and which had to be counteracted by every means.[51]

Whereas in Great Britain the theme of individual provision and education had taken up a broad part of the public air-raid protection campaigns, German recommendations were dominated primarily by the security of the *Volkskörper*. However, correct hygienic conduct was only one side of the coin; on the other side was proper air-raid protection behaviour in the shelters and the self-disciplining of feelings. In dealing with this issue it was suggested that there were at least two serious differences between the fighting front and the home front, between soldiers and civilians. According to the leading physician of the neurological department of the Augusta Hospital in Düsseldorf, Professor Voss, soldiers formed the more robust part of the population in terms of the health of the race; second, civilian reactions to air raids differed considerably from the war situation in the field. 'The soldier,' argued Voss,

> encounters the enemy with the same or better weapons. The knowledge that one could defend oneself is indissolubly linked to the thought of placing of one's own person in the moment of danger. It is completely different with the civilian. He lacks a weapon and therefore also the mental attitude and justified pride bound up with possessing it.[52]

Exposed to danger the civilian must run away and hide, which already weakens his position. But while the soldier is still a soldier after battle, the civilian after the bombs and the night in the shelter once again becomes a private individual attending to his everyday concerns and one who sees all around him many women and children who are not in a position to suppress their 'vital fear'.

In propaganda terms, fighting front and home had indeed merged, but in medical practice the concept of belligerent civilians proved fragile. In the estimation of National Socialist doctors this was due first of all to the fact that the home front was female and thus less stable; and secondly because the endangered *Volksgenossen* lacked the opportunity to strike back at the enemy. They had to bow to their fate and were for the most part defenceless combatants, who had only their good self-conduct as their single but strongest resource. Yet against all expectations, the diagnostic evidence did not confirm the fears, directed principally at women but also some men, that bombardment and shelter life would lead to psychic paralysis, speech impediments or other 'hysterical-functional reactions'. The basis of these medical diagnoses were either conversations that doctors like Voss conducted with patients, or based on the evaluation of patient files drawn up after admission.[53]

In the case of Düsseldorf, the director of the neurological department of the Augusta Hospital came to the conclusion that the number of psychologically damaged patients that had to be treated was relatively small. In his view this was all the more remarkable because air attacks supplied the prerequisites for serious illness and because there was 'no soldierly law' on the home front, unlike at the fighting front, which made flight from the enemy or indiscipline a punishable offence. His diagnosis suggested that the missing mass abnormalities, nervous disorders or panic attacks had nothing to do with the threat of punishment, police persecution or genetic criminality but primarily to do with the 'inner strength' of the *Volksgemeinschaft*. Admittedly, he had observed numerous cases in which patients complained of headaches, sleeplessness, restlessness and feelings of fear. Yet hardly one of them, Voss was happy to conclude, wanted to use the possibility of an air war ailment as an excuse to evade continued work for the war effort.

He found that as a general rule a few tranquilizers were sufficient to overcome the acute state of shock and then – depending upon the degree of disturbance – a few days peace and recovery in a different environment, where the capacity to work could be restored. In his view, anxiety in the shelter or even the experience of being buried alive was not a reason to evade service to the *Volksgemeinschaft*. For the rest, the experience of bombardment exposed how often in peacetime, as a result of far less serious circumstances, the alleged mental state of the individual had been exploited in order to file dubious insurance claims in court. The bombing war showed that 'hysterical reactions' had been attributed much too easily to the effects of an alleged accident, and that compensation claims had been derived from this assumption without justification; thanks to medical-psychological research during the air war, a stop could now be put to the activities of future 'neurosis pensioners', and their 'character failings' ruthlessly exposed. Voss agreed that there had been shocks and terrible events in the bunkers and air-raid cellars of the Reich, but the *Volksgemeinschaft* had proved itself strong enough to handle these. There was no place for the few who had not been strong enough, and no willingness to compensate their weaknesses materially. As early as 1943 Voss evidently had in mind the fact that after the end of the war the question of compensation would arise once more. He thought that this was not a small issue but a serious problem which had to be stamped out during the war, so that the 'strong' did not end up paying for the 'weak'.

Social-utilitarian diagnostics made 'bunker rage' into a phenomenon of the 'sick' part of the *Volksgemeinschaft*; but neither anxiety nor even acute shock produced a state of mind that was out of control, a form of deviant behaviour. They were seen as the understandable reactions to an extraordinarily dangerous situation, but they were not regarded as a legitimate reason to become 'sick' or even to quit work, since the vast majority of the population displayed a 'temperamentally' impeccable conduct, made evident in particular by the astonishingly low number of psychoses. The diagnoses of medical practitioners and psychologists were from their viewpoint evidence of a success story of the healthy 'strength' of the *Volksgemeinschaft* during the air war. Only among children did doctors ascertain a rising number of bed-wetters, evidently due to the fear of air-raid alarms.[54] But it was concluded that even the youngest behaved satisfactorily. The male racial comrade, even more the female, was certainly to be allowed moments of despair, but there was no room for anything more than this in the racial medicine of the bunker.

CONCLUSION

The temporary relocation underground of wartime society which began with the onset of the air war meant a dynamic mobilization of everyday urban life. In the bunkers, air-raid cellars and tunnels, what Jan Philipp Reemtsa has called 'war as a condition of society' manifested itself in a concentrated form. Shelters were spaces where dictatorship and democracy exercised control and disciplined behaviour. They were the subject of propaganda, the sites where protection was promised and conventional gender roles established. Both societies vigorously sought to control access to the shelters and saw in the microcosm of shelter life the harbingers of a new social order, which included the guarantee of safety by the state as well as the social-sanitary compulsion to discipline, cleanliness and obedience. Even though the instruments of repression were less clearly evident in Great Britain than in Germany, there is much to indicate that the respective strategies for solving the problems of war were not only system specific, but at a certain level were part of the communal dynamic typical of the conduct of industrialized war. A fundamental ground for this was the idea that had developed since the inter-war years of a 'totalization' of war, which in Germany and Great Britain was rooted in an acceptance that total war made total mobilization necessary, and that it should be waged not only on distant battlefields but on the home front and with the help of civilians. The transformation of the civilian population into soldiers of the home front represented two things: the precondition and opportunity to be able to wage war from the air on the enemy hinterland, but at the same time a position of potential weakness as the home front seemed to be endangered by unreliable workers and women.

Yet the differences in social practice between 'people's community' and 'people's war' proved to be considerable. War, especially the air war, had as it were shifted the Third Reich into a changed form. One of the attributes of this altered state of society was the radical dynamic that emerged on the one hand from rising societal pressure to conform and on the other hand from newly-created forms of communal self-mobilization and participation in and through the air war. Air-raid cellars and tunnels were therefore central social sites in which conflicts were negotiated and 'solved'. In contrast to the National Socialist dictatorship, British society, despite censorship and the 'state of emergency', had public spaces available in which it could wrestle with forms and strategies for the pacification of social conflict and put the justification for state decisions under critical review. War as a 'state of society' did not make everything happen smoothly. Consensual negotiation processes were in this respect part of the solution, not part of the problem – unlike the situation under National Socialism. The *völkisch* war state had by contrast deliberately rescinded such mechanisms for negotiation and thereby laid the foundation for an ever more radical policy of exclusion and inequality. In the bunkers and air-raid cellars more than in any other site of society at war, protection and compulsion operated directly together; and it was precisely here that the specific National Socialist mixture of racist crisis management, stabilization of dominance and social disintegration manifested itself.

Notes

1   J. P. Reemstma, 'Krieg ist ein Gesellschaftszustand. Reden zur Eröffnung der Ausstellung "Vernichtungskrieg. Verbrechen der Wehrmacht 1941–1944"', edited by Hamburger Institut für Sozialforschung (Hamburg: Hamburger Edition, 1998), 8–13.

2   For example K. K. Patel, *Soldiers of Labor: Labor Service in Nazi Germany and New Deal America, 1933-1945* (New York: Cambridge University Press, 2005).

3   This issue is examined in greater detail in D. Süss, *Tod aus der Luft. Deutschland, Grossbritannien und der Bombenkrieg*, forthcoming (Munich: Seidler, 2011).

4   B. Lemke, *Luftschutz in Grossbritannien und Deutschland 1923-1939. Zivile Kriegsvorbereitungen als Ausdruck der staats- und gesellschaftspolitischen Grundlagen von Demokratie und Diktatur* (Munich: Oldenbourg, 1999).

5   The following is based on R. Blank, 'Kriegsalltag und Luftkrieg an der Heimatfront' in J. Echternkamp (ed.), *Das Deutsche Reich und der Zweite Weltkrieg, Band 9/1: Die deutsche Kriegsgesellschaft 1939 bis 1945. Politisierung, Vernichtung, Überleben* (Munich: Deutsche Verlags Anstalt, 2004), 403-405.

6   On this see the brief pointers in I. Marszolek and M. Buggeln, 'Bunker – Orte, Erinnerungen und Fantasmen' in idem (eds), *Bunker, Zuflucht, Erinnerungsraum* (Frankfurt am Main/New York: Campus, 2008), 10 ff.

7   H. Hammann, 'Der LS-Bunker in der Städte-Planung des Siedlungsverbandes Ruhrkohlenbezirk' in *Baulicher Luftschutz*, 4, 1942, 77-81.

8   Blank, 'Kriegsalltag', 406 ff.; the following draws on this work.

9   G. Graubner, 'Der Wehrgedanke als Grundlage der Stadtgestaltung und Stadtplanung', December 1943, reproduced in W. Durth and N. Gutschow, *Träume in Trümmern. Planungen zum Wiederaufbau zerstörter Städte im Westen Deutschlands 1940-1950*, 2 vols (Braunschweig/ Wiesbaden: Viewig Friedrich Verlag, 1988), ii, 770-776; ibid., 719-729.

10 See the detailed study by M. Foedrowitz, *Bunkerwelten. Luftschutzanlagen in Norddeutschland* (Berlin: Links Verlag, 1998), 9-24.

11 J. R. Gregg, *The Shelter of the Tubes: Tube Sheltering in Wartime London* (Harrow: Capital Transport, 2001), 14.

12 Ibid., 22 ff.

13 J. Newsinger, '"My Country: Right or Left". Patriotism, Socialism and George Orwell, 1939-1941' in P. Kirkham and D. Thoms (eds), *War Culture. Social Change and Changing Experience in World War Two Britain* (London: Lawrence & Wishart, 1995), 29-37.

14 The following section is based on D. Süss, 'Der Kampf um die "Moral im Bunker": Deutschland, Großbritannien und der Luftkrieg' in F. Bajohr and M.Wildt (eds), *Volksgemeinschaft. Neue Forschungen zur Gesellschaft des Nationalsozialismus* (Frankfurt am Main: Fischer, 2009), 124-143.

15 Marszolek, Buggeln, 'Bunker. Orte, Erinnerungen und Fantasmen', 9-25; also M. Thießen, 'Von der "Heimstätte" zum Denkmal: Bunker als städtische Erinnerungsorte – das Beispiel Hamburgs' in ibid., 45-60; also from the perspective of the history of memory of the bunkers S. Wenk (ed.), *Erinnerungsorte aus Beton. Bunker in Städten und Landschaften* (Berlin: Campus, 2001).

16 On the political history of shelter construction in the Third Reich see among others W. Beer, *Kriegsalltag an der Heimatfront. Alliierter Luftkrieg und deutsche Gegenmassnahmen zur Abwehr und Schadensbegrenzung, dargestellt für den Raum Münster* (Bremen: Hauschild, 1990), 108-124; J. Brinkhus, 'Ziviler Luftschutz im "Dritten Reich" – Wandel einer Spitzenorganisation' in D. Süss (ed.), *Deutschland im Luftkrieg* (Munich: Oldenbourg, 2007), 27-40.

17 M. Augé, *Orte und Nicht-Orte. Vorüberlegungen zu einer Ethnologie der Einsamkeit* (Frankfurt am Main: Suhrkamp, 1994); with a focus on the history of the bunker see H. Knoch, 'Transitstationen der Gewalt. Bunker und Baracken als Räume absoluter Verfügbarkeit' in Marszolek and Buggeln, *Bunker*, 309-324.

18 Foedrowitz, *Bunkerwelten*, 117.

19 Ibid., 118.

20 'Erlaß des Reichsministers der Luftfahrt, Inspektion des zivilen Luftschutzes, 7.10.1940: Benutzung der LS-Räume durch Juden' in K. Pätzold, *Verfolgung, Vertreibung, Vernichtung. Dokumente des faschistischen Antisemitismus 1933-1942* (Frankfurt am Main: Fischer, 1984), 270.

21 For example, on Munich see Wolfram Selig and Richard Seligmann, *Ein jüdisches Schicksal*, (Munich: Stadtarchiv München, 1983), 63.

22 V. Klemperer, *Ich will Zeugnis ablegen bis zum letzten: Tagebücher 1933–1945* (Berlin: Aufbau, 1998) vol 8, 14 ff, entry for 20 January, Sunday morning.

23 On this see Foedrowitz, *Bunkerwelten*, 119 ff.

24 On the final phase of the war in Nuremberg see for example W. Wette, R. Bremer and D. Vogel (eds), *Das letzte halbe Jahr. Stimmungsberichte der Wehrmachtspropaganda 1944/45* (Essen: Stadtarchiv, 2001), 365 ff.

25 Aufzeichnungen des belgischen Pfarrers Alphonse Come, entry for 29 November 1944 in Stadt Essen (ed), *Stadtarchiv-Materialien für den Unterricht, Band I: Essen im Luftkrieg* (Essen: Stadtarchiv, 2000), document 31, 85.

26 Foedrowitz, *Bunkerwelten*, 119.

27 Ibid., 121.

28 Stadtarchiv Düsseldorf, IV 1001, Reichsministerium der Luftfahrt, Luftschutz für Ausländer, 13 August 1943.

29 Foedrowitz, *Bunkerwelten*, 121.

30 SD-Berichte vom 10 Februar 1944, Rote Serie, Kulturelle Gebiete in H. Boberach (ed.), *Meldungen aus dem Reich: Die geheime Lageberichte der Sicherheitsdienstes der SS 1938–1945*, 17 vols (Herrsching: Pawlak, 1984), 6318.

31 For an introductory overview see B. Lemke, 'Luftschutzräume im Zweiten Weltkrieg. Strategien-Nutzung-Psychologische Hintergründe' in Marszolek and Buggeln, *Bunker*, 155–169.

32 Ibid, 22 ff.

33 R. Calder, *Carry on London* (London: English Universities Press, 1941), 36–9.

34 *Daily Worker*, 7 September 1940; *Daily Worker*, 10 September 1940.

35 The National Archives, Kew, London (TNA), MH 79/499, Meeting of the Metropolitan Police (MEPO) and Ministry of Health, 6 September 1940.

36 TNA, MEPO, 2/6354, 'Use of Underground Railway Stations as Air-Raid Shelters: Protective Measures and Control, 1941–1943'.

37 T. Harrisson, *Living through the Blitz* (London: Harper Collins, 1976), 119.

38 On the history of Mass Observation see T. Kushner, *We Europeans?: Mass Observation, 'Race' and British Identity in the Twentieth Century* (London: Ashgate, 2004); also D. Süss, 'Krieg, Nation und "Heimatfront". Großbritannien und der Zweite Weltkrieg', *Archiv für Sozialgeschichte*, 47, 2007, 440 ff.

39 Mass Observation, *The Tube Dwellers: The Saturday Book 3* (London: Mayflower Press, 1943), 102 ff.

40 Mass Observation Archive, University of Sussex, (MO-A), File Series 407, 'Sheltering in Middlesborough', 408, Report from Mass Observation on Human Adjustments in Air Raids, 18 September 1940.

41 House of Commons Parliamentary Papers, Ministry of Home Security, Report on an Inquiry into the Accident at Bethnal Green Tube Station Shelter, 3 March 1944, Cmd 6583, January 1945.

42 On this see also J. Bourke, *Fear: A Cultural History* (London: Virago Press, 2005), 236 ff.

43 House of Commons, Parliamentary Debates, Offical Report, 16 March 1943, Vol. 387, Column 1062.

44 TNA, Home Office (HO) 205/236, letter to the Ministry of Home Security, marked 'Bethnal Green', no date but March 1943.

45 House of Commons Parliamentary Papers, Ministry of Home Security, Report on an Inquiry, (Cmd 6583), 12.

46 For the collection of letters see TNA, HO 205/236.

47 MO-A, Topic Collection, Air Raid, TC 23, Box 6/6 H, P. E. Vernon, 'The Conduct of Civil Population in Air-Raids, 30.7.1940'.

48 P. E. Vernon, 'Psychological Effects of Air-Raids', *Journal of Abnormal and Social Psychology*, 36 (1941), 457–476.

49 Ibid., 474.

50 On health conditions in war see the fundamental study by W. Süss, *Der 'Volkskörper' im Krieg. Gesundheitspolitik, Gesundheitsverhältnisse und Krankenmord im nationalsozialistischen Deutschland 1939–1945* (Munich: Oldenbourg, 2003).

51 See among other examples Dr. Schröder, Leitender Stadtmedizinaldirektor Berlin, 'Tuberkulosebekämpfung und Luftkrieg' in *Der Öffentliche Gesundheitsdienst*, 5/6, 1944, 58–60; see also the printing of his own leaflet for tuberculosis patients, ibid., 61.

52 Prof. Voss, 'Beobachtungen aus einer nervenärztlichen Ambulanz im luftbedrohten Gebiet' *Münchner Medizinische Wochenschrift*, 90, 1943, n. 10, 5 March 1943, 185 ff.

53 Peter Feudell, 'Psychische und nervöse Reaktionen der Zivilbevölkerung im Kriege', Diss. med. Leipzig 1944.

54 *Münchner Medizinische Wochenschrift*, 88, 1941, no. 46, 14 November 1941, 1245.

2

The Blackout and the Idea of Community in Britain and Germany

Marc Wiggam

This chapter looks at the role of community in the operation of the blackout. Much of its focus lies in the years leading up to war, where the authorities in Britain and Germany sought to establish not only physical defences against bombing, but a community spirit, or ethic, that would help their populations survive a bombing war. The role of this community spirit is central to a study of the blackout. Within it lie the principles under which citizens of either country were obliged to follow the blackout. As a comparative piece of research, this chapter demonstrates not only the differences in each country's enthusiasm for the blackout, but also the similarities in language and purpose that underlay its operation. Rather than seeing the blackout as a phenomenon discrete to the war itself, it will be seen that pre-war discourses of community and defence played a substantial part in legitimating the blackout amongst the general public. As such, this chapter largely restricts itself to the development of air-raid precautions (ARP) prior to the war, with some comment on its operation during it. What emerges is a consideration of the blackout as being more than a curious and debilitating aspect of the bombing war, but instead as emblematic of the shift to an era of aviation and of total war.[1]

In the early days of the war in Britain, newspapers regularly reported on blackout transgressions amongst the population. The *Bristol Evening Post* ran a story on 7 September 1939 relating the response of an ironmonger in Bournemouth to a policeman who had ordered him to stop showing a light. 'Off back to Germany where you belong,' he told him, 'I have got some work to do, so clear off.'[2] His response, bridling against the obligations of the blackout in a country that saw itself as more free than Hitler's Germany, exemplifies the change the war brought to ideas of individual responsibility. That same day the paper ran an article by Duff Cooper, the former Secretary of State for War and future Minister of Information, who told readers that 'a good first rule for behaviour in wartime is obedience to orders and abstention from criticism, whether it be of the Prime Minister or local air warden.'[3] ARP redefined the idea of the individual's role within the community. This was particularly so in the case of the blackout, where the restrictions were almost entirely universal for the civilian population in both Germany and Britain. The advent of long-range bombing collapsed the distinction between the fighting front and the home front, and to contrast the efforts of Germany and Britain in ARP is to throw into relief not only the political realities of each state's foreign policy, but also its internal politics. This chapter focuses on the latter.

There are two elements to the idea of community that operate within the framework of the blackout.[4] The first is that of the community under threat; that is, the public's fear of attack as a motive force for the development and public assent to the blackout, both in peacetime and in war. The second aspect involves that of the 'social sanction', or the responsibility of a citizen to protect others. Notwithstanding the legal framework which underpins this aspect of the blackout – and which are outside the scope of this chapter – the construction of blackout enforcement as an important element in the defence of the community was fundamental in both countries to how it was understood by the public, and how it was policed. These issues are common to both Germany and Britain, and their roots lie in the years preceding the war.

AIRMINDEDNESS AND THE NATION

The advent of flight brought with it a new realm in which nations could imagine themselves and constitute their political identities. For as much as airspace was now an element of the politics of the state, it was also a space in which the social and cultural politics of the nation could be altered and refashioned. The relationship between the state and the 'airmindedness' of its citizens was therefore every bit as important as the external relationship of the state to its neighbours. Airmindedness is commonly defined as a progressive affirmation of the benefits of aviation. In her study on women and British airspace, Liz Millward regards it as part of a conceptualization of space:

> ... it is the processes and actions of developing the technology, infrastructure, training, finances, legislation, goals and so forth that together produce what is then conceptualized as airspace.'[5]

This conceptualization, while often constructed as a reiteration of existing power structures, is also open to debate and change. Where a nation is described as airminded, it is often within the narrow limits of a positive, progressive attitude to the benefits of aviation, and is therefore not a politically neutral space. To be against aviation, or to be fearful of its consequences, is to be *not* airminded. German advances in aviation before the First World War had left it and France as Europe's foremost airminded nations, much to the chagrin of British commentators at the time. Early discussions within Britain already identified public discipline as a key component of a bombing war, and amid the paranoia of a German invasion, and fears of Britain's naval and imperial decline, 1909 saw Britain experience a wave of 'phantom' airships, apparently drifting across the country unchallenged and menacing the citizenry.[6] The sightings, when reported in the press, so vexed the newspaper magnate Lord Northcliffe that he felt compelled to chastise the nation in print. For Northcliffe, who was visiting Berlin at the time, this apparent spasm of paranoia was nothing less than a national embarrassment. Cabling the *Daily Mail*, the paper ran a two column article by him decrying his fellow countrymen's skittishness, which ended with:

> Germans, who have so long been accustomed to regard Great Britain as a model of national deportment, poise and cool-headed men, are beginning to believe that England is becoming the home of mere nervous degenerates.[7]

The threat of air warfare, and what was assumed to be the febrile character of the British public in the face of it, was of great concern to those who advocated a greater emphasis on aviation in the years leading up to the war of 1914. As a consequence, discipline emerged as one of the key virtues in the discourses that would develop around airmindedness in the interwar years. This skittishness was the product of a genuine fear of the consequences of air warfare, but was also symptomatic of a concern at being outmatched in the air by foreign powers. How advanced a nation was in its aviation industry was both a reflection of its capacity to defend itself, and its place in the rank of modern industrial nations. Airmindedness in this sense encompassed a combination of nationalism and technology.[8] Early debates on aviation in British newspapers and journals in this period were concerned with the country's perceived inability to match its continental neighbours, though, as David Edgerton's study has shown, this perception was based more on material strength than a measure of commitment per se. Thus at the outbreak of war, though British air strength was lower than that of either France or Germany, Edgerton argues that seen as a ratio to the overall strength of each nation's military and naval force, Britain emerged as the more aeronautically inclined power.[9] This was not lost on contemporary observers, as an editorial in the journal *Flight* in June 1914 illustrates:

> The present concentration of the Royal Flying Corps at Netheravon should set at rest the minds of those who still will have it that we are doing nothing – or next to nothing – to bring our aerial defences into line with modern requirements... so far as the records are there to show, it is the largest concentration of aerial strength that has been seen in any army, large or small. On this much we are justified in priding ourselves, and the more so because we felt that our personnel is at least equal to, and probably better than, that of any other of the Great Powers.[10]

What is key here is the relationship between the nation state and technology. The invention of powered flight was exceptionally disruptive to nation states. Where previously the sovereignty of a nation's skies could be regarded as beyond doubt, militarized aviation made this far less certain. It extended the frontline of battle into civilian areas, and with this came a new appreciation of the importance of civilian resolve under bombardment. In the aftermath of the First World War, this crystallized far more quickly in Germany than in the victorious powers. Discussions within government regarding ARP had already begun in the wake of the occupation of the Ruhr by the French in 1923. Bernd Lemke, in his study on the state and preparations for war in the interwar period in Britain and Germany, notes that the tone of the discussions on ARP at this period is one that would last until the German Luftwaffe was dramatically revealed in March 1935.[11] In the immediate aftermath of the First World War it was acknowledged that, given the weakness of the German military, they would not be able to protect the population from enemy aircraft as they had done in the previous war. A memorandum from the Reich Defence Ministry from 1923, outlining the new requirements of ARP, argued that the focus had to be shifted towards a more elaborate system of civilian defence.[12] The memo stated that the occupation of the Ruhr in 1923, and the acquiescence of the major powers during it, meant that a militarily neutered Germany now had to reckon with its more militarized and significantly more powerful neighbours. Germany would have to organize for a war of high explosive and gas bombs dropped on cities from the air, and would therefore have to be secured during peace time so that if war did ever come, the country would be prepared.[13]

This kind of organization would require a fundamental restructuring of how society related to air warfare. In the First World War the organization of ARP in Germany, as well as Britain, had in spite of pre-war efforts ultimately been developed as the war progressed. But the consequences of the rapid development of air warfare after 1918 meant that the German public would have to be significantly more airminded than it had been. This view was strengthened within the German military by the belief that it was the buckling of the will of the home front during the war that had cost Germany victory.[14] The idea of Germany as a weakened power under threat from its militarized and air-capable neighbours would be used to galvanize the nation, with some success, throughout the Weimar period, and with greater success during the Third Reich. Germany's resurgence as a civilian air power and the popular perception of the unjust restrictions made under the Versailles Treaty was later used by the National Socialist regime, when it exploited the fear of bomb attack by neighbouring states as part of its foreign policy, and encouraged civil discipline and unity on the home front.

In 1933, a few months after the takeover of power, a small pamphlet was published outlining the regime's conception of airmindedness; it was written by Dr. Edgar Winter, who was responsible for ARP in the National Socialist Teachers' League. The pamphlet, while dealing with the practical matters of ARP, also detailed the National Socialist world-view with regard to air power, the crux of which remained the same as it had been ten years before: overturning the imposed restrictions of the Versailles Treaty.[15] Airmindedness and ARP were examples of what Herf has called 'the paradox of reactionary modernism': the National Socialist belief in the benefits of technology while at the same time rejecting the ideas of the Enlightenment.[16] This explains how Hitler could both decry the speed of modern life in which, he wrote,

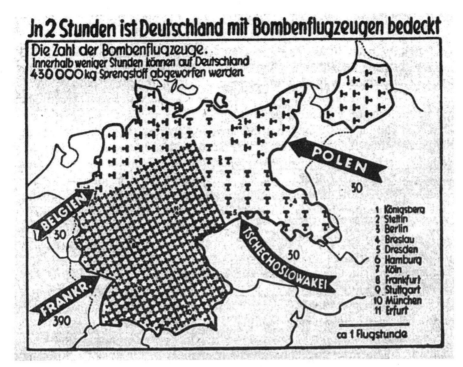

'Germany would be covered with bombers within two hours': German anxiety over air defence before the Luftwaffe, 1933. Dr. Edgar Winter, *Luftschutz tut Not* (Berlin: Verlag fur soziale Ethik und Kunstpflege, 1933), p. 5.

'restlessness and haste mark the thinking of our people', yet at the same time promote aviation – that most modern and potentially disruptive of technologies – as a means of strengthening both the state and the national community.[17] Within Britain, airmindedness was similarly susceptible to political ideology. While competition existed for the definition of airmindedness, broadly defined as that of a pacific internationalism against an imperialistic nationalism, it was arguably the latter that became the dominant discourse in Britain.[18] But being airminded was not the only way of comprehending aviation, and the fear of bombing provided a powerful counter-discourse to airmindedness. Airmindedness became as much about steeling the nation for a bombing war as it was about eulogizing aviation's benefits, and in both countries it promoted unity and collective responsibility in the face of the threat of aerial warfare. As will become clear, fostering this in Britain was far more of a challenge than it proved to be in totalitarian Germany.

MILITARIZATION AND THE COMMUNITY

In March 1936 the film *Things to Come* premiered in Britain. Adapted from H. G. Wells' earlier novel – or rather imagined future history – *The Shape of Things to Come*, Alexander Korda's production mounted an impressive, and still terrifying sequence in which the city of 'Everytown' is bombed to ruins. Preceding it, a father tells his son as he leaves for ARP duties that 'You've gotta do your bit, son. Gotta do your bit!', as the boy beats a march on his drum. The contrast between the film's vision of terror and martial civilian life, and life outside a cinema in Britain in 1936, is stark. British ARP preparations at the time of the film's release were only reluctantly gathering pace. Where the British authorities had avoided for as long as possible the need for public engagement with ARP, German civilian life had become increasingly militarized. The key foundation of the blackout, that of the responsibility to one's neighbour, was formed in this period, and brings into relief sharp differences between Britain and Germany in the way peacetime societies were prepared for the possibility of conflict.

ARP by its nature was invasive, and savoured of war. In no aspect of ARP was this more apparent to the public than the blackout. More than other ARP measures of this period, it was a form of social control. Bunkers, flak batteries and decoy sites were defences that could be constructed from raw materials. But the blackout had to be constructed through the public's assent, and where that was not forthcoming, through the machinery of the state, and through the law. It necessitated a mobilization of the public into a state of awareness of bombing, and in its language and ethic it imagined a 'community' of citizens cooperating in their own defence. J. B. S. Haldane put the case neatly in his 1938 book on ARP: 'If I lose my respirator or go onto the roof during an air-raid I only endanger my own life. But if I leave a light shining through an uncovered skylight I endanger the King in Buckingham Palace and the Prime Minister in Downing Street.'[19] Of course, what was true for the King was true for the Führer, and the dilemma was identical for both British and German citizens. The key difference between Britain and Germany in ARP was the political structure used to prepare it. After taking power the National Socialist Party evolved into an engine of social discipline in all spheres of public life.[20] ARP acquired a central role in the German totalitarian state, and as an element of the *Volksgemeinschaft* – or people's community – embodied an idealized expression of civic responsibility to the state and to the community.[21] Steeling the nation for a bombing war in peacetime would, it was hoped, avoid the collapse of the home front that was popularly believed to have caused German defeat in the First World War. Erhard Milch, state secretary of the Reich Aviation Ministry, wrote in 1937 that German ARP would achieve its goals when

1. the public do not panic in the face of an air raid, even if it were a surprise raid. Nothing strengthens the will to victory more than preparedness.
2. the morale of the nation is not lessened by continuous bombardment.

3. the economic life of the nation, and in particular the war economy, proceeds undisturbed, so that the frontline does not worry over the home front and can commit its full strength to its military tasks.[22]

The militarization of public life under the Nazis stood in marked contrast to British efforts.[23] Though official language spoke of ARP as a duty, much the same as in Germany, it could not take for granted the support of the public. Where political discourse in Germany had effectively been unified after 1933, making it less troublesome to promote ARP as a civic duty, the interwar years in Britain had seen ARP largely underdeveloped due to political inertia, and the resistance expected in familiarizing the public with ARP. It was only the deterioration of the situation on the Continent that spurred efforts to develop ARP. An Air Staff note to the Home Office from June 1935 stated that, in light of recent German manoeuvres and the revealing of their air force, the British public might now be more willing to accept, in their words, 'interference with essential activities' for the purpose of practising blackouts.[24] In Germany, the limiting of public discourse on ARP meant that such a shift in public attitudes was not required and hence, before 1935, while Britain had held no blackout practice, German towns and industry had already held small practices throughout the country.

The social control that the blackout required was contentious from the first trials held in Britain; political dissent could be found on the political left, among the clergy, and from pacifist groups. In a letter to the editor of the *Guardian* in June 1935, the National Council of Civil Liberties – now simply known as Liberty – questioned the legality of blackout exercises and reminded readers that following the blackout restrictions was an entirely voluntary act, with no legal compulsion. It also questioned the motives behind the blackout itself:

> the council is awaiting the results of inquiries which are being pursued by various organizations before declaring its view as to whether the 'black-out' principle is a genuine attempt to protect the civil populations under aerial warfare, or whether it is designed as propaganda for the creation of armament expansion.[25]

If war came, would submitting to the blackout amount to a tacit approval of the war? A Peace Pledge Union pamphlet in 1936 distinguished between war and resisting the preparations for it:

> During a real air-raid, it would not, of course, be right for a pacifist to leave the lights in his house burning; for such action might imperil the safety of his neighbours. But during peacetime the case is clearly different. Blackouts and gas drill are preparations for war, and it is the duty of pacifists to protest, not only in words, but also in action, against such preparations.[26]

This politicized dissent existed alongside views that simply found the blackout trials too much of a nuisance to be bothered with. A Mass Observation report from Bolton in January 1939 surveyed opinion on ARP and found a public confused and often cynical.[27] In the suburbs of London, a Mass Observation interviewer reported that:

> One woman of 65 did not understand the meaning of ARP Another, asked what she thought of ARP, replied: 'I'd rather not say, thanks. It's best to leave it alone'. A third answered: 'I can't be bothered with all that now.' (Turning to greengrocer, also at door): 'I can't be bothered with ARP now, can I, when I've the dinner to get?'[28]

It is difficult to assess how successful German practice blackouts were in comparison during this period. In 1932, early discussions within the *Reichsverband der Deutschen Industrie* identified politicized dissent amongst some industrial workers. Their solution was for the German press to cover Russian advances in air warfare and air-raid precautions, so that workers would 'finally realize that the protection of their own lives is important', and not 'obstinately block' these early attempts at ARP.[29] After the National Socialist takeover of power in 1933, such dissent becomes harder to gauge, and indeed to mount, but there are indications that in spite of the restrictions on freedom during this period, authorities still encountered some resistance. No formal powers to enforce early trial blackouts were issued to begin with, though in 1934 some police forces were using sections of the law related to firefighting to enforce ARP measures.[30] A memorandum disseminated among a German industrial lobby group in 1935 carried a report of the Police Chief of Görlitz criticizing individuals who failed to comply with or sabotaged ARP works, and announcing his intention to use all his powers to prosecute them and make them known through the local press.[31] And in an article that perhaps assumed at least some antipathy to the exercise, the *Deutsche Allgemeine Zeitung* reminded Berlin's residents on the day of a citywide practice in 1935 that it was in their interest to blackout their rooms as completely as possible, and not simply to go to bed earlier than usual.[32] But these small instances of intransigence do not add up to any kind of concerted, politicized resistance, for the simple reason that such dissent was not allowed in Germany.

The collective responsibility for ARP and the blackout was only ever as secure as its collective understanding, and the anxiousness that attended ARP and blackout education in Britain was in marked contrast to Germany, where ARP became increasingly invasive and extended throughout the public sphere during the 1930s. In public spaces throughout the country, *Mahnmale* (ARP monuments) were erected to publicize local branches of the *Luftschutzbund*. These installations took the form of large bombs attached to a plinth, looking rather like exclamation marks, with reminders or slogans inscribed underneath. Major cities hosted exhibitions of ARP measures and equipment, with all sections of society encouraged to attend. Prior to an exhibition in Dortmund in 1935, the area's *Kreisfrauenschaftsleiterin* (leader of the National Socialist Women's League) issued a memorandum exhorting women to visit. Repeating the by now familiar argument of Germany's vulnerability to aerial attack, it stated that:

> No German woman, no German mother who loves her children, her country and her fellow citizens, can afford to miss this opportunity to attend an absorbing exhibition on the aerial threat and air-raid precautions.[33]

These exhibitions made explicit the link between Nazi ethics and ARP. Schools in particular were singled out as ideal places for disseminating good ARP practice. In 1933, the government was already advising school administrators of the benefits of teaching students ARP. Though helpful in mobilizing the spirit of *Volksgemeinschaft* amongst the students, it was also assumed that the benefits of teaching them would extend to the wider community, passing good blackout practice on to their parents.[34]

The German experience contrasts with the voluntarist ethic on which the authorities in Britain had so far relied. During the Czech crisis of September 1938, councils across the country struggled to mobilize their ARP plans, and to recruit volunteers. In Bristol, on 24 September, the council estimated a shortfall of almost 8000 volunteers to carry out its ARP plan adequately.[35] The response by government was to professionalize the service, improving training and, though it remained a voluntary service, instituting a quasi-military system of ranks, uniforms and discipline.[36] This formed a strange paradox: while ARP was promoted as a voluntary civic duty, recruitment and retention of volunteers could only be improved by militarizing it. This was perhaps an acceptance of the fact that ARP made little sense unless set within the framework of an imminent threat. In Germany, propaganda highlighting the danger from neighbouring air forces had been used for a long time to instil an awareness of ARP's importance. By the outbreak of war in 1939, the German *Reichluftschutzbund*, its ARP organization, counted 15 million members;[37] in Britain, ARP counted 1.6 million members. But these figures, when compared, do not necessarily indicate preparedness for war, or even the effectiveness of either organization. Rather, the disparity in membership is more indicative of the far larger political role that ARP and the air threat had played in Germany, and of the desirability to join official bodies and so demonstrate loyalty to the party and state – though this in itself was no guarantee of public assent. Goebbels, writing in the journal of the *Reichsluftschutzbund* in 1939, deplored a widespread response to officials by intransigent citizens who refused to toe the official line: 'The Führer doesn't want a war, so there won't be one. So why should I bother with air-raid precautions?'[38] Such attitudes would change only when the Allied bombardment began.

SOCIAL EFFECTS

It was not until the beginning of the war that the social effects of the blackout could be observed. Pre-war exercises in both countries had been limited by their hours of operation, which in Britain's case frequently took place in the dead of night when few people were awake. Even the most extensive public exercises in Germany, which ran in some cases over a few days, brought a caveat from the undersecretary of state in the Air Ministry, Dr Kurt Knipfer, that enthusiasm over a practice blackout's success, where the light was simply switched off and everything allowed to come to a halt, was unjustified. It was not a case, he claimed, of turning out the lights for a short while, but about learning to live and work under these circumstances.[39] In both countries, pre-war attempts at familiarizing the public with the practical realities of ARP, as opposed to its political or ethical aspects, were consistently deferred in preference to limiting any disruption it would cause. It was not until the wartime blackout began that the changes it brought to community relations became manifest. In the meantime, it had to be based on more abstract notions of community.

In Germany, the idea of the *Volksgemeinschaft* had been actively promoted throughout the public sphere – or at least what constituted a public sphere within a totalitarian state. Notwithstanding the very real tensions that remained buried beneath its political and cultural uniformity, the concept of the *Volksgemeinschaft* was presented as if it were a unified public discourse, closely controlled by the state.[40] The blackout formed one of the elements of the *Volksgemeinschaft*. It helped to reify it, in that its totality and observance required an appreciation of individual responsibility to the community. At the same time, it relied upon the idea of the *Volksgemeinschaft* for its successful operation – creating a symbiosis between the two. When the war began, it was hoped that awareness of the culture of community responsibility would steel the German home front to prevent it from buckling again as it was alleged to have done in 1918.

In Britain, the *Volksgemeinschaft*'s principle of the 'community before the individual' was one that political and cultural élites had to establish quickly once war had broken out. In particular, programme policy makers at the BBC discussed how they could iterate the strength and unity of the nation under wartime conditions. Early discussions were held on how best to mitigate the class differences that the blackout had begun to highlight among the BBC audience. In the early days of the war public entertainment was drastically reduced, both through ARP restrictions and the unwillingness of the public to chance the blackout. With more people at home, their entertainment had to be found, among other activities, through the radio. As a consequence the BBC audience mushroomed, and it became increasingly sensitive to the mood of the nation and its role in the war.[41] A memorandum of 16 September 1939 cautioned against the scheduling of either too many escapist or highbrow items, now that so much of the population – what one document referred to as the

Corporation's expanded and more 'lowbrow' audience – was forced to listen to the radio under blackout conditions.[42] In further memoranda it was argued that the audience might be comforted by widening the scope of programming to reflect 'life in different parts of the country.'[43] As another respondent put it, 'Wales would like to hear the unaffected voice, thoughts and good cheer of the Scotsman, the Northcountryman, the Devonian and the Londoner', and vice versa.[44] By expanding the BBC audience, the blackout formed part of the process by which the nation was represented through its culture, and discussions at the BBC to construct something analogous to the idea of the people's community through its radio programming was part of a wider discourse, propagated by the media and government throughout the war, of a coherent national wartime identity.[45]

Representations of a unified nation at war were, however, susceptible to challenges from lived experience, and the policing of the blackout, and in particular the fines issued to poor and wealthy blackout offenders, could serve to undermine community cohesion. In late 1940, Bow Street magistrates were in particular noted for large fines that, in the view of the Home Office, were apt to cause grievance and undermine the national interest.[46] As one respondent to a Mass Observation survey put it, 'three pounds isn't enough to make Lord Nuffield stop and think, but it's enough to make my mother go without breakfast for a fortnight.'[47] Labour relations were also strained under the blackout, and in a particular case the Trades Unions Congress made representations to the Home Office complaining of Exeter City Council's refusal to upgrade the city's lighting in 1940, in contrast with its neighbour Bristol.[48] Though initial complaints blamed the city's Chief Constable for rejecting the new lighting standard, it was in fact the decision of the council itself to reject the new lighting system on the grounds of cost.[49] But though the maintenance and policing of the blackout and its effect on the community in Britain was undoubtedly a political issue, its organization was free of any one party's influence.

By contrast, in Germany the *Blockwart*, or block warden, who was responsible for the operation of ARP and the blackout in his local area, was a functionary of the National Socialist Party. This explicitly politicized the nature of ARP,[50] and was cemented later in the war in 1944 when Hitler drew the organization and administration of ARP into the Party itself.[51] In an article published in *Die Sirene*, the journal of the *Reichluftschutzbund*, one writer, himself a *Blockwart*, wrote that they should consider themselves 'the ARP-father of the block.'[52] The paternalism enthusiastically promoted by the writer imagined ARP as a 'family'.

In 1940, when it became clear that persistent offences against the blackout were occurring despite the war – and despite the *Volksgemeinschaft* – Hitler ordered the extension of the punishment of blackout offenders to the removal of their electricity for a minimum of eight days. But in an admission perhaps of the scale of the offences, the memo also allowed for the removal of electricity from entire communities for a minimum period of seven days.[53] In this way, Hitler made clear that where the individual had a responsibility to the community, so

'The Block Warden – the father of the Block': visions of the ARP community shortly before the war, 1939. *Die Sirene*, 5, 1939.

too did a community to its neighbours. The persistence of low-level transgressions throughout the war, through complacency and laziness, even when the bombing raids escalated, was an affront to the idea of the *Volksgemeinschaft* and to the authority of the party.

There is, perhaps, an implicit assumption that the end of the blackout would have brought enormous relief. In lifting the blackout, one would not only be free to show a light, but also free of the obligation to conceal it. The end of the war in Germany has left few clues as to how civilians dealt with the cessation of blackout, announced with the country's surrender on 8 May 1945. The eventual collapse of the German state followed from years in which the urban infrastructure was progressively destroyed, assaulted with increasing force by Allied aircraft. This left German civilians with far more to cope with than their British counterparts.[54] Interruptions to the electricity supply were frequent, and any relief that might have been prompted by the absence of the blackout was tempered by continued difficulties in everyday living conditions. On 23 April 1945, a week after the battle for Berlin was launched by the advancing Red Army, local officials in Berlin received a memorandum from the city's Police President, calling for yet tighter control of the blackout. Its content gives an indication of how perverse the restrictions had now become, after the hundreds of bombing raids already experienced and in the face of the city's failing infrastructure:

> Every householder must, in their own interest, secure their blackout ... should any break in the supply of electricity be followed by an air raid, during which the householder leaves the premises, it is best that any lights are turned off and pulled from sockets ... As well as this, upon returning it is advised that blackout materials are checked *before switching on any lights* in case any were damaged during a raid ... Even when the All Clear has been given, bright light should not be allowed to fall on the street, since it is possible that enemy aircraft may still be over the city district.[55]

By this stage, the restrictions could have served little purpose, helping only to bolster what faltering sense of collective will to resist and fight the Nazi leadership tried to instil among German citizens.[56]

Reactions in Britain are far easier to gauge, and what is perhaps interesting among them is the sense of guilt that the use of light now provoked. The blackout in Britain was lifted in stages, as the war drew to a close. On 17 September 1944, the restrictions were relaxed to allow for a greater degree of lighting. But the immediate response to the dim-out, as it was known, was not one of unbridled enthusiasm, but of considerable caution. Years of living under blackout conditions, where any light in the dark meant insecurity, made the population at large hesitant to change, even though commercial enterprises were keen to exploit the new freedom. This paradox was explored in a Mass Observation report from 19 September 1944:

> Practically everyone with whom [the investigator] has spoken continues to enforce the blackout regulations, perhaps not so carefully as in the earlier days of the war, but they haven't taken advantage of the revised regulations. The general feeling is, that the war isn't over yet. When it is, they'll pull down the blackout curtains, and make a bonfire of them.[57]

Others commented that the new freedoms gave them 'the sort of feeling that I had as a child when I picked an apple that wasn't yet ripe and had thrown it away'.[58] One young woman, living with her mother in the Welsh countryside, wrote of the gradual resumption of an almost full blackout in her house:

> September 17 1944
> The beginning of the 'dim out.' I put some different curtains on the bedroom windows but left the rest.

> September 18 1944
> I've just been outside and the light from the living-room through the green curtains seems a blaze of light! I almost felt scared when I saw it, but it does light up the road.

> September 25 1944
> It's no good. We're too used to a blackout. Having no curtains at all on the scullery and bathroom windows made us feel too guilty, naked and unprotected, so I've had to put some back. Mum, knowing there was a light showing outside while I was at choir practice last night, was frightened of being alone.[59]

Though there were, of course, many reasons for this lack of enthusiasm, the duty to the community that had been a focal point of the operation of the blackout during the war remained one of the main reasons for this reticence. The obligations that had been evident to ARP planners in Britain before the war began, yet had been so difficult to promote because of their militarizing nature, had, by its end, become accepted and, to a certain extent, embedded into normative behaviour. The permanence of this behaviour, as the post-war world entered an age of nuclear stand-off, is beyond the scope of this chapter. But by comparing Britain and Germany it is clear that the more militarized a society becomes, the more the state focuses on articulating the bonds of community, and the role the community assumes in defence of the nation. These bonds, however manufactured they may indeed be, formed the basis for the language by which universal prescriptions on individual liberty, such as the blackout, were legitimated.

CONCLUSION

This chapter has sought to reconsider the blackout not only as a phenomenon of the bombing war, but as a reflection of pre-war discourse on the idea of community, on which the blackout system relied in order to function effectively. The blackout was not simply an aspect of civil defence, but a mechanism that redefined the individual's wartime responsibility to the community, and what that community meant. There was a contrast here between Britain and Germany, one a liberal democracy and the other a totalitarian state. Civil defence has a role in constituting the nation state, and defining the community within it. In Germany, pre-war discussion and planning of civil defence was openly committed to these aims. In Britain, where minimal interference from government in daily civilian life was one of the tenets of democracy, this proved to be far more of a challenge. Though it was of course the bombs themselves that provided ultimate justification for the blackout, in both countries the language that legitimated the blackout and the punishment of blackout offences made explicit reference to the obligations of the individual to the wartime community. To return to this chapter's initial discussion of how technology has an impact on the state and the community within it, militarized flight had the consequence of requiring a new way of organizing peacetime communities in preparing for war. In the post-war period, the certainty of annihilation by nuclear weapons was to bring a change in the perception of community and its prospects – or otherwise – for survival. In this earlier age the potential survivability from bombing rested on how firmly the idea of community was embedded in each nation. The blackout, as part of the passive defensive measures, was one of the most important instruments in articulating that sense of community.

Notes

1 I would like to thank the editors for their comments on drafts of this chapter, as well as Professor Jeremy Black and Dr Bruce Haddock for their advice.
2 'More People Fined over Lights', *Bristol Evening Post*, 7 September 1939, 7.
3 'Sound Rules for Behaviour in Wartime', ibid., 6.
4 The use of the word 'community' in this chapter relies on Benedict Anderson's influential idea

of the nation as an 'imagined community', with nationality a culturally generated artefact. ARP is examined within this frame as another mechanism through which nationality – and in particular a wartime nation – is prepared for and constituted.

5 L. Millward, *Women in British Imperial Airspace, 1922–1937* (Quebec: McGill-Queens University Press, 2007), 18.

6 A. Gollin, *The Impact of Air Power on the British People and Their Government, 1909–14* (London: Macmillan, 1989), 49–63.

7 Cited in ibid., 60.

8 P. Fritzsche, *A Nation of Fliers: German Aviation and the Popular Imagination* (Cambridge, Mass.: Harvard University Press, 1992), 6.

9 D. Edgerton, *England and the Aeroplane: An Essay on a Militant and Technological Nation* (London: Macmillan, 1991), 10.

10 Anonymous, 'Editorial Comment – the Army Air Manoeuvres', *Flight*, 6/23 (5 June 1914), 587–88.

11 B. Lemke, *Luftschutz in Großbritannien und Deutschland 1923–1939* (Albert-Ludwigs-Universität, 2001), 127–9.

12 Bundesarchiv-Militärarchiv, Freiburg (BA-MA), RH 43 II / 1295, memorandum, 18 May 1923.

13 Ibid.

14 P. Fritzsche, 'Machine Dreams: Airmindedness and the Reinvention of Germany', *The American Historical Review*, 98/3 (June 1993), 688–9.

15 See Dr E. Winter, *Luftschutz Tut Not* (Berlin: Verlag fur soziale Ethik und Kunstpflege, 1933).

16 See J. Herf, *Reactionary Modernism: Technology, Culture and Politics in Weimar and the Third Reich* (Cambridge: Cambridge University Press, 1984).

17 Cited in R. Overy, *The Inter-War Crisis 1919–1939* (2nd edn.; London: Pearson Education, 2007), 25.

18 Millward, *Women in British Imperial Airspace, 1922–1937*, 20–8.

19 J. B. S. Haldane, *A.R.P.* (London: Victor Gollancz, 1938), 81.

20 R. J. Evans, *The Third Reich in Power* (London: Penguin, 2006), 414–503.

21 A. Nolzen, 'Politische Führung und Betreuung der Bevölkerung. Die NSDAP im Bombenkrieg, 1939–1945', in B. Lemke (ed.), *Luft- und Zivilschutz in Deutschland im 20. Jahrhundert.* (Potsdam: MGFA, 2007), 90–4.

22 E. Milch, 'Was Müssen Wir Tun?', in Dr. Ing. E. Hampe (ed.), *Der Zivile Luftschutz: Ein Sammelwerk aller Fragen des Luftschutzes* (2nd edn; Berlin: Otto Stollberg, 1937), 14.

23 Lemke, *Luftschutz in Grossbritannien und Deutschland*, 67; R. Overy, *The Dictators* (London: Penguin, 2005), 441–82.

24 The National Archives, Kew, London (TNA), HO45/18132, Air Staff note, 27 June 1935.

25 'Letters to the Editor – '"Rehearsals" For Air Raids – Are The "Blackouts" Legal?', *The Guardian*, 15 June 1935, 5.

26 The British Library, WP.8951, Peace Pledge Union pamphlet, 'Three recommendations for members of the Peace Pledge Union', n.d. but circa 1936.

27 Mass Observation Archive, Sussex University, (MO-A) Box 1 Folder 1/A, Casual interviews on ARP, 9 January 1939.

28 Ibid.

29 Bundesarchiv Berlin (BAB), RS36/2715, memorandum of Reichsverband der Deutschen Industrie, 31 December 1932.

30 BAB, R36/2718, memorandum from Reich Ministry of the Interior to the Reichsverband der Deutschen Industrie, 1 August 1934.

31 BAB, R36/2718, memorandum of the Reichsverband der Deutschen Industrie, 29 January 1935.

32 'Die grosse Verdunkelungsübung', *Deutsche Allgemeine Zeitung*, 19 March 1935, 3.

33 Stadtarchiv Dortmund, 113-12, 'Aufruf! Deutsche Frauen, Deutsche Mütter!', circa June 1935.

34 Stadtarchiv Soest, P22 1055, letter 14 March 1935.

35 Bristol Records Office, M/BCC/ARP/1, Air Raid Precautions Committee minute book, minutes for 24 September 1938.

36 T. H. O'Brien, *Civil Defence* (London: HMSO, 1955), 201–18.

37   Lemke, *Luftschutz in Großbritannien und Deutschland 1923–1939*, 407.
38   J. Goebbels, 'Luftschutz-Daemmerung', *Die Sirene*, 2 (1939), 30.
39   BAB, R36/2718, Reichsgruppe Industrie report, 19 July 1935.
40   D. Welch, *The Third Reich: Politics and Propaganda* (2nd edn; London: Routledge, 2002), 60–80.
41   S. Nicholas, 'The People's Radio: The BBC and its Audience 1939–1945', in N. Hayes and J. Hill (eds), *'Millions Like Us?': British Culture in the Second World War* (London: Liverpool University Press, 1999), 68–70.
42   BBC Written Archives, Box R34/3161, internal memorandum on programming, 16 September 1939.
43   Ibid., memorandum BBC West region, 'Broadcast Programmes', 27 September 1939.
44   Ibid., memorandum BBC Wales region, 'Broadcast Programmes', 22 September 1939.
45   S. O. Rose, *Which People's War? National Identity and Citizenship in Britain, 1939–1945* (Oxford: Oxford University Press, 2003), 1–28.
46   TNA, HO45/18628, memoranda, 5, 21 and 30 October 1940.
47   MO-A, 304.2–3 'People's attitude to the blackout', 27 July 1940.
48   After the war's first winter in Britain, a new system of lighting was quickly developed to help minimize the blackout's impact on town and city centres. Its adoption, however, was left to the discretion of Local Authorities, and not all cities chose to adopt this system.
49   Exeter Records Office, ECA ARP Box 19/220, letters between Home Office, Trades Union Congress and Exeter City Council, May 1940, May 1941.
50   For an excellent discussion on the role of the *Blockwart* as intermediary between the public and the state see D. Schmiechen-Ackermann, 'Der "Blockwart"', *Vierteljahrshefte für Zeitgeschichte*, 48/4 (2000), 575–602.
51   BAB, R43 II/665, edict, 25 August 1944.
52   Anonymous, 'Einer von 700,000: Der Unbekannte Luftschutzmann hat das Wort', *Die Sirene*, 5 (1939b), 124.
53   BA-MA, RL/2/II/97, circular letter from M. Bormann (Party Chancellery) to all Gauleiter, 17 August 1940.
54   J. Stephenson, *Hitler's Home Front: Württemberg under the Nazis* (London: Continuum, 2006), 313–43.
55   Berlin Landesarchiv, F Rep. 240/B0058, Bekanntmachung des Polizeipraesidenten, 13 April 1945.
56   U. Beck, *Under the Bombs: The German Home Front 1942–1945* (Lexington: University of Kentucky, 1986), 188–9.
57   MO-A, Box TC23/12/H, A note on the relaxation of the blackout, 17 September 1944.
58   Ibid., Lifting of the blackout, 27 September 1944.
59   Imperial War Museum, Box 82/37/1, Diaries of Miss E. G. Davies, 17–25 September 1939.

3

Evacuation in Italy during the Second World War: Evolution and Management*

Elena Cortesi

International historiography has long designated the Second World War a 'total war'. In many theatres, it represented a political, ideological and also racial conflict aiming at the total annihilation of the opponent. In many countries, too, it acquired the characteristics of a civil war. Almost all belligerents mobilized their economies and societies on an unprecedented scale. Above all, it is regarded as a total war because it was fought *against civilians* on the basis of a premeditated strategy, which rendered civilian populations and the sites of civil life part of the military conflict, and designated them as legitimate, even preferred military targets, in order to ensure a fast and total victory over the enemy. The most common reaction of civilians faced with the violence of war was to escape elsewhere. As populations fled from air raids and from the approaching front lines, evacuation generally occurred spontaneously, although it was often also prompted or ordered by the competent authorities. Although it took place in all the countries involved in the conflict, evacuation has been, and remains at present, an under-researched topic.

The official documents issued by the central and local organs of the Fascist regime – in particular the Ministry of Internal Affairs[1] and the prefectures – as well as the thousands of letters intercepted during the war by the *Provincial Commissions for Postal Censorship*, the diaries, memoirs and testimonies of the time, all delineate the evacuation process as a physical and psychological survival strategy, which was characterized by phases both of escape and return and involved at various times and in different ways millions of Italians.[2] This process also emerges as an important element in the study of the mechanisms that contributed to the decline in the consensus for the Fascist regime.

In Italian historiography, there is no large-scale study of this phenomenon. Only a few texts examine the mechanisms, phases and problems related to the process of evacuation on the basis of specific cases.[3] Numerous contributions have touched upon the theme in various ways, including it among the many dramatic aspects of life during the war,[4] while others have accorded it a central place in their work as a common denominator within a collection of testimonies or in order to analyse the experience of evacuation and its consequences within small groups. They do not, however, examine the spontaneous

*Translated from the Italian by Tania Flamigni and by the editors.

or predetermined aspects which characterized it, or the economic, political and social problems which accompanied it.[5]

A full reconstruction of the process of evacuation in all its elements is, in effect, thwarted by the extreme complexity of factors related to the geographic, economic and social characteristics of the territories from which and towards which evacuation took place; by the different ways in which local authorities intervened; and by the chronological and geographical differences which characterized military developments throughout the peninsula. The scale (and the direction) of escape from the bombed cities was in turn determined by the number and intensity of the air strikes; by the type of shelters built within urban centres for the protection of citizens; by the availability and cost of transport; and by the receptive capacity of the surrounding areas. However, it is possible, thanks to the extensive documentation held in both central and local state archives, to attempt to reconstruct the decisions of the central authorities concerning evacuation, and to observe the movements of Italians from the viewpoint of those authorities. This chapter will identify and explore three main phases of the evacuation process in Italy. It will then analyse the specific case of evacuation of children – one that often required separate attention and different directives and problems.

THE FIRST PHASE

The first phase runs from May 1940 (just before Italy's entry into the war on 10 June 1940) to October 1942. During that period there was an initial partial transfer of the population, starting at the end of May 1940 as a response to the evacuation ordered by the war authorities from an increasing number of territories near the French border. This process was subsequently amplified by the bombing of the large urban centres in the north, which began on the night of 10 June, and soon extended to the south. This was an essentially spontaneous movement, though strongly encouraged by the Fascist authorities, from the cities to the surrounding hills and countryside.

The central authorities of the Fascist regime appear to have seriously underestimated the problems related to evacuation, both directly before and immediately after Italy's entry into the conflict. Although flight from urban centres did not reach a mass scale at once, it gradually increased over the first three years of war. The authorities' failure to plan for evacuation at the outset seems truly surprising, if one considers that evacuation was the centrepiece of the Fascist regime's pre-war civil defence strategy. Indeed, the evacuation of cities with more than 100,000 inhabitants had been discussed in the early 1930s, when the Central Interministerial Committee for Anti-aircraft Protection (CCIPAA) – a body initially (1930–1932) dependent on the Ministry of Interior, and then on the War Ministry – had begun to devise the organizational basis of a civil defence system. The CCIPAA immediately recognized the extreme difficulty, due to logistical, economic and psychological factors, of creating such a system in the larger cities. As early as 1931, the representative of the Committee, the army General Giannuzzi Savelli, suggested that the most effective defence policy would be the reduction of the number of people to be sheltered.[6] Consequently, between 1934 and 1939 the CCIPAA prepared a national evacuation plan, which decreed the forced clearing of the national borders along pre-established routes and indicated 55 main cities to be abandoned in case of war. The remaining cities and most of the smaller towns were designated as receiving areas.[7] While not ruling out long-distance transfers, the exodus of the population was to be organized essentially within each province. The entire process of organization and management of evacuation was left to local authorities; coordination and control were to be carried out by the prefects, while logistics and assistance – that is, actual day-to-day economic management – were assigned to the municipalities.

The city-dwellers to be evacuated were divided into three groups: compulsory evacuees, those who could leave voluntarily and those who were obliged to remain. The first group included, for example, children between the ages of 3 and 10, the elderly over the age of 70, the sick, the bedridden and convicts. It is not clear, however, whether they were to be immediately evacuated at the start of hostilities, or simply ordered to leave when necessary. Among those forced to remain within cities were military staff, war production workers, anti-aircraft personnel, civil servants, service workers and public transport operators. All those who did not fall within these categories had the possibility to choose. Those compelled to evacuate would be assisted by the prefectures, the Party organizations and the municipalities in the receiving areas, while individuals leaving on a voluntary basis had to provide entirely for their own needs. On the basis of this plan, which was sent out to the prefectures at the beginning of 1939, the regime expected the urban population to decrease by half. An evacuation plan was thus ready in case of need, but the likelihood of its being put into practice was considered by the regime to be rather remote. Indeed, in the following months circulars issued by the Ministry of War modified the project by steadily limiting compulsory transfer, while encouraging voluntary departures. In a circular sent out on 6 June 1940, four days before Italy's entry into the war, the category of compulsory evacuees was completely eliminated,[8] while four days earlier another circular invited the prefects to 'facilitate, from this moment on, the voluntary exodus of the population ... giving information about ... the expediency of not waiting until the last minute to reach safe locations.'[9]

Meanwhile, from the last days of May, in view of Italy's imminent entry into the conflict, the regime was forced to deal with the first population transfers caused by the evacuation of increasingly wider security zones near the French border. When, during the nights following 10 June, the first air raids hit the major urban centres in the north-west,[10] military requirements combined with the many difficulties provoked by the lack of a precise management plan and clear assignment of duties, created the first short circuit. Indeed, while the Ministry of the Interior, through a new office (*Ufficio I*),[11] especially created on 10 June, was encouraging the voluntary transfer from the cities of Turin, Cuneo, Aosta, Milan, Genoa and Savona, the War Ministry sent evacuees from the French border to some of the same cities. And while evacuations ordered by the military authorities continued, on 20 June the Ministry of the Interior, facing (after only 10 days) increasing difficulties in managing the first transfers, issued a telegram to the prefects ordering them to limit the voluntary exodus. In addition, those who had already evacuated were to be advised to return to their own homes.

The first practical attempt at managing evacuation was a failure; the 1931 idea of protecting the general population through transferrals had demonstrated its limitations. However, the developments of evacuation policy between June 1940 and the autumn of 1942 seem to have been very few and of little consequence. The 1939 Evacuation Plan and the ensuing circulars represent the only project elaborated by the regime up until November 1942, even though air raids continued on all the major Italian cities in both the north and the south. The only relevant action taken during those three years was the creation, within the Ministry of the Interior, of the Inspectorate for War Services (or, from 16 December 1942 the General Directorate for War Services). Among other duties, this division was charged with the central coordination of the evacuation process, which was thus removed from the competency of the War Ministry.[12]

THE SECOND PHASE

From the end of October 1942, Anglo-American air forces carried out a series of extremely heavy and continuous air strikes across the Italian peninsula. Their number and severity caused what the Fascist authorities labelled 'mass evacuation'. This was not an understatement: hundreds of thousands of Italians left the larger cities, the major industrial complexes and ports, moving mainly to the immediate vicinities, but also, once the receptive capacity of those areas had reached saturation point, to more distant territories, which could provide spaces and structures to accommodate them. The second phase of the evacuation process lasted until October 1943.

Evidence emerging from the documents indicates that the initial reaction of central offices and authorities was a frantic attempt to manage and regulate this process, which was negatively affected by delays, by the urgency of the situation, and by a growing confusion in regard to the strategy to be adopted in order to rescue city dwellers and to protect the cities. In short, what took place in regard to evacuation was a mechanism defined by Italian historian Massimo Legnani as 'retroactive mobilization' (in reference to the Fascist organization of war economy). 'Retroactivity' clearly restricted the efficacy of the programme, although less than at first anticipated, particularly if we consider the shortfalls and improvisation which characterized other important sectors of the Fascist war economy, such as the food industry.

The policies adopted by central government in order to manage mass evacuation were at times hasty and confused, occasionally giving rise to contradictions and to an overlapping of competences, and often required further telegrams and circulars clarifying and setting new directives. However, between the autumn of 1942 and August 1943, they seem to have been fairly efficient, despite some geographical differences due to the varying degree of competence displayed by the local authorities. Indeed, from the end of October 1942 telegrams and circulars with instructions regulating evacuation were issued by the Inspectorate for War Services and by the Cabinet of the Ministry of the Interior on a daily basis (and often even more frequently) touching upon all the organizational aspects of the process: the receptive capacity of provinces and villages, availability of lodgings, bureaucratic procedures related to the distribution of food, assistance for disadvantaged evacuees, and the evacuation of factories, offices, prisons and hospitals.[13] Despite the difficulties encountered during the first month of the war and in subsequent years, the prevailing idea was still the one introduced in 1931: to evacuate cities by encouraging and facilitating voluntary transfer.

On 1 November 1942, new *Norms for the Regulation of Voluntary Evacuation* were finally issued. In part these re-stated the 1939 Plan, but broadened some of its aspects, in particular those related to the reception, lodging and support of the evacuees. It also provided a few basic bureaucratic guidelines, which would allow the regime to follow each movement of the population in order to allocate adequate resources, such as rationed goods and the relevant funds.[14]

After these Norms were issued, they were followed by a number of additional telegrams,[15] adding to or modifying the existing rules. The extent of these changes made it necessary only 20 days later, on 21 November, to amalgamate all the changes into a single circular.[16] This did not, however, end the practice of sending out yet further telegrams to the prefects, and with increasing frequency.

On 2 December 1942, Mussolini, addressing the Chamber of Fasci and Corporations, encouraged the Italian people to evacuate: 'All those who can find lodgings far from the urban centres have a duty to do so.' His statement was reported two days later in a circular by the Inspectorate for War Services addressed to all prefects. The circular summed up the main recommendations concerning evacuation in the following terms:

In his recent speech the *Duce* has once again urged the prompt evacuation of the major urban centres and industrial towns targeted by the enemy's offensive power. Such exhortation, which is for us an order, needs no further comment. ... I trust that the prefects will want to intervene with a vast effort of persuasion in order to stimulate, facilitate and speed up voluntary evacuation.[17]

However, this form of evacuation was to be carried out only by 'that part of the population, whose presence in the great urban and industrial centres targeted by the enemy's offensive, is not justified by any specific reason connected to the present state of war.'[18] A major problem, which until then had been grossly underestimated, was now very evident: the workers of the auxiliary industries were also evacuating *en masse*, together with the personnel of institutions and structures that were necessary to the life of the cities and to the resistance of the 'internal front'. It thus became necessary to order the return of workers to their workplace, and at the same time to urge the prefects to implement as quickly as possible a large scale 'evening evacuation' plan, facilitating the daily commuting of factory workers and employees from their families' evacuation areas to their place of work. The first relevant directives were issued between 4 and 13 December 1942.[19]

However, it was not easy to convince workers and employees to carry out their activities in cities targeted by enemy bombers, and it soon became clear that it was virtually impossible to lodge their families in the outskirts of the cities, as these areas were already saturated with refugees. This state of affairs, which added to the difficulties that the regime was already facing in the attempt to coordinate all the aspects of a massive transfer of population, led to a complete inversion of its evacuation strategy. On 19 February 1943 Umberto Albini (Under Secretary of the Ministry of Interior) wrote to the prefects:

> The situation lately created by the heavy enemy air offensive on urban centres has demonstrated that is it absolutely impossible to transfer to and conveniently lodge in other areas the large masses of people who are evacuating from targeted areas, given the limited receptive capacities, shortages in means of transportation and difficulties with food and other general supplies that are necessary for the assistance of evacuees ... Consequently, on the basis of superior orders, two things are required. The population must continue to stay in the urban centres targeted by the enemy's offensive ... Populations previously evacuated from targeted areas must be urged to go back to their domiciles if their houses have not been destroyed.[20]

On the basis of what occurred during the months that followed (in which the regime never stopped trying, by all conceivable means, to manage the 'evacuation emergency', in order to demonstrate that it still had some cards to play), this directive does not appear as a declaration of complete failure, although it indicates a growing awareness that the situation was getting out of hand. It is not clear why Albini ordered the return of evacuees to the cities, as this would not have reduced the number of transfers, creating instead further movement in the opposite direction, and thus adding to existing problems of transportation, shortages of food supplies, as well as adding further bureaucratic procedures. Two factors were probably decisive: the great difficulties encountered in finding lodgings; and the enormous cost of the economic and material assistance to be provided to evacuees in the locations where they found refuge. However, it is unlikely that these two reasons alone could provide the motivation for an order that would have created management problems as serious as those it attempted to address, and which proved to be unpopular – a problem for a Fascist regime that never lost sight of the issue of winning approval for its decisions and of the problem of consensus.

In any case, only two days later, Albini ordered the prefects to 'suspend' the implementation of the 'instructions imparted' on 19 February and to await further communication.[21] An order was indeed dispatched a month later, on 20 March, confirming the end of evacuation, but not the return of evacuees to the cities.[22] Within the same circular the political and propaganda bodies of the regime were prompted to initiate a specific campaign in which cities were to be increasingly compared to the front line, where civilians were not victims and defenceless targets, but brave fighters:

> The prefects, availing themselves also of the collaboration of the Party, shall endeavour to awaken within the people's hearts a sense of pride in being guardians and defenders of their own homes, enterprises and towns, thus drawing them closer and closer, through an enhanced common feeling of civic virtue and sacrifice, to the fighters who offer and bear all for the supreme ideals of the Fatherland in arms.[23]

The idea of protecting the population by removing it from the urban centres had thus turned into an attempt to convince Italians to resist enemy violence without abandoning their positions. Albini's orders and the patriotic messages, however, had little effect. In the following months the activities of the General Directorate for War Services and the Ministry of the Interior continued to trail behind the inexorable flow of refugees in the effort to find areas that could still receive them.

The landing of Allied forces in Sicily (10–11 July 1943), the arrest of Mussolini (25 July 1943) and the announcement of the armistice (8 September 1943), while representing three crucial dates in the history of Italians at war, did not appear to have any impact on evacuation. These events were not followed by any new, significant directive, change or disruption in the work of the bodies involved. Moreover, until October the advance of the Anglo-American forces up the peninsula caused population movements which are barely traceable in the documents of the Ministry of Interior. Only in the following months did the problem of evacuation from bombed cities almost disappear from the records, while the difficult situation of refugees moving northward from the southern regions became predominant.

THE THIRD PHASE

The third evacuation phase was characterized by a combination of the previous forms evacuation had taken and of the new population movements determined by voluntary escape from the combat zones, where violent ground fighting was accompanied by the massive bombing both of large cities and of railway lines, bridges and main roads across the country. At the same time, there was both the voluntary flight of Fascist family groups and the evacuation ordered by the German authorities for military reasons. In this phase, the process of evacuation became even more significant, both numerically and geographically, than it had been in the phase that preceded it. The General Directorate for War Services abandoned almost completely the use of directives and incentives and started to issue peremptory orders that had to be fulfilled at once. The northern provinces were thus instructed to absorb gradually increasing quotas of refugees, defined by central government and non-negotiable. Some 'province chiefs' (the prefects of the Italian Social Republic – the so-called Salò Republic of 1943–1945), were also asked to organize assembly points for refugees along the routes leading to the north.

The major difficulties faced by the authorities of the Italian Social Republic were caused by evacuations imposed by the German authorities. These transfers occurred along hundreds of kilometres on both the Adriatic and the Tyrrhenian coastlines and ten kilometres inland, but also involved large areas of the Apennines near the main defensive lines, as they were gradually set up, affecting hundreds of thousands of Italians. In most cases, the Germans issued orders directly to the prefectures without consulting the central authorities of the Republic; the latter became aware of the situation once they received numerous telegrams from province chiefs enquiring about possible destinations for the evacuees. The German authorities issued orders and the local authorities had to execute them, while the Ministry of the Interior of the Fascist Republic was required to manage the consequences of those orders. On the one hand, the Ministry of the Interior sought (especially between November 1943 and May 1944), without much conviction, to persuade the Germans to 'defer the transfer of more civilian populations from the areas in which they reside, even if they are located within operational zones';[24] on the other, it desperately attempted to assist the refugees moving northward.

The last transfer of population coordinated by the Italian authorities seems to have been the evacuation of 10,000 refugees towards the province of Verona in November 1944.[25] The last evacuation enforced by the Germans appears to have taken place along the coastline north of the Comacchio Valley in February 1945, that is, during the months (January to April) in which the two opposing armies were stalled on the Adriatic front between Ravenna and the Comacchio Valleys.[26] It thus appears that large groups of civilians were forced to move until only a few days before the end of the conflict on Italian soil. The end of the war, however, did not end the problem of evacuation, but opened its fourth phase, which has not yet been analysed by historians, that of the return home.

THE EVACUATION OF CHILDREN

An important aspect of the process of evacuation which is still unexplored in Italian historiography is that of the evacuation of children. Families who had or wanted to remain in the cities were given the opportunity to evacuate their children. This evacuation was entrusted entirely to the youth organization of the Fascist party, the *Gioventù Italiana del Littorio* (GIL), and, during the Italian Social Republic, to the *Opera Balilla*, involving thousands of children between the age of 6 and 14. A first agreement defining responsibilities was sealed between the Ministry of the Interior and the GIL during the final days of November 1942. The agreement was hastily signed at a time when the Ministry of the Interior was seriously occupied with the evacuation of cities by stimulating voluntary transfer; the evacuation of children was to be carried out on the same terms. On 24 November 1942 the Inspectorate for War Services wrote to the prefects:

> Current circumstances require that particular care be paid to the evacuation of children from urban centres exposed to enemy air incursions. The assistance criteria fall into the general framework of norms already issued regulating evacuation in general and they pertain exclusively to the competence of the prefects. However, the shelter, care and protection of children of both sexes between the ages of 6 and 14 belonging to indigent families, who may have to be transferred from towns hit or threatened by air strikes, will be entrusted to the GIL, which will fulfil its duties with full autonomy. Whereas the evacuation of children must have a voluntary character and must be carried out only upon request by the families concerned, it is necessary to proceed, with the promptness that the current circumstances require, to the completion of a list of those who will have to be evacuated from the main cities and who, in agreement with their families, will be entrusted to the care of the GIL ... At present, the General Command of the GIL has at its disposal Colonies for the lodging of about 12,000 children, a number that is insufficient to satisfy the actual need. Within the various provinces, however, there are other Colonies which, while depending for their surveillance upon the GIL, are the property of other institutions. It is essential therefore that they be made available to the GIL and to this end, when it is not possible to arrive at a direct agreement, you may even resort, if necessary, to their requisition.[27]

The final agreement (which also led to a decree by the *Duce*)[28] was issued on 15 July 1943 to take effect retroactively from 1 January 1943. According to its terms, the GIL was to provide for the care of indigent children who were to be evacuated from locations hit by enemy air strikes, as well as to take care of their maintenance, assistance and surveillance by hosting them in its own Colonies,[29] in other institutes or families. All expenses related to the functioning of the Colonies and the maintenance of the children were to be sustained by the GIL, although the Ministry of the Interior was to reimburse the GIL 20 Italian *lire* for each child on a daily basis. However, only two months after the signing of the agreement, there arose a fierce disagreement between the GIL and the Ministry of the Interior because the latter refused to accept a new demand from the GIL that the sum for maintenance be raised to 30 *lire* to make it adequate. The tension persisted until the end of the war, exacerbated by the failure not only to secure a higher sum but also by the issue of long delays in the payment of those sums due under the original agreement from the Ministry to the GIL.[30]

The documentation held in the central archives clearly indicates that the GIL effectively possessed and used the executive and organizational capacities necessary to fulfil the task it had been assigned, and that it tended to act independently even of the prefects, under whose control it should have been operating. Indeed, the GIL referred to the prefects only when they wanted them to sign the lists of children ready to be evacuated (as established by the agreement), or when it was necessary to proceed to the requisition of a Colony, a measure which only the prefects could order. On the other hand, prefects do not seem to have asked for or desired any further involvement. Despite the effective structures in place for evacuation, the GIL constantly had to contend with two serious problems: the lack of places to accommodate children, and the real shortage of beds, mattresses, linen and blankets, all necessary to make available places actually serviceable. The meagreness of the Ministry of the Interior's financial help further compounded these two problems. Such difficulties increasingly led the GIL to assign children to private institutions and families whom it paid, through an arbitrary decision, 10 *lire* per day for each hosted child. In this way, it could reduce the number of children to be assisted and watched over, while retaining in its own coffers ten out of the 20 *lire* which the Ministry issued for each child. These resources could then be utilized for the children who remained entirely in its care, as well as for the restructuring and furnishing of Colonies.

From a quick overview of the figures (see tables 3 and 4) it emerges that, while the number of children evacuated and lodged in the Colonies in the centre and north of the Italian peninsula is remarkable – about 19,767 children between 1 January and 29 February 1944 – what appears particularly surprising is the number of children hosted by families. The figures reveal, in fact, that an impressive number of Italians were willing to host in their own homes children they did not know.[31] A number of these families could be partly motivated by the ten *lire* they received for each day, and it is possible that peasants and sharecroppers sought in this way to obtain help for agricultural labour. This was a source of help which, even if it involved the very young, was nevertheless important when men were away at the front and only women and children could be relied upon.

CONCLUSION

As the chapter has demonstrated, the regime's central authorities – mostly the state and the Fascist Party – had major responsibility for the ways in which the phenomenon of evacuation developed in Italy. At times they intervened in order to stimulate evacuation, and at other times in order to slow it down or to stop it completely. The process of evacuation, however, also developed independently of the regime's decisions, although throughout the war the authorities, both at a local and at a central level, sought to maintain control over it. In some aspects, and at certain times, they succeeded in organizing and managing it; at other times their efforts failed almost entirely.

Two elements that had a major impact on the efforts of the authorities were voluntary mass evacuations and the German presence. Between the state and the Party it was the state that played the most important role in dealing with them. This was principally because the organization of evacuation needed a strong and experienced bureaucratic management at both central and local level. However, the state inevitably needed the assistance of the Party in order to make use of its efficient youth organizations, as well as its ownership of buildings.

The division of the evacuation process in Italy into three main phases is fundamental in order to understand the phenomenon; however, it runs the risk of simplification. For example, it does not shed light on the role of other institutions, such as the *Ente Nazionale per l'Assistenza ai Profughi e la Tutela degli Interessi delle Provincie Invase* (ENAP, the institution which looked after both the evacuees and the interests of the 'invaded' provinces),[32] or of other organizations, both local and national, devoted to assistance and charity. Moreover, it does not explain the overlapping and confusion between different competences, which emerged at times between various branches of the state, between state and Party, or between these two and other institutions, such as ENAP. Strong and continued tension between state and Party was due to the fact that the Fascist Party (and in the Italian Social Republic the Republican Fascist Party) wanted to claim a greater role in the management of evacuation, because it was considered to have a fundamental impact on the preservation of a consensus for Fascism. All of these many issues and complex political relationships existed throughout the three phases of evacuation analysed here, and cannot be identified with any one of them in particular.

Table 3.1 Statistics of evacuees received in various Italian regions/provinces up until the end of March 1943. *Source:* ACS, MI, DGSG, AG, b. 85, f. 209, sf. 209-1.

Region/ Province	number of inhabitants	evacuees received	Region/ Province	number of inhabitants	evacuees received
Abruzzi			*Marche*		
L'Aquila	365,716	1,187	Ancona	372,229	3,185
Chieti	374,727	1,144	Ascoli Piceno	303,869	2,437
Pescara	211,561	1,187	Macerata	290,057	1,563
Teramo	249,532	841	Pesaro-Urb.	311,916	3,968
Campobasso	399,095	3,659			
Umbria			*Emilia-Rom.*		
Perugia	534,359	723	Forlì	444,528	11,225
Terni	191,559	2,234	Ravenna	279,127	2,412
			TOTAL	4,328,275	36,365

Table 3.2 Statistics of evacuees received in various Italian provinces up until the end of May 1944. *Source:* ACS, MI, DGSG, AG, b. 6, f. without number.

Province	number of inhabitants	evacuees received	Province	number of inhabitants	evacuees received
Alessandria	493,698	62,470	Ferrara	366,611	28,271
Ancona	356,879	18,000	Florence	840,287	150,000
Aosta	226,107	27,136	Forlì	422,831	30,500
Apuania	189,678	1,136	Genoa	831,651	113,488
Arezzo	301,147	15,560	Imperia	162,383	1,362
Asti	245,764	50,000	La Spezia	221,921	40,739
Belluno	210,335	9,310	Livorno	245,787	27,873
Bergamo	584,881	5,818	Lucca	339,991	15,693
Bologna	683,032	92,948	Macerata	277,696	34,740
Brescia	710,642	43,318	Mantua	397,686	26,134
Como	487,277	126,742	Milan	2,001,875	113,730
Cremona	364,842	24,173	Modena	448,429	36,723
Cuneo	619,598	71,359	Novara	389,352	42,194
Padua	632,160	80,000	Siena	260,891	21,514
Parma	373,695	140,000	Sondrio	133,758	6,935
Pavia	481,884	27,508	Teramo	226,414	40,665

Province	number of inhabitants	evacuees received	Province	number of inhabitants	evacuees received
Perugia	514,996	21,350	Terni	179,0,78	20,000
Pesaro	294,360	30,000	Turin	1,168,384	200,000
Piacenza	290,445	8,900	Treviso	560,809	27,000
Pisa	335,187	2,400	Udine	718,245	32,450
Pistoia	202,405	22,202	Varese	382,462	204,200
Ravenna	272,500	14,505	Venice	594,415	56,561
Reggio Emil.	360,909	37,007	Vercelli	359,525	33,198
Rovigo	315,868	15,147	Verona	563,159	12,520
Savona	221,003	3,250	Vicenza	528,256	11,375
			TOTAL evacuees		**2,279,104**

Table 3.3 Statistics of children evacuated and hosted in colonies from 1 January 1943 to 29 February 1944. *Source:* ACS, MI, DGSG, AG, b. 41–43, 109–110.

Town	children evacuated	Town	children evacuated
Ancona	54	Milan	7,332
Apuania	77	Modena	214
Bologna	235	Perugia	101
Cremona	6	Pesaro	11
Genoa	5,075	Rovigo	7
Grosseto	309	Savona	746
La Spezia	785	Turin	3,640
Livorno	876	Vicenza	228
Lucca	71		
		TOTAL	**19,767**

The figures which appear in the documents issued by the various offices involved are in many cases dissimilar, and refer at times to lists of children that can no longer be found in the archive. The figures reported here are therefore only indicative, and in all probability lower than the real ones.

Table 3.4 Statistics of children evacuated from the three main cities of the 'industrial triangle' and hosted by families. Source: ACS, MI, DGSG, AG, b. 41–43, 109–110. In this case too, the figures reported are in all probability lower than the real ones.

City	November 1942	December 1942	January 1943	February 1943	March 1943	April 1943	May 1943	June 1943
Genoa	2	95	218	145	18	11	218	174
Milan	/	4	6	290	1,980	1,336	612	194
Turin	1	67	14	24	10	26	35	11
	3	166	238	459	2,008	1,373	865	379

City	July 1943	August 1943	September 1943	October 1943	November 1943	December 1943	TOTAL
Genoa	6	??	??	??	??	??	887+?
Milan	97	13	13	3	5	3	4,556
Turin	8	1	??	??	??	??	197+?
	111	14+?	13+?	3+?	5+?	3+?	**5,640+?**

Notes

1 More specifically by the Inspectorate for War Services (ISG) created in 1941 and replaced by the General Directorate for War Services (DGSG) in December 1942, the Cabinet and the Under Secretariat of the War Office.
2 See some of the figures in tables 1 and 2.
3 S. Adorno, 'Lo sfollamento a Pesaro', in G. Rochat, E. Santarelli and P. Sorcinelli (eds), *Linea Gotica 1944. Eserciti, popolazioni, partigiani* (Milan: FrancoAngeli, 1986), 281–318; R. Lucioli, 'Sfollamento, mobilità sociale e sfaldamento delle istituzioni nella provincia di Ancona', *Storia e problemi contemporanei*, 15, 1995, 49–64; M. Maggiorani, 'Uscire dalla città: lo sfollamento', in B. Dalla Casa and A. Preti (eds), *Bologna in guerra 1940–1945* (Milan: FrancoAngeli, 1995), 361–393. Data on the timing, locations and local mechanisms pertaining to the process of evacuation can be found in G. Cipollini, 'Il piano di sfollamento totale della provincia di Lucca (maggio-settembre 1944)', *Documenti e studi*, 8/9, 1989, 143-189; E. Cortesi, *L'Odissea degli Sfollati. Il Forlivese, il Riminese e il Cesenate di fronte allo sfollamento di massa (1940–1945): la provincia di Forlì in guerra* (Cesena: Il Ponte Vecchio, 2003).
4 See among others: G. Pedrocco, 'I comuni dell'entroterra pesarese di fronte ai problemi della guerra', in *Linea Gotica 1944*, 263–280; N. Gallerano, 'Gli italiani in guerra 1940–1943. Appunti per una ricerca', in F. Ferratini Tosi, G. Grassi and M. Legnani (eds), *L'Italia nella seconda guerra mondiale e nella Resistenza* (Milan: FrancoAngeli, 1988), 307–23; S. Pivato, *Sentimenti e quotidianità in una provincia in guerra. Rimini 1940–1944* (Rimini: Maggioli, 1995).
5 See for instance: A. Portelli, 'Assolutamente niente. L'esperienza degli sfollati a Terni', in N. Gallerano (ed.), *L'altro dopoguerra. Roma e il Sud 1943–1945* (Milan: FrancoAngeli, 1985), 135–144; F. Koch, 'Lo sfollamento nella memoria femminile. Proposta di lettura di alcuni testi dell'Archivio diaristico nazionale', *L'impegno*, 1, 1993, 32–40; G. Campana and M. Fratesi, *Da Ancona al Cassero. 1943-1945. Tempo di sfollamento* (Ancona: ENDAS, Circolo Culturale Cassero, 1996).

6   On the Central Interdepartmental Committee for Anti-Aircraft Protection see S. Adorno, 'Lo sfollamento a Pesaro', 281–82.

7   See *Piano di diradamento della popolazione civile* and *Elenco delle città alle quali si applica il provvedimento di diradamento* in Archivio Centrale dello Stato (ACS), Ministero dell'Interno (MI), Direzione Generale di Pubblica Sicurezza (DGPS), Affari Generali e Riservati (AGR), A5G IIGM, fascicolo (fasc.) 26, busta (b.) 6, sottofascicolo (sfasc.) 1, inserto (ins.) 1.

8   ACS, MI, DGPS, AGR, A5G IIGM, fasc. 26, b. 6, sfasc. 1, ins. 1, circular n. 135 sent by the Ministry of War (Comando di Corpo di Stato maggiore, Stato maggiore territoriale, Ufficio protezione antiaerea e difesa coste), to the Ministry of Interior (Gabinetto del ministro, Direzione generale della Sanità pubblica, Direzione generale di Pubblica sicurezza), the Fascist Party (Centro nazionale di Mobilitazione civile), the Ministry of Justice, the Ordinariato militare and the Central Direction of Anti-Aircraft Protection, 6 June 1940.

9   ACS, MI, DGPS, AGR, A5G IIGM, fasc. 26, b. 6, sfasc. 1, ins. 1, circular n. 30 by the Ministry of War, 2 June 1940.

10 Turin and Genoa on 11 June 1940; Genoa and Savona on 13 June 1940; Genoa and Milan on 15 June 1940; Milan and Genoa on 16 June 1940.

11 'In order to pass on valuable information we inform you that, because of the present state of war, three new offices have been instituted in this ministry with the following responsibilities, on behalf of the ministry of interior:
    Ufficio I: Evacuation – transfer – relocation of civilian population – refugees – means of transport – blackout – contacts with the Ministry of War and with the Supreme commission of defence.
    Ufficio II: Food – raw materials – contacts with the ministries of agriculture, corporations, communications and with the Under Secretary for war fabrications.
    Ufficio III: political-assistance problems concerning all refugees from the redeemed lands – contacts with the Ministry of Italian Africa and with the Foreign Office'. (Archivio di Stato di Forlì (ASFO), Archivio del Gabinetto di Prefettura (AGP), b. 355, fasc. 32, reserved and urgent circular n. 120.Z 35 from the Cabinet of the Ministry of Interior to the prefects and the governor of Rome, 10 June 1940.

12 Law decree n. 410, 5 May 1941.

13 See the numerous telegrams and circulars held by the Archivio Centrale dello Stato in the following groups of records: MI, DGPS, AGR, A5G IIGM, fasc. 26 – b. from 60 to 66; MI, DGSG, Affari Generali (AG), b. 8, 9, 40, from 44 to 58, and from 75 to 112.

14 ACS, MI, DGSG, AG, b. 95, fasc. 342, circular n. 548–24 *Norme per la disciplina dello sfollamento volontario e del movimento invernale nelle località idrotermali e climatiche* from the Cabinet of the Ministry of Interior to the prefects, 1 November 1942.

15 For archival references related to these telegrams see note 13.

16 ASFO, AGP, b. 372, fasc. 75, circular n. 2979 *Norme per la disciplina dello sfollamento volontario* (which contained the *Norme per la disciplina dello sfollamento volontario* sent to the prefects from the Ministry of Interior on the same day), from the prefect of Forlì to the *podestà*, 21 November 1942.

17 ACS, MI, DGSG, AG, b. 95, fasc. 342–1, circular n. 26179 *Norme sulla disciplina dello sfollamento ed assistenza alle popolazioni sfollate*.

18 Ibid.

19 ACS, MI, DGSG, AG, b. 95, fasc. 342–1, see in particular: circular n. 26179 *Norme sulla disciplina dello sfollamento ed assistenza alle popolazioni sfollate*; telegram n. 26121, ISG to the prefects, 4 December 1942, which ordered prefects to organize immediately everything that was necessary for the evening evacuation; urgent telegram n. 26327, ISG to the prefects, 9 December 1942, which ordered the immediate start of evening evacuation.

20 ACS, MI, DGPS, AGR, A5G IIGM, fasc. 26, b. 60, sfasc. 1, ins. 1, telegram n. 12534–2090, from Albini to the prefects, 19 February 1943.

21 ACS, MI, DGSG, AG, b. 95, fasc. 342–1, telegram n. 13094–2090, from Albini to the prefects, 21 February 1943.

22 ACS, MI, DGSG, AG, b. 95, fasc. 342–1, circular n. 4533, from DGSG to the prefects, 20 March 1943.

23   Ibid.
24   ACS, MI, DGSG, b. 6, circular no. 40/C/2306, Cabinet of the MI to the DGSG, 2 May 1944;
      on 10 May the MI sent an almost identical secret circular to the Chief of German Military
      Administration (ibid.).
25   This can be deduced from a crossing of telegrams between Albini and the province chiefs of
      Verona, Mantua and Vicenza (ACS, MI, DGSG, AG, b. 6).
26   ACS, MI, DGPS, AGR, A5G IIGM, fasc. 26, b. 60, sfasc. 1, ins. 6, communication n. 0733, from
      the prefecture of Ferrara to the General Directorate of the Police of the MI, 26 February 1945.
27   ACS, MI, DGSG, AG, b. 8, circular n. 25371/360–1, from the ISG to the prefects, 24 November
      1942.
28   Decree by Mussolini n. 16037, 17 July 1943.
29   During the Fascist period, and in particular among the Party organisations, the word Colonies
      indicated large buildings created on purpose in order to gather together children and young
      people, so that they could spend periods of holiday (either in the winter or in the summer),
      undertake paramilitary training, or recover from illnesses.
30   Documents on these aspects can be found in ACS, MI, DGSG, AG: b. 2, fasc. 'GIL', 'Assistance
      to evacuated children, October 1943'; b. 3 ONB (Opera Nazionale Balilla), 'Assistance to
      evacuated children, January 1944'; b. 41–42 'Colonies for evacuees – provincial committee
      of Opera Balilla'; b. 43, 'Evacuated children – provincial committee of Opera Balilla'; b. 109,
      'Evacuation of children from bombed cities, care of the GIL'; b. 110 'Evacuation of children
      from bombed cities, care of the GIL'.
31   See for instance the figures in table n. 4. It must be kept in mind that the number of hosted
      children does not correspond to the number of families involved, since the latter could host
      two or three children at a time.
32   Created on 20 November 1943, ENAP had a national directorate as well as provincial branches.
      Documents regarding ENAP can be found in ACS, MI, DGSG, AG. See in particular b. 4,
      fasc. *Ente nazionale per l'assistenza ai profughi e la tutela degli interessi delle provincie invase,
      febbraio-giugno 1944.*

4

'Relieving Sorrow and Misfortune'? State, Charity, Ideology and Aid in Bombed-out France, 1940–1944

Lindsey Dodd[1]

After the defeat of summer 1940, France was partially occupied by the Germans. The majority of the government decided to stay in France and agree an armistice with the invaders rather than to continue fighting from overseas. By remaining, they hoped to bargain for favourable terms in the expected peace treaty, and to protect the country from the ravages of an enemy whose atrocities – real and fabled – during World War One were ingrained in public consciousness. The existence of a government ruling less than half the country from the spa town of Vichy was intended as a temporary measure until the peace treaty was signed. From its outset, therefore, the Vichy government existed to protect the population from worse dangers; war was chaos, and to deprive France of her 'natural defenders' would be 'to deliver her to the enemy',[2] to vengeful occupiers' reprisals, or – equally worrying – subversive elements from within. Yet as time passed, no peace treaty materialized, and in its attempt to retain what autonomy it did have, Vichy was drawn deeper into collaboration with Germany. German use of French ports, factories and other industrial resources, such as the coalfields of the Nord-Pas-de-Calais, power stations and freight transportation networks, made France a target for Allied bombs: what had started as an attempt to protect the population pulled civilians deeper into war. Through all the wartime hardships suffered by the French population, of which air raids became a dramatic feature, Vichy maintained its protective stance, embodied by the paternal figure of the Head of State, Marshal Pétain. Whether that protection was effective or merely rhetorical is another matter. Nonetheless, the role Vichy played in the aftermath of air raids is part of the protective role on which its existence was based, and from which it drew legitimacy.

This chapter examines the work of three agencies which controlled relief to bombed-out French civilians (*sinistrés*). The role of the Vichy government – the French wartime state – will be explored within their work, revealing the bombsite as a contested political territory for competing ideological positions. It does not intend to expose all aid to bombing victims in France as motivated by something less generous than an impulse to 'relieve their sorrow and misfortune'.[3] But it will demonstrate how aid was used in the service of different factions to mobilize support for their own ideological conceptions of the future nation.

THREE VICHYS

When we speak of Vichy and ideology, it is important to note that this 'paradoxical regime' was, in Stanley Hoffmann's words, a 'pluralist dictatorship' – like France's bombsites, a battleground for ideological dominance between varying factions.[4] By abdicating its powers to Pétain, the Third Republic's elected politicians created a political power vacuum into which stepped men of diverse and contradictory tendencies. Three such tendencies – three Vichys – with blurred edges, are identified by Robert Paxton, and have bearing on this discussion.

The first is the Vichy of the traditionalists, the Vichy of Pétain's ambitious reform programme, the National Revolution. From this group came many of Vichy's high-ranking ministers. It set the tone of the regime, even though its power had waned by 1942. France's grandeur was seen in the nation's past; industrialization and modernity had led to a national decline, peaking in the defeat of 1940. The National Revolution prioritized social stability, order, the 'reign of moral virtue' and an 'organic' conception of society, with a strong but severely limited and depoliticized state, the country regulated instead by autonomous communities – of workplace, family, region and nation – giving rise to the National Revolution's motto, Work, Family, Homeland (*Travail, Famille, Patrie*).[5] It sought to remake the nation along traditional lines, squeezing France into a 'socially conservative straitjacket'[6] with the help of the Catholic Church. It excluded those without organic links to French soil, notably Jews, making ideological collaboration with Germany possible. But the Vichy of the traditionalists was internally divided, and the group, despite its high visibility and control over the regime's tone, lacked and eventually lost power, leaving policy-making in the hands of the second group.

The Vichy of the experts, or of the technocrats and bureaucrats, had a growing influence unchecked by parliamentary control, arising from the political power vacuum into which non-elected administrators, civil servants and technical experts stepped in 1940.[7] Vichy was, to quote Marcel Peyrouton, colonial administrator turned Minister of the Interior in 1940, a 'bureaucratic revolution.'[8] Far removed from the traditionalists' non-interventionism, the experts greatly extended Vichy's bureaucratic apparatus. This came in response to the increasingly difficult task of feeding, clothing, and keeping warm, healthy, productive and under control a population suffering severe deprivation, and as part of a conscious effort to modernize the French economy through state management. The experts running France made decisions based on practical rather than ideological grounds;[9] yet this practicality entangled them with the German authorities, tainting their efforts with a willingness to collaborate to maintain and increase economic production for Germany's benefit. This is what Hoffmann describes as *collaboration d'État*: collaboration for reasons of state, which was both involuntary, a necessary part of the maintenance of a semi-autonomous French state, and voluntary, where the technocrats exploited the situation for French gain.[10] Yet some of the experts governing France (such as Paul Marion, Secretary General for Information and Propaganda in 1941) tipped, for ideological reasons, into the third group at Vichy, which also pulled in certain of the traditionalists most wholly steeped in extreme right-wing nationalism.[11]

The third grouping was the Vichy of the fascists. This was also the Vichy of the collaborationists, those who willingly worked with Germany for personal gain or through admiration of the Nazi model.[12] As Laval pushed back the technocrats who threatened his personal power during late 1942 and early 1943, and as traditionalists seeped away from a stumbling National Revolution, the collaborationists finally moved centre stage. In 1940, Vichy did not welcome the extremists of the 1930s; some, like Jacques Doriot, leader of the *Parti Populaire Français* (PPF), were shunned outright;[13] others, like the *Rassemblement National Populaire* (RNP) chief Marcel Déat, desperately plotted for the ear of the influential, notably a reluctant Pierre Laval.[14] The fascist conception of a totalitarian, single-party state, a modern and dynamic nation, was far removed from the traditionalists' ideal society. Its players were also physically distant: Vichy was far less attractive than occupied Paris, where German money bought journalistic influence.[15] Yet fascist ideas were not absent from Vichy: anti-Semitism, anti-communism and anti-liberalism had their own French roots, and the state became increasingly violent and repressive towards its population. Some of the fascists, like Paul Marion, had important posts throughout the regime, but they only controlled key ministries in the last months of the occupation.[16] By late 1943 the independence that Vichy had previously held in terms of policy-making had disappeared; the French state now 'barely existed'; what remained was a rump into which the fascists had clawed a physical presence (Déat as Minister of Work and National Solidarity, Joseph Darnand as Secretary-General for the Maintenance of Order, and later Minister of the Interior, Philippe Henriot in charge of propaganda), but which wielded little autonomous power.[17] French autonomy was indeed so weakened by 1944 that these men were puppets, finding 'Nazi-style solutions' to France's deepening social crisis.[18]

Bombing posed a huge challenge to France, already grappling with growing difficulties of public order and food supply; the welfare structure was undeveloped, although not non-existent. Air raids provoked acute local crises, putting immense pressure on rationing, housing, employment and medical services. France had the skeleton of a public welfare system before 1939: local welfare offices (*bureaux de bienfaisance*) had been created following the French Revolution, attributing the responsibility for the needy to the *communes* (towns, villages). Under the Third Republic the system developed, and in 1888 the High Commission for Public Welfare defined public assistance as a right for those unable to work or deprived of resources. Public welfare for the needy existed from the late nineteenth/early twentieth century, including free medical aid (from 1893), allowances for lone children (*enfants assistés*, from 1904), for the elderly, sick and terminally ill (from 1905) and for women in childbirth and nursing mothers (from 1913 and 1917). Vichy left this system largely intact, with some modifications, although the particular hardships of war meant that it had to innovate, and new forms of assistance developed for refugees and bombed-out civilians, and not just those categorized as needy. So when bombing caused local crises, although a welfare structure existed, it had to evolve. The state had to find ways for those in difficulty to receive more help.[19] The task was so great that other organizations, the 'aid agencies' under discussion here, were created or adapted to help the *sinistrés*.

AID AGENCIES

France was bombed by the Germans during the 1940 offensive, and there-after by the Allies. The RAF raid on the Renault works in the Parisian suburb of Boulogne-Billancourt on 3 March 1942 was the first major attack on an industrial target, the first on the capital, and the largest concentration yet of bombers in time and space. Over two hours 235 aircraft dropped 419 tons of bombs.[20] While the factories were hit, many bombs fell on nearby housing. The raid left 373 civilians dead and 317 injured; furthermore, 9,548 people out of a population of 80,844 were bombed out.[21] Table 4.1 shows relief given in the aftermath, and introduces the 'aid agencies' under discussion. The municipality, one branch of the public authorities, distributed about 2.2 million francs in state allowances to needy bombed-out people, but about 3.4 million in emergency aid from its own coffers.[22] As yet, there was no state provision for emergency financial aid. The préfecture, a second branch of the public authorities, gave an emergency grant of 1.5 million, and also provided priority ration tickets. The Secours National ('National Relief'), the national charity, allocated some financial aid, but its priority was aid in kind. The *Comité Ouvrier de Secours Immédiat* ('Workers' Emergency Relief Committee' – COSI) provided an excep-tionally large sum of money to the *sinistrés*, nearly 9 million francs. These three agencies – the public authorities, the Secours National and the COSI – are the focus of this chapter.

Table 4.1 Aid distributed following the Boulogne-Billancourt raid of 3 March 1942.

The bombing	
Number of dead	373
Number of injured	317
Tons of bombs dropped	419
Number of *sinistrés*	9,548

Financial aid (francs)	
COSI	8,980,000
Municipality of Boulogne-Billancourt	5,622,279
Prefecture (département)	1,500,000
Secours National	2,235,350
Private donations	1,443,176
Metalworkers' union	500,000
Other	450,000
Aid in kind	
Extra ration tickets (from the département)	
Clothing	31,690
Shoes	5,571
Methylated spirits (litre)	1,800
Oil (half litre)	500
Packets of candles	250
Hand soap bars	1,830
Laundry soap bars	1,500
Book of bread tickets	12,990
For a 'tonnage' of coal	1,600
Booklets of meal tickets	9,300
Diverse (from Secours National)	
Items of clothing	43,284
Pairs of shoes	4,068
Packets of cigarettes	8,000
Turnips, carrots, oranges (kg)	17,508
Butter (kg)	900
Lavocine (kg)	500
Soap (kg)	1,000
Crates of chicken	3
Crates of rabbit	7
Sheep	3
Meals (from Secours National)	
Breakfasts	18,200
Lunches	78,034
Dinners	60,143
Hot drinks	118,200

Source: all from AMBB, 6H 72: 'Bombardement par avions effectué le 3 mars 1942', Ville de Boulogne-Billancourt, 15 Feb. 1943; Report comparing raids of March 1942 and April 1943, 19 June 1943; report, sections 'Ravitaillement', 'Secours National' and 'Bons délivrés au 9 avril 1942', 9 Apr. 1942; 'Secours aux sinistrés du 3 mars 1942', 14 Aug. 1944; 'Réponse aux renseignements demandés par Melle Levenez sur les bombardements subis par la Ville de Boulogne-Billancourt', 26 Jan. 1945.

It should be stressed that aid to the bombed-out citizens of France, whether financial or practical, came from other sources too. Table 4.1 includes private donations of 1.4 million francs and a contribution from the metalworkers' union of 500,000 francs. The French Red Cross is not examined here; nor are the Sections Sanitaires Automobiles Féminines ('Women's Mobile Healthcare Sections'), an independent organization of women ambulance crews; nor yet are the Vichyite Équipes Nationales ('National teams'), the youth teams supplying manpower on bombsites. Private donations flooded into the town hall of Boulogne-Billancourt in sums ranging from 20 francs to thousands of francs, from personal savings, workplace collections, charity events and so on. Donations also arrived in Reichmarks from French prisoners of war, their contributions boosted by the favourable exchange rate.[23] A further charitable venture, explored by Michael Schmeidel in Chapter 11, was the adoption of bombed towns by non-bombed towns, a scheme begun by the Comité Lyon-Brest in 1941, but repeated elsewhere.

Secours National was nicknamed the 'charity of charities'. Set up in World War One, re-established under the Daladier government in 1939, and reshaped by Vichy in 1940, it was a vast organization of 43,000 volunteers (by April 1943) and 11,700 employees (by January 1944), with a mission to aid civilian victims of war. It had a monopoly on public appeals to raise money, and controlled the distribution of funds to other bodies. It could also dissolve other charities. On average, about fifty-five per cent of its funding came from the state, in the form of grants and revenue generated from 'public' sources such as the national lottery, or levies on auctioned goods. The rest came from its own fundraising campaigns and private donations. During 1943, public funding of the Secours National reached 65 per cent, and was 3.2 billion francs, three per cent of the state's revenue that year. It was thus a parapublic organization which fiercely supported the National Revolution, and particularly Pétain, its honorary president. The charity was active wherever civilians were affected by war, most notably in the fight against malnutrition, but also helping refugees and the families of prisoners of war; relief for the *sinistrés* was just one of its activities.[24]

The COSI was founded following the Boulogne-Billancourt raid in March 1942. Its honorary president was Fernand de Brinon, its president, René Mesnard. De Brinon was Vichy's representative to the German authorities in Paris and an influential proponent of collaboration, with the title of Secretary of State from the return of Laval to government on 18 April 1942. Mesnard was the secretary of the Centre Syndicaliste de Propagande ('Syndicalist Propaganda Centre' – CSP), and director of the syndicalist newspaper *L'Atelier*. The CSP was an affiliate organization of the RNP, which Déat hoped would become the single party of a French totalitarian state.[25] Mesnard lived the racy lifestyle of the Parisian collaborationists, eventually incurring the Germans' displeasure for his rapid exhaustion of COSI funds.[26] The COSI's leadership reads like a roll-call of the 'collaborationist left', men from syndicalist backgrounds, many drawn from the ranks of anti-communist neo-socialists of the 1930s, most with links to the RNP or Doriot's PPF.[27]

The COSI's (many) critics condemned it as a tool of German propaganda but the Committee itself emphasized that 'it was militant Parisian syndicalists who founded the Committee. Its financial resources came from syndical coffers, which then found themselves insufficient given the extent of the disaster'.[28] The Germans, when asked, donated 100 million francs, money gained 'from the confiscation from Jewish property', originating in a fine imposed on French Jews.[29] A fundraising drive in the Parisian collaborationist media raised a further ten million francs. When Déat entered government in 1944, he allocated the COSI, a private organization, public funding.[30] The COSI's Central Committee in Paris directed numerous local Committees in bombed areas, providing immediate financial aid to the *sinistrés*. While it echoed the RNP's 'genuine concern for workers',[31] and was animated by the activism and dynamism that characterized the Ultra parties,[32] it shared the abhorrent moral character and corruption of the collaborationist world.[33] By October 1943, it had set up 87 local committees and claimed to have aided 65,000 families.[34]

The public authorities – central, departmental, local – had an enormous task to perform in the wake of an air raid, involving numerous government departments and complex systems of attribution. In the opinion of Lille's mayor, 'it is, in fact, the Town Hall which makes the biggest contribution in each of the areas concerning the *sinistrés*', compared to the *département* and state.[35] Municipal authorities bore a heavy responsibility for citizens' wellbeing and had direct contact with them. Following the destruction of Lorient by bombing in January 1943 and the mass exodus of survivors, Laval's government realized it needed to coordinate its post-bombing activity better. At this time, a few months after the Germans' total occupation of France, Vichy's power was waning. Pétain was a figurehead; the National Revolution had stalled. Protecting the population and offering relief after bombing took on a deeper significance, demonstrating that the French state was still active in both zones. It was a positive role that the state could play in citizens' lives, in the face of mounting demands for French forced labour, merciless round-ups of Jews, harsher rationing and civil unrest. In February, therefore, the Service Interministériel de Protection contre les Événements de Guerre ('Interministerial Protection Service against the Incidents of War' – SIPEG) was formed, under Laval's control. It was an 'organ of coordination', intending to unite the work of diverse public bodies, enabling them to 'act quickly and efficiently'.[36] It placed delegates in each *département*, and had two well-publicized emergency trains, dispatched to bombed locations, composed of converted carriages – kitchen, field hospital, baby unit – and stocked with supplies.[37] The effectiveness of SIPEG is unclear: local branches of aid agencies, local initiatives and spontaneous mutual assistance retained their importance in the aftermath of an air raid.

AID AVAILABLE FOR VICTIMS OF BOMBING

The aid available to *sinistrés* from the public authorities developed as bombing increased in severity. It included emergency, short-term and longer-term assistance, and comprised financial and other aid. It evolved out of the state's obligation to provide welfare for the needy; as bombing intensified, it extended to those not categorized as 'needy' but who were temporarily in need, becoming an entitlement for civilian victims of war.

A decree of 2 November 1940 entitled a needy *sinistré* to the same daily *allocation* (allowance) as a refugee, limited to a three month period.[38] Table 4.2 shows the evolution of aid to *sinistrés* from the public authorities throughout the war. A *sinistré* was initially classed as needy if he or she earned less than the maximum total allowance. A fixed additional sum for rent and heating was attributed to those rehoused in privately rented accommodation. Thus a bombed-out Parisian metalworker with a family of wife and two children, one older than 13 years, *could* receive 47 francs per day, including heating and rent

Table 4.2 Evolution of aid provided by the state to civilian victims of bombing (in francs).

November 1940		
Daily allowance (needy only)		*Additional payments (all sinistrés)*
Head of household	10	Rent and heating (daily, per person) 3
Per other adult	6	
Per child over 13 years	12	
Per child under 13 years	7	
September 1942		
Daily allowance (needy only)		*Additional payments (all sinistrés)*
As November 1940		Rent, heating: *as November 1940*
		Emergency assistance
		Part *sinistré*: 60 days' daily allowance
		100% *sinistré*: 100 days' daily allowance
		Funeral expenses
		Up to half, to a maximum of 800 francs
		Moving expenses
		Can be reimbursed, amount unspecified

May 1943			
Daily allowance (needy only)		*Additional payments (all sinistrés)*	
Head of household	15	**Rent, heating and lighting assistance**	
Per other adult	10	1 person	3.5
Per child over 13 years	12	2 people	5.5
Per child under 13 years	10	3 people	7
		4 people	8
		Per extra person	1
		Emergency assistance	
		Part *sinistré*	1,000
		100% *sinistré*	1,500
		Funeral expenses	
		As September 1942	
		Moving expenses	
		Up to 15km: all costs reimbursed	
		Further than 15km: 750 flat rate	

January 1944				
Daily allowance (needy only)			*Additional payments (all sinistrés)*	
	First 3 months	after		
Head of household	19	15	Rent, heating and lighting *as May 1943*	
Per other adult	15	12	Emergency assistance *as May 1943*	
Per child over 13 years	15	12	Funeral expenses	1,000
Per child under 13 years	15	12	Moving expenses	750 flat rate

Sources: Decree of 2 Nov. 1940 (AML 5H10 22: decree detailed in Prefect of the Nord to Deputy Prefects and Mayors of the Nord, 5 Dec. 1940); law of 1 Sept 1942 (*Journal Officiel*, 18 Sept 1942); law of 13 May 1943 (*Journal Officiel*, 12 June 1943); law of 6 Jan 1944 (*Journal Officiel*, 19 Jan. 1944).

benefit; yet as his wage in June 1941 was about 54.5 francs per day, he would not qualify for the allowance. Although this family was poor, the father earned too much to qualify as needy.[39] Nor could the *allocation de sinistré* be added to other welfare benefits, such as family allowance. An unemployed worker would of course qualify as needy; however, Vichy's unemployment benefit, although lower than the *allocation de sinistré*, could be added to other welfare payments (family allowance, housewife's allowance), increasing the total sum received.[40] Official rations fell far short of daily calorific requirements, so people looked to other sources. Some sought food in the countryside, while others made use of the black market. However, prices were high, and prohibitive for those dependent on welfare payments.[41] Furthermore, the amount of the *allocation de sinistré* remained the same from November 1940 to May 1943; during this time official prices had increased by more than half, and all prices – black market included – had more than doubled.[42] Given this level of inadequacy, it is hardly surprising that additional aid was needed.

It took the start of raids on urban industrial targets in spring 1942 to provoke change. By September several innovations had appeared. Emergency financial aid could now be granted to those whose 'domicile was rendered uninhabitable by an act of war':[43] aid was no longer restricted to the needy. It comprised a payment of 60 days refugee *allocation* (at the 1940 rate) for partial *sinistrés*, and 100 days for total *sinistrés*. For the family mentioned above, with 100 per cent destruction, this amounted to 4,700 francs. Funeral expenses would be paid up to 800 francs, as well as contributions of an unspecified amount towards removal costs. This was a move towards allocation based on entitlement rather than neediness. Yet the situation had not improved for needy families. The rate of allowance remained unchanged, but as wages had risen slightly,[44] it became even more difficult for a family to qualify as needy. As official prices had increased by 92 per cent since 1940, and all prices by over 200 per cent, the rate was wholly insufficient to meet a family's food requirements, let alone any other expenses. For needy families, state welfare provision did not suffice, and neighbourly solidarity, or charity, was the alternative.

In May 1943, state emergency aid, available to all, was fixed at 1,000 francs or 1,500 francs per person (the aforementioned family's payment rising to 6,000 francs), depending on the extent of the damage, and the contribution to funeral expenses increased to 1,000 francs. Removal costs were fully refundable up to a distance of 15 kilometres; any further, and a flat rate of 750 francs per person applied. The *allocation de sinistré* (including rent, heating and lighting) for the needy had increased, for a four-person family reaching 55 francs per day.[45] In January 1944, further legislation altered the criteria for 'neediness', and changed the rate of allowances; the family would now receive 72 francs per day for the first three months following the bombing, and 59 francs per day after that. An extra 300 francs per month was introduced for needy elderly people.[46] Throughout the war, the daily allocation remained less than an unskilled metalworker's daily pay, calculated for a family of four; this would not have been the case with bigger families, who may have qualified. However, as Sauvy notes, the gap between revenue and needs widened as families grew, particularly those with teenage children, who suffered most from the calorific deficit of official rations.[47]

The public authorities were the only one of the agencies under discussion which 'officially' sought to continue their aid to the *sinistrés* in the long term. This assistance was intended to re-establish destroyed households. For the most needy, the state would contribute 90 per cent of the cost of new furniture. Longer-term aid was by and large available to all, not just the needy. A furniture allowance was allocated, the sum dependent upon family size and prior insurance policies. New furniture could be loaned and later purchased.[48] The state contributed up to 70 per cent of the costs of rebuilding houses,[49] and from May 1943 architects' fees for rebuilding houses were capped.[50] From July 1941, 'disability pensions' became available for those with permanent injuries.[51] By 1944, pensions for widows and orphans created by bombing had been introduced.[52]

Aid from the public authorities was rooted in the obligation to provide needy citizens with welfare, and the entitlement of war victims to state assistance; aid was therefore not only given to the poorest citizens, but to all who had suffered losses. Aid was based on the idea of re-establishment: getting lives back to a 'normality' in the short term, and rebuilding communities in the longer term. Yet as we have seen, there were problems with the system. The state of neediness was calculated on a salary so low that it excluded many from its remit. The system was complex and slow, entitlement having to be proven, through documentary evidence, interviews and visits, leaving the authorities open to criticism from other bodies, like the Secours National: 'the public authorities have only been able to provide the *sinistrés* with aid which is incomplete in scope and slow in implementation. The *sinistrés* have urgent needs which cannot wait upon administrative procedures.'[53] The lumbering bureaucratic machine, and the insufficiency of its provision, increased the importance of the other agencies.

The Secours National was a complement to the state, supposed to intervene in the aftermath of an air raid only if the public authorities were unable to cope; providing work, food, heating, clothing and health care was officially the remit of the local authorities.[54] Yet the extent of its intervention in these areas testifies to the difficulties the state faced. While the state's aid hoped to re-establish normal life, the role of Secours National was strictly to 'be a stopgap'.[55] Its focus was: 'Accommodation, Food, Clothing the *sinistrés*, Distribution of Cash.'[56]

Concerning food, the assistance of the Secours National was supposed to supplement the state: the municipality and the departmental rationing office should have organized community kitchens and distribution centres. In reality, Secours National was at the forefront of food distribution after an air raid, in the short term through its mobile kitchens, and in the longer term through community restaurants set up permanently in many towns. Clothing the *sinistrés* was the official responsibility of the departmental community wardrobe (*vestiaire*), but again, Secours National played a vital role in the immediate and short term, and organized collections and mending workshops. Finally, the provision of emergency financial aid should have fallen to 'bodies other than the Secours National [which] which are authorized to give cash aid', but, of course, the Secours National helped too.[57] In the Parisian industrial suburb of Argenteuil, for example, the Secours National team arrived half an hour after the end of a night-time raid on 30 April 1942. Soup for 500 people was prepared and distributed, and the mobile kitchen then drove to the worst-hit quarter of the town to feed those as yet unable to leave. A midday meal was prepared for 1,200 people, a children's tea in the afternoon, and an evening meal for 800.[58] As raids increased in scale, so did the quantities of the Secours National's aid until meals were provided in their hundreds of thousands.[59]

In the longer term, *sinistrés* benefited from the Secours National's wider activities. The bulk of its spending was on feeding children in school canteens and distributing vitamin biscuits. It ran holiday camps (*colonies de vacances*) for city children, provided work for the unemployed, assisted mothers and the elderly, and much more.[60] Those assisted could have been *sinistrés*, but longer-term help was not limited to them. Its aid appears as charity, despite a rhetorical obsession with national solidarity, and was not based on entitlement, but on urgency. Its aim was 'to patch things up', not 'to get things back to how they were before'.[61] Yet it too became hampered by the bureaucratic weight of the task it faced, causing one long-serving local delegate to resign in 1944, claiming that the organization had become 'too rigid and centralized, which, at a local level, impedes the accomplishment of the Secours National's mission of charity and solidarity'.[62] A smaller organization, perhaps one with less public accountability, might have fared better.

The COSI's mission was to provide emergency financial relief, which in March 1942 the state – officially – did not. It saw itself as 'an "oxygen bubble" allowing *sinistrés* to catch their breath before carrying on with their lives'.[63] It agreed with the Secours National in June 1943 to limit its aid to cash and removals, although its activity continued to be much broader.[64] Through this wide-ranging aid, it was able to publicize its political intentions.

In the wake of bombing, an immediate sum of money was allocated on the spot to victims by the local COSI. The sum allocated depended on family circumstance, gravity of injury and the extent of bomb damage; for example, a woman widowed in an air raid could receive 2,000 francs, more than an unskilled manual worker's monthly salary, while furniture losses between 50 and 100 per cent would be compensated with an initial sum of 1,500 francs. The beneficiary's file was then sent to headquarters for examination and, if approved, further payment followed. A woman with three children, widowed by an air raid, having lost 100 per cent of her belongings *could* receive 15,500 francs (about 70 per cent of an unskilled metalworker's annual earnings in 1942).[65] In practice, the sums were much lower; the average allocation up to June 1942 per family was around 3,200 francs. The COSI's self-proclaimed achievements must be subject to scepticism, so steeped are they in its propaganda. The COSI also performed furniture removals and storage, did small repairs, helped *sinistrés* find lodgings, exerted 'moral pressure' on unhelpful landlords and provided 'stopgap furniture' (sourced from 'the seizure of Jewish property').[66] But its activities stretched further: it ran parties for bombed-out children, owned two children's residential centres[67] and sought family placements for child evacuees. It took a special interest in elderly workers, made hospital visits and assisted the families of prisoners of war and French workers in Germany, as well as the unemployed. Its social work moved beyond bomb victims and no opportunity was missed to preach its collaborationist message.

The COSI developed an 'unofficial' longer-term activity in favour of bombed-out civilians: 'unofficial' as it was neither within its approved remit, nor was the COSI's name attached to it. During the later part of 1942 the COSI began to set up '*Associations des Sinistrés*', inciting bomb victims to unite and press demands for assistance.[68] Nominally self-governing, the *Associations* relied on the local COSI for material and leadership. In particular, they drew on the legal expertise of the COSI, which was petitioning the government, using the language of justice and entitlement: 'The nation owes you!', Bernard Feuilly of the Management Committee told an *Association* meeting.[69] Civilians should be entitled to the same compensation as military victims:

> A woman widowed by bombing must have the right, like a woman whose husband is killed on the battlefield, to a war widow's pension. An orphan must have the right, like a child whose father is killed in honourable service, to the title and rights of a war orphan [*pupille de la nation*].[70]

Through the *Associations*, the COSI also called for tax exemptions for *sinistrés*, rent reductions, an increase in allowances, permission to recover materials from bombsites and reimbursements for lost furniture based on current prices, not pre-war prices.[71] Much of the work of the *Associations* was to protect and restore private property. By October 1943, there were over 140 *Associations des Sinistrés* in the Northern Zone.[72] Such agitation brought the COSI into direct conflict with the state. Nonetheless on a practical level it continued to work, often grudgingly, with the public authorities and the Secours National, despite the ideological differences between the agencies, each reflecting the different manifestations of the 'three Vichys' outlined above.

AID AND IDEOLOGY

The public authorities, the bureaucratic arm of Vichy, did not attempt to publicize the role they played in the aftermath of bombing, beyond practical instructions to the population. To do so would, perhaps, have emphasized that the state had in fact failed in the task from which it drew some of its legitimacy: protecting the French population from the worst dangers of war. Nonetheless, it seems that here necessity trumped ideology: the aims of the public authorities in aiding bombed-out citizens were pragmatic. The state allocated benefits to bombed-out citizens as an expedient measure in the short term to maintain economic and social stability. The aim was to get work and family lives functioning again as soon as possible. Aid was given not only to the needy: it was a temporary boost to cover unexpected costs, and to permit a continuation of gainful employment. The state allocated building materials to lightly damaged homes for 'rough and ready repairs', to get families rapidly reinstalled.[73] If local temporary accommodation was insufficient, those deemed 'economically without use' would be evacuated; the priority was the working life of the town.[74] The aid available from the public authorities aimed to re-impose normality; its aim was practical re-establishment rather than change, without overt articulation of ideological concerns. It focused on the aid itself not on the act of giving.

In the motivations for giving that animated the public authorities, Vichy ideology is absent: in fact, the public authorities' motivation stemmed from Republican bases which Vichy officially spurned. The new benefits for refugees and sinistrés fell squarely into the republican ideal of welfare provision: as Colette Bec notes, welfare is part of the contractual agreement between governor and governed, 'an obligation for the authorities and a right for the individual'.[75] The state comes to the aid of those who find themselves in need, in no expectation of return from the beneficiary. This contradicts the National Revolution conception of welfare in which help for those in need is provided as a duty by the natural communities of family and workplace. Jackson writes that the National Revolution intended that the 'liberal obsession with rights would be replaced by a stress on duties';[76] yet it was the language of rights which regulated the emergency aid and later the pensions of the victims of bombing: no longer just the needy, but everyone who had experienced loss through the events of war had an entitlement.

The motto of Vichy's National Revolution – Work, Family, Homeland – is, it is true, reflected in the conditions imposed by the state on receiving aid from the public authorities. In the first place, to receive aid a bombed-out person had to be in, or looking for, work. An unemployed sinistré had to be registered at the Office du Travail ('Employment Office') to receive an allowance, but could not claim unemployment benefit and an allocation de sinistré at the same time. Profession was less important, but it did make a difference as only the very lowest earners would have been eligible to receive the allowance. The second element of the motto was family. The family unit formed the basis for the allocation de sinistré: amounts were determined by status within the family (head of household or dependent) and age (for example, children over thirteen years of age received a higher allocation than their younger siblings; adults over 60 but certified unable to work, and all dependent adults over 65 could receive an extra sum). However, some state benefits, such as funeral expenses and moving costs, were a flat rate for all. Unlike Vichy's family allowance, that was intended to act as an incentive for couples to have more children, and so increased exponentially with the number of children in the family, the *allocation de sinistré* was allocated per person, and did not provide increased assistance for larger families. The final part of Vichy's triad of national priorities was *patrie*, or homeland. For much of the war, one had to hold French nationality to claim the *allocation de sinistré*. However, in the early days of the Vichy government, it was possible for German, Italian, Belgian, Dutch or Luxembourgois refugees in France to receive refugee allowances, the earlier equivalent to the *allocation de sinistré*, established before the bombing became more severe. People of other nationalities could not receive financial aid, but could receive aid in kind. But as Vichy became more exclusionist, so did its assistance.

The Vichy of the traditionalists is to be found most clearly within the ideology animating the Secours National. The charity used Pétain to bring in donations, binding itself to his popularity; through its work 'the Marshal comes to ease every distress'. Pétain's propagandists also used the Secours National to spread ideas of his National Revolution north of the demarcation line, where the German authorities did not permit explicitly pro-Vichy propaganda, and the Paris press was hostile. The charity was thus the vehicle for 'pro-Pétain propaganda' in which would be 'attributed to the Marshal all the moral advantages and countless results obtained by the Secours National'. So while publicly the Secours National may have claimed to eschew 'all political and religious concerns', despite its defining link to the state,[77] its propaganda work was undoubtedly political.[78]

The ideology of the National Revolution permeates the Secours National's aims for the aid it offered the *sinistrés*. The Secours National focused on the aid itself and the act of donating to the needy. The aid itself, in food, clothing and money, aimed to prevent social and economic collapse in bombed towns, linked to Vichy's desire for social stability, but without its language of class reconciliation. In an appeal to business and industry, the Secours National called for a 'fraternal' contribution 'capable of bringing about the social calm we so eagerly desire'; 'fraternity' here was not equal brotherhood, but the quelling of a troublesome sibling. This need 'to respect the existing social structure'[79] shows a middle-class organization, acting in charity rather than solidarity, with its own position to uphold as a bulwark against an increasingly desperate working class. For Hoffmann, binding people to their social milieu, without attempting to improve it, was 'an obsessive characteristic' of the National Revolution.[80]

Giving to the Secours National was powerfully linked to the idea of national renewal, likewise a key element in the National Revolution.[81] By giving to bomb victims, citizens inscribed themselves into the national community, as small parts of the organic whole, assisting each other in the spirit of solidarity. Only through this solidarity and the rejection of individualistic behaviour could national renewal come about:[82] 'helping the Secours National', citizens were told, 'is helping France come back to life'.[83] Community solidarity was the essential component, 'without which our country will not be great again'.[84] Within Petain's 'national recovery', the Secours National saw itself as having 'a great part, if not the greatest':[85] through giving, people were creating the new France. The Secours National used the National Revolution's 'sacralizing vocabulary'[86] of suffering and salvation to motivate donors, linking their giving to Pétain's symbolic gesture in 1940: 'by giving the gift of himself to France, Marshal Pétain has spared you the worst suffering'.[87] They should emulate his sacrifice by giving to save the *patrie*, echoing Vichy's anti-individualist rhetoric, suppressing the individual for the benefit of the group.

The conditions governing the receipt of aid from the Secours National also chime with the National Revolution's motto: Work, Family, Homeland. Taken in reverse, the Secours National's assistance was aid for a *national* renewal. Those who did not fit into the newly-styled exclusionist national community were not a priority. While it helped some victims of Vichy's repression, such aid went unpublicized, not fitting into its wider vision; the charity helped alleviate the circumstantial misery of those outside the national community, but did not attack its root.[88] Focusing on who received aid, 'priority is naturally given to large families', echoing the National Revolution's pro-natalism. Being part of a family, rather than a single person, brought greater benefits.[89] Receipt of aid, however, was dependent on a traditional – Catholic – morality, and unmarried couples and divorcees faced discrimination.[90] Potential recipients were divided into the deserving and the undeserving, as in traditional Christian charity and poor relief systems. The deserving were those who fitted more closely the National Revolution's moral ideal. Position within the work community also determined selection for receipt of aid. Certain businesses, such as bakeries, received special help if they were bombed out, but the Secours National limited its help to those businesses 'the resumption of whose work is an essential condition for the resumption of local life'.[91] Part of Secours National's mission was to aid the bourgeoisie and it made special provision for them, directing its personnel to assist those with existing resources, who could be pulled 'from their awkward position once and for all', propping up the social framework.[92]

The intentions that underpinned the COSI's aid share an ideological base with the Vichy of the fascists, the Vichy of the collaborationists; so many of its leaders came from this world that this is hardly surprising. When Jean Ambrogelly of the COSI directing committee stated that its sole aim was 'to serve the unfortunate victims of RAF bombing', he was being disingenuous.[93] Undoubtedly, 'relieving their sorrow and misfortune' was one aim.[94] But the COSI had such a strongly articulated agenda, that aid emerges as a populist means to a political end.

The COSI described its aim in the present as 'the defence of workers' interests'.[95] While its leaders were rarely working-class, and nor indeed were all of its beneficiaries, the COSI saw an opportunity to garner support for its wider goals by bringing together the workers whose traditional organizations had been dismantled by Vichy.[96] It recognized that workers suffered most from air raids, partly as they tended to live near targets but also as they lacked certain knowledge, skills and resources. Its activity sought to address problems specific to bombed-out workers, by providing COSI-managed financial assistance and guidance on dealing with the authorities. The workers had, it claimed, been deprived by a slow and inefficient state, and were discriminated against by a bourgeois Secours National.[97] This placed the *sinistrés* firmly in the hands of those steeped in the COSI's political ideology. In this sense, the COSI's aims were revolutionary: it did not intend to re-establish a pre-bombing status quo, but instead to unite workers to achieve lasting change.

The COSI's broader intentions for the future were also revolutionary, aiming overtly and controversially at radical political change. Its adherence to the ideology of the collaborationist left, seduced by the 'socialism' of national socialism, united present giving and the future France. Worst harmed by war, workers needed peace to thrive; but the COSI placed a condition on its desire for peace: 'There will be no peace in Europe if France and Germany cannot get along.'[98] It therefore followed that working for peace meant working for Franco-German reconciliation; and Franco-German reconciliation would produce a new Europe reorganized 'according to National Socialist ideas', in which France would not be a German vassal, but a respected partner.[99]

The COSI described itself as 'wholly won to Pétain's cause', and echoed certain parts of the National Revolution in its ideology, notably its exclusion of certain elements from the national community. Its attacks on its enemies, however, were conducted with the violence and hatred that characterized collaborationist Vichy. Its activists came from the left, united by 'their original doctrine, fighting against capitalism, the generator of war', but had rejected Marxist socialism, fearing 'the Bolshevik hordes that want to invade Europe and install communism there'.[100] It was anti-capitalism, rather than a notion of national community, however, through which it justified its anti-Semitism and the source of its funding: as 'the French worker has been the victim of Jewish Capitalism, it is therefore natural that the Jew heals the wounds of the French working class'.[101] Anti-communism and anti-capitalism underscored German support, as the Nazis were fighting 'bravely' against bolshevism in a war 'imposed upon us by capitalist financiers in the City and in Wall Street'.[102]

Receiving aid from the COSI was not subject to the same ideological restrictions that the traditionalist Secours National placed upon assistance. In theory – and the COSI's claims must always be treated with scepticism – its aid befitted the realities of working-class life. It recognized the financial vulnerability of working-class wives on the death of a spouse; such women generally suffered 'an emotional loss, but also a material loss'. Widows with or without children could receive money, and mothers were not prioritized. The COSI also considered 'a companion as equal to a widow, as we see things from the human point of view and not the legal point of view'.[103] It appears to have been more sensitive to workers' difficulties, particularly elderly workers. While the state allocated an extra 300 francs per month to those over 65 living alone without income, or in a family deemed needy, the COSI systematically allocated higher sums to the elderly. For example, *sinistrés* over 60 were entitled to double the refurnishing benefit of their younger neighbours.

The COSI presented itself as compassionate, but generous sums were rarely granted. Only two per cent of its spending in November 1942 went on allowances, while 30 per cent was spent on salaries at its headquarters; in June the following year, 2.4 per cent went on allowances and 40 per cent on salaries. The rest was spent on 'general costs at headquarters' and employees' expenses.[104] Furthermore, its objectionable political ideology caused the self-deselection of many in need, and hampered its relations with other relief agencies. 'Not everyone wants German money!' a heckler shouted at a public meeting. Even as they distributed aid at bombsites, COSI personnel were 'subjected to threats and insults'.[105] Furious letters arrived in its mailbox: 'Pooh! Pooh! What a stinking cesspit! What a bunch of rogues! What a COSI!'[106] Many refused its aid on ideological grounds; walkouts were frequent at public meetings. The Bishop of

L'embarquement des petits sinistrés parisiens pour le château d'Hermonville

'Bombed-out Parisian children begin their journey to the château d'Hermonville', after 1942, Bibliothèque de Documentation Internationale Contemporaine (BDIC) et Musée d'Histoire Contemporaine.

Lille forbade his priests to work with it and the local Secours National was at loggerheads with the Committee there.[107] At La Faouet in Morbihan, the mayor refused to be associated with any COSI activities because of its political intentions.[108] When Pétain's representative visited bombed-out neighbourhoods in Rouen in September 1942, the local COSI was not invited to the ceremony; its angry response to this exclusion recognizes the attempt to 'play down our organization's work'.[109] So while its official policy claimed inclusiveness, in reality its political ideology caused many people to turn away from its aid, and other organizations to refuse to work with it.

The French state, the increasingly bureaucratic machine that maintained a functional grip on administrative activities, aided its bombed-out citizens directly, if inadequately, via the public authorities, to re-establish normality now and for the future. Less directly, it funded the parapublic Secours National to provide a stopgap in the short term; the latter supported the ideology of the National Revolution, elements of which were well suited to inspire giving, of oneself and of one's property, to help members of one's community. Yet the state's control was far from total, as the COSI demonstrates. The COSI sought support among the desperate, exploiting need and anger for its wider political aims. The slippage between public and private sources of funding was evident, as was the slippage between public and private motivations for giving: it was not always an intrinsic, philanthropic impulse which inspired aid. Extrinsic pressures pushed giving, and directed what was given, and to whom.

Notes

1   The author would like to thank Professor Andrew Knapp for his invaluable comments on a draft, and for sharing his archival material; Michael Schmiedel was similarly generous in this respect. She would also like to thank the AHRC for funding this research as part of the project 'Bombing, States and Peoples in Western Europe, 1940–45'.

2   Pétain's speech to the cabinet, June 13 1940, in General Émile Laure, *Pétain* (Paris: 1941), quoted in R. O. Paxton, *Vichy France: Old Guard and New Order* (New York: Alfred Knopf, 1972), 16; S. Hoffmann, 'In the looking glass: sorrow and pity?', in *Decline or Renewal? France since the 1930s* (New York: The Viking Press, 1974), 55.

3   Archives Départementales du Nord (ADN), 1W 1290: Commissariat for 'General Information' to Prefect of the Nord, Report on COSI public meeting of 22 November 1942 (speech of Roger Paul), 23 November 1942.

4   S. Hoffmann, 'The Vichy circle of French conservatives', in *Decline or Renewal?*, 3–4.

5   Hoffmann, 'The Vichy circle', 11–12; Paxton, *Vichy France*, 268–9.

6   Hoffmann, 'The Vichy circle', 15.

7   Paxton, *Vichy France*, 193.

8   M. Peyrouton, *Du service public à la prison commune, souvenirs* (Paris, 1950), 84 quoted in Paxton, *Vichy France*, 265.

9   J. Jackson, *France: The Dark Years, 1940-1944* (Oxford: Oxford University Press, 2001), 162.

10   Hoffmann, 'Self-Ensnared: Collaboration with Nazi Germany', in *Decline or Renewal?*, 30.

11   R.F. Kuisel, 'The Legend of the Vichy Synarchy', *French Historical Studies*, 6.3 (1970), 371; D. Drake, *French Intellectuals and Politics from the Dreyfus Affair to the Occupation* (Basingstoke: Palgrave, 2005), 159–61.

12   Hoffmann, 'Self-ensnared', 30.

13   Hoffmann, 'The Vichy Circle', 8; Paxton, *Vichy France*, 253.
14   B. M. Gordon, *Collaborationism in France during the Second World War* (Ithaca, NY and London: Cornell University Press, 1980), 96.
15   Paxton, *Vichy France*, 251-6.
16   Ibid., 231.
17   Jackson, *France*, 232.
18   R. Kedward and R. Austin (eds), *Vichy France and the Resistance: Culture and Ideology* (London: Croom Helm, 1985), 3.
19   J.-P. Le Crom, 'L'assistance publique', in P.-J. Hesse and J.-P. Le Crom (eds), *La protection sociale sous Vichy* (Rennes: Presses Universitaires de Rennes, 2001), 165-7.
20   M. Hastings, *Bomber Command* (London: London, 1999), 147.
21   Slight inconsistencies in death and injury tolls are found in different documentation and publications. Those quoted are drawn from Archives Municipales de Boulogne- Billancourt (AMBB), 6H 72: 'Réponse aux renseignements demandés par Melle Levenez sur les bombarde-ments subis par la Ville de Boulogne-Billancourt', 26 January 1945.
22   For comparison, the town's total expenses during 1942 came to just over 57 million francs. The aid distributed after the 3 March raid was therefore around a tenth of the municipality's annual expenditure (AMBB, 1L 17, 'Rapport sur le compte administratif 1942', 13 December 1943).
23   For example, brothers Jacques and Jean Simon sent 20 francs of their savings for the 'child victims', and Jean Martin in Stalag IV D sent the result of a collection among the prisoners of 360RM (the exchange rate was 20 francs per mark, giving about 7,200 francs (letters of donation in AMBB, 6H 81) – about four months' salary for an unskilled Parisian metalworker, who earned around 1,860 francs per month at this time (A. Sauvy, *La vie économique des français de 1939 à 1945* (Paris: Flammarion, 1978), 128, and Table X, 'Salaires horaires dans les industries des métaux de la région parisienne', 243).
24   Le Crom, 'De la philanthropie à l'action humanitaire'; Le Crom, 'Lutter contre la faim: le rôle du Secours National', in I. von Bueltzingsloewen (ed.) *Morts d'inanition. Famine et exclusions en France sous l'Occupation* (Rennes: Presses Universitaires de Rennes, 2005) 249-62; J. S. Kulok ' "Trait d'union": the history of the French relief organization Secours National/Entraide Française under the Third Republic, the Vichy regime and the early Fourth Republic, 1939–49', University of Oxford, unpublished PhD thesis (2003).
25   P. Ory, *Les collaborateurs, 1940-1945* (Paris: Seuil, 1976), 140, Le Crom, 'De la philanthropie', 225.
26   ADN, 1W 1290: Head of 'General Information' Service (in Lille) to Director of 'General Information' (in Vichy), 7 December 1943.
27   Archives Départementales de la Loire Atlantique (ADLA), 52J 611: COSI brochure, 15 June 1942, 'Comité de patronage', 6; and 'Comité directeur', 15 June 1942; P. Burrin, *La dérive fasciste: Doriot, Déat, Bergery, 1933-1945* (Paris: Seuil, 1986), 397–99, 411, 439.
28   ADN, 1W 1290: Central Police Commissioner to Regional Prefect of Lille, Report on COSI public meeting in Lille on 16 May 1943 (speech of Kléber Legay), 17 May 1943.
29   Archives Municipales de Lille (AML), 5H10 22: COSI leaflet 'Alerte!', undated but probably Spring 1943; Mission d'étude sur l'étude de la spoliation des Juifs de France, *Rapport d'étape*, avr.–déc. 1997, 68-9, cited in Le Crom, 'De la philanthropie', 226, who writes that half of the 950 million francs raised by this fine went to the COSI.
30   Le Crom, 'De la philanthropie', 226.
31   Gordon, *Collaborationism*, 117.
32   ADLA, 52J 611: COSI brochure, 15 June 1942, 'Six semaines d'actions', Roger Auriac, 38; Gordon, *Collaborationism*, 134.
33   Jackson, *France: The Dark Years*, 192.
34   Le Crom, 'De la philanthropie', 224.
35   A *département* is an administrative division of France comparable to a British county, and the territorial basis for the system of state field services headed by the prefects. There were 90 *départements* in France in 1940. AML, 5H10 20: Mayor of Lille to Fernand Martin, 26 June 1944.
36   ADN, 1W 1482: Pierre Laval (Minister of the Interior) to all prefects, 15 February 1943.

37 D. Veillon, *Vivre et survivre en France, 1939–1947* (Paris: Payot, 1995), 270.

38 AML, 5H10 22: Prefect of the Nord to deputy prefects and mayors, 5 December 1940.

39 A year later, this manual worker was earning, according to Sauvy, around 1,860 francs per month (61 francs per day), while a white-collar worker in the Paris metal industry was earning around 2,620 francs per month (Sauvy, *La vie économique*, 128, 243). In his diary, Raymond Ruffin records that in April 1942, a state-employed middle-manager earned around 2,500–3,500 francs per month. At its official price, a kilo of pork cost 17 francs, a kilo of chicken 24 francs, a kilo of butter 45 francs. R. Ruffin, *Journal_d'un J3* (Paris: Presses de la Cité, 1979), 97.

40 Le Crom, 'L'assistance publique', 171–3.

41 Sauvy, *La vie économique*, Table VIII, 'Prix pratiqués au marché noir à Paris', 242.

42 Ibid., 166.

43 Law of 1 September 1942, *Journal Officiel*, 18 September 1942.

44 Wages had been frozen at the declaration of war, but because of high inflation had to be raised, first during 1941, and several times thereafter (Sauvy, *La vie économique*, 201).

45 Law of 13 May 1943, *Journal Officiel*, 12 June 1943.

46 Law of 6 January 1944, *Journal Officiel*, 19 January 1944.

47 Sauvy, *La vie économique*, 203.

48 Law of 12 July 1941, *Journal Officiel*, 16 August 1941.

49 AML, 5H10 20: War Damages Service, 'Obligations des sinistrés' (undated).

50 Law of 13 May 1943; ADN, 1W 1290: Commissariat for 'General Information' (in Lille) to Director of 'General Information' (at Vichy), 15 June 1943.

51 Law of 12 July 1941, *Journal Officiel*, 16 August 1941.

52 AML, 5H10 12: 'Évacués, réfugiés. Voici ce que vous devez savoir', brochure published by SIPEG during 1944, 14 (undated).

53 ADLA, 1690W 146: Prefect of the Loire-Inférieure to deputy prefects and mayors, 19 June 1941.

54 Archives Départementales des Bouches-du-Rhône (ADBdR), 76W 200: Pierre Laval (Minister of the Interior) to all prefects, 9 October 1940.

55 ADLA, 1690W 146: Prefect of the Loire-Inférieure to deputy prefects and mayors, 19 June 1941.

56 Ibid.: Secours National, Social and Administrative Bulletin, 31 March 1944.

57 Ibid.

58 Archives Départementales de la Manche (ADM), 2Z 106: 'Notre Action', no 4, internal publication of Secours national, 15 May 1942.

59 For example, following the raid on the eighteenth arrondissement of Paris, Saint-Denis, Saint-Ouen and La Courneuve on 20 April 1944, the Secours National distributed around 270,000 meals (Mémorial de Caen (MC), FQ 72: Secours National (Paris section) leaflet 'Bilan de Secours au sinistrés', 31 May 1944).

60 MC, FQ 72: Secours National (Paris section), Secours National leaflet 'Où va l'argent?', Occupied Zone 1941, undated (possibly April 1942). During 1941, the biggest expense for Secours National was the Mutual Kitchens (*cuisines d'entr'aide*) (365 million francs), followed by children's vitamin biscuits (95 million francs). In comparison, 15 million francs were spent on new furniture for the *sinistrés*, the same amount on household articles, 9 million on temporary housing structures and 3 million on children's evacuation centres.

61 ADLA, 1690W 146: Monsieur Pichat to regional delegates of the Secours National in the Occupied Zone, 30 May 1941.

62 Ibid.: prefect of the Loire-Inférieure to Marcel Déat (Minister of Work and National Solidarity), 12 May 1944.

63 Archives Départementales du Morbihan (ADMor), 2W 15921: National Police Inspector Montfort to Head of 'General Information' Service (in Vannes), Report of COSI public meeting in Pontivy on 6 June 1943 (speech of Jean Ambrogelly), 8 June 1943.

64 ADN, 1W 1290: COSI, 'Bulletin mensuel', June 1943, 5.

65 Sauvy, *La vie économique*, 243.

66 ADLA 52J 611: COSI brochure, 15 June 1942, 'Les autres tâches du COSI', Robert Letourneur, 19, 15 June 1942.

67   One of which was renamed Centre Philippe Henriot following the collaborationist minister's murder at the hands of the Resistance in June 1944 (Archives Nationales, Paris, F7 14901a: René Mesnard to Joseph Darnand, 4 August 1944).

68   ADN, 1W 1290: Central Police Commissioner to Regional Prefect of Lille, report on COSI public meeting in Haubourdin, 26 September 1942.

69   Ibid.: Commissariat for 'General Information' to Prefect of the Nord, report on COSI public meeting of 22 November 1942, 23 November 1942.

70   ADLA, 52J 611: COSI brochure, 'Les unions des sinistrés, Jean Ambrogelly, 28, 15 June 1942.

71   ADN, 1W 1290: Commissioner for 'General Information' to Deputy prefect of Dunkirk, Report on COSI public meeting on 27 September (speech of Jean Ambrogelly), 28 September 1942.

72   ADMor, 2W 15921: COSI poster, 'Aux Sinistrés Lorientais', October 1943.

73   AML, 5H10 12: 'Évacués, réfugiés. Voici ce que vous devez savoir', brochure published by SIPEG during 1944, 14 (undated).

74   AML, 5H10 22: Regional prefect of Lille to Mayor of Lille, 14 January 1943.

75   Colette Bec, Assistance et République (Paris: Éditions de l'Atélier, 1994), 15, quoted in Le Crom, 'L'assistance publique', 165.

76   Jackson, France, 149.

77   ADBdR, 76W 200: Departmental Secours National delegate Félix Prax to Presidents of Departmental Mutual Aid Committees, 11 November 1943.

78   ADLA, 1693W 129: Police Commissioner for 'General Information' (in Nantes) to Prefect of the Loire-Inférieure, 1 June 1943.

79   Kulok, '"Trait d'union"', quoting Archives de la Ville de Paris, 24W 1, 'Rapport moral sur l'activité de la Direction sociale du SN', 1941, 15, 68.

80   Hoffmann, 'The Vichy Circle', 14.

81   Kulok, '"Trait d'union"', 227.

82   ADBdR, 76W 200: Departmental Secours National delegate Félix Prax to Presidents of Departmental Mutual Aid Committees, 11 November 1943.

83   Ibid.: Félix Prax to potential donors, letter (undated) and leaflet 'Le Bilan du Secours National pour 1943', April 1944.

84   MC, FQ72: Secours National leaflet, 'Luttez avec nous', undated (after March 1942).

85   ADM, 2Z 106: 'Notre Action', no 4, internal publication of Secours national, 15 May 1942.

86   Kulok, '"Trait d'union"', 231.

87   MC, FQ72: Secours National (Paris section), advertising flyer for portraits of Pétain at 5 francs each, sold to raise money for the Secours National (undated).

88   Kulok, '"Trait d'union"', 194–208.

89   ADLA, 1690W 146: Pichat to regional Secours National delegates in Occupied zone, 30 May 1941.

90   Le Crom ('De la philanthropie', 201) cites a woman who was 100 per cent bombed out, but received only four plates and two forks from the Secours National as she was a divorcée.

91   ADLA, 1690W 146: Pichat to regional Secours National delegates in Occupied Zone, 30 May 1941.

92   Kulok, '"Trait d'union"', 68, and 168 for establishment of 'Mutual Aid Restaurants for the Middle Classes'.

93   ADLA, 52J 611: COSI brochure, 'Les unions des sinistrés', Jean Ambrogelly, 28, 15 June 1942.

94   Commissariat aux renseignements généraux (Kervarec) to prefect of the Nord, 23 November 1942, report on COSI public meeting of 22 November 1942, speech of Roger Paul, ADN, 1W 1290.

95   ADLA, 52J 611: COSI brochure, René Mesnard, 'Le COSI et les organisations syndicales', 11–12, 15 June 1942.

96   The Confédération générale de travail had been outlawed in November 1940 (Jackson, France, 297).

97   ADN, 1W 1290: Central Police Commissioner to Regional Prefect of Lille, report on COSI public meeting in Lille on 16 May 1943, (speech of René Mesnard), 17 May 1943.

98   Ibid.: Police Commissariat for 'General Information (in Lille) to Prefect of the Nord, report on public meeting of COSI on 26 July 1942 (speech of René Mesnard), 27 July 1942.

99   Ibid.: Commissariat aux renseignements généraux (Lille) to Prefect of the Nord, report on confidential note from local COSI to Sonderführer Eggert concerning potential COSI/PPF integration, 18 September 1942; Commissariat aux renseignements généraux to Prefect of the Nord, Report on COSI public meeting of 22 November 1942 (speech of Roger Paul), 23 November 1942.

100   Ibid.: Central Police Commissioner to Prefect of Nord, report on COSI children's party on 11 March 1943 (speech of Kléber Legay), 12 March 1943.

101   Ibid.: Commissioner aux renseignements généraux to Deputy prefect of Dunkirk, Report on COSI public meeting on 27 September (speech of Jean Ambrogelly), 28 September 1942.

102   Ibid.: Central Police Commissioner to Prefect of Nord, report on COSI children's party on 11 March 1943 (speech of Kléber Legay), 12 March 1943; ADLA, 52J 611: COSI brochure, 'Les unions des sinistrés', Jean Ambrogelly, 28, 15 June 1942

103   ADLA, 52J 611: COSI brochure, 'Service d'allocations', Mme Noualhaguet, 15, 15 June 1942.

104   René Mesnard received 75,000F per month, plus 125,000 each quarter from the German Embassy (Le Crom, 'De la philanthropie', 225); ADN, 1W 1290: COSI, 'Bulletin mensuel', June 1943, 5.

105   ADMor, 2W 15921: National Police Inspector Montfort to Head of 'General Information' Service (in Vannes), report on public meeting in Guemene sur Scorff on 7 June 1943, 8 June 1943; ADN 1 W 1290: Commissariat aux renseignements généraux (Lille) to Prefect of the Nord, 21 July 1942.

106   ADN, 1W 1290: message typed on the back of a COSI tract, August 1942.

107   Ibid.: Commissariat aux renseignements généraux (Lille) to Prefect of the Nord, 21 July 1942.

108   ADMor, 2W 15921: National Police Inspector Montfort to Head of Commissariat aux renseignements généraux (Vannes), report on public meeting in La Faouet on 7 June 1943, 8 June 1942.

109   Archives Municipales de Rouen, 4H 141: Monsieur Linant, Secretary of Rouen COSI to Mayor of Rouen, 25 September 1942.

PART II

Cultural Responses to Bombing

5

The Defence of Works of Art from Bombing in Italy during the Second World War*

Marta Nezzo

In Italy, research on the protection of works of art during the Second World War has emerged noticeably late. Paradoxically, the availability of a large number of memoirs (produced by both ministerial functionaries and superintendents) has for a long time inhibited critical analysis. Almost dazzled by adventurous and heroic (though certainly also valuable) stories by some of the protagonists of the time, only recently have scholars begun to compare sources and to undertake archival work. Among the scholars who worked on these subjects, a special mention should be made at least of Maria Marta Boi and, in a more recent period, Elena Franchi, Ilaria Sgarbozza and Francesca Iannetti.[1] This chapter will be principally concerned with the activity of the Superintendencies for Monuments and for Galleries based in Venice. These two bodies played a crucial role in protecting works of art, as is clear from the various shelters set up in the Veneto region from 1940 to 1945, particularly the Abbey of Praglia, in the province of Padua.[2]

The Veneto can be regarded as a paradigmatic region as far as the protection of works of art is concerned. Unlike southern and central Italy, the Veneto was affected by the war throughout its whole course. Here can be found each of the phases and all of the procedures involved in the defence of works of art, together with their successes and failures, from the initial plans for the protection of both the movable and immovable artistic heritage issued by the Fascist government between 1940 and 1943, to the new directives promulgated by the Italian Social Republic (the so-called Salò Republic) during the years 1943–45. Moreover this region, or more precisely the city of Padua, hosted from 1943 the Republic's Ministry of National Education and the new General Direction of the Arts, which simultaneously had to confront both the threat of Allied bombing and the menace of German depredations. This explains the focus of this chapter on the experience of the Veneto.

*Translated from the Italian by Richard Pierce and Stuart Oglethorpe.

PRE-WAR APPROACHES TO CONSERVATION: FROM INTERNATIONAL TO NATIONAL

During the Second World War, the monuments in Italy that could not be moved were subject first to the visual and symbolic alteration made by defensive structures aimed at protecting them, and then to the irreversible damage wrought by bombardment. Movable works of art, on the other hand, survived as if in a state of suspension, consigned to the limbo of continuous mobility. A perpetual motion of paintings, jewellery and sculptures, from the city centres to the outskirts and countryside and back again, was the apparently schizophrenic manifestation of the defence of works of art, an unceasing task once defined as a 'Sisyphean labour.'[3]

These predicaments occurred in Italy due to the particular and multi-level nature of the types of warfare developed there. Leaving aside the controversial pro-Nazi stance the country espoused in the pre-war period (for example, its participation in the Spanish Civil War, the racial laws, and the Axis alliance), two basic phases can be delineated: that of aggressive acts (against France and Greece in 1940 and Yugoslavia in 1941), which resulted in Italy being bombed but not invaded, and then the months following the summer of 1943, after the Anglo-American invasion of Sicily and the illusion of an armistice, which led to the Allied advance from south to north, the German occupation and retreat and the civil war. From the standpoint of the preservation of works of art, each of these phases presented problems and required different solutions.

On an international level, the first codification of modes of warfare that incorporated safeguards for the belligerents' artistic patrimony dates to The Hague conventions of 1899 and 1907. Tragically, these were emptied of all meaning by the increased destructive potential of weaponry used in the First World War. In the period following the 1914-1918 conflict, given the damage to Reims, Louvain and Venice (where Austrian bombing between 1915 and 1918 resulted in the destruction of Tiepolo's ceiling of the Scalzi church near the railway), new solutions were sought. At The Hague in 1922-1923 an international commission of jurists tried to establish rules for the conduct of aerial warfare, and even touched upon the theme of the 'open city.'[4] Soon afterwards the matter was taken up by the League of Nations: from 1926 onwards, the *Institut International de Coopération Intellectuelle* (International Institute of Intellectual Cooperation) sought to mitigate – on a cultural level – the excesses of ever growing chauvinism.[5] One of its instruments was the *Office International des Musées* or OIM (International Bureau of Museums), which was established in 1927 and, through the periodical *Mouseion*,[6] coordinated the efforts of the various nations to preserve and administer their museum collections. In this context, in October 1932 the assembly of the League of Nations recommended 'educational action on the part of the governments as the safest means of ensuring respect, in all circumstances, for the testimony of past civilizations.'[7]

At the outset this recommendation fitted in well with the prevailing constructive and peaceful climate. But as early as 1934 the OIM took upon itself the task of describing a less reassuring atmosphere, inviting individual governments to prepare forms of material protection of their artistic heritage should any emergencies arise. This was a sinister sign of things to come, whose meaning soon became evident with the outbreak of the Spanish Civil War. In 1937 the periodical *Mouseion* called upon persons responsible for the management of fine arts throughout Europe to reflect realistically on the possibly catastrophic consequences of a new conflict,[8] and between 1937 and 1938 the OIM hastily drew up plans for a multilateral convention to promote the defence of works of art in each nation, even suggesting that works should be temporarily entrusted to neutral countries.[9] Italy took part in these proceedings,[10] but Giuseppe Bottai, the Minister of National Education, rejected the pact, pointing out the difficulties involved in transferring masterpieces to the border while the country was being mobilized. He especially feared the loss of national identity that such a transferral would provoke, since in case of defeat large numbers of works of art would risk being confiscated as war reparations.[11] For this and other reasons, the international agreement failed and therefore, when the Second World War broke out in 1939, the artistic patrimony of Europe remained vulnerable. The OIM hastily published in the September–October 1939 supplement of *Mouseion* all the various pre-existing international conventions and unilateral governmental declarations concerning the emergency protection of works of art; it also proposed a preliminary report of the unilateral measures already adopted in Belgium, the Netherlands, Switzerland, Greece, France, Great Britain, Germany and Egypt, as well as Norway and the other Scandinavian countries.[12] The supplement suggested the demilitarization of the sites of artistic importance and the conveyance of movable objects far from the theatre of war and possible military targets. Lastly, the OIM published *La protection des monuments et oeuvres d'art en temps de guerre* (The Protection of Monuments and Works of Art in Wartime),[13] a manual that not only provided a juridical history of the subject, but also furnished detailed information on various defensive techniques, from shelters to fire-fighting procedures and the strengthening of buildings in order to protect windows. The illustrative material was based on photographs of the protective measures taken in war-torn Spain and on several Italian plates (illustrations of a remarkable colour and size), most of which concerned measures adopted in World War One.[14] The description of the packing methods is meticulous, but the related images only partially cover the subject matter, showing boxes and crates for paintings as well as bags filled with sand used to protect buildings. Simple diagrams give instructions on how to fortify the storehouses at a ground level and underground. This was a true gallery of fear and hope, completed by the addition of the text of the planned international convention, which had failed to win support.

In Italy the first consultations between the Ministry and superintendencies concerning possible plans for protection took place at a very early stage: in the Veneto region they date from 1930–31.[15] At this time the superintendent of medieval and modern art in Venice, Gino Fogolari, complained that it was impossible to protect in any truly effective manner such structures as the Scrovegni Chapel and St. Mark's Basilica, because the protective measures against shrapnel adopted in World War One – 'buttresses, sandbags …, protective covering made of algae or other soft material' – now seemed inadequate.[16] Less dramatic, in his opinion, was the situation regarding movable objects: mindful of the tragic events of 1915–1918, he had already instructed his inspectors 'to keep ready the lists of the objects, divided according to their importance and the planned procedure for gathering and taking them far away'.[17] With time, a precise salvage hierarchy was established, consisting of three categories according to the works' quality and transportability.[18] With regard to the places where the works were to be sheltered, Fogolari immediately excluded Venice due to the city's lack of cellars, while he planned to distribute them in various depots in the countryside. As early as 1931, he thought of the Villa Nazionale of Stra, the Praglia Abbey and former Convent at Carceri (all in the province of Padua) as probable places for safekeeping.[19]

A more detailed inquiry into the possible means for protecting works of art from aerial attacks was ordered by the Ministry of National Education (in connection with OIM's advice and the preparations being made for the Ethiopian campaign) only in 1935, after the publication of the *Regolamento per la protezione antiaerea del territorio nazionale e della popolazione civile* (Regulation for the anti-aircraft defence of national territory and the civilian population).[20] However, according to the official reports compiled after the Ministry's inspections,[21] the superintendencies' actual preparations for an 'unexpected' war were generally considered insufficient. Indeed, the theoretical defence plan was not matched by parallel logistical support capable of meeting the need for the rapid evacuation of works of art. In short, the means were lacking. The problem related more to government delays in getting the various departments (Ministry of Finance, of Public Works, and of National Education) to agree, on the allocation funds, rather than to the local bodies responsible for care of the works.[22] This uncertainty was to continue for a long time, as can be seen in complaints and requests for funds and guidance sent to the National Superintendence of Fine Arts by the Committee for Air-raid Protection in 1936,[23] by the prefectures in 1937,[24] and by Fogolari in 1938 and subsequently.[25] At a theoretical level, the planning of protective measures was to be left with the superintendencies throughout the second half of the 1930s, and without any effective response from Rome until at least 1939.

A booklet entitled *Istruzioni per la difesa antiaerea* (Instructions for Anti-Aircraft Defence), published and distributed by the Ministry of National Education in 1937, contains only a few rather generic lines concerning the protection of the artistic and scientific heritage. The movable works of art were 'to be taken away and put in safe places, preferably in towns of little importance inland'; as far as the monuments were concerned, orders were given to 'construct defensive works, reinforce isolated elements, wall up arcades, inter-columniations and doorways, make barricades with sandbags, and, if possible, cover the entire monument with temporary structures'.[26] Equally vague were the instructions imparted by the Law of War and Neutrality of 8 July 1938.[27] Only in February 1939 did a ministerial ordinance specifically ask the superinten-dents to 'state the sum needed to acquire the necessary means of anti-aircraft protection and packing material for the movable works of art'.[28] In conclusion, funds began to arrive only at the start of the war, in very limited amounts and for the most urgent needs.[29]

The whole question of emergency protection for works of art was bound up with the formulation of the more comprehensive and well-known Law Concerning the Protection of Objects of Artistic and Historic Value, which dealt with the conventional problems of artistic conservation and which was finally signed and promulgated by Bottai in June 1939. The law had taken two years of hard work to formulate, largely thanks to its sophisticated juridical character, but it became one of the first victims of the changes brought about by Italian intervention in the European war on 10 June 1940. The potential effec-tiveness of Bottai's law was undermined, not only by the operational regulations that came into force, but by the decision to adapt its provisions to war purposes by a supplementary ordinance issued in July 1940, which effectively nullified its impact. The governance of the emergency protection of works of art came to be based on a very slender legal foundation.

THE PRACTICE OF CONSERVATION, 1939–42

On 6 June, with hardly any advance notice, the superintendents received a new order to move works of art from cities and towns. Although the alert lasted for some time, the effects differed widely from region to region: for example, after the war, reports of a total lack of preparation came from Carlo Ceschi about Liguria,[33] and from Emilio Lavagnino for Umbria.[34] However, wherever possible, the works from museums and private collections began to be packed. As for the protection of immovable objects, a very limited selection was made and very few monuments were covered:[35] for example, in the Veneto region these monuments included among others the façade of St. Mark's, the arches of the Ducal Palace, and Sansovino's loggia in Venice, as well as the Scrovegni Chapel in Padua.

The protection consisted either of bags filled with river sand placed on a framework made of fireproofed wood or of masonry, or facing made up of cases, again filled with sand, or yet again, covering consisting of hanging mattresses. These protective structures were in turn covered on the top with roofs and slabs, and asphalt-covered cases were placed on the sides.[36] The lists of the covered sites in the Veneto bear the following clarification: 'All the measures adopted for the protection of the ... immovable works of art are effective only for protection against shrapnel, and not against direct hits'.[37] The workmen were careful 'not to place the bags against the works ... but always to leave an aerated intervening space between them'; to 'use very dry river sand, not sea sand, in order to prevent any possible damage that might be wrought by salinity'; and again, to 'avoid contact between the supporting or protective walls and the old structures by means of sheets of paraffin paper and tarred cardboard'.[38] The visual impact made by the monuments with 'defensive cladding' was, psychologically speaking, depressing indeed, while the actual protection had very little effect. Therefore those responsible for the works often preferred to mark the roofs of the buildings with a conventional sign that showed the bombardiers that they were of artistic value.

For the transport of movable works of art, just as had happened in 1915–1918, rolls of material one metre in diameter were prepared for wrapping round canvases, as well as boxes and crates for painted panels and other rigid objects. The ordinary staff were accompanied by numerous honorary inspectors, who were often chosen from among the directors of the various civic museums.[39] As for the shelters, the choice was based on the safety requisites repeatedly indicated by the OIM: a necessary distance from industrial and military structures, as well as from communication routes and railways, and the required width and relative dryness of the rooms available for use as repositories. It has been calculated that there were about one hundred storehouses in Italy,[40] among which mention should be made of the 37 in Tuscany and the ones in Sassocorvaro and Carpegna in the Marche region, which became famous thanks to the audacious acts of Pasquale Rotondi and Emilio Lavagnino.[41] From October 1940 these repositories also housed a few works from Venice, taken from the Ca' d'Oro, the Museo Orientale and the Gallerie dell'Accademia (Academy Galleries), including Giorgione's *Tempest*. This operation, determined by the Ministry, reiterated the First World War model of protection: to move key works of art far away from the national border.[42] This time, however, a limited selection was considered[43] as superintendencies thought for some time that the danger to be faced would be exclusively from the air. Fogolari wrote:

> We must not be too heavily influenced by what was done in the previous great war. Then, protection from air attacks had to be supplemented by provision for rescuing what might have been of great value to the potential enemy invader; while now we just need to plan for aerial bombardment, with our region no more vulnerable than any other to these dangers.[44]

Appropriate places in which to house books, documents[45] and works of art were also set up in the Veneto region, which even hosted material from the jurisdiction of the Mantua superintendence (such as the artistic patrimony of Verona);[46] as had been planned for since 1931, the main depository was the former Olivetano convent of Carceri (for the province of Venice), which, as time went on, was joined by the Villa Salom at Brugine (for Padua, Venice and Rovigo), the Villa Camerini in Montruglio (for Vicenza), the Villa Gradenigo (for Bassano), the Gipsoteca or gallery of plaster casts at Possagno (for Treviso), the Certosa (Carthusian monastery) of Vedana (for Belluno).[47] In the case of minor works of art, or those difficult to move, it was decided from the start that rather than transfer them it was best to keep them where they were, though in reinforced buildings: for example, in Venice some halls and rooms in the Correr Museum, the Palazzo Rezzonico, the Palazzo Pesaro and others were used for this purpose. However, from the outset, the pace by which protective measures were pursued was bound up with the course of Italian military strategy, which was closely linked with the fortunes of the German war machine. Thus, the loss of Addis Ababa in April 1941 and the Axis invasion of Yugoslavia the same month prompted an intensification of the programme for removing works of art; yet by the following autumn the tension had eased and the programme slowed down.[48]

Allied raids, which were ceaseless (albeit not yet devastating) in southern Italy, largely spared the north until late 1942.[49] The Ministry, along with the superintendencies, dedicated its efforts to a self-aggrandizement that smacked of propaganda with the publication of *La protezione del patrimonio artistico nazionale dalle offese della guerra aerea* (The Protection of the National Artistic Patrimony against Aerial Attacks), a richly illustrated volume that came out very early, in 1942, with an unequivocally triumphant tone. Surprisingly, the book did not focus on the value of war as such but focused instead on the quality of the civil society that had answered the call to arms. The exploitation of monuments as a form of national identity – which had aimed between 1915 and 1918 at consolidating a sense of national identity – now underwent a marked evolution. The spectacular photographs of the defence of Italian artwork, whether expressed through their transfer to places of safety or through their protective covering, extolled the cultural and political maturity of the civil institutions involved; it was no longer the army, an amorphous national body, which protected the arts, but the Fascist state itself, with all its juridical and administrative creatures. In 1942 the tone of military aggressiveness, and the condemnation of the barbarous destruction by the Allies, were both scaled down. Rather, in his introduction to the volume, Marino Lazzari, the Director General of Fine Arts, praised the work of the superintendents and other officials, paradoxically calling attention to the great opportunity for preservation that had presented itself thanks to the war. He wrote:

> Teams of restorers … are at work, and, while the workmen are preparing the wrapping, the canvases are being restored, cleansed of the dust and mould that might, in the enclosed space of the rolls or crates, damage the surface of colour; the restored colour is being consolidated, the blisters are being smoothed, and protective gauze is being pasted onto the painting in order to prevent the colour from peeling off. And, at last, it is time to set off: we already know that the shelter selected is quite safe, the technicians know the place like the back of their hands, they know what the average humidity of the rooms is and what difference in temperature there is between summer and winter and between day and night. Everything has been foreseen, studied and arranged beforehand.[50]

The difficulties involved in protecting the immovable works allowed Lazzari to laud the newly established *Istituto Centrale del Restauro* (Central Restoration Institute), the pride and joy of the Ministry, whose task was to check periodically 'the environmental conditions created by the protective apparatus around the frescoes'.[51] It was not enough, according to Lazzari, to protect the building from the danger of collapse:

> Fire, the gases produced by a nearby explosion, the water itself from the pumps used to extinguish the fires ... all undermine the fragile existence of those highly precious paintings. ... The protection itself may become lethal: the coverings could favour humidity, deprive the natural respiration process of the wall of its air. It is therefore necessary to cover and protect, but not to seal off; and to prevent any possible alteration in the chemical and physical conditions of the colour and the plasterwork. ... Suitable solutions have been found: incombustible and impermeable materials that will allow air to pass through special vents and yet constitute an impenetrable barrier for fire and water.[52]

These words and the photographs that accompanied them were designed to show that the situation was under control.

Works for the antiaircraft protection of the façade of St. Mark's Basilica in Venice. Direzione Generale delle Arti (ed.), *La protezione del patrimonio artistico nazionale dalle offese della guerra aerea* (Florence: Le Monnier, 1942).

But it was in 1942 that the fortunes of the Axis Powers began to decline. Aside from the setbacks in North Africa and in Russia, the RAF, which had begun area bombing over Germany in the spring, applied the same technique in northern Italy that autumn. Genoa was attacked six times in October and November; Turin received seven raids in November and December. These raids had devastating effects both on civilian morale and on the historical and artistic patrimony.[53] Put on the alert by the government, all the superintendencies were once again in a state of agitation.

Such attacks also worried the authorities in Venice, where, in October-November 1942, it was decided to remove the numerous works of art that were still in the city, 'beginning with the horses of St. Mark's, Tintoretto's *Paradise*, etc.'[54] To this end, a new, huge repository was made operational: the Praglia Abbey.[55] The presence of a shooting range and troops there made this complex a moderately noticeable target, but the urgency of the situation prevailed. In fact at first the superintendents appreciated the military neighbours, who they thought 'could increase the safety of the site', and only at a later stage did they begin to request the total demilitarization of the zone.[56] Once the transport of the works had already begun, measures were taken to ensure the security of the convent with a telephone system, stocks of sand and lightning conductors and new electrical wiring. The superintendencies placed their own caretakers there on a permanent basis.[57] The transferral of the sculpture pieces was truly impressive: busts, statues made of stone (as well as wood, bronze, terracotta and alabaster), altar frontals, portals, windows and above all the architectural elements and the frameworks for funerary monuments, including virtually all the famous mausoleums in the Santi Giovanni and Paolo Basilica. Besides the shipments that came directly from Venice, Praglia received groups of works that had already been deposited in Carceri, in order to reduce the stock in the latter depot. These shipments were not conducted by servicemen, but rather by specialized delivery firms. The sentry duty was carried out by security guards who were especially paid for this service.[58] Thus the logistical organisation consisted almost entirely of civilians and in all probability drew on the inherited experience gained earlier by mounting major temporary exhibitions, for which Italy had become famous. The fact that the organisation was funded by the Ministry also reveals the great difference between the new system and the experience of the Great War, when the army had assumed responsibility. The difference was due to the growing strength of the official organisations now responsible for the fine arts, made evident by the role of the superintendencies in drawing up lists of essential artwork and in regularly checking their condition.

THE PRACTICE OF CONSERVATION, 1943–45

But this state of equilibrium was itself soon interrupted. The Allied invasion of Sicily in July 1943 changed the military situation, and with it the emergency protection system: the danger of air raids was now complemented by that of land warfare, which would expose the storehouses of works of art in the rural areas to both shelling and pillage. The first consequence was therefore an increase in surveillance, given the probability of the rapid advance of the enemy troops. In 1943, with the fall of Mussolini in July, the armistice in September and the foundation of the Italian Social Republic, the country was plunged into civil war. Carlo Alberto Biggini became the head of the new Ministry of National Education, which was set up in Padua.[59] His task was to deal with the air raids, the demands of the Germans, and the land battles. But he had other problems too: for example, he was aware that he could not exercise the same influence on all the superintendencies, or on the old functionaries at the General Direction of the Arts, still based in Rome and largely autonomous. As we shall see, these limitations would have serious consequences. Furthermore, Biggini both feared and distrusted the Nazi protectorate, and hoped to be able to establish a less problematic relationship with the surviving Fascist authorities.

In the meantime, the situation of Italy's immovable artistic heritage began to take on a tragic aspect. Among the countless disasters (for example, as noted above, in Liguria and Piedmont), it is worth remembering the four raids on Milan in August 1943, which unleashed a terrible fire that lasted for a week, aggravated by the lack of water.[60] Damage to monuments was devastating. In the south too, during and after the Allied landing, air raids became particularly heavy. Apulia and Campania, subjected in the summer of 1943 to bombing by both the Allies and the Luftwaffe, suffered most. The Church of Santa Chiara in Naples, for example, was hit by incendiary bombs which left only the external walls intact; the frescoes, pictures and sculptures, none of which had been removed, were all lost. From the autumn of 1943, the Ministry reports are thus explicit not only about the most drastic destruction, but also signal the collateral effects of the bombardments, such as the continuous exposure to bad weather of the interiors of historic buildings whose roofs had been destroyed.[61]

So far as the non-movable architectural heritage was concerned, the Veneto suffered most between 1944 and 1945. However, as early as October 1943, the superintendents were facing both aerial bombing and land combat (which had already had such dramatic consequences in World War One) and insistently called for the return of the movable works of art to the cities. The accounts of the overall management of the problem are quite explicit. In an anonymous note sent to Minister Biggini (which he agreed with), it is possible to read:

> Now that the war is being fought inch by inch on our national territory and without any immune or less jeopardized areas, [the] shelters situated for the most part in the countryside run the risk of finding themselves ... in the very midst of the battlefield. The imminent danger regarding the material integrity of the works is accompanied by that of theft on the part of individuals, or worse, of confiscation either ordered or tacitly authorized by the commanders of the troops engaged in battle.[62]

There was thus a palpable sense of fear concerning German requisitions. Given this new state of affairs, the objectives of the emergency defence of works of art were reformulated as follows:

> Guarantee the material preservation of the works until the end of the war; guarantee Italian possession rather than that of foreigners, be they allies or enemies. Having said that, it is self-evident that the dispersion of the works in shelters, which at any moment may become strategic or tactical points, is far more dangerous than storing them together in a large city.[63]

Summing up, there were at least two aspects to the problem – aerial attacks and theft – and they suggested opposite solutions: gathering together the works of art in a few demilitarized cities might have spared them from air raids, but at the same time it could facilitate confiscation by the Nazis. At first, one possible compromise seemed to be to concentrate the works of art in Rome and Venice, where both the Germans and Allies were to be notified immediately, in the uncertain hope that the works would be spared. Certainly Rome was an ideal choice, because it might have made possible asylum in the Vatican City,[64] but the idea that Venice might have been a suitable refuge[65] in the autumn of 1943, in a city almost entirely lacking in dry underground storage facilities, was evidently of dubious value.[66] In November 1943, however, National Superintendent of Fine Arts Marino Lazzari (outraged by the Germans' removal of works at Montecassino) wrote to Alessandro Pavolini, former Minister of Popular Culture and now head of the Republican Fascist Party at Salò:

> This paradoxical situation must be urgently resolved. I do not doubt that the Germans want more than just to save the works. It is a fact, however, that a group of very valuable objects, taken by foreigners [the Germans] from their shelter, is now being moved across Italy without the office responsible for its reception having been given due notice or even knowing where it will arrive. The German authorities must understand that none of us is reckless and irresponsible enough to want Italian art treasures to be captured by the British and Americans, and that we too want these treasures out of the war zone, and therefore in the North; but that we should be the ones to take them from their shelters, protect them en route, and decide on the most suitable destination. ... The issue of the general depot in Venice, which I have discussed with Biggini – and he agrees – must be resolved positively and as soon as possible. This is the only guarantee we still have of being able to carry out an independent, Italian operation, and to remove, once and for all, this problem, which has nothing to do with politics, from the political arena. I am putting this sacred matter in your hands and asking you to take the utmost care of it. We are dealing with the only possession that we Italians still have, and as it is a spiritual one it must be saved at all costs.[67]

Uncertainty ruled: the documents indicate that only a few days later the National Superintendence was considering bringing all the works of art together in one place, in Rome.[68]

When in October 1943 paintings and sculptures were again moved – this time from their rural shelters to the cities – the procedure was not uniform. In the Veneto, only certain repositories were emptied: the one in Carceri immediately, while in Praglia the storehouse not only remained active until April 1945, but even continued to take in works of art, for example from the Vicenza area. Moreover, in December 1943 institutional upheaval affected the administrative personnel of the National Superintendence of Fine Arts, weakening its network of control: most of the Roman officials either did not recognize, or were not recognized by, the new Italian Social Republic. Thus Lazzari, at the head of the sector for the former Fascist-monarchist government, was dismissed together with several inspectors,[69] and was replaced by Carlo Anti, the former Chancellor of the University of Padua. And the official headquarters of the Direction itself was transferred to Padua, in direct contact with the Ministry.[70]

In the midst of this chaotic situation there was yet another countermanding order: the new minister Biggini summoned all superintendents and on 9 January 1944, quite unexpectedly, he suspended the transferral of works of art to the cities.[71] The halt imposed by Biggini provoked the indignation of the officials operating in Central Italy, who had hoped the works of art would find asylum in the Vatican City; some rebellious ones – such as Rotondi and Lavagnino – carried out the planned transferral of works of art to Rome, earning the formal condemnation, but also the moral approval, of the Superintendence of Fine Art in Padua. On 25 January 1944 Pasquale Rotondi wrote in his diary:

> I had the impression that [Anti] was not at all unhappy about the dispatch of works of art to the Vatican. His idea ... is that the defence of movable heritage needs to be intensified. He is therefore trying, on the basis of an international convention, to have one of the cities in central Italy (Assisi? Florence?) declared an 'open city' and so host the most important works. In the meantime, according to him, I should avoid gathering many works in the same shelters, and try to spread them throughout the territory under the surveillance of churches, in agreement with the bishops of the Marche ... (But how can he not see the risks of such an adventure?)[72]

However, the Ministry now seemed firmly opposed to the transferral of works of art from Central Italy to the north,[73] perhaps because this could have encouraged the expatriation of Italian works of art to Germany.[74] Indeed, in the summer and autumn of 1944 Nazi pillage increased, especially in Tuscany, and in early 1945 the same fate awaited the Ravenna area, in a criminal itinerary that marked the path of the retreating German troops.[75]

The situation in the Veneto was different, partly because most of the anxieties were directed at the course of the land campaign, partly because the Ministry might have thought that its presence in the region would be enough to check the danger of thefts. It would almost seem that at this stage of the war the National Superintendence of Fine Arts felt that the effective defence of the artistic heritage, both movable and immovable, could no longer be planned or managed against the chief danger, that of air raids. This would explain the apparent lack of continuity in the ministerial guidelines and even the appeals to spare the historic towns and areas made by Resistance leaders to the Anglo-American troops.[76] We now know that, at least from 23 February 1944, the commanders of the Allied Air Forces attempted to balance military needs with respect for monumental sites. This resulted in a tragic classification of heritage sites: those that were absolutely to be avoided unless specifically authorized by the Allies (category A), those that were to be avoided if possible (category B), and those that could be bombarded and attacked without any qualms (category C). At the top of the list, only four cities were a step away from safety: Rome, Florence, Venice and Torcello.[77] Padua, Verona and Vicenza were included in the unfortunate category C, and in fact these cities were bombed,[78] while the *Serenissima* was spared; but in 1944 the officials of the Italian Social Republic probably knew nothing of these instructions, and in any case they could not control the movements of German troops, which of course were targets for the Allies.

In the Veneto region the concentration of works of art was largely completed,[79] but only after the fall of Rome in June 1944, that is to say, when it became quite clear that Allied armies would advance northward. So, partly as a reaction

Fascist propaganda condemns Allied bombing for the destruction of Andrea Mantegna's frescoes in the Eremitani Church in Padua on 11 March 1944. *La guerra contro l'arte* (Milan: Domus, 1944).

to the appeals of the superintendents, priority was given to the movement of the works to Venice.[80] In conclusion, the artistic treasures of Italy suffered tremendous damage on the part of all the belligerents.[81] As the superintendents had foreseen from the start,[82] the protection of non-movable objects was revealed to be a palliative solution – if not useless, certainly a rather modest one. Plans to evacuate movable objects, by contrast, were successful: the initial shelter in countryside stores and afterwards the continuous moving around of pictures and sculptures (literally escaping from the bombs), were the key to safety. That said, no precautions could be taken or strong resistance made Nazi theft. Even today a long list exists of works of art which disappeared never to be found again.[83] Furthermore, on top of the material damage there was ideological abuse. In September 1944, the publisher *Domus* brought out a photographic book entitled *La guerra contro l'arte* (The War against Art),[84] in which another desecration was committed in the name of propaganda. The photographs (provided by the superintendencies and specialized studios, as well as by the National Socialist *Kunstschutz*, responsible for the artistic patrimony in occupied territories)[85] present certain monuments in their intact state, at times with their protective covering, side by side with photographs of the same monuments reduced to rubble. Thus the lost architectural heritage, with many of the sites now in Allied hands, retained a ghostly presence, phantoms marked by a white cross to indicate their artistic death. This was not a call to arms but rather to hatred, and art, which was already a victim, now became its principal instrument.

Notes

1   M. M. Boi, *Guerra e beni culturali (1940–1945)* (Pisa: Giardini, 1986); E. Franchi, 'Una "doverosa ma non convinta obbedienza". La protezione del patrimonio artistico a Pisa durante la seconda guerra mondiale', *Polittico*, 2 (2002), 233–251; F. Iannetti, 'Il "lavoro di Sisifo": interventi per la difesa delle opere d'arte mobili durante la seconda guerra mondiale' and I. Sgarbozza, 'Venezia 1935-1945. La difesa della città dai pericoli degli attacchi aerei', in P. Callegari and V. Curzi (eds), *Venezia: la tutela per immagini. Un caso esemplare dagli archivi della Fototeca Nazionale* (Bologna: Bononia University Press, 2005), 137–46; 129–36; E. Franchi, *Arte in assetto di guerra: protezione e distruzione del patrimonio artistico a Pisa durante la seconda guerra mondiale* (Pisa: ETS, 2006). I also would like to mention the conference *Proteggere l'arte, proteggere le persone. Bologna 1940-1945*, Bologna, Oratorio di S. Filippo Neri, 23-24 November 2007 – see proceedings *Bologna in guerra. La città, i monumenti, i rifugi*, ed. L. Ciancabilla (Bologna: Minerva, 2010) and the exhibition *Brera e la guerra* held in Milan at Brera on 10 November 2009 – 21 March 2009 – see catalogue *Brera e la guerra. La pinacoteca di Milano e le istituzioni museali milanesi durante il primo e il secondo conflitto mondiale*, ed. C. Ghibaudi (Milan: Electa, 2009). Although not strictly on Italian questions, it is worth mentioning the wider reflection on the European situation in N. Lambourne, *War Damage in Western Europe. The Destruction of Historic Monuments During the Second World War* (Edinburgh: Edinburgh University Press, 2001).

2   M. Nezzo, 'Praeterea Archiva, Bibliothecae, Musea, Pinacothecae ac praestantissima cuiusvis Artis opera in Domo nostra asylum ac tutamen habuerunt' in *L'Abbazia di Santa Maria di Praglia* (forthcoming: Abbazia di Praglia). Superintendencies in Italy were created at the

beginning of the 20th century. They are still administratively decentralized organs, generally distributed on a regional basis, and entrusted with the co-ordination of protection of works of art. Their denomination and format have changed with time. During the period covered by this chapter, the Superintendencies operating in a certain territory were generally three: the Superintendence for Monuments (for the protection of non-movable objects and buildings), the Superintendence for Galleries and Works of Art (for movable objects) and the Superintendence for Antiquities (for the archaeological patrimony), all dependent on the General Direction of the Arts. The latter was part of the Ministry of National Education. Until the beginning of 1941, the Superintendencies for Monuments and for Galleries based in Venice were directed by Gino Fogolari, who had been involved in the protection of the historical-artistic patrimony during the First World War. When he died in January 1941, Ferdinando Forlati became director of the Superintendence for Monuments and Vittorio Moschini of the Superintendence for Galleries. For information on superintendents see Ministero per i Beni e le Attività Culturali, Direzione Generale per il Patrimonio Storico Artistico e Etnoantropologico, Centro Studi per la Storia del Lavoro e delle Comunità Territoriali (ed.), *Dizionario biografico dei soprintendenti storici dell'arte, 1904–1974* (Bologna: Bononia University Press, 2007).

3   The definition is by P. Bucarelli, author among other works of a chronicle of the war period: *1944. Cronaca di sei mesi* (Rome: De Luca, 1997).

4   See 'Conference de la Haye. Le code de la guerre aérienne', *Revue des deux mondes*, 1 September 1923. For more information see Boi, *Guerra e beni culturali*. About the defence of works of art during the wars, see G. Vedovato, 'La protezione del patrimonio storico, artistico e culturale nella guerra moderna', in *Congresso internazionale della Société international pénal militaire et de droit de la guerre* (Florence: Palazzo Vecchio, 17 May 1961 – off-print); F. Panzera, *La tutela internazionale dei beni culturali in tempo di guerra* (Turin: Giappichelli, 1993); F. Maniscalco (ed.), *La tutela del patrimonio culturale in caso di conflitto* (Naples: Massa, 2002).

5   About the IICI see J.-J.Renoliet, *L'UNESCO oubliée: la Société des Nations et la Coopération intel-lectuelle. 1919–1946* (Paris: Publications de la Sorbonne, 1999); M. C. Giuntella, *Cooperazione intellettuale ed educazione alla pace nell'Europa della Società delle Nazioni* (Padua: CEDAM, 2001).

6   About the periodical see Annamaria Ducci, 'Mouseion', *Annali di critica d'arte*, 1 (2005), 287–313.

7   For a history of OIM activity aimed at protecting monuments, see 'Commentaire du Projet', in 'La Protection des monuments et oeuvres d'art en temps de guerre', *Mouseion*, 47–8 (1939), 202–14, 202.

8   J. Renau, 'L'organisation de la défense du patrimoine artistique et historique espagnol pendant la guerre civile', *Mouseion*, 39–40 (1937), 7–66; 'La protection des monuments et objets histor-iques et artistiques contre les destructions de la guerre. Proposition de la Société néderlandaise d'archéologie' (1919), *Mouseion*, 39–40 (1937), 81–9.

9   'Avant-projet de Convention internationale pour la protection des monuments et oeuvres d'art au cours des conflits armés proposeée par L'Office International des Musées', *Société des Nations. Journal Officiel*, XIX, 11 (November 1938); also in 'La Protection des monuments et oeuvres d'art en temps de guerre', *Mouseion*, 47–8 (1939), 180–201.

10   Many well-known figures sat on the committee: A. Geouffre de La Pradelle (Professor of International Law, University of Paris), E. McLagan (Victoria and Albert Museum, London), S. de Madariaga (OIM); Commander Moineville (Ministére de l'Air, Paris), F. Pellati (National Superintendence of Fine Arts, Rome), N. Politis (Greece), Captain Sas (General Staff, Holland), F. Schmidt-Degener (Rijksmuseum, Amsterdam), A. Stix (Kunsthistorisches Museum, Vienna), H. Verne (Musées Nationaux, Paris); C. de Visscher (Court of International Justice); and E. Foundoukidis (OIM).

11   G. Bottai, 'La Protection des chefs-d'oeuvre de l'esprit', *Nouvelles Littéraires* (12 February 1938), 8; Bottai, 'La Tutela delle opere d'arte in tempo di guerra', *Bollettino d'arte*, 31, s. 3, 10 (April 1938), 429–430, re-published in Bottai, *La politica delle arti. Scritti 1918–1943*, ed. A. Masi (Rome: Editalia, 1992), 141–3.

12   'Conventions internationales en vigueur et autres déclarations de Gouvernements concernant

la protection des Monuments et oeuvres d'art au cours des conflits armés' and 'Les mesures de protection prises dans différents pays contre les dangers de la guerre', *Mouseion. Supplément mensuel* (September-October 1939), 5–22.

13   *Mouseion*, 47–8 (1939).

14   The Italian photographs have been published in U. Ojetti, *I Monumenti italiani e la guerra* (Milan: Alfieri e Lacroix, 1917).

15   Archivio Centrale dello Stato, Rome (ACS), Ministero della Pubblica Istruzione (MPI), Direzione Generale Antichità e Belle Arti (DGA), Divisione (Div.) II, 1934/40, b. 69, fasc. *Venezia. Soprintendenza monumenti. Elenchi opere d'arte e progetti per la difesa del patrimonio artistico*, G. Fogolari to Ministry of National Education (MNE), Direzione Generale Antichità e Belle Arti (National Superintendence of Fine Arts) (DGA), 31 December 1930.

16   ACS, MPI, DGA, Div.II, b. 69, fasc. *Venezia. Soprintendenza monumenti. Elenchi opere d'arte e progetti per la difesa del patrimonio artistico*, G. Fogolari to MNE, Ministerial Committee, 24 June 1931.

17   ACS, MPI, DGA, Div. II, b. 69, fasc. *Venezia. Soprintendenza monumenti. Elenchi opere d'arte e progetti per la difesa del patrimonio artistico*, G. Fogolari to MNE, DGA, Div. II, 7 May 1931.

18   See Direzione Generale delle Arti (ed.), *La protezione del patrimonio artistico nazionale dalle offese della guerra aerea* (Florence: Le Monnier, 1942). The effective implications of this hierarchy are explained in letters in ACS; for example see ACS, MPI, DGA, Div. II, 1934/40, b. 102, fasc. *Venezia. Soprintendenza alle gallerie. Elenco opere d'arte salvaguardate*, U. Pasquinelli (Provincial Inspector, Air Raid Protection, Prefecture of Treviso) to MNE, DGA, 2 December 1935.

19   ACS, MPI, DGA, Div.II, 1934/40, b. 69, fasc. *Venezia. Soprintendenza monumenti. Elenchi opere d'arte e progetti per la difesa del patrimonio artistico*. G. Fogolari to MNE, Ministerial Committee, 24 June 1931.

20   Law decree of 5 March 1934: *Regolamento per la protezione antiaerea del territorio nazionale e della popolazione civile* (Rome: 1934). The Ministry published circulars on this topic: 107/31 December 1934 and 16/19 February 1935. For more information, see Franchi, *Arte in assetto*, 27.

21   ACS, MPI, DGA, Div. II, 1940/45, b. 73, fasc. *Protezione antiaerea del Patrimonio artistico. Ispezioni alle Soprintendenze del Comm. De Tomasso*, M. De Tomasso, 'Protezione del materiale artistico mobile dai pericoli della guerra aerea. Relazione' (May 1935). See also ACS, MPI, DGA, Div. II, 1934–40, b. 57, fasc. *P.A.A. Progetti per la difesa dei monumenti e opere d'arte e rapporti con i Comitati provinciali*, 'Riservatissima. S.E. il Capo del Governo ha approvato il piano d'azione', 8 June 1935.

22   ACS, MPI, DGA, Div. II, 1934–40, b. 57, fasc. *P.A.A. Progetti per la difesa dei monumenti e opere d'arte e rapporti con i Comitati provinciali*, C. M. De Vecchi (Ministry of National Education) to F. Baistrocchi (Under Secretary of State for War), 15 July 1936.

23   Ibid. C. Tironi (President, I. P.A.A. Central Committee) to MNE, DGA, 27 June 1936.

24   ACS, MPI, DGA, Div. II, 1934/40, b. 102, fasc. *Venezia. Soprintendenza alla gallerie. Elenchi opere d'arte salvaguardate*, Alliaudi (Prefect of Vicenza) to MNE, 12 April 1937.

25   Ibid., G. Fogolari to MNE, DGA, 20 April 1938.

26   'Protezione del patrimonio artistico e scientifico e degli ingenti valori', in *Istruzioni per la difesa antiaerea* (Rome: Istituto Poligrafico dello Stato, 1937).

27   Law Decree of 8 July 1938, n. 1415, 'Approvazione dei testi della legge di guerra e della legge di neutralità', Supplement to *Gazzetta Ufficiale*, 211, 25 September 1938.

28   Circular no. 376, 8 February 1939, in Iannetti, *Il 'lavoro di Sisifo'*, 137.

29   ACS, MPI, DGA, Div. II, 1934/40, b. 57, fasc. *Richiesta fondi per acquisto materiale imballaggio opere d'arte e per acquisto materiale equipaggiamento squadra di I intervento*, General Director of Fine Arts, 'Appunto per il signor Ministro', 28 August 1939.

30   Law 1039 of 1 June 1939.

31   For more information, see M. Serio, 'La legge sulla tutela delle cose di interesse artistico o storico', in V. Cazzato (ed.), *Istituzioni e politiche culturali in Italia negli anni Trenta* (Rome: Istituto Poligrafico e Zecca dello Stato, 2001), vol. 1, 329–441, 342–4.

32   Law 1041 of 6 July 1940. See also ACS, MPI, DGA, Div. II, 1934–40, b. 57, fasc. *Legge per la protezione del patrimonio artistico della nazione in caso di guerra*, 'Progetto di legge per le cose di interesse artistico, storico o in genere culturale e degli archivi, in circostanze straordinarie'.

33   Carlo Ceschi was superintendent for monuments in Liguria from 1939 to 1953. See his criticism in *I monumenti della Liguria e la guerra* (Genoa: Istituto di Studi Liguri, 1949).

34   At the time Emilio Lavagnino was Inspector at the Ministry of National Education, General Direction of Fine Arts. See his diary 'Diario di un salvataggio artistico. Dicembre 1943 – Maggio 1944', *Nuova Antologia*, 109 (1974), 509–47.

35   Although the number of protected monuments in the different regions might appear to be substantial, they in fact represented only a very small proportion of a very large cultural heritage. The application of those defences was therefore almost negligible.

36   Direzione Generale delle Arti (ed.), *La protezione del patrimonio*, 109–10.

37   ACS, MPI, DGA, Div. II, 1934/40, b. 69, fasc. *Venezia. Soprintendenza monumenti. Elenchi opere d'arte e progetti per la difesa del patrimonio artistico*, Ferdinando Forlati (Superintendent for Monuments, Venice) to MNE, DGA, 29 July 1940.

38   Ibid. Within the limit of financial possibilities, the defensive claddings were continuously maintained and restored throughout the whole conflict.

39   Direzione Generale delle Arti (ed.), *La protezione del patrimonio*, 113.

40   Boi, *Guerra e beni culturali*, 3.

41   At the time Pasquale Rotondi was Superintendent to Galleries at Urbino. For a short description of the activities by Lavagnino and Rotondi see later, 18. It is also worth mentioning both their memoirs and the work of scholars on the latter subject: E. Lavagnino, 'Migliaia di opere d'arte rifugiate in Vaticano', *Strenna dei romanisti*, 7 (Rome: Staderini, 1946), 82–8; P. Rotondi, 'Capolavori d'arte sottratti ai pericoli della guerra ed alla rapina tedesca', *Urbinum*, July-August 1945, 1–35; E. Lavagnino, 'Diario di un salvataggio artistico' in P. Bucarelli, *1944. Cronaca di sei mesi* (Rome: De Luca, 1997); S. Giannella and P. D. Mandelli, *L'Arca dell'Arte* (Milan: Editoriale Delfi, 1999); A. Lavagnino, *Un inverno. 1943-1944* (Palermo: Sellerio, 2007).

42   ACS, MPI. DGA, Div. II, 1934/40, b. 102, fasc. *Mezzi per il trasporto delle opere d'arte in caso di guerra*, Ministry to Superintendent of Art Galleries, Venice, 26 November 1939.

43   Ibid. fasc. *Venezia. Soprintendenza Gallerie. Elenchi opere d'arte salvaguardate*, G. Fogolari to MED, DGA, 29 January 1940.

44   G. Fogolari to the Prefect and President of the provincial committee for air raid protection, Venice, 20 April 1938, see above.

45   On libraries, archives and the relevant superintendencies, see A. Paoli, *Salviamo la creatura: protezione e difesa delle biblioteche italiane nella seconda guerra mondiale* (Rome: Associazione Italiana Biblioteche, 2003); A. Capaccioni, A. Paoli and R. Ranieri, *Le biblioteche e gli archivi durante la seconda guerra mondiale: il caso italiano* (Bologna: Pendragon, 2007).

46   Although geographically in the Veneto region, Verona was under the superintendence of Mantua rather than that of Venice.

47   V. Moschini, 'Vicende di guerra delle opere d'arte venete', *Arte Veneta*, 1 (January-March 1947), 60–4; 61.

48   Moschini, 'Vicende di guerra', 61–2.

49   G. Bonacina, *Obiettivo Italia. I bombardamenti aerei delle città italiane dal 1940 al 1945* (Milan: Mursia, 1970), 100. The situation in the south rapidly became serious in 1943. At the time of the liberation of Naples, the city had already been subject to 131 Allied raids and to five German raids. See also Boi, *Guerra e beni culturali*, 33.

50   Direzione Generale delle Arti (ed.), *La protezione del patrimonio*, vii.

51   Ibid, viii.

52   Ibid, ix.

53   It is estimated that, throughout the war, Genoa was subject to 83 air raids and to three naval bombardments. Even considering only the city centre, 234 historic buildings were either damaged or destroyed. Turin, which had already suffered terrible damage to its archival and book patrimony by the end of 1942, experienced the further devastation of 31 churches and 77 palaces by the end of the war. For more information see Boi, *Guerra e beni culturali*, 117, 121–6.

54   Moschini, *Vicende di guerra*, 62. For an account of the removal of the horses of St. Mark's, see
M. Tortora, 'Da Piazza S. Marco a Praglia. Un Leone e quattro cavalli', *Il Popolo d'Italia*, 21 April
1943. See also Nezzo, 'Praeterea Archiva'.

55   ACS, MPI, DGA, Div. II, 1934/40, b. 102, fasc. *Venezia. R. Soprintendenza alle Gallerie.
Ricoveri*, G. Bottai to Superintendence of Art Galleries (Venice), telegram, 16 November 1942.
For more about Praglia see Nezzo, 'Praeterea Archiva'.

56   Nezzo, 'Praeterea Archiva'.

57   Ibid.

58   Ibid.

59   Biggini was minister between 6 February and 25 July 1943, and retained this position under the
Salò Republic. For more details, see L. Garibaldi, *Mussolini e il Professore. Vita e diari di Carlo
Alberto Biggini* (Milan: Mursia, 1983); M. Borghi, 'Il Ministero dell'Educazione Nazionale
durante la Repubblica Sociale e l'operato di Carlo Alberto Biggini', in L. Scalco (ed.), *Tra liberazione e ricostruzione. Padova, 8 settembre 1843-2 giugno 1946* (Padua: Editoriale Programma,
1998).

60   25 per cent of Milan was razed to the ground, while 35 per cent experienced minor damage. Of
the 27 churches listed among the protected monuments only five were not hit' (Boi, *Guerra e
beni culturali*, 128).

61   ACS, MPI, DGA, Div. III, 1945/48, b. 257, fasc. *Rapporti con le autorità germaniche per la
tutela delle opere d'arte*, '[Nota] consegnata al Ministro Biggini che approva, il 10 ottobre 1943'.
The disaster continued as the armies moved northwards, through the unfortunate junction at
Montecassino. In Lazio, Rome was subject to a less tragic fate compared with other cities, with
the exception of the devastation of San Lorenzo; the historical-artistic patrimony of Tuscany
was subject to heavy bombardment, particularly in the summer of 1944. The ruin of the
Florentine bridges, as it is well known, was due to the Germans.

62   Ibid.

63   Ibid.

64   On 12 November 1943, after long negotiations, the papacy agreed to State-owned works of
art being moved into the Vatican. M. De Tomasso, Promemoria, in ACS, MPI, DGA, Div. III,
1945/48, b. 257, fasc. *Rapporti con le autorità germaniche per la tutela delle opere d'arte*.

65   As repositories were selected Palazzo Ducale, Ca' Rezzonico, Gallerie dell'Accademia, Palazzo
Pesaro, Palazzo Pisani, Seminario Patriarcale (V. Moschini to the Fire Brigade headquarters,
5 February 1945, in ACS, MNA, DGA, Div. II, 1934/40, b. 101, fasc. *Venezia. Ricoveri per le
opere d'arte. Fasc. II. Carte dal 1943*).

66   Between August 1943 and April 1945 a series of pleas were made by Italian religious and
political authorities to both the German and Italian military authorities to have Venice declared
an 'open city' (ACS, MPI, DGA, Div. II, 1934/40, b. 100, fasc. *Venezia. Protezione antiaerea.
Città aperta. Allontanamento obiettivi militari*).

67   ACS, MPI, DGA, Div. III, 1945/48, b. 257, fasc. *Rapporti con le autorità germaniche per la tutela
delle opere d'arte*, Lazzari to Pavolini, 26 October 1943.

68   'Appunto per il viaggio a Padova del sig. direttore generale', no date but probably November
1943.

69   Lavagnino, *Diario di un salvataggio artistico*, 517.

70   The forced retirement of many functionaries was formally explained by their refusal to move
to the new destination. Some of them continued to work as if nothing had happened. Among
them was Emilio Lavagnino, who wrote ironically in his diary on 21 January 1944: 'I never
worked so much as since I retired' (Lavagnino, *Diario di un salvataggio artistico*, 521).

71   Evidence on this meeting is not entirely consistent: the best substantiated is the account
according to which Biggini halted the centralization operation, following up the order with
a circular; this however has yet to re-emerge (Note of 13 January 1944, in Lavagnino, *Diario
di un salvataggio artistico*, 519-20; A. Lavagnino, *Un inverno. 1943-1944*, 55). The ministerial
decision probably allowed for dispensations: according to Moschini (Superintendent for the
Venice Galleries), at that meeting 'the security position was reviewed for the various centres
where works of art from galleries and museums in general were being brought together'. He,
however, used this review to pursue centralization, ordering the transfer of some works to

Venice from an outlying storehouse (ACS, MPI, DGA, Div. II, 1934/40, b. 101, fasc. *Venezia. Ricoveri per le opere d'arte. II. Carte dal* 1943, V. Moschini to the town council of Bassano del Grappa, 21 January 1944). Forlati (Superintendent for Venice's monuments) also mentioned the meeting in neutral tones: 'the Minister wisely gave clear and well-considered orders which can be summarized thus: use every means possible to hasten provision for and protection of monuments and works of art; manage state money with strict honesty and economy' (ACS, MPI, DGA, Div. II, 1934/40, b. 100, fasc. *Riservato. Venezia. Soprintendenza Monumenti. Documenti contabili delle anticipazioni fondi per la Protezione Anitaerea*, Forlati to MNE, DGA, 20 October 1944). The 'politicized' and 'anti-collaborationist' accounts drawn up between the summer and autumn of 1944 by Romanelli-Argan, De Tomasso and Lavagnino, discovered in the State Archives, convey a more complex situation. Once again, this evidence is not consistent. An objective reconstruction of the protective activity by the Salò Republic – in the shape of Biggini and Anti – is still being undertaken. To add to the papers in the State Archives, the diaries of Anti himself are in fact kept in the city museum of Padua; after years of fruitless requests, it is hoped that these will soon be available for consultation. In the meantime, the recent volume *Diari e altri scritti di Carlo Anti*, edited by Girolamo Zampieri (Verona: Accademia di Agricoltura, Scienze e Lettere, 2009) is unfortunately an unacceptable substitute.

72   Note by Pasquale Rotondi, 25 January 1944, in *L'Arca dell'arte*, 131–6. In these pages, Rotondi witnessed Biggini's discomfort: he found it difficult to talk to Mussolini because he was always surrounded by German officials, as if he was under surveillance.

73   The ministerial position was in effect very unclear and seemed to change with each emergency: on the one hand we know that in August 1944 works from Bologna, Ravenna and Forlì were to be brought to Venice (ACS, MPI, DGA., Div. II, 1934/40, b. 101, fasc. *Venezia. Ricoveri per le opere d'arte. II. Carte dal* 1943, V. Moschini to Superintendent of Bologna Art Galleries, 21 August 1944); on the other hand, however, Biggini and Anti, on the grounds that transport was dangerous, were to obstruct the transfer of Tuscan artistic heritage north as much as possible (Notes of 15 May and 12, 16 June 1944, in Garibaldi (ed.), *Mussolini e il professore*, 171; 250; 275; ACS, MPI, DGA, Div. III, 1945–48, b. 257, fasc. *Antichità e Belle Arti*, E. Lavagnino, [Relazione], August 1944). On the transfers, see also Boi, *Guerra e beni culturali*, 4.

74   It is likely that the minister suspected (or already knew about) the existence of storages in the Gau Tirol, where the Germans gathered works of art stolen from Italy. See R. Siviero, *L'arte e il nazismo* (Firenze: Cantini, 1984); Boi, *Guerra e beni culturali*, 5–10.

75   L. Morozzi and R. Paris (eds), *L'Opera da ritrovare. Repertorio del patrimonio artistico italiano disperso all'epoca della seconda guerra mondiale* (Rome: Istituto Poligrafico e Zecca dello Stato, 1995). See also R. Siviero, *Seconda mostra nazionale delle opere recuperate in Germania* (Florence: Sansoni, 1950).

76   'Lettera di Pietro Nenni per indurre i piloti, nel limite del possibile, a non colpire i monumenti', in Fondazione Cassa di Risparmio di Padova e Rovigo, *Bombardamenti aerei sulla città di Padova e provincia* (Padua: Tempio-Museo dell'Internato Ignoto, 2005), 30.

77   Boi, *Guerra e beni culturali*, 95.

78   Padua was subject to 40 air raids, with extended artistic damage. In particular, Mantegna's frescoes in the Ovetari Chapel at the Eremitani Church were completely destroyed. Verona was bombed 30 times, with consistent monumental losses, among which was the devastation of the Porta dei Leoni (of imperial Roman age); the situation was further worsened by the German destruction of its bridges, which damaged the churches near the river. The 15 raids on Vicenza provoked catastrophic damage to the historic part of the city – for example, the Cathedral was almost entirely destroyed, the Eratenio theatre was completely ruined and the Palladian factories were damaged.

79   The exception of Praglia is important.

80   ACS, MPI, DGA, Div. II, 1934/40, b. 101, fasc. *Venezia. Ricoveri per le opere d'arte. II. Carte dal* 1943, V. Moschini a MNE, DGA, 12 June 1944. For more information see Nezzo, 'Praeterea Archiva'.

81   For a summary of losses on the national territory Boi, *Guerra e beni culturali* remains fundamental; in order to have a sense of the nature of the damage it is also worth consulting

the volume *La Ricostruzione del Patrimonio artistico italiano*, ed. Direzione Generale delle Antichità e Belle Arti (Rome: La Libreria dello Stato, 1950).

82   See above, footnote 38.

83   Morozzi and Paris (eds), *L'Opera da ritrovare*.

84   *La guerra contro l'arte* (Milan: Domus, 1944). Photos by the Superintendencies of Florence and Venice and by Hans Gerhard Evers (German *Kunstschutz* in Italy).

85   About *Kunstschutz* in Italy, see E. Kubin, *Raub oder Schutz? Der deutsche militärische Kunstschutz in Italien* (Graz-Stuttgard: Leopold Stocker Verlag, 1994).

6

'The photograph my skull might take': Bombs, Time and Photography in British and German Second World War Literature

Lara Feigel

In the winter of 1940, Stephen Spender experienced a 'tremendous' bombing raid which seemed powerful enough to 'destroy the whole of London'.[1] He described his first impressions of the bombing in unreal, photographic terms in his 1945 poem, 'Rejoice in the Abyss'.

> When the foundations quaked and the pillars shook,
> I trembled, and in the dark I felt the fear
> Of the photograph my skull might take
> Through the eye sockets, in one flashlit instant
> When the crumbling house would obliterate
> Every impression of my sunlit life
> With one impression of black final horror
> Covering me with irrecoverable doom.[2]

Dreading the apocalyptic flash of the bomb, Spender fears the flash of the camera, with its unnerving power to suspend and destroy time. The photograph like the bombs obliterates past and future, trapping the scene in an eternal present that is itself immediately in the past. The black horror is 'final' and 'irrecoverable'.

Accounts of the Blitz in both Britain and Germany frequently figure the bombs as photographic and cinematic. This is partly a question of lighting effects: the flash of the fire and searchlights illuminated against the blackout. But in seeing the bombs as photographic, these 1940s writers seem to be engaging more fundamentally with 1920s and 1930s ideas about the nature of photography. In particular there is often a sense that war shares the photograph's ghostly capacity to turn presence into absence, rendering the world in the strange tense of the has-been-there.

This essay will explore the use of photographic images in 1940s British and German literature responding to the Second World War civilian bombing. In Britain, it will focus on Elizabeth Bowen's 1949 *The Heat of the Day* and stories and poems by Henry Green, William Sansom and Stephen Spender, who all worked as firemen during the war. In Germany, it will look at Hans Erich

Nossack's 1943 *Der Untergang* (*The End*), stories by Wolfgang Borchert and an account of the bombing of Hamburg by Gretl Büttner. It will consider the use of camera-eye narratives as a form of witnessing and the presentation of the air war itself as inherently photographic. This is not so much a comparison of the two national literatures as an exploration of the strikingly similar imaginative responses of writers in the two countries.

The photographic rendering of war has political implications. In seeing war as a photograph, these writers are detaching themselves from the world around them, abnegating political responsibility and experiencing the destruction as essentially apolitical. The extreme, often self-conscious aesthetics seem to counteract or negate politics. This is why the British and German bombing literature is so often similar, despite the totally different political contexts and war experiences. At the same time, to photograph war, either literally or textually, is a political act. In framing these moments and bearing witness, these writers are necessarily engaging with 1940s politics.

'I AM A CAMERA'

In both Britain and Germany, the 1920s and 1930s were decades of photography and cinema. During the 1930s, the Left in both countries saw both as potentially radical media, with the power to redeem society. In his influential 1936 'The Work of Art in the Age of Mechanical Reproduction', the German political theorist Walter Benjamin celebrated the loss of aura in technologically reproduced images. He claimed that the photographic 'work of art' was at last emancipated from its 'parasitical dependence on ritual'. 'Instead of being based on ritual, it begins to be based on another practice – politics.'[3] In England, photojournalists like Bill Brandt were making the most of photography's capacity to represent the working classes and Auden was lauding photography as '*the democratic art*', extolling 'amateur snapshots' as 'the only decent photographs.'[4]

The enthusiasm for photography was part of a more general enthusiasm for reportage, and for factual witnessing. 'I am a camera with its shutter open', Christopher Isherwood famously announced in his 1930 Berlin diary, 'quite passive, recording not thinking.'[5] In 1937 the novelist Storm Jameson demanded that the socialist writer should turn himself into a mechanical camera. 'As the photographer does', she wrote,

> so must the writer keep himself out of the picture while working ceaselessly to present the *fact* from a striking (poignant, ironic, penetrating, significant) angle ... His job is not to tell us what he felt, but to be coldly and industriously presenting, arranging, selecting, discarding from the mass of his material to get the significant detail, which leaves no more to be said, and implies everything.[6]

Spender, fearing the photograph his skull might take, is quite different from

Jameson's ideal witness. The kind of detached witnessing that she describes was arguably impossible, even in the 1930s. Isherwood would later state that

> what I really meant by saying 'I am a camera' was *not* I am a camera all the time, and that I'm like a camera. It was: I'm in the strangest mood at this particular moment … I just sit and register impressions through the window – visual data – without any reaction to it, like a camera.[7]

Isherwood suggests that he was using the image of the camera to express a subjective state. In wartime, when the writer-observer is himself cowering from the bombs, objectivity becomes even harder. The writer is necessarily implicated in his world, feeling and fearing as he observes. For 1940s writers, the assumption of a camera eye often functions instead as a way to escape the facts; to go beyond the significant detail to a detached visual spectacle. The camera can also, as in Spender's case, serve to express an existing detachment; an existing sense that the world as it is experienced is already mediated by the camera. For Spender, the fire is already photographic partly because it has already been photographed.

This sense that the world was already photographic – that, as Baudrillard would later put it, the 'hyperreal' 'signs of the real' precede the real – is prevalent in both Britain and Germany in the 1930s and 1940s.[8] In an essay about Picasso's *Guernica* written in 1938, Spender states that Picasso's picture was not a response to personal horror but to 'horror reported in the newspapers, of which he has read accounts and perhaps seen photographs.'[9] 'This kind of second-hand experience', he adds, gleaned from the media, 'is one of the dominating realities of our time':

> The many people who are not in direct contact with the disasters falling on civilization live in a waking nightmare of second-hand experiences which in a way are more terrible than real experiences because the person overtaken by a disaster has at least a more limited vision than the camera's wide, cold, recording eye, and at least has no opportunity to imagine horrors worse than what he is seeing and experiencing.[10]

In Spender's formulation, war mediated by camera consciousness is in fact worse than actual war. Keith Williams has labelled the Spanish War the 'first fully modern media conflict', in the sense that people away from the conflict learnt about events on the battlefield almost as they took place.[11] Due to recent advances in photography, news photographers at the front line were able for the first time to take 36 photographs before needing to reload their cameras. The cameras themselves were more portable than ever before, making the photographer almost as mobile as the soldier, and subject to the same dangers.[12] These photographs did not merely depict the war. In a sense they *were* the war. They were weapons rather than mere representations; weapons used to incite the foreign involvement that was so crucial to both sides.[13] Robert Capa's controversial September 1936 *Loyalist Militiaman at the Moment of Death* typifies the hyperreal aspect of the Spanish Civil War. It is now believed that the soldiers were playing around with their rifles for Capa's benefit, hoping to help him manufacture some convincing shots. According to Capa's biographer, Richard Whelan, the soldiers 'fired, and by doing so attracted the enemy's attention.'[14] Federico Borrell Garcia, the soldier in question, stood up so that Capa could photograph him from below. But just as Capa was about to press his shutter release, a hidden enemy machine gun opened fire. If we accept Whelan's explanation, the photograph becomes all the more potent, straddling the real and the hyperreal. The photographer has entered the war as a killer as well as a victim, initiating conflict.

Similarly, Hitler's regime frequently staged political events for the sake of photography or cinema. The masses need illusion', Hitler said in 1938, observing the crowds flocking to the cinema, 'but not only in theatres or cinemas. They've had all they can take of the serious things in life.'[15] According to Paul Virilio, Hitler transformed Europe into a cinema screen, and his spectacular rallies were created foremost in order to be filmed.[16] Thus Leni Riefenstahl was given an unlimited budget for *Triumph of the Will*, her 1936 film of the week-long Nazi rally, and the rally itself was created as a film set. Hitler's architect Albert Speer was loaned 130 anti-aircraft searchlights (almost the entire German strategic reserve) to create 'the feeling' of a 'vast room, with the beams serving as mighty pillars of infinitely high outer walls.'[17] 'The result,' he said later, 'was to make the architecture of the building emerge sharply outlined against the night, and at the same time to make it unreal'.[18] In his 1965 diary he professed himself to be 'strangely stirred by the idea that the most successful architectural creation of my life is a chimera, an immaterial phenomenon.'[19] What is more, this immaterial 'cathedral of light' was created largely for the purposes of being filmed. Events in the 1930s created a world that people became used to experiencing as spectacle, losing sense of the line between photograph and actuality; between the real and its representation.

PHOTOGRAPHIC FIRE

In the British and German bombing raids, the hyperreal, already photographic aspect of life became particularly marked. Fearing the picture his skull might take through the eye sockets, Spender experiences the bombing preemptively as a photograph. British and German writers recording the bombing retained the need to witness events, providing accurate reportage. At the opening of his account of the Hamburg bombing, Nossack states that he feels he has been given 'a mandate to render an account': 'if I do not bear witness now, it will gradually fade like an evil dream.'[20] At the same time, though, these writers were more victims than witnesses. Even when Nossack or Sansom begin by witnessing, the assumption of the camera eye ends up involving a detached, dream-like aestheticism. They are too implicated in the situation they describe to remain neutral. In 'Rejoice in the Abyss', Spender is the victim of his own camera consciousness; he is helplessly passive in the face of this picture of total destruction. In his poem 'A Man-made World', he depicts the figures in the shelter as trapped in a camera-like 'black, malicious box' waiting for 'the man-made toys / To begin their noise.'[21]

At the same time, the assumption of a neutral camera-eye is complicated by the fact that the scene exists photographically before the writer begins to observe it. Viewing the scenes in the photographic hyperreal, 1940s writers are unable to be camera-eye witnesses. This is made explicit in William Sansom's 'The Witnesses', a story told by a ghostly crew of witnesses:

> We, the witnesses, were of course present throughout the episode, although it would be difficult ever to determine whether what we saw was the final truth or indeed if we viewed the matter in its right perspective at all, for at the time there was a great deal of smoke blurring the air.[22]

In self-consciously ascribing the narrative voice as a plural, chorus-like witness, Sansom undermines the concept of witnessing itself. He draws attention to the fallibility of the objective perspective; the witnesses see a fireman floating 'in mid-mist' but are aware that he is actually sitting astride a broken wall.[23] Photographic vision is shown to be rendered inaccurate by the cinematic effects of the bombing. The witnesses venture into more subjective territory when they invent a feud between the pump operator and the fireman as a prelude to the fireman throwing himself away from the wall. This moment, the climax of the story, takes place in a 'malicious instant of blinding light' in which 'everything flash[es] into being ... like objects switched suddenly onto a screen'.[24] In the witnesses' account, the fireman's gesture follows a sinister smile from the pump operator, who then sets about attempting to murder the fireman by increasing the pressure of his pump. But the narrative voice makes clear that this is mere speculation: 'We never saw the pump operator's hand move the throttle'.[25] The story ends with the suggestion that both the firemen and the witnesses have been deluded by the visual: 'A moment's fear transformed into a smile of hatred by the fireman's brain, the unreliable agent that informed us, the witnesses, his eyes'. The fireman's own eyes here are described as unreliable agents. But the ambiguous syntax also enables Sansom to suggest the unreliability of the witnesses themselves who have acted as his eyes, reflecting him back to himself. They, like him, have been blinded by the light; seduced by the 'brilliant red glare' of the fire.[26]

Both British and German writers record their sense of themselves as the inert spectators of an already cinematic vision. 'London burning, a grandiose spectacle,' wrote E. M. Forster to Isherwood recording the first night of the Blitz. 'I am certainly very sad and apprehensive.'[27] In her account of the bombing of Hamburg, the German writer Gretl Büttner describes the flames on the tower of the town hall as igniting like 'a tremendous neon billboard.'[28] For Nossack, the same raids are all the more photographic because he experiences them at a distance. He sees the searchlights 'nervously' scanning the sky, forming 'geometrical figures' with the other shafts of light.[29] In a 1941 short story, Henry Green goes further in seeing the searchlights as joining 'to create a slowly-moving giant tripod with nothing, nothing in their beams.'[30]

Trained to frame scenes photographically, these 1940s writers are sensitive to the natural photographic framing provided by the war. Searching for a man who has fallen down a manhole, Green figures the hole itself as a screen. The 'cinema light' of the firemen's 'electric torches' illuminates (or projects) the man's figure, fifteen feet below.[31] Like the cinema image, this man looks 'flat' in the 'shrouded' torch light, 'grotesquely caught up, dreadfully still, most like a rag doll made full size he was so limp'. In Hamburg, Gretl Büttner finds her gaze moving, camera-like, from the dislocated limbs to the no-longer human, in their atrocious, menacing faces.[32]

Photography and cinema dismember by nature. In 1923 the experimental Russian filmmaker Dziga Vertov extolled his own butchering kino-eye in terms that resonate disturbingly with the bombed bodies. 'From one person I take the hands ... from another I take the legs ... from a third, the most beautiful and expressive head.'[33] In 1921 the French filmmaker Jean Epstein delighted in the 'anatomical' tragedy possible in cinema, where a head 'swells with an extraordinary intensity.'[34] For Büttner, surveying the German ruins, the butchering has already taken place. There is no need of a camera to create close-ups. Here already are the torn-open mouths, the protruding eyes.[35]

Büttner's figures are photographic not just because they are dismembered but because they are suspended in time. The countenances are contorted by a 'last, unresolved cramp', caught at the moment when 'a monstrous, mighty scream rose up in painful, distressed accusation'.[36] Looking at them, she wonders helplessly 'what expression lay on the faces, what were those eyes looking at, what were the cramped hands holding on to, what were those opened lips trying to say?'.[37] For Büttner each face is like a mirror of 'inconceivable, incomprehensible eternity'.[38]

The bomb's power to suspend time is literal. In Wolfgang Borchert's story 'The Kitchen Clock', the clock rescued from a bombed house is eternally stopped at 2.30. 'When the bombs drop,' an onlooker announces, 'the clocks stop. It's because of the blast.'[39] In Elizabeth Bowen's The Heat of the Day the ghostly timelessness of wartime London is accentuated by the 'shock-stopped clocks.'[40] Their lack of time-telling becomes a kind of bizarre presence, so that Stella and Harrison come face to face in 'the unbounded night in which no clock struck.'[41]

It is in their unnerving capacity to still time that the bombs are at their most weirdly photographic. The photograph's ability to suspend – or to dismember – time is a key feature in early-twentieth-century photographic theory. In 1927 Benjamin's colleague Siegfried Kracauer described the photographic smile as the 'arrested', 'rigid and perpetual' smile of the mannequin in the beauty parlour.[42] For Kracauer, the beautiful girl caught in the frozen smile is at once the ghost of a young girl and the old woman she will or has already become. According to Kracauer, the turn to photography is the 'go-for-broke game of history'; a game that has already failed because in freezing and immortalizing moments in order to defy death, photographers implicitly reveal their own fear of death. The photograph, 'seemingly ripped from the clutch of death, in reality ... succumbs to it.'[43]

In wartime, the photographic, visual aspect of the bombs serves to highlight their deathliness. The bombing is photographic because it is unreal and deadly and at the same time is unreal and deadly because it is photographic. In William Sansom's story 'The Wall', the moment of destruction is 'a timeless second' before the wall falls down towards them, wreaking deathly destruction.[44] In this 'simple second' his brain digests 'every detail of the scene.' 'New eyes' opening at the sides of his head, he, like Spender, becomes a camera: 'from within, I photographed a hemispherical panorama.' The 'shutter' closes on his mind so that the 'picture appear[s] static to the limited surface senses', even though he knows on one level that the scene is moving.[45]

Like Sansom, Bowen is explicit in seeing the bomb's deadly freezing of time as photographic in the scene where the lovers Stella and Robert first meet. Their relationship begins with a glance in which they see 'in each other's faces a flash of promise'.[46] The blue of Robert's eyes, as they glance at Stella, is intensified by the 'mirror-refracted lighting' and he fixes his gaze on the 'one white lock' in her hair as he studies her. At this point Stella turns to wave goodbye to the friend who has brought her across the room and her 'gesture of goodbye' freezes as a photographic memory in their minds so that 'Remembered, her fleeting sketch of a gesture came to look prophetic; for ever she was to see, photographed as though it had been someone else's, her hand up'. At this point, she turns back to Robert and they fix their eyes 'expectantly on each other's lips.' But the words remain unheard and therefore unspoken; time is stilled by the bombs. Outside 'the barrage banged, coughed, retched; in here the lights in the mirrors rocked.' There is a 'direct hit, somewhere else', and 'in here' it is the 'demolition of an entire moment': 'What they had both been saying, or been on the point of saying, neither of them ever now were to know.' The words, lost, begin to have 'the significance of a lost clue'.[47] This is a scene that fulfils the fate of the photograph in Kracauer's essay, attempting and failing to resist death. Their relationship is posited in the past before it has a chance to begin. Their first meeting is photographically indexed as a gesture of goodbye and their first words remain unspoken. Their experience is consigned to the deathliness of memory before it has a chance to live.

Caught in moments of frozen time, both the dead and the living become ghosts. Büttner's suspended, dismembered figures seem to call out to her as she observes them. Green's fallen man may be alive but he takes on the appearance of a ghostly projected rag doll. Spender, after mentally photographing the bombed scene around him, goes out into the icy night where he sees 'The dead of all time float on one calm tide.' He realizes that the 'walls of brick and flesh' are merely 'transitory dwellings of the spirit / Which flows into that flooding sky of death.'[48] The bombs, through their destructive ease, have revealed both houses and bodies to be transitory, rendering the dead as tangible (or intangible) as the living.

'The dead', says the narrator of *The Heat of the Day*, 'from mortuaries, from under cataracts of rubble, made their anonymous presence – not as today's dead but as yesterday's living – felt through London.'[49] Bowen's living experience today as a 'tomorrow' the dead had expected – 'for death cannot be so sudden as all that.' They are caught in just that ghostly absent presence that Roland Barthes has associated with photography, which he sees as existing in the intractable tense of the 'that-has-been.'[50] Wolfgang Borchert's stories and poems are pervaded by ghosts. In his story 'There are Voices in the Air – At Night', an old man complains about the voices in the night who prevent him from sleeping.[51] He attributes the voices to 'the dead, the many, many dead' who 'jostle each other in the air at night' with nowhere to go, preying on the living.[52]

The bombs, unlike the photograph, render the viewers themselves as ghostly as the viewed scene. The eponymous fireman of Sansom's story 'Fireman Flower' experiences the bombing from the start in visually photographic terms. Entering a bombed house, he finds that the blinding, 'dead light' of the smoke sometimes clears to reveal brief glimpses of 'some object': a drape of wallpaper, a pile of plaster.[53] Framed briefly, these objects take on the qualities of ghosts, seeming to emerge out of a 'half-remembered episode from the dreamed past'. Flower becomes drunk on the fire and starts to hallucinate. Raising his head he sees faces smiling out of the fireglow, 'wholly sensual.'[54] The photographic quality of the fire begins to extend to its temporality when Flower sees his own reflection in a mirror. At first he thinks he is another fireman, and stops dead. He then sees that it is 'the ghost of himself'; 'the reflection of his past masqueraded as the darkling ghost of the future'. Here Kracauer's photographic timeframe is reversed. Where Kracauer's young girl poses as a figure from the past but in fact reminds us of the future, Flower's reflection poses as his future but serves only to resuscitate his past.

Flower escapes into a wardrobe and, hacking his way through, emerges into a fantasy room where he is greeted by the ghost of an old friend. The friend takes it upon himself to point out the relics of Flower's past arrayed around the room (his father's bowl, his mother's sewing bag, his own French grammar) and then recounts the story of a shared picnic from long ago. Lulled into sleepiness, Flower wonders if the afternoon is lost, but finds that it is returning: 'The photograph was brilliantly clear, a bright circle of summer yellow framed by the grey mists of memory'. Indeed, he finds that 'the past was more real than the present because the picture was clearly defined.'[55] The photographic wartime present has evoked the clearer photographs of the past, rendering Flower himself ghostly in the present.

THE AESTHETICIZATION OF POLITICS

In 'Fireman Flower', Sansom detaches his story from the political realities of the Blitz. If the victim of the bombing becomes a ghost, surrounded by ghosts, it is easy to see the bombing itself as an inevitable, dreamlike experience, rather than as the result of enemy action in a political war. In the second that the flash of the bombs becomes the flash of a camera, the experience is aestheticized and the personal experience is detached from the national. Recording the November 1943 bombing of Berlin, Albert Speer observed that

> I had constantly to remind myself of the cruel reality in order not to be completely entranced by the scene: the illumination of the parachute flares, which the Berliners called 'Christmas trees', followed by flashes of explosions which were caught by the clouds of smoke ... no doubt about it, this apocalypse provided a magnificent spectacle.[56]

Stephen Spender saw Borchert's ghostly stories as exhibiting this entranced detachment. 'The war which he described', Spender later wrote, 'is not the one for which German leaders bore, in the opinion of the rest of the world, a certain responsibility.'[57] Spender himself recalled the war as a time when 'we lived in a trance-like condition', witnessing events as 'in a dream.'[58] According to the literary critic Adam Piette, British Blitz literature by writers like William Sansom and Henry Green tends to:

> defuse the bombardment as Luftwaffe action. The bare fact of real German bombers dropping sticks of bombs on real Londoners is translated into solitary politics and aesthetics, as though the enemy did not exist. The apocalypse falls from the empty sky into the waiting imagination, which claims it for its own.[59]

This gap between politics and aesthetics is made explicit in Nossack's *The End*. Nossack could be seen as evading the question of politics in order to avoid the question of blame. If the fire blazes in a political vacuum, there are no Allied aggressors and therefore no Nazis. Near the opening of *The End*, he describes his frequent desire in the early raids for it to 'get really bad', which could imply he wants Germany to be liberated by its enemy.[60] But he presents his desire for 'apocalpyse' as a natural, inevitable desire, 'entertained', he says, by everyone who wanted to 'test themselves.' This desire for an apocalypse as the final test resonates with Spender's account of the raids in his autobiography. He recounts welcoming a particularly heavy raid as 'the end I seemed now to have been awaiting all my life.'[61]

However, although Nossack does not claim to remember politics when faced with apocalypse, he does interrogate his own abstract sense of the photographic beauty of the fire, together with his sense of himself as an atemporal ghost. He is explicit in separating the 'horror of the night' from the visual effects of the raid, which is 'almost lovely to look at', like 'gazing' at sparks on 'a clear blue sea'.[62] He also sees the stilling of time created by the bombs as necessarily dampening political engagement. Because 'we were outside of time', he writes, 'everything we did immediately lost its meaning'. He presents the atemporality created by the bombs as a type of ghostly sanctification. The 'infinite behind man wafted unhindered into the endlessness before him and hallowed his countenance for the passage of what is beyond time'.[63]

At the same time, Nossack makes clear that 'this paralysis of the will' had to be recognized as a 'disease'. The disease deadens so that each time he emerges from the haze of the city he is 'devastated, numb, and depleted, like a poet who has held converse with demons'.[64] He presents this state as necessarily apolitical. 'During those days, if by chance a newspaper came into our hands, we didn't bother to read the war bulletins ... Whatever happened outside of us simply didn't exist.' In this context, they give little thought to the enemy. He does not hear a 'single person curse the enemies or blame them for the destruction'.[65] It is this apolitical sense of a war without an enemy that perhaps explains the bizarre similarities between the British and German literature. Despite the obvious differences in scale between the London Blitz and the bombing of Hamburg, the waiting imagination in the two countries claimed the bombs to similar effect.

Nossack's explicit sense of the ghostly withdrawal from politics occasioned by the bombs can be helpful in explaining the problematic politics of Bowen's *The Heat of the Day*. Here, in a book published only four years after the end of the war, Bowen makes Robert, the hero of the book, a traitor, spying for the Nazis. Critics then and now have unsurprisingly found this problematic, seeing Bowen herself as either a flawed novelist or a fascist sympathizer. Critics who see her as flawed wonder why she could not make him a Communist sympathizer instead.[66] It would be more palatable, and leave less of an awkward hole in the novel. Alan Sinfield has taken the opposite approach and suggested that Bowen whole-heartedly endorsed Robert's decision. In his view, Bowen was also troubled by the increasing power of the masses and the tendency for democracy to cater for the lowest common denominator.[67]

Reading Bowen alongside Nossack helps us read the politics as part of the photographic strangeness of the novel. If we see the whole book as operating in a death-driven, eerily de-animated world, the political itself is undermined by a history that operates as memory. In committing himself to the fascists, Robert is behaving logically in a world he experiences as a living death. Showing Stella photographs from his childhood he finds that each time he returns to them 'I'm hit in the face by the feeling that I don't exist – that I not only am not but never have been'.[68] In wartime, this feeling extends to the rest of his life, which has itself become photographic. 'What country,' he asks Stella, 'have you and I outside this room? Exhausted shadows, dragging themselves out to fight'.[69] It is, then, as a ghost that Robert makes his decision to sympathize with the Nazis, who are never named as such. They seem to exist in Robert's mind like the enemy does for Nossack merely as a vague, almost supernatural other. Stella herself comments on the shadowiness of his explanation: 'You know, Robert, for anybody *doing* anything so definite, you talk vaguely. Wildness and images'.[70]

In his 'Work of Art' essay, Walter Benjamin sees fascism as aestheticizing politics and states that the Left must counter this by politicizing aesthetics.[71] He suggests that photography and cinema are the media best placed for this process. But it seems that there was something inherent in the experience of being bombed that aestheticized what we might expect to have been a political experience. The bizarre but seemingly commonplace sense of the bombs as a photograph combined with and strengthened the sense that the bombs placed the victims outside time and therefore outside history.

THE POLITICIZATION OF AESTHETICS

In 2004, Susan Sontag chastised Baudrillard for claiming that contemporary, postmodern war took place in the realm of the hyperreal:

> To speak of reality becoming a spectacle is a breath-taking provincialism. It universalizes the viewing habits of a small, educated population living in the rich parts of the world, where news has been converted into entertainment ... It assumes that everyone is a spectator. It suggests, perversely, unseriously, that there is no real suffering in the world. But it is absurd to identify the world with those zones in the well-off countries where people have the dubious privilege of being spectators ... just as it is absurd to generalize about the ability to respond to the sufferings of others on the basis of the mindset of those consumers of news who know nothing at first hand about war and massive injustice or terror.[72]

Sontag might also have levelled her criticism at Spender, writing about the 'second hand' nature of the Spanish Civil War, or at Nossack or Bowen, exploring the visual effects of the bombs. To see the Second World War as a photographic spectacle was to forget the presence of the wounded body. Louis MacNeice, describing the enlivening 'spectacle' of the 'fantasy of destruction' created by a night of London bombing, was careful to point out that 'people's deaths were another matter'.[73] Those were the deaths that must be remembered if writers were to remain politicized amid the bombing.

An attempt to restore both bombers and victims to history was made by Bertolt Brecht in his wartime photomontages. This series of collaged photographs and poems, assembled and written between 1937 and 1945, was collected together in Brecht's *Kriegsfibel*, or *War Primer*, first published in the GDR in 1955. In a sense we can see these montages, by their nature, as performing an opposite movement to the photographic texts. Where the texts render the experience of war photographic, aestheticizing politics, the montages bring out the politics inherent in any photograph of war, politicizing aesthetics. In 1931 Brecht had condemned photojournalism, stating that its tremendous development had 'contributed practically nothing to the revelation of the truth about the conditions of this world', instead acting as 'a terrible weapon *against* the truth'.[74] Throughout the War Primer, Brecht reminds us of the political choices involved in the act of photographing war. He insists on the presence of the governments behind the bombs that are themselves behind the suffering of the civilians.

Jennifer Bajorek has seen Brecht as responding to Benjamin's sense of the radicalism of the photographic image, which Benjamin links to a Marxist conception of history.[75] In his 1940 'Theses on the Philosophy of History', Benjamin states that 'the true picture of the past flits by. The past can be seized only as an image which flashes up at the instant when it can be recognized and is never seen again.'[76] According to Benjamin, the historical materialist must make the most of this phenomenon, seizing hold of the memory 'as it flashes up at a moment of danger', reinterpreting the entire past in the light of the present.

In the Second World War, the flash of the bombs brings with it the flash of history, in that the bombing is a political phenomenon with historical causes. Where for Sansom this flash is a 'malicious instant of blinding light', for Brecht, it is crucial, in the moment of danger, to remember the perpetrators of the photographic vision of destruction. In collage 23 in the English edition, Brecht draws attention to the transience of this vision. The photograph depicts the bombing of an unknown city and Brecht does not attribute the landscape to Britain or Germany, although it follows shots of civilians taking cover in the London Blitz. Brecht makes clear that the bombing happens so fast that in reality, as in a photograph, it is in the past even as it takes place. 'A cloud of smoke told us that they were here', he says, suggesting that the bombers make their presence felt only through their subsequent absence.[77] Aerial bombardment, like photography, is an absent art. The bombers, like the photographic subject, leave only an indexical trace of their presence, and in this case the trace of the bombs is captured as photograph. The quatrain finishes:

> They were the sons of fire, not of the light.
> They came from where? They came out of the darkness.
> Where did they go? Into eternal night.

The questions, combined with the unsatisfactory answers, remind us to look beyond the trace to its history, preventing us from accepting the bombs as vision.

In collage 25, Brecht introduces a Swedish photograph of the ruins of the 1940 bombing of Berlin, which depicts a veiled woman, bent over to stare at the rubble. 'Stop searching, woman,' the quatrain commands:

> you will never find them
> But woman, don't accept that Fate is to blame.
> Those murky forces, woman, that torment you
> Have each of them a face, address and name.[78]

Here Brecht directly challenges the attitude of people like Nossack, Borchert or Spender, who divorce the destruction from politics, accepting the raids as an apocalyptic dream. He reminds the woman that the planes may seem like murky spectacles but are in fact driven by individual human beings, each with his own background and history.

Brecht himself did not experience the bombing. It is perhaps his more detached perspective on the destruction that enabled him to remain politicized in a way that writers like Nossack and Borchert could not. Witnessing it only in the photographic hyperreal, he is anxious to restore actuality to the nightmare – to turn the photographs into logical text. His brief record of the 1943 Hamburg attack in his diary is filled with facts, and devoid of the visual descriptions we find in eye-witness accounts. 'Hamburg is being destroyed', he writes. 'There is a column of smoke above it twice as high as the highest German mountain, 600 m. The bomber crews need oxygen apparatus. There have been raids every 12 hours for 72 hours.'[79]

In her study of psychoanalysis and literature in Second World War Britain, Lyndsey Stonebridge suggests that it is in the literature of the period that the psychoanalytic trauma produced by the war is found. Psychoanalysts who expected the Blitz to result in thousands of traumatized victims were surprised by the low numbers of reported cases. Instead, Stonebridge writes, 'the kind of psychoanalysis that [they] sought is probably best found in the fiction of the period'; the 'compelling strangeness of the 1940s novel.'[80] Looking at the British and the German bombing literature side by side, it is striking how similarly strange and dreamlike the two literatures are. Despite two very different experiences of the war, and two very different political situations, the victims of the bombs who turn writers in both countries seem to aestheticize the war around them in similar ways. Most marked is their shared tendency to view it photographically in both its visual and its temporal aspects. In aestheticizing politics through photography, these writers have wrested photography from reportage. In the 1940s, to photograph is not so much to witness as to haunt, or be haunted. It is left to Brecht, and to subsequent historians and critics, to fulfil Benjamin's injunction to respond by politicizing art.

Notes

1   S. Spender, *World Within World* (London: Hamish Hamilton, 1951), 308.
2   Stephen Spender, 'Abyss', *Citizens in War – and After*, foreword by Herbert Morrison (London: Harrap and Co, 1945), 52–3. The poem is reprinted in revised form as 'Rejoice in the Abyss' in Spender, *New Collected Poems* (London: Faber and Faber, 2004), 243–4.
3   Walter Benjamin, 'The Work of Art in the Age of Mechanical Reproduction', 1936, in H. Arendt (ed.), *Illuminations, Essays and Reflections*, trans. H. Zohn (New York: Schoken Books, 1968), 224.
4   W. H. Auden, letter to Erika Mann Auden, in W. H. Auden and L. MacNeice, *Letters from Iceland* (London: Faber and Faber, 1937), 137.
5   C. Isherwood, *The Berlin Novels* (London: Vintage, 1999), 243.

6   S. Jameson, 'Documents', *Fact*, volume 4, July 1937, 15–16.
7   R. Wennersten, 'An Interview with Christopher Isherwood', quoted in S. Wade, *Christopher Isherwood* (London: Macmillan, 1991), 12–13.
8   J. Baudrillard, *Simulacra and Simulation*, trans. S. Faria Glaser (Ann Arbor: The University of Michigan Press, 1994), 2.
9   S. Spender, *Guernica*, 1938, in V. Cunningham (ed.), *Spanish Civil War Verse* (Harmondsworth: Penguin, 1980), 418–20.
10   Ibid.
11   K. Williams, *British Writers and the Media, 1930–45* (London: Macmillan, 1996), 3.
12   See C. Philips, Introduction to R. Whelan, *This Is War: Robert Capa at Work* (New York: International Center of Photography, 2007), 9.
13   See C. Brothers, *War and Photography: A Cultural History* (London: Routledge, 1997), 2.
14   Whelan, *This Is War*, 75.
15   Quoted by P. Virilio, *War and Cinema: The Logistics of Perception*, trans. P. Camiller (London: Verso, 1989), 53.
16   Virilio, *War and Cinema*, 53.
17   A. Speer, *Inside the Third Reich*, trans. R. and C. Winston (London: Sphere Books Limited, 1970), 59.
18   A. Speer, *Spandau, The Secret Diaries*, trans. R. and C. Winston (London: Collins, 1976), 428.
19   Speer, *Spandau*, 428.
20   H. E. Nossack, *The End: Hamburg 1943*, trans. J. Agee (Chicago: University of Chicago Press, 2004), 2.
21   S. Spender, 'A Man-made World', 1949, in *New Collected Poems*, 245.
22   W. Sansom, 'The Witnesses', in *Fireman Flower and Other Stories* (London: Hogarth Press, 1944), 81.
23   Ibid., 82.
24   Ibid., 85.
25   Ibid., 86.
26   Ibid., 85.
27   Quoted by P. Stansky, *The First Day of the Blitz: September 7, 1940* (New Haven: Yale University Press, 2007), 69.
28   G. Büttner, 'Zwischen Leben und Tod', Anlage zum internen Polizeibericht vom 1.12.1943, in V. Hage (ed.), *Hamburg 1943, Literarische Zeugnisse zum Feuersturm* (Frankfurt am Main: Fischer Taschenbuch Verlag, 2003), 24; my translation.
29   Nossack, *The End*, 7.
30   H. Green, 'A Rescue' (1941), in *Surviving: The Uncollected Writings of Henry Green*, edited by Matthew Yorke (London: Chatto and Windus, 1992), 77.
31   Green, 'A Rescue', 79.
32   Büttner, 'Zwischen Leben und Tod', 30.
33   D. Vertov, 'Kinoks, a Revolution', 1923, in A. Michelson (ed.), *Kino-Eye, The Writings of Dziga Vertov*, trans. K. O'Brien (London: Pluto Press, 1984), 17.
34   J. Epstein, 'Magnification', 1921, in R. Abel (ed.), *French Film Theory and Criticism: A History/ Anthology 1907–1939* (Princeton: Princeton University Press, 1988), 235.
35   Büttner, 'Zwischen Leben und Tod', 30.
36   Ibid.
37   Ibid., 31.
38   Ibid.
39   W. Borchert, 'The Kitchen Clock', in *The Man Outside: The Prose Works of Wolfgang Borchert*, trans. D. Porter (London: Hutchinson International Authors Limited, 1952), 169.
40   E. Bowen, *The Heat of the Day*, introduction by R. Foster (London: Vintage: 1998), 99.
41   Bowen, *The Heat of the Day*, 141.
42   S. Kracauer, 'Photography', 1927, in T. Y. Levin (ed.), *The Mass Ornament: Weimar Essays*, (Cambridge, Massachusetts: Harvard University Press), 48.
43   Kracauer, 'Photography', 59–61.
44   Sansom, 'The Wall', in *Fireman Flower*, 109.

45   Ibid., 111.
46   Bowen, *The Heat of the Day*, 95.
47   Ibid.
48   Spender, 'Abyss', 54.
49   Bowen, *The Heat of the Day*, 91.
50   R. Barthes, *Camera Lucida: Reflections on Photography*, trans. R. Howard (New York: Hill and Wang, 1981),77.
51   W. Borchert, 'There are Voices in the Air – At Night', in *The Man Outside*, 23.
52   Borchert, 'There are Voices', 24. The German text reads: 'Die Toten sind es, die vielen vielen Toten'; 'Sie drängeln sich nachts in der Luft' (56).
53   Sansom, 'Fireman Flower', in *Fireman Flower*, 133–134.
54   Ibid., 143.
55   Ibid., p 149.
56   Speer, *Inside the Third Reich*, 288.
57   Spender, introduction to Borchert, *The Man Outside*, v.
58   Spender, *World Within World*, 284.
59   A. Piette, *Imagination at War: British Fiction and Poetry 1939–1945* (London: Papermac, 1995), 46.
60   Nossack, *The End*, 12.
61   Spender, *World Within World*, 308.
62   Nossack, *The End*, 16–17.
63   Ibid., 29.
64   Ibid., 36.
65   Ibid., 34.
66   In 1949, the novelist Rosamond Lehmann wrote to Bowen: 'What bothers me a little is that I cannot see why he shouldn't have been a Communist and therefore pro-Russian, pro-Ally, rather than pro-enemy'. Quoted in V. Glendinning, *Elizabeth Bowen: Portrait of a Writer* (London: Weidenfeld and Nicolson, 1997), 151.
67   A. Sinfield, *Literature, Politics and Culture in Postwar Britain* (London: Continuum, 2004), 19–21.
68   Bowen, *The Heat of the Day*, 117.
69   Ibid., 267.
70   Ibid., 282.
71   Benjamin, 'The Work of Art', 242.
72   S. Sontag, *Regarding the Pain of Others* (London: Hamish Hamilton, 2003), 98–9.
73   L. MacNeice, 'The Morning after the Blitz', 1941, in A. Heuser (ed.), *Selected Prose of Louis MacNeice* (Oxford: Clarendon Press, 1990), 117.
74   Quoted in Reinhold Grimm, 'Marxist Emblems: Bertolt Brecht's *War Primer*', *Comparative Literature Studies* 12.3 (1975), 266.
75   See J. Bajorek, 'Holding Fast to Ruins: The Air War in Brecht's *Kriegsfibel*', in W. Wilms and W. Rasch (eds), *'Bombs Away!' Representing the Air War Over Europe And Japan* (Amsterdam, Rodopi, 2006), 97–110.
76   W. Benjamin, 'Theses on the Philosophy of History', in Benjamin, *Illuminations*, 255.
77   B. Brecht, *War Primer*, translated and edited by J. Willett (London: Libris, 1998), no. 23. This collage is no. 21 in the German edition (Brecht, *Kriegsfibel* (Berlin: Eulenspiegel Verlag, 1955)).
78   Brecht, *War Primer*, no. 25 (no. 22 in the German edition).
79   Brecht, *Journals 1934–55*, edited by J. Willett, trans. H. Rorrison (London: Methuen, 1993), 287.
80   L. Stonebridge, *The Writing of Anxiety: Imagining Wartime in Mid-Century British Culture* (Basingstoke: Palgrave Macmillan, 2007), 17.

7

Religion and Bombing in Italy, 1940–1945

Claudia Baldoli

> The history of Italy is essentially a religious history, and the hand of Providence … is clearly visible in every single one of its pages.[1]

This quotation is from the principal wartime Catholic daily newspaper of northern Italy, and was written at a particularly difficult time: in July 1943, the war, which had until then hit Italian cities from the sky, now also threatened from the ground. It was Italy's destiny, according to the Church, to have to endure the most difficult trial. The enemy was admittedly too powerful, and in a country where anti-aircraft defences had never been able to protect the population, the only solution was to rely on supernatural forces.

THE CHURCH REPLACES THE STATE

The day after Mussolini's declaration of war, the bishop of Bergamo instructed his diocese on how to react: 'a grave decision has been taken for the nation. Our duty as Catholics is the following: to obey.' For Catholics, obedience had to be reinforced 'by an internal discipline of the spirit'. He thus exhorted the faithful to conduct an 'honest, good and saintly' life 'in order to deserve God's justice.'[2] A week later, the archbishop of Turin addressed his clergy in a letter which outlined the three principal lines of conduct they must observe during the conflict: confide in God, co-operate with the authorities and help the population. Since Turin was bombed less than 24 hours after Mussolini's declaration of war, he insisted on the need to remind the population to observe the blackout, and suspended all outdoor religious processions.[3]

All over Italy, the Catholic Church collaborated with the regime by providing the population with information about shelters, anti-aircraft regulations, gas masks and other wartime requirements. From early on in the conflict the Clerical-Fascist newspaper in Milan, *L'Italia*, accused the British of targeting civilians rather than military objectives. An article on the bombing of Milan, Turin and Alessandria on 17 August 1940 listed the names of those killed or injured, and concluded: 'This list, in large part women and children – and among them there is an entire peasant family – shows which industrial and military objectives the enemy aircraft has reached.'[4] Bishops of bombed cities wrote letters to both local and national newspapers to express their support for civilians. Bombed populations were united in the name of the fatherland but also, in the Catholic view, in the name of the Gospel – as bishops under-lined when officiating at public funerals of bombing victims in the churches.[5] Following an agreement between UNPA (National Union for Anti-aircraft Protection) and the bishoprics all over Italy, from July 1940 church bells came to serve as alarm systems in towns which did not possess sirens, or in areas of cities where sirens could not be heard well enough.[6] The new use of church bells was interpreted in a militant fashion by patriotic Catholics, as *L'Italia* made clear: 'when the fatherland in arms calls, even the bells descend from their heavenly towers.'[7]

The relationship between the Church and the state had much improved during the First World War and especially under Fascism, after the difficult times of the Liberal age. Priests appeared increasingly integrated into public life, and the theatrical Fascist *piazza* gave the Church visibility.[8] Clerical writings of the 1920s and 1930s demonstrate a belief in the triumph of the Christian mission over socialism. In 1940, the faith in victory, the blessing of the dead, the adhesion of the Church to patriotic ceremonies and national myths could rely on an established symbolism. This situation began to change in the autumn of 1942, when the first RAF experiments in area bombing on Italian soil brought the war into large numbers of civilian homes. From that point onwards, the Church began to lose its patriotic fervour.[9] The content of priests' preaching began to change: the victorious hymns of 1940 were replaced in 1941 by sermons on the safety of soldiers, and in 1942 by heartfelt prayers for the country to be spared the horrors of air attack.[10]

After raids on Genoa, Milan and Turin had caused hundreds of casualties, Mussolini went on Italian radio on 2 December 1942 and demanded that all civilians should evacuate the industrial cities of northern Italy nightly.[11] This increased panic and lowered morale, as Italians realized that evacu-ation represented the only anti-aircraft 'solution'. Indeed, Arthur Harris, the commander-in-chief of Bomber Command, was surprised that 300,000 people, half the population of Turin, abandoned the city *en masse*, but he found that the panic was even greater in Milan after a daylight raid 'by fewer than one hundred Lancasters'.[12] The Allies took advantage of Italy's inadequate preparation for war, presenting themselves in the propaganda as liberators and holding Mussolini responsible for the war. Italians' reactions to bombing included forms of non-compliance with the militarization of society, the tendency to blame disaster on the Axis rather than on the enemy, and the spread of rumours that challenged the regime's propaganda.[13]

In this situation, the presence of the Catholic Church began to fill the gap left by the regime's inability to protect bombed cities. Priests blessed shelters, placed crucifixes in them, and visited bombed towns to bring words of comfort to survivors. These actions came to be perceived, albeit unconsciously, as an important part of Italy's civil defences. For example, as early as November 1940 the prefect of Turin informed the Ministry of the Interior that priests had begun to sell plastic images of the local Madonna della Consolata, and that about 100 people had bought them and inserted them, embellished with flowers and candles, on the walls of blocks of flats and shelters for protection. The prefect worried that this could be a symptom of depression and of 'morbid religious feeling' among the population.[14] By 1943 reliance on religious protection was made evident by scenes that had become typical all over Italy. Don Giovanni Vitrotti, a priest from Alpignano near Turin, provides one such example in his diary in May 1943: 'I've just finished blessing people's homes. Families who built a shelter asked me to go and bless it.'[15] At the opposite end of the peninsula, the bishop of Taranto, Ferdinando Bernardi, described in his 'public' diary on 26 August 1943:

> Terrible enemy air incursion on Taranto ... hit the station, workers' homes beyond Porta Napoli and Tamburi. Even before the end of the alarm, the archbishop with his secretary immediately goes to visit the hit areas, to comfort the wounded, those who suffered losses, providing all possible help in those terrible moments, stopping among the ruins at the most pitiful cases.[16]

Sometimes the activity of priests was reported in diary form by Fascist spies. In July of the same year, a monthly report from Turin noticed:

> The archbishop during the same night, just after the air raid, went through the city streets bringing his word to hearten and encourage; he made many visits to damaged churches [and hospitals], where he comforted the wounded, finding for them words of spiritual help; subsequently at the cemetery he gave absolution to the dead.[17]

Priests also played an important role in assisting evacuees. In January 1943 Agostino Gemelli, founder of the Catholic University and president of the Vatican Academy of Science, instructed Italy's priests on their duties towards evacuees from bombed cities in an article in the *Rivista del Clero Italiano* (journal of the Italian clergy). The bishop of Naples, Alessio Ascalesi, considering that his advice would be helpful to village priests in the surrounding province (which had continued to host evacuees from the city), published Father Gemelli's article in the local church bulletin. Priests were asked to focus on the religious problems provoked by the arrival of evacuees, who were defined as 'souls to be saved'.[18] Five months later, the Neapolitan bulletin again reflected on this issue, reminding its priests that the evacuees lived in painful conditions and could easily fall prey to a sense of discomfort that might lead to 'dangerous lapses'.[19] Similar problems were experienced in central Italy when all its regions had been bombed in 1944. In Cesena province, evacuations continued until all the country churches that hosted evacuees were inundated. There, a local priest wrote in his diary, 'the good and the bad from the city arrived. A general mixing up of peoples.'[20]

The importance of the Church's role in replacing the state became particularly evident when Rome was bombed. A former member of the Roman Resistance explains in a memoir how the Fascists arrived in San Lorenzo after the raid of 19 July 1943, but were ignored by the population. Soon afterwards, however, news arrived that the Pope was on his way.[21] The report of the Pope's appearance in San Lorenzo by the Vatican newspaper suggests how Pius XII was replacing the Duce in the hearts of the Romans: the pope's visit to the bombed areas was his first outing from the Vatican since May 1940. Along the route, crowds surrounded his car, and the news spread that he was approaching San Lorenzo. 'One hundred, one thousand arms' reached out to touch 'the sacred and adored hand of the Pope.' He blessed the wounded, the victims, their families, the city and the whole country: in the midst of tragedy, claimed *L'Osservatore Romano*, this mystical symbol generated new energy.[22] The scene was repeated after successive raids in August 1943, when the Vatican press emphasized that a large blood stain had appeared on the Pope's white robe – the touch of the injured.[23] By 1944, following many attempts to make Rome an open city,[24] the Pope had become the only reference point for the Roman population, a symbol of peace and security. By that time, the Church had understood who was winning the war and even when it locally accused the bombers of barbarism, it never mentioned who they were. For example, a letter from the bishops of Piedmont to the clergy and their faithful in Easter 1944 made reference to 'savage air raids', the 'devastation of churches', the 'ruin of populous cities' and the 'agony of unarmed populations', but did not accuse anyone in particular.[25] The Church in the German-occupied North began officially distancing itself from the Fascist Republic, encouraging the population to take a non-political stance.[26]

RELIGION AND DEFEATISM

Once war had been declared the Church was expected to collaborate, which meant that priests had to put any idea of universal fraternity aside. God must be asked to favour the fatherland and grant Italy victory. The Pope made clear that any peace must be a just peace: in January 1941 an article in *L'Osservatore Romano* attacked pacifism, restating that the Pope had never 'talked about peace for its own sake'.[27] However, the attitude of the clergy was not the same everywhere, and Fascist informers continued to report on priests who appeared to be lukewarm towards the war, or who expressed hostility towards the German ally. In October 1940 the Ministry of the Interior informed Italy's prefects about religious prints priests sent to soldiers, in which they hinted at the horrors of the war and the dangers for the civilian population. At times they invoked peace and included considerations inspired by feelings of fraternity towards the enemy. Clearly such impulses were 'inopportune at a moment like this', so it was asked 'that censorship should be strengthened and that any intercepted dubious correspondence regarding religion should be reported.'[28] Although the Church did not criticize the regime and collaborated with the authorities during the raids, by the autumn of 1941 Catholic newspapers were progressively confiscated and controls on religious preaching increased. This was not always due to the content of the preaching, but mostly to the reactions of the faithful, who tended to interpret any expression of Christian fraternity as encouragement to pacifism.[29] Moreover, Fascist informers tended to construe aspects of the Church's attitude as potentially defeatist.[30]

On 13 April 1942, Turin's Chief of Police informed the prefect that the Turin diocese had celebrated the 'week of the young woman'. Priests' speeches, he assured him, did not go beyond religious matters; the archbishop celebrated mass in the courtyard of the Valentino Castle to 15,000 of the faithful, reminding them of their Christian duty 'for the glory of God and the good of the Fatherland.'[31] However, at less public occasions, priests often preached a different message. For example, in the church of San Carlo, only one month before the 'week of the young woman', the Dominican Don Guaschino proclaimed that, 'men among themselves, according to natural law, must understand each other and hold each other's hands – man to man, city to city, nation to nation.'[32] In April, a more general comment on the behaviour of the clergy sent by the Chief of Police to the prefect observed that some priests 'hinted inopportunely at peace and of the harsh conditions imposed by the war, not only with an expression of Christian fraternity, but also with a pacifist mentality.'[33]

Even more so than priests, grass-roots clerical organizations worried the Fascists – groups of religious women in particular. In January 1943, the women of Catholic Action in Cagliari disseminated a printed version of Pope Benedict XV's speech at the time of the First World War.[34] A 1943 prayer modified the *Ave Maria*, adapting it to the times. It revealed both the scorn to which the regime's anti-aircraft measures were subject and the longing for peace among the Catholic population:

> Ave Maria full of grace
> Please make the siren never sound again
> So that the aeroplanes will no longer come
> Please let me sleep until tomorrow
> Blessed Virgin Saint Mary
> Please make the British lose their direction
> And if a bomb falls down here
> Blessed Virgin please save me
> Please make the anti-aircraft more careful
> Less deaf and less slow
> Make it peer at the blue sky
> Make it sleep less and shoot more
> Make the fighters rise and fly
> Rather than remaining always on the ground
> And just going up and down

When the enemies have already left
Good Madonna who can see everything
Make my walls remain intact
And if anything must fall
Give me wings to fly
Blessed Virgin Queen of the sea
Make me wake up tomorrow
With the news which everyone likes
That there are no more [ration/party] cards
And we are at peace
Amen.[35]

Often priests were pacifist because their communities were. When the bishop of Naples asked for 'peace with victory' during a procession, the people responded with the cry: 'peace anyway and at any cost'.[36] In St Peter's Square, where the Roman crowds went to listen to the Pope's speech on 12 March 1944, as the Pope asked 'both belligerents' to preserve Rome, women began shouting 'peace, peace, Germans out'.[37]

BOMBING AND THE MORAL QUESTION

The view expressed by *L'Italia* from 1941 was that war, although a painful event, could not be opposed as it was 'a consequence of the sin that continuously sows the path of humanity with thorns.'[38] In concert with its previous policies, the Catholic Church during the war fought a battle against the decline in moral values. The conflict aggravated a situation that had caused anxiety during peacetime. The interpretation of bombing as divine punishment, to which humanity had to submit before peace could return, became widespread in the Catholic press from autumn 1942, when bombing began to destroy entire areas of cities. This interpretation was openly endorsed by the Pope after the raids on Milan and Genoa. On 16 November, he addressed a public letter to the archbishop of Genoa in which he asked Catholics to avow that the tragedy that had hit Genoa would be a source of greater spiritual good: 'may the mourning have the sentiment and value of healthy penitence, to expiate the guilt that has generated so much disorder in the world and provoked divine punishments.'[39]

The need to renew moral habits and reinforce faith in order to end the war was a concept that was passed down by the Church hierarchy to local priests. After the major raids of autumn 1942, Piedmontese priest Don Astegiano confided to his diary the conviction that good works could move God's charity. It was necessary, he wrote, to 'banish evil deeds from our lives.'[40] Don Murzone, assistant to a Catholic Women's association, emphasized that raids had mostly hit the big cities, 'where guilt mostly triumphs'. He argued that there was not much that country priests could do in order to save the cities;

they could, however, have an impact on the evacuees, who continued to arrive in the villages: 'if our country villages are good, they can healthily influence the evacuees from the cities.'[41]

In March 1943 the Vatican newspaper reflected on the bombing of churches in Italian cities, and wondered: 'Were they satisfying the ends for which God wanted them?' What would Bernini, Palladio or Giotto think about the decline in moral habits? And what about the emptiness of churches in present times? It was not surprising that God had decided to 'try us in this manner too, with the ruin of His own houses' now left empty as a simple reminder of a past splendour.[42] In the same month, the official bulletin of the bishop of Naples invited local priests to reflect on their city reduced to ruins: 'From any tragedy we can always draw admonishments to improve our spiritual life. Indeed, these ruins allow us to meditate that among the causes of so much pain there could be some which concern us closely.'[43] Two months later, the church bulletin of Taranto reminded people that 'we all have our burden of guilt.'[44] In August 1943 a priest from Cesena commented in his diary on a letter the local bishop had sent to his diocese. The bishop insisted there was no point in imploring God for his blessing until present habits were reformed: a true statement, thought the priest, who was alarmed by the presence of women in swimsuits on the coast and wearing short dresses when cycling.[45] The link between the return to peacetime and the reform of female habits became increasingly recurrent in priests' preaching. According to the Vatican press, the first step towards the present tragedy had already been made in the eighteenth century: resistance to bombing in 1944 signified a return to the Church's struggle against the Enlightenment.[46]

As fear of bombing increased, popular religiosity tended to express itself mostly through 'external' signs, as people did everything they could in order publicly to propitiate saints and Madonnas. Although the role of priests was to try to persuade the faithful that they also needed to deepen their inner religiosity, the interpretation of war as divine punishment and the question of morality remained distant from the population's needs and beliefs. In Suzzara, a Lombard village just south of the river Po, which experienced bombing in the summer of 1944, local priest Don Giorgio Buzzacchi recorded in his diary that many people offered him money in the hope that he would stage public religious events, while he continually urged that the most efficient way to obtain peace was 'to conduct a truly Christian life.'[47] The clergy realized that request for inter-cession and miracles did not necessarily reflect deep faith, and a discrepancy persisted between official Catholic preaching and popular religiosity.

ASKING FOR SUPERNATURAL HELP

In March 1941, a Fascist informer from Modugno in Apulia warned the Ministry of the Interior that war weariness was receiving no other relief than the illusion of religious aid, the hope that God listened to prayers and penitence, 'just as when the people invoke water at prolonged times of drought, or the end of the rain when it has rained for months.'[48] Recourse to supernatural help against the bombs increased after the first area bombing raids on the industrial northern cities in autumn 1942. Most of this took the shape of Marian devotion – the most important in Italy since the Middle Ages. In particular, the interpretation of natural cataclysms and political-social upheaval as supernatural phenomena, for which miracles were evoked, had been reinforced in post-unification rural Italy by the Church in its struggle against modernity and the secular state.[49] Throughout Catholic Europe, the 'century of progress' witnessed uncontrolled growth of Marian visions, which often alarmed the clergy.[50] The Virgin represented the most physical aspect of religion, the one that most closely involved the sphere of emotions and feelings. The importance of this cult during the war years was evident from the variety of events that took place which were linked to it; there was also a precedent for this phenomenon in the Great War, when the Virgin Mary had been 'a constant presence' in Catholic countries.[51]

In November 1942, some Milanese citizens wrote to the archbishop asking him to organize public collective prayers and to officiate at religious functions in order to protect the city and the Lombard region from the tragedies that had befallen Genoa and Turin. The archbishop refused to organize a public procession but instead proclaimed one hour of adoration to the Madonna in a city sanctuary, in order to divert the bombs away from the sky over Milan. However, he reminded his petitioners that a modification of behaviour, with the rejection of immoral habits, would have helped the propitiation.[52] In January 1943 in Venice – a city itself untouched by bombs during the war, except for a raid on the port in 1945, but close to the industrial area of Porto Marghera – the population met in St Mark's square, where the Cardinal Patriarch renewed a vow made to the Madonna 26 years earlier, which had allegedly saved the city from destruction during the First World War.[53] A prayer for Turin published by the Pope a month earlier was taken by the city archbishop as an invitation to gather and invoke the Madonna.[54] The Madonna of the Consolata was the one to whom the Turinese turned when they needed protection, and ceremonies to propitiate her had begun in Turin as early as June 1940.[55] While Church authorities repeated that without moral renewal peace could not be achieved, the Catholic masses hoped, more simply, that the Madonna could divert bombs away from their homes. Another Madonna to whom Italians prayed for help during the war was the Regina di Pompeii; mothers, wives and families visited her sanctuary all year, asking for safety. In June 1942, the sanctuary bulletin reported that the traffic became daily more intense: 'the exceptional cold of the past winter has not diminished the influx of visitors, nor has the coming heat of this summer.'[56]

Famous images of the Madonna in important sanctuaries were removed and taken to safer places whenever there was a risk that sanctuaries would be bombed. However, sanctuaries were chosen as shelters because it was believed that the images of the Madonna they contained would protect the faithful from the bombs. According to one of the most popular legends of wartime Pompeii, the bishop decided to move the famous image of the Regina to a safer place while the population sheltered in the sanctuary. Shortly afterwards, on 13 September 1943, Pompeii was bombed for the first time. The population asked the bishop to return the Madonna; he did, and the town was no longer bombed.[57] Pompeii was one case in which the protection of the Madonna had been 'experienced', in the words of the sanctuary's official calendar. While the town suffered considerable damage (though very few victims), nothing happened to the sanctuary 'despite being surrounded by falling bombs'.[58] The diary of a nun who lived in the sanctuary, Sister Maria Giuliana Perillo, describes how the town's population moved to the sanctuary after the air raid, and refused to return home.[59] Similarly, Don Placido Romano Zucal recorded in his memoirs the months he spent in 1944 in Santa Maria del Monte (Cesena) while the Benedictine church (which contained a statue of the Madonna and had been a site of pilgrimage for centuries) was crowded with evacuees. However, as was the case with other churches, including the famous abbey of Montecassino, Santa Maria del Monte was devastated in raids by airmen described by Zucal as 'flying Lutherans'.[60]

After the Anzio landings in January 1944, the Pope decided to transfer to Rome a picture of the Madonna del Divino Amore contained in the Sanctuary of Castel di Leva, a traditional pilgrimage site south of the capital. The image was brought to a church in the city centre, and the usual May pilgrimages to the sanctuary moved to the new site. During the battle for Cassino, as the bombing and fighting resounded in the peripheral areas of southern Rome, the population adhered with enthusiasm to the Pope's invitation to pray to the Madonna for the safety of the city. So many people went to visit the Madonna during May that it became necessary to move the image to the large church of St Ignazio. On 4 June 1944, the day of the liberation of the capital, a vow was made in the church by the Roman faithful gathered there: if the Madonna saved the city, they promised they would 'correct their moral conduct, renew the Sanctuary, and carry out charity work in Castel di Leva.' The vow was made quickly because the curfew started at 7pm and the population had to leave; at the same time as the Romans were making their vow, the Germans began to leave the city and at 7.45pm, the Allies entered peacefully. The next day, thousands of Romans went spontaneously to St Peter's square to express gratitude to the Pope, and on 11 June Pius XII went to St Ignazio to thank the Madonna as the 'Saviour of the *Urbe*'.[61]

Although the Madonna was the most celebrated – both in general terms as the Virgin and in the shape of local Madonnas – people also asked patron saints for help, just as they had done throughout the centuries in the case of wars and natural disasters. In Taranto, one of the first cities to become a target of British bombing because it was a major base for the Italian fleet, tributes to the patron saint were particularly widespread. In the spring of 1941 the population gathered in the cathedral to ask St Cataldo's intercession to protect the city

– something the saint had done throughout the centuries, as a long article in the local church bulletin explained. The church of Taranto asked St Cataldo to shorten the war through a 'true peace based on justice', emphasizing that this was not an expression of pacifism.[62] Pilgrimages to St Cataldo were organized by all the city dioceses in the spring of 1942 and the city's archbishop, Bernardi, claimed that the population unanimously attributed the defence and protection of the city to the saint.[63] Having experienced more bombs than Taranto, a

'The venerated Madonnina del Borgo after the recovery among the ruins which had buried her'. *In Memoriam. Dove passò la guerra: la tragica notte a Madonna di Campagna*, pamphlet on the bombing of 8 December 1942 (Turin: Stabilimento Tipografico Ajani Giovanni e Canale Giacomo, 1943).

desperate Milanese population implored in December 1942 for the intercession of St Ambrose, the city's patron saint who had allegedly helped in the defeat of the German emperor Barbarossa at the time of the northern Communes in the twelfth century.[64] The Pope, expressing his sorrow for the December raid on Milan, asked for the 'powerful intercession of the Madonna and of your protector Saint'.[65] He addressed a similar blessing to the people of Naples after the raid there in December, when he recalled the protection of the Madonna and of St Gennaro, 'always so close to you'.[66]

A widespread belief concerned bombed churches in which only the sacred image of the Madonna or of a saint had remained intact. In Turin following the raid of 8 December 1942, the church in the area of Madonna di Campagna was destroyed, but under the ruins the statue of the Madonna was found intact.[67]

Again in Turin, following the raids of February 1943, a mass was held in the basement of a destroyed church, where a huge cross had remained untouched. The people, kneeling amid the ruins, took Holy Communion while they stared at the miraculous cross.[68] In April 1943 the bishop of Naples informed his clergy that although the bombs had damaged the cathedral, the temple of St Gennaro inside had not been hit, thanks to the saint's protection.[69] Two months later, the image of the Madonna del Fuoco in Forlì remained intact when a fire destroyed the sanctuary; the image was moved to the cathedral where, according to L'Osservatore Romano, 40,000 citizens took part in the procession begging the Madonna to protect the city.[70] Processions to do penance and propitiate the Madonna followed a few days later in Agrigento, Amalfi, Anagni, Santa Agata dei Goti near Caserta, Teramo and Garfagnana in Tuscany.[71] The sheer number of participants was impressive. In Verona, a procession of penitence for peace in the spring of 1943 gathered, according to the prefect, more than 50,000 people.[72] Although sometimes the local clergy organized these events, often they were promoted by the faithful, or were much bigger than expected due to mass participation. The clergy did not know how to deal with religious rituals which inevitably raised collective expectations – principally, by 1943, the end of the war and of the regime.

MIRACLES AND PROPHECIES

Italy's most famous twentieth-century saint is the Capuchin priest Padre Pio, who established his monastery in a village in Apulia, San Giovanni Rotondo – still one of the most important sites of pilgrimage in the country – and allegedly developed stigmata during the First World War. His cult soared after Italy entered the war in 1940. Particularly after the first defeats of the Italian army and the realization that the anti-aircraft defences did not work, Italians began to send letters to Padre Pio asking for his intercession. Before 1939 Padre Pio received around 9,000 letters a year, a figure that grew to 12,000 in

1940, to 15,000 in 1942, and to more than 20,000 by 1945.[73] With the intensification of bombing after the armistice in September 1943, a rumour spread
across Italy that God had granted Padre Pio the gift of levitation. This miracle
had a precedent in Apulia in the seventeenth century with St Giuseppe da
Copertino, another Capuchin monk, who had been seen to levitate. As a result
it seemed plausible that Padre Pio could fly and intercept the enemy's bombs.
With the exception of Foggia, which was repeatedly bombed between May
and September 1943, the area of Apulia where he lived in Gargano received
no raids, and this convinced many that the rumour must be true. For decades
after 1944, the supporters of his case for beatification were even able to find
RAF pilots who were willing to confirm that it was indeed an apparition of a
flying Padre Pio which had stared at them so directly that they abandoned the
mission and returned to their bases without dropping bombs.[74] Such a story has
precedents in the early Middle Ages, when popes apparently repelled barbarian
invaders simply with the power of their gaze. The lethality of technology
involved in the air war provoked behaviour and legends that were, as Eric
Leed wrote of the Great War, 'reminiscent of archaic mentalities'.[75] The belief in
Padre Pio also shows that, even before the regime fell, the crisis of war marked
the collapse of legitimacy of Mussolini and the King, and transferred it to new
reference points, with the Catholic Church replacing the cult of the Duce and
the House of Savoy.

Just as during the Great War soldiers believed that survival in the inferno
of the trenches could only come from a miracle,[76] so civilians in cities did
not see any other possibility to survive air bombardment. In both wars, a way
of thanking the Madonna for granting safety, and at the same time a way of
relating a miracle, was the *ex voto* in the shape of paintings or letters to church
bulletins.[77] The *ex voto* had a double function: it was a (material) offer to the
religious institution dedicated to a certain Madonna, and communication of the
event. The *ex voto*, canonized by a centuries-long Christian tradition, is made
after the Madonna has provided the requested favour. The images portrayed in
sanctuaries and the letters in church bulletins transformed a private experience
into a public one.[78] It could also be argued that writing (or drawing) about the
traumatic experience of bombing was a way of coming to terms with it. For
example, a letter from a survivor of a raid in Soverato (Catanzaro) to the church
bulletin of Pompeii described just such a miraculous event:

On 29 October 1941 at noon, we were having lunch when we heard bombs falling near
our home. Immediately we got up invoking the Madonna of Pompeii and, terrified, we
ran to a different room. As soon as we got there, a bomb fell just near the stairs, which
were damaged while a splinter penetrating the external wall reached us, with a rain of
glass and stones. We can say that it was because of a true and miraculous inspiration
of the Madonna that we moved to shelter inside the house rather than running out to
the stairs, where we would have probably died. For this and for other celestial favours,
I send a humble offer.[79]

Ex-voto painting in the Basilica of Consolata, Turin: 'To the Consolata Virgin Mary with grateful hearts for the protection granted during the aerial bombing of 12 June 1940 and with certain hope to be assisted again by Her in any adversity. The tenants of homes in Turin, via Priocca n.10, n.12'.

Courtesy of Santuario Basilica La Consolata, Turin.

Miracles were often related to prophecies. In April 1942, Chief of Police Carmine Senise informed the country's prefects about a miracle that occurred in the church of St Maria in Monticelli in Rome, where a soldier saw the image of Jesus moving his eyes. People recalled a similar event that had happened just before the end of the First World War, and saw this as a propitiatory sign that the war would soon end. This rumour began to spread among the population and the soldiers, raising hopes that were totally unjustified by concrete events.[80] The Church was very wary of prophecies: in the case of the prophecy of Don

Bosco, one of the most successful of the war – according to which the war would end when Turkey entered it – the Vatican newspaper warned in 1944 that there was no proof that such prophecy could be applied to the current conflict.[81]

All these phenomena – prophecies about the coming peace, miracles and apparitions of the Virgin – evidenced a relationship between emotions and morale: hope in the supernatural was an expression of fear, which could undermine morale when it influenced collective behaviour. During the Italian Social Republic, the German authorities were particularly concerned by the apparition of the Virgin at Ghiaie di Bonate (Bergamo) to a seven-year-old girl on 13 May 1944 – just as in the case of Fatima on 13 May 1917 during the First World War. The Madonna made 13 appearances to the girl up to 31 July 1944, predicting that the war would end in three months. Despite the disruption of public transport and the real danger of air raids, tens of thousands of people from all over northern Italy visited the village, a fact interpreted by the Waffen-SS as a sign of defeatism among Italians. The Germans searched for the girl, but she was hidden in a convent by nuns. In his first official communication on the affair, on 20 May, the bishop of Bergamo warned clergy to remain cautious about the miracle; four days later, he forbade priests from going to the village and on 30 June he stated that no sufficient proof existed of the authenticity of the visitations.[82] A Turin industrialist, Carlo Chevallard, wrote in his diary that rumours of the Bonate vision spread throughout northern Italy particularly after the bombing of the Dalmine steel factories (also near Bergamo) on 6 July 1944, which killed 257 workers. In Turin, this was associated with another mysterious event which also occurred on 13 May (described by Chevallard as possibly a phenomenon of collective hallucination): the sun began to turn at high speed 'on its own'. People began to provide their own interpretations, some of which were related to the end of the war and could be connected with the miracle of Bonate. Both the apparition of the Virgin and the phenomenon of the revolving of the sun were expected to occur again on 13 July. The Fascist station Radio Tevere (which pretended to broadcast clandestinely from Rome, but was in fact based in Milan) decided to broadcast a programme on 16 July about these miracles, making fun of the events that had moved – as Chevallard noted – hundreds of thousands of people.[83] However, there was little the Fascist authorities could do at a time when the population expected miracles to happen and was ready to endorse them. Like other wartime rumours, miracles were created by believers, as Paul Fussell put it, 'out of their dire need'.[84]

CONCLUSION

Analysis of Catholic writings in different cities in northern, central and southern Italy during the war suggests that the Church proposed an interpretation of bombing as divine punishment, which required the clergy's respect for and collaboration with the state authorities. Bishops' letters in diocesan bulletins explained what the Church authorities expected from the lower clergy: an extraordinary commitment in assisting the population in bombed areas and in salvaging the country's moral values. Although the Church suspended public processions when Italy entered the war, after the raids during the winter of 1942-3 recourse to supernatural help increased, and was expressed through thousands of people taking part in processions, the multiplication of *ex votos* to the Madonna, and the spread of rumours regarding miraculous events. For official religion, and even more so for popular religion, the sky is by definition where signs of divine intervention manifest themselves. In 1940-5 the sky was where the most terrifying wonders of the air war occurred. On the one hand, the destructive modernity of bombing made people fear that little could be done to protect themselves; on the other, the hope of survival justified belief in 'wonder-working power' that had provided thaumaturgic remedies in previous centuries.[85] Although the link between bombs and religious signs cannot be interpreted as conscious indications of defeatism or anti-Fascism, the beliefs of the masses could barely be controlled by either the state authorities or the Church, and reflected feelings of fatalism, resignation and the lack of faith in the regime. The Church sought to avoid any link being made between religious events and forms of pacifism or anti-Fascism, and insisted on aspects of penitence. Nevertheless, despite its cautious attitude, and thanks to its presence both during and after the raids, the Church came to replace the regime as the point of reference for survivors and evacuees. In the same way, the Madonna, patron saints and Padre Pio came to replace Italy's ineffective anti-aircraft defences.

Notes

1   'Questa nostra Italia', *L'Italia*, 8 July 1943, 1.
2   'Un nobilissimo appello del Vescovo di Bergamo', *L'Italia*, 12 June 1940, 2.
3   *Rivista diocesana torinese*, XV, 6, 20 June 1940.
4   'Le vittime dell'incursione aerea nemica su alcune città dell'Italia settentrionale', *L'Italia*, 17 August 1940, 3.
5   See for example 'Nobile lettera del Card. Boetto alla cittadinanza genovese', *Il Corriere della Sera*, 13 February 1941.
6   'La protezione degli edifici destinati al culto contro bombardamenti aerei', *Bollettino Ecclesiastico di Napoli*, XXI, 7, July 1940, 176.
7   'Le nostra campane', *L'Italia*, 18 July 1942, 2.
8   On the Fascist *piazza*, see M. Isnenghi, *L'Italia in piazza. I luoghi della vita pubblica dal 1848 ai giorni nostri* (Milan: Mondadori, 1994), 301-29.
9   M. Fincardi, 'Pastori di profughi. La dispersione bellica e la ricomposizione delle comunità locali nella memorialistica dei parroci', in B. Gariglio and R. Marchis (eds), *Cattolici, ebrei ed evangelici nella guerra. Vita religiosa e società, 1939-1945* (Milan: Angeli, 2007 – 1st ed. 1999), 250-1, 243-4.
10 M. Franzinelli, *Il clero del duce, il duce del clero. Il consenso ecclesiastico nelle lettere a Mussolini (1922-1945)* (Ragusa: La Fiaccola, 1998), 201.
11 B. Mussolini, *Opera Omnia*, vol. 31, *Dal discorso al direttorio nazionale del P.N.F. del 3 gennaio 1942 alla liberazione di Mussolini: 4 gennaio 1942-12 settembre 1943* (Florence: La Fenice, 1960), 118-33.

12 A. Harris, *Bomber Offensive* (London: Greenhill Books, 1990 – 1st edn. 1947), 141.

13 C. Baldoli and M. Fincardi, 'Italian Society under Anglo-American Bombs: Propaganda, Experience, and Legend, 1940-1945', *The Historical Journal*, 52, 2009, 1017–38.

14 Archivio di Stato di Torino (AST), Prefettura, Gabinetto, b. 524, Prefect of Turin to Ministry of the Interior, 29 November 1940, 'Manifestazioni religiose nei rifugi antiaerei'.

15 G. Vitrotti, *Cronistoria Alpignanese, 1932-1968* (Turin: Editrice STIP, 1970), entry for 15 May 1943, 65.

16 'Diario di S. E. Mons. Arcivescovo – dal mese di Agosto 1943 a Febbraio 1944', *Rivista Diocesana di Taranto*, IX, 1–2, January–February 1944, 8.

17 AST, Prefettura, Gabinetto, b. 509, 'Relazione mensile sull'attività del clero nel mese di luglio 1943', entry for 13 July.

18 'Il parroco e gli sfollati', *Bollettino Ecclesiastico di Napoli*, XXIV, 2, February 1943, 23.

19 'Il parroco e gli sfollati', *Bollettino Ecclesiastico di Napoli*, XXIV, 7, July 1943, 111–13.

20 Don L. Bagnoli, *Gli anni difficili del passaggio del fronte a Cesena* (Cesena: Comune di Cesena, 1986), entry for 28 May 1944, 81.

21 C. Capponi, *Con cuore di donna. Il ventennio, la Resistenza a Roma, via Rasella: i ricordi di una protagonista* (Milan: Il Saggiatore, 2009; 1st edn. 2000), 79.

22 'Il Santo Padre tra i fedeli della Sua Diocesi di Roma colpiti dall'incursione aerea', *L'Osservatore Romano*, 21 July 1943, 1.

23 'Il Santo padre nelle zone colpite dall'odierno bombardamento di Roma', *L'Osservatore Romano*, 14 August 1943, 1; 'Il Padre', *L'Osservatore Romano*, 15 August 1943, 1.

24 U. Gentiloni Silveri and M. Carli, *Bombardare Roma: gli alleati e la città aperta, 1940-1944* (Bologna: Il Mulino, 2007).

25 'Lettera degli arcivescovi e vescovi della regione piemontese al clero ed al popolo nella Pasqua 1944', *Bollettino Mensile della Parrocchia di S. Giulio, Torino*, XV, 6–7, June–July 1944.

26 Conferenza Episcopale della Regione Triveneta, *Notificazione* (Venezia: Libreria Emiliana Editrice, 20 April 1944), 8–9. On the attitude of the Vatican throughout the war, see G. Miccoli, 'Pio XII e la guerra', in M. Franzinelli and R. Bottoni (eds) *Chiesa e guerra. Dalla benedizione delle armi alla 'Pacem in terris'* (Bologna: Il Mulino, 2005), 393–416.

27 'Vittorie spirituali', *L'Osservatore Romano*, 1 January 1941, 1.

28 Archivio di Stato di Genova (ASG), Prefettura, Gabinetto, Sala 21, b. 220, Ministry of Interior to prefects of the kingdom, 15 October 1940.

29 G. Tuninetti,' Strategie pastorali, guerra e Resistenza nella diocesi di Torino: l'opera dell'arcivescovo Maurilio Fossati e dei suoi principali collaboratori', in Gariglio and Marchis (eds), *Cattolici, ebrei ed evangelici*, 122–4.

30 G. Vecchio, *Lombardia 1940-1945. Vescovi, preti e società alla prova della guerra* (Brescia: Morcelliana, 2005), 144.

31 AST, Prefettura, Gabinetto, b. 509, Head of Police of Turin to Prefect of Turin, 13 April 1942.

32 Ibid., 'Brani della predica tenuta il 2 marzo 1942. XX nella chiesa di S. Carlo da padre Guaschino dell'ordine dei domenicani'.

33 Ibid., Head of Police of Turin to Prefect of Turin, 1 April 1942.

34 Archivio Centrale dello Stato, Rome (ACS), Ministero dell'Interno, A5G Seconda Guerra Mondiale, b. 26, Ministry of the Interior to Prefect of Cagliari, 'Cagliari – preghiera per la pace', 19 January 1943.

35 Ibid. 'Ave Maria del tempo di guerra', no date but probably spring 1943.

36 ACS, Ministero dell'Interno, A5G Seconda Guerra Mondiale, b. 28, confidential report from Naples to the Ministry of the Interior, 8 January 1943.

37 Capponi, *Con cuore di donna*, 214.

38 'Cristiani in guerra', *L'Italia*, 29 September 1941, 1.

39 'La confortatrice parola del Santo Padre al popolo di Genova', *L'Italia*, 20 November 1942, 1; see also 'Il paterno conforto e le riconfermate sollecitudini del Sommo Pontefice per le vittime e le rovine delle incursioni aeree', *L'Osservatore Romano*, 6 December 1942, 1.

40 *Note sul diario di don Massocca* (Virle Piemonte), unpublished typescript.

41 Don G. Cinotti, *Briciole di storia piemontese* (Romano Canavese: Tipografia Ferrero, 1977).

42 'Pianto sulle chiese che crollano', *L'Osservatore Romano*, 4 March 1943, 1.

43   'I presenti disastri ed il nostro miglioramento spirituale', *Bollettino Ecclesiastico di Napoli*, XXIV, 3, March 1943, 45.

44   'Nell'ora più grave della patria', *Rivista Diocesana di Taranto*, VIII, 5-6-7, May-June-July 1943, 33-35.

45   Don Bagnoli, *Gli anni difficili*, entry for 21 August 1943, 47.

46   'La Chiesa e la guerra', *L'Osservatore Romano*, 16 February 1944, 1.

47   Don G. Buzzacchi, 'Diario da Parrocchia di S. Michele Arcangelo in Villa Saviola', in Don L. Boselli, *Bicicletta da donna col passo da uomo* (Suzzara: Edizioni Bottazzi, 1991), entry for 21 July 1944, 147.

48   ACS, Ministero dell'Interno, A5G Seconda Guerra Mondiale, b. 27, 'Relazione del fiduciario n. 21', 14 March 1941.

49   For the apparition of the Virgin in the Po Valley at the end of the 19th century, see M. Fincardi, '"Ici pas de Madonne". Inondations et apparitions mariales dans les campagnes de la vallée du Pô', *Annales*, 50, 1995, 829-854.

50   D. Blackbourn, *The Marpingen Visions: Rationalism, Religion and the Rise of Modern Germany* (London: Harper Collins, 1995; 1st edn. 1993), 210.

51   A. Becker, *War and Faith: The Religious Imagination in France, 1914-1930* (Oxford, New York: Berg, 1998; French ed. 1994), 62.

52   'Una solenne funzione religiosa per propiziare la Vergine sulla città di Milano', *L'Italia*, 26 November 1942, 2.

53   'Il patriarca e il popolo di Venezia rinnovano il voto del Cardinale La Fontaine per la salvezza della città dalle insidie della guerra', *L'Osservatore Romano*, 10 January 1943, 6.

54   'La consacrazione dell'archidiocesi torinese al Cuore Immacolato di Maria Santissima', *L'Italia*, 22 December 1942, 2.

55   'Funzioni propiziatorie alla Consolata di Torino', *L'Osservatore Romano*, 15 June 1940, 2.

56   *Il Rosario e la Nuova Pompei*, LIX, 3, May-June 1942, 87.

57   Personal interview with the sanctuary's archivist, Don Antonio Maiello, 12 July 2009.

58   'Un mese sotto l'incubo del pericolo', *Calendario del Santuario e delle Opere di beneficenza cristiana di Pompei*, 1944, 32.

59   Archivio Storico Diocesano 'Bartolo Longo' del Santuario di Pompei, I, 753, 'Testimonianza di Suor Maria Giuliana Perillo delle Figlie del S. Rosario di Pompei', unpublished typescript.

60   Don P. R. Zucal, *Clausura violata* (Cesena: Stilgraf Editrice, 2004), 12.

61   C. C. Canta, *Sfondare la notte. Religiosità, modernità e cultura nel pellegrinaggio alla Madonna del Divino Amore* (Milan: Angeli, 2004), 154-6.

62   'S. Cataldo protettore di Taranto', *Rivista Diocesana di Taranto*, VI, 5-6, May-June 1941, 65-71.

63   '10 Maggio: S. Cataldo', *Rivista Diocesana di Taranto*, VII, 3-4, March-April 1942, 18.

64   'La protezione di S. Ambrogio su Milano e sulla patria tutta', *L'Italia*, 8 December 1942, 3.

65   'Paterne parole di conforto di Pio XII ai milanesi', *L'Italia*, 9 December 1942, 1.

66   'La commossa benedizione del Santo padre al Clero e al Popolo di Napoli', *L'Italia*, 15 December 1942, 1.

67   'Dove passò la guerra. La tragica notte a Madonna di Campagna', *La Stampa*, 8 December 2002.

68   'La S. Messa domenicale in un sotterraneo', *L'Italia*, 16 February 1943, 2.

69   'Notificazione al Clero ed al Popolo dell'Archidiocesi', *Bollettino Ecclesiastico di Napoli*, XXIV, 4, April 1943, 50.

70   'Quarantamila forlivesi ai piedi della Madonna del Fuoco', *L'Osservatore Romano*, 14-15 June 1943, 4.

71   'Manifestazioni di penitenza e di propiziazione', *L'Osservatore Romano*, 18 June 1943, 4.

72   ACS, Ministero dell'Interno, A5G Seconda Guerra Mondiale, b. 27, prefect of Verona to Ministry of the Interior, 12 April 1943.

73   S. Luzzatto, *Padre Pio. Miracoli e politica nell'Italia del Novecento* (Turin: Einaudi, 2007), 279.

74   Ibid., 290.

75   E. J. Leed, *No Man's Land: Combat and Identity in World War I* (Cambridge: Cambridge University Press, 1979), 128; 115.

76   A. Gibelli, *L'officina della Guerra. La grande guerra e le trasformazioni del mondo mentale*

(Turin: Bollati Boringhieri, 2009, first edn. 1991), see in particular chapter on the 'new mental landscape'.

77 See for example the ex votos to thank the Madonna della Consolata for protection from bombing, Provincia di Torino, *Gli ex voto della Consolata. Storie di grazia e devozione nel santuario torinese* (Turin: Provincia di Torino, 1982), 142–9.

78 P. Caggiano, M. Rak and A. Turchini, *La madre è bella* (Pompei: Pontificio Santuario, 1990), 103–4.

79 *Il Rosario e la Nuova Pompei*, LIX, 1, January–February 1942, 12.

80 ASG, Prefettura, Gabinetto Sala 21, b. 220, Chief of the Police Senise to prefects of the kingdom, 28 April 1942.

81 C. Chevallard, *Diario, 1942-1945. Cronache del tempo di guerra*, edited by R. Marchis (Turin: Blu Edizioni, 2005), entry for 12 May 1944, 244; 'Profezie di guerra', *L'Osservatore Romano*, 15 March 1944, 1.

82 G. Cortinovis, *Le apparizioni della Madonna a Ghiaie di Bonate nel 1944* (1984); Vecchio, *Lombardia 1940-1945*, 221–3.

83 Chevallard, *Diario, 1942-1945*, entry for 17 July 1944, 299–300.

84 P. Fussell, *Wartime: Understanding and Behavior in the Second World War* (New York: Oxford University Press, 1989), 45.

85 M. Bloch, *The Royal Touch: Sacred Monarchy and Scrofula in England and France* (London: Routledge, 1973; French edn. *Les Rois thaumaturges*, 1961), 242.

8

'Defend us from All Perils and Dangers of this Night':[1] Coping with Bombing in Britain during the Second World War

Vanessa Chambers

the men took cover as usual ... and sat and talked – mostly doubtful jokes and stories and, in the hardboiled way of Yard workers, they cursed and blasphemed ... the foreman went to see the damage and came back and said, 'I hope to God there is not another – it looks as if we are trapped now.' As he spoke there was a worse crump, and then a deathly silence ... torches dropped from nerveless fingers on to the floor, and by their light he saw the 'round' of knees as men instinctively dropped to kneel on playing cards or newspapers. He saw clenched or clasped hands and a glimpse of grey hollowed cheeks, and then a calm steady voice rose, 'Father, into Thy hands we commend our spirits,' and the Lord's Prayer started. Gerald recognized the voice as belonging to about the dirtiest-mouthed and hardest-swearing man in the shop.[2]

Thus Nella Last, a Mass Observation diarist known to the organization as 'housewife 49', wrote in 1941 about Barrow shipyard workers. These so-called 'hardened', irreligious yard men sought refuge and consolation in prayer when trapped in a shelter by an exploding bomb. This type of reaction was not limited to shipyard workers. My recent research[3] and analysis of a variety of primary source material across Britain and Northern Ireland reveals that many people turned to a range of 'supernatural'[4] resources or props during the Second World War, in particular during the blitzes and sustained bombing campaigns. While this impact of bombing on the Home Front has been largely unexplored in the historiography of the Second World War, this chapter argues that the anxiety occasioned by the war and the unpredictable nature of life on the Home Front caused many people to turn to a variety of supernatural resources. Focusing on this aspect of the social and cultural impact of bombing in the UK and Northern Ireland during the Second World War allows an alternative understanding and interpretation of the impact of bombing to that of the prevailing 'we can take it' view.[5] As author and historian Constantine FitzGibbon noted in 1958 in his account of the Blitz: 'the whole of the British propaganda machine was concentrated on one theme: London can take it. Reading the very heavily censored newspapers of the time, the impression one gets is of endless cockney jokes, of grim determination, and of utter self-confidence in the face of dastardly and unfair attack'.[6]

While some recent scholarship has touched very briefly on popular belief during the Second World War, general views seem fairly dismissive and it has not been considered specifically as a result of bombing. One recent commentator wrote of recourse to the supernatural during the war as 'miscellaneous beliefs [which] rarely constitute an articulate and alternative world-view' and argued that 'their significance should not be overstated'.[7] Others, while accepting that people did turn to supernatural props, consider it is difficult to determine the level of belief.[8] This may be so, but there is certainly evidence in primary sources that belies the former view. For example, a middle-class teacher and settlement worker, Phyllis Warner, wrote articles on the home front for the *Washington Post* during the war, and in the early days of the London Blitz she revealed that most people 'find ourselves soundlessly muttering some form of words over and over during these bad periods, usually some childhood prayer or line of a hymn'.[9] While it is impossible to quantify popular belief, sources reveal that a significant number of people sought recourse to supernatural beliefs which had a significant impact on their lives, especially during bombing; it helped them feel safe in times of anxiety, danger and adversity, and provided succour and comfort in times of loss, death and bereavement. Some turned to fortune-tellers or mediums, others sought refuge in religion, prayer or in so-called 'lucky rituals', or both. Some heeded advice of astrologers in the increasingly popular newspaper horoscope columns, who undertook to tell them where best to shelter during bombing. Others, like Mass Observation's Nella Last, relied on tarot cards to calm them during anxious moments.[10] People resorted to such popular beliefs in order to try to understand their situation, to gain reassurance, to try to foreknow their future or to attempt to keep themselves or loved ones safe. Joanna Bourke, in her recent cultural history of fear, states that this took many forms, but one way or another 'most people dealt with their fears through 'magic thinking'.[11]

PRAYER: A PROP OR A LAST RESORT?

During the Second World War many people kept diaries or journals recording their observations, worries, concerns and general day-to-day thoughts during the momentous events unfolding around them. Mention of prayer, religion, superstition and aspects of popular belief is often to be found in these diaries and journals, but has mainly been overlooked by historians examining the social history of the Second World War. Author, playwright, journalist and one time Beauty Editor for *Women's Own*, Ursula Bloom was just one whose wartime memoirs survive and can be used to help build up a picture of what life was like for people in Britain during the dark days of blitz and bombing. Writing of March 1941, when bombs rained down on London, Bloom hesitantly revealed that she derived comfort and help from reciting her old childhood prayers. She wrote, 'During this time, and perhaps it sounds absurd to mention it, my great help, and the thing that composed me most, was the old prayer of my childhood which seemed completely suitable for this horror':[12]

Lighten our darkness, we beseech thee, O Lord;
and by Thy great mercy defend us from all
perils and dangers of this night ...

Clydeside resident Thomas Kearns described in a letter how prayer had helped him during bombing in March 1941: 'On the night of the 13th March the sirens sounded around 9 p.m ... The gunfire started and this made us a bit panicky naturally ... They peppered away, never a lull in all this time, we prayed and prayed and God must have heard our prayers and at the break of day, after 9½ hours we received the 'all-clear'.[13] Mass Observation found similar instances of people turning to prayer during bombing: so-called 'non-believers' used prayer to help them get through air raids.[14] Mass Observation's Tom Harrisson argued later, however, that prayer did not play a big part in helping people through the crisis of bombing[15] and recently Helen Jones has stated that momentary 'crisis-praying' did take place, but suggests that 'hard evidence' of this is difficult to find.[16] On the contrary, diaries, memoirs and personal accounts contain many examples of people turning to prayer, religious chants or hymns to help them get through the bombing. James Bell, sheltering during a raid in Exeter recalled:

There was a raid on, bombs were falling, guns were blasting away 'bang ... bang ...'. Glass was breaking, and ceilings, and chimneys falling. The noise was deafening – then we heard a string of bombs fall that was close, now closer, oh God this one must be for us. Father's voice was praying through the racket 'Lord we place ourselves into Your safekeeping. Lord Jesus save us.'[17]

A Birmingham man trapped under wreckage for nine hours before being rescued exhibited a response that might be considered typical for people in a desperate situation. He began to pray when he felt all was hopeless: it was the only thing he had left, a last resort: 'The smoke began to get down my throat, then I felt a trickle of water falling on me. I realized that firemen were at work with the hoses. But it was hopeless! I began to pray'.[18] As John Wolffe has argued in his study of religion and national life, 'people at home were affected by the war in an unprecedented manner, above all through bombing and evacuation. Such experiences could evoke religious responses'.[19]

Given the success of events such as national days of prayer that were regularly held during the war, perhaps this response is not surprising.[20] These were arranged by the Archbishop of Canturbury with approval of the King and ordered by the Privy Council on behalf of the Church of England, and were also fully supported by the National Free Churches. The first such day was organized for Sunday 1 October 1939, only a month after war was declared and was described as 'a means by which the State expresses its recognition of God and of the need of Divine help and guidance'.[21] The second event, on 26 May 1940, saw 'far larger [congregations] than is ordinarily seen' attending services up and down the country.[22] One Plymouth diarist, Mr Hurrell, made the following entry for 26 May 1942:

> Day of National Prayer requested by the King throughout the Empire. A united service held at Hooe Church at 3 p.m … The church full with people and chairs brought in from Church Hall to seat the overflow of congregation – several chairs brought between the Choir and altar rail.[23]

In his sermon broadcast to the nation, The Archbishop of Canterbury stated that 'the act of prayer now and repeated continually day by day … will bring calmness, courage, self-control.'[24] Somewhat ironically, the beginning of the London Blitz and the intensification of air attacks coincided with the next national prayer day, 8 September 1940, the Sunday after the anniversary of the start of the war. By the time of the third anniversary day of prayer in September 1942, a working day, The Times reported that millions of people joined in the 'national act of rededication' either by attending one of the church services throughout the land or by listening to loud speakers outside the overflowing churches. At some churches, large queues formed an hour before the service was due to begin. Even important war work was stopped for 15 minutes and 'workers in groups thousands strong gathered in their canteens in the great factories' to take part in the service broadcast on the wireless.[25]

THE IMPACT OF RELIGIOUS SYMBOLS: MORALE, ENDURANCE AND REASSURANCE

Notwithstanding the obvious success of and apparent need for National Days of Prayer, the church itself was often found wanting in terms of providing the help and support that people needed during and after bombing. While John Wolffe notes 'signs of a transient religious vitality' during the War,[26] and Helen Jones finds some evidence to support this view,[27] Tom Harrisson argued that organized religion played a minor role in helping to comfort people and had little to offer in terms of coping strategies.[28] Clearly parish life was in any case fragmented, due both to bomb damage to churches and to men and women departing for the front or leaving to work in agriculture and industry. Stephen Spinks, in his study of religion in Britain since 1900, commented that the extent of disruption meant that without church or congregation, many a minister 'found his life's work brought to a calamitous end.'[29] Michael Snape, in his recent study of religion and the British army in the First and Second World Wars,[30] agrees that bomb damage to church building influenced the perception of growing secularization during the Second World War.[31]

Nevertheless, bomb-damaged churches and religious statues and windows left standing amidst the ruins do seem to have had an impact on people, and some were considered superstitiously as a lucky sign. Any event slightly out of the normal could be interpreted as a miraculous sign. Ursula Bloom wrote of:

> a most extraordinary vision. It was of a crucifix and was seen last night over the Ipswich neighbourhood. A most miraculous sight for the whole sky changed with it, and I think this is undoubtedly true, for too many saw it. Some said that it was very comforting. Surely a religious vision *must* be of good omen.[32]

St Patrick's church in Ballymacarrett, Belfast was left with gaping holes in the roof and severe structural and internal damage after bombing. However, according to the *Belfast Telegraph* of 8 April 1941, the stained glass window of Christ and the Apostles, which remained intact along with the undamaged altar, were testament to the fact that 'God after all was still on the side of the city'.[33] In Plymouth, reassurance was derived from the undamaged statue of Jesus amid the devastation to St Peter's church following bombing in August 1941.[34]

Such sources confirm that people obtained great comfort from traditional religious icons and symbolism and adopted these during bombing as part of their coping strategies in a superstitious manner. Undoubtedly the most potent example of this belief was St Paul's Cathedral in London. Having survived the early part of the London Blitz, it very nearly succumbed to bombing during the night of 29 December 1940 when the City of London was firebombed in what became known as 'The Second Great Fire of London'. Had it not been for an energetic team of firewatchers and firemen, St Paul's would have been destroyed. Its almost miraculous escape amid complete ruins became a symbol of hope, of comfort and of superstition to many people and came to symbolize the heart of the City. A woman from Bethnal Green in London, for example, is quoted as saying:

> I went up on the roof with some of the firemen, to look at the City. And I've always remembered how I was choked, I think I was crying a little. I could see St Paul's standing there, and the fire all around, and I just said: 'Please God, don't let it go!' I couldn't help it, I felt that if St Paul's had gone, something would have gone from us. But it stood in defiance, it did. And when the boys were coming back, the firemen said: 'It's bad, but, oh, the old church stood it.' Lovely, that was.[35]

Historian John Wolffe notes that Winston Churchill was aware of the importance to morale of St Paul's which had become symbolic of national resistance, endurance and belief in the future. Its emergence from the fire, smoke and devastation around it seemed miraculous and was a massive boost to morale.[36] Phyllis Warner noted, 'The escape of St Paul's is amazing: completely encircled by ruins, it stands superbly and dauntlessly the same – Thank God'.[37] Indeed, arguably the most evocative photograph of the war, and certainly one much used today as a representation of the Blitz, was Herbert Mason's photograph of the dome of St Paul's on 29 December 1940 and published in the *Daily Mail* that New Year's Eve. Of that photograph, he is quoted as saying:

> an artificial wind sprang through the heat caused by the fires, parted the clouds, the buildings in the foreground collapsed, and there revealed in all its majesty was St Paul's, a hauntingly beautiful picture which no artist could recapture.[38]

SPIRITS IN THE SKY: SPIRITUALISM AND THE AFTER-LIFE

St Paul's was haunted indeed, as far as one munitions worker was concerned. In a small booklet published just after the London Blitz, A. E. Cook described in great detail how he saw a multitude of angels all in white in the sky, coming from every direction, but converging on the golden cross on the top of the dome of St Paul's. These were, he insisted, the spirits of people killed in bombing raids:

> With the light now failing fast, my gaze turned in the direction of the ruins of St Thomas's Hospital ... I thought I saw angels, all in white, coming from that direction, and making for some point behind me. And, yes! As, wondering, I looked around, I saw them coming from every part of London – north, south, east and west ... I saw plainly that they were converging on one point; and, further, I saw what that point was. Behold, standing out above the huge town and all its mists, a CROSS! ... it was the Cross on the topmost point of St Paul's Cathedral. No wonder those angels were going there – that great emblem of God! Those angels ... were loved ones that had been taken away from us, but who, nevertheless, are still with us; yes, they and thousands of others ... are still with us, watching over London, watching over Coventry, watching over Plymouth, watching over Bristol; watching over all those towns of ours that have felt the ruthlessness of German bombing.[39]

Notwithstanding the above, there was no major collective surge towards spiritualism, such as that experienced during the First World War and during the inter-war years, and numbers of spiritualists declined during the early years of the Second World War.[40] Historians seeking to explain the decline in numbers of spiritualists during the Second World War, and to differentiate between the public reaction to mass bereavement during the First and Second World Wars, have offered varying explanations. Geoffrey Nelson, in his 1969 study of spiritualism, claimed that the very public failure of prophecy (many spiritualists were vociferous in 'no war' prophecies right up to August 1939) caused lasting disillusionment and 'bitter disappointment' among many spiritualists, though he also argued that this was just one of the factors causing decline: wartime restrictions, evacuations and general wartime disruption also played a part.[41] Jenny Hazelgrove offers an entirely different theory based on the increasingly callous, light-hearted and indifferent language used by soldiers of the First World War, and again in the Second World War, regarding the dead. She suggests that society's perception of death and attitudes towards the dead had changed in the inter-war period due to growing secularism and to medical advances, which caused sharp contrast between spiritualist values and the growing modern desire to see death as an ending. The 'weakening of stable mourning codes and ritual helped to produce a new prohibition on grief', and during the Second World War people were discouraged from individual displays of grief and mourning lest this adversely affected public morale.[42] The 'stiff upper lip' attitude may have helped the war effort, but, Hazelgrove argues, may also have accounted for the decline in spiritualist numbers, as their representation of a lasting after-life came to be perceived as increasingly improbable.[43] More likely is David Cannadine's conclusion that the lower numbers of fatalities, and the fact that the Second World War was not such a major shock as the previous conflict, meant that there was no collective surge towards spiritualism during and after the Second World War as there had been during and after the First World War.[44]

Nevertheless, there is much evidence to suggest that spiritualism and associated beliefs continued to play an important role during the Second World War.[45] As the war continued, the public perception of spiritualism was aided by the growing preoccupation of the film industry with the 'Great Beyond'. Many popular cinema films of the later war years featured the after-life and other supernatural themes[46] and were extremely popular with the British cinema-going public.[47] Newspapers remarked on the cinema's fascination with this subject. The *Daily Mail* attributed it to a general preoccupation with the supernatural, with people more likely to reflect on the possibility of an after-life during the anxiety of bombing and wartime.[48]

YOUR FUTURE IN THE STARS: ASTROLOGY AND NEWSPAPER HOROSCOPES

This anxiety, particularly during bombing, caused many people to place reliance and faith on newspaper horoscope columns. These columns had begun following the birth of Princess Margaret in August 1930, when the popular British newspaper *The Sunday Express* published a forecast for the new princess by popular astrologer R. H. Naylor, along with a general forecast for those born in August. This proved an instant success. Thus began the craze for newspaper astrology that became the horoscope column. These became increasingly popular during the war and some people used them to plan their every action. For example, one 30-year-old woman from Mill Hill appeared to arrange her whole life around the predictions of Lyndoe, the astrologer in the *People*. She stated:

> Astrologers are often right. Look at Lyndoe. I read him and study him regularly and find it a great help ... I really have great faith in him ... I plan by him. If he said I'd get

run over on a certain day if I went out, I would never leave the house even to go into the garden.[49]

During bombing raids some astrologers took it upon themselves to advise people about where they should shelter. In *Predictions* magazine, Naylor published a 'new sort of astrological guidance for air raids' which advised people specifically on how they should behave in air raids, depending upon when they were born. Those born in January, for example were advised 'not to rely too much on underground shelters, nor to be too nervous about taking their chance in a hollow in the open', but people born in November were advised that they were safest sheltering in the open.[50]

The authorities, aware of this growing reliance, were concerned that 'believers [might] be prompted by their astrological faith to take action which may not only be contrary to Government policy, but may also jeopardize their own safety'. Some, it was rumoured, had already based their decision on whether to bring back evacuated children on such astrological advice.[51] As a result, the Ministry of Home Security (Intelligence Branch) set up an extensive investigation into the effect of newspaper astrology on public morale. The subject was brought to the attention of the War Cabinet Defence Committee when the Financial Secretary to the Treasury expressed concern that 'the illusions disseminated in this way had a harmful effect on public morale and on the war effort'; he called for 'strong action [to] be taken to put a stop to this form of journalism'. Investigation of the effect of newspaper astrology on the public mind, and on the success rate of astrologers' wartime predictions, was the result of these concerns. A Sub-Committee was set up to investigate the effect of astrology on the public morale.[52] The Sub-Committee's report reached similar conclusions to Mass Observation findings:

1. About two thirds of the adult population of England glances at or reads some astrological newspaper feature regularly or occasionally.
2. About four out of ten members of the public have some interest in, or belief in, astrology.
3. A small proportion of people, at the most one in ten and probably of a neurotic type, make astrology a major interest in their lives and allow it to play some part in forming their conduct ... It would appear that the decline in religious belief among people ... has provided the astrologers with a favourable field for their operations.[53]

While the report may have dismissed one in ten of the population as a 'small proportion', in statistical terms this would potentially have represented a huge number of people who were influenced by their horoscopes enough to let them guide their conduct during air raids. The number (two thirds) of the adult population who read their horoscopes was even greater. This disposition was represented in the 1943 novel, *Shaving through the Blitz*, in which during a lull in the bombing, one shelterer remarked that an astrologer had told her that blue was her unlucky colour and she remembered that the night of the land-mine, she had been wearing blue.[54] Astrology's increased popularity during bombing and wartime can be considered as a response to anxiety and uncertainty and the need for people to find order and reason amid chaos. As historian Angus Calder noted in 1969, the phenomenon of people turning towards religion and prayer to help them during the war 'was clearly related to the quickening of interest in astrology'.[55]

WALKING UNDER LADDERS: LUCKY CHARMS AND SUPERSTITIONS

So-called 'lucky' charms were also relied upon by some people to help them during bombing raids. Mass Observation observers noted that 'lucky' items such as amulets and horseshoes were widely available on the high street. Woolworths sold 'Good luck amulets' for threepence and Boots displayed horseshoes and other 'lucky' items in their windows.[56] Ursula Bloom related in April 1941 how her maid, Rosa, relied on a small angel her mother had given her years before. The angel was lost during a bombing raid and Rosa became extremely distraught:

> Rosa ... came crying out of her shattered room full of glass. She complained only that she had lost the angel that her mother had given her years ago. She stood there crying and saying that she must have the angel. The fact that she was still alive did not impress her, the angel was her worry, and in the chaos and the darkness we could do nothing about it for her.[57]

All sorts of objects, not just religious items, could be deemed lucky. Indeed, more secular events could also be considered lucky, such as the belief noted by Mass Observation that people would be safe as long as the King and Queen remained in London.[58] As one anxious mother noted, 'as long as they're here you can feel sure things are alright'.[59] Similarly, in the First World War evidence suggests that soldiers had farthings sewn into their braces and worn over the heart. The coin represented the Monarch, who represented God, so the soldier was indirectly seeking God's protection by positioning this over his heart.[60] Michael Snape has compared the religious and popular belief of British soldiers in both conflicts and finds much continuity of belief among soldiers, for example in the widespread fatalism exhibited in both wars, and in the quasi-religious belief in the magical properties of Bibles and in prayer itself, used as talismans rather than in the traditional religious sense.[61]

There is even evidence to suggest that for some people, the carrying of gas masks took on a superstitious nature and they were treated as a sort of lucky charm, instead of just providing protection from possible gas attacks.[62] For others, it appears that the superstitious noting down of each and every raid might have offered a form of comfort.[63] There are several examples of diaries that break off from normal chit-chat type entries and during the war contain just lists of when raids started and finished. The pocket book of Plymouth builder's labourer, William Reed, for example, details the 611 times the siren sounded in Plymouth. Every single raid is meticulously listed with the time the siren went, to the all-clear, beginning with 28 June 1940 to 30 May 1944, including the Plymouth blitz period of March/April 1941 during which much of Plymouth and Devonport was destroyed.[64] Similarly, the diary of Devonport dockyard worker, J. S. Wellington, contains small details of both daily life and important events before the raids started, but then simply lists the start and finish of bombing raids on the Plymouth area and casualties.[65] Just as some repeated a set of words like a charm or mantra to allay fear and anxiety, this repetitive noting down of each and every raid can be interpreted as having the same purpose and of having a calming effect. Superstition, after all, has been defined as 'an irrational belief that an object, action or circumstance not logically related to a course of events influences its outcome'.[66]

New technology caused new superstitions to develop. For example, people held a superstitious belief that bombers were deliberately able to target specific buildings or even individuals – that somehow it was personal. There were those who attempted to camouflage shelter roofs with branches, believing that the bombers could see them from the air and would deliberately target them. East-Enders sheltering in a school believed the bombers had seen them trekking there and would deliberately bomb it later.[67] For Liverpudlian fire-fighter, A. E. Randall, it was the 'damned, insistent, menacing, rhythmic drone of the Nazi bombers coming nearer and nearer' that made him believe it was personal. It sounded, he wrote, 'for all the world, as if they were looking for you'.[68] This belief was clearly widespread enough to be considered and evaluated seriously by the War Cabinet. A top secret review of the London Blitz to the War Cabinet in May 1941 concluded that 'There is no evidence that for the most part the attacks were directed against specific objectives' and later in the report that 'individual targets could not be picked out'.[69]

Old superstitions, however, took on new significance during bombing, for example the belief in 13 as unlucky: Phyllis Warner noted 13 December 1940 as 'an unlucky date'[70] and Wembley housewife, Mrs. R. E. Uttin, noted in her diary entry for 30 January 1941: 'Bill has been asked to stay at the Exchange on Monday and fire-watch there. They are a group of ten and three paid watchers – an unlucky number, I wonder?'[71] Mass Observation carried out a survey in 1941 on superstitious belief and concluded in the resulting report that women were particularly susceptible to superstition, with 86 per cent of women surveyed admitting to being influenced by superstition and around 50 per cent of men acknowledging they were influenced.[72] A variety of supernatural type props and beliefs were being relied upon by many people during the difficult days of the Second World War and especially during bombing amid a climate in which such belief became fairly widespread. For example, in 1940 during a fifteen-minute observation of people walking under a ladder, an observer noticed that ninety-eight people passed by the ladder. Only five (men) actually walked under it, the rest carefully walked round it.[73] In one small stretch of London's premium shopping area, Oxford Street, between Tottenham Court Road and Selfridges, another observer noted three sandwich men advertising private clairvoyants and three men selling the magazine *Prediction*.[74]

CONCLUSION

Robert Mackay, in his examination of civilian morale in Britain in the Second World War, notes that during the Blitz people became familiar with sudden, violent death. Few were spared the experience of a 'near miss'. To live through an experience in which, all around, others were being killed or injured was to carry a burden of fear that one's own survival was uncertain.[75] As the examples in this chapter have shown, people's response to this uncertainty and anxiety was often to turn to a variety of supernatural resources and props such as chanting, repetitious noting of dates, prayer, astrology or superstition to help them get through the dark days of bombing and to give them hope for the future. This widespread belief in fortune-telling, superstitions, astrology and the like that took place during the Second World War was not entirely new as similar responses were noted during the First World War. However, with the onset of strategic and long-range bombing, the nature of war changed irrevocably and this had an impact on people, on morale and on their responses. Strategic and long-range bombing brought new aspects of total war to the population, and civilians were considered increasingly as legitimate targets. Anyone might be at the mercy of bombing campaigns: merely being in the wrong place at the wrong time could result in injury or death. Chance or fate therefore played a much greater role in deciding whether people lived or died. The idea that a shell or bullet had a person's name or number on it, which in the First World War related mainly to soldiers in the trenches,[76] had meaning to a much wider group in the Second World War – not just to combatants but to non-combatants too. As a bus driver in London observed wryly to Phyllis Warner, 'Well, if the bomb hasn't got your number on it, it won't get you anyway'. Feeling scared, she repeated those words 'like a charm' she said, all the way home to comfort herself. She explained, 'in these days it's the Londoner's only possible philosophy'.[77] As the following popular prayer shows, turning to such supernatural props was another weapon in the armoury of support that people utilized during bombing:

God is our refuge
Don't be afraid
He will be with you
All through the raid

When bombs are falling
And danger is near
He will be with you
Till the all-clear[78]

Just as companionship, singing in the underground, cups of tea and the 'we can take it' spirit are aspects of the impact of bombing in Britain during the Second World War, so too is the recourse to and comfort derived from superstition, from belief in luck, chance, fate and the ability to foretell the future. These beliefs were important. They helped people cope during the dark and dangerous days when bombs rained down and the unpredictable nature of war caused anxiety and fear. As the examples in this chapter have shown, such beliefs provided comfort and succour and hope for the future and deserve a place in the history of the impact of bombing in Britain during the Second World War.

Notes

1   'Evening Prayer: The Third Collect for Aid against Perils', *Book of Common Prayer and Administration of the Sacraments and other Rites and Ceremonies of the Church: According to the Use of the United Church of England and Ireland: Together with the Psalter or Psalms of David* (Oxford: Samuel Collingwood & Co, 1836), 47.

2   R. Broad and S. Fleming (eds), *Nella Last's War: The Second World War Diaries of Housewife, 49* (London: Profile, 2006), 143.

3   Research for this article was undertaken during a one-year research fellowship at the University of Exeter as part of the AHRC-funded project on the impact of bombing on peoples and states during the Second World War in Britain, France, Germany and Italy 1940–45. I would like to acknowledge and thank the AHRC for providing the funding for this project. I would further like to thank the project leader, Professor Richard Overy, for providing guidance, help and support for this research. Thanks also to my fellow project team members.

4   The definition of 'supernatural' used throughout this article is based on the *Oxford English Dictionary* (1996) definition: 'forces above and outside the laws of nature and to synergize a variety of beliefs such as astrology, fortune-telling, so-called "lucky" charms/objects, prayer'.

5   For alternatives to the 'we can take it' view see for example A. Calder, *The Myth of the Blitz* (London: J. Cape, 1991); S. Hylton, *Their Darkest Hour: The Hidden History of the Home Front 1939–1945* (Stroud: Sutton, 2001); M. Connelly, *We Can Take it! Britain and the Memory of the Second World War* (Harlow: Longman, 2004).

6   C. FitzGibbon, *The Winter of the Bombs: The Story of the Blitz of London* (New York: Norton, 1958), 176.

7   M. Snape, *God and the British Soldier: Religion and the British Army in the First and Second World Wars* (Abingdon: Routledge, 2005), 243.

8   H. Jones, *British Civilians in the Front Line: Air Raids, Productivity and Wartime Culture, 1939–45* (Manchester: Manchester University Press, 2006), 166–7.

9   Imperial War Museum (IWM), 3208 95/14/1, P. Warner, 25 September 1940.

10 For examples, see *Nella Last's War*, 74, 98, 198.

11 J. Bourke, *Fear: A Cultural History* (London: Virago, 2006), 251.

12 U. Bloom, *War isn't Wonderful* (London: Hutchinson, 1961), 75.

13 The Mitchell Library, Glasgow, 'The Blitz on Clydeside: Clydebank & Kilman St., Maryhill 13 & 14 March 1941', Ref. B5 letters from Thomas Kearns to Patrick McDiamid, 28 March 1941.

14 Mass Observation Archive (MO-A), *Puzzled People: A Study in Popular Attitudes to Religions, Ethics, Progress and Politics in a London Borough* (London: Victor Gollancz, 1947), 56–9.

15   T. Harrisson, *Living Through the Blitz* (London: Collins, 1990), 307.
16   Jones, *British Civilians in the Front Line*, 166.
17   J. Bell, 'The Exeter Blitz', *Exeter Memories*, http://www.exetermemories.co.uk/EM/Story_12. html.
18   'Buried in the ruins of B.S.A.', 19 November 1940, quoted in M. F. Minton, *A Tribute to the Heroes of the Birmingham Air Raids 1940-1943* (Studley: Brewin, 2002), 119.
19   J. Wolffe, *God and Greater Britain: Religion and National Life in Britain and Ireland,1843-1945* (London: Routledge, 1994), 251.
20   There were nine National Days of Prayer during the War: 1 October 1939, 26 May 1940, 8 September 1940, 23 March 1941, 7 September 1941, 29 May 1942, 3 September 1942, 3 September 1943, and 3 September 1944.
21   *The Times*, 16 September 1939.
22   *The Times*, 27 May 1940.
23   Plymouth & West Devon Record Office (PWDRO), MS1416/1/6/119, Ref. 1476/2, Diary of H. J. Hurrell of Hooe and Turnchapel.
24   *The Times*, 27 May 1940.
25   *The Times*, 4 September 1942.
26   Wolffe, *God and Greater Britain*, 251.
27   Jones, *British Civilians in the Front Line*, 166.
28   See Harrisson, *Living Through the Blitz*, 307-8.
29   G. S. Spinks, *Religion in Britain since 1900*, (London: Andrew Dakers, 1952), 224.
30   Snape, *God and the British Soldier*, 4.
31   For recent debates on secularization in the twentieth century, see for example S. Williams, *Religious Belief and Popular Culture in Southwark c. 1880-1939* (Oxford: Oxford University Press, 1999); C. Brown, *The Death of Christian Britain* (London: Routledge, 2001).
32   Bloom, *War isn't Wonderful*, 173.
33   *Belfast Telegraph*, 8 April 1941, quoted in R. Davison, 'The German Air Raids on Belfast of April and May 1941 and their Consequences' (unpublished PhD thesis, Queens University of Belfast, 1979).
34   The *Western Independent*, Plymouth, 17 August 1941.
35   FitzGibbon, *The Winter of the Bombs*, 214.
36   Wolffe, *God and Greater Britain*, 254.
37   IWM, 3208 95/14/1, P. Warner, February 1942.
38   H. Mason, quoted in FitzGibbon, *The Winter of the Bombs*, 210-11.
39   A. E. Cook, *A Munition Worker's Visit to London after the Blitz of 1940-1941: His Impressions and Resolution and a Revelation* (London: Arthur H. Stockwell, 1943).
40   See G. Nelson, *Spiritualism and Society* (London: Routledge, 1969).
41   Ibid.,162.
42   J. Hazelgrove, *Spiritualism and British Society between the Wars* (Manchester: Manchester University Press, 2000), 270-3.
43   Ibid.
44   D. Cannadine, 'War and Death, Grief and Mourning in Modern Britain', in J. Waley (ed), *Mirrors of Mortality: Studies in the Social History of Death* (London: Europe, 1981), 234.
45   Ibid; G. Nelson, *Spiritualism and Society* (London: Routledge, 1969), 161.
46   *Song of Bernadette*, directed by Henry King, 1943; *A Guy Named Joe*, directed by Victor Fleming, 1943; *The Uninvited*, directed by Lewis Allen, 1944; *Between Two Worlds*, directed by Edward A. Blatt, 1944; *Halfway House*, directed by Basil Dearden, 1944; *Blithe Spirit*, directed by David Lean, 1945.
47   For example, in a website about the origin of babies' names, *Song of Bernadette* is credited to a surge in the use of the name 'Bernadette', especially among Catholic families, though this information is unconfirmed. See 'Think Baby Names' on www.thinkbabynames.com/keyword/0/popular/2.
48   *Daily Mail*, 24 March 1944.
49   MO-A, TC8, Astrology & Spiritualism 1938-47, Box1/A, June 1941, Mill Hill.

50 R. H. Naylor, *Predictions*, September 1940.
51 The National Archives, London (TNA), Home Office (HO) 199/454, Ministry of Home Security (Intelligence Branch): *The Effect of Journalistic Astrology on the Public Mind (Morale)*, Extract from Ministry of Information Home Intelligence Report No. 45, August 1941.
52 TNA, HO 199/454, Extract of the Minutes of a Meeting of the War Cabinet Civil Defence Committee, 7 January 1942.
53 Ibid., Extract of the Minutes of the War Cabinet Civil Defence Executive Sub-Committee, 19 January 1942.
54 G. W. Stonier, *Shaving Through the Blitz* (London: J. Cape, 1943), 41.
55 A. Calder, *The People's War: Britain 1939-45* (London: J. Cape, 1969), 480–1.
56 MO-A, TC8, Astrology & Spiritualism 1938-47, Box1/A, Bolton, 25 July 1940.
57 Bloom, *War isn't Wonderful*, 77.
58 MO-A, file Report 150, 'Air Raid Fear', 21 May 1940, 2.
59 Quoted in Bourke, *Fear*, 252.
60 See V. Chambers, 'A Shell with my Name on It: The Reliance on the Supernatural During the First World War', *Journal for the Academic Study of Magic*, 2, 2004, 79–102.
61 See Snape, *God and the British Soldier*, 32–3.
62 FitzGibbon, *The Winter of the Bombs*, 29.
63 See S. Roud, *The Penguin Guide to the Superstitions of Britain and Ireland* (London: Penguin, 2003), 75–6 for an explanation on the use of written words as protective charms.
64 PWDRO, Ref. 1961, Pocket book of W. Reed, Plymouth.
65 PWDRO Ref. 2173/1, J. S. Wellington Diary No. 2 from 1913–1957.
66 Definition of 'superstition', www.yourdictionary.com.
67 FitzGibbon, *The Winter of the Bombs*, 51.
68 IWM 1/23(33), A. E. Randall, *One Night of Hell! Extracts from Diary of A. F. S. Man, Night of Merseyside's Big Blitz*, May 3–4 1941, 3.
69 TNA, CAB/67/9/44, *Air Raids on London, September–November 1940. Memorandum by the Home Secretary and Minister of Home Security*, 5 May 1940.
70 IWM, 3208 95/14/1, P. Warner, 13 December 1940.
71 IWM 88/50/1, Mrs R. E. Uttin, 'Journal kept by a Wembley housewife mainly between January 1941–December 1945 but with a few later entries (1947–1956) and beginning with a retrospective account of her experiences during the first months of the London Blitz'.
72 MO-A, PR 975, 'Report on Superstition. Part B. Observing and Feelings About Superstition', 26 November 1941, 1.
73 Ibid.
74 Ibid., Kilburn, 29 July 1940.
75 R. Mackay, *Half the Battle: Civilian Morale in Britain during the Second World War* (Manchester: Manchester University Press, 2002).
76 Chambers, 'A shell with my Name on it'.
77 IWM, 3208 95/14/1, P. Warner, 26 October 1940.
78 A popular people's prayer, often discussed in memories of the Second World War. See for example J. Bell, *The Exeter Blitz*, http://www.exetermemories.co.uk/em/_story/story_12.php.

PART III

Society in the Bombing War

9

The Blitz Experience in British Society 1940–1941

Juliet Gardiner

In August 1941 the British Association of Architects, Surveyors and Technical Assistants published a sixpenny illustrated booklet with a rather odd title. It was called 'Why Wait for the Blitz?' which was puzzling because by August 1941 the waiting was definitively over – the Blitz had come and had indeed passed three months previously, though at the time no one knew that for sure, and there were indeed more and dreadful aerial horrors still to come.[1]

The puzzle did not end with the title for the content was an odd jumble of technical information and social exhortation. The technical information was primarily concerned with such things as the density of concrete best able to withstand bomb damage, the possibility of incorporating reinforcing 'skins' into the construction of windows to resist bomb blast, roof replacements that would, if not repel incendiary bombs, at least make it harder for them to lodge and smoulder dangerously, and hints about how 'first-aid' could be applied to bomb-damaged homes by cannibalizing materials from properties rendered uninhabitable by air raids.

The social exhortation consisted of a series of robust declarations that the people of Britain's war-besieged towns and cities were getting a raw deal, they were having to 'take it' in conditions that were unacceptable, as they had been throughout the previous decade: a combination of red tape and central government and regional and local authority parsimony was militating against the proper provision of services for victims of the Blitz. Under photographs of what looks like the notorious Tilbury shelter (which had still been functioning as a margarine warehouse), adjacent to Liverpool Street Station in the East End of London was the disclaimer:

> it is not our fault [that we have reproduced this photograph] of squalid conditions in public air-raid shelters. The files of the Ministry of Information were ransacked for more relevant and cheerful photographs – well-organized rest centres, first-aid posts, and canteens; crowds of grateful people receiving assistance and advice. The search was fruitless …[2]

The booklet, which had previously been printed as a series of articles in the *Architect's Review*, the more technical and least modernist of the profession's journals, concluded by promoting a scheme devised by a Mr O. N. Arup (whom we now know better as Ove Arup) for the building of reinforced-spine construction concrete housing in Clydeside for the working classes which would give them proper protection in wartime and a decent standard of housing in peacetime. This explains the title of the booklet, 'Why Wait for the Blitz?', with its implicit subtitle 'before giving the people of Britain a better deal'.

In so many ways this modest booklet epitomizes an important facet of the prism through which it is possible to try to assess the 'Blitz experience' and to try to gain an understanding of that experience in Britain: a powerful combination of indictment, stoical practical action and leverage for change. In sum, those eight intense months of bombing served as a mirror to British society, but also as a manifesto for the need to change that society in many ways – political, social, economic, cultural and scientific.

The experience of evacuation has been the subject of fruitful and exhaustive analysis; the Blitz itself much less so. This chapter seeks to explore different ways of viewing the experience of bombing. It is not intended here to offer a contribution to the 'myth of the Blitz' debate – in essence the notion that the British people were entirely united during the bombardment, that they 'took it' with equanimity and steadfast resolve, that class barriers came crashing down as debutante and dustman shared a common experience. The deconstruction of this facile picture has been dealt with effectively by Angus Calder,[3] and subsequently added to with scant profit,[4] and in any case forms only one strand in the debate that can be had about experience of the Blitz in Britain.

MORALE IN THE BLITZ

Of course, 'morale', which is the foundation of the 'myth', *is* one of the key components of any discussion about the Blitz, since morale was one of the targets pursued by the German Air Force along with military installations, ports and factories concerned with war production, the war economy and the administration of Britain. The resolve of the British people to carry on the fight – the fight from which Hitler had periodically offered a way out via a negotiated peace or surrender – was an aiming point of the incendiary and high explosive bombs and all the other lethal devices dropped from the air on Britain from 7 September 1940 until 10 May 1941.[5]

Morale was regarded as hard to define at the time. One of the founders of Mass Observation thought it was 'the woolliest concept of the war' and far too variable and complex for definition,[6] while a Barrow-in-Furness housewife, Nella Last, worried 'what *is* morale – and have I got any, or how much more could I call on in need, and where does it come from and what is it composed of?'[7] Stephen Taylor, a physician who had trained at the Maudsley hospital and was the Ministry of Information's Director of Home Intelligence felt professionally bound to try to define it, and pronounced that morale must be 'ultimately measured not by what a person thinks or says, but what he [and presumably she] does and how he does it.'[8] From the official perspective, low morale in wartime might include 'panic, hysteria, grumbling about those in authority, scapegoating, absenteeism', while 'high morale' was likely to encompass 'cheerfulness, cooperation, high productivity, volunteering'.[9]

This question of morale had been in the forefront of government minds throughout the so-called 'phoney war' from September 1939 until the invasion of the Low Countries and the fall of France in May–June 1940, since it was predicted to be so frail, particularly among the inner city poor, that the war might be lost for want of it. When the test of war did come for the civilian population in September 1940, it was invariably those people who were its first and most frequent victims.

As Robin Woolven, Edgar Jones and their colleagues have pointed out, morale was not just a response to air raids, but to a range of other factors such as the availability of food, the cost of living and other extraordinary conditions of wartime such as the blackout, and of course the progress of the war itself.[10] But the Blitz – continual and concentrated bombing raids – gave an intensity of focus to these concerns, since this was the war that everyone had been expecting; and though there were privations and regulations to be grumbled about, the Blitz was real warfare: it brought the danger, death and destruction of the battlefield to the home front. The Blitz made sense of a state of war that the long drawn out phoney war had begun to question. The logic of evacuation, of the blackout, of ARP duties, which had come to seem increasingly tiresome, even unnecessary, was now clear and accepted. The test of total war was a test not just of individuals, but also of the government, of the provisions that were in place for the defence of Britain and its citizens. Throughout the Blitz, morale would be inextricably linked to notions of protection, defence and organization – as well as that of repelling of the enemy. On the one hand the bombing conjured into being the model of the innate gumption of the British people (the preternaturally cheery Cockney in particular); the official rhetoric was of 'taking it', of 'keeping calm and carrying on'. Yet reports showed that when morale did break down the causes were invariably the failure of the authorities to deal effectively with the consequences of the bombardment. This perception fed into the freight of the 1930s carried by a great many, who recalled that the government had manifestly not been able to protect at least three million of its people from the vicissitudes of the slump and unemployment, and had shown an apparently uncaring face to their plight. This explains the visceral character of publications such as 'Why Wait for the Blitz?'

Despite the ill-thought-out attempts of the Ministry of Information in the early days of the war to raise morale,[11] the government took the question very seriously, recognizing that the war could be as well lost on the home front as the battleground if civilians fell into such a state of panic, lassitude or anarchy that war production would be brought to a standstill and troops required to subdue or contain the population rather than fight the enemy. The ARP services were briefed in June 1937 that their primary aim was not the protection of individuals or property from destruction, but 'the maintenance of the morale' of the people, while plans were made for some 17,000 regular troops and 20,000 reserve constables to be drafted into London to stop a mass exodus and uncontrollable panic as Londoners tried to get away.[12]

Various organizations monitored morale: from August 1940 regular weekly reports were prepared by the intelligence branch of the Ministry of Home Security, based mainly on reports from a variety of local sources including the police and civil defence officials. But these were entirely unscientific and vague, the subjective reports of individuals who had something of a vested interest in suggesting that morale was holding steady, and that their particular organization was coping effectively with the challenges that the Blitz brought. The regular reports of the Ministry of Information, mainly staffed by a cacophony of journalists, broadcasters, poets, academics and lawyers, rather than career civil servants, were more apt to report incidents of panic, and that other pervasive result of the Blitz, exhaustion, which could make people 'nervy' in the language of the time. It was left to Mass Observation, an organization set up by an ornithologist turned anthropologist, a journalist and a poet in 1937, to take the pulse of the British people, to first use such words as hysteria, dislocation, panic, depression, crying, screaming, fainting, in reports on Coventry after the raids there on the night of 14–15 November 1940.[13]

Yet if the Ministry of Home Security – a wartime extension of the Home Office, both under the same minister (from October 1940 Herbert Morrison, former leader of the LCC and Labour MP for Hackney) – had a vested interest in producing reports of steadfast morale, MO was accused of the opposite. The Ministry of Home Security, suspecting MO of being politically unreliable, had initially been reluctant to use the organization to report on morale. Since the journalists Ritchie Calder in the Daily Herald (and the New Statesman) and Hilde Marchant in the Daily Express repeatedly used evidence of low morale as an indictment of government and local authorities, the government feared that the presumed left-wing bias of the self-selecting and almost solidly middle-class people who volunteered as observers would do the same. Moreover, it was assumed that MO had a vested interest in turning in reports that suggested that the population of blitzed towns and cities was in danger of serious disaffection, since such intelligence would keep MO in work, as a necessary monitor of volatile morale. It was even feared that such reports might contribute to lowering morale, despite the fact that they were not released to press or public.

Taking the Ministry of Information's own indices, what could be taken as evidence of low morale? And if it clearly was not always a serious or prolonged feature of a post-raid situation, what were the factors that produced it? Mass Observation drew some clear conclusions in the case of the raid on Coventry: the attack had been extremely intense and bombs had been concentrated on the city centre, so evidence of the raid was clear for all to see. Coventry was a relatively small city of some 238,000 people, of whom 569 were estimated to have been killed in the November raid and over 1,200 badly injured, so everyone was likely to have known at least one person who had been killed, injured, missing or rendered homeless by the raids. In contrast, in London, given its size, even at the height of the Blitz in September–October, on 29 December 1940 and during April–May 1941, there were many areas that would be largely unaffected by a particular raid. Although Coventry had experienced raids prior to November, this one, code-named 'Moonlight Sonata', had not been expected. Utility services and communications had been seriously disrupted so the people of Coventry felt unable to resume their normal life and felt cut off from the rest of the country.[14] It was precisely the unexpected and concentrated nature of the raids and the feeling that proper provision had not been made that later affected Clydeside in March 1941 when it was subjected to intense and destructive bombardment.

The morning after a bombing raid on Coventry, 1940. (Photo by Fox Photos/Getty Images).

COPING WITH BOMBING

It was not only the number of bombs that fell and the death and damage sustained that affected morale: it was also the impact on people's lives in the immediate aftermath. Two eminent scientists, the physicist J. D. Bernal and the zoologist Solly Zuckerman, were sent by the Ministry of Home Security to two other blitzed cities, Birmingham and Hull, to report on post-raid morale and its effect on productivity. They found that while morale was relatively high in Birmingham, in Hull the people were 'torpid and apathetic'.[15] They decided the difference was largely situational and historic. Birmingham was a prosperous city of small industries which meant it was easier for production to resume, and regular employment and good wages meant that workers were more inclined to remain in post, whereas Hull had suffered high rates of unemployment in the 1930s. The heavy raids, repeated over several nights in the spring of 1941, seemed like a further body blow to a city whose *raison d'être* had been eroded over a decade.[16]

Part of the problem of the government's tests of low morale was that the symptoms could equally be regarded as evidence of entirely rational behaviour. Like the treatment of stroke victims, the first 36 hours after a raid were regarded as crucial. If during that time Blitz victims found that facilities for feeding, clothing and accommodating them were grossly inadequate and that rest centres, which had been envisaged as places of short term respite, were, in the absence of any other place to go, having to cater for 'bombees' for days rather than hours, and that the only food available for 48 hours or more was tea and bread and margarine, and that there was confusion and endless bureaucracy about finding somewhere to stay, having homes patched up, even a change of clothes, it was hardly surprising that people became depressed and disempowered. Indeed they *were* disempowered, as Tom Harrisson, one of the founders of MO, revealed in his salutary description of the bureaucratic blind alleys faced by a young mother whose sailor husband was away at sea, who had lost one of her three children in an air raid and whose home and small shop had been rendered uninhabitable.[17]

Local authorities had over-calculated and over-prepared for deaths and serious injuries, laying in thousands of papier-mâché coffins and requisitioning swimming pools as temporary mortuaries, and clearing hospital wards in anticipation of hundreds of casualties. Meanwhile, they had grossly underestimated the damage to houses and utilities and, in general, had made inadequate arrangements for the supply of building materials, for sorting out communal feeding arrangements and requisitioning houses in which to billet the homeless. Even so the scale of the dead after an intense raid such as the one on Coventry, or those on Merseyside, or Clydeside, could confound the local authority which found that it neither had the manpower to dig the hundreds of graves required, nor coffins for those victims whose bodies were not claimed by relatives. In Bradford, for example, any corpse not claimed after 48 hours was buried in a hessian shroud, and in Hull, where 920 bodies needed to be buried between March and September 1941, shrouds, rather than individual coffins, were used for some 200 victims buried in a mass grave. Frequently there were few actual bodies to be buried, but only unidentifiable fragments of corpses, and in response to this local authorities organized mass burials in communal graves (for which a government grant could be obtained). However practical this was, it was reported to have had a deleterious effect on local morale since mass burial carried the stigma of workhouse 'pauper' burials. Both the Home Office and the Ministry of Health tried to assuage this sensitivity by using military rhetoric for such funerals, since 'we are all soldiers now', and encouraging the use of the Union Jack as a pall on the coffins that were available.[18]

Similarly, going underground can be seen as an entirely rational if visceral response to aerial attack, although there were two terrible tube disasters during the Blitz: one at Balham station on 14 October 1940 in which 64 people were killed; the other at Bank on 11 January 1941 when the death toll was 112. The government had initially refused to allow the underground system to be used for shelter during raids, though this is what had happened during the Zeppelin attacks in the First World War. This was partly because of the necessity of keeping the trains moving to transport supplies and troops, and remove the dead and wounded. It was also because it was feared that tube shelterers would adopt a troglodyte mentality, refusing to re-emerge once the raids were over and that this would seriously affect productivity. The lessons of Barcelona during the Spanish Civil War had suggested that the way to keep the civilian population as safe as possible was to build deep shelters to accommodate the entire population of towns and cities considered vulnerable to attack. The scientist J. B. S. Haldane campaigned tirelessly for such provision, dismissing government insistence that the best policy was dispersal in a raid.[19] However, it was not just governmental short-sightedness that accounted for this reluctance: economic implications also played an important part. It would have been necessary to build many miles of underground tunnels to shelter the whole population of London, Liverpool or Glasgow and the other menaced cities, and there was neither the time, nor the resources, nor the necessary manpower to embark on such an elaborate and comprehensive programme.[20]

The efficient output of war material was a paramount government concern since there was no point in conscripting a large fighting force if it could not be sufficiently equipped with planes, battleships, tanks and weapons. The war could be lost on the home front as well as on the battleground. It was essential to keep factories at full production. Thus the fear of absenteeism was a very real one during the Blitz. After the experience of an intense air raid, it was feared that workers and their families would simply flee from the cities into the countryside and refuse to return to work, and that war production would grind to a halt. Indeed, there were mass exoduses from bombed urban areas. Yet despite slurs about 'the Funk Express' and 'yellow buses' carrying civilians out of cities such as London, Clydebank, Liverpool, Hull, Belfast and Plymouth, trekking away from danger by whatever form of transport could be found or on foot, when it had been proved that protection in the cities was inadequate, was a rational response. Families might trek out into the countryside as night fell, but frequently a large proportion of men would return daily to their places of work, as happened for example at John Brown's shipyard on Clydebank after the devastating raids there.[21]

THE PSYCHOLOGY OF BOMBING

Panic and clinical neurosis had been identified before the war as possible key indicators of low morale. It had been anticipated that these would rise dramatically in the event of air raids, and on the advice of a neurologist and a psychiatrist, both of whom had clinical experience with troops in the First World War, hospitals known as 'Neurosis Centres' were opened on the outskirts of those major cities expected to be targets for the German Air Force. However, these facilities were found not to be needed: it was discovered that most trauma-tized victims recovered with only minimal medical intervention, and eventually the centres were largely turned over to military use.[22] Nevertheless, a note of caution needs to be entered here: it is very hard both to qualify and to quantify incidences of mental suffering, such as depression and persistent anxiety, which were present in numerous different forms that were not always recognized or treated sympathetically by the medical profession at the time. No adequate data exist on those admitted to hospital or seeking help from their doctor during this period, and even if the numbers could be logged, it would be no easy task to deconstruct the true reason for a patient's presentation, or the persistence of their symptoms, nor to assess whether, before the existence of the National Health Service, some who would have liked to seek help were inhibited from doing so for reasons of cost.

What does exist is evidence of wartime trauma in the work of various psychoanalysts including that of Anna Freud and Dorothy Burlingham, who worked with children who had been involved in air raids and in some cases had been bereaved by war. The effect of these experiences could lead to tragic cases of compulsive neurosis.[23] Psychoanalysts such as Edward Glover and Melitta Schmideberg argued that psychological effects could be a slow-burning fuse, not instantly apparent,[24] though in general the conclusion was that those who were mentally stable before their traumatic experiences, recovered their equilibrium relatively quickly, while those who suffered anxiety neurosis as a result of the Blitz had invariably exhibited such symptoms previously in some form or other.[25]

The other issue that attracted the interest of psychology was fear. An unnamed psychologist writing in *Picture Post* on 5 October 1940 drew a distinction between what they called reasonable fear – being afraid because there was something to be afraid of – and 'chronic fear' when 'something is interfering with the normal process by which one is accustomed to danger'. The doctor's recommendation for this condition was based on the commonsense prescription that sufferers should find a way to fight back against fear. It was suggested that they could volunteer for ARP service, or join the WVS, or dig for victory, all activities which it was claimed would 'drain tension away'.[26] This was an individual version of the relief Londoners felt when, on the third night of the Blitz, anti-aircraft guns could be heard for the first time, even though the anti-aircraft artillery commanders recognized full well that this was essentially an exercise in reassurance rather than warfare: the likelihood of the guns scoring a hit on a German plane was minimal, while the danger of damage from falling shrapnel was considerable.[27] Nevertheless, it was the feeling of helplessness and passivity which proved so destructive of psychological stability – the gesture of fighting back was essential for civilian morale and resolve.

RESPONSES TO THE BLITZ

The role of the press was a complicated one during the Blitz: for supposed reasons of security blitzed targets were not usually named for several weeks (Coventry was one exception), and when they were it was with a lack of precision. Streets and individual buildings were not identified, nor addresses allowed in obituary notices, and those for people who had lived in a particular street might be spread out over several weeks so that it would be impossible to know which town had been a target by scanning the obituary columns. But, as is now fully recognized, there is little more disempowering than lack of information: people outside London in particular resented the fact that their suffering did not seem to be recognized. Hull presented an acute version of this feeling of non-recognition, invariably referred to as 'a north-east town', or a 'northern coastal town', which the residents felt belittled their place in the grim taxonomy of death and destruction. One result of the absence of reliable information was a great inflation of the numbers of dead and injured reported by word of mouth. It also gave rise to other rumours, among which was a particularly persistent and pernicious one which suggested that civil defence workers were being ordered to concrete over air-raid sites before all the bodies had been recovered, in order to save on resources and to prevent the lowering of morale which a lengthy excavation process was supposed to have had.

According to various Mass Observation reports, provided that a victim had not been injured, nor had family or close friends killed, nor their home destroyed, the most morale-lowering effect was the serious disruption of services. Crowd disturbances were noted when shops failed to open. Almost 12,000 gas mains were fractured during the attacks on London, and all London's gasworks were damaged to some degree or other. After the raids of 10–11 May 1941, more than 200,000 customers were without gas for more than a week as a result (and gas was more widely used than now for cooking and heating and even light), and a total of 959 roads were closed due to craters, debris, dangerous buildings or unexploded bombs.

Wartime letters and diaries reveal that exhaustion was another entirely predictable cause of low morale during the Blitz, which involved nights on end without proper sleep. This might have been a gift to advertisers who were able to put this down to insufficiently deep sleep, and recommend the purchase of Horlicks or Ovaltine as a bedtime drink, but not to citizens who were still expected to turn up for work after a few hours of snatched and fitful sleep.

There are other sieves through which the Blitz experience in Britain must be filtered: one is the reconfiguring of the role of local authorities in relation to central and regional government when it became obvious in the first days of the Blitz that some were simply unable to cope with the magnitude of the devastation. The responsibility for war preparations had been devolved to local authorities without the necessary devolution of money to make this realistic, and it was clear that several were simply overwhelmed, either because their preparations had been inadequate and/or because they were experiencing a level of attrition that was beyond the aggregate of particular local resources and local capabilities. Stepney in East London was just such an example where the borough ARP controller, despite the support of the local council, was replaced by the Town Clerk of the nearby borough of Islington as a result of allegations of gross incompetence levelled by the Regional Commissioner and the Minister of Home Security.[28] This kind of tension raised pertinent questions about what the relations between central and local government would be when peace came, but these were issues that were never fully resolved, since it became less contentious to talk of 'wartime expediencies', and let the matter lapse.[29]

Another approach is to suggest that the Blitz experience complicated rather than simplified notions of the bonding of communities under threat, particularly with stories of crimes committed in the confusion of air raids. This is exemplified by the experience of ARP area wardens like the Reverend Markham whose parish was in Walworth, a poor area of south-east London, who soon realized that important though it was to get the emergency services to bomb incidents, it was almost equally important to get any damaged property secured against looters as rapidly as possible.[30] The Blitz also witnessed an increase in anti-Semitism – or at least the open expression of anti Semitism – in the East End of London during the time that raids were heavy and nightly recourse to public shelters was usual. This was not a new phenomenon, nor one confined to the East Enders – from Harold Nicolson to George Orwell, references to the Jews as avaricious, cowardly or self-interested were frequent. The tensions were given an added intensity by the Blitz – so much so that the Board of Jewish Deputies felt it incumbent to commission a non-Jew to investigate the allegations.[31]

'The background to this war, corresponding to the Western Front in the last war, is the bombed city', wrote the poet Stephen Spender, and the full impact of the unique nature of the Blitz, its sheer irrational surrealism, was forcefully represented both in art and literature.[32] It should not be forgotten that for all Tom Harrisson's robust common sense, there was a strong surrealist streak running through the intentions of MO in the early days, particularly those of Charles Madge, and indeed the poet David Gascoyne, who was closely involved from the start, and who saw the Crystal Palace fire in 1936 as but the start of an engulfing conflagration of which the Blitz was the climax. This slightly sinister, anxious, macabre quality is hauntingly captured in the writings of Elizabeth Bowen, in particular, her short story 'The Demon Lover', or in her novel *The*

Heat of the Day. It is present in Graham Greene's *Ministry of Fear* or *The End of the Affair* (which was later filmed with exactly that other-world camera shots of the floating detritus of war and relationships), in Henry Green's bitter novel *Caught*, in Rose Macaulay's *The World My Wilderness.*[33]

In art it pervades the unsettling images of the surrealist photographer Lee Miller;[34] or the 'instant ruins' that the artist John Piper discovered in the Blitz (though he once had to take shelter in a Coventry solicitor's office, fearing the local people would be incensed that he was painting detritus, rather than trying to help deal with it). His paintings, it has been argued, 'became for Britain what Picasso's *Guernica* had been for Spain ... a symbol of national resistance to Hitler.'[35] It pervades Henry Moore' drawings of armies of silent ghost-like forms, the sculptor's representations of people sheltering in the underground;[36] it is even present in the stage set photographs of Cecil Beaton of a strange depopulated, deracinated metropolis in which he described 'desolation full of vitality' in the strange Piranesi forms of the blitzed buildings.[37]

CONCLUSION

But to square the circle: there was a persistent feeling, which surfaces in Home Intelligence reports, Mass Observation surveys and the letters and diaries of individuals, that the Blitz was at one and the same time a terminus and an opportunity: it was a terrible, cleansing, purifying experience that was cathartic in some ways in its destructiveness – a kind of revenge on the previous decade that had to become an atonement. As the *Blitzkrieg* – the lightning war across Norway, the Low Countries and France – had in effect swept away Chamberlain and the 'gang of old muttons', who had treated and connived, so the Blitz had gone some way to sweep away the industrial shame and social inequality that was Britain in the 1930s. Bombs fell more heavily on working-class areas, as these tended to be clustered round docks and factories, prime targets for the bombers, and such areas sustained more damage as the dwellings were more shoddily built of cheaper materials than those in more prosperous areas. An informal slum clearance programme was achieved by the bombing, far in excess of the cautious legislation of the 1930s. It was almost a realization of John Betjeman's cruel 1937 poem 'Come, friendly bombs, and fall on Slough/It isn't fit for humans now',[38] as the chief planning officer for Coventry rejoiced at the tabula rasa that his city had become as a result of the raids, offering an opportunity for full scale replanning on a scale that would never have been able to be so radical and comprehensive given normal peacetime conditions.[39]

Underlying this was the aspect much stressed by Richard M. Titmuss in his volume in the official history of the Second World War series, of an informal social contract forged in extreme circumstances. A people who had largely proved that they could 'take it' could expect fortitude and sacrifice to be rewarded, Titmuss hoped, by a more equitable treatment from the nation they were defending;[40] that one meaning of the transitive verb 'to blitz' meaning 'to destroy by aerial bombardment' would be replaced by a more modern one, 'to deal with something energetically; to concentrate a lot of effort on something to get it done.'

Notes

1   *Why Wait for the Blitz?* (Ninth Annual Report of the Association of Architects, Surveyors and Technical Assistants), August 1941.
2   *Why Wait for the Blitz?* (unnumbered pages).
3   A. Calder, *The Myth of the Blitz* (London: Jonathan Cape, 1991).
4   For example C. Ponting, *1940: Myth and Reality* (London: Hamish Hamilton, 1990) and S. Hylton, *The Darkest Hour: The Hidden History of the Home Front, 1939–1945* (Stroud: Sutton Publishing, 2001).
5   Morale was not only under attack during the Blitz. The 'Battle of the Atlantic', aimed at starving the island nation of supplies (including food), was intended to have the effect of lowering the resolve of the British to resist, as were subsequent aerial attack from 'tip n' run' raids, the so-called Baedeker raids in 1942, the 'little blitz' in 1943–4 and finally the V1 and V2 attacks of 1944–5.
6   T. Harrisson, quoted in P. Addison, *The Road to 1945: British Politics and the Second World War* (London: Jonathan Cape, 1994), 121.
7   R. Fleming and S. Broad (eds), *Nella Last: A Mother's Diary, 1939–45* (London: Profile Books, 2008), 135.
8   Quoted in I. McLaine, *Ministry of Morale: Home Front Morale and the Ministry of Information in World War II* (London: Allen & Unwin, 1979), 9.
9   R. MacKay, *Half the Battle: Civilian Morale in Britain during the Second World War* (Manchester: Manchester University Press, 2002), 3.
10 E. Jones, R. Woolven, W. Durodié and S. Wessely, 'Civilian Morale During the Second World War: Responses to Air Raids Re-examined' *Social History of Medicine*, 17, 2004, 464.
11 Campaigns included the deeply resented poster 'Your Courage, Your Cheerfulness, Your Resolution, Will Bring Us Victory', and much derided characters such as 'Miss Leaky Mouth', 'Mr Glum Pot', 'Miss Teacup Whisperer' etc. to warn against 'the dangers of rumour'.
12 T. H. O'Brien, *Civil Defence* (London: HMSO, 1955), 71–3.
13 University of Sussex, Mass Observation Archive (MO-A) File Report 495 'Coventry: the effects of the bombing'.
14 On the Coventry raids see N. Longmate, *Air Raid. The Bombing of Coventry, 1940* (London: Hutchinson, 1976); T. Lewis, *Moonlight Sonata* (Coventry: Coventry City Council, 1990); D. McGrory, *Coventry at War* (Stroud: The History Press, 2007).
15 S. Zuckerman, *From Apes to Warlords, 1904–46. An Autobiography* (London: Hamish Hamilton, 1978) 140-8.
16 MO-A, File Report 640 Hull: effects of air raids.
17 Quoted in McLaine, *Ministry of Morale*, 131–3.
18 J. Rugg, 'Managing "Civilian Deaths due to War Operations": Yorkshire Experiences During World War II', *Twentieth Century British History*, 15, 2004, 152–73.
19 J. B. S. Haldane, *A.R.P.* (London: Victor Gollancz, 1938); R. Clark, *J. B. S. The Life and Work of J. B. S. Haldane* (London: Hodder & Stoughton, 1968), 119–29.
20 Deep shelters were finally sanctioned by Herbert Morrison in a broadcast on 3 November 1940. See B. Donoghue and G. W. Jones, *Herbert Morrison: Portrait of a Politician* (London: Weidenfeld & Nicolson, 1973), 289. However, the first, at Stockwell in south London, was not open to the public until 9 July 1944. See J. Gregg, *The Shelter of the Tube: Tube Sheltering in Wartime London* (London: Capital Transport, 2001), 89.

21   I. M. M. Macphail, *The Clydebank Blitz* (West Dumbartonshire Libraries and Museums, 1974), 63–4.

22   Jones, Woolven et al., 'Civilian Morale', 474–6.

23   *The Writings of Anna Freud*, vol. III, *Infants Without Families: Reports on the Hampstead Nurseries, 1939–1945*, in collaboration with D. Burlingham (Madison, CT: International Universities Press,1973).

24   E. Glover, 'Notes on the Psychological Effects of War Conditions on the Civilian Population. III. The 'Blitz' – 1940–41', *The International Journal of Psycho-Analysis*, 23, 1942; M. Schmideberg. 'Some Observations on Individual Reactions to Air Raids' *The International Journal of Pyscho-Analysis*, 23, 1942.

25   C. Berg, *War in the Mind. The Case Book of a Medical Psychologist* (London: The Macaulay Press, 1941).

26   *Picture Post*, 5 October 1940, 27.

27   F. Pile, *Ack-Ack. Britain's Defence Against Air Attack during the Second World War* (London: George Harrap, 1949), 131–4.

28   R. Calder, *The Lesson of London* (London: Secker & Warburg, 1941), 61, 124–8; E. D. Idle, *War Over West Ham. A Study of Community Adjustment* (London: Faber & Faber, 1943), 61–3; G. Alderman, 'M. H. Davis: the Rise and Fall of a Communal Upstart', *Jewish Historical Studies* 31, 1990, 249-68.

29   W. A. Robson, 'Reform Our Local Government', *Picture Post*, 15 February 1941, 24–6; 'The Regional Commissioners', *Political Quarterly*, 12, 1941, 144–53.

30   IWM Department of Documents, 912/5/1, the papers of the Reverend J. G. Markham, 30.

31   A. Julius, *Trials of the Diaspora. A History of Anti-Semitism in England* (Oxford: Oxford University Press, 2010), 324.

32   Cited in B. Foss, *War Paint: Art, State and Identity in Britain 1939-1945* (New Haven: Yale University Press, 2007), 33.

33   A. Wilson (ed.), *The Collected Stories of Elizabeth Bowen* (London: Penguin, 1983); E. Bowen, *The Heat of the Day* (London: Penguin, 1962); G. Greene, *The Ministry of Fear: an Entertainment* (London: Penguin, 1973); idem, *The End of the Affair* (London: Penguin, 1975); H. Green, *Caught* (London: Hogarth Press, 1943); R. Macaulay, *The World My Wilderness* (London: Virago, 2000).

34   E. Carter (ed.), *Grim Glory: Photographs by Lee Miller and Others* (London: Lund Humphries, 1941); M. Haworth-Booth, *The Art of Lee Miller* (London: V&A Publications, 2007).

35   M. Harries, S. Harries, *The War Artists* (London: Michael Joseph, 1983), 180–94; A. Ross, *Colours of War* (London: Jonathan Cape, 1983), 36–52; D. F. Jenkins, *John Piper: The Forties* (London: Philip Wilson Publishers/Imperial War Museum, 2000).

36   J. Andrews, *London's War: The Shelter Drawings of Henry Moore* (London: Lund Humphries, 2002).

37   C. Beaton, *The Years Between. Diaries, 1939-44* (London: Weidenfeld & Nicolson, 1965), 587–9; idem, *History Under Fire. 52 Photographs of Air Raid Damage to London Buildings, 1940-41*, with a commentary by J. Pope-Hennessy (London: B.T. Batsford, 1941).

38   *John Betjeman's Collected Poems* (London: John Murray, 1958), 22.

39   N. Tiratsoo, 'The Reconstruction of Blitzed British Cities, 1945–55: Myths and Reality', *Contemporary British History*, 14, 2000, 27–44; J. Hasewega, 'The Rise and Fall of Radical Reconstruction in 1940's Britain', *Twentieth Century British History* 10, 1999, 137–61.

40   R. M. Titmuss, *Problems of Social Policy* (London: HMSO, 1950), passim.

10

The Allied Air War and German Society*

Stephan Glienke

The Second World War saw the realization of Giulio Douhet's vision, expressed in the early 1920s, of what the aeroplane might be capable of achieving in war. In the words of one of the first historians of the bombing war, Hans Rumpf, the Second World War witnessed 'a form of strategic air warfare which, through the provision of heavy bomber fleets directed like a great machine against indiscriminate enemy targets, strove to achieve the complete physical destruction of the enemy's population and material life.'[1] The traditional historiography also accepts the image of modern war as decisively defined by air warfare against an industrial society, above all by looking at the destruction of armaments capacity, human and material resources, industry and the built environment. The German master narrative of the air war, in particular, is dominated by the violent experience of the bombing of the centres of German urban life and industry. German historical research supplies us with an almost unmanageable number of micro-studies of individual cities during the air war,[2] often of single raids.[3] This might well lead the unwary reader astray into seeing the air war from the perspective of the bombed locality, viewed as a sequence of individual events, affecting a single location. The fate of people in the air war is presented in such accounts in a narrow temporal and spatial framework. They fail to illuminate the time before and after the raids. In particular, the indirect effect of air attacks on the population and areas not directly hit remains obscure, and the fate of small towns and villages is all too often neglected within a culture of memory and memorialization which, though lively enough, is none the less locally focused. Yet recent research on the evacuation of civilians from cities threatened by air attack has shown that the effects of the air war reached out well beyond the main targets into the hinterland and the rural areas.[4] These too require the historian's attention in order to obtain a proper impression of the consequences of the air war for the whole of society.

THE QUESTION OF 'EFFECT' IN THE AIR WAR

What impact did the Allied air war have on the German population, and how many Germans were affected by it? There are two contrasting approaches to this question. For Olaf Groehler, the proportion of the population affected by

*Translation from German by Richard Overy.

wartime bombing is taken as a constant: the air war as such touched only a defined segment of the German people.[5] Peter Heinl, on the other hand offers a psychological perspective, arguing that the air war in one way or another fundamentally affected the whole German population.[6] Groehler, of course, also admits that there were extensive effects beyond the target areas but his focus nevertheless clearly lies on the direct area of attack and the *direct consequences* of the raid. He neglects the *indirect effects* of attacks on the unbombed region around the target zone and the far-reaching impact on German society of bombing. Heinl, however, rightly recognizes the *far-reaching effects* of wartime events on society, though his explanation remains rather vague. The claim that all Germans were affected in one way or another by the air war points in the right direction, but is still too undifferentiated. For a closer investigation of this subject of research it first appears necessary to define the forms of 'effect' in relation to the direct and indirect complex of events. If we define 'effect' as the form and way in which people's daily lives and affairs are influenced and defined by the Allied conduct of the air war, this already implies different degrees of effect. It will be explained in what follows that events from the air war at the local level spread out not only into neighbouring areas but also into the more distant regions of the Reich.

DIRECT IMPACT – IMMEDIATE EFFECT

Although direct results of attack were most clearly visible in the stricken cities, they also spread out into the surrounding area. Moreover, the effect of the attacks in the targeted cities was not limited to the moment of a certain operation, but extended far beyond it in time.

In total, 41,400 tons of high explosive and incendiary bombs were dropped on Germany in 1942; this grew to 206,000 tons in 1943 and finally increased to 1,202,000 tons in the year 1944. In the first four months of 1945, which brought the total destruction of the city centres of Nuremberg, Würzburg and Dresden, a further 471,000 tons were dropped.[7] In all the major cities of Germany, this increase in the number and severity of raids from 1942 onwards entailed the massive destruction not only of industrial installations but also of residential quarters. In Hamburg alone, 253,000 dwellings out of a total of 450,800 were destroyed, amounting to 56 per cent of the total housing stock.[8] The city of Kassel had 225,694 inhabitants and approximately 65,000 dwellings before the major attack of October 1943, in which around 10,000 people were killed. When the Americans entered Kassel there were only around 40,000 inhabitants and 19,000 dwellings.[9] More than a quarter of all houses in Germany were damaged, around 14 million people lost a part of their possessions through bombing, and between 17 and 20 million were without electricity, gas or water at some point or other because of the bombing. Almost nine million were compelled to evacuate through air raids.[10] The suggested figures for deaths in the air war vary between 305,000[11] and 410,000.[12] Ian Kershaw estimates that approximately one-third of the population suffered from the *direct effects* of the bombing war.[13]

The heavy attacks presented the municipal authorities with almost insoluble tasks. A single raid on the night of 8/9 October 1943 faced the city authority in Hanover with the problem of finding shelter for 250,000 people whose homes had been destroyed. Berlin already had 400,000 homeless by October 1943; a few months later, in March 1944, this had reached 1.5 million.[14]

All these people had to be looked after. They needed clothing, accommodation and above all food. Action squads from the fire services were called out to fight the numerous fires and to cool down the ruins with water to prevent the fires from rekindling.[15] Special units cleared the streets, medical emergency care had to be set up,[16] public field kitchens and emergency accommodation arranged, ruined plots cleared of rubble, stones and debris and bomb craters filled in. Units of the armed forces cleared the area and rescued those who were buried. These and many other tasks for local officials all had to be co-ordinated by the municipal authority. Rescue squads made only slow progress because of fires and destroyed or blocked streets. Numerous unexploded bombs or bombs with delayed-action fuses made the activity of the helpers especially dangerous.[17] Gas or water supplies were often hit, making the work even more difficult and risky. The prevailing shortage of fuel and damage to roads slowed down the job of clearing the area. The transport of furniture rescued from the ruins was delayed; so was the arrival of help from other towns. In Bremen in January 1943 the State Office remarked:

> The exceptional shortage of fuel and the as yet insufficient conversion of vehicles to generator gas has led to this, that the transfer of rubble from the bomb-damaged areas cannot be undertaken in order to restore the industrial zones which Bremen so desperately needs.[18]

In Frankfurt am Main in October of the same year, there were not enough lorries or workers available to transfer the regional offices of the city administration into emergency accommodation.[19] In Kassel and Krefeld the problem was met by demanding the assistance of forced labour and military workers.[20] To guard stored furniture and emergency supplies it was necessary to appoint personnel to oversee the security of the goods and their distribution to those who needed assistance. Further delays were caused by the search for suitable storerooms. Additional costs arose for the city administration in the targeted cities because of both these problems.[21]

In Bremen in January 1943 alone, 2,104 men were put to work clearing the streets and ruined plots, while throughout the city 8,200 workers were occupied in rescue work and the reconstruction of 1,703 buildings.[22] Despite this there was frequently not enough labour available for the renovation of damaged streets and buildings. As a result the authorities often fell back on convicts or the occupants of concentration camps, and here too personnel had to be found to guard them.[23]

After a raid, damaged machinery had to be repaired or replaced and industrial sites cleared of ruined buildings. Many firms were compelled as early as 1940 and 1941 to introduce ten- or twelve-hour shifts and weekend working. Besides the damage to production facilities and the finance and time spent on putting machine tools back in order,[24] war production was also indirectly affected by the attacks when workers lost their homes or relatives. If their homes were destroyed, they and their families had to be found new accommodation by the city administration along with numerous applications submitted for clothing, furniture and foodstuffs. If their homes were only damaged, they had to apply for building materials to repair them. Not uncommonly the local administration itself suffered destruction and dispersal. For example, in October 1943, after considerable damage from air attacks, the buildings of the city administration of Frankfurt am Main were usable either to only a limited extent or in many cases not at all. The administration was transferred to the outskirts.[25]

After a raid, people needed the local administration more than ever, but if it had been moved, they found it hard to know where to go, and at what time. With public transport running a reduced service at best, thanks to damaged streets, wrecked trams or platforms,[26] or failure of the electricity supply, the bombed-out often needed hours to reach a particular authority. The NSDAP Ortsgruppe in Bremen Sebaldsbrück reported the complaint of a man who had had to wait three and a half hours for a coal allocation certificate. One bomb victim complained in January 1944: 'If I want to have a house, people say to me, if you have no furniture, then we cannot supply you with a place to live in, then I go off and concern myself with furniture, which I am supposed to have first if I want to get somewhere to live.'[27] A similar problem was reported by the Ortsgruppe in Bremer 'Wasserturm':

> A bomb victim has to organize formalities with the local office, the city office etc., but is not in a position to manage all that in a day as the individual offices in most cases are open from 8.30 or 9.00 until 12.00 or 13.00. As a result the person affected, 90 per cent of whom work in armaments, is compelled to leave several days free before midday in order to sort out the matter.[28]

Generally people expressed their incomprehension that individual administrative offices should be scattered across the whole city area. As a result interpersonal relations increasingly suffered; offices were short-staffed, and the overworked officials had often suffered themselves from the raid. During the hours of waiting people voiced their annoyance out loud in the office corridors about the uncouth treatment they received and the lengthy processing of their applications.

At the same time, every raid increased the administration's workload and costs. The supply, accommodation, compensation and evacuation of the bomb victims had to be organized, damage reported, and city statistics brought up to date. More and more bombed-out people needed help, while the officials themselves had often lost homes, relatives or friends.[29] The local National Socialist propaganda authorities in Bremen noted in a morale report in February 1944:

> It is certainly understandable that under such great pressure the tone of the bureaucrats and officials who are getting things done is not always exemplary. It must nevertheless be asked that they pay more attention to the spiritual state of the bomb victims and try to do everything to help them in a satisfactory way.[30]

Often just trying to negotiate these official pathways cost the survivors of the attacks days; this was potential work time, which the firms now lost. Those who had not themselves been directly affected or whose homes were hardly damaged had to make their way back to work at once, after a sleepless night of air alarms or bombing raids, on an often failing public transport system.[31] At a time when there was a notorious shortage of personnel in every area of municipal and economic activity,[32] it proved extremely difficult for both the local authorities and the firms to overcome the consequences of air raids themselves.

THE INCLUSION OF OUTSIDE RESOURCES, REGIONS AND PEOPLE

The first concern in a newly-bombed city was to supply the surviving population with food, shelter, clothing and medical care. Emergency accommodation was prepared and food and consumer goods frequently established outside the city limits. At central points, spread out over the city area, dressing stations for medical aid and public soup kitchens were set up. Stores of foodstuffs, clothing and furnishings were laid in beforehand. In order to build up stocks of supplies for the impending disaster, the city authority in Vienna ordered large quantities of shoes from Hungary; Cologne supplied itself from occupied France; and the city administration in Hamburg bought shoes from Belgium and France. In collaboration with the armed forces, shoes (among other things) were bought up in unoccupied Vichy France and transported across occupied France to Germany, where these could be distributed to the needy population after the air raids.[33] For example, the city administration of Kassel had stored foodstuffs and other consumer goods and provisions in the surrounding area, allowing a good level of supply for the city after an air raid.[34]

When fleeing a bombed locality, the population often chose nearby areas that were so far untouched. The police in Osnabrück had already reported in August 1942 that despite a ban on doing so, people found overnight accommodation in the suburbs or the countryside, returning in the morning to work in the city. With the help of the police, the city administration tried to keep people in the city by carrying out checks at stations and on the streets, but they were unable to prevent the evening flight. The authorities' concern was that during a night raid many houses would be empty, and that afterwards there would be too few people to help in putting out fires and incendiary bombs.[35] After a big raid thousands of inhabitants often flooded out of the city, frequently on foot or by bicycle because the trains had stopped, pushing handcarts, wheelbarrows and prams along the damaged streets. Streaming along main roads to the surrounding towns, people then used the railway stations there to journey further on.[36]

Heavy raids with large-scale use of incendiary bombs often overwhelmed local fire defences. It was therefore usual that firefighters from surrounding cities and communities came to help. In Frankfurt am Main, for example, after a major raid in October 1943, fire defence units from Gelsenkirchen were involved, as well as emergency services from Mainz, Hanau, Bad Homburg and Aschaffenburg.[37] Similarly, after a big raid on Frankfurt on 22 March 1944, the Red Cross drew units from Weimar, Stuttgart and Bonn, while the armed forces brought in assistance from Worms.[38] After the first heavy night attacks on Cologne, lorries were brought in from the whole of the surrounding area from as far away as Gummersbach to help the Cologne emergency services to remove the rubble, furniture and refugees and to supply the survivors.[39] But these mutual assistance arrangements could go wrong. During another major raid on the night of 12/13 August 1944, the Frankfurt emergency services were not in place; they had already set out for Darmstadt earlier that night because of another heavy Allied raid there.[40]

Skilled craftsmen were also frequently brought in from outside to repair damage. For example, in Bremen glaziers from Hildesheim were set to work in January 1941.[41] The city authority had not only to co-ordinate such large groups of workers, often from distant cities, but also to house and feed them. This brought particular problems because of the strained supply situation immediately after a heavy air raid.[42] In October 1942 the city of Osnabrück already had problems supplying the workers who had travelled there with enough blankets;[43] two months later, blankets intended for bomb victims had to be distributed to outside craftsmen, building workers and carpenters.[44] Soldiers who had been called in to help voiced aloud their dissatisfaction with the state of their provisions, particularly towards the end of the war. An armed forces' propaganda officer reported from Nuremberg in February 1945 that the soldiers allocated for clearance and repair work complained that for the whole day they had to do the heavy work of clearing streets and bomb sites but their provisions had for some time been inadequate. In the evening they had to queue for several hours for the one hot meal of their day.[45]

Some people travelled from the surrounding areas and from other cities to view the bomb damage. For example, inhabitants came from Lippe, which remained completely spared by the air war, to inspect the damage to Bielefeld. In the summer of 1940, Fritz Geise from Lage made a Sunday excursion to look at the destruction in Bad Lippspringe.[46] An unusual case in this respect was that of Ilse von A. who, following the massive raids on Hamburg in the summer of 1943, during which around 40,000 people were killed, travelled there to look at bomb damage. On arrival she pretended to be a bomb victim, who had lost everything in the raids except for the clothes on her back, and was repeatedly invited inside by people who took pity on her. Once she had gained admittance to these homes, she stole money, jewellery and clothes from her hosts. Ilse von A. was eventually sentenced to a year and three months in prison by the Special Court (*Sondergericht*) in Hanover on 8 February 1944.[47] But everyone, whether emergency workers, craftsmen, or simple onlookers, reported on bomb damage when they returned home.[48] Their stories were spread abroad by their families, friends and colleagues and even reached the fighting forces through letters sent to the front.[49] Soldiers also learned from comrades returning from leave about conditions at home and in turn shared that knowledge in their own letters home.[50] Soldiers caught in air attacks while on leave unanimously expressed the view that the helplessness experienced in the air raid shelter was more difficult to bear than combat at the front. These private reports not only contributed to permanently undermining belief in final victory but also in the reliability of German propaganda.[51]

INDIRECT IMPACT

Cities and towns were bombed all across Germany, both large and small.[52] Nevertheless, of the approximately 90 million Germans, the great majority suffered direct bombardment either sporadically or never. If a bomb dropped on their town or village, it was often by chance. But while air attacks were directed at selected cities, the air routes to major targets covered more and more of the German Reich. Even if the Allied bomber squadrons aimed for the priority points in the larger cities – industrial installations important for the war effort – the surrounding area, including suburbs and a wider circle of small townships, was also always hit. Some bombs would be dropped in error; others, surplus to requirements, would be jettisoned after the attack in order to save fuel for the return flight, as happened on 6 October 1942, when several high explosive bombs fell on the small town of Uphusen after a raid on nearby Emden.[53] In autumn 1943 after an RAF attack on Berlin, bombs were jettisoned on the village of Libehna, fully 120 kilometres from the actual target area.[54] Friedrich Pohlmann recorded an air attack by Allied bombers on Gummersbach where bombs fell within a ten-kilometre radius over the small town and the neighbouring area. The attack was actually aimed at Siegen, thirty kilometres away, but the squadron had lost their orientation because of bad weather and by mistake attacked the small town in the Bergland.[55] Allied bombers might also be diverted from their main target by German fighter attacks. They jettisoned their bombs in flight, often a long way from the actual target area.[56] In all these tangential regions the population had to ask itself if the next attack would be on them.[57]

In order to avoid the threat from German night fighters, the RAF undertook numerous evasive actions; sometimes parts of an attacking force separated themselves from the main group and flew to the target by different and confusing routes; at other times aircraft undertook diversionary attacks in order to disguise the actual target of the main attack for as long as possible. For example, during an attack on Berlin, air-raid alarms were sounded in large parts of present-day Lower Saxony, in Bremen and in parts of North Rhine/Westphalia and Brandenburg. For the population living there this meant a further inter-rupted night's sleep and a further night in the air-raid cellar or bunker. On clear nights, British bomber squadrons attacking Berlin guided themselves along the river Weser, flying directly over Bremen, at the mouth of the river. Further south the route to Berlin led over Hanover, Brunswick, Magdeburg and Potsdam. Anti-aircraft guns and searchlights stationed in these cities made the operation audible and visible in the wider area around, which could also be damaged by shrapnel from anti-aircraft shells. Even in the small village of Polle, lying directly under the flightpath along the Weser, the population suffered from attacks directed at more distant Berlin, or Hanover, Magdeburg or Brunswick.[58]

The compulsory blackout also had an influence on daily life. However, from April 1940 the air-raid alarm, which had to be sounded regularly at the approach of every aircraft, had a more persistent effect. For example, Lippe, in North Rhine/Westphalia, though not itself a target, lay under the flight corridor of Allied aircraft heading for, or returning from, central Germany and Berlin. Since the object of attack of the approaching bombers could only be estimated imprecisely, attacks on the area around Bielefeld and Herford also prompted regular alarms. By the end of 1944 Lippe had experienced 731 air alarms, 293 of them during 1944 alone, with the emphasis on the months from October to December.[59]

The private economy also suffered in many ways from the attacks. As early as May 1940 the city administration in Münster observed a fall in industrial production of ten per cent; the main cause was the workers' general lack of sleep. In 1943 in Münster public air-raid alarms were sounded 209 times, in the first nine months of 1944 the figure reached over 300 alarms, and from autumn 1944 constantly increased in almost all areas of the Reich. During the three-month period from January to March 1945, Münster counted 329 air-raid alarms; the inhabitants had to spend around 293 hours in the bunkers and cellars, more than for the whole of 1943.[60] The steel industry was hit particularly badly by alarms because the blast furnaces had to be slowly restoked after every stoppage before production could resume. At the beginning of December 1940 the Hoesch Works in Dortmund had recorded a production loss of 1,480 tonnes of pig iron and 1,926 tonnes of raw steel. The Hoerder Works, an important supplier for tank production, showed a production loss of 705 tonnes of pig iron and 2,536 tonnes of raw steel.[61]

Constant overflights by Allied bombers provoked a mixture of wonder, anxiety and anger. On 20 August 1943, the SD branch in Bad Neustadt reported that as people from the surrounding area watched Allied bomber units flying towards Schweinfurt,

> at first scarcely one of the people thought about looking for an air-raid shelter when the enemy squadrons appeared, and they watched the progress of the flyers in amazement. Only later did people give vent to their feelings and criticized the air protection measures and above all the lack of our defence. Throughout they stressed that the enemy flyers on their way to Schweinfurt clearly demonstrated how defenceless we are at the moment and that air superiority lies exclusively in the hands of the enemy.[62]

In May 1944 Ingeborg T. wrote a letter to her husband Wilhelm at the front about her constant anxiety caused by the threat of the bombs:

> Dear Bill, At the moment it is once again unbearable: day and night ceaseless alarms. This tears so much at nerves that are anyway already shattered, that I'm afraid I will go mad if the war with all its terrible consequences does not end soon ... Yesterday and today the bombers were in Münster, at midday today in Hamm. When will it be Soest's turn? I dare not go out of the house, I don't dare to settle down to sleep. I drift along in constant crisis and torment.[63]

This letter demonstrates another level of the 'impact' of the air war: people's lives were not just influenced by the overflight of their own region, with all its anxiety and worry. Reports which came in from other areas already subject to attack about the scale of the raid, the level of destruction there and the number of fatalities frightened the population in regions not yet attacked. In this case the reports stirred up anxiety for the future in the towns and small villages in the surrounding areas.[64]

Each night the populations of these regions did not know whether they would be attacked directly or fall victim to a bomb jettisoned or carelessly dropped. There was no way they could know. They had to come to terms each night with the possibility it would be their turn for attack, with their valuables already prepared in the hallway – to have them close to hand in case of need – and they had to prepare themselves psychologically so as to be forearmed in case of an attack. The Berlin schoolteacher Lilo G. gave an impressive description of this situation in her diary in January 1944:

> You rightly observe that the nerves are slowly destroyed. Every evening you wait for the alarm. In the night you awake with a start because you believe that the siren has sounded. Then if it sounds, you go weak at the knees, you hurry, put things on (shirts, three pairs of stockings etc., because whatever you have on is sure to be saved).[65]

The Allies already exercised command of the air over broad areas of Germany in 1942 but the heavy attacks were carried out principally against cities in north and northwestern Germany, among others Hamburg, Lübeck, Rostock,

Cologne, Essen and Bremen. Small attacks followed against cities in south Germany, which though not on the same scale as those on north Germany or in the Rhineland, also had observable effects, particularly psychological. The advance of Allied bomber fleets southwards carried the war further and further into the German hinterland and made it clear that almost no-one was secure from the threat of bombing, even if they liked to imagine themselves to be immune. Gisela Neuhaus, for example, described in her memoirs how again and again Allied bombers flew over Dresden, but had never attacked the city. Almost no-one sought out the shelters during an alarm. People had said: 'We are certainly safe, Dresden will never be attacked.'[66] On 13/14 February 1945 Dresden was finally attacked and 25,000 people died.[67]

SPREADING INFORMATION AND RUMOURS

In order to prevent panic in the population, the Ministry of Propaganda and Popular Enlightenment only allowed the press to give information to the public about selected raids. The city authorities were also instructed not to publish damage reports or lists of the dead, and also to refrain from public appeals to the citizens for clearance work, since this could supply the enemy with information about the effects of the attack.[68]

The strategy of 'information in doses' was supposed to work against the demoralization of the German population, while at the same time evoking the idea of the 'people's community' (*Volksgemeinschaft*) and stirring up hatred against the enemy.[69] Instead of reporting the suffering of the civil population, propaganda concentrated on the detailed presentation of the destruction of German cultural and architectural monuments. After the cathedral at Cologne was badly damaged in a raid on 29 June 1943, an attempt was made to mobilize the population by stirring up hatred against the enemy who had bombed one of the outstanding monuments of German culture and history. In a national press campaign the 'instigators of the destruction of the cathedral of Cologne' were judged to be 'as brutal as gangsters'[70] against 'the values of irreplaceable European culture'.[71] By using controlled information about the destruction of buildings of cultural value, the Propaganda Ministry hoped to deflect attention from the lack of detailed information about raids, to enhance the believability of those who supplied the news and to combat the formation of rumours.[72] But the SD (Sicherheitsdienst) confirmed that concern expressed for damaged or destroyed cultural buildings in reporting the raids was 'mostly not shared' by those who read them. Sympathy was directed more towards the victims and their homes.[73] An industrial worker from Suhl expressed this in pithy terms: 'Better the destruction of Cologne cathedral than 100 people dead.'[74] The SD in Halle also cited a female worker for whom the cathedral was less important: 'but the poor people who have lost their lives were not mentioned; passed over in silence. The individual apparently has no more value in today's Germany!'[75]

In the presentation of the damage to the cathedrals in Cologne and Münster, both in the reports for the armed forces and in the press, people often saw, particularly in the cities threatened by the air war, a trivialization of the heavy damage in the residential quarters, but above all of the victims.[76] It was precisely the fate of inhabitants in the cities threatened by air attack that interested people in the regions not directly affected by the air war. Increasing restrictions on press reporting led people to seek their information from alternative sources. Here private correspondence, whether to friends, relatives or to the fighting front, was of outstanding importance.[77] Despite the postal censor, this means of exchange of information and the formation of opinion could not be effectively controlled. The scale of this correspondence is difficult to estimate. In June 1943, the Reich Interior Ministry gave the number of people living in the areas threatened by air attack as 26 million. Assuming at least a potential active correspondence with friends and relatives throughout the country and at the front, it becomes obvious why the postal censor was not capable of effectively stopping the spread of information in private letters.

Above all, the experiences reported by the evacuees left a lasting impression on the local population in the areas that had not been affected, and resulted in spreading fear of an intensification of the air war.[78] What was heard was repeated in the air-raid cellars and bunkers, in trains, in queues in front of shops and at work. The regime reacted by imposing penalties on those who talked, but even this, imposed with a degree of sensitivity to the circumstances, could not stop the rumours. The reported experiences were seldom reliable. For example, a rumour appeared after the major raid on Wuppertal on 24 January 1943 that '10,000 to 20,000' people had been killed. In fact in this attack 1,800 people died.[79] In holding back details of raids and focusing on ruined cultural buildings, the regime not only failed to dam the demand for news about what had happened, but invited people to draw their information from private reports from bombed regions, or from second-hand accounts or rumours.

A regular flood of rumours arose in the summer and early autumn of 1943. The accounts spread abroad particular horrors – that phosphorous 'rained from heaven' and people in Wuppertal were 'burnt like human torches in the windows and on the street, where they got stuck in the glowing surface of the roads.'[80] Technically this was not possible, yet the accounts were believed and passed on. The Propaganda Ministry attempted with explanatory articles to steer people in a different direction: it was not possible, so it was asserted, to spray burning phosphorous from an aircraft, and what people had seen were the flares used for the approaching bombers. The 'phosphorous bombs' were presented simply as what they were: a standard liquid incendiary bomb, whose content consisted of a mixture of oil and an artificial resin. But rationality could not set aside the conviction that burning phosphorous fell from the skies.[81] Thus the Munich police explicitly reported a 'phosphor psychosis' which, among other things, led to the fact that many local self-protection communities filled in their cellar windows with bricks so that phosphorous could not flow in. The result was that the blast effect from explosive bombs simply pushed the new bricks on top of the people who had sought shelter in the cellar. This happened during the night of 2/3 October 1943, when 25 people were seriously injured and two people killed in the Munich Brudermühlstrasse.[82]

The psychological shock in the population following Operation Gomorrah against Hamburg, Germany's second-largest city, was particularly persistent. In just a week in July–August 1943, some 40,000 people were killed through Allied air attacks and the so-called 'firestorm' generated by the incendiaries; broad areas of the inner city were completely destroyed. The shocking accounts of people from Hamburg left a deep impression on the population of Bavaria, who had already had a taste of the horrors of air war through attacks on Munich, Augsburg and Nuremberg. After the catastrophe in Hamburg in the summer of 1943 there was a regular exodus from Munich.[83] The president of the city's Higher Provincial Court reported in November 1943 that a 'larger number of the citizens of Munich had sought refuge with relatives or acquaintants near and far in the surrounding area, [and] in the summer had even stayed overnight in the open many times, returning to the city in the mornings.' This led to an extraordinary burden on rail traffic but also to a weakening of the local workforce for protection duties since among the people who abandoned the city in the evening were many men capable of being mobilized to carry them out.[84]

Glaziers at work in Hamburg, July 1943, repairing windows. Courtesy of Staatsarchiv Hamburg.

Public soup kitchen, Hamburg, July 1943. Courtesy of Staatsarchiv Hamburg.

EVACUATION AND RURAL AREAS

After the intensification of Allied air attacks in 1942 and 1943, and with concrete for building bunkers in short supply, the leaders of the Third Reich relied increasingly on the evacuation of the 'surplus' population from the major cities, leaving behind only those needed to work in industry and supply essential to the war. Since it was not possible in wartime to overcome the housing shortage caused by air raids, the regime saw evacuation as a way to ensure that the remaining stock of housing could be allocated as accommodation for essential industrial workers. In the meantime, propaganda pointed people to the post-war period and promised a rapid reconstruction of the cities. In view of the particularly heavy destruction in the Rhineland, many people no longer believed that they, or even their children and grandchildren, would ever experience 'the revival of the cities'. They calculated that reconstruction would take at least 30 to 50 years.[85] In October 1943 the Frankfurt professor, Adolf L., wrote in a letter to his family in Mannheim that he could 'not even imagine how our shattered cities can be rebuilt again.'[86]

The Reich Interior Ministry calculated in late June 1943 that out of the 26 million people in the cities threatened by air attack, it was necessary to evacuate 25 per cent, that is to transfer 6.5 million from the city to the countryside or small towns. When a month later 40,000 people lost their lives in the heavy raids on Hamburg, the National Socialist leadership ordered the evacuation of all schools from the Hansa city and the equally heavily hit Ruhr area. A short time later millions of women, children and the elderly left the air war regions and were brought to those areas of the Reich which had so far been spared the horrors of the air campaign.[87] Towns and villages throughout the Reich served as reception areas for the evacuees, as for example in Upper Bavaria, the designated reception zone for bomb victims from North Westphalia. Refugees from the air war from other northern and northwestern cities which were exposed to heavy attacks also arrived. Hamburg refugees from attacks of summer 1943 were brought to Bayreuth, Danzig and West Prussia;[88] for refugees from Aachen and Cologne the regions of Saxony and Lower Silesia were allocated.[89] Up to the end of the Second World War, an estimated nine million people were compelled to leave their homes in the cities and to move to the countryside. An opinion research project in 1952 indicated that 41 per cent of the Germans asked had experienced heavy bombing and 21 per cent had been bombed out with their families.[90] The extensive evacuation measures for millions of people intervened decisively in a private sphere hitherto untouched by the war. Millions of people in the whole area of the Reich were now affected indirectly by the bombing war and its consequences, without being themselves immediate victims of bombing. The trek of the bombed-out brought the air war into the countryside and allowed broad segments of the 'people's community' to become involved in the experiences on the home front in the cities. To justify their own misfortune and neediness, the bombed-out gave elaborate accounts of their fate and of the dangers of the air war. The result could be ambiguous. The SD in Linz reported in July 1943 that the inhabitants, faced with the suffering of the victims of the bombing war, could feel a 'certain satisfaction and even thankfulness' that they had been spared a similar misfortune. On the other hand, the fear grew that they too would become the object of enemy air attacks.[91]

The evacuation, however, led to fundamental social problems and conflicts. In cultural terms, there was a confrontation between the values and behaviour of city and village, and a favourable reaction was in no way guaranteed on either side. More materially, the relocation presented both the home authorities and the authorities on the spot with the task of distributing provisions. At least in the initial phase, bottlenecks often arose which exacerbated the indignation of the local population against the townspeople, but also the dissatisfaction of evacuees.[92] Particular complaints concerned the short supply of vegetables and firewood,[93] as well as the tardy provision of furniture, household goods and cooking utensils for evacuees.[94] Sometimes the sheer number of evacuees in relation to the original population could lead to problems. The town of Gronau, with around 3,000 inhabitants, was told in April 1944 to take 850 evacuees from Hanover.[95] In March 1944, the 4,000 inhabitants of Duderstadt had to take in around 3,000 evacuees from the same city.[96]

Local conflicts often arose between evacuees and the local population. For example, in Clausthal-Zellerfeld Liselotte B. had taken a married couple into her three-room apartment. Some time later, an additional homeless married couple with two children were allocated and Liselotte B. found herself barred from her own home.[97] The hotel owner L. complained about the three secondary-school teachers from Hanover evacuated to Clausthal and placed in her hotel. They were originally supposed to sleep in one room, but then each took a hotel room for themselves and occupied three rooms with a total of seven beds. Frau L. turned to the local police but despite police instructions the three men refused to leave the hotel and take up the alternative quarters prepared for them. In another case, Annelise B. took an elderly married couple into her three-room apartment and gave them both two of the rooms while she kept one of the rooms to store her furniture in. The tenants then got access to the third room and Frau B. was also denied entry to her own property.[98]

Evacuees also complained about those who gave them shelter. In Dassel in May 1944, a woman from Hanover complained about harassment from her host and demanded alternative accommodation.[99] In April 1944 the evacuee Frau C., who had been transferred with five children to Hameln, grumbled about the malicious behaviour of her landlady, who denied her and her children entry to the air-raid cellar during an air-raid alarm because there was food stored there. In one case the local mayor and the official delegated by the Hanover city administration for the evacuees were called in to clear up a conflict. In the end, the evacuee Frau R. brought the matter to court and charged her landlady with defamation.[100]

After the first Allied air attacks, Goebbels had talked almost gloatingly about the 'people's community', which in his view as a result of the disastrous air raids would inevitably arrive at the point where the individual, whatever his social position, would be subsumed into a mutual solidarity, so that the classless society talked of in official propaganda would be transformed into a kind of 'emergency community'.[101] How little weight the idea of the 'people's community' conjured up by Goebbels actually had is illustrated by the inability of host communities to feel sympathy for evacuees. In the rural areas, and particularly in Bavaria, the massive influx of evacuees and the evident worsening of the supply situation led to hostility from the local population.[102] For example, Dora D. retained a vivid memory of what little understanding she had met with after her parents had sent her away from Berlin to relatives in Naumburg an der Saale. In December 1943 the apartment block where she lived with her family had been bombed. In Naumburg she was teased by her classmates for being a coward because she ran to the air-raid shelter whenever the siren sounded.[103] Lilo B. from Mellenbach wrote in a letter on 25 April 1944:

> Today I've again seen so much poverty, it is much worse for many than it is for us. Today 50 evacuees came from Düsseldorf and Mönchengladbach. All of them young women with small children. The youngest was eight weeks old. We were at the station, coffee and cakes were handed out. This necessity for accommodation – quite a few women turned back, who were simply not accepted by the people here. Tomorrow

some want to go back. One woman had the door slammed in her face when she arrived with her small child at the place she had been allocated, and this woman had lost her husband on the Eastern Front only a short time previously. It is a shame.[104]

CONCLUSION

If during the course of the First World War the experience of shortages and hunger was stamped on popular memory, the German memory culture of the Second World War is dominated by the experience of the air war, the evacuation necessitated by air raids, and the flight from Germany's eastern regions, all elements, for many, of a personal lived experience. The story of the air war is composed of diverse levels of social, regional, local and individual experience, of which the current memory culture must be understood as a reflection Events such as the Hamburg firestorm in the summer of 1943[105] or the big raid on Kassel in October 1943[106] serve as objects of local collective identification and at the same time as a frame of reference that reaches beyond its connection with the locality and becomes the focus of projection, against a background of shared local experiences, for the entire social experience of the Allied conduct of the air war.[107] This is confirmed by the fact that in the post-war period the Hamburg raids of summer 1943 were emphasized in the official political memory as a symbolic event for commemoration in West Germany, while the country-wide memory culture in East Germany principally concentrated on the air raid on Dresden in February 1945; other heavy raids, among them the attack on Magdeburg on 16 January 1945 with nearly 2,500 dead, as well as local memory culture in general, were subordinated to the commemoration defined by the state.[108]

This highlights again the principal problem with the positions taken by Groehler and Heinl outlined at the start of this paper. As night fell on Germany, no-one could foresee which area would be attacked. Those affected by air raids were therefore not limited to those whose city was the eventual target. The very different personal effect on people in the different regions calls for a differentiated engagement with the material. To grasp the direct and indirect impact of the air war it is essential to define the different forms of effect and to categorize the different regions appropriately. In addition, individual situational problems as well as generationally specific aspects must be considered; so too allegiance to particular social classes, the shared experiences stemming from a specific residential area, the character of an individual and the predispositions that arise from it for the possible wartime experiences to come. Consideration of the social, individual-sociological, individual-psychological, life-historical, social-psychological and geographical aspects is a necessary precondition for forming a comprehensive picture of the effects of Allied air war strategy on German society in the Second World War. Above all, it is important to recognize that an air operation affected not only the target area, but also sections of population not directly menaced. No doubt the results of the passage of ground forces bound for their main battlefields is much more directly visible than the overflight of bomber squadrons, which, unlike troops of marauding soldiers living off the land, leave no trace of devastation behind them on their way to their targets. Yet they did leave traces among the populations below.[109]

People in many regions of the Reich were confronted only indirectly by the air war, but directly by its consequences. The overflight, with the accompanying air alarm, followed often by several hours waiting in the air-raid cellar or bunker and the consequent loss of sleep (even without a single bomb falling), means that direct links can be established even when Allied bombers actually made an attack a considerable distance away. Through the *direct impact* of air attacks, an estimated 405,000 people died in the whole area of the Greater German Reich, including Austria. Their death affected several million dependants, relatives and friends. Among the survivors, many suffered injuries which they would carry with them for the rest of their lives and which influenced both them and their families and friends, touched not directly by the bombs, but by the suffering of someone close. Then there were the nine million evacuees, and the further millions who had to find room (or rooms) for them, willingly or not. More people still, though themselves not drawn directly into danger, were made fearful through accounts and rumours of the air war. Emergency workers were summoned from several hundred kilometres away. Fire defence units travelled from neighbouring regions following heavy attacks. Military units were requested for clearing bombsites, and craftsmen and workers from the wide surrounding area for carrying out repairs. Then emergency supplies came from the rest of the Reich area. Often as a result of the experiences in other cities, and even before the onset of heavy attacks, consumer goods and provisions, in particular clothing and furniture, were bought up from the rest of the Reich and even from occupied Europe. In this way, the surrounding areas were tied in to the air protection measures as storage sites for emergency stocks. The effects of the Allied air war were therefore far more complex than might appear from minute-by-minute accounts of individual attacks, and it is this perspective that requires further research.

Notes

1 H. Rumpf, 'Der Irrweg des Bombenkrieges', *Wehrwissenschaftliche Rundschau*, 10, 1960, 549.

2 There are numerous examples of local case studies, some of them about a raid on a small area of a city. See for example R. Siebert, *Bomben auf Querum vor 50 Jahren. Den Toten des 21 Februar und 8 Mai 1944 zum Gedenken* (Brunswick: Friedenszentrum Braunschweig, 1994). For studies of a city or area see G. Bergander, *Dresden im Luftkrieg – Vorgeschichte, Zerstörung, Folgen* (Weimar: Böhlau, 1994, 2nd ed.); I. Permooser, *Der Luftkrieg über München 1942–1945: Bomben auf die Hauptstadt der Bewegung* (Munich: Wittek, 1993); H. Schnatz, *Der Luftkrieg im Raum Koblenz 1944/45*, vol. 4 (Boppard am Rhein: Kommission des Landtages für die Geschichte des Landes Rheinland-Pfalz, 1981).

3　W. Dettmer, *Die Zerstörung Kassels im Oktober 1943* (Fuldabrück: Hesse, 1983); W. Fischer-Pache and G. Jochem, *Der Luftkrieg gegen Nürnberg: Der Angriff am 2. Januar 1945 und die zerstörte Stadt* (Neustadt an der Aisch: Schmidt Verlag, 2005).

4　K. Klee, *Im 'Luftschutzkeller des Reiches": Evakuierte in Bayern 1939–1953. Politik, soziale Lage, Erfahrungen* (Munich: Verlag Oldenbourg, 1998); M. Krause, *Flucht vor dem Bombenkrieg: 'Umquartierungen' im Zweiten Weltkrieg und die Wiedereingliederung der Evakuierten in Deutschland 1943–1963* (Düsseldorf: Droste Verlag, 1997).

5　O. Groehler, *Bombenkrieg gegen Deutschland* (Berlin: Akademie-Verlag, 1990), 295.

6　P. Heinl, 'Invisible Psychological Ruins: Unconscious Long-Term War Trauma', paper at a workshop on 'War, Bombing and Trauma in World War II in Comparative Perspective', Reading University, 13 March 2009. See too P. Heinl, *Splintered Innocence: an Intuitive Approach to Treating War Trauma* (Hove: Brunner-Routledge, 2001).

7　L. Gruchmann, *Der Zweite Weltkrieg* (Munich: Deutscher Taschenbuch Verlag, 1975, 3rd ed.), 198, 280 ff., 414.

8　Krause, *Flucht vor dem Bombenkrieg*, 90.

9　W. Dettmar, 'Kassel im Luftkrieg' in *Leben in Ruinen. Kassel 1943–1948 im Gedenkjahr der Stadt Kassel zur Erinnerung an ihre Zerstörung am 22 Oktober 1943* (Marburg: Jonas Verlag, 1993), 11–22, here 17.

10　I. Kershaw, *Der Hitler-Mythos. Führerkult und Volksmeinung* (Stuttgart: Deutsche Verlags Anstalt, 1999), 247.

11　Ibid., 247.

12　K. A. Erdmann, *Die Zeit der Weltkriege. Gebhard: Handbuch der deutschen Geschichte*, vol 4, part 2 (Stuttgart: Deutscher Taschenbuch Verlag, 1976, 9th ed.), 807. Olaf Groehler gives a figure of 406,000 in 'Der strategische Luftkrieg und seine Auswirkungen auf die deutsche Zivilbevölkerung' in H. Boog (ed.), *Luftkriegführung im Zweiten Weltkrieg: Ein internationaler Vergleich* (Bonn: Verlag E.S. Mittler, 1993), 344.

13　Kershaw, *Der Hitler-Mythos*, 247.

14　N. Gregor, 'A *Schicksalsgemeinschaft*? Allied Bombing, Civilian Morale and Social Dissolution in Nuremberg, 1942–1945', *The Historical Journal*, 43, 2000, 1056.

15　See for example Kempowski-Archiv, Akademie der Künste Berlin, Bio 6/2001, undated diary entry, July 1943 by Frieda Hartz.

16　Staatsarchiv Osnabrück, Best. Dep 3 b XIX, no. 78, Johannes Garrels, 'Vernehmungsprotokoll vom 1 October 1942'.

17　Staatsarchiv Bremen, Best. 4, 113 19.b., letter from Carl Hagens to Martin Spockler, 14 January 1941.

18　Ibid., Bremisches Staatsamt: Tagebuch der Stadt Bremen, entry for 31 January 1943.

19　Institut für Stadtgeschichte, Frankfurt am Main, Signatur 3.812, Magistratsakten, report from Municipal Nutrition Office to the mayor, 10 October 1943.

20　T. Ewald, C. Hollmann and H. Schmidt, *Ausländische Zwangsarbeiter in Kassel 1940–1945* (Kassel: Verlag Gesamthochschulbibliothek, 1988), 155, 157; R. Feinendegen and D. Pützhofen (eds), *22 Juni 1943, als Krefeld brannte: Augenzeugenberichte von der Bombennacht* (Krefeld: Verein für Heimatkunde Krefeld, 1993), 160.

21　Staatsarchiv Osnabrück, Best. Dep 3 b XIX, no. 82, Ortsgruppenleiter NSDAP Osnabrück, proposal from 18 August 1942; letter from Osnabrücker Lagerhausgesellschaft to OB Osnabrück, 20 August 1942.

22　Staatsarchiv Bremen, Best. 4, 113 19. b, Bremisches Staatsamt: Tagebuch der Stadt Bremen (manuscript), January 1943.

23　Stadtarchiv Hannover, HR 39 no. 102, letter from the Stadtbauamt Hannover to the rector of the Technical High School, Hannover, 24 May 1941.

24　R. Blank, 'Wartime Daily Life and the Air War on the Home Front' in R. Blank (ed.), *Germany and the Second World War, Vol IX/1, German Wartime Society 1939–1945: Politicization, Disintegration and the Struggle for Survival* (Oxford: Oxford University Press, 2008), 429.

25　Institut für Stadgeschichte, Frankfurt am Main, Signatur: 3.812, Stadtkämmerer report of 5 October 1943.

26 Staatsarchiv Bremen, 3-N.7.no 162, NSDAP-Ortsgruppe Seebaldsbrück, morale report of the Kreispropagandaleitung NSDAP, 12 February 1944.
27 Ibid.
28 Ibid., 3-N.7, no 162, NSDAP Ortsgruppe 'Wasserturm', morale report of the Kreispropagandaleitung, 12 February 1944.
29 Ibid.
30 Staatsarchiv Bremen, Best. 3-N. 7., no 162 [28], Kreispropagandaleitung der NSDAP, morale report from 12 February 1944.
31 Bibliothek für Zeitgeschichte, Sammlung Sterz, letter from Frau H. (Karlsruhe), 1 June 1942: 'For two days there was no longer a road until it was cleared again. Firefighters were here for two days from every city, almost everything has burnt'.
32 See for example R. Müller, *Stuttgart zur Zeit des Nationalsozialismus* (Stuttgart: Konrad Theiss Verlag, 1988), 440.
33 Stadtarchiv Hannover, HR 39 n. 102, discussion between mayor of Hannover and the finance advisory committees, protocol of meeting on 28 November 1941.
34 Stadtarchiv Kassel, Best. S8 B13, US Army, 'Background Report of German Cities (Kassel)'.
35 Staatsarchiv Osnabrück, Best. Dep 3 b XIX, no. 82, circular letter from Captain Schmidt (security police), 19 August 1942.
36 Institut für Stadtgeschichte, Frankfurt am Main, S5/236, no. 10, Siegfried Heisig diary.
37 Institut für Stadtgeschichte, Frankfurt am Main, Magistratsakten Signatur 3.812, state councillor Dr. Müller, entry for 6 October 1943.
38 Ibid., S5/236, no. 10, letter from Siegfried Heisig to his son, 10 April 1944.
39 Deutsches Tagebucharchiv, Emmendingen, Signatur 948/1, memoirs of Friedrich P., 211.
40 Ibid., S5/199, Hans Drüner chronicle, entry for 13 August 1944.
41 Staatsarchiv Bremen, 9 S 9–25, letter from Carl Hagens to Martin Spockler, 14 January 1941: 'From our house, bombs smashed up a factory and three private houses and in the whole quarter many windows were destroyed. Glaziers had to be brought in from Hildesheim, and they replaced the most important windows in the houses on account of the cold.'
42 Staatsarchiv Hannover, HR 39 no. 102, letter from city building council to city councillor Bakemeier, 20 October 1941.
43 Staatsarchiv Osnabrück, Bes. Dep 3 b XIX, no. 80, minute from 12 October 1942.
44 Ibid., circular from 17 December 1942.
45 W. Wette and R. Bremer, D. Vogel (eds), *Das letzte halbe Jahr: Stimmungsberichte der Wehrmachtpropaganda 1944/45* (Essen: Kartext Verlag, 2001), 367.
46 A. Ruppert and H. Riechert, *Herrschaft und Akzeptanz. Der Nationalsozialismus in Lippe während der Kriegsjahre. Analyse und Dokumente* (Opladen: Verlag Leske & Budrich, 1998), 83.
47 Niedersächsisches Hauptstaatsarchiv, Hannover, Hann. 171a Hann. Acc. 107/83, no. 789, case against Ilse von A., judgement of 8 February 1944.
48 See for example Staatsarchiv Bremen, Az. 7.500–KT–269, Adolf Meier, Diary 3, 26 ff.
49 Museum für Kommunikation Berlin, Feldpostsammlung 3.2002.1317, letter from Mrs Schädel to her husband, Paul Schädel (Eastern Front), 31 August 1942: 'Tomorrow we will have had three years of war and still there is no end in sight. Yesterday spoke with von Stiller and he has just returned from Mainz and says that three quarters of Mainz has disappeared, it was frightful.'
50 Bibliothek für Zeitgeschichte, Sterz collection, letter from Obergefreite Alfred M. (Paris), 12 July 1942.
51 The SD in Kitzingen reported in November 1943 that many people who had seen the damage caused by Allied air attacks in Schweinfurt would no longer believe the propaganda that war production had not suffered any 'heavy damage'. People living in the country were of the opinion that it had become pointless to work any longer since everything would certainly be destroyed soon. See SD Kitzingen, report of 8 November 1943 in M. Broszat, E. Fröhlich and F. Wiesemann (eds), *Bayern in der NS-Zeit: soziale Lage und politisches Verhalten der Bevölkerung im Spiegel vertraulicher Berichte* (Munich: Oldenbourg, 1977), 658.
52 See for example the attack on the Friesian town of Esens in G. Rokahr, *Der Bombenagriff auȷ Esens am 27 September 1943. Annäherung an ein schwieriges Thema* (Esens: Söker Verlag, 2003).

53 Bunkermuseum Emden, www.bunkermuseum.de/tagebuecher/lehmann_01.pdf, Alfred Lehmann, war diary, entry for 6 October 1942.

54 On this see M. Michel, 'Bombenangriff dauert über eine Stunde', *Naumburger Tageblatt*, 19 July 2009.

55 Deutsches Tagebucharchiv Emmendingen, Best. 948/1, Friedrich Pohlmann 'Erinnerungen', 215; Erich Heinemann, *Da kam ein stolzer Reiter. Jugendjahre in Hildesheim 1939–1945* (Hildesheim: Verlag Gerstenberg, 1995), 18, diary entry for 19 July 1940: 'Tonight it broke. We were lying in bed despite the air-raid alarm. But now we could all suddenly sit up. The bombs had fallen in open country near Himmelsthür. Certainly jettisoned. But mother was of the view that it was serious, in future we absolutely had to get up with the alarm.'

56 As observed by the deputy Gauleiter Hannover-Ost in his letter to the Party Chancellery, 12 December 1944, Bundesarchiv Berlin, NS 19/2193.

57 Bibliothek für Zeitgeschichte, Sammlung Sterz, O-Gefr. Karl P., letter of 28 October 1943.

58 See for example the 1952 memoir of teacher Hans Prigge, Hauptstaatsarchiv Hannover, ZGS 1 no. 78.

59 A. Ruppert and A. Riechert, *Herrschaft und Akzeptanz. Der Nationalsozialismus in Lippe während der Kriegsjahre. Analyse und Dokumentation* (Opladen: Keske & Budrich, 1998), 82.

60 W. Beer, *Kriegsalltag an der Heimatfront. Alliierter Luftkrieg und deutsche Gegenmassnahmen zur Abwehr und Schadensbegrenzung, dargestellt für den Raum Münster* (Bremen: Hauschild, 1990), 102.

61 R. Blank 'Wartime Daily Life and Air War on the Home Front', 429.

62 SD-Aussenstelle Bad Neustadt (Gau Mainfranken), report from 20 August 1943 reproduced in M. Broszat, E. Fröhlich and F. Wiesemann (eds), *Bayern in der NS-Zeit. Soziale Lage und politisches Verhalten der Bevölkerung im Spiegel vertraulicher Berichte* (Munich: Oldenbourg, 1977), 646.

63 I. Hammer and S. zur Nieden (eds), *Sehr selten habe ich geweint. Briefe und Tagebücher aus dem Zweiten Weltkrieg von Menschen in Berlin* (Zurich: Schweizer Verlagshaus, 1992), 159, letter from Ingeborg T. to Wilhelm T., 31 May 1944.

64 Staatsarchiv Osnabrück, Best. Slgt 54 n. 1. See also the memoir of Alexander D. (hectographic manuscript, Königswinter, 1994), 98.

65 Hammer, zur Nieden, *Sehr selten habe ich geweint*, 289, Lilo G. Diary, entry for 3 January 1944.

66 Kempowski-Archiv, Bio 3774-10, Gisela Neuhaus, 'Spring, wenn du kannst', 1.

67 'Abschlussbericht der Historikerkommission zu den Luftangriffen auf Dresden zwischen dem 13 und 15 Februar 1945', Landeshauptstadt Dresden, 17 March 2010, 67.

68 Hauptstadtarchiv Hannover, Best. Hann. 122a no. 7058/7059, circular letter from the Reich Ministry of Interior to the provincial governments, 4 January 1943.

69 M. G. Steinert, *Hitlers Krieg und die Deutschen. Stimmung und Haltung der deutschen Bevölkerung im Zweiten Weltkrieg* (Düsseldorf: Econ Verlag, 1970), 365; W. A. Boelcke, *Wollt Ihr den totalen Krieg? Die geheimen Goebbels-Konferenzen 1939–1943* (Herrsching: Pawlak Verlag, 1989), 345.

70 H. Jenkner, 'Herostraten-Ruhm', *Der Angriff*, 2 July 1943.

71 Anon., 'Untilgbare Kulturschande', *Der Angriff*, 2 July 1943.

72 W. Hagemann, *Publizist im Dritten Reich* (Hamburg: Hansischer Gildenverlag, 1948), 173.

73 SD report on internal questions, 2 December 1943 (Red Series) in H. Boberach (ed.), *Meldungen aus dem Reich. Die geheimen Lageberichte des Sicherheitsdienst der SS 1938–1945* (Herrsching: Pawlak Verlag, 1984), vol. 15, 6093.

74 Bundesarchiv-Berlin, NS 6/406, SD Weimar, report of 6 July 1943.

75 Ibid., NS 6/406.

76 SD report on internal questions, 22 July 1943 (Red Series) in Boberach (ed.), *Meldungen aus dem Reich*, vol. 14, 5516.

77 See for example Bibliothek für Zeitgeschichte, Sammlung Sterz, letter from Josef Sch. (Munich), 28 April 1944.

78 See report from the Kreisschulungsamt, Rothenburg o.d. Tauber, 20 October 1943, reproduced in Broszat, Fröhlich and Wiesemann (eds), *Bayern in der NS-Zeit*, 583.

79 I. Permooser, *Der Luftkrieg im Raum München 1942–1945* (Munich: Wittek, 1993), 194.

80 Bundesarchiv-Berlin, NS 6/407, SD Schwerin, report for 29 June 1943.
81 K.-H. Mistele, 'Kriegsgerüchte' in K. Guth and T. Korth (eds), *Lebendige Volkskultur. Festgabe für Elisabeth Roth zum 60. Geburtstag* (Bamberg: Verlag Meisenbach, 1980), 146.
82 Permooser, *Der Luftkrieg*, 194.
83 Bundesarchiv-Berlin, R22/3379, Oberlandesgerichtspräsident, Munich, report of 26 November 1943.
84 Ibid.
85 SD-Berichte zu Inlandsfragen vom 22 Juli 1943 (Rote Serie) in Boberach (ed.), *Meldungen aus dem Reich*, vol. 14, 5517.
86 Letter from Prof. Adolf L. (Frankfurt am Main), 3 October 1943, Bibliothek für Zeitgeschichte, Stuttgart, Sammlung Sterz.
87 See for example the measures in Munich in April 1944 in K. Klee, *Im 'Luftschutzkeller des Reiches'. Evakuierte in Bayern 1939-1953. Politik, soziale Lage, Erfahrungen* (Munich: Oldenbourg, 1999), 145 ff.
88 Forschungsstelle für Zeitgeschichte in Hamburg (ed.), *Hamburg im 'Dritten Reich'* (Göttingen: Wallstein Verlag, 2005), 662.
89 M. Krause, *Flucht vor dem Bombenkrieg. 'Umquartierung' im Zweiten Weltkrieg und die Wiedereingliederung der Evakuierten in Deutschland 1943-1963* (Düsseldorf: Droste Verlag, 1997), 34.
90 Ibid., 15.
91 Bundesarchiv-Berlin, NS 6/408, SD Linz, report from July 1943.
92 Stadtarchiv Hannover, HR 39 no. 106, 'Sprechtag für umquartierte Einwohner der Stadt Hannover in Duderstadt', report of 19 April 1944.
93 Ibid., Ibid. See, among others, complaints over the provision of vegetables in the town of Dassel in Lower Saxony, whose 2,000 inhabitants had to accommodate 525 evacuees. 'Sprechtag umquartierter Hannoveraner in Dassel und Umgebung (Kreis Einback)', report of 25 May 1944. Similar complaints were voiced in Duderstadt over the supply of vegetables and wood for fuel. 'Sprechtag für umquartierte Einwohner der Stadt Hannover in Duderstadt', report of 24 March 1944.
94 Ibid., Ibid. In Göttingen evacuees complained about the failure to consider the distribution of fish and also about the shortages of household utensils. See 'Sprechtag für umquartierte Einwohner der Stadt Hannover in Göttingen', report of 17 April 1944. In Dassel communal kitchens were set up to cope with the lack of opportunity for cooking. See 'Sprechtag umquartierter Hannoveraner in Dassel und Umgebung (Kreis Einbeck)', report of 25 May 1944.
95 Ibid., Ibid., 'Sprechtag für umquartierte Einwohner der Stadt Hannover in Gronau', report of 4 April 1944.
96 Ibid., Ibid., 'Sprechtag für umquartierte Einwohner der Stadt Hannover in Duderstadt', report of 24 March 1944. In Kreis Hameln-Pyrmont with around 70-75,000 inhabitants, around 12-15,000 were brought from Hannover. See 'Sprechtag für umquartierte Einwohner der Stadt Hannover in Hameln', report of 19 April 1944.
97 Ibid., Ibid., 'Sprechtage in Clausthal-Zellerfeld', report of a trip to Hannover, 3 March 1944.
98 Ibid., Ibid., 'Niederschrift über den Sprechtag für evakuierte Hannoveraner am 23 Mai 1944 in Clausthal-Zellerfeld'.
99 Ibid., Ibid., 'Sprechtag umquartierter Hannoveraner in Dassel und Umgebung (Kreis Einbeck), report of 24 May 1944.
100 Ibid., Ibid., 'Sprechtag für umquartierte Einwohner der Stadt Hannover in Hameln', report of 19 April 1944.
101 H. Mommsen, 'Kriegserfahrungen' in U. Borsdorf and M. Jamin (eds), *Über Leben im Krieg. Kriegserfahrungen in einer Industrieregion 1939-1945* (Reinbeck bei Hamburg: Rowohlt, 1989), 12.
102 See Stadtarchiv Hannover, HR 39 no. 106, 'Sprechtag für umquartierte Einwohner der Stadt Hannover in Bad Pyrmont', protocol of 24 March 1944. On Bavaria see Broszat, Fröhlich and Wiesemann (eds), *Bayern in der NS-Zeit*, 595.
103 Tagebuch- und Erinnerungsarchiv, Berlin Treptow, Sammlung 'Nationalsozialismus, Krieg und Kriegsende: Erinnerungen, Berichte', Dora D. 'Erinnerungen', recorded 2002.

104   Bibliothek für Zeitgeschichte, Sammlung Sterz, letter from Lilo B. (Mellenbach), 24 April 1944.

105   M. Thiessen, *Eingebrannt ins Gedächtnis. Hamburgs Gedenken an Luftkrieg und Kriegsende 1943 bis 2005* (Munich: Dölling und Galitz Verlag, 2007).

106   There is no case study available on the local culture of memorial in Kassel, but the author's first researches in the Kassel Stadtarchiv and in the yearly runs of local newspapers indicate that the air attack of October 1943 on Kassel has had a similar impact in the local memory culture.

107   P. L. Berger and T. Luckmann, *The Social Construction of Reality* (New York: Doubleday, 1966); J. Habermas, *Der philosophische Diskurs der Moderne* (Frankfurt am Main: Suhrkamp, 1985); R. Grathoff, *Milieu und Lebenswelt: Einführung in die phänomenologische Soziologie und die sozialphänomenologische Forschung* (Frankfurt am Main: Suhrkamp Verlag, 1989).

108   J. Arnold, '"Nagasaki" in der DDR – Gedenken in Magdeburg' in J. Arnold, D. Süss and M. Thiessen (eds), *Luftkrieg. Erinnerungen in Deutschland und Europa* (Göttingen: Wallstein Verlag, 2009), 239–55.

109   Bibliothek für Zeitgschichte, Sammlung Sterz, letter from Reverend Heinrich M. (Hettingen), 26 March 1944: 'This week there were again powerful squadrons of enemy fliers in Frankfurt/M. and for hours on end they flew over our township and also disturbed us with heavy attacks and gruesome fireworks. Many hundreds of aircraft also flew over our village by day for further attacks on the city'.

11

Orchestrated Solidarity: the Allied Air War in France and the Development of Local and State-Organized Solidarity Movements

Michael Schmiedel[1]

After Rouen in Normandy had received its worst raid of the war at the hands of American and British bombers on 18 April 1944, the head of the Vichy regime, Philippe Pétain, addressed a message to the French people: 'It is at this moment, when our country is completely disarmed, that our former allies turn against us. My thoughts are always with you. Your pain is also mine.'[2] Pétain's message made two things clear: first, the war experience in France was not only heavily influenced by the German occupation but also by the Allied air raids that came as a consequence of it. Everywhere in France the population was threatened by bombing. The menace increased especially in 1943 and 1944 when Allied heavy bombers attacked not only industrial and military targets throughout France but also, from March 1944, transport and communication lines in order to prepare for the landing in Normandy in June. Second, Pétain's words suggested that despite the hardships, the Vichy state sought to help its bombed-out citizens, to promote solidarity among the French, and to use the raids to reinforce links with a population increasingly alienated from the regime.

One dimension of solidarity in the face of Allied bombing lay in the development of solidarity movements between French towns. There were two aspects to this. First, there were mostly local and private initiatives to bring together bombed-out towns and communities which had as yet been spared. Of these, the *Comité Lyon-Brest*, under which Lyon, as yet undamaged, acted as 'godparent' (*parrain*) to bomb-stricken Brest, is a perfect example. The second was the introduction of a scheme, developed and enforced by the Ministry of Interior, called *Adoption des communes sinistrées*, the adoption of war-damaged cities, a programme aimed at controlling locally-generated adoption projects and extending them across the whole of metropolitan France and even to Algeria. Encouraged by the adoption projects, large parts of the French population proved willing to make financial donations for their fellow countrymen in bombed cities. The mechanisms of fundraising, and the origins of the gifts, showed how the willingness to donate encompassed many sectors of society without stopping at traditional social boundaries. But it is also clear that these collections were exploited for propaganda purposes in order to create a national solidarity centred around the ideology of the Vichy regime and the head of state, Philippe Pétain.

BOTTOM-UP: THE *COMITÉ LYON-BREST*

The Breton port of Brest became a regular target for British, then American, bombers from summer 1940, thanks chiefly to its role as a base for big German surface warships and later for U-boats as well.[3] Lyon, by contrast, though one of France's most important metropolitan areas, was spared (like most of the rest of the south) until the spring of 1944.[4] Its population therefore knew of the devastation caused by Allied air attacks only from second-hand accounts. This was true even of Lyon's archbishop (and Catholic Primate of France), Cardinal Gerlier. On 22 August 1941 Canon Courtet, parish priest of Saint-Louis in Brest, invited Gerlier to visit the bombed town with a view to Lyon adopting it. He enclosed a number of photographs, including the wreckage of a big Catholic girls' school. Gerlier's first visit, which included both a tour of Brest and church services and prayers, took place that autumn.[5] After his return, he delivered a plea for help addressed from Courtet to the municipality of Lyon. The message was also supported by Brest's mayor, Victor Eusen, and by the town's diocesan bishop, Adolphe Duparc of Quimper and Léon.[6] On its receipt, Georges Villiers, mayor of Lyon, proposed to a public session of his municipal council on 8 December 1941 that Lyon adopt Brest. Villiers justified his proposal firstly in terms of solidarity. Lyon, as yet largely undamaged by the war (and not as yet occupied by German troops) had a duty to adopt a city in the north where war and occupation had already made a deep impact. It was also crucial, he continued, to re-establish relations with cities beyond the demarcation line drawn under the armistice of 1940, which had effectively divided the country into two almost sealed-off zones.[7] The adoption of Brest would be seen as a strong bond between the French population in the two zones, and Lyon could serve as a model of solidarity in face of air attack. After a brief debate the motion was adopted unanimously.[8]

Just a month after the adoption had been agreed by the Lyon city council, Georges Villiers, accompanied by a municipal delegation, visited Brest, where he presented the municipality with a first cheque of one million francs in aid of the air-raid victims.[9] The Lyon delegation was given a very warm welcome and the mayor's representative, Masson, praised in his welcoming remarks the generosity of the Lyonnais: 'What you have done for us is not only a gesture of solidarity, it is even more: it is an act of charity.'[10] The official reception was followed by a tour through the bombed areas of the city, allowing Villiers to see with his own eyes, like Gerlier a few months before, the destruction caused. On his return to Lyon, he encouraged the establishment of a permanent committee to supervise and co-ordinate all twinning activities and to serve as a liaison bureau for all the associations involved.[11] On 17 January 1942 the *Comité Lyon-Brest* started work. The committee consisted chiefly of municipal personnel, but also includes representatives of the Catholic Church and the Chamber of Commerce. Their most important task now was to establish and reinforce contacts between Brest and Lyon, to draft a priority list of projects to be supported and to organize and co-ordinate ideas, services and support that were proposed to the committee by private and Catholic associations. Soon the committee was supervising a wide range of activities: a big charity event, the *Journées de Brest*, was organized in Lyon, where the committee wooed visitors for donations. This event alone brought in another one million francs which were handed over to the special envoy sent from Brest for the occasion.[12] As far as the City of Lyon was concerned, the initial municipal gift of one million francs in January 1942 was repeated in 1943 and 1944, and topped up with an additional 500.000 francs in 1942 and more than 600.000 francs in 1943. The authorities in Brest distributed most of the money as direct cash payments to bombed-out townspeople. Donations for Lyon's adopted town came from clerical dignitaries as well as from municipal personnel: City Hall division heads urged employees to donate for the population in Brest. Donations also came from private sources, and from schools and colleges.[13] Cheques from schools were often accompanied by personal letters from the children who organized the collections, who reassured their companions in Brest that their suffering was not forgotten and that they were prepared to share their hardship. Compassionate sympathy with the difficult situation in Brest was clearly present in the letters as was an obligation to show solidarity and help its population.[14]

Besides financial aid, the committee also organized the collection and transport of donations of food and clothes. The donations of clothes were especially important and a number of consignments were met en route for Brest. The collections were generally organized on the initiative of private or charitable associations and financially and logistically supported by the *Comité Lyon-Brest*. The same went for the support for Brest's municipal library, which had been wrecked in the bombing. In Lyon a 'committee of friends of the Brest library' (*Comité des amis de la bibliothèque de Brest*) was founded in order to finance the reconstruction and the acquisition of new books. This initiative was also put under the supervision of the *Comité Lyon-Brest*, which acted more and more like an umbrella organization. In March 1945, after Lyon and Brest had already been liberated, the municipality in Lyon voted once again to support their adopted town and decided to pay for two lorries that could be used to counter the difficulties in supplying the population in Brest. The price of the two lorries, which were ordered from the Lyonnais producer Berliet, stood at 680.000 francs, not including the transfer to Brest.[15]

Equally important for the *Comité Lyon-Brest* was public relations, a measure that was also meant to increase revenue from donations. Because the Lyon-Brest partnership was backed by the municipality and the mayor, there was no difficulty in obtaining coverage in the Brest and Lyon newspapers. In addition, the committee published its own brochure, again to increase publicity and public attention. The booklet *Brest, notre filleule* (Brest, our godchild) combined articles on the committee's work, its history and especially on the solidarity between the two cities that outlasted the end of the war in 1945.[16] The committee also engaged in co-operation with the press: in spring 1944 a glossy magazine appeared as a fund-raiser for the committee's work. Nothing in the coloured magazine indicated the air war and its harsh consequences; on the contrary, it contained love stories and styling tips for the modern French lady. Many Lyon businesses, moreover, advertised in its pages.[17] To attract the public's attention, the *Comité Lyon-Brest* itself advertised in different newspapers and magazines. To prepare the *Journées de Brest* at the end of May 1943, both the public and businesses were therefore targeted with advertisements to donate directly to the mayor, who was pictured in an expectant pose.[18]

Besides activities for public relations, the coordination and supervision of various initiatives and fundraising, two more issues were of major importance for the committee: personal exchange and symbolic politics. Frequent official journeys between the two cities developed after Gerlier's and Villiers's initial trips to Brest. By the end of June 1942 the first return visit took place when Brest's mayor Eusen was welcomed in Lyon by regional prefect Angeli, who had himself been in 1937 prefect of Finistère,[19] the *département* in Brittany where Brest is situated. On their way back the Brest delegation stopped over at Vichy where they had an informal meeting with Pétain.[20] Another delegation from Lyon visited Brest in March 1943. There the representatives of the two cities celebrated the partnership in a symbolic ceremony to rename a street in Brest town centre 'rue de Lyon'. Just one month later, Cardinal Gerlier paid another visit to Brest and participated in the central ceremonies for the town's symbol *la Recouvrance*.[21] Again, just two months after Gerlier's visit, Lyon received another delegation from Brest who had been invited to attend the *Journées de Brest*. A little book was published about this journey shortly afterwards, where the itinerary was described in detail.[22] The reader was given an insight into how the events developed, what ceremonies were organized in favour of the adoption, and the biggest gathering, which had taken place at the central park in Lyon, *Tête d'Or*. The stay in Lyon was described as cordial and uncomplicated; there was not even any problem getting home after dark when the curfew imposed by the Germans had come into effect.[23] In August of the same year the new mayor of Lyon, Pierre Bertrand, who had replaced Georges Villiers in February, paid his inaugural visit.[24] Shortly before Christmas 1943, Mayor Eusen could also finally unveil a new street sign, renaming a major street in Lyon smart second *arrondissement* as 'rue de Brest'.[25] This symbolic gesture was already held up by Bertrand in May as a sign of further solidarity and a suitable sequel to the example of Brest.[26] The symbolic importance of the renaming was once again underlined by the presence of Cardinal Gerlier.

Before Eusen had left Lyon, the mayor had given an interview to the *Lyon Républicain*, and the complete front page of the Christmas edition in 1943 was dedicated to the activities of the *Comité Lyon-Brest*. The mayor urged the people of Lyon via the *Lyon Républicain* to take care especially of the children of Brest, because they were the country's only future.[27] This took up a theme present since the start of the adoption process. Already after his first visit to Brest, Georges Villiers declared bombed-out children to be one of his priorities.

He even told the Lyon council that he had already had numerous offers of accommodation from Lyon families, although he admitted that not every child could be saved from this 'perpetual nightmare' of air raids. But he called for at least 500 families in Lyon to be found to take in one of the children; in the end 300 came forward.[28] While in Lyon the authorities were still discussing how to organize such an exchange, and creating the first reception centres in order to coordinate the influx of children, the Brestois newspaper *Ouest-Éclair* published on 18 February 1942 a call to all heads of households whose families were affected by the Allied raids. This stated that now there were so many families ready to welcome one of the children, there was no turning away: 'You have no further right to hesitate', parents were told. Now it was urgent to take the children outside the threatened areas and hand them over to foster families in Lyon.[29]

The whole evacuation initiative, however, ended in complete failure. Few Brest families followed the call to evacuate their children. On 21 March 1942, the first convoy to leave Brest consisted of only 28 children; a second the following day carried only 15.[30] The timing of the first convoys, however, was unfavourable: it came just one month after the two German battleships *Scharnhorst* and *Gneisenau* had left Brest, giving the town a respite from Allied air attacks.[31] Not just in Brest, but also in Lyon, the members of the *Comité Lyon-Brest* had expected far more children. Therefore the authorities started yet another campaign to promote the evacuation scheme. The president of the committee in Lyon, Joseph Nicol, a financial manager, himself declared that his family would offer a 13-year-old girl from Brest a temporary new home.[32] But this appeal also died away unheard. When the third convoy to leave Brest assembled on 7 July 1942, the 22 children on the train were almost outnumbered by official representatives from the municipality and charity organizations on the platform.[33] The long distance – over 1,000 kilometres – from their home, and with it homesickness, were initially seen as the main reasons for low attendance. Under these circumstances many parents had no wish to be separated from their children.

But even the few children from Brest soon caused deep worries among authorities and foster parents. Shortly after the first evacuations, parents in Brest complained of not receiving any news from their children, whereas in Lyon the families insisted that they regularly sent letters to Brest or encouraged the children to do so themselves. This often inexplicable difficulty of getting news through led a number of families in Brest to try to bring their children back home. Then worried parents complained to local authorities about the lack of control in the repatriation of the children. Other parents went to Lyon on their own initiative without informing either the authorities or the foster parents. This attitude, and the authorities' inability to stop this behaviour, poisoned relations between the families in Brest and Lyon more and more. In return the foster parents also complained about the children. They were characterized as impertinent and uneducated, some of them even as little thieves. One child was accused of having stolen a precious ring, two five-dollar notes and a 1,000-franc note from his foster parent.[34] Under these circumstances the foster parents thought it impossible to keep the child for even one more day. In the course of 1944 another problem arose with the extension of the Allied air campaign to the whole of occupied France. Now many foster parents in Lyon could no longer offer what the children from Brest came for: protection against air raids. Some of the foster parents themselves had to leave their homes and find refuge in the countryside. Villiers's 'perpetual nightmare' had now reached Lyon too, and there seemed to the parents in Brest no further point in sending their children away. Thus ended this attempt to show a sign of tangible solidarity. In the end even the authorities had to admit that the number of evacuated children had not even reached one sixth of the 500 expected.[35]

What failed with the evacuation programme on an interpersonal level was working very well on an indirect level: solidarity expressed by donations of money, food and clothing was not only easier to organize for the local authorities, but most of all it mobilized far more people. Likewise political relations and symbolic acts developed well. The numerous reciprocal visits between Brest and Lyon, between both state and municipal representatives and Catholic priests from Cardinal Gerlier down, were especially remarkable. The aspirations of both came together in symbolic acts which were solemnly celebrated as a sign of national solidarity. Thus indirect and symbolic solidarity was a promising formula in order to organize help and to generate a feeling of social and national cohesion which would bind French society together in the face of Allied air raids.[36]

TOP-DOWN: THE *ADOPTION DES COMMUNES SINISTRÉES*

Local adoption projects, as in Lyon and Brest, soon attracted the attention of the government in Vichy.[37] There lay an opportunity to use these local activities to create a strong bond between state and citizens, while at the same time there was the possibility of raising urgently needed funds for the bombed-out towns. For the ambitious but cash-strapped *État Français*, this was a chance to demonstrate its capacity to act, to coordinate and to orchestrate these solidarity movements at low cost to the regime itself.

Indeed, Lyon was not the only city that had adopted a heavily damaged town. Other organizations and associations had already come up with their own initiatives to adopt bombed-out communities. These were quickly picked up by the Ministry of the Interior, which sent out its first circular on the matter to all prefects on 26 January 1942. This stated that Marshal Pétain, being very touched by these demonstrations of solidarity, had decided that these efforts should lie from now on in the hands of the government. Though private and local initiatives were greatly appreciated, strong arguments in favour of state control were brought forward. It was necessary to increase the efficiency and effectiveness of the solidarity movements. Only the state could ensure this. Furthermore, the government knew best how to organize and distribute help effectively on a national level. The purpose was to concentrate all solidarity efforts under one roof so that they could 'bear their full fruits'.[38] To underline its demand for control, the Ministry of the Interior prescribed a set of rules that the prefects had to comply with. First of all, the Ministry called for an overview of all adoption activities, now officially called *Adoption des communes sinistrées*. In addition there was a detailed four-part questionnaire. Prefects were invited to give an overview of partnerships already in place within their *départements*; to list towns and cities that could eventually be linked; and to supply a guide to all the towns and local communities affected by the war, with a detailed description of the damage and its causes.

The questionnaire thus served a double purpose: to get a first inventory of all initiatives already undertaken, and to establish a standard procedure for adoption that would guarantee the government's control over the whole programme. A further circular in October 1942 again advised prefects to submit detailed reports to the Ministry of the Interior. Rejecting allegations that the measures imposed were stifling local initiatives, the circular nevertheless pointed out that official procedures offered the only possibility of ensuring the distribution of help and organizing adoptions. From January 1943, moreover, the prefects had to report in detail every quarter on the *Adoption des communes sinistrées*.[39] The hitherto conciliatory tone changed from February 1943, when the Ministry of the Interior dispatched yet another circular, under the impact of the previous month's fierce raids on Lorient.[40] With the 'aggravation of raids', the circular said, prefects were now given a proactive role: to look for towns that could be linked.[41] Discussion of partnerships therefore became more intense in the following months. The authorities sensed a sincere willingness among local communities to adopt bombed towns, if only there were appropriate financial support. To address the financial issue there were discussions about different models for raising more money. The ideas extended from direct state sponsorship for local initiatives, the celebration of special adoption days within the whole *département*, to the idea of an extraordinary tax over a period from five to ten years.[42]

However, the most important source of income for adoption projects still came from private donations. The Vichy regime never introduced any compulsory measures to raise money for the programme. It was therefore crucial for the regime to coordinate fundraising campaigns held across the country. In order to achieve this the Ministry made clear that all fundraisers had to be recognized by the Secours National, the most important organization for helping French war victims.[43] The Secours National was a forceful semi-private organization that enjoyed a monopoly – at least of oversight – over all charity activities related to the war.[44] It had to approve all charity events, and most of the time the donations collected were distributed afterwards by the Secours National to victims.[45] Hence local representatives of the Secours National had to be involved in the planning of the partnership committees; campaigns for adopted towns could not be allowed to interfere with the nationwide activities of the Secours National. The *Comité Lyon-Brest* therefore coordinated its activities, especially charity events, with the local Secours National, while the municipal administration took care that the collections they asked from their employees did not interfere with one another.[46]

The *Adoption des communes sinistrées* programme was not limited just to bringing together towns bombed by the Allies. Some communities had already been bombarded during the invasion of 1940 and were equally in need. Most towns brought together by the adoption programme, however, had suffered at the Allies' hands. Indeed, the government's intervention had some effect on the number of adoptions. Soon after the circular of 26 January 1942, the number of partnerships increased significantly. In the Rhône *département*, Villefranche was twinned with Chablis in Burgundy, Caluire-et-Cuire with Toul in Lorraine, and Tarare with Gâvres in Brittany. In the case of Le Havre the municipality even extended the programme beyond metropolitan France, successfully seeking adoption by Algiers.[47] The mostly working-class industrial town of Saint-Etienne, which like Lyon escaped major Allied raids till Spring 1944, adopted Abbeville, a town on the Somme which had been badly hit by the Luftwaffe in the campaign of 1940.[48]

The activities initiated under the umbrella of the adoption scheme were similar to those of the *Comité Lyon-Brest*. Most of the administrations transferred money to their adopted town, but small towns could not be as generous as big cities like Lyon. Tarare and Villefranche could only afford to transfer 50,000 francs and 40,000 francs respectively to their twinned towns. But they were innovative when it came to organizing charity events. On 26 June 1943, Villefranche put on a formidable sports gala, organized by nine different associations, in order to help Chablis. Donations from this event, where the world and French fencing champion was a major attraction, were collected. The whole of Villefranche was mobilized and all 23 schools sent a group of their pupils to participate.[49] Elsewhere towns transferred not only money but also directed personal help to their adopted town. In the spring of 1943 the youth associations in Angers showed their solidarity in sending out groups of youngsters to help with the clearance of debris in Saint-Nazaire.[50]

On the site in Saint-Nazaire, the youngsters were congratulated by Colonel Bonhomme, Pétain's personal representative, on their 'formidable effort of national solidarity.' Colonel Bonhomme was specially assigned to this job, and spoke in Pétain's name during numerous trips in 1942 and 1943. In April 1943 he attended the opulent celebrations of the adoption of Saint-Nazaire by Angers, and of Trigniac by Cholet. Besides Bonhomme, representatives of almost all the municipal services, charity associations as well as the Catholic Church were also present. The official part of the ceremonies took place in Nantes, but the programme also included an excursion to Saint-Nazaire for the participants to see with their own eyes 'that the city was completely destroyed by a series of air raids, the most savage the country had known since the start of hostilities.[51] Colonel Bonhomme's presence at such celebrations helped attract nationwide attention for the *Adoption des communes sinistrées* programme. At the same time it was a moment to be seized by Vichy propaganda[52] to exploit the notion of solidarity for its own purposes. National solidarity, went the message, had to be organized nationally; French society was pictured as characterized by national unity where citizens stood together against Allied attacks. The government in Vichy itself was described as the co-ordinator of effective help, while Pétain was portrayed as a guardian behind whom the French nation could find cover. It was certainly not accidental that the propaganda evoked a connection to similar partnerships following the First World War; at that time there were already towns from the hinterland that helped other towns in the devastated war zones in the north and east of France.[53] Vichy propaganda tried relentlessly to draft a scenario where Pétain and the *État Français* appeared as protectors of a country under attack from its former allies (but ancient enemies). According to this tableau, the government took care of its citizens, giving assistance to the nation in need and comforting air-raid survivors. This interpretation was personified in Colonel Bonhomme's incessant tours, during which he left out almost no hospital where he could shake hands with victims and provide them with warm words from Pétain, chocolate and other gifts that were hard to find in wartime France. Obviously a team of the Information Ministry was always present at these occasions, along with selected journalists.[54]

Bonhomme's itinerary and the places and occasions where he appeared in public were carefully chosen and intended to show that the regime cared about its people and could act independently from the German occupying forces.[55] They also aimed to portray the regime and its leaders as guardians of the civilian population, an interpretation expressed in the concept of the partnerships. Cities that adopted another destroyed town called themselves 'godparent' (equally used in the female and male term: *marraine/parrain*) while the towns adopted were called 'godchild' (*filleule*). What started as a local initiative like the partnership between Lyon and Brest, originating in the mediation of the Catholic Church, was soon reframed as a symbol of national solidarity in the sense of the Vichy regime. In the end the *Comité Lyon-Brest* too fell under the control of the *Adoption des communes sinistrées* programme and submitted regular reports about its activities to the Ministry of the Interior.[56]

With regard to the increasing numbers of partnerships set up after the Ministry of the Interior took over the *Adoption des communes sinistrées* scheme, the policy of the regime paid off. The stakes were not high and the Vichy regime had only to apply low-level administrative acts and a celebrity special envoy. With these minimal efforts the Vichy regime could orchestrate impressively the solidarity of the French population, gain control over the programme, develop it further and exploit its activities for its propaganda. At the same time the civilian population also benefited from the scheme; the victims in the destroyed towns in particular accepted financial help and the donation of food and clothes as a gesture of genuine charity to help them cope with their everyday lives. The partnerships also served as a sort of moral reassurance that even in these dangerous times help was available.

CONCLUSION

The Vichy regime was not alone in seeking to use air raids to reinforce links between society and the state. In Germany, Nazi propaganda sought to include the victims of the Allied bombing into a mythical (and, of course, racially defined) *Volksgemeinschaft*.[57] In Britain, the far more inclusive 'Myth of the Blitz' described by Angus Calder owed much to the efforts of Churchill, the BBC and journals such as *Picture Post*.[58] But inter-community solidarity expressed by the *parrainages* was a uniquely French invention, drawing both on post-World War One precedents and on spontaneous initiatives within French society, in which the Catholic Church, in the case of the *Comité Lyon-Brest*, was a key player.

The solidarity showed to French victims of the Allied air war thus had two faces. On the one hand there was sincere sympathy and compassion to those in distress. On the other hand the solidarity was orchestrated, and its conductor was the Vichy regime. Under the common threat of Allied bombers, Vichy propaganda stage-managed the image of a society where everybody was welded together, citizens and victims, but also the population and the state. This external threat, which for once did not come from the Germans but from France's former allies, was exploited to create the idea of a population that gathered behind the state and was thus safe. National solidarity and the patriotic sense of unity had no limits in this conception; it involved all social classes and age groups, its lubricant being money and other donations.

The Allied air war and its effects on the French population were therefore the basis of a socialization that was orchestrated by the authoritarian Vichy regime. This found its expression especially in the bringing together of numerous delegations, and the development of strong bonds between the representatives of twinned towns, as in Lyon and Brest. What started as charitable initiatives on a local level were soon controlled by the Ministry of the Interior. The Vichy regime was clearly aware that these activities had the potential for a successful propaganda campaign. With Colonel Bonhomme the regime sent out someone who knew exactly how to play his role and appeal constantly to French national unity.

The experience of Allied air attacks thus had the power to establish new forms of movements committed to helping each other overcome the consequences that bombing brought on French society. The perception of violence, physically as well as in a representative collective form transferred and created by the mass media, led to a transmission of these violent experiences into social energy, expressed in various forms of solidarity movements. All these movements incorporated a notion of 'national solidarity' which was quickly seized by the Vichy regime in order to exploit these feelings for their own purposes; although many of the initiatives had developed from a private and local basis, the movements for helping bombed-out citizens and communities in France have to be seen as an 'orchestrated solidarity' where the Vichy regime aspired to control the whole process in order to use it for its own propaganda purposes.

Notes

1   The author would like to thank Professor Andrew Knapp for his invaluable comments and his editorial help. He would also like to thank Lindsey Dodd for her comments and for sharing her archival material so generously.
2   Philippe Pétain, 'Message du 21 avril 1944', in Barbas, Jean-Claude (ed.), *Philippe Pétain. Discours aux Francais, 17 juin 1940–20 août 1944* (Paris: Editions Albin Michael, 1989), 322.
3   Jean-Yves Besselièvre, 'Les bombardements de Brest (1940–1944)', *Revue Historique des Armées*, 2, 1998, 97–107.
4   The most destructive attack on Lyon took place on 26 May 1944, when more than 700 civilians lost their lives. See Gérard Chauvy, *Lyon 1940–1947* (Paris: Perrin, 2004), 235.
5   See 'Quelques vues des derniers bombardements. April–July 1941', in Archives de l'Archidiocèse de Lyon (AAL) (without signature). Other photos show Gerlier leading a procession in Brest which was attended by a huge crowd (AAL 11 II 236/9).
6   Archives Municipales de Lyon (AML), 1 C/702050, Comité Lyon-Brest, *Brest – notre filleule* (Lyon: Éditions Sève, 1945).
7   See É. Alary, *La ligne de démarcation* (Paris: Perrin, 2003).
8   AML, *Bulletin Officiel Municipal: Procès-verbaux des déliberations*, 21 December 1941, 'séance du 8 décembre 1941, 137: Adoption d'une proposition de M. le Maire tendant à accorder à la ville de Brest le parrainage de la ville de Lyon'.
9   Archives Départementales du Rhône (ADR), 3958 W120, Préfecture, Cabinet, Adoption des communes sinistrés (1942).
10   Archives Municipales et Communautaires de Brest (AMCB) 4 H4/29, Allocution de M. Masson, 7 January 1942.
11   AML, *Bulletin Officiel Municipal: Procès-verbaux des déliberations*, 25 January 1942, 'séance du 12 janvier 1942', 139.
12   See ADR, 3958 W120, Préfet du Rhône, 'Rapport trimestriel sur l'adoption des communes sinistrées', 26 April 1944.
13   See AML, 799/WP/003 for the register of donations for the Comité Lyon-Brest from September 1943 as well as individual receipts of money transfers for the whole year of 1943.
14   See AMCB, 4 H4/29, Lettre, Collège moderne, 7 January 1944 (and other letters in the same file).
15   AML, *Bulletin Officiel Municipal: Procès-verbaux des déliberations*, 4 February 1945, 'séance du 19 janvier 1945', 20; *ibid.*, 15 April 1945, 'séance du 26 mars 1945', 86.
16   AML, 1 C/702050, Comité Lyon-Brest, *Brest – notre filleule*.
17   AML 1 C/205071, *Lyon – Brest. Album consacré au prestige de la qualité française. Edité au profit du Comité Lyon-Brest.*
18   AMCB 4 H4/29: 'Your factory may be working poorly, but it's still working. Think of the ones in Brest! Take part in the *Journées de Brest* and send your personal gift to the mayor. He'll be expecting it!' (*Le Soir de Lyon*, 25 May 1943). Another advertisement went as follows: 'When you come home tonight, you'll find your wife and children. In Brest, they come home to nothing: their homes have been destroyed and their families scattered' (*Le Salut Public*, 26 May 1943).
19   See R. Bargeton (ed.), *Dictionnaire Biographique des Préfets. Septembre 1870–mai 1982* (Paris: Archives Nationales 1994), 54.

20 AMCB 4 H4/29, 'Lyon-Brest … sous le signe du Maréchal', *Ouest-Eclair*, 2 July 1943.

21 This journey was also documented in many photographs that can be found in AAL 11 II 239/6.

22 AML 1 C/4673, *Brestois à Lyon* (Brest: Imprimerie commerciale et administrative, 1943).

23 Ibid., 22.

24 Villiers had been dismissed by the Vichy government on (well-founded) suspicions of Resistance sympathies. See Géraldine Prompt, 'Le renouvellement des élites municipales à Lyon 1935–1953', *Rives nord-méditerranéennes*, 1, 1998 (http://rives.revues.org/document143. html, accessed 26 August 2009).

25 See *La Vie Lyonnaise*, 8 January 1944.

26 AML, *Bulletin Officiel Municipal: Procès verbaux des délibérations*, 20 June 1943, 'séance du 8 juin 1943', 78: 'Attribution du nom de la ville de Brest à une rue où une place de Lyon'.

27 *Lyon Républicain*, 23/24/25 December 1943: 'Le maire de Brest nous declare'.

28 AML, *Bulletin Officiel Municipal: Procès verbaux des délibérations*, 25 January 1942, 'séance du 12 janvier 1942', 139: exposé de M. le Maire sur son voyage à Brest.

29 AMCB 4 H4/29, 'Comité Lyon-Brest: Évacuation des enfants', *L'Ouest-Eclair*, 18 February 1942.

30 Ibid., '28 enfants brestois sont partis hier pour Lyon', *L'Ouest-Eclair*, 22 March 1942; 'Second convoi des enfants', ibid., 23 March 1942.

31 See R. Huguen, *La Bretagne dans la Bataille de l'Atlantique 1940–1945. La stratégie du Bomber Command appliquée à la Bretagne* (Spézet: Coop Breizh, 2003); J.-Y. Besselièvre, «Les bombardements de Brest (1940–1944)», *Revue Historique des Armées*, 2, 1998, 97–107.

32 AMCB 4 H4/29, 'Lyon-Brest … sous le signe du Maréchal', *L'Ouest-Eclair*, 2 July 1942.

33 Ibid., '22 petits brestois s'allèrent hier à Lyon', *L'Ouest-Eclair*, 8 July 1942.

34 AMCB, 4 H4/33, Letter to Monsieur Eusen, Président de la Délégation Spéciale de Brest, Lyon, 31 March 1944.

35 AML, 1 C/702050, Comité Lyon-Brest, *Brest – notre filleule*.

36 This became especially important when the financial and material aid provided from the state proved to be more and more insufficient. See Lindsey Dodd, chapter 4 in this book.

37 See H. Rousso, *Le régime de Vichy* (Paris: PUF, 2007); J. Jackson, *France: The Dark Years 1940–1944* (Oxford: Oxford University Press, 2003), 139–235.

38 ADR 3958 W120, Circulaire no. 20, 'Le Ministre, Secrétaire de l'Etat à l'Intérieur à Messieurs les Préfets. Objet: Adoption des communes sinistrées', 26 January 1942.

39 Ibid., Circulaire n. 202, 'Le Chef du Gouvernement, Ministre Secrétaire d'Etat à l'Intérieur à Messieurs les Préfets. Objet: Adoption des communes sinistrées', 16 October 1942.

40 See E. Florentin: *Quand les Alliés bombardaient la France* (Paris: Perrin, 1997), 88–101; P. Le Melledo, *Lorient sous les bombes. Itinéraire d'un Gavroche lorientais* (Le Faouet: Liv'éditions 2003).

41 ADR 3958 W120, Circulaire no. 72. Le Chef du Gouvernement, Ministre Secrétaire d'Etat à l'Intérieur à Monsieur le Préfet Régional de Lyon. Objet: Adoption des communes sinistrées, 15 February 1943.

42 See Archives Nationales, Paris, (AN), F/1c III/1198, 'Synthèse des Rapports Mensuels des Préfets de la Zone occupée', April 1943.

43 ADR 3958 W120, Circulaire no. 142, 'Le Chef du Gouvernement, Ministre Secrétaire d'Etat à l'Intérieur à Messieurs les Préfets. Objet: Adoption des communes sinistrées', 13 May 1943.

44 See J.-P. Le Crom, 'De la philanthropie à l'action humanitaire', in P.-J. Hesse and J.-P. Le Crom, (eds), *La protection sociale sous le régime de Vichy* (Rennes: Presse Universitaires de Rennes, 2001), 183–236; J. Kulok, 'Trait d'union: The history of the French relief organization *Secours National/Entr'aide française* under the Third Republic, the Vichy regime and the early Fourth Republic 1939–1949', D. Phil. thesis, University of Oxford, 2003.

45 On the tasks of the Secours National see L. Dodd, chapter 4 in this book.

46 In 1942 the staff of the municipal roadworks division was asked to donate for the Secours National. The following year the collection was designated for the Comité Lyon-Brest. The amount for the two collections was almost the same. See AML 937 WP185, 'Service de la Voirie, Division de la voie publique, Collecte organisé au profit du Secours National (1942) et sinistrés de Brest (1943)'.

218 BOMBING, STATES AND PEOPLES IN WESTERN EUROPE 1940-1945

47 AN, F/1c III/1188, 'Rapport Mensuel d'Information. Préfet de la Seine-Inférieure', February 1942.
48 See AAL (no code no.), *Semaine Religieuse, Diocèse de Lyon*, 7 January 1944.
49 ADR 3958 W120, 'Le Maire de Villefranche-sur-Saône à Monsieur le Préfet, Rhône', 5 July 1943, and the enclosed coloured agenda card for the event.
50 AN 2 AG22, 'Angers au secours de sa filleule Saint-Nazaire', *Le Matin*, 28 April 1943.
51 Ibid., 'L'adoption des cités martyrs de Saint-Nazaire et de Trigniac par les villes d'Angers et de Cholet', *Le Petit Courrier*, 9 April 1943.
52 For a general overview on the activities of Vichy propaganda see L. Gervereau and D. Peschanski (eds), *La propagande sous Vichy 1940–1944* (Paris: BDIC, 1990); D. Rossignol, *Histoire de la propagande en France de 1940 à 1944. L'utopie Pétain* (Paris: Presses Universitaires de France, 1991); F. Denoyelle, *La photographie d'actualité et de propagande sous le régime de Vichy* (Paris: Editions CNRS, 2003).
53 AML, *Bulletin Officiel Municipal: Procès-verbaux des déliberations*, 21 December 1941, 'séance du 8 décembre 1941', 137. During the first session in Lyon when the partnership with Brest was discussed there were remarks on Lyon's twinning with Saint-Quentin and Laon in 1918. I have been unable to find scholarly studies of these early *parrainages*. However, records do exist, for example, on http://www.crdp-reims.fr/memoire/bac/1gm/dossiers/reconstruction. htm (accessed 16 March 2010; for Reims) and on http://actualites-grande-guerre.blogspot. com/2009/12/une-ville-filleule.html (accessed 16 March 2010; for the smaller commune of Trucy (Aisne)).
54 Within ten months from October 1942 to August 1943, Bonhomme visited 53 towns, many, like Paris, twice or even more often. Constantly on the road, he sometimes 'did' five towns in a single month. See AN 2/AG/21, 'Deplacements, colonel Bonhomme en représentation du Maréchal Pétain, octobre 1942–septembre 1943'.
55 In fact the German occupiers neither supported nor obstructed the activities within the adoption scheme. Thus most of the delegates who travelled from Brest to Lyon and vice versa were granted permits to travel and to cross the demarcation line before it was (officially) abolished in March 1943.
56 See ADR 3958 W120, 'Mairie de Lyon à la Préfecture, Rhône. Rapport trimestriel sur l'activité, Comité Lyon-Brest, 4ème trimestre 1943', 6 January 1944.
57 See D. Süss, 'Nationalsozialistische Deutungen des Luftkrieges', in Id. (ed.), *Deutschland im Luftkrieg. Geschichte und Erinnerung* (München: Oldenbourg, 2007), 99–110.
58 A. Calder, *The Myth of the Blitz* (London: Jonathan Cape, 1991), 120.

12

The True Cause of the 'Moral Collapse': People, Fascists and Authorities under the Bombs. Naples and the Countryside, 1940–1944*

Gabriella Gribaudi

BOMBING IN ITALY

Six weeks before Italy's entry into World War Two, the British Chiefs of Staff planned a bombing campaign against major Italian cities in the conviction that this would prove decisive in forcing the country to surrender. Italy was judged to be a vulnerable enemy due to its economic weakness, its poorly developed anti-aircraft defences, its lack of military preparation, but above all because the 'Italian psyche was unsuited to war'. It was believed that systematic bombing would easily depress the morale of the Italian people: it was therefore necessary 'to destroy the morale of the Italians with heavy attacks at night and, with suitable weather conditions, during the day against the four most important industrial cities'. The objectives were to be chosen in order 'to increase the moral effects over as wide an area as possible'.[1]

The RAF's early raids against specific industrial and military targets in continental Europe, executed with a very small bomber force, proved ineffective, and from February 1942 the strategy shifted to the area bombing of cities, with a view to wrecking the morale of civilians and particularly of industrial workers.[2] By late 1942 Italy, which was clearly in a state of crisis following the defeat of its forces in Africa, seemed to be the easiest target. It was hoped that intensive raids would provoke a crisis among its ruling classes:

> The attack should be concentrated against a selection of the most important cities and naval bases. The provisional list is: Milan, Rome, Naples, Turin, Genoa, Taranto, Spezia and Brindisi ... the monthly scale of attack on Italy should be about 4,000 tons a month. This is comparable with the average weight of attack delivered on Germany over the past three months.[3]

Between October and December 1942, the main Italian cities sustained large-scale area bombing. In October and November, Genoa, Turin and Milan were

*Translated from the Italian by Colum Fordham.

hit, while Naples was bombed in December. The population clearly became a hostage of war: it was constantly told that it had to separate its destiny from that of Mussolini and Germany, and to rebel and commit acts of sabotage in order to save itself. Together with the bombs, the civilian population was bombarded with thousands of leaflets containing messages to Italians. The latter were described as a pacific people who had been driven to war by the Fascist regime, and must therefore rebel against their dictator. Mussolini, together with the Nazi ally, were the sole culprits for the deaths caused by aerial warfare. And if the population failed to separate its own fate from that of the two dictators, this would be tantamount to signing its own death warrant, as emphasized in a leaflet dropped by the RAF in May 1943:

> Hitler and Mussolini have condemned Italy to becoming a 'no man's land'. No man's land: this term is used by strategists to define the desolate sector situated between two fronts of combat.... You will learn what it means to become no man's land, the centre of a battlefield fought over with modern weapons ... what has happened so far is nothing compared to what Hitler and Mussolini are about to bring to your country. If we tell you that Italy will become 'no man's land', we are being perfectly serious; your country will be exposed to bombardment, machine-gunning, and wholesale disorganization; numerous houses will end up in flames, and corpses will litter cities and the countryside. Cold in winter, infections during the summer, dismay and hunger will multiply.[4]

The language could not be more explicit. This leaflet carried an intimidatory message which was designed to instil fear and which threatened a tragic fate to its readers. And indeed, the situation had deteriorated by August, as the second major wave of raids on Italian cities gathered pace.[5] The Fascist regime had collapsed on 25 July, but the new government headed by Marshal Badoglio had declared that Italy would continue to fight the war alongside their German allies. The bombardment would therefore have to continue with even greater intensity. Such intentions were expressed in a document produced by the Northwest African Strategic Air Force Command on 1 August 1943, with the significant title of 'Psychological Bombardment Operation Designed to Drive Italy to Surrender':

> It is firmly believed that now is the time for decisive blows to be dealt against the ragged nerves and crumbling morale of the Italian people, especially during this period of readjustment and reorganization caused by the collapse of Mussolini's regime. This can be done by properly displaying the devastating power of the Strategic Air Force. To make it even more impressive and terrifying, they should be given a list of specially selected Italian cities which are to be systematically isolated and totally destroyed. Operations against these cities should be periodic and spaced between other operations.... These cities should be carefully selected so that all of Italy will feel the tremendous effect of such a war. This list should contain cities such as Rome, Naples, Florence, Genoa and Venice as these cities are nearest to the heart of the Italian people.[6]

The strategy of moral collapse was accompanied throughout the war by bombardment aimed at blocking the economic and military activities of the enemy country and by tactical raids linked to naval and land operations. Amongst the various types of 'precision' bombing, we can distinguish between raids carried out on factories which had begun when Italy entered the war, those linked to Allied landings (Sicily, Salerno, Anzio), and ground support

Naples, September 1943. Bombing of the port and of the area of Santa Lucia, via Caracciolo, Riviera di Chiaia: NARA, 342-FH-3A-25340. Courtesy of US National Archives.

operations close to the front lines. Tactical raids in support of the three major landings took a heavy toll on southern Italy. Many cities and towns suffered devastating attacks, and in some cases were razed to the ground, because they were situated on the banks of a river, near a bridge of strategic importance, or because they were considered important railway or road junctions or the location of factories. The scale and relative inaccuracy of 'precision' daytime bombing meant that its results were almost identical to those of area bombing: collective memory has classified both within the category of 'carpet-bombing'.

This chapter analyses the geographical area that stretches from the bay of Salerno, where the Allies landed on 9 September 1943, to southern Lazio, the site of one of the longest and bloodiest battles of the war on the western front (the battle of Cassino, October 1943–May 1944). This geographical area can be defined as an illustrative example for studying ordinary people's experience of bombing in the Second World War. Naples, the largest southern city and one of the largest in Italy, as well as being of critical military importance because ships with soldiers and supplies for North Africa left from its port, was the most heavily bombarded city in Italy. Campania and southern Lazio were also subjected to air raids linked to the Salerno and Anzio landings, and the advance of Allied troops until the long battle of Cassino.[7]

Detailed analysis of Naples and Campania should enable us to respond to several questions which are of crucial importance for research on the war and air raids in particular: What was the experience of the population in the towns and cities that were bombed? What was the relationship between the authorities and the population? What contradictions emerged? What were the internal contrasts within the populations? The Allies' approach to the bombing campaign in Italy briefly outlined above clearly shows the conviction that air attacks would play a decisive role in the country's collapse. Was this really the case? Did the air raids distance Italian citizens from the regime?

From the documents and testimonies of the time an evident link emerges between the progressive growth of hostility towards the Fascist regime and the continual evidence of ineptitude offered by its ruling classes to a population distressed by the sufferings of war. The authorities' loss of legitimacy proceeded simultaneously with food deprivations, queues at food shops, the dangerous and disorganized shelters and the evident inefficiency and lack of responsibility of those who represented the state institutions. Social fractures widened (poor versus rich, city dwellers versus country people), but so did the gap between local communities and the 'leader', who was unable to protect the people he claimed to govern.[8]

STRATEGIC AND TACTICAL BOMBING: NAPLES AND THE LANDING AREA

Naples was struck by air raids right from the start of the war in June 1940, but the first raids were little more than demonstrative. The real raids arrived in waves in autumn 1940, in the summer and autumn of 1941 and in the winter of 1941–2. In this first period, RAF bombers struck the towns and cities of the bay of Naples. The main targets were industrial districts and the districts of the old historic centre overlooking the sea and the port, which was to remain a key objective until the liberation of the city.

From December 1942 to September 1943, Naples and Campania were attacked by bombers of the United States Army Air Forces, which were assigned the task of striking southern Italy from North African bases. This period coincides with the intense campaign of carpet-bombing that was intended to bring about the collapse of the Fascist regime. Most of the raids took place during the day in accordance with the procedures favoured by the Americans. These raids were particularly devastating. As a consequence, collective memory recalls the British RAF almost as the gentlemen of the air while only the Americans were associated with carpet-bombing. In oral memory the two periods are distinctly separated by the massive bombing raids of 4 December 1942, and the recollection of the greatest hardships, destruction and loss of life is linked to the 'American period'. In reality, as we shall see, the records indicate an increasing crescendo of hardship, fears and discontent beginning from the winter of 1940–1, and this was to continue for the rest of the war.

The period from June to July 1943 was marked by raids in preparation for the Allied landings. The Sicilian cities had already been ravaged by the bombings, and these were followed by the towns and cities of continental southern Italy, and in particular the region where the landings took place on 9 September 1943. The most ferocious raids took place in Campania on 9 September 1943, the day after the armistice, when the population was celebrating the end of the war.[9] This time the strategic objectives were those points considered to be of crucial importance to the German retreat. After the first heavy bombings, many of the inhabitants of the bay of Naples were evacuated to provincial towns without realizing what lay in store for these areas (chosen as safe havens); after the armistice, they found themselves at the epicentre of the war. The list of air-raid victims across the province of Naples included numerous families who had fled there from the city. For the whole of September the towns and cities that lay between the bay of Salerno and the fortification lines that the Germans were constructing along the roads and railway lines – which were to witness the retreat of the Wehrmacht and the advance of the Allied troops – were devastated by continuous raids.

After 8 September the violence of the bombing was compounded by that of the German troops who occupied Italian territory and fought against the Allied advance in Campania. There was to be further destruction and yet more victims. It was a brutal period, full of uncertainty. Italian institutions were on the verge of collapse. The terrible predictions in the British leaflets were coming true and Campania had become a no man's land. In Campania and in southern Lazio, Allied air raids continued until the German Gustav line was destroyed and abandoned. Naples, on the other hand, which had been liberated on 1

October 1943, was hit by three German attacks, the last of which took place on 15 March 1944 when no one expected it. It was one of the most serious raids of the war. German raids claimed at least 470 victims according to official statistics, even though there is virtually no recollection of the event in the city's collective memory.

VICTIMS

How many victims did bombing claim in Naples? It is almost impossible to give a precise number. Journalist Aldo Stefanile suggests 20,000, without providing the sources on which he based his estimate.[10] In a note dated 1 June 1943 and addressed to the head of wartime affairs at the Italian Ministry of the Interior, the prefect estimated the number of victims in the province of Naples at 1,499, including 1,388 victims in the city of Naples. But this figure does not even correspond to the total number of victims on the lists provided on each occasion by the prefecture itself. If a total is calculated from the official lists contained in the reports made until 21 September 1943, then the figure goes up to about 3,100, to which the 470 victims of the German raids need to be added. With enormous difficulty, given the number of inhabitants and the quantity of civil status registers, I have tried to calculate the number of victims during the most tragic year of the war, 1943, and I have estimated a total of about 6,000.[11] However, it is necessary to add the lists for 1940, 1941 and 1942 to this figure. If it is borne in mind that many bodies were not buried, and many people were reported missing, or were never reported or only reported much later, then the figure worked out from the city council registry lists would appear to be mistaken. I am therefore unable to establish how many victims there were of bombings in Naples and its surrounding province, but I would argue that the prefecture's figures are definitely a considerable underestimate.

To the direct victims of air attack we should add deaths caused by typhus or by other infectious diseases, by the cold or by hardship. The case of children can be examined by way of example. We can begin by examining the 'normal' records of the municipal section of a poor district from 29 July to 12 August 1943. Over a period of 15 days, 51 deaths are registered, including 29 children under the age of four, among them a child aged ten months, another four years old, yet another ten-month-old baby, a baby of only 16 days, a one-year-old, two babies aged seven months, a two-year-old and a four-year-old. It is a well-known fact that children are the first victims in these circumstances but reading the list has a profound effect and is a useful exercise in historical understanding. It is worth analysing a few lists. On 15 April 1943 among the 66 victims at Torre del Greco there were six siblings aged from three to 13. During the night of 14–15 December 1940, in a 'minor', 'precision' attack, the victims included Angela Miele, aged 41, and her four children aged from one to 17. On 14 March 1944 in piazzetta San Gregorio Armeno n. 2, Elena Capaldo died with her four children aged 6, 5, 3 and 2.[12] Her husband, the only one to escape, had lost his whole family in a single fleeting moment of the war.

We can examine another case, chosen from among the towns that were targeted by the bombings linked to the advance of the Allies. Teano is a small town in Campania which stood between two German fortification lines, the Barbara line and the Bernhard line, and along the line of the Allied advance, in other words at the epicentre of the fighting. The town was bombed between 6 and 22 October 1943. Among the 110 victims of the raids who appear in council records (we have no way of knowing the number of unburied bodies, which remained among the ruins and whose disappearance was recorded years later), there were 61 girls and boys aged between five months and 14 years old (22 were under five), more than 55 per cent; among the adults (19–55 years old), women made up 70 per cent.[13]

On 25 November 1943 two brothers-in-law, Claudio Trifiletti and Francesco Adinolfi, came to the council to report the total disappearance of both their families, crushed under rubble in piazza Duomo on 6 October. Trifiletti had simultaneously lost his mother, two sisters, his wife and four children.[14] Most members of the destroyed families had previously lived in Naples and had been evacuated to their ancestral homes to avoid raids on the city. This was the fate of many other Neapolitans who could not have known that the whole region would become a war zone.

Although many Neapolitan victims were killed by collapsing buildings, others were crushed in shelters by crowds seeking escape from the bombs, or died from the epidemics that resulted from the appalling sanitary conditions in which they lived. An important part of the problem was shelter provision. Most shelters in Naples were made, with minimal additional work, from the ancient hollows that lay beneath the city. Of these, some had been the refuge of early Christians, others dug out over the centuries from the quarrying of tuff stone for building, while still others were made from the Bourbon waterworks; they were connected by incredibly long tunnels that stretched throughout the bowels of the city. The underground, with its stations, formed another shelter widely used by Neapolitans. Everywhere there were long, steep flights of steps, underground tunnels and passages where hordes of people thronged, fleeing in panic; a person could easily trip and a disaster ensue. There are endless episodes, as emerges from the records of the prefecture which reports about 20 cases of shelters collapsing and multiple deaths caused by pressing crowds of people. This is one description provided by an anonymous informer in October 1941:

The seriousness and violence of the enemy air raids alarm all parts of the population, who flee in a chaotic rush towards the entrances of the public shelters, fully aware now that the makeshift private shelters do not offer any guarantee of safety, without any proper strutting or adequate support. Everyone says that it is necessary to increase the number of entrances to these public shelters, which provide greater safety. In the poorer areas – between Montecalvario and S. Ferdinando – there is a shelter capable of taking thousands of people, but there is a completely inadequate number of entrances, and the people remain outside during the bombings waiting for their turn to enter. At the entrance in vico d'Afflitto wild scenes could be observed: children rolling on the ground, people suffocated by the violent pressing of the crowds as they came from all the surrounding streets and lanes. In the darkness scuffles broke out which degenerated into furious fights, creating indescribable panic which lowers the morale of the population who say their lives are not being protected by the authorities.[15]

A letter dated 15 November 1941 describes life in the air-raid shelters: sick people and invalids carried by volunteers moved by the spirit of humanity, hundreds of children who 'lie on the floors of public and private shelters on a few rugs or rags, and spend the entire night in cold, damp rooms with stale air which is detrimental to the health and development of these delicate young souls'. On 21 November another informer added further details:

> The public complain that the long air raids force them to spend nights in shelters which lack the most basic sanitary facilities, with no proper toilets and no drains; the stench makes the air, which is already rarefied by the considerable number of people sheltering there, almost unbreathable. People complain that they have to spend the night standing since there are no benches or anything else on which to sit. They complain of the lack of water and everything that could be useful for first aid, despite the many cases of women and children fainting due to the lack of necessary nutrition.... Following the continued and prolonged enemy raids the inhabitants of working-class neighbourhoods such as Vicaria and Mercato complain about the lack of shelters and the lack of places to sit in any of them. Indeed, on recent nights it has been possible to observe that certain public shelters ... are crowded with people so that after a few hours the air becomes rarefied and the temperature increases to an extent that breathing is almost impossible. The lack of benches to sit on, toilets and adequate running water lowers the depressed morale of the population who are forced to relieve themselves as best they can at the expense of their decency.[16]

In autumn 1943 thousands of homeless families lived on a regular basis in the shelters. As many as 11,930 people lived everyday in the bowels of the city.[17] The commission that conducted the inquiry into the homeless compiled a list of 41 shelters crammed with evacuees in the old quarters of Naples, the area which had been most heavily bombed and had the highest concentration of people with no alternative resources (without relatives with large houses who could shelter them and without the possibility of renting other accommodation). There are several particularly striking cases. The shelter in via Foria n. 76 was inhabited by '43 families affected by the disaster, all of them lacking financial means and accommodation, making a total of 211 people'; in the same street at n.106, 108 and 122 there were as many as 107 families with a total of 876 people; at Montecalvario in the shelter in vico Tofa and vico Lungo Trinità degli Spagnoli there were 400 families with 2,000 people overall; the shelter in the

Petraio, the steps of San Nicola da Tolentino and corso Vittorio Emanuele (the station and the gallery of the central funicular railway station) were home to 150 families with 2,000 people overall, and the shelters of San Lorenzo between piazza San Gaetano, via Nilo, via Tribunali and Porta San Gennaro housed about 230 families with about 1,900 people.[18]

The writer Anna Maria Ortese, in her account written immediately after the war, described the situation of roughly 3,000 homeless people housed in the port in the Granili, the old Bourbon warehouses for wheat: an infernal maze of gloomy, foul-smelling rooms, seething with humanity who had been made sick and dirty by poverty, by the dark and by the almost total lack of sanitation. Men and women appeared in the half-light of a few lamps situated between doors 'made of planks, sheets of metal, pieces of cardboard or faded curtains', 'larvae of a life where the wind and the sun once existed' but of which 'they had almost lost all memory'.[19] It was in these conditions that the typhus epidemic spread. The victims of typhus should therefore be included as part of the 'side effects' of the bombings. In order to deal with the epidemic the Allies created a commission, which produced a report on its causes and suggested the measures to defeat it. The report began in this way:

> The city had suffered very severe damage. The gas, electricity, water and sewage systems were out of action and a considerable number of people lived more or less permanently in air-raid shelters. It was evident that these factors, operating in a depressed, malnourished, unwashed populace of nearly a million, were ideal for the occurrence and rapid dissemination of infectious disease.... During the period October 1943 to February 1944, there were 1,500 known cases of typhus in Naples and its immediate vicinity. Little information could at first be obtained as to the occurrence of cases in previous months. The initial focus of infection was probably the Russian Front. Contact cases occurred later in the prisons and in the shelter population. No vigorous effort had been made to combat the threatened outbreak at its inception. In the late summer an almost complete disruption of essential services and disorganization of medical arrangements made control almost impossible with the facilities then available to the Italians. By this time the shelter population had increased and the louse incidence in the population was very high. Air raids during October augmented the difficulties.[20]

In a report dated 4 April 1944 the Allied medical commission presented an official figure of 1,841 cases of typhus, with a mortality rate of 15 per cent, which increased to 50 per cent among those aged over 50. The epidemic reached its peak in January 1944. There are accounts of hospitals where it was impossible to provide treatment; indeed, there was an extremely serious risk that even the doctors might become ill: the Cotugno hospital, which specialized in infectious diseases, had undergone semi-occupation by the armed forces, had been bombed and had no windows left at all. Nearly all the houses and public buildings in the city had no windows during the particularly cold winter of 1943–4. The Allies had taken drastic measures to combat the epidemic. The most well-known and widely used solution was DDT. Disinfestation centres with insecticide were opened in various quarters, in the railway station, the hospitals, the port and the refugee camps. Italian doctors and nurses were taken on; teams had worked in the shelters during the nights. About 60,000 people had been treated every day and by the end of February about 250,000 people had been disinfected; 60,687 people had been inoculated with the vaccine.[21]

GROWING DISCONTENT

Even though the Fascist regime's propaganda machine worked throughout the war to tone down the most tragic news, to conceal the air raids[22] and to minimize the defeats of the army, discontent grew from 1940 on. This is clear from the reports of prefects, chiefs of police and *Carabinieri* who were forced, against their will, to take note of the situation and inform the Ministry of the Interior. From the very beginning of the war the civilian population was aware of the inefficiency of the anti-aircraft defences. This situation was common to all Italian towns and cities, and protests were equally widespread. The records and archives in Naples reveal that there was continual criticism. An informant wrote the following in July 1941:

> For an entire night the enemy had full control of the skies of Naples with the chance of striking and hitting the most inaccessible sites. The public is not informed about our defences. Nevertheless they realize that the defences are almost non-existent and are anxious that this is happening in a city which has already been the target of enemy raids and therefore deserving of greater and much more serious guarantees. Twenty-four hours after the first bombings it should have been possible to avoid the disaster of the refineries and the ammunition dumps. There would have been time but the necessary foresight was lacking. This is the general mood; mistrustful opinions and views are not just held by the lower classes but also by the middle and upper classes. A judge I know told me yesterday, 'Not only do we have to resign ourselves to the inefficiency of rationing but also to the inefficiency of our defences'. This judge (president of the Court of Appeal) is not only someone who is concerned with order but a passionate Fascist who yearns for the victory of our forces. One cannot close one's eyes to certain kinds of evidence.[23]

The awful performance of anti-aircraft defences and the growing pessimism of the population were underlined by several informants in October of the same year. The population observed that enemy aircraft could fly unopposed for hours, selecting their targets and seriously damaging the economic structure of the city. Informants stressed that mistrust in the regime was growing, and that the propaganda from Radio London and from the Allied leaflets (which described the faults of Fascism and invited Italians to abandon it) was increasingly popular.[24] Evident hints of such mistrust appeared in the anonymous letters sent to the authorities, held among the prefect's files:

> 'We Neapolitans want to be defended by our soldiers and not by senile militiamen shooting haphazardly'; 'For the anti-aircraft defences we want soldiers and not money-grabbing Fascists'; 'The population of Naples must be defended by soldiers and not by Fascists'; 'It is shameful that not one English plane has been shot down. This depends on the anti-aircraft militia. It would be better if these money-grabbing militiamen were replaced once and for all by soldiers'.[25]

Besides the criticism of anti-aircraft defence, reports by anonymous informants provide a record of the unrest and protests against the inefficiency of the rationing system, the scarce food rations, the delay in delivering them and the queues. The reports became even more serious and concerned in December 1942 following the massive area bombing raids aimed at inflicting a decisive blow on the morale of Italian civilians. References are made to hours and hours of queuing, rationed goods delivered with more than a month's delay, and numerous protests by women. The famine and inadequate functioning of the rationing system occupy pages and pages of censored letters.

Despite their cautious tone, confidential reports could not avoid admitting the increasing disenchantment with the regime and its propaganda. The population was becoming aware that the war was being lost, and capable of evaluating the relationship between reality and propaganda. All the reports invariably mentioned that the population's morale was particularly low as a result of the news coming from the fronts. And when things did go well, as in April 1941 in Africa, it was clear to Italians that most of the credit went to their German allies:

> There is new faith in the certainty of final victory …; however, it is noted that these opinions exalt the contribution of our ally and its military potential with too much emphasis, losing sight and almost devaluing the immense effort and huge sacrifices that we have made.[26]

The war unmasked the regime's propaganda and revealed its lies, the empty rhetoric of Fascism:

> Our contribution to the war against the enemies of the Axis is judged to be almost insignificant. It is observed that this costs us considerable losses, especially in terms of material resources, in the Mediterranean, due to the continuous combined attacks of submarines and torpedo bombers; and it is feared that very soon, as a result of the deficiency of the merchant navy, it will prove impossible to reinforce and supply our troops in North Africa. The raid on the port of Gibraltar by our assault forces has created an excellent impression; however, the propaganda that the radio and press

continue to make about the raid is not appreciated because it is not judged to be proportionate to the actual results.[27]

There was growing awareness of both the ineptitude and irresponsibility of the Fascist ruling class. On 27 March 1943 an emblematic incident took place in Naples when a ship full of ammunition exploded in the port. A fire had started in the morning, probably as a result of a technical error, and had not been brought under control; it continued all day until the explosion in the afternoon. The technicians and the various authorities concerned had either failed to intervene or had reciprocally put off taking decisions. In the end the explosion had the effect of a terrible bombardment. The following is the report of the episode by the chief of police:

> Nothing was done to sink the ship by flooding it, when initially the extent of the fire might have made this possible by opening the safety valves near the engines. And even if this had not been possible due to the shallow water, no attempt was made to tug it offshore which could have been done without great problems, since the ship was not anchored but moored with tow-ropes which could easily have been cut. What should be emphasized is the indecision shown by the port authorities, the lack of coordination and sense of responsibility, and the inadequacy of the initiatives that were taken.... Precious time was wasted as a result of doubts and indecision; neither was there any proper evaluation of the tragic effects that the explosion might have had, so that the only precaution taken was to evacuate the area within a radius of 500 metres, while it would have been possible to avoid many victims in the city if only the authorities concerned had given the order to sound the alarm sirens.... I must also add that the officer on duty at the Provincial Committee of Anti-aircraft Protection at the prefecture asked for information about the first explosions which were clearly heard in the city both from the Dicat (Anti-aircraft Defence Militia) and from the Harbour Office which replied, I would venture to say, in an almost superficial manner.[28]

In the letter enclosed with the reports, the fire-fighting officer sent by the commanding officer to confer with the Harbour office and the Port Authorities at 14.35 reported that he could not find any senior officer in their offices. At the Operations Office of the Port Authorities, where he and the Military Commissioner of the ship *Caterina Costa* had pointed out the seriousness of the situation, they had been told that 'without orders from senior offices, it was not possible to take any decision.'[29] The rest of the document is a description of people rushing to and fro across the port, carrying useless messages and trying to make the authorities take decisions that were never taken.

After this long series of omissions, the ship exploded at 5.30 pm 'scattering burning wreckage and a huge number of projectiles in a wide radius all over the city'.[30] Naples was covered by

> a hail of incandescent detritus, as sharp as guillotine blades.... A hail of iron and fire, a hail of red-hot fuses, bullets, cartridge and shell cases, a hail of metal sheets, pieces of

tanks, shapeless metal forms wrenched from the ship and its load, from wharves and from houses rained down on the streets. A piece of ship ended up on the bridge of the Maddalena, where two rows of houses collapsed, burying the inhabitants. It was the most savage and terrible devastation of the whole zone of Granili, Caserma Bianchini, Lavinaio and Borgo Loreto.[31]

The entire city was affected. Nearly all the glass in doors and windows was broken; the force of the explosion caused partition walls and ceilings to collapse in many houses, but the damage done to the districts closest to the port and the number of victims in these areas resembled a full-scale bombing raid. The inspector of the Office of Works calculated that 50,000 buildings had been damaged.[32] The historic basilica del Carmine was seriously damaged, a fire broke out in the State Archive, the wharves of the port exploded, and damage was also caused to the bonded warehouses as well as the factories and plants of the industrial zone which had already been the targets of regular bombing raids; the gasometer was seriously damaged, causing interruptions to the supply of gas throughout the city. In some areas, lighting was cut off and tramlines were rendered unusable. The central railway station and the Circumvesuviana station were seriously affected and there was an undetermined number of victims among people packed into trains or waiting on platforms. The backdrops of three theatres collapsed and the ceiling of a cinema fell in. It was Sunday and the venues were crowded; there were dead and injured. The report of the commanding officer of the fire brigade refers to numerous bodies of victims 'collected in the railway station, the port and in the streets, and transported to various storage rooms'.[33]

The city was left on its knees as if it had endured an incredibly heavy air raid. An anonymous informant reported that 'the citizens of Naples are still stunned by yesterday's sudden accident and many keep on talking about it and are critical, believing that the blame lay with people and not with fate'.[34] For the civilian population this was just the latest demonstration that they were in the hands of incompetent adventurers who were leading them to ruin. This is implied once again by the comment of the prefect himself:

> It is obvious that the series of distressing episodes has caused the general public to feel profoundly discouraged and to have the sensation that they were at the mercy of events. The latest tragic event, which could possibly have been avoided or at least attenuated by rapid decisions and precise orders, fully confirms the opinion of the citizens of Naples.[35]

FROM AUTHORITARIANISM TO ANARCHY: FASCISTS, THE AUTHORITIES AND THE CIVILIAN POPULATION

The explosion of 27 March 1943 illustrates an important point: it was not only air raids that detached the Italian public from the regime. Their alienation was accelerated by the fact that despite the defeats, the regime continued to indulge in self-celebration. The Fascist dead received different treatment compared with other victims. During a night raid on 20/21 July 1941, for example, seven blackshirts of the anti-aircraft militia who had died were given solemn funerals. The corpses, arranged on four lorries, had been taken from the chapel of the mortuary to the cemetery, followed by relatives, civilian and military authorities, Fascist party officials and representatives of all sections of the army. At Corso Garibaldi the procession came to a halt in front of a stand where the prince of Piedmont, the mayor and senior officials awaited and the customary rite of the Fascist roll-call of the dead took place.[36]

For the whole period of the war the victims from the military and the Fascist party would be honoured with solemn public ceremonies, while civilians began to die in huge numbers. A gulf gradually formed between ordinary people and the representatives of the regime, and widened steadily. The records from the prefecture reveal further significant traces of apprehension. An emblematic case can be found in documents dating from January 1941. A member of the regime applied for and received an exceptionally generous sum of 10,000 *lire* as compensation 'for losing furniture and other household objects of particular value during a raid'. However, the request was followed by telegrams from the Minister of the Interior and letters from anonymous informants who denounced not only the iniquity of paying such a large sum to a well-off person, given the huge number of homeless people, but also the discovery, in the apartment made roofless by the bombs, of an incredible store of foodstuffs. Even a month after the event an informant claimed that the gossip had not subsided and that people still talked of the scandal, of the food reserves removed from general consumption by a Fascist and of further injustice perpetrated by the authorities who, instead of sending the person into internal exile, as would have happened to anyone else, rewarded him with special compensation.[37]

In 1943 after three years of terrible bombing, with brothers, fathers, husbands and boyfriends either prisoners or missing, the aversion to war and to those that had led Italy into the war had now spread throughout most of the population. This is documented by many studies.[38] There are significant traces in the oral evidence which refer to abuses of power by the Fascists and to neighbourhood arguments between those in favour of or against the war, despite the fear of denunciation by informers. Both oral history and the documentary evidence of the period provide a picture of an extremely tense situation full of potential conflict, not just between the authorities and the population but also among the population, sometimes leading to divisions along class lines. An interesting piece of oral evidence tells us, for example, about the tension between the inhabitants of 'bassi' (basement flats) and those of the upper floors of the same building in the historic centre of the city: the young family members of the 'bassi' were opposed to Fascism and the war while the 'respectable' members of the upper floors defended the regime. Oral evidence is, in this case, substantiated by the written records: it was the young popolano (a member of the working classes) critical of Fascism who was typically killed by German soldiers during the Neapolitan uprising.[39] The places and victims of the uprising in September 1943, mainly members of the working classes in working-class quarters, provide further confirmation of the situation.

As is well-known, the state and all its institutions collapsed after the armistice. The army disbanded. However, the whole of Italian society was abandoned. In some cases, it was the informal structures of society that still resisted and made up for institutional collapse: for example, during the Naples uprising, it was the neighbourhoods, families and groups of friends who acted as the basic social structure during the fighting. Elsewhere, where evacuation and the flight of the inhabitants had temporarily destroyed all forms of social organization, there developed extremely serious conflicts among the population. The most serious was the one that involved the provincial capitals which were destroyed in the bombings of September 1943 and abandoned by the inhabitants. For example, the city of Benevento was entirely cleaned out by crowds of looters, many of whom came from provincial towns to take possession of the property of the inhabitants who had fled.[40] All forms of civil authority had disappeared. The Germans carried out raids themselves and incited others to do likewise. In the case of Benevento we also find records of the presence of supporters of the occupying forces: local Fascists who had extremely close relationships with local criminals. The siege of Benevento is very much alive in the collective

Benevento after the raids of August–September 1943. Photo by Luigi Intorcia, courtesy of Archivio Fotografico Intorcia.

memory of the city. I could find countless oral testimonies, but there are also memoirs of the time such as the diary of priest Rocco Boccaccino:

> The deserted ruins of the city were filled with German troops and plunderers who came in hordes from nearby places, or individual looters who came out of temporary shelters. The houses that were still standing were scoured from top to bottom and the things that were the fruit of hard labour and an entire lifetime were extracted and taken away from the ruins. Furniture and fittings and pieces of household linen hung from half-destroyed balconies or were caught in electric wires, the remains of everything that had been chucked down by the looters. And it was not a rare sight to see in the streets, which were not entirely blocked in the upper part of the city, wagons and carts full of stolen goods. This represented the most disgusting and disgraceful scene: a moral catastrophe that was worse than the surrounding ruins. Lying in wait at the end of various streets were others who preyed on the plunderers. These were gangs of boys and adults who attacked the looters returning with the spoils on their shoulders and in carts and despoiled them of their booty.[41]

Demolished buildings, refugees fleeing and wandering in search of food like souls in torment, poor people from the countryside heading towards Benevento to plunder the property of refugees, looters who attacked other looters: it was an apocalyptic vision. At Avellino other looters were discovered and reported. They were put on trial and sentenced. A whole family ended up in prison: they could boast noble origins and included a baron, his wife, his daughter-in-law and two maids, accused of looting the house of their neighbour, a judge who, by virtue of his job, managed to find the culprits.[42] As at Benevento, country people arrived at Avellino with sacks, carts and all sorts of other forms of transport and took away as much as they could.

Avellino was bombed for the first time on 14 September 1943. More than in other towns and cities, the inhabitants felt they were safe; they thought they did not represent a strategic objective and had managed to avoid the violence of the war. They therefore remained inside their houses, in the streets, in the market and in their workplaces, intent on carrying out everyday tasks. More raids would follow on 15, 17, 20 and 21 September. According to one local historian, there were about 1,500 victims.[43] At the same time, as had happened in other towns and cities in ways we have already seen, the German occupiers of the area were particularly brutal; the troops themselves began the looting of property and supplies. Like Benevento, the city was completely abandoned by the public authorities. On the day of the bombing the mayor was on 'authorized leave', the prefect was on a special mission, the chief of police had fled for fear of being deported by the Germans and the military command was in complete disarray. Many of the wounded died without medical help; a man whose wife had died of festering wounds denounced the head of the hospital who had fled fearing further air raids, leaving the sick in the care of a few brave but unskilled nuns. Many of the corpses lay unburied. The list of omissions and cases of neglect of duty is a very long one. As in other cases, one image that stands out is that of a bishop 'in the street helping the dying and burying the dead'.[44]

At Benevento as at Avellino, the authorities demonstrated a complete lack of responsibility. Their inefficiency and cowardliness exacerbated the state of abandonment of the local population who were caught between Allied bombing and German violence. Ordinary people, on the other hand, appear in the dual role of victims and looters, highlighting another phenomenon that accompanied the flight and evacuation of people caught on the front lines: looting among the ruins, the plundering of abandoned houses (the exact opposite of the striking examples of solidarity that also occurred, as in the case of the Neapolitan uprising against the Germans) in which people gave vent to long-standing resentment (country people against town dwellers, the poor against the rich), giving rise to ancient rituals of sacking the homes of the enemy; however, this situation also presented opportunities to common criminals, adventurers and social outcasts who sometimes took the first steps in their careers among the ruins of war in a society that had been left entirely to its own devices.

CONCLUSION

The war rapidly led the Fascist state and its institutions into crisis. The Allies viewed air raids, which hit a population unsuited to war, according to a traditional stereotype of the character of the Italians, as one of the central causes of the Italian collapse. In reality, right from the start of the war, the civilian population was confronted by the inadequacy of the regime on all fronts: the internal front, where the regime was incapable of defending citizens from air raids and guaranteeing a minimum level of provisions, and on the military front, marked by a continuous series of defeats. The war highlighted the distance between the regime's grandiose dreams and actual possibilities, revealing all its limitations and ineptitude.

As has been so masterfully shown by Marc Bloch with regard to the French defeat,[45] a nation at war reveals more clearly the cultural and structural traits of the ruling élite inherited from peacetime. The inability to plan for the future, the negligence, the superficiality, the lack of consideration for the fate of ordinary people and the irresponsibility of the ruling classes did not begin with the war and, unfortunately, would not cease with the end of the war. The same dynamics were to lead to the complete break-up of the army and to the flight from Rome of the king and the new government on 8 September.[46] The experience of the population during the bombings was made worse by the inefficiency, incapacity and corruption of the regime's ruling class. This was essentially the true cause of the 'collapse of morale'.

Notes

1 The National Archives, Kew, London, (TNA), AIR 2/7197, 'Operations Against Italy by Bomber Sqdns', 'Note on Air Offensive against Italy', 3 May 1940.

2 Air Chief Marshal Sir A. Harris, *Despatch on War Operations* (TNA, AIR 14/4465, reprint London: Frank Cass, 1995), 192.

3 TNA, CAB 120/292, letter from C. Portal to the Prime Minister, 29 November 1942. In a subsequent letter, dated 1 December 1942, Italy was identified as the main target of the moment.

4 Archivio di Stato di Napoli (ASN), Prefettura, Gabinetto, b. 1224/1. RAF leaflet of May 1943.

5 On 4 August Naples; on the night of 7–8 August Turin, Milan and Genoa; 12–13 August Turin and Milan; 13 August Rome; between 14 and 16 August again Milan; 19 and 25 August Foggia; 23–24 August again Naples; 27 August Catanzaro.

6 Air Force Historical Research Agency (AFHRA), Maxwell Air Force Base, Montgomery, Alabama, microfilm A 6013–1621. Headquarters Northwest African Strategic Air Force, APO 520: 'Psychological Bombardment Operation designed to drive Italy to surrender'. Reuben Kyke Jr, Colonel GSC. A-5 to Major General J. H. Doolittle, 1 August 1943.

7 I reconstructed the history of the civilian population during the Second World War, in this area, more fully in G. Gribaudi, *Guerra totale. Tra bombe alleate e violenze naziste. Napoli e il fronte meridionale 1940–1944* (Turin: Bollati Boringhieri, 2005).

8 On the theme of the collapse of the state and the accelerated loss of legitimization of the ruling classes unable to protect the population, see P. Macry, *Gli ultimi giorni. Stati che crollano nell'Europa del Novecento* (Bologna: Il Mulino, 2009), which engages with considerations by G. Agamben, *La comunità che viene* (Turin: Bollati Boringhieri, 2001).

9 The planning of the bombings can be found in the D-Day orders in AFHRA, microfilm A 6013–1621, NASAF Headquarters, APO 520, US ARMY, 2 September 1943.

10 A. Stefanile, *I cento bombardamenti di Napoli* (Naples: Marotta, 1968).

11 Registers of deaths, Naples City Council. I took into account the central register and the registers of the districts with hospitals or cemeteries.

12 The lists of the victims of the two bombings are in ASN, Prefettura, Gabinetto, b. 1224/1 and b. 1227.

13 City Council Archive of Teano, Register of the dead, 1943.

14 Ibid.

15 ASN, Prefettura, Gabinetto, b. 1221/1, anonymous letter of 23 October 1941 (my translation).

16 Ibid. (my translation).

17 ASN, Prefettura, Gabinetto, b.1227, Questura of Naples, 13 February 1944, subject: 'public shelters'.

18 Ibid. There were 41 shelters in the districts of Stella, the Port, Mercato, Fuorigrotta, Vicaria, Pendino, S. Ferdinando, Montecalvario, Vasto-Arenaccia, S. Carlo all'Arena, Poggioreale and S. Lorenzo.

19 A. M. Ortese, *Il mare non bagna Napoli* (Milan: Adelphi, 1994 – first edn. Turin: Einaudi, 1953).

20 TNA, WO 220/414, Allied Force Headquarters, Typhus Commission, 'Notes on the civil typhus outbreak. Italy 1943–44'.

21 Ibid., Headquarters, Allied Control Commission, Public Health Sub-Commission, Typhus Control Section, APO 394, 4 April 1944.

22 See the prefect's note on 11 November 1940: 'The Ministry of Popular Culture telephoned ordering the newspapers to avoid using the headlines "the bombardment of Naples" or anything similar but instead to entitle the page with the most important news of the day's bulletin' (ASN, Prefettura, Gabinetto, b. 1221/1).

23 ASN, Prefettura, Gabinetto, II Deposit, I Category, Provisional orders, b. 53, Anonymous letter dated 12 July 1941 (my translation).

24 Ibid., Anonymous letter dated 23 October 1941.

25 Ibid., This is the text of 19 letters collected in the last days of October 1941 (my translation).

26 Ibid., Report of the *Carabinieri*, Caserta, 23 April 1941 (my translation).

27 Ibid., Report of the *Carabinieri*, Naples, 24 September 1941 (my translation).

28 ASN, Prefettura, Gabinetto, b. 1130/45, Report of the prefect to the Ministry of Interior, 31
    March 1943 (my translation).
29 Ibid., Report of the Engineering Officer Della Morte to the commander of the 54th Fire Brigade
    about the fire on the cargo boat *Caterina Costa* (my translation).
30 The words of the prefect from the above-mentioned report dated 31 March (my translation).
31 A. Stefanile, *I cento bombardamenti di Napoli*, 88 (my translation).
32 ASN Prefettura, Gabinetto, b. 1330/45, Phonogram of the Chief inspector of the Civil Engineers
    to the Prefect, 29 March 1943 (my translation).
33 Ibid.
34 Ibid., sheet with confidential information dated 29 March 1943 (my translation).
35 Ibid., prefect's report mentioned above.
36 Ibid., letter from the Chief of Police to the Prefect, 23 July 1941 (my translation).
37 It should be emphasized that the hatred of hoarders was one of the strongest motives behind
    the reprisals of September and October 1943, when, during the anti-German insurrection, the
    population attacked the local Fascist authorities. The best-known case is that of the secretary
    of the Fascist Party of Ponticelli, who was killed by the crowd following a German retaliation
    of 29 September 1943 (ASN, Corte di Assise di Napoli, sentence of 9 August 1946). See also
    Gribaudi, *Guerra totale*, 266–70.
38 See R. De Felice, *Mussolini l'alleato*, vol. 2, *Crisi e agonia del regime* (Turin: Einaudi, 1990); P.
    Cavallo, *Italiani in guerra. Sentimenti e immagini dal 1940 al 1943* (Bologna: Il Mulino, 1997);
    S. Colarizi, *L'opinione degli italiani sotto il regime. 1929–1943* (Rome-Bari: Laterza, 1991); A.
    Lepre, *L'occhio del duce. Gli italiani e la censura di guerra* (Milan: Mondadori, 1992); A. Lepre,
    Storia degli Italiani nel Novecento: chi siamo, da dove veniamo (Milan: Mondadori, 2003).
39 Interview to Antonio Mari, in Gribaudi, *Guerra totale*, 284–6.
40 Benevento, a provincial capital, had been the target of repeated bombings since July 1943. In
    September repeated raids had reduced the city to a mass of rubble.
41 The priest's diary was first published between September and November 1978 in the weekly
    magazine *Messaggio d'oggi*, on the 35th anniversary of the bombings, and was reprinted in
    1993: R. Boccaccino, *Benevento nella terribile estate del '43* (Benevento: Edizioni Messaggio
    d'oggi, 1993), 39.
42 V. Cannaviello, *Avellino e l'Irpinia nella tragedia del 1943–44* (Avellino: Tipografia Pergola,
    1954), 61.
43 Ibid., 30–37 (my translation).
44 Ibid., 69 (my translation).
45 M. Bloch, *L'étrange défaite: Témoinage Ecrit en 1940* (Paris: Société des Éditions Franc-Tireur,
    1946).
46 E. Aga-Rossi, *Una nazione allo sbando. L'armistizio italiano del settembre 1943* (Bologna: Il
    Mulino, 1993).

PART IV

Friend or Foe? Popular Perceptions of Bombing

13

Anglo-American Air Attacks and the Rebirth of Public Opinion in Fascist Italy*

Marco Fincardi

THE FRAGILE REPRESENTATION OF ITALY AS A GREAT POWER

The Fascist regime equipped itself in the 1930s with powerful means of mass communication. The technical tools and the language of propaganda were perfected in order to make the rhetoric of military conquest both popular and shared, according to the principles of the totalitarian state.[1] In the Italy of the time, what is understood as 'public opinion' did not exist; free expression and the circulation of non-conformist views were unimaginable, due to the regime's monopoly of all means of communication, the close check by the Fascist party on every form of public meeting, and a pervasive system of police control and political espionage.[2]

Well in advance of the Second World War – having experimented with terrorist bombing and strafing by Italy's air force in various war zones in Africa and Spain[3] – the Italian ruling classes were fully aware of the potential role of aerial bombardment in deciding military victory in a European conflict. The aeroplane itself was presented as a perfect image of the modernity and military effectiveness of the regime, and was continually used in Fascist propaganda to represent the strategic superiority of Italy's ascendant fighting forces; these would surpass the military strength of France and Great Britain, which was portrayed as outdated.[4] The debates in the British press, which expressed fear of their country being outclassed by the European powers that invested in rearmament, were also exploited: extracts were published with the aim of giving Italians the mistaken impression that military supremacy in the air would be easily achieved.[5]

And yet the Italian political and military authorities, and equally the industrialists, who took lucrative government orders for the production of military aircraft and equipment for anti-aircraft defences, did not provide the armed forces with the means necessary for a modern military power to conduct aerial warfare. Both the weapons in use and the methods for producing them were antiquated: throughout the war, large-scale planned mass production of

*Translated from the Italian by Stuart Oglethorpe.

Propaganda postcard (1941) depicting a powerful Italian anti-aircraft battery hitting an enemy plane and targeting another with its searchlights. In fact, Italy's anti-aircraft defences were equipped throughout the war with scarce, aged and ineffective weapons. Archivio iconografico del Museo della guerra di Rovereto, fig.13304.jpg.

combat and bomber aircraft never came into being.[6] Because of this failure of responsibility by an entire civil and military ruling class, Italy entered the Second World War without an air force capable of attacking Britain, but above all lacking strong defences, both active and passive, against aerial attacks: the aircraft detection systems were rudimentary and ineffective, and the population was kept ignorant of the impending threat.[7]

Italians were to a large extent unconvinced of the aims of a war conducted in partnership with Nazi Germany.[8] In the second week of the war an accident occurred that was truly emblematic, and fatal for Italo Balbo, Marshal of the Air Force. Balbo, a charismatic former leader of the early Fascist squads, had become the regime's key figure in promoting the role of the air force.[9] This leader and aeronaut, and governor of Libya from 1934, was shot down by Italian anti-aircraft artillery while landing in a three-engined S70 at Tobruk airport after a British raid: an extraordinary event, which instantly exposed the inaccuracy and disorganization of the anti-aircraft system. The solemn state funeral arranged for him did not dispel the feelings of dismay regarding his death, nor the widespread suspicion that his elimination might have been planned by Mussolini.[10]

Nevertheless, the Fascist regime continued to release reassuring propaganda, which led to a considerable underestimation of the danger of aerial bombardment, even after the first unopposed British raids on Italian cities. By dropping bombs and printed propaganda, the British air attacks, which started on the second day of Italy's war, were to put the morale of the population seriously to the test, although in 1940 and 1941 these attacks were neither intense nor frequent.[11] British propaganda leaflets were therefore limited in this phase, and bore messages that had only a minimal impact on the psychological stability of Italian society. However, these raids were already enough to induce a strong sense of insecurity among the public,[12] who realized they were essentially without protection; the anti-aircraft system, where it existed, showed itself to be almost useless, with few installations and a range of fire that only reached low altitudes. Fighter aircraft were few in number, and unable to intercept and challenge the enemy bombers; these were much faster, impervious to light shelling, and better equipped with flight instruments and armaments. Moreover, Italian fighters were very vulnerable and completely unsuitable for night combat. Italy's lack of modern systems of aircraft detection meant that neither enemy aircraft nor their final destinations could be easily predicted. As a result, if the inaccurate detection systems identified even a single plane approaching Italian airspace, warning telephone calls would cause half of Italy's sirens to be sounded. This resulted in continual and generally pointless alerts, with obvious consequences: damage to industrial production and exhausting psychological stress for the urban population, whose sleep was disturbed almost every night. The clear technological gap between Italy and its enemies had a distressing impact on the armed forces, and on civil society, which struggled to maintain its spirits, mindful of the disturbing technical capabilities of the Wehrmacht and the Luftwaffe, which had already rescued the Italian ally in several war theatres, but only to assume the command of operations and to relegate the Italian military to a humiliating subjugated position.

THE LOSS OF CREDIBILITY OF THE FASCIST REGIME

The home front began to experience an irreversible collapse of morale in the autumn of 1942, just after the conquest of Libya had allowed the RAF to launch a programme of strategic bombardment on the Italian peninsula, using new heavy bombers like the Lancaster. Moreover, while the British bombers usually approached their targets at night for safety reasons, from December 1942 the arrival of the United States' Flying Fortress and Liberator aircraft, flying from bases in Egypt and Algeria, made the raids continual in daytime as well, and gave them an impressive coverage: they could reach targets of greater importance, and had a decisive impact on a strategic level. This new type of daytime bombardment from high altitude by the Americans, despite its claims of accuracy, became the most feared among the population. The impression created was that it was the American planes, rather than the British, that caused indiscriminate and ruthless destruction, the more so because the British civilian population, like its Italian counterpart, had been subjected to bombing.[13] On the military level, however, what counted was that the British and American air forces, attacking together, reinforced their total air supremacy across the whole region, and made the tragedy of bombardment a common experience for local populations, especially in southern Italy.[14] During this phase, the scarcity and poor quality of air-raid shelters and the improvised nature of evacuation plans, compounded by the dire shortages of food and other supplies, fostered a perception of the incompetence, negligence and corruption of the regime's authorities. These were believed to be responsible for all the difficulties and exposures to danger that the population suffered. This was a result not only of the spectacular and destructive attacks, but also of the Allies' psychological warfare techniques. Millions of propaganda leaflets dropped on Italian cities explained the benefits of the raids as a means to end the war more quickly, to such an extent that by the autumn of 1942 they had instilled in the Italians a clear perception that there was no chance of victory.[15] After Italy entered the war, the arrival from the skies of appealing messages from the enemy, and the start of various Italian-language broadcasts by enemy radio stations,[16] put an end to the political monopoly of information which had lasted for some 15 years: this represented a sudden and powerful change for the stability of a totalitarian system. From then on, faced with Italy's obvious military disaster and exposed to a system of mass communication that was more credible than that of the Fascist dictatorship, a growing number of Italians saw the regime's propaganda as increasingly discredited. From the end of 1942, as military defeats in Africa and Russia became apparent, people began to translate their doubts and murmurs into openly voiced dissent.[17] The army had to seek careful forms of control over the soldiers at the front to prevent them being affected by this collapse in morale, which in particular hit civilians and military units away from operational areas.[18]

An example of successful propaganda was the British exploitation in 1942 of the alleged Italian involvement in the bombing of southern England in

1940–41. Indeed, in autumn 1940 Italian propaganda had dwelt on accounts of the largely peripheral involvement of the Italian air force in the bombing of London and other southern British cities from improvised airfields in Belgium.

Nel 1940

"Ho chiesto ed ottenuto dal Fuehrer una diretta partecipazione alla battaglia contro la Gran Bretagna con velivoli."

RISULTATO ...

Nel 1940/41

100,000 uomini, donne o bambini uccisi o gravemente feriti — una casa su cinque danneggiata — in INGHILTERRA.

Nel 1943

Ogni fabbrica, che lavora per questa guerra tedesca, — ogni obiettivo militare — in procinto d'essere polverizzato — in ITALIA.

Valeva proprio la pena di chiedere il permesso del Fuehrer per questo ?

Leaflet dropped all over Italy by the RAF at the end of 1942, which justifies the raids on Italian cities by blaming Mussolini personally for his request to Hitler to take part in the bombing of London in the summer of 1940. Archivio Centrale dello Stato, Ministero degli Interni, A5G Seconda Guerra Mondiale, b. 21, f. 7.

Mussolini himself had been quick to boast publicly about this operation as one of his personal successes. British city-dwellers, who during the Blitz had suffered casualties and destruction inflicted by the Luftwaffe, had no way of knowing about those imaginary parallel raids by Mussolini's planes; but such boasting had for a short period served to boost Italian spirits, although many were left with the fear that British reprisals might be horrendous.[19] However, such an unwise campaign by the Fascist press became a formidable weapon for British propagandists when a new phase of the war opened in 1942, as soon as the RAF had had the chance to repair and enlarge their airfields in Malta and northern Africa. In the increasingly sophisticated leaflets dropped by the British and American bombers over the country,[20] it was easy to accuse Mussolini of criminal irresponsibility for having wanted the earlier bombing of London and Coventry; this made the bombardment now being suffered by Italians, who had no means of resistance, seem an inevitable retaliation.[21] Italians, who still remembered Fascist claims regarding the Blitz on English cities, also being terrorized by bombing, were thus impelled to unload their collective moral responsibility directly onto the Duce. This argument, which justified British bombing, entered everyday conversations among Italians even in the air-raid shelters, as recorded by the secret informants of the Fascist police.[22]

The evacuation of several major cities, recommended by Mussolini from autumn 1942 in one of his speeches to the nation, raised to a maximum the difficulties, worries and exasperations caused by the war during the cold season.[23] Meanwhile, Fascist propaganda sought to conceal the reality and to give Italians a skewed perception of relative strengths in the air and on the sea. An Italian book on the theory of wartime propaganda, referring to the situation in the spring and summer of 1942 (when Italy became a constant air target, with its air force almost out of action and its navy in permanent shelter in the ports of Taranto and La Spezia) resorted to the subterfuge of trying to suggest that the British were in a state of military disadvantage:

> With the additional aim of seeking to frighten Italy, from July 1941 Churchill announced a heavy bombardment of Italy, not excluding Rome, to give Londoners, who were particularly badly hit at that time, the idea that their enemies would also be hit hard. On several occasions, in fact, various Italian cities – generally of no military significance – were made the targets for RAF aeroplanes; when they have the chance, these still have no hesitation in striking the residential districts and hospitals of our cities. However, the only results achieved have been the deepening of our people's hatred for the enemy, and the increased engagement of all our efforts in achieving final victory ... British propaganda, at a loss for subject matter, now hardly ever focuses on its own navy and air force, and restricts itself to contentious points of little interest, or to stories that are too divorced from reality to be believed by anybody.[24]

In a memoir written some years later, taking a rather excessive pleasure in paradox, the magistrate and legal expert Salvatore Satta expressed his indignation at the Anglophile attitudes of his fellow citizens, which he described as 'general feelings among the people' but 'particularly strong' among the middle classes:

> In the secrecy of people's homes, where the eyes of a regime functionary could not penetrate, the news items put out with subtle skill by London were discussed, weighed up and obsessively analysed, and on these depended the peace in our hearts and the very tranquillity of our families.... In the exhausting progression of the war there were days of euphoria and days of prostration: the former exactly corresponded with British good fortune in their attacks, and the latter with the sudden and unexpected good fortune of our own forces, or with a draining lack of progress for the operations.... What then occurred during the brutal bombing raids is something that the human mind struggles to understand, and only the words of a Tacitus can describe: populations that were decimated, worn away and dispersed, and, far from having a spark of revolt against their cruel enemy, seemed to forget their own downfall in favour of delighting in the enemy's revered might: a widespread satisfaction regarding the general ruins, with a total indifference towards generations of achievement which had collapsed in a single moment; the first thought of any survivor was to reassure himself that factories and vehicles that could be used in the war were among the ruins, and when this had not happened, to find some way of justifying the inaccuracy of the strikes and the senseless slaughter.[25]

According to this former Fascist lawyer, such a way of viewing wartime events had become 'the rival to the ridiculous monopoly of patriotism assumed by those in power'.[26] Most inclined to give voice to this dissenting view, first of all, would have been (according to Satta) a minority of large landowners, businessmen, speculators and Jews, who saw in Britain a political system that was ideal for the defence of their own private interests. However, there was also a less precisely identifiable bourgeois mass which – even at the cost of accepting the destruction of their own country as a positive fact – saw Britain as the best model of a liberal society, forgetting that British governments had for a long period applauded Mussolini's regime, and that the crusade against him could therefore only be explained in terms of rivalry for the control of the Mediterranean. Several police informers confirmed this particular preference of the ruling classes for a rapid British invasion, strongly desired in order to avert what they feared much more: the arrival of the Red Army in Italy, after the Battle of Stalingrad.

WAITING FOR THE WINNERS/LIBERATORS

Italian society, brought into and kept in the war for years in conditions of longstanding and serious insecurity, did not react against the enemy air forces; these both bombed and at the same time dropped leaflets advising on how to oppose the dictatorship, which was charged with direct responsibility for the tragedy. The Italians in part absolved the Anglo-Americans of responsibility for the losses and destruction which the latter continued to scatter everywhere, while there was widespread and increasing rejection of any message that came through the regime's official channels, which lacked credibility and were therefore assumed to be misleading.[27] In March and April 1943, strikes spread across most of the factories in Piedmont and Lombardy. They were among the most significant strikes in Axis-occupied Europe so far. They were not covered in the press, but the residents of these regions deluded themselves that such an extraordinary protest by the working class could truly convince the British bombers to stop their raids on Turin and Milan;[28] while, by contrast, various representatives of the upper classes were afraid that fresh bombing and the continuation of the war might give rise to a communist revolution, which only the speedy arrival of the British army could avert. The population exhibited a growing anti-Fascist defeatism and an increasingly unequivocal support for the Anglo-American air forces, thus becoming the first in Europe to accept their image as 'liberators', while Fascist propaganda had for years portrayed them as examples of criminal and bloodthirsty barbarism. Even the Anglo-American bombers were seen in an ambivalent light: deliverers of an underhand death but at the same time almost friends, or at least less dangerous than the Fascists and Germans, who were forcing the Italians to carry on with a pointless war effort that could only worsen their defeat.[29]

A great many Italians, who no longer feared being reported by the regime's police, now casually expressed the belief that the national radio and newspapers only reproduced the deceptions of Fascism. It became normal to look forward to the arrival of liberators in British and American uniforms; among the workers, there was also a fervent wish for the arrival of the Russians, who were seen as preferable because – far off as they were – at least they were not bombing Italian factories and cities. On the streets and in workplaces, criticism and insults were frequently directed at Fascist militants, who previously had been greatly feared. The regime's counter-propaganda at that time sought to spread the belief that the aerial bombardment by the Anglo-Americans was not only inhuman, but also the technological expression of a barbarism with the covert racist aim of annihilating the ancient Latin civilization and that of all continental Europe, destroying its churches and historical monuments along with its peoples, for whom it was preparing complete enslavement. The Minister of Popular Culture, Alessandro Pavolini, when giving the regular secret directives to the press on 26 October 1942, admitted that painting the enemy in such dark tones might be counterproductive, but still indicated that a similar approach should be taken:

> With regard to both past and, presumably, future air raids, the approach of the press has been by and large correct. Thundering phrases against British savagery, barbarism and so forth must be avoided, as in fact we ourselves have bombed London: aerial warfare is what it is. Better to present these raids as the papers have already done; portray them as an expression of American and British hatred for Italy, with the aim of reinforcing

what is, after all, the spontaneous reaction of the great majority of the Italian people ...
Continue to highlight enemy planes shot down, the effectiveness of the anti-air attack
artillery, and so on.[30]

Six months later, following a change of ministers, and shortly before the regime
collapsed, the tendency to report the fictitious shooting down of enemy aircraft
still persisted. This even provoked criticism in an important militant Fascist
periodical about the ineffectiveness of deliberately mendacious military information, which was designed to reassure the public, but which people were
naturally sceptical of:

> It is too transparent a game and in the long run people are bored by it, if not actually
> annoyed... Old and new phrases from a pseudo-strategic repertoire have now lost
> meaning through their usage. The public always catches on, and the Italian public (at
> least as intelligent as any other) has caught on too.[31]

However, the Fascist party was progressively losing its ability to react as
summer 1943 approached: the dictator and other leaders were now thought of
by the nation as public enemies, authors of misfortune and hateful frauds, as
reported to Mussolini by the various bodies for internal espionage.[32] Repressive
action by the police was toned down and lost its deterrent effect, while a real
conspiracy was taking shape inside the institutions. The destruction and losses
from the continual bombing seemed to the people to be an expiation for their
guilt in having believed in Mussolini's imperial rhetoric; it also fed their hopes
that this succession of tragedies would soon bring the collapse of the Fascist
dictatorship, the termination of an unwelcome alliance with the Germans, and
the end of a war in which only an extremist minority still believed. The final
solemn speech to the nation, to prepare it for entrenchment around Fascism
and the monarchy in expectation of an imminent Anglo-American landing in
Italy, was given on the radio on 24 June 1943, from the Campidoglio fortress:
not by the discredited Mussolini, but by the philosopher Giovanni Gentile, the
most important intellectual of the period. With great rhetorical emphasis he
invited his fellow citizens to a desperate but proud clash of civilizations, down
to the last man, drawing an extreme contrast between the spiritual superiority
of the Latin race and the obvious great technological superiority of the Anglo-
Saxons, who were materially wealthy but lacking in humanity. Gentile declared
that even if destroyed, but not accepting defeat, Rome would in time emerge as
the moral victor of this total war:

> The enemy, who has savoured the most bitter taste of defeat, has with all the terrible
> weight of his violent engines poured destruction over the weakest area of the opposing
> front, the territory held by us; he has ruined our cities; he has committed acts of cruelty
> towards our hearths and homes.... And the enemy may have hoped that this rupture
> would have weakened us and persuaded us to leave open a breach in the European

front, which he must still crash against, after the pointless massacres of his sport in the air, if he wants to start to win the war that he has unleashed on every continent and ocean. The response to these heroes of the sport in which the sexes mingle, but not one glimmer of military honour shines, has been given by our populations: bombed, strafed, physically and mentally tormented day and night for months on end with every kind of difficulty and unspeakable misery caused by each raid, between the terror of death and the trials of evacuation, hungry and thirsty, they continue to curse the ruthless enemy and to long for the salvation of the Fatherland. Not one cry of protest against those alleged to be responsible for the war; not one attempt to have it over; not one sign of tired or flagging spirits.... Can we really be afraid that this immortal Italy, resplendent in the eyes of the whole world, might die beneath raids by the intoxicated pilots of flying fortresses, if it is alive in our hearts?[33]

ITALY INVADED AND LACERATED

On 10 July, when the papers and radio announced the start of the invasion of Italy with the landing in Sicily, reactions in the country were confused; however, most of the population and the military accepted this event with fatalism, or sometimes with ill-concealed approval. On 19 July, to slow up Axis supplies to this new southern European front, over 600 American planes bombed Rome for the first time,[34] devastating the most important rail and air centres; near to the main station they struck the surrounding residential area and the basilica of San Lorenzo. This action made a huge impression, but from many Italian cities the outlying authorities reported widespread reactions of joy to the announcement that bombs had fallen near the palaces of the Duce and the king, in the city that served as a symbol for Fascist mythology.[35] Ennio Flaiano, a young journalist and well-established writer, remembered in 1945:

> Italians were pleased: the Romans must finally have understood the nature of war. It was then said, in jest, that in a city in northern Italy they had considered hiring a few planes to repeat the gesture. This would not have been a surprise: Rome represented all the hatred of Fascism, and it seemed right that it should be punished. Thus when the city was bombed there was a chorus of approval. Even the Fascists were content. The weekly paper of the GUF (Fascist university groups) had indeed called out not long before asking (against the papal manoeuvres aimed at saving the city from air attacks) that Rome too be granted the *honour* of being bombed.[36]

One week later, Mussolini's fall and his disappearance from the public sphere generated a wave of patriotic enthusiasm and the mistaken belief that all the promises of the Anglo-American propaganda were about to come true. Once Mussolini's dictatorship was over and his party suppressed, and once the occasions of military confrontation between the Italian and Anglo-American armies had stopped with the withdrawal from Sicily, this attitude of collaboration with the enemy air forces, which were dropping bombs and leaflets, continued even through August 1943, when the belief that the war and bombing of the cities could suddenly stop was dispelled. The Italian population continued to give a triumphal welcome to the 'liberators', who after Sicily occupied much of southern Italy, Sardinia and Corsica, meeting resistance only from the Wehrmacht.[37] Meanwhile Anglo-American propaganda leaflets encouraged Italians to regard the Badoglio government as dangerously untrustworthy; the government was trying to negotiate the surrender of the Kingdom of Italy with the British and withdrew its troops from combat zones, but without openly declaring the break with Berlin. In precisely this phase, in order to force Badoglio and the king to dissolve the Axis alliance and to accept an unconditional surrender, the worst raids of the whole war were carried out over Milan and Turin by Bomber Command, with the aim of setting both cities alight using 'area bombing'. The new provisional government appointed by the king and the ruling classes, who showed themselves unable to create alternatives to a Fascist regime of which they had until recently been organic components, were gripped by the fear that there would be popular uprisings against them, due to the sudden and marked turn for the worse in the terror bombing of civilian targets, and the aggressive provocation of Anglo-American propaganda. Worries about hostile reactions from the Catholic world, and about the growing sympathies that both lower classes and intellectuals demonstrated towards the Soviets (the only ones who had not brought the war to Italian territory), contributed to a limitation of further terroristic bombardments on Italian cities.[38] The rhythm of bombing raids was only slowed with the preparations for signing the unconditional surrender; it was then resumed and continued – in an Italy occupied by opposing armies in the south and north – until the end of the war, with notably debilitating effects on the morale of the population, by now fatalistically resigned to the tragedies that came from the sky, and less likely to count on the promises of propaganda. Even then, however, air-dropped leaflets remained an important weapon and channel of one-way communication until 1945, while the bombing of cities and ports continued, carried out by both the Anglo-Americans and the Germans.

Only a very small number of Italian intellectuals welcomed the idea of commitment up to the last drop of blood in a clash of civilizations or races, as expressed by Gentile. The majority (like the majority of Italian society) opposed the German invader and the unpopular Republican Fascist Party; however, it was generally a passive resistance. Only a minority of Italians took part in an organized resistance which fought Nazi-Fascism and established a direct collaboration with the Anglo-American air forces, receiving weapons and protecting and hiding the pilots of planes shot down by the Germans. However, the continuation of air raids after the end of the regime and after the armistice gave rise to a shared sense of scepticism towards the democratic values and declarations of friendship of the 'liberators'. Moreover, following the landings in Sicily, Taranto and Salerno, the Anglo-American armies were quickly weakened by the massive transfer of ships, aircraft and troops to the Pacific theatre and above all to Britain to prepare for the Overlord landings. Such a sudden decrease disappointed the Italian population, which had mostly remained a spectator of the events, but feeling certain to be liberated from the Germans by 1943. At the end of the summer of 1943, having completely lost faith in the authority of the state, many of the high- or middle-ranking officials from what had been the organization of the dissolved Fascist regime chose not to align themselves either with or against the German occupiers, taking a politically sceptical and inert position. At the end of 1944, Satta, the former Fascist lawyer, who hid in the countryside to avoid either supporting or opposing the Italian Social Republic (the so-called Salò Republic), compared modern total warfare to a colossal Moloch: it was fascinating for its destructive capabilities, and freely worshipped for its potential to wipe out not so much soldiers, but civilized life itself, in a cruel and unnecessary demonstration of technological power, 'destroying in an instant so much life and beauty'.[39]

> Nothing is more mundane and wretched than this war, in which everything is reduced to a ratio of forces; victory inevitably goes to whoever has the greater destructive capability, and can therefore demonstrate his brutality most fully.... It seems to be the result of a macabre piece of accountancy: a specified number of tons of bombs, the calculated sacrifice of *n* hundreds of thousands of men and the 'Coventrization' of a given area of the earth's surface have produced that outcome, and necessarily so, for the simple reason that the defenders did not have as many bombs, planes and men. As a result, this and other similar feats are all the same to us of this era, and are now of no interest other than for the impact they might have on the duration of the war.... The German, who in his racial frenzy submits hundreds of thousands of people to appalling agonies, kills hostages, sets villages alight, spreads terror among peaceable populations; the Briton who leaves his remote lands and travels thousands of kilometres to raze cities and villages to the ground, machinegun women and children, these are not monsters: they are the ministers of a god who does not forget, who demands revenge as the price of his love. Thus nothing is more unreasonable than the charges of atrocity that adversaries regularly throw at each other, and nothing more absurd than the trial that the victor wishes to inflict on the vanquished for the massacres he has carried out.[40]

From this opportunistic perspective, only the great powers were acknowledged to have committed war crimes, as if Italy – due to its military weakness – had only been the victim of mass violence, whether it was practised by the Germans or the Anglo-Americans. In this way the ruling classes, who had seen the Fascist state and its armed forces melt away, hid behind this condition of passivity from 1943, in order to portray themselves as victims rather than aggressors, and thus deny any personal responsibility for the Fascist wars conducted from the beginning of the 1930s.[41] Among them prevailed a self-absolution for any repression and violence carried out by Italian arms towards populations bombed by the kingdom of Italy's air force, or occupied by the Italian army during ten years of constant military operations in Africa and Europe;[42] a widespread stereotype was constructed according to which their country had neither possessed nor used the modern technology for mass destruction. Part of the population and of the intellectual class – in particular in northern Italy, where from September 1943 the armed resistance against the Nazi-Fascists evolved – expressed itself in a confrontational and polemic manner against the historical mystifications of these ruling classes. However, the continuity of Italy's social structures – immediately reinforced between 1943 and 1945 by the Anglo-American occupiers – made it difficult to cleanse the past compromises with Fascism. A shared coherent memory, which could explain the ways in which the popular rejection of the dictatorship occurred, also did not emerge, although the process of detachment was clearly documented by the very organs of the regime that were entrusted with social control.

Notes

1 See N. Tranfaglia, *La stampa del regime 1932-1943. Le veline del Minculpop per orientare l'informazione* (Milan: Bompiani, 2005); M. Argentieri, *Il cinema in guerra. Arte, comunicazione e propaganda in Italia. 1940-1944* (Rome: Editori Riuniti, 1998); G. Isola, *Abbassa la tua radio per favore ... Storia dell'ascolto radiofonico nell'Italia fascista* (Scandicci: La Nuova Italia, 1990); G. Santomassimo, 'Propaganda', and 'Consenso' in V. De Grazia and S. Luzzatto (eds), *Dizionario del fascismo* (Turin: Einaudi, 2005), vol. 2.

2 See J. Habermas, *Storia e critica dell'opinione pubblica* (Rome-Bari: Laterza, 1977); S. Colarizi, *L'opinione degli italiani sotto il regime. 1929-1943* (Rome-Bari: Laterza, 1991), 3–5; Colarizi, *La seconda guerra mondiale e la repubblica* (Turin: Utet, 1984).

3 See R. Gentili, *Guerra aerea sull'Etiopia 1935-1939* (Florence: Edai, 1992); N. Labanca, 'Dominio e repressione. I crimini di guerra nelle colonie italiane', in L. Baldissara and P. Pezzino (eds), *Crimini e memoria di guerra,* (Naples: L'ancora nel Mediterraneo, 2004), 260–70; G. Rochat, *Le guerre italiane 1935-1943. Dall'impero d'Etiopia alla disfatta* (Turin: Einaudi, 2005), 7–8, 44–6, 65–70, 112–15; F. Pedriali, *Guerra di Spagna e aviazione italiana* (Rome: Ufficio storico dell'Aeronautica militare italiana, 1992); J. Villarroya i Font, *Els bombardejos de Barcelona durant la guerra civil (1936-1939)* (Barcelona: Regidoria de drets civils-Publicacions de l'Abadia de Montserrat, 1999); D. and J. Serra, *La guerra quotidiana: testimonis d'una ciutat en guerra* (Barcelona: Columna, 2003); S. and E. Albertí, *Perill de bombardeig! Barcelona sota le bombe (1936-1939)* (Barcelona: Albertí, 2005); X. Domènech and L. Zenobi (eds), *Quando piovevano bombe. I bombardamenti e la città di Barcellona durante la guerra civile* (Barcelona: Generalitat de Catalunya, 2007).

4 See Labanca and M. Di Giovanni, *Fantasmi di guerra totale. Studi di storia della guerra chimica* (Florence: Forum per i problemi della pace e della guerra, 1999); Di Giovanni, 'L'aviazione e i miti del fascismo' in P. Ferrari (ed.), *L'aeronautica italiana* (Milan: Angeli, 2004), 203–27; Di Giovanni, *Scienza e potenza. La modernizzazione della guerra tra mito, immaginario e ideologia. Italia 1935-1945* (Turin: Zamorani, 2005).

5 A British book that warned of this risk was purposely published twice, the second time in 1940: J. Montague Kenworthy, *Nuove guerre e nuove armi* (Milan: La Prora, 1931).

6 See F. Minniti, 'La politica industriale del ministero dell'aeronautica. Mercato, pianificazione, sviluppo (1935-1943)', *Storia contemporanea*, 1-2, 1981, 5–55; 271–312; N. Della Volpe, *Esercito e propaganda tra le due guerre* (Rome: Ufficio storico stato maggiore dell'esercito, 1992); M. Knox, *Hitler's Italian Allies: Royal Armed Forces, Fascist Regime, and the War of 1940-43* (Cambridge: Cambridge University Press, 2000); Ferrari (ed.), *L'aeronautica italiana*; G. Alegi, 'Aeronautica', in De Grazia and Luzzatto (eds), *Dizionario del fascismo*, vol. 1 ; Rochat, *Le guerre italiane 1935-1943*, 10–15.

7   N. Della Volpe, *Difesa del territorio e protezione antiaerea (1915-1943)* (Rome: Ufficio storico dello Stato maggiore dell'esercito, 1986).

8   L. Rizzi, *Lo sguardo del potere: La censura militare in Italia nella seconda guerra mondiale 1940-45* (Milan: Rizzoli, 1984); I. Dalla Costa (ed.), *L'Italia imbavagliata. Lettere censurate 1940-43*, (Treviso: Pagus, 1990); A. Cecchi and B. Cadioli, *La posta militare italiana durante la seconda guerra mondiale* (Rome: USSME, 1991); E. Cortesi, *Reti dentro la guerra. Corrispondenza postale e strategie di sopravvivenza (1940-1945)* (Rome: Carocci, 2008).

9   See Rochat, *Italo Balbo aviatore e ministro dell'aeronautica 1926-1933* (Ferrara: Bovolenta, 1979); M. Isnenghi, 'Italo Balbo ovvero il volo fascista' in O. Calabrese (ed.), *Italia moderna. Immagini e storia di un'identità nazionale* (Milan: Electa, 1983), vol. 2, 111-26.

10 Rochat, *Italo Balbo* (Turin: Utet, 1986); C. M. Santoro (ed.), *Italo Balbo. Aviazione e potere aereo* (Rome: Aeronautica militare, 1998).

11 See S. Harvey, 'The Italian War Effort and the Strategic Bombing of Italy', *History*, 70, 1985, 32-45; R. Overy, *Bomber Command 1939-45* (London: Harper Collins, 1997); G. Bonacina, *Obiettivo: Italia. I bombardamenti aerei delle città italiane dal 1940 al 1945* (Milan: Mursia, 1970); M. Gioannini and G. Massobrio, *Bombardate l'Italia. Storia della guerra di distruzione aerea 1940-1945* (Milan: Rizzoli, 2007); A. Rastelli, *Bombe sulla città. Gli attacchi aerei alleati: le vittime civili a Milano* (Milan: Mursia, 2000); M. Patricelli, *L'Italia sotto le bombe* (Rome-Bari: Laterza, 2007).

12 N. Gallerano, 'Gli italiani in guerra 1940-1943', *Italia contemporanea*, 160, 1985, 82-93; Gallerano, 'Gli italiani in guerra 1940-1943. Appunti per una ricerca', in F. Ferratini Tosi et al. (eds), *L'Italia nella seconda guerra mondiale e nella Resistenza* (Milan: Angeli, 1988); P. Cavallo, *Italiani in guerra. Sentimenti e immagini dal 1940 al 1943* (Bologna: Il Mulino, 1997); M. Fincardi, 'Le parabole del fronte interno', in Isnenghi, G. Albanese (eds), *Il ventennio fascista. La seconda guerra mondiale* (Turin: Utet, 2008).

13 See G. Gribaudi, *Guerra totale: tra bombe alleate e violenze naziste. Napoli e il fronte meridionale, 1940-1944* (Turin: Bollati Boringhieri, 2005), 89-93; Gioannini and Massobrio, *Bombardate l'Italia*, 270-278.

14 G. Chianese, *Quando uscimmo dai rifugi* (Rome: Carocci, 2004); Gribaudi, *Guerra totale*; U. Gentiloni Silveri and M. Carli, *Bombardare Roma: gli alleati e la città aperta, 1940-1944* (Bologna: Il Mulino, 2007).

15 C. Baldoli and M. Fincardi, 'Italian Society under Anglo-American Bombs: Propaganda, Experience and Legend, 1940-1945', *The Historical Journal*, 52, 2009, 1017-38.

16 See M. Piccialuti Caprioli, *Radio Londra 1939-1945* (Rome-Bari: Laterza, 1979); P. Fussell, *Wartime: Understanding and Behaviour in the Second World War* (New York: Oxford University Press, 1989); P. Ortoleva and C. Ottaviano (eds), *Guerra e mass media. Strumenti e modi della comunicazione in contesto bellico* (Naples: Liguori, 1994); A. Mignemi (ed.), *Propaganda politica e mezzi di comunicazione di massa* (Turin: Gruppo Abele, 1995).

17 The framework developed for other contexts by the economist Hirschmann can also be applied to this phase of the Italian war. See A. O. Hirschmann, *Exit, Voice and Loyalty: Responses to Decline in Firms, Organizations, and States* (Cambridge, Mass: Harvard University Press, 1970); and Id., *A Propensity to Self-Subversion* (Cambridge, Mass: Harvard University Press, 1995).

18 N. Della Volpe, *Esercito e propaganda nella seconda guerra mondiale. 1940-1943* (Rome: Ufficio storico stato maggiore dell'esercito, 1998).

19 Colarizi, *L'opinione degli italiani sotto il regime*, 339-43.

20 See A. Pizarroso Quintero, *Stampa, radio e propaganda. Gli Alleati in Italia 1943-1946* (Milan: Angeli, 1989), 25-34, 46; L. Mercuri, *Guerra psicologica. La propaganda anglo-americana in Italia 1942-1946* (Rome: Archivio trimestrale, 1983); P. Jammes, 'Essai de repertoire des tracts lancés par avion pendant la guerre 1939-1945', *Vieux papier*, 19, 1946; J. C. W. Field (ed.), *Aerial Propaganda Leaflets: a Collector's Handbook*, (Field: Sutton Coldfield, 1954); *A Complete Index of Allied Airborne Leaflets and Magazines 1939-1945* (a catalogue of all the propaganda dropped from the air by the British and Americans, compiled by an official, presumably in July 1945). From this last publication, the Psywar Society of Leeds has extracted a *Catalogue of Allied Leaflets Dropped in North Africa to German and Italian Troops and Civilians 1940-1943*.

21 Gentiloni Silveri and Carli, *Bombardare Roma*, 94-7.

22 Colarizi, *L'opinione degli italiani sotto il regime*, 364–67, 384–6.

23 Cortesi, *L'odissea degli sfollati, 1940–1945: la provincia di Forlì in guerra* (Cesena: Il Ponte Vecchio, 2003), 66–107.

24 V. Araldi, *La guerra delle parole. Il fallimento della propaganda inglese* (Bologna: Cantelli, 1942), 169–170, 200–1. See also Fondazione Luigi Micheletti, *L'Italia in guerra, 1940–1943. Immagini e temi della propaganda fascista* (Brescia: Fondazione Micheletti, 1989).

25 S. Satta, *De profundis* (Milan: Adelphi, 1980 – 1st edn. 1948), 71–3.

26 Ibid., 73.

27 See F. Coen, *Tre anni di bugie* (Milan: Poan, 1978); N. Tranfaglia and B. Maida (eds), *Ministri e giornalisti. La guerra e il Minculpop. 1939–43* (Turin: Einaudi, 2005), xxiv–xxvi.

28 Colarizi, *L'opinione degli italiani sotto il regime*, 393.

29 Sèe A. R. Perry, '"Era il nostro terrore". Un'indagine sul mito di Pippo', *Italia contemporanea*, 225, 2001, 589–604; C. Bermani, 'L'immaginario collettivo di guerra: il mito di "Pippo"', in *L'aeronautica italiana*, 229–65; Baldoli and Fincardi, 'Italian society under Anglo-American bombs'.

30 Tranfaglia and Maida, *Ministri e giornalisti*, 304–5.

31 V. Zincone, 'Stampa e propaganda in tempo di guerra', *Civiltà fascista*, 10, 1943, 526.

32 See G. B. Guerri, *Rapporto al duce* (Milan: Mondadori, 2003); Gallerano, 'Il fronte interno attraverso i rapporti delle autorità (1942–1943)', *Il Movimento di liberazione in Italia*, 24, 1972, 4–32; A. M. Imbriani, *Gli italiani e il duce (1938–43)* (Naples: Liguori, 1992); A. Lepre, *L'occhio del duce. Gli italiani e la censura di guerra 1940–1943* (Milan: Mondadori, 1992); Lepre, *Le illusioni, la paura, la rabbia. Il fronte interno 1940–1943* (Naples: Liguori, 1989); S. Luzzatto, *Il corpo del duce* (Turin: Einaudi, 1998).

33 G. Gentile, 'Discorso agli italiani', in B. Gentile (ed), *La vita e il pensiero*, vol. IV, (Florence: Sansoni, 1951), 74–5, 80.

34 Gentiloni Silveri and Carli, *Bombardare Roma*, 103.

35 Gioannini and Massobrio, *Bombardate l'Italia*, 338–9; Colarizi, *L'opinione degli italiani sotto il regime*, 408–10.

36 E. Flaiano, *Il Risorgimento liberale*, 19 July 1945.

37 Gallerano, 'L'arrivo degli alleati', in Isnenghi (ed.), *I luoghi della memoria. Strutture ed eventi dell'Italia unita* (Rome-Bari: Laterza, 1997), 455–64.

38 Gentiloni Silveri and Carli, *Bombardare Roma*, 176, 184.

39 Satta, *De profundis*, 88.

40 Ibid., 85–87.

41 See S. Setta, *Profughi di lusso. Industriali e manager di Stato dal fascismo alla epurazione mancata* (Milan: Angeli, 1993); R. Palmer Domenico, *Processo ai fascisti* (Milan: Rizzoli, 1996); H. Woller, *I conti con il fascismo* (Bologna: Il Mulino, 1997); Isnenghi, *La tragedia necessaria* (Bologna: Il Mulino, 1999); P. G. Zunino, *La Repubblica e il suo passato* (Bologna: Il Mulino, 2003); G. Oliva, *Le tre Italie del 1943* (Milan: Mondadori, 2004); Fincardi, 'L'incerto colore: i due dopoguerra in Italia', in S. Pivato and M. Ridolfi (eds), *I colori della politica. Passioni, emozioni e rappresentazioni nell'età contemporanea* (S. Marino: Guardigli, 2008), 129–43.

42 L. Borgomaneri (ed.), *Crimini di guerra. Il mito del 'bravo italiano' tra repressione del ribellismo e guerra ai civili nei territori occupati* (Milan: Guerrini e Associati, 2006).

Chapter 14

Muted Applause? British Prisoners of War as Observers and Victims of the Allied Bombing Campaign over Germany

Neville Wylie

By late 1944 some 180,000 British & Commonwealth prisoners of war (POWs), plus a further 45,000 from the United States, occupied ringside seats on the Allied bombing of Germany. When set alongside the millions of German civilians, POWs of other nationalities, internees and forced labourers caught up in the bombing, Anglo-American POWs represent a very small audience indeed. As victims, too, their experience was hardly exceptional: the 1,000 British POWs estimated to have been killed by the bombing is scarcely remarkable when compared to the 80,000 foreigners thought to have lost their lives as a result of Allied air action, far less the 410,000 German civilians who shared their fate. Nevertheless, the prisoners' perspective on the events is a distinctive one, and helps foreground certain features of the bombing experience not captured by other participants. As the title of this paper suggests, prisoners' attitudes towards the bombing offensive was ambivalent. Every bomb dropped on Germany brought them one step closer to home, but also exposed them to mortal danger. Bombing also threw up some awkward questions about the prisoners' place in the war, their relationship with the German authorities and with the German civilian population at large, whose suffering they not only witnessed but for which they were also, in part, responsible.

Though small in numerical terms, it would be wrong to assume that British POWs viewed the events through a single lens. Prisoners' experience could be shaped by a huge variety of factors, from their social background, religious beliefs, length of captivity or the arm of the services they belonged to. Officer and NCO prisoners – which included all pilots and aircrew – were, for the most part, detained in permanent camps, often located some distance from urban conurbations, and only ventured beyond the perimeter fence on carefully supervised 'parole walks' or when relocated to new camps. 'Other rank' POWs by contrast were held in work detachments and spent most of their time away from their base camps. Though some were billeted in rural areas, most worked in industrial areas and therefore faced the same dangers that confronted other sections of Germany's industrial work-force. It was only in the final months of the war, when the prisoners were moved to camps away from the front to prevent them from being liberated by the advancing Allied forces, that these distinctions broke down. The prisoners' military background also had a bearing on how they experienced the bombing. Knowing only too well the hazards involved in approaching a target, RAF prisoners were often distinctly 'jumpy', as one army observer put it, whenever planes were heard overhead, and spent a good deal of time 'praying to free pilots not to press their buttons until they got near the fires'.[1] Even here, though, experience was not uniform. One POW recalled the surprise of two recently downed US pilots at seeing British prisoners rush to the shelters whenever US aircraft were spotted in the area. It was only when the camp was bombed, two days after their arrival, that the pilots realized that their faith in the accuracy of Allied bomb-sights was sadly misplaced.[2]

INTRODUCTION

Notwithstanding the disparities that marked the experience of individual POWs, this paper offers some observations about how the bombing, in particular the growing presence of Allied aircraft above Germany, shaped prisoners' perceptions of their own captivity and their place in the war, and how it affected the prisoners' relations with their captors and civilian population. Before doing so, two general comments need to be made. First, for the vast majority of POWs, the bombing was only one – albeit important – element in the broader experience of captivity. Although prisoners' lives were affected by British air raids from an early date – many spent their first days in German hands clearing bomb damage caused by British aircraft – bombing only became a prominent feature in prisoners' lives from the autumn of 1943, when the fortunes of war had already tipped decisively in the Allies' favour. Inevitably, the meaning prisoners attached to the appearance of Allied aircraft was coloured by their general reading of the war situation. Secondly, for 'long-timers', which included the 80,000 men captured during the campaigns of 1940/1, the arrival of significant numbers of Allied aircraft coincided with the end of what many referred to as the 'static' period of captivity.[3] During the middle years of the war, in the absence of any immediate hope of an early end to the conflict or repatriation on the grounds of health or length of captivity (the first Anglo-German exchange did not occur until October 1943), most POWs were compelled to adjust to a form of existence that bore little relation to the world existing beyond their camp. The psychological impact of captivity, and the attendant problems associated with 'barbed wire disease', was perhaps less noticeable for 'other rank' prisoners whose work took them out of their camps for long periods each day. But once the initial trauma of their capture had worn off, most devoted their energies towards overcoming the appalling monotony and drudgery of POW life.

Prisoners' coping strategies varied greatly, but P. J. C. Dark, who was captured at St Nazaire in March 1942, offers a useful insight into the process when he spoke of prisoners' lives bifurcating into two forms of existence. One, he suggested, recognized the physical constraints imposed by captivity – the roll-calls, barbed wire, sentries and watchtowers – and the surreal vacuum it created to those hemmed in within its boundaries; the other took advantage of the regularity and minimal impact of the guards' intrusion into the prisoners' day-to-day lives and saw prisoners focusing on those activities – from gardening to reading, theatre-going to sporting pursuits – that offered a partial substitute for the kind of lives they had enjoyed at home. The former saw the prisoner 'contending with the physical world of his incarceration'; the latter, which Dark argued tended to predominate, 'was a daydream ... relating one to the outside [world]'. Over time, prisoners' sensitivity towards their past lives and the existence of the world beyond the wire gradually ebbed. 'One is aware there is a life outside', Dark recalled, 'but nearly all the beyond is danger, and only in the remote distance lies freedom'.[4] Prisoners coped, then, by creating a form of surrogate normalcy, recreating as best they could the trappings of a peacetime world to replace the reality they had lost on entering captivity. For this purpose, it is important to note that the appearance of Allied bombers occurred at precisely the time that the 'normalcy' in prisoners' lives came under pressure. Overcrowding, especially after the transfer of POWs from Italy in late 1943 and onset of fighting in France in June 1944, coupled with the sharp deterioration in the level of rations reaching POWs in the second half of 1944, meant that prisoners found it increasingly difficult to apply themselves to the kinds of pursuits that had provided such emotional and psychological release in the past.

THE BOMBERS AS LIBERATORS

These two points need to be borne in mind in deciphering the emotions expressed by POWs at the sudden presence of Allied bombers above them from late 1943. Few diarists failed to record their impressions on encountering Allied aircraft for the first time. For most, it was the throbbing sound of the aircraft engines at night, and the wail of the air-raid sirens heralding their approach, that first signalled the presence of friendly forces. On these occasions, though a wave of excitement invariably rippled through the barracks, the lack of *visual* contact and the fact that men experienced the event in the silence of the night, either on their own or in small groups, created what one POW called a 'strange kind of excitement': an exhilaration at the novelty of the sound, and what it meant for Allied war fortunes, mixed with a sense of melancholy and homesickness.[5] The situation is captured in the sketch by W. S. A. Clough-Taylor – 'Listen! Here they come!' – which featured in the spring 1945 edition of the *Quill*, a camp magazine produced by officers at Oflag IX A/H, Spangenburg.

POW diaries suggest, however, that it was the visual spectacle of 'silvery streaks' darting across the sky, as one POW put it, that ignited prisoners' enthusiasm and boosted their morale.[6] One of the best descriptions of these events

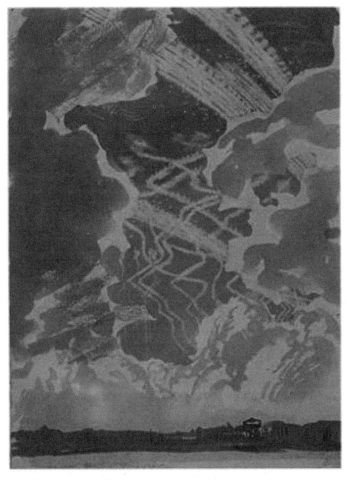

John Worsley, 'Heavies' over Germany: Spring 1945', watercolour. Worsley painted this picture while an inmate of Marlag-Milag camp. The painting well illustrates the way in which the appearance of Allied planes over Germany transformed POWs' perceptions of, and relationship to the 'world beyond the wire'. Imperial War Museum, London. Art LD 5125.

is provided by J. Ellison Platt, an inmate of Oflag IV C, Colditz. Planes had been heard above Colditz castle since the autumn of 1943, and by the spring of 1944 nightly air-raid warnings had become so frequent that they created 'no stir except an odd cheer from the irrepressible'. On 28 May, however, the sound of Leipzig's flak batteries opening up sent prisoners rushing to the windows, and soon had men standing three to four deep, watching the attack unfold. Suddenly, Platt wrote, there was such a crescendo of howling and cheering as I have not heard since I sat with the football crowds at Wembley, for someone at the north window had spotted a formation of bombers with fighter escort that, having passed over the target and unloaded, had turned and were coming in our direction. For fifteen minutes [as the planes passed over the camp] there was such excitement as will only be equalled when the news of the invasion reaches us.... The bombers were the first Liberators and Fortresses most of us had ever seen and were certainly the first friendly planes most of us had seen (though we had heard many) since we were taken prisoner.... If ever dull monotony was shattered, it was so today. British air supremacy has passed out of the realm of newspaper reports into mass formations of bombers with an umbrella of fighters, sailing into our sight as unmolested as though they flew over America, or any country of the British Empire. I have never known this camp so jubilant as on this Whitsunday 1944.[7]

Platt's account hints at some of the range of emotions triggered by the sight of friendly planes. Prisoners were frequently struck, like Platt, by the technological sophistication of the aircraft on display. The heavy four-engine bombers and their long-distance escorts far outshone the antiquated equipment most had known before their capture. The impudence shown by the bomber streams in traversing German skies at will inevitably underscored the upswing in Allied war fortunes and exhibited a sense of agency and independence so obviously lacking in the prisoners' lives up until that date. Diary accounts frequently portrayed the bomber crew as carefree youngsters. Even in late 1944, when Allied planes were regularly spotted above western and central Germany, prisoners could still be struck by the 'pretty patterns' made by the vapour trails; like 'the marks left by a child who has been playing with chalk on a slate', as one inmate of Stalag Luft I, Barth recalled.[8] 'The bombers', an N.C.O. prisoner wrote in his diary on 28 November 1944, 'are shooting across the sky like shoals of tadpoles while their escorting fighters loop and criss-cross, and gambol like lambs in the spring'. These 'inspiring sights' had an immediate effect on the prisoners' psychological state. [9] 'Morale', noted one officer POW on seeing a stream of bombers heading towards Augsburg in March 1944, 'went up 50 per cent by this amazing sight, like the thermometer in our room when the fire is lit, only then it is about 1,000 per cent.'[10]

The effect of the bomber formations on the prisoners was, however, more profound than simply administering a much needed shot in the prisoners' arm. At a fundamental level, the appearance of Allied bombers irrevocably changed the way British POWs viewed their place in the war. The bombers transformed the prisoners' relationship with the world beyond their camps and resuscitated a sense of time that had been largely lost to those inured to the monotonies of life in captivity. For one thing, the bombers brought the war back into the prisoners' lives. 'The war that had vanished in Corinth four years before had suddenly returned to our very doorstep', noted one POW on seeing Allied aircraft above his camp in early 1944.[11] 'We have suddenly seemed to enter into the picture of war', noted another diarist at the same time, 'due solely to the increase in the number of air raid warnings that come our way.'[12] Prisoners could finally dare to contemplate, and even make preparations for, their first days of freedom. The sight of Allied aircraft also helped turn what had hitherto been an unchanging, almost inert, landscape beyond the prisoners' enclosures into a vibrant arena of action, pregnant with meaning, movement and almost infinite possibilities. For the first time, the 'real' world no longer had to be imagined or artfully reconstructed, but could be seen, smelt, sensed and heard. Far from the bombers 'freezing' time – fixing the hands of clocks at the bomb's first strike – for British prisoners, the bombers' arrival jolted time back on to its axis. The planes brought an end to the 'interminable weekend' of POW life – 'an endless Saturday and Sunday that never succeeds on getting round to Monday', as one POW put it – and reconnected prisoners with the 'real' world, governed not by roll-calls and dinner-times, but by events hewn by the actions of their compatriots.[13]

The impact is perhaps most noticeable in the content of prisoners' diaries and log books, which had up until then largely dealt with mundane events, camp distractions and the omnipresent pre-occupation with food. With the onset of the bombing campaign, diaries became alive. The process was particularly pronounced in the Far East, where the appearance of Allied aircraft in late 1944 frequently encouraged prisoners to return to their diaries after months of neglect.[14] But even in Europe, diary entries expanded, sentence length increased, and prisoners began meticulously noting the duration and frequency of air raids, or estimating the number of aircraft passing overhead. Red-letter days were no longer confined to the arrival of relief parcels or mail from home. Camp magazines and newspapers reflected this trend, featuring sketches, paintings, poems and stories relating to the bombing, and connecting the prisoners' lives with events taking place beyond the perimeter fence. Food remained an abiding topic of conversation, but it now featured in the prisoners' attempts to connect with their compatriots, piloting the planes above them. What struck Platt on the morning after the Whitsun demonstration of Allied airpower was the knowledge that the bombers 'were manned by men who spoke our tongue, men who had enjoyed an English tea and [who] would – at least, most of them – be back home in a few hours enjoying an early English breakfast'.[15] 'At tea yesterday', another POW noted after catching sight of Allied planes for the first time, 'I suddenly wondered how many of those crews – probably very young lads – were sitting down to a damn good and well-deserved meal in their Mess at home, only a few hours after we had seen their machines over us ...'.[16] Captain J. M. Kinross, who had been captured in Crete in the spring of 1941, echoed these sentiments. After witnessing one of the early raids on Hamburg in October 1941, he noted how 'strange' it was 'to think of one's own people up there above; these pilots would be returning to their breakfasts in a few hours' time. Imagine an English breakfast again and reading the papers, jokes in the mess – for them an unnoticed everyday affair not to be given a moment's thought – to me the longed-for climax of all these miserable months'.[17]

'FRIENDLY FIRE'

The events therefore had an energizing effect on British POWs that was probably only matched, as Platt predicted, by news of the opening of the second front in June 1944. Yet if the arrival of Allied bombers helped reconnect the prisoners with the war and instil a sense of pride in the uniform they wore, it inevitably had an unsettling effect too. The war may have come to their doorstep, but the prisoners' capacity to influence the climactic events was no greater than it had been before. 'Goon baiting' – the most common technique used to undermine German authority – inevitably came to look rather juvenile when set beside the aerial duels played out in the skies above Germany. Newly minted POWs, many aircrew themselves, were often puzzled by the 'childish' antics and sullen outlook of 'long-timers'.[18] Even escaping – the most direct form of defiance open to POWs – diminished in importance after the murder of the 'great escapers' from Stalag Luft III in March 1944 prompted London to discourage its men from planning mass break-outs. For many POWs therefore the very novelty of aerial bombing, on the scale seen in 1944, went to underline their own powerlessness and lack of agency.

Likewise, while the bombers' arrival brought the prisoners demonstrably closer to the moment of liberation, it also increased the danger of death or serious injury. No exact figures exist for the number of British POWs killed by 'friendly fire' in Germany, though the figure of one thousand deaths, given by Wynne Mason, New Zealand's official historian of POWs, seems plausible. According to reports reaching London from the Swiss government and International Committee of the Red Cross, the worst single incident involving the death of British POWs was the bombing of a camp near Epinal, France, which claimed the lives of 400 Indian prisoners. An attack on a train at L'Aquila, Italy, ferrying POWs into Germany in December 1943, killed another 140. By the autumn of 1944, London had evidence of some 651 deaths through Allied air action since mid-1943: 166 in Italy, 400 in France and 85 in Germany, the latter between May and August 1944. Though the figures for L'Aquila and Epinal were unconfirmed, the accuracy of the figures for Germany can probably be relied upon. The increasing frequency of raids on Germany inevitably meant that the death rate was set to climb. In August, Stalag VII B suffered a 'St Bartholomew's massacre' when the lead American aircraft in an attack on a nearby aircraft factory mistakenly dropped a bomb marker in the middle of the British compound: the resulting bombardment left seven dead and many injured.[19] Corporal Robert Prouse, a Canadian captured at Dieppe, recalled that by November 1944 there was 'seldom a moment that heavy bombers with fighter escorts were not seen overhead', and counted no fewer than 115 air-raid warnings for his camp, Stalag IX C, in December alone.[20] This month also proved the most costly to date. The number of *reported* fatalities crept up from six in October and eight in November, to 48 in December, largely the result of the bombing of Arbeitskommando E793 on 2 December, which led to the deaths of 28 men, with a similar number seriously injured.[21] 'But for the fact that only 500 of the camp's complement of 1,169 were in the camp at the time', noted camp leader R S M Sherriff, 'the casualties would almost certainly have been far greater.'[22]

A considerable (though again unknown) number of deaths was caused by tactical air attacks. The psychological impact of these low-level attacks on POWs was probably greater than the earlier 'strategic' bombing, partly because of the prisoners' enfeebled state by this stage of the war – brought on by weeks of forced marches on inadequate provisions – and partly because, with the end of the war literally days away, the loss of one's friends was that bit harder to bear. The majority of British and American POWs were held in Poland and the eastern provinces of Germany and were therefore largely unaffected by the Allied strategic bombing campaign over 1943 and 1944; it was only in early 1945, when they were evacuated westwards to avoid falling into the hands of the advancing Soviet forces, that these men saw the Allied air forces first hand.[23] Though numerous permanent camps and work detachments were bombed, it was when prisoners joined the throng of displaced people on the open road, moving from one camp to another, that the danger of attack from the air reached its peak. Prisoners whose columns avoided the attention of Allied aircraft counted themselves lucky: by the spring of 1945, some camp captains simply refused to allow their men to leave the camps in daylight for fear of being attacked.[24]

Tragically, it was the final month of the war that saw the greatest number of deaths from 'friendly fire'. Three of the worst incidents occurred in a single week. Six prisoners, the majority from the naval camp, Marlag Milag, were killed on 12 April when a pair of US Thunderbolts strafed their column as it worked its way towards Lübeck. Two days later, the evacuation of Oflag VII B, Eichstätt, was stopped in its tracks when eight men were killed and a further 42 wounded within hours of leaving the camp. Only 20 minutes before, the prisoners had raised a cheer at the sight of a solitary US fighter which had circled the column waggling its wings. As a result, when eight Thunderbolts began strafing a convoy of lorries on a parallel road 800 yards away, most prisoners viewed the event with more interest than concern and were 'gawping upwards' when the planes suddenly levelled their gunsights on the column of ambling men. In the words of one survivor, 'Black Monday' was 'the most tragic, terrifying and emotional day of my life'.[25] Worse was in store for evacuees from Stalag 357, Fallingbostel, who lost 37 men dead and many more severely injured to a Typhoon attack on 16 April.[26] By the end of the month, over a quarter of all Red Cross relief trucks operating out of the north German port of Lübeck had been destroyed by Allied air attacks.[27]

All prisoners who endured the appalling final weeks of the war in German hands attest to the constant fear of being ambushed by low-flying aircraft. Dr. Borrie, whose Lazaret was evacuated by train to Stalag VIII B, Lamsdorf, in Upper Silesia in February 1945, spoke of the terror on hearing that 'sickening drone overhead'. 'Because there now seemed a faint hope of freedom', he recalled, 'our anxiety was at its peak. Each carried with him months of privation and uncertainty – lasting memories. Now, 2,000 men sweated side by side under lock and key, an unprotected target on a moonlit railroad'.[28] Each man dealt with this fear in their own way. The sense of excitement and curiosity that greeted the first sightings of bombers in late 1943 and early 1944 thus gave way to mounting anxiety. In early January 1944 Sergeant Nell was so euphoric at feeling the ground shake beneath his feet that he labelled anyone showing fear a 'yellow rat'.[29] Such insensitivity was, however, relatively rare, and usually reserved for those like Nell whose camp escaped the attention of the passing planes. POWs who experienced bombing first hand often found that their words came to carry more weight with their peers than those who had not.[30] Colonel Arnold of the US Army Air Corps recalled a raid on Stalag XIII B, Nuremberg, in which a wave of panic swept through the compound, leaving prisoners 'crying, yelling, wailing and praying'.[31] By late 1944, according to Robert Prouse, 'no one ridiculed or blamed these men'; instead, most 'went out of their way to talk with them and to sympathize, trying to get their minds away from the growing thoughts of impending doom'.[32] Rumours of friendly fire incidents – often with wildly inflated death tolls – spread quickly in POW compounds, heightening the sense of apprehension.[33] Captain Casdagli, whose own camp was fortunate in avoiding direct attack, recorded in his diary on 26 December 1944 news of an attack on a 'local Stalag' which had left 48 prisoners dead and another 200 injured. On New Year's Eve, he reported the return of a fellow officer whose nerves were 'all to hell from the bombing' after an eight week spell in a German military hospital in Limburg.[34]

HUMAN SHIELDS AND *LYNCHJUSTIZ*

Probably the most significant consequence of the increased presence of Allied bombers over Germany was the impact on the prisoners' relations with the German authorities and population at large. This was, to some extent, entirely in keeping with the broader historical experience of wartime captivity: prisoners' treatment tends to deteriorate the closer they come to the front line. A case could be made for seeing the relative benevolence in German treatment of British POWs before June 1944 as a function of the passivity of British belligerency before this date. In extending the battleground to Germany's 'home front', the Allied air offensive inevitably compromised the prisoners' security and damaged their relations with their captors.

That the bombing offensive led to a decline in the treatment of British POWs was at one level, however, entirely deliberate. Though Germany had traditionally penalized British POWs in reprisal for alleged infractions of London's obligations under the 1929 POW convention, the enunciation of the 'commando order' in October 1942 – stipulating that British commandos were to be liquidated on capture – started a process that saw the German leadership progressively use British POWs in retaliation for Britain's illegal methods of war.[35] As early as August 1943, the Luftwaffe proposed constructing new camps in built-up areas to provide what it called a 'certain security' against further raids. London, it was suggested, could be allowed to learn of the new camps' existence through the arrival of POW death notices.[36] Though the proposal was never acted upon, the temptation to use British POWs as a 'human shield' did not disappear: in December 1944 Hitler considered holding 5,000 Allied airmen in central Berlin for this very reason. Two months later, his propaganda chief, Josef Goebbels, demanded the execution of several thousand Allied POWs in retaliation for the obliteration of Dresden on 12/13 February 1945. The fragmentary evidence we have on Hitler's attitude towards Allied POWs in the final months of the war likewise suggests that, besides officer POWs and the so-called *Prominente* – the scions of British aristocracy – it was RAF prisoners who the Führer wanted to use as bargaining chips in negotiations with the Allied authorities, or as victims of a final, gruesome 'blood-payment' before the eclipse of his regime.[37]

If Hitler ever believed he could distract the Allied bombing campaign by threatening the lives of British POWs, he was mistaken. At no time did the British or US governments ever permit concerns for the safety of their prisoners to dictate military choices. Quite the reverse: Britain's service chiefs were explicitly instructed *not* take to such considerations into account when planning military operations. When the matter came up for discussion in late 1944, a consensus quickly emerged that little could be gained from expressing 'righteous wrath in public' over the deaths of Allied POWs in German hands, not least as this would only underscore the extent to which the Allied bombing targeted Germany's civilian workforce. It was, moreover, 'questionable' whether German POWs were entirely safe from danger during the flying bomb attacks on southern England at the same time.[38] Though anxiety was voiced at the mounting number of fatalities among British and American POWs, at no time did the deaths of other nationalities ever provoke comment in Whitehall. On 6 February 1945, four days before the attack on Dresden, the chiefs of staff concluded that – in contrast to the Japanese, who were believed to have deliberately exposed prisoners to air attacks in Thailand – 'Germany has not used Prisoners of War to render legitimate targets immune'. News of Hitler's musings over the fate of British POWs in the wake of the Dresden bombing reached London in early March, but no one believed a change of policy would influence the Führer's views. Indeed, by this stage of the war, it was generally held that anxieties over the wellbeing of their men ought to be kept secret, lest they merely encourage Nazi extremists to turn against the defenceless prisoners.[39]

Though incidents certainly occurred, the evidence of the deliberate placing of POWs near strategic targets in an effort to deter – or punish – Allied attacks is not sufficient to demonstrate official intent to use Allied POWs in this way. Instead, decisions appear to have been taken at a local level. On one occasion POWs were held at gunpoint in central Braunschweig during a bombing raid on the city. Memoir literature attests to numerous instances in which prisoners' lives were endangered by their being denied entry to air-raid shelters, confined to their barracks or prevented from constructing suitable trenches or shelters in the camps. Prisoners were frequently left to fend for themselves during air raids, seeking shelter among the rubble or fleeing from the target area. Though London considered lodging a general protest in late 1944, officials ultimately decided to keep their powder dry for use in specific cases. As early as mid-1944, however, there were twenty-six camps, including most of the principal camps holding British POWs, and numerous hospitals thought to be either dangerously close to military installations or lacking in adequate air-raid shelters.[40] This number did not include the many hundreds of work detachments, whose location was unknown to the Swiss diplomats and Red Cross delegates, and where the majority of fatalities appear to have occurred.

Where more malevolence can be shown behind official German policy was in the encouragement given to public attacks against downed airmen. As early as mid-1943, the police were instructed not to intervene to protect Allied airmen from the fury of German civilians.[41] Attacks on Allied pilots certainly took place from this date, but the number and intensity dramatically increased after the early summer of 1944, when the regime took further and more public steps to promote *Lynchjustiz*. In a widely reported article in the *Völkischer Beobachter* on 27 May 1944, Josef Goebbels praised the actions of some Saxon farmers who had spent their Whitsun afternoon hunting down and murdering an Allied pilot who had allegedly strafed a group of children at play.[42] Reports of similar incidents began appearing in the German and neutral press over subsequent weeks. As early as the first week of June, decrypted German signals traffic confirmed that Berlin was deliberately publicizing incidents of 'spontaneous' mob violence against downed pilots in the hope of intimidating Allied aircrew and discouraging low-level attacks.[43]

Whether or not Goebbels' initiative was quietly suppressed by the *Wehrmacht* and *Luftwaffe* authorities, as General Alfred Jodl later claimed at Nuremberg, there is little doubt that many Allied airmen lost their lives to angry mobs before they could reach the sanctuary of a POW camp. The post-war American court at Dachau heard over 200 cases against individuals involved in *Lynchjustiz*, while British investigations unearthed the names of at least 125 airmen who had died in this way.[44] Conservative estimates of the number of fatalities start at 350, though some scholars have put the figure as high as 1,500 (700 USAF and 800 RAF). Given the frequency with which ill-treatment crops up in the diaries and memoirs of Allied aircrew, a figure of 700 seems plausible.[45] If lynching cannot be considered the norm, threatening behaviour of German civilians certainly was. Many airmen came perilously close to death or serious injury at the hands of irate civilians. The experience of Squadron Leader Arct, a Spitfire pilot shot down in September 1944, can be taken as typical. On his capture, Arct's first port of call was the Luftwaffe interrogation centre at Oberursel, near Frankfurt am Main. Arriving at Frankfurt's main station just after an RAF raid on the city, Arct and his two fellow RAF prisoners attracted such hostility that their guards felt it necessary to avoid the city centre and continue their journey by train and tram. Even at the outskirts of the city, however, Arct's guards had to overpower a labourer, who drew a pistol on the prisoners, and beat back an angry crowd. They could do little, though, to stop two soldiers veering their car towards the prisoners with the intention of running them over. Arct was hit by the bumper but fortunately sustained only minor bruises. 'But for our guards', Arct later recalled 'we would probably have had a pretty rough time at the hands of these hoodlums'.[46]

Although it was often the intercession of the local police, *Volkssturm* or *Wehrmacht* units that saved Allied pilots from the wrath of local thugs or Nazi officials, post-war investigations do not lead to any firm conclusions on the matter.[47] All too often it was members of the uniformed services that were guilty of executing Allied POWs. The number of recorded incidents in which civilians were *solely* responsible for the death of Allied pilots is relatively small. Civilians were invariably complicit in killings, orchestrated by members of the armed services.[48] Typical was the murder of three unidentified RAF airmen, rounded up after a raid on Essen on 12/13 December 1944 who were, like Arct two months earlier, surrounded by an angry crowd on their way to the railway station. On this occasion, the prisoners' escort, led by a Hauptmann Erich Heyer, did little to calm the situation; one of the corporals injured an airmen in the head with a shot from his revolver, while Heyer was reported to have shouted, 'These are the dogs who have killed our wives and children. Kill them!' The airmen were promptly thrown off a bridge; one was killed by the fall, while the remainder were beaten to death by the civilian crowd.[49]

Officially, *Lynchjustiz* was only sanctioned for those individuals guilty of strafing civilians, commuter trains and hospitals, or firing upon German pilots as they descended to the ground by parachute.[50] Though such details were no doubt lost on those bent on avenging the loss of their homes and loved ones, a distinction ought to be drawn between the treatment meted out to downed aircrew, and that shown to regular prisoners – even RAF prisoners – based in permanent camps. Downed pilots were invariably caught injured, alone and close to the scenes of their 'crime'. Once they had passed into official hands and registered as POWs, the opportunity for individuals to take the law into their own hands diminished. Having killed three crew members of a downed Liberator on 4 March 1945, Adolf Franz Haan's SS unit found it impossible either to prise the fourth member of the crew, Flt Lt Macdonald Moor, from the hands of the Graz police authorities, or convince them to shoot the airman themselves.[51] Most civilians only encountered British POWs as part of a larger work detachment or marching column, when the men could derive some protection from the safety of numbers. Nonetheless, by the final years of the war it is clear that British uniforms no longer afforded the same guarantee for good treatment as they once had. 'Since obliteration bombing began', reported an army captain after his repatriation in October 1943, 'the civilians whom prisoners meet travelling in trains from one prison camp to another are perhaps a shade less ready to start conversation.'[52] By early 1945, Swiss diplomats were reporting that the bombing of German cities was creating an increasingly 'ugly mood' against British prisoners.[53] When Capt Stuart Mawson RAMC emerged from his air-raid shelter to tend to injured civilians after the bombing of Leipzig on 22 February 1944, it was only his Red Cross armbands that spared him from some 'nasty incidents'. Elsewhere in the city, vengeful citizens stoned British POWs employed to clear fallen debris.[54] The only firm conclusion that can be drawn from these incidents is that members of the Luftwaffe and permanent camp guards were generally more sympathetic towards the prisoners than their colleagues in the other services. A sense of mutual respect between the air services appears to have influenced the behaviour of Luftwaffe personnel.[55] In the case of the permanent camp guards, not only was it their job to protect the prisoners, but they were rarely in the position to abuse their power without fear of consequences. Incidents of maltreatment and neglect were rife during the final months of the war, but so too were examples of prisoners helping their elderly guards survive the gruelling marches, and avoid death or serious injury through air attacks.[56] Cold and cannon fire were indiscriminate in their effects on a marching column.

The demonstration of Allied firepower inevitably had the effect of upsetting the established routines, expectations and boundaries that had been constructed between the prisoners and their captors and overseers. As Jonathan Vance has shown, camp authorities were rarely able to impose their will arbitrarily on the prisoners: a bargaining process was always at work mediating the interests of the two parties.[57] The arrival of Allied aircraft inevitably opened up new areas for negotiation. In some cases, the result was detrimental to the prisoners. In Oflag VII B, Eichstätt, attempts to have prisoners return to their barracks during air raids got off to a bad start when, on the very first air raid, two officer POWs were shot for disobeying their guards' commands. It took several weeks before a workable set of regulations was agreed upon between the commandant and the prisoners' camp leader, the senior British officer.[58] Even when arrangements were put in place, the pandemonium created by the sudden appearance of Allied aircraft invariably prevented the German authorities from enforcing normal regulations. Naturally, sentries took no joy in the sight of Allied bomber formations, and resented egregious displays of gloating or revelry on the part of their captives. Some of the shooting incidents at Eichstätt and other camps were probably inspired by such sentiments, though the violent suppression of the celebrations that occasioned the arrival of two Mosquitoes above Stalag Luft I on 22 April 1944 was at least justified on the grounds that the camp authorities feared the event was being used to cover an escape attempt.[59] Enforcing blackout restrictions and air-raid precautions proved increasingly difficult. Corporal Robert Prouse so loathed descending into the flea-invested dungeons that served as air-raid shelters at Stalag IX C that he tried to hide himself above ground whenever the air raid siren went off. On 1 December 1944, his entire hut received twelve days 'Strafe' for failing to head for the shelters when required.[60] As the frequency and duration of the air raids intensified – in March 1945 alone, Prouse's working party was ordered to the shelters on 170 occasions, lasting a total of 235 hours – the guards' authority gradually declined. Outside prison camps, the breakdown of order was even more observable. The meticulous arrangements to segregate prisoners of different nationalities, or limit their contact with forced labourers, foreign workers or the civilian population, often collapsed. For many prisoners, the air raids offered fleeting moments of freedom, allowing them to interact with other individuals on equal terms. It is indicative of the extent to which racial boundaries disintegrated under the pressure of the bombing that as early as the spring of 1943, the OKW began publicizing evidence of exemplary behaviour and good discipline amongst POWs during the aerial attacks.[61]

BOMBING AND POW ATTITUDES TOWARDS THE GERMAN POPULATION

Where the strategic bombing had a transformative effect on the experience of British POWs was in its effect on the prisoners' relations with the German civilian population. In a startlingly candid post-war account of a daylight raid on Uelzen railway station, where his work detachment was employed clearing bomb debris, Jim Sims remarked that he and his colleagues were not 'unduly upset by POWs killed in the raid'. It was, he claimed, the 'dead children [that] upset us. We had some sympathy for the German women and children, but it all seemed such a waste'.[62] British prisoners tended to recognize that they were, at least partially, responsible for the bombing. POWs remained members of the British armed forces, and it was for their benefit that the RAF was wreaking such havoc on the German people.[63] Attitudes on this point clearly varied. Though conscious of the moral ambiguity of aerial bombing, Captain Kinross's account of the bombing of Hamburg in October 1941 left little doubt as to where his own loyalties lay: 'God! how I envied [the pilots], high up, riding over the shell bursts, cool and impersonal, picking out their targets. How callous, how beastly this bombing of civil towns, cruel, impersonal, murderous – what wouldn't I give to be up with them!'[64]

But by late 1943, prisoners' diaries reveal a growing sense of unease at the relentless and indiscriminate destruction they observed around them. On 17 March 1944, a day after watching a flight of bombers pass overhead on their way to bomb Augsburg, Captain Mansel admitted that while he was still enthralled by 'yesterday afternoon's wonderful entertainment', he could not help 'reflecting on the horrible side of it and the madness of war'. For Dunkirk veterans like Mansel, Britain's embrace of area bombing was unsettling precisely because it was at odds with the kind of values that they had known before their capture. 'No doubt [the bombing] wouldn't seem quite so mad', Mansel ruminated, 'if we weren't sitting here to all intents and purposes out of sight of war altogether and if we could see some of the bomb damage at home, let alone a modern battle-field'.[65] As the bombing raids intensified over 1944, prisoners found it harder to explain away their misgivings. There was something fundamentally wrong about being able to read the pages of the German newspaper, the *Camp*, by the light of burning cities.[66] Even those officers and NCOs whose contact with the German civilian population was limited found the sight of such destruction unsettling. The view afforded on a raid on Potsdam from Pilot Ron Walker's hut at Stalag III A, Luckenwalde, 'was so awe-inspiring' that it made him shake and feel physically sick. Though such acts would, he thought, 'undoubtedly finish the war ... I had to wonder whether any nation had the right to employ such a diabolical means'.[67]

The moral dilemma confronting prisoners was illustrated in a poem by Lt Col D. G. Adams, a Dunkirk veteran from the East Surrey Regiment, who witnessed the bombing of Kassel from the safety of Oflag IX A/H, Spangenburg, on 22/23 October 1943. Though the depiction of events is probably imaginary – there is no reason to believe he was in Kassel at the time – the sentiments it conveyed were no doubt sincere;

Slowly the sound of the battle departs;
Only the smoke and the fires remain,
The Fighters of fires, and the funeral carts,
And the weeping of countless, comfortless hearts
That follow their train.

Surely my soul with a joy should awaken,
Soul that has known the enemy's guile;
Father and Mother homeless and shaken,
Home of my own destroyed, freedom forsaken?
Vengeance is slow, but it comes – and is vile![68]

Like Adams, for most of 1944 Sergeant Nell observed the bombing from afar. His detailed diary entries of his time at Stalag IV B, Mülberg, show very clearly the conflicting emotions provoked by the bombing. In fact Nell, a professional soldier with pre-war service on the North West frontier, never fully came to terms with the moral ambiguity of the situation, even after experiencing the bombers' destructive power first hand when his camp was bombed on 3 December 1944. His diary frequently talks of the 'deliciously devastating rumble of exploding bombs' and of his enjoyment in 'listening joyfully in the

darkness' as the 'sirens warbled merrily'.[69] He occasionally recorded his delight
at the thought of making 'good [i.e. dead] Germans' and of the bombing being
dragged out until Germany's 'absolute exhaustion'; 'Sterilization to the last Nazi!
Needs must …!'.[70] In early October 1944, with the weather deteriorating and
the bombing offensive unrelenting, he sought to justify his views on military
grounds: 'Whole residential areas have been blotted out. This seems inhuman
but all war is inhuman so what does it matter! And at this stage of the war
– and the year – the bombing of residential areas is almost as important as
bombing industrial areas'.[71] But try as he could to rationalize the events, he
ultimately found it impossible to ignore his own discomfort at the suffering
caused or, indeed, hide his embarrassment at the pleasure he took in witnessing
such unprecedented destruction. His anger was increasingly directed against
'the bastards who are ruling this country [and who] are afraid for themselves,
knowing that their lives will end when the war does'.[72] 'I'm sure some of us felt
uneasy about our jubilance', he wrote on 28 November:

> It is winter and cold and where once stood homes and ordered living there is now
> dereliction and virtual desert and dead and maimed people. And terrified screaming
> children. During the periods of silence we could hear the low rumbling of the devas-
> tation taking place in the distance – Germany crumbling.[73]

It was only in early 1945, when his own material situation had deteriorated,
that a coldness began to enter his diary entries.[74] 'We ought to feel sorry for the
thousands of people being made homeless', he wrote on 3 March, 'but, at best,
I think we're indifferent. Man's inhumanity to man! But it's reciprocal. We're
trying to exist on a diet, per day, of a little bread, a couple of potatoes, a mug-full
of thin soup, and a little margarine (ersatz). Also there would be some jam but
we've had none of this during the last two weeks'.[75]

There was, of course, something paradoxical in the bombing's impact on
prisoners' attitudes. If the havoc wrought by the bombing erased the boundaries
separating prisoners from the German civilian population and put prisoners
into contact with German civilians as never before, it was the horror brought in
the wake of such indiscriminate destruction that enabled prisoners' to sympathize with their luckless captors and their families. 'During the air raids we met
a lot of people from Graz', recalled Ray Dalton; one such person, a local girl
from Graz, would become his future wife.[76] Dalton belonged to a very small
minority of British POWs who became romantically engaged with German
women during the war, but Allied air activity was probably an important
contributory factor in the fourfold increase in the number of cases brought
against German women for fraternizing with foreign prisoners between 1941
and 1942.[77] POWs did not, however, need to be romantically involved with
German civilians to empathize with their plight, or feel unease at their own
complicity, however marginal, in the dreadful events around them, notwithstanding the fact that the majority of POWs employed in work detachments

were soldiers, not airmen. When private 'Dusty' Ayling's detachment was caught up in a raid in early November 1944, he instinctively helped a mother carry her children to the nearest shelter, and comforted them as bombs rained down. Ayling's reaction was no doubt triggered by a sense of shared humanity, but after the event he could not help feeling that his behaviour had 'served as good propaganda in counteracting in a small way the picture of British soldiers depicted as flat-nosed, cauliflower-eared murderers of women and children'.[78] A similar mixture of sentiments may have prompted the inmates of Stalag IV B to follow the lead given by one of the camp padres, Revd R. G. McDowall, and offer sanctuary to local German families after the camp was liberated by Russian forces in late April.[79]

If British POWs looked upon the German population with growing sympathy, there is little doubt that they were also won over by the display of stoicism and resilience shown by the German civilian population. Stuart Mawson, who had lived through the London Blitz, felt that the tremendous exertions he saw after a devastating raid on Leipzig had little to do with national characteristics. 'After a raid on such an oppressive scale', he argued, 'the feeling of relief of the survivors at still being in one piece releases a great wave of pent-up energy directed at picking up the pieces and starting again'.[80] Others, however, sought to explain it in terms of the effects of Nazi brain-washing or the workings of the 'Teutonic mind'. 'Dusty' Ayling caught the prevailing mood when he described the German reaction to a raid on Weissenfels on 14 September 1944, which left the factory at which he was employed entirely crippled. 'The Huns', he wrote,

> have to be admired, for immediately 'all-clear' sounded, remote control from Berchtesgaden caused these well-indoctrinated ants to swarm everywhere with that intense, highly strung quick way peculiar to the Teutonic mind, and all controlled, willingly or unwillingly, by the terrific power of that little bastard of a corporal, to repair the damage and get back to *Produktion*. 'When we have only a handful of potatoes to eat', they said, 'we shall fight and work on', and so they did, day and night. Had to admire it. Imagine the Wops and the frog-eaters sticking to it like that![81]

The German authorities were by no means blind to the positive impact such encounters had on the outlook of British POWs. Of the numerous initiatives taken by the regime to influence the views of British prisoners – from the stationing of 'public relations' officers in British compounds in late 1943, to the efforts to recruit disaffected Irishmen, anti-communists, or American and South African prisoners from German 'stock' to Hitler's side – it was probably the exposure of prisoners to Allied bombing that had the greatest effect on their attitude towards the war and the German people. Parole walks to residential districts recently visited by the RAF rarely failed to register an impression on those prisoners involved. The two 'rest' camps, opened for British POWs in June 1943, at Zehlendorf and Steglitz, were both sufficiently close to Berlin for prisoners to gauge something of the horror being inflicted upon the city. Even more explicit was the effort taken to ensure that those prisoners repatriated home during the war were made aware of the terrible human and material damage inflicted by the Allied bombing campaign. The hospital trains ferrying sick and wounded prisoners to neutral territory were deliberately routed through bombed-out areas to emphasize the point.[82]

CONCLUSION

By the time the war drew to a close, the Allied strategic bombing campaign had left an indelible mark on the lives of British prisoners in German captivity. Whether this experience, though, and the sentiments it engendered influenced broader societal attitudes is difficult to say. There is certainly no evidence to suggest that those repatriated during the war had an appreciable influence on official thinking, least of all on bombing policy. The prisoners' impact on Britain's collective memory of the bombing offensive is equally obscure. Though the army was wary of stationing former POWs in Germany after the war lest they try to settle old scores, prisoners of war have historically shown more generosity towards their former foes – and gaolers – than other sections of the uniformed services.[83] After 1918 POWs took the lead in tackling the problem of Franco-German antagonism, and in the main British prisoners appear to have born few grudges against the German population after their return home in 1945. But with most former POWs devoting their energies towards drawing a line under the 'wasted years' of their captivity and with relatively few going on to positions of major social or political responsibility, the prisoners' voice on such issues as the treatment of post-war Germany barely figured in the public debate.[84] In struggling to readjust to civilian society, most POWs preferred to bury painful memories – and awkward questions – about the Allied bombing campaign. Most came to accept the torrent of escape literature that dominated the 'narrative' of imprisonment after the war, and which conveniently passed over both the 'reality' of camp life, and the unparalleled level of destruction the prisoners had witnessed around them. There was, moreover, a natural reluctance to show ingratitude to the memory of those bomber crews who risked their lives to bring the war to a close and hasten the prisoners' liberation. The prominence given to bombing in the prisoners' diaries and logbooks is not reflected in the memoirs or semi-fictional accounts published after the war.[85] This 'selective amnesia' is perhaps only being challenged today. The BBC's recent oral history programme on the 'people's war' has found former POWs freely reflecting on their memories of the bombing campaign, and offering an insight into some of the moral and ethical ambiguities of the position they occupied half a century ago. It is, no doubt, a cathartic experience for those involved, but for historians, offers a window on to one of the hidden stories of the Second World War.

'LISTEN! HERE THEY COME!' (SPRING, 1945)

W. S. A. Clough-Taylor

W. S. A. Clough-Taylor, 'Listen, here they come!' (1945).
Source: E. G. Beckwith (ed.), *Selections from The Quill. A collection of prose, verse, and sketches by Officer Prisoners-Of-War in Germany, 1940–1945* (Country Life. London, 1947). *The Quill* was one of a number of periodicals produced in POW camps during the war. Bombing and the effects of bombing frequently featured as subjects of short-stories, paintings and poems. The original copies of *The Quill* are held in the Department of Documents, Imperial War Museum, London.

Notes

1   M. Duggan (ed.), *Padre in Colditz. The diary of J. Ellison Platt MBE* (London: Hodder & Stoughton, 1978), 293, entry for 14 February 1945. For a similar incident in late May 1944, this time involving US POWs, see Brigadier A. Crook, *Barbed-Wire Doctor. One Doctor's War* (Edinburgh: Pentland Press, 1996), 79.
2   G. C. Bateman, *Diary of a Temporary Soldier* (privately published, 1986), cited in R. J. Aldrich *Witness of War: Diaries of the Second World War in Europe and the Middle East* (London: Doubleday, 2004), 552.
3   J. Borrie, *Despite Captivity. A Doctor's Life as POW* (London: William Kimber, 1975), 203, September 1944.
4   P. J. C. Dark, unpublished manuscript, Imperial War Museum, London (IWM.) Dept. of Docus. 94/7/1.
5   Duggan (ed.), *Padre in Colditz*, 218, entry for 1 September 1943.
6   Borrie, *Despite Captivity*, 223. See also E. G. C. Beckwith (ed.), *The Mansel Diaries: The Diaries of Captain John Mansel, Prisoner-of-War – and Camp Forger – in Germany 1940–1945* (Privately published, 1977), 115, entry for 25 February 1944.
7   Duggan (ed.), *Padre in Colditz*, 256, entry for 28 May 1944.
8   R. Kee, *A Crowd is Not Company* (London: Phoenix, 2000), 184. The first appearance of planes above Singapore on 5 November 1944 had a similar impact on Far East POWs: see S. M. McQuaid, *Singapore Diary. The Hidden Journal of Captain R. M. Horner* (Stroud: Spellmount, 2006), 148, entry for 5 November 1944 and J. N. Farrow, *Darkness before Dawn. A diary of a Changi POW, 1941–1945* (Peterborough: Stamford House, 2007), 351, entry for 5 November 1944.
9   D. Nell, *POW. The Diary of a Prisoner-of-War* (St Albans: MechAero Publishers, 2004), 121–2 entry for 28 November 1944.
10   *The Mansel Diaries*, 118, entry for 16 March 1944.
11   Borrie, *Despite Captivity*, 210.
12   *The Mansel Diaries*, 115, entry for 25 February 1944.
13   W. S. Churchill, *My Early Life. A Roving Commission* (London: Thornton Butterworth, 1930), 273–312 (esp. 273). Flying Officer Harold J. Dothie, 'A wartime log', Library and Archive of Canada, Ottawa. MG30 E398.
14   See for example C. Twomey, *Australia's Forgotten Prisoners. Civilians Interned by the Japanese in World War Two* (Cambridge: Cambridge University Press, 2007), 119.
15   Duggan (ed.), *Padre in Colditz*, 218, entry for 1 September 1943.
16   *The Mansel Diaries*, 118–19, entry for 17 March 1944.
17   Capt. J. M. Kinross, 'Raid on Hamburg (October 1941)' in E. G. Beckwith (ed.), *Selections from The Quill. A Collection of Prose, Verse and Sketches by Officers Prisoner-of-War in Germany, 1940–1945* (London: Country Life, 1947), 74–7 (especially 75).
18   IWM, Docus 03/10/1, Capt G. E. Stoker MC, memoir, 'Rothenburg and the Medical Board', 4. See also IWM, Docus. P370, Mjr. E. Booth, 'The Diary of a Prisoner of War', 176, entry for 8 July 1944, where he admits that long-timers often behaved 'like children but without the charm'.
19   Aldrich, *Witness of War*, 552.
20   A. R. Prouse, *Ticket to Hell via Dieppe. From a Prisoner's Wartime Log 1942–1945* (Exeter: Webb & Bower, 1982), 125, 128.
21   The National Archives, Kew, London (TNA), FO 916/889, Evelyn Smith (War Office, Directorate of Prisoners of War) to Gardner (Foreign Office, Prisoners of War Department), 14 October 1944, memo by War Office Directorate of Prisoners of War for Foreign Office, Prisoners of War Department 'Casualties among British P.W. due to Allied air attacks', 30 December 1944; TNA, FO916/1185, memo by War Office Directorate of Prisoners of War for Foreign Office, Prisoners of War Department 'Deaths of British Prisoners of War due to Allied Air Raids', 1 February 1945.
22   TNA, FO 916/1185, Regimental Sergeant Major Sherriff (Camp leader, Stalag 344) to Swiss legation, Berlin, 8 December 1944.
23   A. Kochavi, *Confronting Captivity. Britain and the United States and their POWs in Nazi Germany* (London and Chapel Hill: University of North Carolina Press, 2005), 203–24.

24   H. Bucklebee, *For You the War is Over. A Suffolk man recounts his prisoner-of-war experience* (Sudbury: Don Fraser, 1994), 51. I. R. English and H. Moses, *For you, Tommy, the War is Over. The experience of the Durham Light Infantry Prisoners of War during World War II* (Sunderland: Business Education Publishers Ltd, 2006), 143.

25   J. Torday (ed.), *The Coldstreamer and the Canary. Letters, memories and friends of Roger Mortimer. POW No. 481, 1940–45* (Birkenhead: Birkenhead Press, 1995), 149. Of the 42 injured, two died later that day, taking the death toll to ten. See TNA, FO916/1184, memo by CIC Depot Troops. Chief of POWs, 25 April 1945, 'Low bombing attack on marching group of British Officer Prisoners of War'.

26   J. Nichol and A. Rennell, *The Last Escape. The Untold Story of Allied Prisoners of War in Germany, 1944–1945* (London: Viking, 2002), 297–302. D. Rolf, *Prisoners of the Reich: Germany's captives, 1939–1945* (London: Leo Cooper, 1988), 239–43.

27   National Archive and Records Administration, College Park, Maryland, USA (NARA), RG84 Bern Box 91 Johnson, US minister, Stockholm, to State, 26 and 27 April 1945.

28   Borrie, *Despite Captivity*, 223.

29   Nell, *POW*, 63, entry for 20 January 1944.

30   S. Mawson, *Doctor after Arnhem. Witness to the Fall of the Third Reich* (Stroud: Spellmount, 2006), 146.

31   Cited in Nicol and Rennell, *The Last Escape*, 233.

32   Prouse, *Ticket to Hell via Dieppe*, 129

33   Prouse received news on 25 November of the death of 250 POWs, though their nationality was never ascertained (*Ticket to Hell via Dieppe*, 125).

34   IWM, Docus. P463, Mjr. A. F. Casdagli, unpublished Diary, entry for 26 December 1944.

35   See N. Wylie, 'Captured by the Nazis: "Reciprocity" and "National Conservatism" in German policy towards British POWs, 1939–1945', in C-C. Szejnmann (ed.), *Rethinking History, Dictatorship and War. Essays in Honour of Richard Overy* (London: Continuum, 2009), 107–24.

36   Bundesarchiv-Militärchiv, Freiburg (BA–MA), RW4/765 Oberbefehlshaber der Luftwaffe Führungstab I c to OKW Kgf, 9 August 1943 (and reply of 13 August); WFSt/Qu. F. H. Qu. Vortragsnotiz für Chef OKW, 3 Sep. 1943.

37   According to Gottlieb Berger, the SS general in charge of POWs at the end of the war, Hitler wanted the *Prominente* executed, rather than be allowed to fall into Allied hands. For a discussion of this and the other issues raised in this paragraph, see N. Wylie, *Barbed Wire Diplomacy. Britain, Germany and prisoner of war diplomacy, 1939–1945* (Oxford: Oxford University Press, 2010), 237–64.

38   TNA, FO 916/889, see FO minutes, W. St. C. Roberts, 25 July 1944; Alexander Cadogan, 26 July 1944.

39   Ibid., AMSSO to SACSEA, 6 February 1945; TNA, CAB122/678 COS (45) 37 Meeting, 6 February 1945. Paradoxically, POW casualties suffered during the attack on Nonpladuk on 3 December 1944, which aroused Mountbatten's suspicions over Japanese policy, were considered by POWs themselves as comparatively light because of the slit trenches provided for their protection. See E. E. Dunlop, *The War Diaries of Weary Dunlop. Java and the Burma–Thailand Railway, 1942–1945* (London: Lennard, 1987), 369, entry for 3 December 1944.

40   TNA, FO 916/889, memo 'P/W camps in Germany and France in Dangerous Areas contrary to Article 9 of Convention', June 1944; TNA, FO916/1184,W. St. C. Roberts (FO) to C. J. Warner (US embassy, London), 16 March 1945.

41   Bundesarchiv Berlin-Lichterfelde, NS6/350 Martin Bormann, Rundschreiben 125/44g, 30 May 1944; NS19/344, memo by Frack for Himmler, 10 August 1943.

42   J. Goebbels, 'Ein Wort zum feindlichen Luftterror', *Völkischer Beobachter*, 27 May 1944. H. Heiber, *Goebbels* (London: Robert Hale, 1972), 321.

43   TNA, HW 5/705, CX MSS C279 OKW Propaganda IA to Propaganda Army Groups C, F, E, 2 June 1944. For mounting Swiss concerns, see Swiss Federal Archive, E2200 Berlin (56) 3 vol. 14 bis, Feldscher, head of the Swiss special interests division, Berlin to A. de Pury, Berne, 4 July 1944.

44   M. G. Steinert, *Hitler's War and the Germans* (Athens: Ohio University Press, 1977), 236–7. R. G. Reuth, *Goebbels* (London: Constable, 1993), 326. R. Siegel, *Im Interesse der Gerechtigkeit.*

Die Dachauer Kriegsverbrecherprozesse 1945–1948 (Frankfurt a. M: Campus, 1992), 113–19. *Trial of the Major War Criminals before the International Military Tribunal, Nuremberg* vol. 15 (Nuremberg: IMT, 1947), 418–20, Jodl testimony.

45   T. Bower, *Blind Eye to Murder. The Pledge Betrayed: America and Britain and the denazification of post-war Germany* (New York: Doubleday, 1982), 230, 236. O. Clutton-Brock, *Footprints on the Sands of Time. RAF Bomber Command Prisoners-of-War in Germany 1939–1945* (London: Grub Street, 2003), 473. B. Grimm, 'Lynchmorde an alliierten Fliegern im Zweiten Weltkrieg', in D. Süss (ed.), *Deutschland im Luftkrieg* (Munich: Oldenbourg, 2007), 71–84 (75).

46   Squadron Leader B. Arct, *Prisoner of War. My Secret Journal* (London: Webb& Brower, 1988), 28–31.

47   See William F. Miller, 'A Letter to My Grandchildren', www.merkki.com/millerbill.htm (accessed 8 August 2009) which recalls members of the *Wehrmacht* intervening to prevent him following the fate of one of his crew and being shot by an angry civilian.

48   See Grimm, 'Lynchmorde', 80–4. Clutton-Brock, *Footprints on the Sands of Time*, 198–224.

49   Clutton-Brock, *Footprints on the Sands of Time*, 210.

50   Institut für Zeitgeschichte (IfZ), Munich, MA208, Stellv, Chef WFSt. Vortragsnotiz, 6 June 1944. and minutes, Keitel and Jodl, n.d.

51   See IfZ, Gf 03 22 Landgericht Frankfurt v. Obstltn d. Schutzpolizei u. SS Adolf Franz Haan, relating to the attempted murder of Flt Lt Macdonald Moor on 4 March 1945.

52   IWM, Docus. 03/17/1, Capt R. F. Campbell, unpublished memoir.

53   TNA, CAB 122/690, UK legation, Berne, to FO, 27 February 1945.

54   Mawson, *Doctor after Arnhem*, 133.

55   IfZ, ZS158, interrogation of Generaloberst d. Luft. Hans-Jürgen Stumpff, Oberbefehlshaber Luftflotte Reich, Berlin, 20 January 1948.

56   A similar situation appears to have played out in the Far East. Though there were incidents of ill-treatment – notably the murder of 800 men, locked into the hold of the *Lisbon Maru* when it was struck by a torpedo on 1 October 1942 – awareness of the common danger facing anyone caught on board a ship in the open sea encouraged a more sympathetic outlook from the Japanese guards. See Don Peacock's description of his sea voyage from Ambon to Java in September 1944: *The Emperor's Guest. The Diary of a British Prisoner-of-War of the Japanese in Indonesia* (Cambridge: Oleander, 1989), 146–51.

57   J. Vance, 'The Politics of Camp Life: The bargaining Process in Two German Prison Camps', *War & Society*, 10/1 (1992), 109–26. S. P. Mackenzie, *The Colditz Myth. British and Commonwealth Prisoners of War in Nazi Germany* (Oxford: Oxford University Press, 2004), 108–13. It was not uncommon for commandants who lost the confidence of the POWs elected representatives to be removed from their posts.

58   *The Mansel Diaries*, 115, entry for 25 February 1944. For fatalities in similar situation at Stalag Luft VII, see reminiscences of Sgt Philip Potts in V. F. Gammon, *No time for fear. True accounts of RAF airmen taken prisoner, 1939–1945* (London: Arms and Armour, 1996), 196.

59   See recollection of Gwilym Peake in Gammon, *No Time for Fear*, 172–3. The camp recorded twelve escape attempts that month. See BA–MA, RL23/91, Stalag Luft I, Luftwaffe Bautruppen/Einheiten für Wach- und Sicherungsaufgaben. In Thailand, E. E. Dunlop recorded that 'some soldiers laughed at Nipponese soldiers running to shelters and were taken to the guardroom and punished. This was their own fault'. Dunlop, *War Diaries*, 326, entry for 4 February 1944.

60   Prouse, *Ticket to Hell via Dieppe*, 125, 133.

61   See BA-MA, RH49/30, Anlage zur Befehlsammlung Nr. 23. 5 April 1943, which reported the good discipline shown by French and Soviet POWs during recent attacks on Karlsruhe, Düsseldorf, Neuss and Bremen.

62   Cited in S. Longden, *Hitler's British Slaves, Allied POWs in Germany 1939–45* (London: Constable, 2005), 252.

63   Nell, *POW*, 137: 'It is disturbing when borne in mind that their horror is being caused by our side. And it must go on before it can end' (entry for 17 January 1945).

64   It should be noted that Kinross wrote his account with a wider audience in mind. Kinross, 'Raid on Hamburg (October 1941)', 75.

65 *The Mansel Diaries*, 118–19, entry for 17 March 1944. Note the discomfort expressed in the following diary entry: 'Padre Dacres showed me a book on Dresden, a lovely city. Last night, he said sadly, they dropped 14,000 tons of bombs on Dresden, a saturation attack "to aid the Russian advance": senseless destruction, with appalling loss of life' (Borrie, *Despite Captivity*, 213).

66 Gunner Leonard Bellas (Stalag III E), diary entry for September 1943, vol 3, www.bbc.co.uk/ww2peopleswar/stories/66/a6395466.shtml (accessed 20 August 2009).

67 Cited in Nicol and Rennell, *The Last Escape*, 196.

68 Lt Col D. G. Adams, 'Night Raid on Kassel: a reflection' (22–23 October 1943), in Beckwith (ed.), *Selections from The Quill*, 178–80.

69 Nell, *POW*, 77, 25 May 1944; 122, 28 November 1944.

70 Ibid., 86–7, 28 June 1944; 115, 4 November 1944.

71 Ibid., 105, 8 October 1944.

72 Ibid., 96, 24 August 1944.

73 Ibid., 122, 28 November 1944.

74 Other prisoners too, tired of the raids: 'These raids are becoming a bore, as far as we are concerned, as it means that we have to spend the best part of every day indoors'. Lt D. F. Parkinson, 'Extracts from A Diary of 1945', printed in Torday, *The Coldstreamer and the Canary*, 141.

75 Nell, *POW*, 153, 3 March 1945.

76 Cited in E. Petschnigg, *Von der Front aufs Feld. Britische Kriegsgefangene in der Steiermark 1941-1945* (Graz: Verein zur Förderung der Forschung von Folgen nach Konflikten und Kriegen, 2003), 236.

77 See BA-MA, RW5/314, OKW KTB, 11 February 1943, and in general, J. Stephenson, *Women in Nazi Germany* (London: Longman, 2001), 47–8.

78 IWM, Docus 78/35/1, E. Ayling, 'Eleven More Months. The journal of private soldier, POW', entry for 7 November 1944.

79 A. Gilbert, *POW. Allied Prisoners in Europe, 1939-1945* (London: John Murray, 2006), 312.

80 Mawson, *Doctor after Arnhem*, 142.

81 Ayling, 'Eleven More Months', entry for 14 September 1944.

82 Politisches Archiv des Auswärtigen Amtes, Berlin. R40796 Report by General Consul Reinhardt (AA), 'Die Rapatrierung vom Mai 1944', 26 May 1944.

83 For official policy, see recollections of Les Allan, founder of the National ex-POW Association, cited in Longden, *Hitler's Slaves*, 327.

84 For POWs reluctance to embrace public responsibilities and attitudes towards Germany, see Rolf, *Prisoners of the Reich*, 288–91.

85 Kurt Vonnegut's, *Slaughterhouse Five or the Children's Crusade. A Duty-Dance with Death* (London: Jonathan Cape, 1970) is a notable exception. For diaries, see T. Mallon, *A Book of One's Own. People and their Diaries* (London: Picador, 1985), esp. 1–40 and 166–206, and Aldrich, *Witness of War*, 1–17.

15

Criminals or Liberators? French Public Opinion and the Allied Bombing of France, 1940–1945

Simon Kitson

Writing in 1945, Jean-Paul Sartre summarized French attitudes towards Allied bombing raids:

> The young pilot, passing over our heads in his machine, was linked by invisible threads to England or America, and so the sky seemed full of the great, free world. But the only messages he carried were messages of death. It will never be realized how much faith we had to have in our Allies to go on loving them, and to wish for the destruction they carried out on our soil, and to salute their bombers, in spite of all, as the true expression of England.[1]

Sartre's quote highlights the complexity of French reactions towards the Allied air forces. Air raids brought a mixture of excitement, hope, curiosity, fear and panic. This multifaceted set of feelings is the central topic of this chapter: how ordinary French men and women reacted to attacks carried out by those who, until June 1940, were their official Allies, who were never their declared enemies and who were their potential liberators. This account will demonstrate how until the summer of 1943 the bombing campaign was remarkably popular, before showing the greater degree of hostility which set in thereafter.

WELCOMING THE BOMBERS, 1940–43

On the Allied side, W. H. B. Mack of the British Foreign Office warned in the run-up to the first major raid on the Renault factory at Boulogne-Billancourt outside Paris in March 1942 that it would have a negative effect on most French civilians since they were 'apathetic and gutless'.[2] Foreign Office reports, however, rapidly changed this assessment once the attack had taken place, claiming that the raid had been surprisingly well received. They suggested that 'An accurate raid on an essential factory in France is far more potent proof of British power than a heavy raid on Hamburg ... of which the effectiveness is doubted in occupied territories.'[3] A sense of the popularity of raids is also found in accounts from Allied aircrew. For instance, William Simpson, who spent much of 1941 in a French hospital following a crash, wrote that he received numerous visits from French women eager to express their enthusiasm for the RAF: 'The most enthusiastic of all were the women from the towns which had been attacked the most by the RAF, and the others were jealous of them and asked when it would be their turn to have the privilege of British bombs dropping on their towns.'[4]

Resistance sources often confirm the popularity of these early raids. The Resister Robert Nivelle assessed the situation as follows: 'If the French people have mourned the inevitable deaths, they waited each evening with hope in their hearts for the coming of the Allied aircraft.'[5] Amazingly, the BBC received letters from French people asking for more raids on their country: one received in the spring of 1942 asked plaintively: 'When will you come to pay us a call? We are all so pleased when we hear the sympathetic droning of the RAF motors overhead.'[6] The March 1942 editions of the Resistance newspapers *Combat* and *Libération* justified the deadly raids on Paris, writing that 'these French workers fallen on the field of battle are the victims of the policy of collaboration.'[7] The Resistance did, however, call on the Allies in the latter stages of the Occupation to place greater faith in sabotaging specific targets using ground-based units which would not cause as much collateral damage or the same level of casualties as the bombing.[8]

Initial popular acceptance of bombing sorties features frequently in German reports. The March 1942 raid on the Renault factory was by far the largest raid to that date and in fact, by killing some 373 civilians, surpassed the death toll of any single raid on Germany up till that point in the war. Nevertheless, the German Military Commander in France explained that even though French public opinion 'regretted the victims, it does see in this attack a legitimate act of war that has as its aim the weakening of the German war effort through the destruction of vital plants.'[9] A November 1942 report noted that most French people saw the bombings as entirely legitimate and aimed exclusively at the Germans.[10]

Vichy tended to see popular reaction in a similar vein. After raids on Paris, the Prefect of the Manche wrote: 'One might have expected the majority to react with disapproval to the bombings of 3 March, but it appears that it has attracted more people to the British cause than it has alienated.'[11] In October 1942 the Prefect of the Seine-Inférieure complained in the wake of the first American attack on Rouen that after an initial burst of anger the 'odious nature of the British [sic] attack was forgotten with a disconcerting ease, even by the families of the victims.'[12] Vichy authorities reported that the number of casualties of raids was increased by the large numbers of people who stayed in the streets to wave their handkerchiefs and cheer the bombers.[13]

Memoirs and diaries written by ordinary people who lived through the occupation also generally highlight that the raids were well accepted. Although she personally became very critical of Allied bombing, France-based Englishwoman Ninetta Jucker observed: 'Much as they had to suffer from bombing and bombardment, the population of such towns as Le Havre and Saint Nazaire were remarkably pro-ally.'[14] Schoolgirl Liliane Schroeder highlighted in her diary her confidence in the Allies, reporting that 'Among our friends there is not a single person who goes to the shelter, such is the impression that the English don't come to do [us] any harm.'[15] Antonia Hunt, a teenage English girl in France at the time, remembers that while she was in hospital following an appendix operation, the nuns who were acting as nurses were tremendously excited by the raids and opened the windows to cheer the Allied aircrew.[16] From the particularly desperate viewpoint of a persecuted teenage Jew, Micheline Larès-Yoël remembered:

> Even the sound of the bombs was a relief. You felt joy after the storm had calmed down observing that none of the bombers was burning in the sky! Just as a prisoner revels in a friend's face on the other side of the bars, you gorge yourself on this proximity with men who have come to free you, yourself amongst others, who have come from a country where persecution is not practised.[17]

To understand this tolerance towards the bombing we need first of all to get a sense of public opinion towards the Allies. The analysis by the *Contrôle Technique*, Vichy's postal censor, of the intercepted personal correspondence of ordinary citizens stated at the end of July 1940 that, in spite of the British destruction of the French fleet at Mers-el Kébir, the majority of the population hoped for an Allied victory.[18] This was confirmed in subsequent reports such as that written in September which added the caveat that 'this was not through an instinctive love for the British but rather because this victory would rid us of the Germans.'[19] Pro-Allied support did not exclude some serious reservations about the British, traditional rivals who had failed to commit sufficient resources to the campaign of May-June 1940, who had rapidly fled the battle, leaving the French to cover their retreat from Dunkirk and who had then sunk a large part of the French navy.

Alongside the Allies representing the best chance for freeing their country from a hated occupier, there was also the fact that the French population was subjected to an extensive and hugely successful pro-Allied propaganda campaign. The collaborating Vichy regime's Prefect of the Gironde reckoned in April 1941 that the only 'propaganda which has any effect is British or pro-British propaganda.'[20] There were around five million radio sets in France during the occupation.[21] Vichy sources estimated that by the beginning of 1942 more than three million of these were regularly tuned to the BBC.[22] Little wonder, then, that the Germans noted: 'the BBC rules the airwaves'[23] or that the Free French observed: 'there are three governments in France: Germany, Vichy and British radio. The latter is listened to much more than the two former.'[24] In addition Allied airforces engaged in an extensive operation of dropping propaganda leaflets for civilians; 676 million leaflets were dropped on France alone between 1940 and 1944.[25] *Le Courrier de l'Air*, the most extensively dropped of the leaflets, always reminded its readers in the top corner that it was 'brought by your friends in the RAF.'

The RAF held a special place in this pro-Allied stance.[26] Writing in 1941, André Maurois suggested 'The Royal Air Force was very popular with us. At the beginning of the war, when France herself had so few aeroplanes, the exploits of the British Air Force reassured our soldiers.'[27] A colour referred to as 'RAF blue' had been considered the height of fashionable Parisian dress in the spring of 1940.[28] If the service suffered a temporary loss of prestige as a result of its poor showing during the Battle of France, it appears this was rapidly regained after the Battle of Britain, which seemed to provide the first evidence that the German threat might be countered. Amongst the political graffiti that covered French walls after defeat was praise for the RAF. On 4 November 1940, for instance, the words 'Long live the RAF' were scrawled on walls in Grenoble.[29] In Marseille, graffiti wishing for the death of Hitler and Mussolini was accompanied by the words 'long live de Gaulle and the RAF.'[30] These three letters frequently accompanied the V for Victory graffiti on walls from the spring of 1941.

Support was also seen in behaviour towards downed aircrew. The commune of Thurmeries in the Nord was punished in July 1941 for having 'demonstrated hostility' towards German patrols trying to discover downed aircrew. Bars were closed, radio sets were confiscated and 12 local residents were taken hostage for a month as a result.[31] In September 1941, the Germans took hostages from a village near Dunkirk as punishment for the behaviour of the population towards a captured Canadian pilot: he had been cheered and many local girls had tried to kiss him.[32]

A funeral held at the Breton village of Lanester near Lorient in December 1940 was just one of many examples where the burial of an Allied airman on French soil attracted several thousand mourners who would shout 'Long Live England.'[33] When aircrew were buried in the Breton village of Viré in the summer of 1942, the authorities tried to limit attendance to Germans and Vichy officials. Unfortunately for them the streets of the village were lined with 2,000 locals who had come to pay their respects and for days afterwards the graves of the aircrew were drowning in flowers.[34] Initially such funerals had been authorized by local Wehrmacht commanders eager to show that they were abiding by noble principles of war such as the respect of the enemy's dead. By the end of 1942 the Germans were generally trying to stamp down on such events. In November of that year *Sicherheitspolizei* (security police) officials barged into the Prefect's office in Vannes (Morbihan) ordering him to put a stop to one such funeral because a crowd of several hundreds was forming.[35] In Calvados in early 1943, the Germans surrounded the cemetery where a large crowd had formed to pay their respects to a Canadian airman. Around 15 of the demonstrators were subsequently arrested.[36]

Roughly 2,000 downed aircrew managed to make it to safety through occupied France, despite the death penalty imposed on those who helped them.[37] Such a large-scale operation, dependent on the spontaneous help of the population, would have been difficult without an instinctive degree of support. Not everyone agreed to assist them, it is true. Near Honfleur in August 1942, the seven-man crew of a British bomber bailed out; six were captured by German patrols while the seventh was denounced to the Gendarmerie by the person with whom he had taken refuge.[38] But many were prepared to help, whether by providing food and shelter or by putting aircrew in touch with evasion networks.[39] The risk of doing so was amply demonstrated by the death sentence carried out against Marcel Weiss in the Eure in July 1943.[40] This is all the more remarkable given that these aircrew frequently crashed in the very areas which they had just been bombing. During intensive raids in May 1943 the Prefect in the Finistère area of Brittany had to remind the local population repeatedly of the penalties for assisting Allied airmen.[41]

Central to these positive reactions was the desire that Allied activity would oust the hated German occupier from France. Undoubtedly there was a large dose of optimism in early assessments that raids in 1940 on ports or factories used by the Germans represented a step towards liberation.[42] But at that time of desperation, some shred of hope was needed, however unrealistic it appeared to be. There seemed little possibility that France could be liberated from within, and the sight in late 1940 of French POWs being transported across the Rhine from temporary camps in France confirmed that the Germans were in no hurry to make peace. France would have to rely on the Allies to remove the occupier, and with the air raids representing the only real offensive actions the British were carrying out, the RAF became the single focus of all hope in the Allied cause. In July 1941 an inhabitant of Dunkirk drew strength from the British raids: 'We're happy to be disturbed in this way, it brings the beautiful day of our liberation closer.' The letter-writer found it comforting that whereas the previous year they had seen only German planes heading for Britain, now there were far more British ones heading in the opposite direction.[43] Raids served as a reminder that the Allies had not forgotten France, and for all the damage inflicted on the French, they did simultaneously undermine the German war machine.[44] They seemed to highlight German weakness.[45] If the Allied bombers were getting through in such large numbers it was because the German defences were inadequate. The stunned, shocked or panicked reactions of the German soldiery when attacks took place helped undermine their image of strength.[46]

Indeed, one thing that is certain is that, paradoxically, the main propaganda victims of the Allied air raids were the Germans, whose unpopularity increased as a result. With reference to Allied bombing, any excuse was used for criticizing the Germans. They were condemned when they used air-raid sirens too often, as this was said to make people *blasé* about taking cover.[47] More often, though, it was for *not* sounding the siren that they were attacked.[48] This failure can be explained by a desire to avoid interrupting work in factories producing German war material.[49] The absence of alarms increased the level of civilian casualties by giving people no time to reach safety.[50] Rumours suggested Occupation troops had actually prevented factory workers from entering air-raid shelters, a story probably grounded in the fact that the Germans wanted to avoid civilians sharing soldiers' shelters.[51] It is true that the Germans did not help their image by appropriating for their own usage hospital air-raid shelters which had previously been designated for patients, as happened in Athis-Mons (Seine-et-Oise).[52] Elsewhere they were criticized for using factories or placing weapons in close proximity to civilian populations.[53] When bombs hit the Longchamp races in April 1943, the Germans were held accountable because they had set up an anti-aircraft battery in close proximity to the racetrack.[54] Above all, the Germans themselves were considered responsible for the bombings because it was their continued presence in France which had made them necessary in the first place.[55] A letter from a Monsieur Petit in Vichy to a Marseille-based relative expressed it thus: 'Germany is held responsible for the continuation of the war, and therefore for all the difficulties, hardships and miseries caused by this continuation, and in this particular case, the Germans are reproached for having left Paris defenceless against the enemy bombers.'[56] Blaming the Germans allowed an outlet for any negative feelings about raids.

German propaganda, which was generally ineffective in France, was powerless to stop this. Their claims that the Allies were targeting civilians only served to remind the public of how Stukas had deliberately attacked columns of helpless refugees in 1940.[57] When the Germans underlined the civilian deaths around the Renault plant in March 1942 this caused outrage: no one had forgotten the 200 dead occasioned when the Germans had bombed the Citroën and Renault factories on 3 June 1940.[58] Indeed, rumours circulated that there had actually been two separate bombings of Renault in March 1942, one conducted by the Allies which was confined to the factory and an entirely separate one in its wake where German bombers had wreaked destruction on civilians.[59] Similar rumours were commonplace for other raids too.[60]

THE TIDE TURNS: 1943-4

Although the Allied raids were initially popular, one category of people was instantly hostile: French prisoners of war in Germany. Their political attitude was usually far more favourable to the Vichy regime, and sometimes even to the Germans, than that of the average French person. Several reasons explain this. First, they were cut off from the harsh realities of an Occupation where the Germans frequently broke legal conventions regarding behaviour in wartime. POWs' dealings with ordinary Germans were more frequent than those of their compatriots back home and generally conformed to the Geneva Convention.[61] POWs were a major propaganda target for a Vichy government careful to control the information available to these prisoners. Nor should it be forgotten that many POWs captured around Dunkirk felt suspicion towards the British, sensing that the French had been left holding off the enemy while their ally fled back home. In the summer of 1941 a prisoner expressed disbelief that French people seemed so favourable to British bombings, and worried that his compatriots would be exploited by the British in the same way they 'did to us at Dunkirk.'[62] From Oflag IV B, a general wrote critically of British raids on Paris:

'Always the same bandits as at Dunkirk ... I don't think that anyone should doubt the mentality of these people who haven't changed since Joan of Arc.'[63]

Beyond the POW milieu, criticism of Allied bombing was relatively muted up till the summer of 1943. After that date a greater degree of hostility towards air attacks was evident. By April 1944, for instance, the Lyon branch of the Postal Censor was reporting that of the private letters it had opened in the previous week, 13,150 had made reference to air raids. Of these, 54 per cent were described as neutral, 42 per cent as negative or fearful, and only four per cent positive.[64] Overly literal interpretations of these statistics are best avoided: after all, many people knew that private correspondence was being intercepted and read by the authorities, leading to a reticence about expressing overtly pro-Allied remarks.[65] But the general decline in popularity of raids is obvious from most sources after summer 1943.

Behind this increase in hostility was the significant intensification of raids. This came about not only with the approach of D-Day but also because in August 1942 the US Air Force became active in Europe, causing a change of strategy. Now bombing raids were carried out around the clock – with the British tending to bomb at night and the Americans bombing during the day – making the experience that much more unrelenting for civilians. There was also the question of altitude. What had happened previously was that in response to a request from the Vichy government, Churchill had agreed at a cabinet meeting of August 1941 that British bombers would drop their bombs from a lower altitude in France than they did in Germany.[66] The Americans observed no such precautions and were frequently accused of dropping their bombs from too high an altitude. This is a point made explicitly in the memoirs of Nicole Roux, a teenager during the occupation: 'We particularly feared the American Flying Fortresses, which flew very high ... they dropped their bombs quite blindly, often missing their target; the British bombers frightened us less, they dived down to hit their targets, they took risks; they were less dangerous for civilians.'[67] Of course, civilians on the ground may have exaggerated the extent to which bombing from high altitude limited visibility: after all, even at lower altitude visibility at night-time could be limited. In reality, night-time raids tended to be less costly of civilian lives because civilians were not so likely to be wandering near targets like railway marshalling yards.[68] The image of the deadliness of US Air Force raids compared to those of the RAF stuck. In Chambéry, inhabitants contrasted the American bombing of their town on 26 May 1944, which caused 200 deaths, with the considerably more accurate RAF attack on a ball-bearing factory 50 kilometres away in Annecy on the night of 9/10 May.[69]

The intensification of raids encouraged people to be careful about what they wished for. Earlier in the Occupation, encouraging Allied bombers had been relatively simple for a public unaware of how this bombing activity would eventually affect them personally. When in December 1940 the Allies began attacking industrial targets, with a raid on an aircraft factory in Bordeaux, very few would have felt remotely worried or threatened by such an attack. The number of French civilians then in direct German employ was very small and it was therefore easy to celebrate the raids for striking at symbols of collaboration.[70] By August 1943, 40–50 per cent of French production was going to Germany.[71] This meant that a large proportion of the population was employed in some capacity by the occupier, and many therefore would have felt directly concerned by any extension of the raids. Not only may this have caused them to fear for their own safety but it would also have given them an empathy for those employed in a similar way.

Once the raids intensified and spread further into the country, the grim reality of what it was like to be under bombardment would have sunk in more. For those on the ground, bombings produced a mixture of negative sensations: panic, disgust, anguish, stress and downright fear. Philippe Bertin described the frightful scenes which confronted witnesses to bombings: 'We daren't look round. It's hell. Everything destroyed.... A festering smell, the smell of death.'[72] Mutilated and carbonized corpses littered streets.[73] Sixteen-year-old Renée Fouques claimed in 2004 that she had been haunted for 60 years by memories of the screams of her dying neighbour trapped under the rubble.[74] Edmond Duméril witnessed the bombing of Nantes: 'A terrible, inhuman racket, like the grating of an express train on a metal bridge, like a waterfall of cauldrons and saucepans falling from the sky, forced our hearts into our mouths.... The children are screaming; my wife and I understand each other with a glance: we are about to die.'[75]

Air-raids brought disruption and a transformation of daily life. Hundreds of thousands of buildings, including many houses, were damaged. It has been suggested that overall 18 per cent of all of France's buildings were seriously damaged or destroyed.[76] Levels of destruction varied considerably between towns. Out of 8,000 buildings in St Nazaire, around 5,000 were totally ruined.[77] While Le Havre was 82 per cent destroyed, France's makeshift capital in Vichy, on the other hand, was never hit.[78] In Paris, many of the suburbs were very badly damaged but the centre of the city was not greatly affected. Homelessness was an inevitable consequence of the bombing campaign.[79] Large-scale evacuations took place,[80] generally in difficult circumstances because of the lack of transport.[81] Some were just temporary, as those dwelling in targeted cities would evacuate their homes at night and take refuge in the countryside or in shelters.[82] Others were more permanent transfers of populations and led to difficulties of accommodating refugee populations in host communities.[83] A Dunkirk resident, Edmond Perron, recalled that during the Nazi occupation he changed home 12 times to escape the bombings.[84] Daily life was disrupted. People were woken from sleep by sirens and air raids.[85] Essential services such as telecommunications, water, gas, electricity and public transport were cut on many occasions.[86] Unemployment was also a consequence of bombings as devastated factories closed their doors or reduced production.[87] There should be no doubt that the bombings caused widespread suffering and considerable disruption to daily life.[88] By 1944, even parts of France such as Montpellier, which had not received regular raids, saw airforce activity as their single most pressing concern.[89]

Raids also brought death. Estimates for the number of French civilians killed vary between 56,000 and 67,000, in other words roughly equivalent to casualty figures for Britons killed by German raids on the UK.[90] Loved ones realized that such deaths were often horrific. Schoolgirl Renée Roth-Hano was deeply affected by the loss of her classmate Monique Jamet, whom she had seen laughing and playing only a few days before. Renée noted:

> I can't get Monique out of my mind. Wasn't she hit by a bomb? Did she die instantly? Or was she burned in the fire? God, the flames were so high! Maybe she got buried under the rubble and suffocated to death? ... I wonder if she called for her mother. Mademoiselle Lucienne once told me that one always calls one's mother when in pain or in danger.... It's so unfair that she died in this way, for nothing. She was just a little girl – a brave little French girl who studied hard in school and was waiting for the war to end. Why couldn't anyone save her?[91]

Expanding the raids meant that more people were likely to be victims or to suffer their effects. Complaints about the choice of targets were expressed with increasing frequency.[92] In the early part of the Occupation, when there had been less firepower available to the Allies, they needed to be especially selective in their choice of targets.[93] Confusion about the objective of a particular raid set in once there was a diversification of the types of intended targets. In 1940 most raids had been aimed at naval installations, known to harbour German battleships or U-boats. Then, from late 1940, factories began to be targeted. Progressively, power stations, marshalling yards and railways were added to the list, on a massive scale after 1943. A raid aimed at docks or a factory known to be producing military equipment for the Germans was easily comprehensible. But some of the towns targeted in Normandy in 1944 were hit not because they contained any obvious military target per se but rather because the Allies were trying to block 'choke points' through which German reinforcements might move, or else to clear a particular pathway to ensure their own break-out.[94] There was always likely to be a gap in understanding between the military strategists, aware of the full picture, and the population on the ground who could only guess at what the Allies were thinking.

Even when people did understand the target, criticisms were aimed at the lack of accuracy. There were many reasons why bombs missed their designated target. Faulty intelligence could cause the target to be badly identified. Flak might disorientate aircrew and spotlights could blind them.[95] Nervous, inexperienced crews sometimes dropped their bombs too soon as they were worried about flying into the flak. Technical factors added their own weight to the inaccuracy of the bombers: initially they did not have very precise navigational tools.[96] Criticisms of inaccuracy did not just come from those who were hostile to the Allied cause. Having suffered numerous Allied bombings the teenager Renée Roth-Hano began to lose patience and confided to her diary:

> Before returning to bed, I look out of the window one last time. I feel like shouting to our Allies, flying above in the sky, that we are their friends, for goodness' sake, and that they should be able to distinguish us from the Germans, their enemies. How can they drop bombs on innocent people?'[97]

Clearly, some had unrealistic expectations of the degree of accuracy which bombers could achieve.

The use of the word 'futile' to describe raids was far more common in 1943–4 than it had ever been in the first two years of the Occupation.[98] Beyond just a misunderstanding of the reasons for selecting a particular target, there was also the fact that airforce activity, which had been so central to perceptions of Allied strengths in the early years, became less so once the tide of war shifted in the Allied favour. By that stage Allied victory seemed inevitable, and likely to be achieved not by isolated air activity but rather by the combined use of the different branches of the armed forces.[99] With the Allied landings in North Africa, Corsica and Italy as well as the Russian advances after Stalingrad, perceptions of the Allies had become more multi-dimensional. The war was being won on the ground as well as the air. This allowed the luxury of criticizing air strikes without calling into question one's overall support for the Allied cause. Many frustrated French civilians found themselves questioning the purpose of the intensive raids of 1943 if they were not to be accompanied by an immediate Allied landing.[100] In July 1943 the Prefect of the Maine-et-Loire *département* noted that recent bombings had been judged severely because 'scepticism is growing about the allied landings which are announced so often.'[101] The unending nature of the attacks took their toll on nerves, leading to exhaustion.[102] In April 1944, Vichy's postal censor intercepted private letters expressing their writers' extreme bombing fatigue: 'It's every day and every night now. I'm in a continual trance and if this continues I'll go mad.'[103] A month later another stated pessimistically: 'It's over: I no longer believe in anything! We will certainly all be dead before this ends, only the end of the world can save us from this!'[104]

Stoking up the flames of these criticisms was Vichy propaganda. From as early as 1940, Vichy attempted in propaganda and through the behaviour of its officials to exploit any negative feelings.[105] Government newspapers and newsreels gave top billing to the effects of bombing raids using emotive language to highlight the suffering.[106] The authorized press made no attempt to set the bombing raids in their wider context. Thus, for example, when Brest was badly hit in 1940 newspapers did not mention that the attack was linked to the build-up of German forces in the area, or indeed the considerable damage done to the Germans themselves.[107] State propaganda tried to equate raids to a long-term problem with the British and Americans. The eternal image of

'Murderers always return to the scene of their crimes', French anti-Allied
propaganda poster linking Joan of Arc's death in Rouen in 1431 to the Allied
bombing of the city in 1944.
Courtesy of Bibliothèque de Documentation Internationale Contemporaine (BDIC) et
Musée d'Histoire Contemporaine.

Joan of Arc was invoked when Rouen, the city in which Joan had been burnt on English orders in the fifteenth century, fell victim to yet another deadly raid in April 1944. Posters showed a forlorn Joan kneeling on the rubble with the caption: 'Murderers always return to the scene of their crimes.'[108] Vichy propagandists made a cartoon for cinema audiences depicting Mickey Mouse, Donald Duck and Popeye flying American planes over France, dropping bombs and leaving death and destruction in their wake. It was even hinted that Popeye's enthusiasm for the bombing was based on the fact that the French had better spinach than the Americans.[109] Victims of bombings were promoted to martyr status through remembrance ceremonies in cathedrals and churches. After the Renault raid of March 1942, Vichy declared a day of national mourning.[110] In the aftermath of raids, state officials would tour the bombed area, visit the hospital beds of the injured and attend funerals of the dead in acts of political recuperation.[111] These propaganda efforts appear to have borne little fruit in the first three years of occupation.

It seems that in 1944 Vichy did at last find some propaganda mileage in the theme of bombing. When Head of State Pétain visited Paris following an April 1944 bombing of the city which had killed 600 (chiefly in the neighbouring suburbs), he was greeted by large cheering crowds who probably appreciated that he had been trying to keep France out of the war.[112] Vichy's Propaganda and Information minister, Philippe Henriot, achieved some success in 1944 with his radio broadcasts within which the theme of the destruction brought by bombing was a major component.[113] Henriot branded the Allies as 'criminals' rather than 'liberators' for their bombing raids. His broadcasts were attracting people to Vichy radio to such an extent that the Resistance assassinated him to limit his influence.

CONCLUSION: CONDITIONAL ACCEPTANCE

In reality, however, one should note that even in the period from summer 1943 to summer 1944, French attitudes to Allied bombing were not systematically negative. There was a series of what might be termed 'variables of acceptance' of specific raids. The British Foreign Office had predicted in March 1942 that bombings would be accepted if they satisfied three criteria: '(1) powerful and (2) well directed and (3) reasonably economical of civilian life.'[114] Raids which were clearly well targeted and caused few casualties continued to be tolerated even in the latter stages of the Occupation. A letter intercepted by the Postal Censor in Clermont-Ferrand highlighted the acceptance for accurate raids: 'The town has been bombed four times, three times by the British which was quite acceptable because they were relatively accurate, but the fourth time it was done by the Americans in daylight on a beautiful sunny day. The village closest to their target suffered more damage than the target itself.'[115] Beyond just the level of casualties and the degree of accuracy there were other factors which affected how well received a particular raid was. Operations which took place on symbolic dates, such as Bastille day, New Year's Eve or Mother's Day, tended to be roundly condemned regardless of the damage they did.[116] It was not just casualty statistics that shaped perceptions but also the type of victim, sacred status being accorded to children and the sick. When hospitals and schools were hit, they provided fodder for criticisms.[117] The types of bomb used for missions affected degrees of acceptance: there was outrage when incendiary bombs were used and delayed action bombs spread great fear among the population.[118]

It should be further noted that although air raids could cause very real anger, they did not ultimately undermine the public's wish for an Allied victory.[119] The prefect of the Normandy *département* of Calvados commented in May 1944 that while public opinion viewed the possibility of an imminent invasion with great fear, 'it continued to wish for it as a necessity.'[120] Given that much of the hostility was based on fear that oneself or one's loved ones would become victims, it is legitimate to suppose that much of it was short-term. Once the fear died down, some of the anger would recede. In the same prefect's report it is observed: 'The bombings are generally criticized when they happen, and if some people adopt a strongly hostile attitude to the Anglo-Americans, in the following days these people look for excuses for them.'[121] Allied troops did find remnants of anger in some of the towns they liberated.[122] However, anger did not stop the population in most parts of France from eagerly waving American and British flags alongside the tricolour during the Liberation.[123] From Liberated France air-force personnel also reported some positively favourable reactions. Bomber Command noted in September 1944: 'No one who has visited France in RAF uniform can fail to be impressed by the lack of rancour shown, even by those who have directly suffered. Indeed, far from rancour, the wholehearted welcome extended, seemingly especially to anyone in RAF blue, is spontaneous and genuine'.[124] Air Chief Marshal Harris decided to repay the French for this welcome and the support that had been offered to escaping aircrews by setting up a special benevolent fund within the service for children who had suffered as a result of air-force activity.

It is clear that the Allied raids continued to represent an awkward and embarrassing question in Franco-Allied relations after the Occupation ended. If hundreds of thousands of French people were homeless in 1945 it was often because their homes had been destroyed by the bombs of France's liberators. Some 60,000 civilians had also perished in Allied air-force operations. In liberated Le Havre the newspaper *Havre Matin* gave vent to its frustration at the level of death and destruction, proclaiming on 13 September 1944 'We awaited you with joy, we greet you with mourning'.[125] However, there was generally relatively little public condemnation of bombing raids after the Liberation. After all, the reason why the country had been targeted was because its factories and workers had been employed by the Occupier. This was not something on which the French wished to dwell as they tried to create an image of France as 'a nation of Resisters'.[126] Often collective memory resigned itself to a semi-silence on this question. It is true that plaques commemorating the dead were erected in parts of France but rarely did they mention which side had perpetrated the bombing raids, thereby leaving open the question of whether the guilt lay with the Allies or the Germans.[127] There were, however, specific towns which made a virtue of their suffering under the Allied bombs, perhaps as a way of underlining that their dead were killed in a battle zone and thereby implying that they were somehow linked to the ultimately victorious Allied campaign in the region. Thus two communities in the Nord-Pas-de-Calais (Le Touquet and Couderkeque), one in Normandy (Biéville) and one in the Champagne region (Saint Oulph) renamed streets to include the words 'Royal Air Force' in their title. The street which received the worst bombing in St-Étienne changed its name from the rue de St Chamond to the rue des Alliés, a local resident stating that this was to show the Allies that the city bore no grudge.[128] Amazingly, one of the central avenues in devastated Caen was renamed in honour of Air Chief Marshal Sir Arthur 'Bomber' Harris.[129] Henri Calef's 1945 film *Jéricho*, which included scenes of France being bombed, opens with a dedication to the RAF and closes with a lorry full of Resisters singing 'It's a Long Way to Tipperary' as an RAF Mosquito burns on the ground, before the image fades to a caption reminding viewers of RAF aircrew killed 'on the soil of France, for the cause of freedom'. Plaques, streets named in honour of the RAF and a film dedicated to the Air Force were voluntary constructions of memory designed to show that many had continued to regard the Allied bombings as legitimate. However, in the town of Lorient, a grim tourist site acts as an involuntary preservation of a different memory.[130] The submarine pens, the very reason the British destroyed the town, are still almost intact today, as post-war authorities decided it would cost too much to destroy them and found them useful for sheltering French submarines. This reminder of the limitations of bombing lends its voice to those who during the occupation singled out some raids as futile.

Sartre's quotation, which opened this chapter, highlighted just how complicated was the interaction of the French public with the Allied bombers. A wide range of sources underline that initially bombing operations were not only tolerated but actually welcomed and encouraged. Raids served as a reminder that France had not been forgotten and thereby offered the smallest glimmer of hope that one day the country might be liberated. Because they were small-scale and localized, it was easy to cheer them on, as few French people would have felt threatened. Before 1943, it seems the raids promoted both the popularity of the Allies and hostility towards the Germans. Many took advantage of any opportunity to demonstrate their support: pro-RAF graffiti, waving at planes, helping downed airmen or attending the funerals of dead aircrew. French POWs in Germany were a rare category immune to this enthusiasm. From the summer of 1943 the general mood began to change. The bombing intensified significantly as the Allies began to prepare for D-Day and as the American Air Force joined the campaign. Operations were now taking place around the clock and could just as easily target the south as the north of the country. Increasing numbers of

French people were affected by raids which disturbed everyday life and caused widespread death and destruction. Although attitudes generally became more negative, not all raids were systematically criticized. There were 'variables of acceptance' of a particular raid based around its accuracy, its perceived purpose, the level of destruction, the number and category of the victims and the way in which the operation was carried out. Since the range of targets had diversified, there was more chance of the purpose of a raid being misunderstood. Many individual raids might seem futile, especially as they were not accompanied by the long-hoped-for Allied landings. Despite an increase in negative attitudes about aerial bombing, this did not generally deter French people from enthusiastically cheering the arrival of Allied troops in 1944. Nor did it prevent a film-maker dedicating a post-war film to the RAF, or several towns from renaming streets in honour of their Liberators or the RAF.

Notes

1   J.-P. Sartre, 'Paris under the Occupation', in J. G. Weightman, *French Writing on English Soil* (London: Sylvan Press, 1945), 129.
2   The National Archives, Kew, London (TNA), FO 371/31999, W. H. B. Mack, 'RAF bombing of the Renault Factory', 6 March 1942.
3   TNA, FO 898/311, 'Psychological aspects of bombing during the spring and summer', 14 April 1942.
4   W. Simpson, *One of our Pilots is Safe* (London: Hamish Hamilton, 1942), 129.
5   R. Nivelle, *And Yet France Smiled* (London: Hachette, 1944), 28.
6   Archives Nationales, Paris (AN), F 90/21620, Anonymous letter sent to the BBC from Creil on 6 August 1941. Letter from May 1942: T. Brooks, *British Propaganda to France* (Edinburgh: Edinburgh University Press, 2007), 86.
7   AN AJ41/46, 'Note n. 46 au sujet de l'activité séditieuse des partisans de l'ex-Général de Gaulle', 15 April 1942.
8   R. Kedward, *La vie en bleu: France and the French since 1900* (London: Penguin, 2005), 298–9.
9   AN AJ 40/444, Situation report for February-March 1942; Paris, 23 March 1942.
10 AN AJ 40/897, Grosskommandant von Paris, November 1942.
11 AN AJ 41/376, Manche, Prefect's monthly report, April 1942.
12 AN AJ 41/390, Seine-Inférieure, Prefect's monthly report, October 1942.
13 AN AJ 41/356, 'Note de renseignements concernant la zone occupée', 24 July 1941.
14 N. Jucker, *Curfew in Paris* (London: The Hogarth Press, 1960), 84.
15 L. Schroeder, *Journal d'Occupation, Paris 1940–1944: chronique au jour le jour d'une époque oubliée* (Paris: de Guibert, 2000), 131.
16 A. Hunt, *Little Resistance: A Teenage English Girl's Adventures in Occupied France* (London: Leo Cooper/Secker and Warburg, 1982), 98–9.
17 M. Larès-Yoël, *France 40-44: Expérience d'une persécution* (Paris: L'Harmattan, 1996), 47.
18 AN AJ41/25, Postal Censor's monthly synthesis, 20 June–20 July 1940.
19 Ibid., Postal Censor's monthly synthesis, 25 October–4 November 1940.
20 AN AJ41/372, Gironde, Prefect's monthly report, April 1941.
21 C. Lévy, 'La Propagande' in J.-P. Azéma and F. Bédarida, *La France des années noires* (Paris: Seuil, 2000), vol. 2, 60. Brooks, *British propaganda to France*, 54.
22 I. Ousby, *Occupation* (London: Pimlico, 1999), 237.
23 A. Mitchell, *Nazi Paris* (Oxford: Berghahn, 2008), 30.
24 AN F60/1689, CNI, 'Etat de l'Opinion', May 1941.
25 T. Brooks, *British Propaganda to France*, 38; Y. Le Maner, 'Presse parachutée' and J.-L.

Crémieux-Brilhac, 'Propagande française et britannique' in F. Marcot (ed.), *Dictionnaire historique de la Résistance* (Paris: Robert Laffont, 2006), 685-8.

26 AN AJ 41/25, Postal Censor's monthly synthesis, June–July 1942.

27 A. Maurois, *Why France fell* (London: John Lane, 1941), 127.

28 D. Veillon, *Fashion under the Occupation* (Oxford: Berg, 2002), 13.

29 AN AJ 41/46, Résultats des enquêtes effectuées sur le territoire des 14e et 15e Division Militaire, 2 April 1941.

30 Ibid., Italian Armistice Delegation to French Delegation to the Armistice, 29 April 1941.

31 AN AJ 41/383, Nord, Prefect's monthly report, August 1941.

32 Ibid., Nord, Prefect's monthly report, September 1941.

33 AN AJ 41/381, Morbihan, Prefect's monthly report, January 1941; L. Capdevila and D. Voldman, 'Rituels funéraires de sociétés en guerre (1914–1945)' in S. Audoin-Rouzeau et al. (eds), *La violence de guerre, 1914–1945* (Brussels: Complexe, 2002), 296-7; A. Morize, *Resistance, France 1940–1943* (Boston: France Forever, 1943), 26; AN 3AGII/333, BCRA, 'Extraits des RG, semaine du 13 au 20 septembre 1943'.

34 Capdevila and Voldman, 'Rituels funéraires', 296.

35 AN AJ 41/381, Morbihan, Prefect's monthly report, November 1942.

36 F. Marcot et al. (eds), *Dictionnaire historique de la Résistance* (Paris: Robert Laffont, 2006), 929. Some funerals of aircrew continued into late 1943: see: AN 3AGII/333, BCRA, 'Extraits des RG, semaine du 13 au 20 septembre 1943'.

37 The exact statistics are open to question, ranging from around 1975 to 4000: M, Middlebrook and C. Everitt, *The Bomber Command War Diaries* (London: Penguin, 1990), 712; E. Florentin, *Quand les Alliés bombardaient la France* (Paris: Perrin, 1997), 445.

38 AN F60/1508, Rapport du Capitaine Epinoux, Commanding the Gendarmerie section at Pont L'Evêque, 12 August 1942.

39 TNA AIR 14.1021, Air Chief Marshal Harris, 23 September 1944.

40 AN AJ 41/325, 'Exécutions 3e trimestre, Etat complémentaire'.

41 AN AJ 41/372, Finistère, Prefect's monthly report, May 1943.

42 Larès-Yoël, *France 40–44*, 47.

43 AN F60/1690, CNI, letter sent from Dunkirk, 15 July 1941.

44 Bundesarchiv, Freiburg (BA)-MA Wi IA 3/187 '*Bericht über Luftangriff auf Paris* 3 March 1942' by *Der MBF Kommandostab Abt* Ia, Paris, 10 April 1942. AN AJ 40/444, MBF Situation report for February–March 1942, Paris 23 March 1942. E. Alary, *Les Français au Quotidien* (Paris: Perrin, 2006), 521.

45 AN AJ 40/444, Situation report for January–March 1943, Paris 22 April 1943; situation report for April–June 1943, Paris 21 July 1943.

46 J. Galtier-Boissière, *Mon journal pendant l'Occupation* (Garas: La Jeune Parque, 1944), 136, entry for 12 June 1942.

47 AN F7/14926, Postal censor's weekly report, 11–17 November 1943.

48 Archives Municipales de Rennes 6/H/23, Maire de Rennes à M le Directeur des Services Techniques du Ministère de l'information, 18 December 1943.

49 BA-MA RM 45 IV 1600, *Luftflottenkommando* 3, *Führungsabteilung* IA/LS, 25 July 1944.

50 AN F60/1508, Le Président du Conseil Municipal de Paris à M l'Ambassadeur de Brinon, 4 March 1942. J. Guéhenno, *Journal des années noires* (Paris: Gallimard, 1947), 281, entry for 4 March 1942.

51 AN AJ 41/388, Haute-Saône, Prefect's monthly report, March 1942.

52 AN AJ 41/391, Seine-et-Oise, Prefect's monthly report, May 1941.

53 N. Roux, *C'est la guerre, Les Enfants!* (Cherbourg-Octeville: Éditions Isoète, 2007), 64.

54 The mayor of the eighth *arrondissement* wrote in his monthly report for April 1943 that the inhabitants of this district were 'looking for extenuating circumstances for the aggressor [the Allies]' and that instead of blaming the Allies for killing French civilians they blamed the German anti-aircraft batteries placed nearby in the bois de Boulogne for attracting Allied bombs. Archives de la Ville de Paris (ADVP) 1052/67/1 1 (0662, 0663), Le Maire du VIIIème Arrondissement à Monsieur le Préfet de la Seine, 16 April 1943.

55 AN AJ 41/375, Loiret, Prefect's monthly report, June 1943.

56 AN F7/14927, Postal Censor, Intercepted Letter of 10 March 1942.
57 Archives de la Préfecture de Police (APP), 'Rapport', 16 March, 1942. See also Galtier-Boissière, *Mon journal*, 124, entry for 4 March 1942.
58 G. and W. Fortune, *Hitler Divided France* (London: Macmillan, 1943), 35.
59 Florentin, *Quand les Alliés bombardaient*, 54.
60 AN F7/14926, Clermont-Ferrand, Postal Censor weekly report, 12–19 May 1944; AN AJ 41/25, Postal Censor monthly synthesis, June 1941.
61 Y. Durand, *Les Prisonniers de Guerre* (Paris: Hachette, 1994), 13.
62 AN AJ 41/25, Postal censor, monthly report, June 1941.
63 Ibid., Postal censor, monthly report, June-July 1942.
64 The Contrôle Technique from the Limoges office dated 1 April 1944: 509 negative references, 69 positive, 419 expressing a fear of their extension. For Lyon on the same date there were 13,150 intercepted letters which made reference to bombing. Of these 7,066 were described as neutral references, 2,358 as negative, 577 made excuses for the bombers, and 3,149 expressed fears about the extension of the bombing campaign: Ibid., Postal Censor, weekly statistical report, Limoges, 22–28 March 1944; AN F7/14926, Postal Censor, weekly statistical report, Lyon, 22–28 March 1944.
65 AN F7/14930, Postal Censor report, letter from Pierre Bonnoure of Lyon to Constantin Dobrescu in Vichy, 23 September 1941.
66 See TNA FO 371/28541 for discussion of this decision.
67 Roux, *C'est la guerre*, 71; Jucker, *Curfew in Paris*, 76. AN F60/1690, CNI – La situation en France, moral et ambiance de la population en France, 2 May 1944. Local populations appreciated the risks the British took: AN F60/1690, European Intelligence Section, BBC, intelligence report dated Paris, March 1942.
68 AN AJ 41/356, Le Préfet du Finistère à Monsieur le Secrétaire General à l'Intérieur, 25 July 1941.
69 S. London, 'The Bombing of Chambéry', Master's thesis, University of New Brunswick, Canada, 1993, 92.
70 Fortune, *Hitler Divided France*, 34.
71 J. F. Sweets, *Choices in Vichy France* (Oxford: Oxford University Press, 1994), 175; J. Jackson, *France: the Dark Years* (Oxford: Oxford University Press, 2001), 234.
72 P. Bertin, *Histoires extraordinaires du jour le plus long* (Rennes: Éditions Ouest-France, 1994–2004), 94.
73 Madame Marie, *Carnet de Bord. Des pensionnaires sous les bombes* (Alençon: Imprimerie alençonnaise, 1949), 35.
74 J. Lichfield, 'The day Allied bombers destroyed my home town', *The Independent*, 5 June 2004.
75 E. Duméril, *Journal d'un honnête homme pendant l'occupation* (Thonon-les-Bains: Éditions de l'Albaron, 1990).
76 D. Voldman, *La Reconstruction des villes françaises de 1940 à 1958* (Paris: L'Harmattan, 1997), 25–35.
77 Florentin, *Quand les Alliés bombardaient*, 108.
78 A. Knapp, 'The Destruction and Liberation of Le Havre in Modern Memory', *War in History*, 14, 4, 2007, 477.
79 AN AJ 41/390, Seine département, Prefect's monthly report, 5 October 1943.
80 Around 200,000 people fled their homes in Lower Normandy in the summer of 1944 to escape the bombs: Alary, *Les Français au Quotidien*, 529. See A. Kemp, *6 juin 1944. Le débarquement en Normandie* (Paris: Gaillard, 1994), especially 168–171; AN 3AGII/333 BCRA, 'Bombardement de Clermont-Ferrand', 17 September 1943.
81 Alary, *Les Français au Quotidien*, 510; see Letter from Fernande Aveline, 11 June 1944 in *Paroles du Jour J* (Paris: 2004), 80.
82 AN AJ 41/356, 'Rapport du Capitaine Lefort, commandant la section de gendarmerie de Chalons sur Marne sur les explosions au camp de Mourmelon', 21 June 1941.
83 R. Gildea, *Marianne in Chains* (Basingstoke: Macmillan, 2002), 307. Kedward, *La Vie en Bleu*, 299.
84 Florentin, *Quand les Alliés bombardaient*, 19.

85   Ibid., 19 and 61.
86   D. Petit, *La Vie quotidienne d'une Nazairienne de 1939 à 1944* (Saint-Nazaire: Association Mémoire et Savoir nazairiens, 1944), 53; Marie, *Carnet de Bord*, 37.
87   Alary, *Les Français au Quotidien*, 519. See also Archives de la Préfecture de Police (Paris), Rapport de quinzaine, 4–17 April, 1943.
88   M. Carrier, *Maréchal, nous voilà … 1940–1944* (Paris: Éditions Autrement, 2004), 104; M. Rouchaud, *The Time of our Lives* (New York: Pantheon, 1946), 271; W. D. Halls, *The Youth of Vichy France* (Oxford: Oxford University Press, 1981), 44.
89   P. Laborie, *L'Opinion française sous Vichy* (Paris: Seuil, 1990), 318–19.
90   The *Journal Officiel* gave the figure of 56,896 in 1948 (*JO*, 26 May 1948). The national statistics bureau, INSEE, gave a figure of 60,000 in 1950: INSEE, *Mouvement économique en France de 1938 à 1948* (Paris: 1950), 197. Florentin gives an unsourced figure of 67,078 deaths: Florentin, *Quand les Alliés bombardaient*, 446.
91   R. Roth-Hano, *Touch Wood: A Girlhood in Occupied France* (New York: Macmillan, 1988), 241–2, entry for 6 June 1944.
92   AN F7/14926, Postal Censor's Weekly summary, Limoges, 17–23 February 1944. AN AJ 41/384, Nord, Prefect's monthly report, 5 October 1943.
93   L. Dodd and A. Knapp, '"How many Frenchmen did you kill?" British Bombing Policy Towards France, 1940-1945', *French History*, 22, 4, 2008, 469–92.
94   D. Voldman, 'La destruction de Caen en 1944', *Vingtième Siècle, Revue d'Histoire*, 39, July–September 1993, 14.
95   Florentin, *Quand les Alliés bombardaient*, 20, 33, 41, 171, 223.
96   Ibid, 19.
97   Roth-Hano, *Touch Wood*, 240, entry for 6 June 1944.
98   AN F7/14926, Limoges, Postal Censor's weekly report, 9–16 March 1944.
99   AN AJ 41/372, Gironde, Prefect's monthly report, August 1943.
100 *Gazette de Lausanne*, 'Impressions de France: le déclin de l'Anglophilie', 25 February 1944.
101 AN AJ 41/376, Maine-et-Loire, Prefect's monthly report, 5 July 1943.
102 Alary, *Les Français au Quotidien*, 513.
103 AN F7/14926, Clermont-Ferrand, Postal censor, weekly report, 31 March–7 April 1944.
104 Ibid., Clermont-Ferrand, Postal censor, weekly report, 12–19 May 1944.
105 D. Veillon, *Vivre et survivre en France, 1939–1947* (Paris: Payot, 1995), 263.
106 *Le Petit Parisien*, 11 March 1942. J. Sainclivier and B. Le Marec, *L'Ille-et-Vilaine dans la Guerre* (Roanne: Éditions Horvath, 1986), 66.
107 Florentin, *Quand les Alliés bombardaient*, 12.
108 http://laureleforestier.typepad.fr/blog_de_laure_leforestier/images/2008/04/22/assassins_2. jpg.
109 This can be viewed in Claude Chabrol's film *L'Oeil de Vichy*.
110 Morize, *Resistance, France 1940–1943*, 79; D. Voldman, 'Les civils, enjeux du bombardement des villes' in S. Audoin-Rouzeau et al. (eds), *La violence de guerre, 1914–1945* (Brussels: Complexe, 2002), 164; Veillon, *Vivre et survivre*, 266.
111 Alary, *Les Français au Quotidien*, 519.
112 *L'Illustration*, 6–13 May 1944, 157–65.
113 AN AJ 41/388, Haute-Saône, Prefect's monthly report, March 1944. AN AJ 41/375, Loiret, Prefect's monthly report, April 1944. AN AJ 41/380, Meuse, Prefect's monthly report, May 1944. For intercepted letters reacting to Henriot's broadcasting see AN F7/14933.
114 TNA FO 371/31999, W Strang, letter of 13 March 1942.
115 AN F7/14926, Postal Censor's weekly report, Clermont-Ferrand, 28 April–5 May 1944.
116 AN F7/14926, Postal Censor's weekly report, St Amand, 21–28 July 1943. Sainclivier and Le Marec, *L'Ille et Vilaine*, 66.
117 Sainclivier and Le Marec, *L'Ille et Vilaine*, 66.
118 AN F7/14926, Postal Censor's weekly report, Limoges, 2–8 March 1944; Florentin, *Quand les Alliés bombardaient*, 17.
119 Kedward, *La vie en bleu*, 298-299.
120 AN AJ 41/366, Calvados, Prefect's monthly report, May 1944.

121 AN AJ 41/366, Calvados, Prefect's monthly report, May 1944.

122 M. Boivin, G. Bourdin and J. Quellien (eds), *Villes normandes sous les bombes (juin 1944)* (Caen: Presses Universitaires de Caen, 1994).

123 J.-P. Husson, *La Marne et les Marnais à l'épreuve de la Seconde Guerre Mondiale* (Reims: Presses Universitaires de Reims, 1995), vol. 2, 77.

124 TNA AIR 14/1021, Air Chief Marshal Harris, 23 September 1944.

125 Knapp, 'The Destruction and Liberation of Le Havre', 489.

126 S. Kitson, 'Creating a Nation of Resisters? Improving French Self-Image, 1944–46', in M. Riera and G. Schaffer (eds), *The Lasting War* (Basingstoke: Palgrave, 2008), 67–85.

127 http://www.danaxtell.com/france/Bombardement/SaintEtienneBombardement-AmericanView.html.

128 APA (Association pour l'autobiographie et le Patrimoine Autobiographique, Ambérieu-en-Bugey, France), APA 60, testimony from Dr Raymond Gerest, written in 1954–5.

129 I owe the reference to Caen to Andrew Knapp.

130 http://www.blavet.co.uk/keroman%20submarine%20base%20lorient.htm.

16

A Comparative Approach to Newsreels and Bombing in the Second World War: Britain, France, Germany

Olivier Dumoulin

The sirens sound. Schoolchildren, factory hands, housewives, office workers, one and all don their gas masks. Whirring planes overhead lay down a blanket of protective smoke. Cellars open to receive their refugees. Red Cross stations to succour the stricken and the wounded are opened at improvised shelters; underground vaults yawn to receive the gold and securities of the banks; masked men in asbestos suits attempt to gather up the fallen incendiary bombs. Presently the anti-aircraft guns sputter. Fear vomits; poison crawls through the pores. Whether the attack is arranged or real, it produces similar psychological effects. Plainly, terrors more devastating and demoralizing than any known in the ancient jungle or cave have been re-introduced into modern urban existence. Panting, choking, spluttering, cringing, hating, the dweller in Megalopolis dies, by anticipation, a thousand deaths. Fear is thus fixed into routine: the constant anxiety over war produces by itself a collective psychosis comparable to that which active warfare might develop. Waves of fear and hatred rise in the metropolis and spread by means of the newspaper and the newsreel and the radio programme to the most distant provinces.[1]

Like many Europeans of my generation, I have an indirect, polyphonic and somehow disharmonic representation of air raids. I have in mind my mother's account of her refusal, when the Paris suburbs were bombed on the night of 19–20 April 1944,[2] to get down into the darkness of a shelter, because she was so excited by her first reading of Proust. I remember, too, my father's recollection of Allied raids over his concentration camp at Melk, in Austria.[3] Many years later, I learned with surprise of my wife's grandparents' complaints about the damage caused to their farm in Normandy by Allied attacks on a nearby V1 base.[4] As in Pirandello's plays or in Akira Kurosawa's *Rashomon*, each point of view implies a different memory and a different representation. Such testimonies are shared with millions of Europeans. But the subject of this paper is the representation of bombing in non-fiction films, and particularly newsreels.[5]

AIR RAIDS AS CULTURAL CONSTRUCTS

Lewis Mumford's quotation above suggests that some representations of the bombing of civilians seemed constructed, perhaps ready-made, when the Second World War broke out. Already the few raids of the First World War, plus episodes such as Guernica, the British attacks on insurgent Kurds in Iraq,[6] or the Japanese bombing of Shanghai had given real examples of the consequences of air attacks on civilians.[7] These elements give some credit to the hypothesis that the bombing of civilians was well enough publicized to support quite strong representations before the Second World War. More than that, Paul K. Saint-Amour argues that novelists frequently projected, as Mumford did, the catastrophic consequences of air raids on cities far beyond what they already knew. So 'they were contributing to a memory and dread of aerial bombing that not only figured prominently in interwar public discourse and the concurrent urban imagination, but also constituted the *locus classicus* for a kind of proleptic mass-traumatization, a pre-traumatic stress syndrome whose symptoms arose in response to an anticipated rather than an already realized catastrophe.'[8]

One may therefore question the way already pre-constructed visions of bombing interacted with their material consequences. Despite the significant differences between the aims and the execution of raids on Britain, France and Germany, and the differences in the numbers of victims, a comparative approach is legitimate. Nevertheless this statement has to be discussed because historians know, for instance, Marc Bloch's testimony about the fear that air attacks, despite his usual courage, caused him in June 1940: obviously the great historian had not acquired yet a 'bombing culture'. The goal of this chapter is to understand how, to what extent and through which formal devices the French, British, and German newsreel corporations constructed representations of the bombing of civilian objectives. The purpose is not to demonstrate their (obviously) opposed political and ideological points of view, but to elucidate how they set about their task. Did they require the same rhetoric? Did they share, or try to make their audience share, the same kinds of emotions? Did they give air raids the same place in the hierarchy of news? The hypothesis mentioned above of a possible European anticipation of the 'air terror' suggests that there might have been at least some elements of a common approach.[9]

The careful viewing of hours and hours of newsreel is our central source. The potential stock is very large. In Britain, five firms competed for the attention of cinemagoers at the start of the war: Gaumont-British, Movietone, Pathé, Paramount, Universal. In France, until August 1942, the occupied zone watched the *Actualités mondiales* released by the German authorities from November 1940, while the 'free zone' had *France-Actualité-Pathé-Gaumont*: in August 1942 these two systems merged into *France-Actualités*, run by Vichy under German supervision with an agreement to use shots taken from the *Deutsche Wochenschau*. Finally, in Germany four newsreels, the *Ufa-Tonwoche*, the *Deulig-Tonwoche*, the *Tobis-Wochenschau* and the *Fox Tönende Wochenschau*, were submitted to the control of the Ministry of Propaganda and Popular Enlightenment in the 1930s. In September 1939 they were merged into one, which took the name of *Deutsche Wochenschau* in June 1940. From 1938, Goebbels made the viewing of a newsreel compulsory before the feature film. Cinema doors, moreover, were supposed to be closed after the start of the newsreel, barring entry to spectators intending to avoid it by arriving late.[10]

With 243 weekly newsreels for Germany, around 380 for France and some 729 for Great Britain, the three countries' combined production represents roughly 444 hours to watch and analyse if we estimate the average length at 20 minutes.[11] A complete viewing would require a team, though coverage of the hours would not in itself guarantee an exhaustive examination of the subject. The present approach is more selective and focuses on key moments: the Blitz and the V1 period for Great Britain, and the years 1943 and 1944 in France and Germany. The dates were chosen to include both massive attacks and relatively calm weeks. Proceeding this way, I am looking for the '*topos*', the 'master narrative' of 'bombing rhetoric' and then for the moments when this repetitive narration fell apart. Much can be learned through newsreel rhetoric, both about the intentions of official narratives and about their reception. Such a problematic is not only legitimate *per se*, but it may contribute to a better understanding of the 'morale'[12] of those who knew about air raids through the media.

THE ROLE AND SIGNIFICANCE OF NEWSREELS

If we assume that, in spite of the massive character of air attacks, most people in Britain, France and Germany were not direct victims, or even witnesses, of raids, it is evident that for many the facts were reconstructed through others' representations, transmitted by word of mouth, newspaper narratives, radio news, and last but not least by newsreels. The popularity of newsreels is strongly attested in all three countries. This was clearly the case in France and Britain during the First World War.[13] At the beginning of the 1930s, when 'talkies' took over the screen, this success seemed greater than ever. Various media, for example the *Daily Sketch* newspaper in 1934, noted their tremendous popularity.[14] Even critics of the bias of newsreels involuntarily give some evidence of their popularity.

Of course, when the war came this positive reception was subject to variations, depending on the type of audience and on the circumstances. For instance the first comments of a Mass Observation inquiry underline the gap between the reactions and emotions of the audiences which suffered directly from the bombings and the others:

> Shots of air-raid damage have been included in nearly half the observed newsreels. The reaction to these is noticeably different in London and the provinces, the first time that any such variation has been noticed. In London the shots have been received in rather

an uninterested silence; the only shot that has caused adverse comment was where injured people were seen being brought out of a damaged house, creating a personal touch. In the provinces, however, reports come mainly from Watford, Oxford and Stockport, all fairly undamaged areas; there has been a high degree of comment on these shots, and some signs of horror.[15]

If the Mass Observation reports seem to describe the weakening of audience reactions towards newsreels, it appears that at least early on in the conflict newsreels were highly successful. Even at the end of the war, despite their declining appeal, it was still a commonplace throughout Europe to celebrate the popularity of the newsreeel:

> Every day hundreds of reporters armed with their cameras rush in pursuit of the news. Every day hundreds of thousands of metres of film are running through their shooting devices; thousands of people are working in this industry, and for millions of people, the image of our time is as the newsreels represent it to them.[16]

As for German newsreels, even the enemy was convinced by the quality of the *Deutsche Wochenschau*. Siegfried Kracauer's report, sponsored by the Rockefeller Foundation and published by the Museum of Modern Art, was originally written to support American war aims and denounce the fake appearance of authenticity of the *Deutsche Wochenschau*.[17] In fact Kracauer's work was compelled to recognize their unique capacity to make images speak for themselves.[18] In neutral Switzerland, the war news of the *Deutsche Wochenschau* provoked the same flattering appreciation as in the United States of an impressive spectacle with high technical quality, and deeply moving realism.[19]

Within the Axis, *Deutsche Wochenschau*'s combination of efficiency and seduction was clearly demonstrated by the Golden Lion awarded at the Venice festival of 1941. Inside the Reich, for a fairly long period, even when the circumstances in 1942–4 could generate a strong scepticism towards official propaganda, the Security Service of the Reich (*Reichssicherheitsdienst*) continued to send positive feedback about the popular reception of the *Deutsche Wochenschau*.[20] In his diary, Goebbels, who himself supervised the newsreel drafts every Sunday evening before they were released on Monday, celebrated their efficiency. On Sunday 31 January 1943 he wrote: 'This evening we are finishing the *Deutsche Wochenschau* which is dealing with various topics; according to the SD they are very much appreciated. By contrast, the radio is much more criticized.'[21] These Sunday work sessions were repeated week after week and were supplemented by additional sessions if events justified it. Sometimes Goebbels complained about the quality, as he did following five air raids on Berlin in November 1943, but even though he postponed their release, he was eventually convinced of their value. Even when, after five air raids over Berlin since 22 November 1943, Goebbels complained about their quality and postponed their release, he was still convinced in the end.

In occupied France, the authorities felt obliged to show the cinema newsreel with the house lights on in order to discourage catcalls, laughter and other kinds of demonstrations disrespectful to the government or the occupying forces. Nevertheless these responses do not cast doubt on the authenticity of the newsreel. For example, when French spectators whistled at the head of government Pierre Laval getting out of his car, shouting 'look at his car, it's powered by petrol not charcoal gas', the audience interpreted the shots very differently from the desired response, but these reactions imply there was no doubt on the issue of the film's authenticity.[22]

Newsreels were also successful because the cinema was probably attracting a larger audience than ever before. It was, after all, among the rare leisure activities that remained widely frequented during the war by German, British and French people. A regular evening at the cinema usually included two feature films, a sequence of newsreels and sometimes some short propaganda movies. Politicians were fully aware of the importance and, probably, the effect of newsreels. In England, the weekly audience grew from 19 million in 1939 to a peak of 30 million in 1945. In spite of economic difficulties and air raids, only ten per cent of cinemas closed, and 32 per cent of adults visited the cinema at least once a week.[23] The danger of air raids often seemed forgotten. In Germany, even when the government had to ban almost all public leisure, Goebbels decided to maintain theatre and cinema because they were the last opportunities to divert and control the mind of the masses.[24]

THE FRANCO-GERMAN COMPARISON

On the French side, *France-Actualités* resulted from a merger in August 1942 of several pre-existing newsreel companies. This was supposed to symbolize the renascent unity of France and its territory. It was quite logical, therefore, that France should be a central feature of its content. In the first issue, ten out of twelve topics dealt with France, including a feature on the significance of the new newsreel for national unity.[25] The pattern of each newsreel was always the same, showing the latest news from France first, with a good deal of sport and entertainment, then the international news, and finally the war news. The German presence steadily declined, though the *Deutsche Wochenschau* still provided many of their shots. Anti-Semitism lost the key place in the week's news that it had occupied from 1940 to 1942, but air raids became more and more important: their geographical distribution even dictated Marshal Pétain's travels through the country. The denunciation of damage and human losses caused by the Anglo-American attacks allowed a position that was hostile to the Allies, without being openly supportive of Nazism. From this point of view, it is easy to understand the proportion of the *France-Actualités* weekly newsreel dedicated to air raids on civilians.

Under different and suggestive titles, 'La France meurtrie', 'Guerre aux civils', 'Bombardement' and 'Le calvaire continue', the bombing of civilians more often than not ranks first in the headlines.[26] On 21 April 1944 the reporting took the shape of a special issue after the weekly news. Lasting four minutes (total footage for the rest of the week, war news included, represented 13 minutes and 30 seconds), it was a cinematic presentation of Philippe Henriot's speech after the latest raids on Paris and Rouen.[27] Even without any special section or particular issue, coverage of the raids was substantial: four minutes on 9 April 1943, one minute on 28 May 1943 after the bombing of a district in Bordeaux, one minute about the Rennes raid of 4 June 1943 and so on. Even when the topic was not directly mentioned, viewers were still kept aware of the raids through descriptions of the welcoming of child evacuees in the countryside,[28] or the celebration of the merits of the Red Cross in the rubble of a bombed town,[29] or through the use of images of rubble to illustrate a speech by Pétain about the turmoil through which France was passing.

For Germany the picture was quite different, for obvious reasons. If the denunciation of the Anglo-American raids gave a rare opportunity to turn Vichy France into an innocent victim, for the Reich the publicity given to the Allied raids was ambivalent. On the one hand it might cement the national feeling against such a cruel enemy, but at the same time it implied a recognition of the losses, the relative impotence of the Luftwaffe and the progress of the Allied forces. Such an ambiguous situation is clearly visible in the evolution of Goebbels' diary. In 1943, even when circumstances seemed unfavourable, Goebbels maintained his feeling of self-satisfaction with the *Deutsche Wochenschau*: it was very much appreciated, according to the SD, unlike the radio broadcast on 31 January 1943; still very satisfactory on 4 April; colourful and varied on 14 November. Even the aftermath of the five raids on Berlin at the end of November 1943 did not prevent Goebbels from hoping to make positive propaganda from the aerial battle of Berlin through clever editing of the *Deutsche Wochenschau*. Only after August 1944 did Goebbels begin to complain about the lack of good images in such an unfavourable situation.[30] At last, speaking of the prospect of an everlasting war, the *Reichminister* stressed the difficulties of filling the news with topics that might attract the audience's interest and attention.[31]

THE COMMON THEME: VIOLATED CHURCHES

One specific theme runs through the newsreels of all three countries when they deal with bombing: churches. In German newsreels, for instance, the images impose a very specific view of the damage caused by raids. In first place stands the assault against religion. This was evident on one of the first occasions when the bombing of a German city was given detailed treatment in a long film sequence of approximately five minutes out of a 23-minute newsreel released on

30 June 1943. One of the first weeks the bombers' assaults on a German city are detailed, a long sequence, roughly 5 minutes in a *Deutsche Wochenschau* lasting 23 minutes and 14 seconds, was released on 30 June 1943.

Even if we aim to underline the similarities between the three countries, we have first to pinpoint here the characteristic device of the *Deutsche Wochenschau*: each sequence is framed as a dramatic and chronological development with a real sense of narration. In a newsreel of August 1943, the first things represented are the shouts of alarm, then an image of the alerts given out by the air defence centre, then shots of anti-aircraft fire flashing in the darkness, and of civilians hastening towards the shelters. Then comes the aftermath of the raids, which lasts three minutes, more than a half of the sequence. It begins with the blazing Protestant chapel of Krefeld: 'shots taken shortly after a terror attack by British-American bombers.' Then, after two minutes dedicated to a picture of the efficiency of the emergency services (organized by the authorities), the sequence comes back to the church. From the church and its rubble, the spectator's eyes are driven to the wrecked treasures of the city's fine arts museum, to end with the restarting of the city's electric facilities. The sequence concludes with these words: 'Great is the suffering of the population in the west German air-war region, but its will to resist the British-American air-raid terror has not been broken.' Beyond the celebration of the German civilians' heroic resistance, the *Deutsche Wochenschau* constantly stresses one theme: from wrecked churches to destroyed museums, culture appears as the main victim of the apparently indiscriminate destruction. Returning the argument the Allies used so much in the First World War, the fight for culture is central: 'Even terror cannot alter the cultural life of our Nation' claims the *Deutsche Wochenschau*, showing soldiers on leave and munitions workers coming to the Bayreuth festival at the Führer's invitation.[32]

Week after week German propaganda against the 'air terror' showed images of ruined or damaged churches, shattered stained glass windows, and wrecked treasures of sacred art: these were a crucial part of its rhetoric. Commentaries were few, and seldom emphatic or bombastic. The impressive sequences are supposed to speak for themselves: a ruined church remains a true scandal, a major evidence of the foe's inhumanity.

In an enlightening review of Jörg Friedrich's book *The Fire*,[33] Richard G. Moeller concludes: 'Again and again, Friedrich's ledger of destruction begins with churches and cathedrals, symbols, he implies, of a nation whose citizens believed in God, not the Führer, and in his descriptions of bombing raids it is the religious calendar, not weather patterns or Allied estimates of German defences, that seems to determine the timing of bombing missions.'[34] The same, strikingly, holds for the message conveyed by *Deutsche Wochenschau*. From every angle the *Deutsche Wochenschau* transmits a message of national unity built on a national identity at the core of which stands German culture, and at the nucleus of that, Germany's religion. On 6 July 1943, for instance, in the *Deutsche Wochenschau*, Cologne cathedral,[35] heavily hit 'by the bombs of the British terrorist pilots', is covered in a sequence of over a minute. The commentary stresses that 'the British terrorists bombarded the Hanseatic town on the Rhine, with its venerable monuments and unique art treasures, which had been made, on their own admission, almost invisible by dense cloud cover.' Long shots of the rubble support the following comments: 'The bombs broke through the vault, causing havoc inside the cathedral. Built over a period of six and a half centuries and considered sacrosanct by the entire civilized world, the cathedral was destroyed by the British air-raid barbarians in just a few minutes.'[36]

The Ariadne's thread running through the *Deutsche Wochenschau*, through its depictions of the destruction of churches, is the binary representation of a timeless fight of the 'civilized world' against 'barbarians'. Again and again, Goebbels' team knitted together German identity, religion and, last but not least, culture. Of course one could object in a very materialistic way that the rubble of great monuments is more impressive than that of anonymous buildings, and that in Western Europe the best-known monuments are quite often churches. Obviously this is true and the *Deutsche Wochenschau* also shows other types of buildings destroyed by the 'air terrorists'. The case of Cologne cathedral might be also interpreted in specifically German terms. The final phase of the construction of this Catholic edifice was undertaken, from 1840, with the support – financial as well as verbal – of King Friedrich-Wilhelm IV, a Protestant Prussian. Ever since, Cologne cathedral had stood as one of the national symbols of the nascent German state.[37]

This specific explanation could work if Cologne had received unique attention. In fact, it represents one among scores of destroyed church sequences featured in the *Deutsche Wochenschau*. These require another explanation. The coverage may be interpreted as a simple *topos* of civilian raids without any peculiar meaning. But we may read this obsession with churches in a very different way. If we follow Carlo Ginzburg's 'clue paradigm',[38] this characteristic is both a common basis for this kind of propaganda but at the same time a unique feature in itself. Like fingerprints in criminology, like the fingernails of Leonardo da Vinci's characters, the church reduced to rubble would appear as a necessary figure of any cinematic representation of air raids on civilians but also expresses a particularity of place and time, evident to the viewer. This explains why ruined churches are central images in the newsreel treatment of the bombing in all three countries. Such a point of view implies that wrecked churches are among the usual visions of raids whatever the country.

This line of thought, suggested by German newsreels, is clearly confirmed if we turn to their British and French counterparts. In France, 'Les bombardements' or 'La France meurtrie' became a regular entry in weekly newsreels from quite early in 1943. Apart from shots from the front supplied by *Deutsche Wochenschau*, the raids are often all that *France-Actualités* showed of the war. Usually these shots were classified in two different categories: the efforts of the government to repair the damage and to assist the wounded on the one hand,

and the mourning of the dead and the denunciation of the Allies' massive and indiscriminate bombardment on the other. Of course the question of the destruction of churches was raised, even if most of the time churches appeared first as the place of funerals for the victims.[39] Even if the rubble of houses was the most frequent vision, shots of wrecked churches, and more broadly allusions to religion, were frequent.

First of all the fortunes of France are emphasized as a form of martyrdom, whether through the title of the section or via comments such as 'le calvaire continue'[40] or 'une nouvelle cité martyr: St Omer'.[41] Sometimes the choice of shots is even more explicit: on 28 May 1943, for instance, while a bombed district of Bordeaux was evacuated, the operator and the editor selected a five-second shot of a sculpture of a crucified Christ sliding slowly from the wall to the ground, probably as a metaphor of France under the raids. This tendency to point out the sacrilegious dimension of the raids implied a malign purpose on the part of the Allies. This connotation is highly evident in the commentary on the heavy raid on Bruz, a small village near Rennes in Brittany, which reminds us that the raids took place at the end of a solemn communion day.[42] Here the commentary underlines the fact that the raids could have resulted in the mass slaughter of the parish children. As Jörg Friedrich was later to argue, the comments quite often imply that the calendar of raids was dictated by the liturgical calendar: for instance with a formula such as 'Whitsun celebration: bloody celebration' on 2 June 1944.[43]

In such a context it is rather predictable that the destruction of churches played as least as important a part in *France-Actualités* as it did in *Deutsche Wochenschau*. The most noticeable feature is undoubtedly the place given to the bombing of Rouen. The special issue on the raids of 21 April 1944 began with nightly shots of the blazing Parisian suburbs, then the rubble of the suburbs by day, while the third sequence was dedicated to Rouen after the raids of 19 April 1944. After a panoramic view taken from the heights of Mont Saint Aignan, the rubble of the Justice Hall and of the 'wonderful' cathedral are the main scenes. After shots of the rescue of survivors, the newsreel comes back to the cathedral, 'one of the most moving of France', with shots of the nave and its destroyed vault. A week later the speech given by Henriot, at the public funerals in Paris, concluded by alleging that Sacré-Coeur in Paris, as well as Rouen Cathedral, had been scandalously transformed into military objectives. This new claim is accompanied by renewed shots of the cathedral.

Other examples are numerous but it is enough to accept the idea that, in *France-Actualités* as in *Deutsche Wochenschau*, the will to show the horror of civilian raids was necessarily expressed through the denunciation of attacks against culture and particularly religion. Of course in the case of a regime which presented itself, in part, as revenge against the secular Third Republic, such insistence might appear predictable. In the case of Philippe Henriot, who came into politics through General de Castelnau's *Fédération Nationale Catholique*, this explanation seems obvious.

But once again, such circumstantial and ideological explanations are not adequate to explain the common dimension of the bombing rhetoric in Germany, in France and in Britain too. Even by focusing only on the Movietone weekly, the same trope is revealed. Once more one monument stands for nearly all the others. Even though the newsreel alluded to the fate of a number of churches in London or to the damage close to Canterbury cathedral in 1942, the cathedral of Coventry is the central example. Immediately after the raid of 14 November 1940 the cathedral occupied a privileged place in the narrative of the Coventry raid. One third of the original shots, and a quarter of the final version, were devoted to the fate of the cathedral, which also closed the report.[44] In the newsreel review of the year 1940, the cathedral was the only monument outside London selected to represent the Blitz.[45] A section in the newsreel of 22 March 1941 describes a visit to Britain by the Australian Prime Minister, Robert Menzies: his tour leads him to Coventry where half the sequence (nearly one minute) is dedicated to the cathedral, a description of it before the raid by the Cathedral Provost, the Very Reverend Dick Howard, and a tour of the ruins.[46] Last but not least, when Winston Churchill visited the martyred city, there were two sites deserving particular attention: the aircraft factories and the ruined cathedral.[47]

A common polemical culture thus prepared the three countries to manipulate to a considerable degree, though in very different contexts in other respects, the fate of churches and of cathedrals in particular. This type of rhetoric had obvious precedents. In the first months of the First World War the myths and reality about the 'German atrocities' gave rise to the fiercest controversy, which involved intellectuals, scholars and professors. The seminal part played by the *Manifesto of the Ninety-Three*, signed by the elite of Germany's science, arts and social science communities in defence of Germany's military actions, is well known.[48] A speedy French reply to the German text protested not only against alleged German murders and rapes of civilians, but to an equal degree against crimes against civilization committed in Louvain and Reims. If slaughtering children and raping women were the crimes of the modern 'Huns',[49] the firing of Reims cathedral, the place where for centuries French kings had been crowned, was one of the main pieces of 'evidence' of the Germans' attacks against culture.

This exchange launched a competition between French and German scholars to demonstrate where the true cradle of Gothic art was and who the real defenders of art and civilization were. In this struggle the fate of churches and museums became a central stake. The French medievalist Joseph Bédier used German soldiers' diaries to demonstrate the reality of the alleged 'atrocities', and was in turn attacked by German intellectuals who used their philological skills to refute Bédier's interpretations. In part, this was a bitter professional quarrel by former international colleagues over proper critical method.[50] But the debate went further than that: from the beginning scientists, scholars and artists drew the contrast between barbarism and civilization.[51] The *Société Nationale des Antiquaires de France*, on 23 September 1914, declared that 'the German, without any military need, has burnt and deliberately destroyed the cathedral of Reims.... On learning of such a monstrous crime, the civilized world has been taken by astonishment. The lights of the fire of Louvain and Reims will remain indelible.'[52] The *Société de l'école des Chartes*, the association linked to France's élite training school for archivists, joined the protest shortly after, at its meeting of 5 November, against what it called unforgivable acts of barbarity. On 30 October 1914 the *Académie des Inscriptions et Belles-Lettres* voted a very similar text putting on the same level the 'atrocities' and the raids on the cathedrals of Malines and Reims.[53]

The very words of the French protests of 1914 are echoed by the later *Deutsche Wochenschau* accusations about Cologne Cathedral. On the British side, we have evidence that propaganda followed the same path as in France; better than that, it can be traced in newsreel. In a film released in March 1916, 'Ypres – the shell-shattered City of Flanders', abundant evidence of the unparalleled destruction the city had suffered is given, and most of the sequences, despite the general destruction, are dedicated, once more, to the local cathedral.[54] The full titles of the film tell the story: 'General panorama of the City', 'The remains of the Grande Place (City Square)', 'All that remains of the Cloth Hall', 'The exterior of the Cathedral', 'The Western Door', 'The interior of the Cathedral', 'The broken organ left behind amidst the ruins.' Among the newsreel's seven sequences, four are dedicated to the fate of the cathedral. So in a very revealing way, the British newsreel of 1916 paved the way for the 1943 sequence of the *Deutsche Wochenschau*. And in the same way, the early British propagandists chose deliberately to concentrate on a highly symbolic piece of evidence.

Rouen, Coventry and Cologne cathedrals, therefore, were all made into propaganda symbols after suffering damage or destruction through bombing. The *Deutsche Wochenschau*'s insistence on showing attacks on churches is a commonplace piece of rhetoric, which serves to denounce the cruelty of raids on civilians. Beyond the peculiarities of some 'sites of memory' (such as Rouen cathedral's connection with Joan of Arc, an easy evocation to stress British inhumanity, or the symbolic national value of Cologne cathedral), we have sought to demonstrate that the argument for the special place of the church was not simply rooted in a common Christian faith, but can also be seen as a legacy of propaganda themes of the First World War. On this shared ground of propaganda polemics, newsreels – whether democratic or authoritarian – seem to speak the same language and to express the same images.

POINTS OF CONTRAST

However, in our efforts to decipher the conception and meaning of these sequences, we have to take into account the propaganda context in which they were made. Newsreels follow their own logic but they are also a piece in the jigsaw puzzle composed by propaganda. For instance, Rémi Dalisson reminds us that the 'hommage aux victimes des bombardements de 1942' was among the five circumstantial festivals created by Vichy in order to promote the regime's ideology.[55] Saturday 7 and Sunday 8 March 1942, after the severe raid of 3 March on Boulogne-Billancourt, were decreed national days of mourning. Every big city organized ceremonies to express compassion for the victims and to expiate the former alliance with Britain. Paris was the centre of the most impressive demonstration. The ceremony in Notre-Dame saw all the religious, civil and military authorities come to pay tribute to 'the innocent victims of the barbarity of our so-called Allies'.[56] It is easy to identify there the framework within which the various film sequences of 'la France meurtrie' or 'Bombardement' take their due place.

Similarly, if we try to understand precisely how the symbol of Coventry cathedral was generated, we unveil a process peculiar to British circumstances. In spite of its Gothic architecture, St Michael of Coventry, built in the fourteenth century, is not at first sight a national landmark as Reims cathedral is for anyone in France; it only became a cathedral in 1918. Nevertheless it is indisputable that newspapers, photographers and artists constructed the symbol very quickly indeed. Under the title 'Coventry – Our Guernica', the *Birmingham Gazette* celebrated the rubble of the cathedral as a symbol: 'The proud spirit of Coventry Cathedral yesterday stood over the grim scene of destruction below.'[57] Soon after, in an article in the *New York Herald Tribune*, illustrated with a photograph shot eastwards across a pile of rubble to the apse, it became the 'voiceless symbol of the insane, the unfathomable barbarity which had been released upon western civilization.'[58]

But if the way journalists described the event refers to the rhetoric outlined above, only the British information and propaganda programme fully explains the treatment given to Coventry. The cathedral's status in wartime martyrology was due in no small part to the extension of a scheme, launched in autumn 1939, called 'Recording Britain.' This engaged artists such as John Piper to paint Britain's national heritage, now endangered by war. More than that, it was no accident that John Piper, whose famous paintings would contribute to the cathedral's symbolic status, was already walking through the rubble on 15 November, the very day after the raid.[59] Just six days earlier, the War Artists Advisory Committee (WAAC), under Sir Kenneth Clark, had commissioned him to paint bombed churches.[60]

In the case of Nazi Germany the common 'bombing rhetoric' was directed in a very specific way and on several levels. As far as the choice of symbol is concerned, the national dimension is obvious, as we noted in the case of Cologne. If we consider the peculiarity of the *Deutsche Wochenschau*, we have to notice that the common rhetoric is embedded in a global device which clearly distinguishes the Nazi newsreel from the others: it is a narrative, not a series of sections on the newspaper model. Each sequence is built up as a tale, and this succession of tales is organized in a general one which makes a continuum. Starting most of the time from the daily life of the German *Heimat*, it reaches military action in a kind of spiral movement. This scheme is specific to the *Deutsche Wochenschau*.

CONCLUSION

Before completing a systematic examination of the whole stock of sources, other topics may be explored to understand how newsreels constructed a common war culture and how they built up a specific representation of the bombing experience. In a different direction it would be fascinating to discover if the track suggested by Pierre Laborie about the Spanish Civil War for France before 1939 ('The Spanish mirror transformed Frenchmen into spectators of their own battles, of their own anxiety or of their own hopes')[61] holds in war newsreels: for instance the extent to which the shots of Allied raids on Caen, in June 1944, are used by the *Deutsche Wochenschau* as a substitute for the raids on Germany, which for the German public are visually less and less bearable.

These comparisons lead us to the view that to understand the ways in which contemporary propaganda interpreted bombing, we have to work in at least three directions. First of all, these newsreels are obviously the product of an ideologically oriented framework, which they display with different styles. But at a second level we have shown that the images and stereotypes associated with bomb damage are very similar. Deprived of their linguistic specificity and of a few material details, newsreels of bombed civilian areas could be switched very easily from one country to another, and from the Axis to the Allies. Several elements in our analysis, moreover, reveal the long shadow of the propaganda contests of the First World War. This phenomenon suggests the idea of a single war culture, built up progressively from 1914 to 1945. It can be seen as a common culture based on more or less identical stereotypes and clichés: in a paradoxical but logical way, the two sides, while pursuing their military duel, represented their conflict through the same set of iconic cinematic images. Wrecked churches and ruined cathedrals stand as a symbol for the murder of civilization: this is not only a cliché for a Christian Europe, it is also the direct heritage of the propaganda battles of the First World War. Indeed, the German newsreel of the First World War has been read as the primitive paradigm on which German and foreign war newsreel were framed for years.[62] Hélène Puiseux has argued that the pioneering work of the early German film tycoon Oskar Messter in modelling the newsreel from 1914 set the code and the rituals of the war newsreel from 1914 to present-day television.

Nevertheless, a final path has to be explored: the close connection between different media. To what extent, for example, did newsreels and feature films rely on the same shots, on the same rhetoric? And to what extent did the cinematic view of air raids differ from those of the radio and the press? Peter Marvick has argued that 'the different media should neither be isolated from one another nor be seen as operating independently upon society.'[63] This chapter has dealt mainly with the second hypothesis, that of the shared culture of war, but we believe that other approaches to the history of wartime media would shed further light on how the bombing of towns and civilians in the Second World War was reconstructed through the newsreel.

Notes

1   L. Mumford, *The Culture of Cities* (New York: Harcourt, 1938), 275, quoted by P. K. Saint-Amour, 'Airwar prophecy and interwar modernism', *Comparative Literature Studies*, 42.2, 2005, 130.
2   These precise data are, of course, an historian's reconstruction.
3   He was probably alluding to the bombing of Melk on 8 July 1944.
4   Located in Pommeréval, their farm was very close to the site of the Val Ygot, at Ardouval in the Eawy Forest in Seine-Maritime; this V1 site was repeatedly and heavily bombed between December 1943 and June 1944.
5   O. Dumoulin, 'Et le Reichminister inventa la réalité semaine après semaine (L'authenticité selon le *Deutsche Wochenschau*)', in S. Crogiez (ed.), *Dieux et hommes, Histoire iconographie des sociétés païennes et chrétiennes de l'Antiquité à nos jours*, Mélanges en l'honneur de Françoise Thélamon (Rouen: PURH, 2005), 659–75.
6   See A. Harris, *Bomber Offensive*, (London: Greenhill Books, 1990 (1st edn. London: Collins, 1947), 34.
7   D. E. Showalter, 'Plans, Weapons, Doctrines: the Strategic Cultures of Inter-war Europe', in R. Chickering and S. Förster (eds), *The Shadows of Total War: Europe, East Asia, and the United States, 1919–1939* (Cambridge: Cambridge University Press, 2003), 60; R. J. Overy, 'Air Power in the Second World War: Historical Themes and Theories', in H. Boog (ed.), *The Conduct of the Air War in the Second World War: an International Comparison* (Oxford-New York: Berg, 1992), 7–28; S. Lindqvist, *A History of Bombing* (New York: The New Press, 2001).
8   Saint-Amour, 'Airwar prophecy', 131.
9   Newsreels have been analysed with care in various famous examples such as A. Aldgate, *Cinema and History: British Newsreels and the Spanish Civil War* (London: Scholar Press, 1979). In France, the works of S. Lindeperg are of great interest: see S. Lindeperg, *Clio de 5 à 7. Les actualités filmées de la libération : archives du futur* (Paris: CNRS Éditions, 2000).
10 The producing company, DW Gmbr, was founded on 21 November 1940. Among the numerous books and articles on this topic are G. Albrecht, *National-sozialistische Filmpolitik*, (Stuttgart: Ferdinand Enke, 1969); U. Bartels, *Die Wochenschau im Dritten Reich: Entwicklung und Funktion eines Massenmediums unter besonderer Berücksichtigung völkisch-nationaler Inhalte* (Frankfurt am Main: Peter Lang, 2004); D. Welch: *The Third Reich: Politics and Propaganda* (London: Routledge, 1993).
11 This average length was subject to variation. For instance, the regular *Deutsche Wochenschau* had a 40-minute standard at the beginning of the war. When the conflict ceased to be a succession of triumphs, for instance during winter 1941–1942, it was cut to 20 minutes which remained, more or less, the standard until the last issue. *France-Actualités* from August 1942 to August 1944 lasted between 8 and 22 minutes. J.-P. Bertin-Maghit, *Propagande, France 1940–1944* (Paris: Nouveau Monde, 2004). B. Bowles, 'German newsreel propaganda in France, 1940–1944', *Historical Journal of Film, Radio and Television*, 24, 1, 2004, 45–67. B. Bowles, 'Newsreels, ideology, and public opinion under Vichy: The case of "La France en marche"', *French Historical Studies*, 27, 2, 2004, 419–63. J. Charrel, 'Entre pouvoir allemand et pouvoir français: les actualités cinématographiques en France (1940–1944)', *Sociétés et représentations*, 12, 2001/2, 63–70. When viewing for an analytical purpose, the length of a cinematic source should be multiplied by at least four.
12 For Goebbels, this generic noun includes the two following categories: 'Haltung' (bearing, conduct, observable behaviour) and 'Stimmung' (feeling, spirit, mood). The analysts of

Goebbels' propaganda stressed this categorization very early: see L.W. Doob, 'Goebbels' Principles of Propaganda', *The Public Opinion Quarterly*, 14, 3, 1950, 419–42.

13   L. Veray, in *Les films d'actualité français de la Grande Guerre* (Paris: S.I.R.PA./A.F.R.H.C., 1995), quotes E. Juvey's article 'Le journal de guerre' in *Le Film*, 2, 25 March 1916, 7, which notes that every cinema manager was eager to obtain war newsreels because of their popularity.

14   N. Pronay, 'British Newsreels in the 1930's: their policies and impact', *History*, vol. 57, 189, February 1972, reprinted in L. Mac Kernan (ed.), *Yesterday's News: The British Cinema Newsreel Reader* (London: British Universities Film and Video Council, 2002), 138–60.

15   Mass Observation Archive, File Report 524, Memo on Newsreels 11.12.40, report from 28 November 1940, http://bufvc.ac.uk/wpcontent/media/2009/06/mo_report_524.pdf, Reproduced with the permission of Curtis Brown Group Ltd on behalf of the Trustees of The Mass-Observation Archive © Trustees of Mass-Observation.

16   H. Laemmel, 'La mission des actualités cinématographiques', *Cinéma d'aujourd'hui. Congrès international du cinéma à Bâle* (Geneva and Paris: Éditions des Trois Collines, 1945), 183, quoted in G. Haver, *Les lueurs de la guerre: Écrans vaudois 1939-1945* (Lausanne: Payot, 2003), 240.

17   S. Kracauer, *Propaganda and the Nazi War Film* (New York: The Museum of Modern Art, Film library, 1942) and Id., 'The Conquest of Europe on the Screen – The Nazi Newsreel, 1939-40', *Social Research*, 10, 1/4, 1943, 337–57. On this topic see C. Delage, 'Luis Buñuel et Siegfried Kracauer au service de la propagande anti-nazie du Museum of Modern Art. De New York à Nuremberg', Actes du colloque *Les Européens dans le cinéma américain. Emigration et exil* (Paris: Presses de la Sorbonne Nouvelle, 2003), 239–48; D. Culbert, 'The Rockefeller Foundation, the Museum of Modern Art Film Library, and Siegfried Kracauer, 1941', *Historical Journal of Film, Radio and Television*, 13, 4, 1993, 495–511.

18   More than simple newsreel, the films analyzed by Kracauer are documentaries on war made out of edited shots of newsreel: *Blietzkrieg im Western*, *Feuertaufe* (Baptism of fire) and *Feldzug im Westen* (Victory on the Western front). See T. Sakmyster, 'Nazi documentaries of Intimidation, Feldung in Polen (1940), Feuertaufe (1940) and Sieg im Westen (1941)', *Historical Journal of Film, Radio and Television*, 16, 4, 1996, 485–514.

19   G. Haver, *Les lueurs de la guerre*, 273. These commentaries come from the *Feuille d'avis de Lausanne* during 1941.

20   K. Hoffman, 'Propagandistic Problems of German Newsreels in World War II', *Historical Journal of Films, Radio and Television*, 24 1, 2004, 133–42. She quotes on this topic Heinz Boberach (ed.), *Medlungen aus Dem Reich. Die geheimen Lageberichte des Sicherheitsdientes der SS 1938-1945*, 16 vols (Herrsching: Pawlak, 1984), 27. Composed of 30,000 members of the NSDAP, this service transmitted hundreds of reports stating that after the Führer's speeches nothing had more effect on the population.

21   J. Goebbels, *Journal 1943-1945* (Paris: Tallandier, 2009), 57, entry for 31 January 1943. All quotations from Goebbels's diary are taken from this French translation.

22   The source for this information is Bowles, 'German Newsreel Propaganda in France, 62'; the interpretation, however, is my own.

23   A. Aldgate and J. Richards, *Britain can Take It: British Cinema in the Second World War* (London and New York: Tauris, 2007 – 3rd edn.).

24   Goebbels, *Journal 1943-1945*, 39, entry for 23 January 1943.

25   *France-Actualités*, n. 1, 21 August 1942 spoke of itself as an 'invisible link of unity', which for the first time since the tragic year 1940 will bring together the children of renascent France from the two zones and the Empire' under the authority of the French State and of its chief, Marshal Pétain. All issues of *France-Actualités* were viewed on the website of the Institut National de l'Audiovisuel (INA): http://www.ina.fr/histoire-et-conflits/seconde-guerre-mondiale/video/.

26   *France-Actualités*, respectively 19 March 1943; 21 May 1943; 23 July 1943; 24 September 1943.

27   Henriot, the most famous extreme right-wing speaker on Radio-Paris, was appointed Information and Propaganda Secretary of State from January 1944.

28   On 30 April 1943, *France-Actualités* featured the arrival of evacuees from the Paris suburbs to a location near Guéret, in the rural Limousin.

29   *France-Actualités*, 4 June 1943.

30 Goebbels, *Journal 1943–1945*, 614, entry for 17 September 1944.
31 Goebbels, *Journal 1943–1945*, 658, entry for 3 December 1944.
32 *Deutsche Wochenschau*, 675, 11 August 1943, vol 11, disk 2, total length 18 mn and 47 s, Sequence 3, Heimat, Bayreuth 1.22.
33 J. Friedrich, *The Fire: The Bombing of Germany, 1940–1945* (New York: Columbia University Press, 2006); original edition, *Der Brand: Deutschland im Bombenkrieg 1940–1945* (Munich: Propylaeen, 2002).
34 R. G. Moeller, 'On the History of Man-Made Destruction: Loss, Death, Memory, and Germany in the Bombing War', *History Workshop Journal*, 61, 2006, 103–34.
35 *Deutsche Wochenschau*, 6 July 1943, Sequence 2, 0,35 minute to 1,44 minute.
36 *Deutsche Wochenschau*, 6 July 1943, Sequence 2. The quotation is taken from the English subtitles given in the IHA edition of the *Deutsche Wochenschau*.
37 T. Nipperdey, 'La cathédrale de Cologne, monument à la nation', in *Réflexions sur l'histoire allemande* (Paris: Gallimard, 1992), 222–45; original 'Der Kölner Dom als Nationaldenkmal', in *Nachdenken über die deutsche Geschichte. Essays* (Munich: C. H. Beck, 1986).
38 C. Ginzburg, *Clues, Myths, and the Historical Method* (Baltimore: Johns Hopkins University Press, 1989).
39 See *France-Actualités*, 9 April 1943 (funerals at Suresnes, in Paris, at Saint Honoré d'Eylau and in Antwerp); 16 April 1943 (funerals at Boulogne-Billancourt); 28 April 1944 (funerals at the Sacré-Cœur in Paris with a speech by Philippe Henriot).
40 *France-Actualités*, 24 September 1943.
41 *France-Actualités*, 21 May 1943.
42 *France-Actualités*, 19 May 1944. The newsreel claimed 100 dead, but a more recent account puts the figure at 183, including 51 children (in a village of 600 people), who had gathered in the church for a communion service. The attack fell wide of its target, an ammunition dump near Rennes. See M. Coutel, *Bruz sous les Bombes: un Village Breton dans la Guerre* (Rennes: Éditions La Part Commune, 2005).
43 *France-Actualités*, 2 June 1944.
44 British Movietone Digital Archive, Sound Story no. 40012, http//www.movietone.com.
45 British Movietone Digital Archive, 'Review of the Year 1940', Sound Story n. 36259, http//www.movietone.com.
46 British Movietone Digital Archive, 'Menzies In Coventry', Sound Story n. 40538, 116 seconds, 22 March 1941, http//www.movietone.com.
47 British Movietone Digital Archive, 'Premier's V tour', Sound Story n. 41374, 72 seconds, 2 October 1941, http//www.movietone.com.
48 'An die Kulturwelt ! Ein Aufruf', *Berliner Tageblatt*, 4 October 1914.
49 See J. Horne and A. Kramer, *German Atrocities, 1914. A History of Denial* (New Haven: Yale University Press, 2001).
50 J. Horne and A. Kramer, 'German "Atrocities" and Franco-German Opinion, 1914: The Evidence of German Soldiers' Diaries', *Journal of Modern History*, 66, 1, 1994, 1–33.
51 A. Rasmussen, 'La "science française" dans la guerre des manifestes, 1914–1918', *Mots: Les langages du politique*, 76, 2004, 9–24.
52 *Bibliothèque de l'école des chartes*, 75.1, 1914, 469–70.
53 Académie des inscriptions et belles-lettres, *Comptes-rendus des séances de l'année*, 58, 6, 1914, 577–8.
54 N. Reeves, 'Film Propaganda and its Audience: The Example of Britain's Official Films during the First World War', *Journal of Contemporary History*, 18, 3, 1983, 463–94. Reeves analyses a film kept at the Imperial War Museum film Archive, IWM 206. The argument is also developed in N. Reeves, *Official British Film Propaganda during the First World War* (London: Croom Helm, 1986).
55 R. Dalisson, 'La propagande festive de Vichy: Mythes fondateurs, relecture nationaliste et contestation en France de 1940 à 1944', *Guerres mondiales et conflits contemporains*, 207, 2002/3, 5–35. For a more comprehensive study, see R. Dalisson, *Les Fêtes Du Maréchal: Propagande Festive et Imaginaire dans la France de Vichy* (Paris: Tallandier, 2008).
56 *Journal de Rouen*, 10 March 1942, quoted in Dalisson, 'La propagande festive de Vichy', 13.

57   L. Campbell, *Coventry Cathedral: Art and Architecture in post-war Britain* (Oxford: Clarendon Press, 1996), 8-9.
58   Quoted by R. T. Howard, *Built and Rebuilt: The Story of Coventry Cathedral, 1939–1962* (Coventry: Council of Coventry Cathedral, 1962), 18.
59   J. Piper, *Coventry Cathedral, 15th November 1940* (Manchester: Manchester Art Gallery, 1940).
60   F. Spalding, 'John Piper and Coventry, in War and Peace', *The Burlington Magazine*, 145, 1204, 2003, 489. I am indebted to this article for all the references about Coventry Cathedral. For a comprehensive study on Piper see F. Spalding, *John Piper, Myfanwy Piper: Lives in Art* (Oxford: Oxford University Press, 2009). The understanding of Piper's paintings in the surrounding of the destroyed cathedral is almost inseparable from the fact that Piper had already seen 'Guernica' three times: in Paris in July 1937, in the winter 1938–39 at the Burlington New Galleries and then at the Whitechapel Gallery in London.
61   P. Laborie, *L'Opinion française sous Vichy* (Paris: Seuil, 1990), 164.
62   H. Puiseux, *Les figures de la guerre: représentations et sensibilités, 1839–1996* (Paris: Gallimard, 1997), 184-5.
63   P. Marvick, 'Print, Pictures and Sound: The Second World War and the British Experience', *Daedalus*, 111, 4, 1982, 153.

Postscript

17

From War Talk to Rights Talk: Exile Politics, Aerial Bombardment and the Construction of the Human Rights Project during the Second World War[1]

Jay Winter

It is impossible to understand the current human rights regime in Europe without attending to the crucible years of the Second World War and after. In this study, I want to highlight the way in which exile politics during and after the Blitz in London provided the framework for the emergence of a new international regime of human rights. Out of protests by governments and individuals in exile over the targeting of civilian populations by Nazi forces, and crimes being committed daily on the Continent from 1939 on, there emerged an approach to war aims which placed human rights at the heart of the post-war international order. The men and women who drafted these documents did so at a time when no one could have predicted an Allied victory in the war. And yet during those desperate hours, during the Blitz and in its aftermath, a new human rights regime was born.

Such an outcome was unprecedented and to a large degree unanticipated. And yet it gives a new meaning to the notion that the Second World War was a war of liberation. Not in Poland, not in Czechoslovakia, not in Hungary, caution historians of Eastern Europe. One form of imprisonment succeeded another. But if we adopt a longer time horizon, perhaps the notion of the 1939-45 conflict as a war of liberation can be defended, and not just for the remains of the Jewish population of Europe who survived the Final Solution. Theirs was liberation pure and simple. The human rights regime of the 1940s was both an overground and an underground river; on the surface it froze during the Cold War. But there were other slower, more indirect ways in which human rights liberated Europe. May 1968 was a plea in many registers for liberation, from South America to Vietnam. The Prague spring of the same year gave liberation a human (and socialist) face; even after it was suppressed, Charter 77 resumed the struggle, without socialism. So did Solidarity in Poland, and so did the Helsinki accords of the 1970s, yielding a trade-off between the recognition internationally of the Soviet Union's western borders and Western surveillance of human rights violations in the Soviet Union itself. It would be absurd to claim that human rights brought down the Soviet empire, and yet the courage of Soviet dissidents was part of a much wider process begun, I believe, decades earlier. The *longue durée* does matter in international history, as the story of the unfolding of the human rights movement in the mid-twentieth century and after shows.

Who were the carriers of this message? Who were the human rights activists of the generation of the Second World War? Some were lawyers; others were military men in exile. Others still were ex-soldiers, veterans of the Great War who found a way to continue the struggle they endured in one war in the harsh conditions of another. Among them was the French jurist René Cassin, whose contribution to this story is important to note.

It may be surprising that I focus on the role of old soldiers. The primary reason for proverbial raised eyebrows at this claim is the tendency of scholars to work from an American or from a German perspective to probe the political outlook and pressure of veterans' groups over the last century. In that approach, veterans are overwhelmingly patriotic, conservative or reactionary. Their experience of war or of preparation for war makes them authoritarian, illiberal, or natural supporters of right-wing or extreme right-wing political parties and movements.[2]

What happens if we choose a different approach, a French one, and juxtapose it to the conventional view? In some respects, there is evidence of right-wing or extreme right-wing tendencies among some French veterans, like Jean Marie Le Pen of the *Front National,* or the inter-war *Croix de feu,* or among the OAS terrorists (Organisation de l'Armée Secrète) who tried and failed several times to kill de Gaulle after his *volte face* on Algerian independence in 1959. But in other respects French history provides a long and well-documented alternative narrative that today remains in the shadows. It tells a story of a different kind, that of a mass movement of pacifist veterans, millions of them, who from the 1870s to 1940 saw military service as the shield of the Republic.[3] It arises in the late nineteenth century in the cry of Jean Jaurès for *La nouvelle armée.* It moves to the left in revulsion over the anti-Republican and Catholic cabal which aimed to convict, imprison and forget Colonel Dreyfus. It rails against the use of troops as strike-breakers, but virtually to a man, answers the call-up of 1 August 1914 and fights to the bitter end. Thousands of 'trouble makers' on the left to be arrested so that mobilization can go forward peacefully in 1914 could not be found. Why? Because they had already joined up.[4]

During the war itself, many of these men worked to create a veterans' movement with two central objectives. The first was decent treatment for the wounded and a decent pension for the demobilized. The second was the abolition of war. Perhaps 60 per cent of the roughly eight million men who served in French forces joined these organizations. These were not the voices of parliamentary politics, but of an extra-parliamentary movement, the membership of which came from small market towns and villages – what we call *La France profonde.* Their voices were heard throughout the inter-war years and beyond, and while they were never univocal, they carried an unmistakable pacifist message.[5]

In the short term, their cause failed miserably. Betrayed by their own illusions, by their belief in reaching out to ex-servicemen in Italy and Germany, even to Mussolini and Hitler themselves, they were left in 1940 with a taste as of ashes. Their story is one of political bankruptcy, to be sure.

And yet that is not the end of the story. Out of the veterans' movement to outlaw war came another crusade, one privileging the rights of soldiers, of the wounded and the unemployed, within the framework of human rights. Drawing on elements of the French revolutionary tradition, and the Universal Declarations of Human Rights of 1789 and 1793, veterans and other democrats in exile created a new form of the human rights message, one which arose out of the catastrophe of the Second World War. The passage from the struggle for dignity in and after one world war to an even more profound and long-lasting commitment to human rights after a second world war is the subject of this chapter.

Veterans' politics found a home in the new League of Nations. The International Labour Organization (ILO), was founded by the League with the aim of ensuring the right to work of all those disabled in the war. Here is a central theme of the whole sweep of this story. It starts with the victims of war and ends with the claim that rights belong not only to victims but to us all.

On 2 September 1921, there was in Geneva an international veteran discussion of work for war invalids. René Cassin represented the largest French veterans' movement, *Union Fédérale*, with two million members, and it was at this venue that he and his colleagues met for the first time enemy veterans from the defeated Central Powers. Such contacts convinced Cassin that veterans had to work together with their former enemies and within the League of Nations if their voice was to be heard in international affairs.

With this aim in mind, he took the initiative in establishing an international veterans' organization, CIAMAC, which met for the first time at Geneva in September 1926.[6] This body emerged from earlier discussions among veterans from both sides in the war, men who were committed to coming together to discuss matters of common interest. The German delegates from the *Reichsbund* affirmed their commitment to republican values. They accepted the need to pay reparations and to contribute to the reconstruction of devastated regions, all as steps to reassure Allied ex-servicemen that they too wanted to preserve the peace. Italian, Polish, Austrian and British delegates joined them, and went on in later meetings to share information through the ILO on questions of pensions, work placement, and on medical and orthopedic assistance for veterans. Belgian and Yugoslav veterans joined in these discussions. When the Dawes Plan regularized reparations payments, the political conditions were ripe for more formal discussions about the formation of an international organization of veterans' associations. Initially 80 delegates from ten nations and 20 associations came to the inaugural meeting, and committed themselves to working for the principle of mandatory arbitration of international conflicts. Here was a body unattached to their governments, able to speak out with the moral authority earned by military service and sacrifice. Annual meetings were held in the later 1920s in Vienna, Berlin, Warsaw and Paris. They had no difficulty in integrating German delegates, whose commitment to peace was unquestioned. It was harder to bring Soviet veterans to the table, since the war had been entirely eclipsed by the 1917 revolution.

This set of initiatives was part of the political culture surrounding the League of Nations. Veterans like Cassin argued that repairing the physical damage caused by the war was a first step towards repairing the moral damage it caused. Their task was political education at home and the lessening of enmity between former enemies. They were committed to making the League of Nations as powerful as possible an obstacle to war. That is why their distance from foreign offices was essential: these men spoke over the heads of governments to the millions of men and women whose lives and families had been disfigured by war. They spoke to youth who did not know what war was, and urged them to join in their international crusade for peace.

Their main aim was what we have come to term 'moral rearmament'. By this Cassin meant that those who knew war had to educate the public as to the horrors of violence and the absolute necessity of saving the new generation from the catastrophe of another war. This could not be done within the boundaries of one country alone, or solely among the victors. That is why he bypassed the objections of the more conservative Inter-allied Veterans' Federation (FIDAC), which had no truck with the idea that German and Austrian veterans had to be brought into the conversation. Bridges had to be built, but with prior agreement on certain clear principles about the way to preserve the peace.[7]

All these efforts were marked by both the strengths and the weaknesses of the League of Nations. Disarmament exposed them all. Cassin served on the French delegation to the League of Nations for 14 years, from 1924 to 1938, and much of his work in this body concerned arbitration and disarmament. He therefore had a front-row view of the fragility of an institution which challenged the supremacy of state sovereignty as a principle of international political order. If a more robust League of Nations or any similar venture were ever to succeed, it would do so only after a sea change had occurred in both academic and popular notions of the indivisible sovereignty of the state, and of the power of the duly elected statesman, acting like a *châtelain dans son château*.

The League had made a start, in particular by outlawing the use of biological and chemical weapons, and by making it a war crime to deliver such weapons from the air on civilian populations. In Geneva, both before and after the Nazi seizure of power, there were efforts to limit the horrors of aerial warfare, by defining what constituted an undefended town, what appropriate warning meant, and what level of civilian casualties were to be deemed excessive.[8] A draft Convention on these matters proposed in 1938 remained just that, a draft.

By then the depredations of what René Cassin termed the Leviathan state had exposed the essential flaw in the theory of unlimited state sovereignty.

Anyone with eyes to see could follow the argument, so painfully etched into the minds first of Germans, then of Czechs, and then of Austrians, and after 1939 into the minds of a vast occupied population stretching all across Europe. Human rights emerged as a fundamental formulation of war aims at this, the darkest moment of the war. But it is important to note how many individuals were active long before the war in the effort to provide an alternative view of state sovereignty. And that view ultimately bore fruit in the 1948 Universal Declaration of Human Rights. The ideas behind this document emerged before the war, but the war made them stand for what the Allies were fighting for.

AFTER 1940

Exile politics in general, and human rights politics in particular, emerged out of catastrophe. In 1940, Cassin watched the collapse of France from an office in the Ministry of Information. He realized that as an anti-fascist and a Jew, he was a marked man. He returned to his home in the south of France, paid his taxes, and decided to embark on an Australian troop ship to England. He never heard the call to arms of de Gaulle of 18 June 1940, but responded to it on arrival in London on 29 June. He told de Gaulle that he was a veteran, founder of the veterans' movement, and a Jew. He put himself, as a jurist and as a Frenchman, at the disposal of de Gaulle's embryonic movement. De Gaulle called him a godsend. Why? Because de Gaulle had 36 hours left to prepare a document for Churchill establishing his credentials and that of his movement, *France Libre*, as a French government in exile. Churchill was prepared to recognize – and, of equal importance, to fund – de Gaulle's movement if he could claim *de jure* status as the representative in exile of the French Republic. Cassin drew up the document which provided this crucial legitimation, later ratified on 7 August 1940, and the cornerstone of the French Resistance movement.[9]

The significance of this juridical service was of the highest importance, which de Gaulle recognized by making Cassin one of his ministers (or commissioners) in exile. Cassin had responsibility for education and justice, and sat on all the major committees of the French resistance movement in London. He represented de Gaulle on missions to Lebanon and to Africa, showing that the Republic was alive in its empire. He ran the central bureau of *France Libre* throughout the worst months of the Blitz. And it was in London that he met a group of exiles with similar inclinations, men who saw that human rights had to be part of a radically new post-war international order. Nikolas Politis, Foreign Minister of Greece and Edouard Benes, Foreign Minister of Czechoslovakia, were two of the men he had met in Geneva and who like him had to escape to London to avoid execution. Alongside other legal scholars like Hersch Lauterpacht, these men helped convert discussions about war aims into discussions about human rights.

The paradox at the heart of my argument was that as the possibility – perhaps the probability – of Nazi victory emerged in 1940 and 1941, a number of exiles in London, under Nazi aerial bombardment, began to construct a vision of an entirely different post-war world. Many of them did so in shelters, during the long nights of the Blitz; others developed their ideas in terms of the maltreatment of occupied populations. The outcome was the same; these men and women constructed a blueprint for the future, through which the warfare state would be turned into a welfare state, and in which the defence of human rights came before the defence of national interest.

Consider the poignancy of the setting: in shelters, tube stations and basements scattered around the city, exiles huddled with Londoners amidst the dust and damp hoping each time the foundations shook that that tremor was the worst. To while away the time, or simply to keep the faith, men like Cassin and Benes engaged in thought experiments, moments of fancy which brought their minds not to the stark reality of a city under bombardment, but to the outlines of a world after the war, one they might very well never get to see. And that world was one configured by them, and by others at the same time, as fundamentally different from the present order. It was a world in which human rights came before *raison d'état*, where international law came before *Machtpolitik*, and where no state could ever again claim, with the Nazis, that it was *un châtelain dans son château*, able to do with *their* Jews or *their* socialists whatever they chose to do. Aerial warfare described the warfare state, red in tooth and claw. Another kind of international order had to be constructed, one in which each state's legitimacy rested on its respect for the human rights of its citizens and those of its neighbours. What a vision emerged in those dark nights, one which flew in the face of reality, and expressed to a world at war what I have termed a minor utopia, a vision of a world where people had the right to die one at a time.

WARFARE STATE OR WELFARE STATE: ST JAMES'S CONFERENCE I

Human rights are always defined by their violation. People come to see what they might be by facing their utter destruction. That is what the Blitz meant, and what the military ascendency of Nazi power represented. By the late spring of 1941, the Nazis had begun the construction of what they termed a new European order, whatever the fate of Britain. This Nazi version of a European Union of the future was composed of a German core and a periphery dominated by collaborators in every occupied country.

To counter the notion that the collaborators were the lawful rulers of occupied Europe and that they, under German and Italian leadership, were forging a new Europe, the British decided to hold a war council of her Allies. This meeting, held in St James's Palace in London on 12 June 1941, brought together representatives of her Empire, her Commonwealth, and her Dominions, alongside leaders of governments in exile from countries under Axis control. Poland, the Netherlands, Belgium, Luxemburg, Czechoslavakia and Norway were all represented at the Prime Ministerial level. General Sikorski spoke for Poland; Jan Masaryk was there as foreign secretary of Czechoslovakia; Trygve Lie as foreign secretary of Norway. Paul-Henri Spaak represented Belgium as foreign minister in its government in exile. Churchill met the participants in the Portrait Gallery of the Palace. There he told them and the world that 'whatever are the movements of the Nazis worldwide, it is in the fortress formed by the British Isles where the final outcome of the struggle between liberty and tyranny will take place'. And alongside him were men and women equally determined to see this monumental struggle through to victory.

The accord all the delegates signed affirmed three points. The first was that the struggle will continue until 'victory is won'. There would be no compromise or negotiated settlement. The second was that there will be no peace until German forces cease to oppress or threaten to oppress free peoples, that is until the Nazi regime is destroyed. The third is that 'enduring peace' will come only after 'the menace of aggression' is lifted, so enabling 'free peoples' to 'enjoy economic and social security'. To this end the signatories promised to work together and with others 'both in war and in peace'.[10]

Ten days later the war took a turn which ultimately led both to victory in 1945 and to the implementation of Allied plans for the post-war world. The Nazis invaded the Soviet Union, and despite spectacular victories in the weeks after the invasion, it was clear that Britain was not alone, and neither were the governments in exile who had met at St James's Palace a few days before. It is clear too that the entry of the Soviet Union into the war was a decisive moment in the slow but steady tilt of the United States towards the Allies. On 9 August 1941, Churchill and President Franklin D. Roosevelt met on board USS Augusta at Naval Station Argentia in Placentia Bay, on the southern coast of Newfoundland, then still a British colony. FDR let it be known that he was going to New England on a fishing trip. Instead he met his Chiefs of Staff and Churchill for their first but by no means their last council of war. It was Churchill who landed the biggest fish of all.

There could be no doubt as to the American position, formulated in the document they released on 14 August, when Churchill was back in Britain. The key point was in the sixth of the common principles to which they agreed. This read as follows:

Sixth, after the final destruction of the Nazi tyranny, they hope to see established a peace which will afford to all nations the means of dwelling in safety within their own boundaries, and which will afford assurance that all the men in all lands may live out their lives in freedom from fear and want; ...[11]

Here, four and a half months before the Japanese attack on Pearl Harbor, the United States effectively declared war on Nazi Germany. When Hitler received a cable with this text attached, he exploded. What followed thereafter is still a matter of controversy, but who could doubt that just as in the First World War, the United States was going to join the Allies, and convert a European war into a world war? Hitler had promised that should the Americans so decide, the Jews of Europe would pay the price. And so they did.[12]

ST JAMES'S CONFERENCE II

The second time there was an inter-Allied conference of exiles and allies in St James's Palace, six weeks later, the entire political landscape had changed. The war was now one of left versus right on a global scale. In September 1941, it was time to bring the Atlantic Charter to bear on Allied war aims and on preparations for the world after the war and for the war crime trials which would ensue. All the governments in exile had abundant evidence of Nazi war crimes against subject peoples. To announce to their citizens suffering under Nazi occupation that retribution would come one day, they provided both hope to the oppressed and a warning to the Nazis that justice would be done. Here is the first clear sign of Allied willingness to hold war crimes trials after the war.

Anthony Eden, the newly appointed Foreign Minister, presided at this second inter-Allied conference. This change at the top was clearly to the advantage of the Free French. The previous British Foreign Secretary, Lord Halifax, was at best tepid towards de Gaulle, whereas Eden, who had served like Cassin in the Great War, spoke reasonable French and admired de Gaulle. The other major newcomer was Ivan Maisky, representative of the Soviet Union, whom Cassin had known in Geneva at the League of Nations a decade before.[13]

In his address to the conference, Cassin made sure everyone knew that this was not the first time Germany had invaded countries with which it was at peace. 'Hitler', he said, 'has merely revived, in a more monstrous and brutal form, William II's dream of world domination':

> Invaded three times in less than a century by an adversary bent on death and destruction, France can see no safeguard for this independence and freedom, or for that of maritime communications, outside the framework of an effective organization of international security, an essential element of which is preliminary disarmament, the destruction of the military machine and the limitation of war potentialities in countries which have never ceased to threaten her and are still liable to do so.
>
> The French also consider as necessary to the establishment of a real peace the practical ratification of the essential liberties of man and the concerted utilization, in view of the economic and social securities of peoples, of technical progress creative of fresh wealth.
>
> Indeed when peace has come, constant respect for the law of solidarity will impose itself on all. In the future it alone will enable us to avoid a repetition of those catastrophes which rend the unity of the human race.[14]

'The essential liberties of man' was Cassin's way of pointing towards the need to make human rights a bulwark of peace. Here he spoke for the exile community as a whole.

The primary business of the second St James's meeting was to ratify and adapt the Atlantic Charter to serve as a succinct statement of Allied war aims. For Cassin, that meant France, along with all other countries, had the right to choose its preferred system of government. It also meant that something stronger than the League of Nations had to carry the burden of preventing war in the future. What would strengthen such a new institution would be a clear and comprehensive statement as to the universality of human rights. It was here, in London in September 1941, long before the war was won, that the quest for a new and practical human rights regime began.

ST JAMES'S CONFERENCE III

The ferocity of Nazi occupation intensified in the autumn of 1941. Both Churchill and Roosevelt issued statements condemning the execution of hostages. After the Japanese attack on Pearl Harbor on 7 December 1941, and the German declaration of war on the United States four days later, they joined with 23 other nations in signing the United Nations Declaration on 1 January 1942, affirming their commitment to the destruction of the Nazi regime.

The evolution of Allied thinking on the post-war world reveals a strong division between Britain, the United States and the Soviet Union, who ran the war, and governments in exile representing occupied populations. The Great Powers wanted to postpone any precise commitments on how such judicial proceedings would operate. Governments-in-exile had no such luxury. They needed to show captive populations that their national sovereignty was still intact and that after the war, there would be a national reckoning on war crimes. Such proceedings did not at all preclude the establishment of an international tribunal, planning for which developed in the second half of the war. The first step to this end was the St James's conference of 13 January 1942. Sir Anthony Eden, British Foreign Secretary, welcomed the delegates, but stood aside from its deliberations, which were chaired by General Sikorski of Poland. The conference issued a declaration signed by representatives of nine occupied countries. Here is the text they agreed:

> Whereas Germany since the beginning of the present conflict, which arose out of her policy of aggression, has instituted in occupied countries a regime of terror characterized in particular by imprisonments, mass expulsions, execution of hostages and massacres,
>
> And whereas these acts of violence are being similarly perpetrated by Allies and associates of the Reich and in certain countries by accomplices of the occupying power,
>
> And whereas international solidarity is necessary in order to avoid repression of

these acts of violence simply by acts of vengeance on the part of the general public and in order to satisfy the sense of justice of the civilized world.

Recalling that international law and, in particular, the convention signed at The Hague in 1907 regarding laws and customs of land warfare do not permit belligerents in occupied countries to perpetrate acts of violence against civilians, to bring into disrepute laws in force or to overthrow national institutions,

The undersigned representatives of the government of Belgium, the government of Czecho-Slovakia, the Free French National Committee, the government of Greece, the government of Luxembourg, the government of The Netherlands, the government of Norway, the government of Poland and the government of Yugoslavia

1. Affirm that acts of violence thus perpetrated against civilian populations are at variance with accepted ideas concerning acts of war and political offences as these are understood by civilized nations;
2. Take note of the declaration made in this respect on October 25 1941, by the President of the United States of America and the British Prime Minister;
3. Place among their principal war aims punishment through the channel of organized justice of those guilty and responsible for these crimes, whether they have ordered them, perpetrated them or in any way participated in them;
4. Determine in the spirit of international solidarity to see to it that (A) those guilty and responsible, whatever their nationality, are sought for, handed over to justice and judged; (B) that sentences pronounced are carried out.

The key point here is the third point: that the framing and carrying out of war crimes trials emerged as a central element in the formulation of war aims. Signing the document for France was Charles de Gaulle, who attended while Cassin was on special mission in Syria.[15] For de Gaulle, the task was not only to seek retribution; it was also to 'take measures to ensure that a renewal of such crimes should be made impossible'.[16]

It was from this point that thinking about retribution and about the shape of the post-war international legal order came together in a kind of double helix. The liberation of subject peoples and the punishment of those responsible for monstrous acts during the war presented one key element of what the Allies were fighting for. The other part of war aims was the affirmation of positive principles on which the peace would be secured, and that is where human rights came in.

Here we have reached something of a parting of the ways. The Second World War was fought to restore the territorial integrity of individual states occupied and humiliated by German military power. This was its essential character, be it with reference to France or to the Soviet Union. But the very depredations of Nazi occupation set in motion forces seeking to replace the bankrupt system of the League of Nations with an international order of a different kind. The notion that state sovereignty was inviolable and sacrosanct was contaminated by the Nazis and their allies. No state could be permitted to do what the Nazis had done first to its own citizens and then to the rest of Europe, and then to justify its acts on the grounds that sovereignty was indivisible and untouchable as a principle of international life. That is why the Second World War was the occasion for the search for a dual approach to reconstruction after the war. First came the need to restore the dignity of those states whose regimes had been destroyed by the Nazis. Territoriality came first. But secondly, there emerged a growing consensus among the Allies on the need to reconstruct the international order on a different basis, one which rested on commitments which went beyond state sovereignty. Out of that search the United Nations emerged, and so did a set of human rights commitments flowing from the adoption of the Charter of the UN in 1945 to the passing of the Convention on Genocide and the Universal Declaration of Human Rights in 1948.

THE INTER-ALLIED COMMISSION ON WAR CRIMES

The period between the third St James's conference and the formation of an inter-Allied commission on war crimes was the time when the Holocaust was at its height. But even though hundreds of thousands of Jews were being murdered daily, it was the death of one man, and the retribution it brought in its wake, that moved the Allies into action. On 27 May 1942, a group of Czech parachutists, trained in Britain, fatally wounded SS General Reinhard Heydrich, head of all security policy and protector of Bohemia and Moravia. In revenge, the Nazis exterminated all the inhabitants of one village – Lidice – near the site of the assassination. Czechs in London demanded that the British formally associated themselves with the January 1942 St James's declaration on punishing war criminals. This they were unprepared to do, though they did issue a formal repudiation of the Munich agreement, hardly an answer to Czech demands for justice.

In June 1942 in Washington, Churchill and Roosevelt discussed the question of setting up a war crimes commission. Harry Hopkins, Roosevelt's special adviser, drafted a paper on the work of such a commission in taking evidence and in reporting to the United Nations on egregious violations of human rights, naming those responsible. He also urged the appointment of commissioners of undoubted international standing, who would not be national representatives so much as representatives of the alliance against Hitler. Churchill agreed with the plan, approved by the British War Cabinet on 6 July 1942. They were willing to go along, in order to contain public pressure to punish war criminals, a current of opinion that grew with reports of Japanese atrocities against British soldiers in the Pacific theatre. What they had in mind was that those accused of war crimes be tried in and by the countries in which the alleged crimes took place. They wanted the restoration of national courts rather than the creation of an international tribunal. Once again, we see the importance of the restoration of territoriality in the development of war crimes policies, as an alternative to extra-territorial judicial proceedings. The fact that the one prepared the ground for the other was one of the unintended consequences of the war and the monstrousness of Nazi crimes.

The Allies did not choose at this time to define what were Nazi war crimes, preferring instead to fall back on older, commonly accepted definitions of the laws of war in the Geneva Conventions. With this understanding, the Cabinet Committee for the Treatment of War Criminals was established. On 7 October 1942, Lord Simon, the Lord Chancellor and chief legal officer in Britain, announced to the House of Lords that the Allies would set in motion an inquiry into the appropriate form to bring to justice war criminals 'irrespective of rank'. The same day, President Roosevelt stated that there would be trials of a relatively small number of people, those he termed 'the ringleaders responsible for the organized murder of thousands of persons and the commission of atrocities which have violated every tenet of the Christian faith'.[17]

On 20 October 1943, Cassin was appointed French delegate to the inter-Allied commission on war crimes. He sat with colleagues from those governments-in-exile which had signed the third St James's declaration. This document now became official Allied policy. Once again, London became his adopted home and the site of some of his most important wartime work, this time undertaken on behalf of the incipient United Nations. Complicating this work was the lack of consensus on the purpose of this commission. The Soviet Union started trying war criminals as soon as they liberated territory from the Nazis. In December 1943, they held trials and public executions in Kharkov.[18] At the same time, Lord Simon had made it clear in the House of Lords that the Allies intended not mass trials but ones limited to a relatively small number of people in positions of power. British law changed, though, to permit the prosecution of accused criminals whose alleged crimes took place in other countries. French law, Cassin observed, was not as advanced as British law in this respect.[19] Further difficulties arose from American doubts about the nature of the work of the commission of experts, on which Cassin himself sat.

Still, on 18 January 1944, Sir Cecil Hurst, the President of the Permanent Court of Justice in the Hague, as chair, convened the Commission, even though the Soviet Union had not named a delegate. With new American backing from Herbert Pell, formerly US ambassador to Portugal and Hungary, three sub-committees were formed. The first committee, chaired by the Belgian jurist de Baer, addressed dossiers on war crimes presented by individual nations. Between 9 and 16 February 1944, they examined the first 16 dossiers presented by France. Several were deemed sufficiently complete to present to the whole commission, which could name individuals as those to be handed over to Allied authorities for trial. By May 1944 about 100 such individuals were on this list.

The second sub-committee was chaired by Ambassador Pell, and examined procedural questions. He probed national differences in the definition of war crimes, and their handling by civil or military courts, as well as the politically charged question of the character of an international criminal court. The third commission, headed by the Polish jurist Stephan Glaser, dealt with difficulties in legal thinking on collective responsibility for crimes, as well as the viability of the defence of innocence on the grounds of following higher orders. The outcome of these deliberations was limited by the chair's reluctance to go beyond his government's position of wait and see on matters of international justice. Still, the commission agreed to grant the right of lawyers or others to take evidence under oath in any country for the purposes of obtaining evidence of the commission of war crimes committed in another country. They also noted that the pace of atrocities had actually increased in the period of the commission's work, and renewed their determination to make public the intention of the United Nations to bring war criminals to trial, wherever they might be found.[20]

Cassin summarized his own contribution to this commission in uncharacteristically bold terms. He claimed credit for the convening of the third St James's conference, a claim which could have been contested by the Czech and Polish delegations. He also claimed the leading role in preventing the sidetracking of the Commission into limited technical questions of the law. As French delegate, he turned attention time and again to the urgent matter of framing war crimes tribunals, a position which reflected the way *France Libre* aided the Resistance in occupied France itself. But there was another, more personal level to this part of his work. Cassin learned on his return to France in 1944 that 25 members of his family, including his 88-year-old uncle Samuel and his sister Yvonne and her husband, had been deported from Drancy and killed. He himself had been stripped of his French nationality by Vichy and sentenced to death in absentia. All his property had been sequestered. He was not outside the problem of restoring the legal order and securing justice for those guilty of monstrous crimes. For the Nazis and for Vichy, Cassin and Jews like him were part of the problem, and now in the months of preparation for the return of the Republican order, he insisted on being part of the solution to the legal and moral morass produced by Nazi occupation.

In the following months in and out of London, Cassin assembled and framed numerous reports for the Commission on crimes committed in France and against French citizens. These included maltreatment of French prisoners of war, black and white, in Germany; the machine gunning of civilians during the *exode* of 1940; and the role of German soldiers and the Gestapo in the transit camp of Drancy, from which French Jews and other Jews found in France were deported to Auschwitz.[21] Above all, he pressed the commission, and succeeded in persuading them, that they had a responsibility to act on behalf of millions still under Nazi persecution, who awaited the day of their liberation as the first day of judgment.

On 4 April 1944, the Commission received from the constituent member states lists of all men in the SS, the Gestapo, the army or in other leadership positions in each occupied nation, with the intention of seeing who among them would stand trial for war crimes.[22] This was the key step before setting up trials of those whom the Germans had to hand over to Allied authorities at the Armistice, as suspects in war crimes prosecutions.

What Cassin had helped accomplish here was important in both the French and the international realms. For the *Comité Français de la Libération Nationale*, here was one means to re-establish the Republican judicial order, and to limit the role of *l'épuration sauvage*, or local vigilante justice. For the Allies as a whole, here was one way to approach the transnational character of crimes without precedent. The first step was to hand over those guilty of crimes against French men and women in France, and the second was to try those guilty of transnational crimes, which came later to include genocide, a word only just invented by Rafael Lemkin at the time.[23] What mattered was to see a pattern at the core of the Nazi order, one which used terror and murder to execute a plan of domination of Europe and beyond. This is what made the criminality to be judged after the end of the war a collective act. Individuals were guilty of crimes against infants, children, the elderly, deported from Drancy to Auschwitz or starved or worked to death in other camps. That is true, but the nature of the crime went beyond individual culpability. It reached the German conception that law did not touch them in their new order; indeed, to them, there were no laws of war but only the rule of force. Even if they were to lose the war, their crimes would have so weakened the countries they conquered, they might have reasoned, that Germany could prepare for the next war from a favourable position even when defeated.

Hence the task was no less than the creation of some kind of common international law to restore the ties that judicial systems provide against injustice and cruelty. That reconstruction had to be both political and legal, since the Nazis destroyed extant legal systems *tout court*, and the kind of national culpability that the Nazis fixed on the Jews could not be fixed on the German race *per se*, but on those among them guilty of crimes established by the rules of law and evidence. By resuscitating justice through the arrest and trial of putative war criminals, countries like France, humiliated by occupation and collaboration, could thereby recover their political dignity. But the enormity of the crimes committed meant that legal steps had to be taken to restore what Cassin termed 'the laws of humanity', the sanctity of which must be protected against 'future aggressors'.[24]

Part of the achievement of Cassin and this group of exiles was to keep up the pressure on Britain, the United States and the Soviet Union to set up an international court to try major war criminals. To do so would be to drive home to the world at large the revolutionary character of Nazi crimes, and the way these crimes undermined the concept of the rule of law *per se*.[25]

There was injury to the international order to repair as well. To reach that goal, the Allies had to consider drafting a transnational legal code,[26] stating what the laws of humanity are, and how nations which, like Hitler's Germany systematically violate them domestically are a threat to international peace. Here is the link between war talk and rights talk, between protests against the inhumanity of the Nazis and the construction of a transnational code of behavior limiting what states can do against other states and against their own citizens.

POST-WAR

The story of the emergence of human rights thinking in the early days of the United Nations is complex, and cannot be treated *in extenso* here. The important point is that there were many voices in this debate, some imperialist, some simply chauvinist, and others committed to a new regime of human rights. Cassin was one of them, and it would be foolish to claim his was the loudest or the most profound. But it is perverse to ignore it entirely, as Mark Mazower does; cynicism is rarely a synonym for wisdom.[27] The UN in its infancy was a house of many mansions, certainly no magic palace, but it gave room for those who believed that the defence of human rights was the foundation of peace. That argument is an ongoing one.

The London exiles – veterans of the Blitz and much else besides – were there in San Francisco, in Geneva, in Lake Success and in Paris, where the work of establishing a new human rights regime was carried out. René Cassin was among them. His standing in *France Libre* enabled him to join Eleanor Roosevelt, Charles Malik, John Humphreys and others in the United Nations in drafting the Universal Declaration of Human Rights in the period 1945–48. He wrote the preamble himself, and it was Cassin who made the final changes and read out the document to the United Nations assembled in Paris on 10 December 1948.

It took some time, but this group of old friends and battle-hardened human rights warriors eventually saw that the opening of the Cold War made it impossible for the United Nations Human Rights Commissions to act with any coherent authority. As a consequence, they transferred their efforts to creating an institution higher than that of state sovereignty within the project of European unification. In 1950, a European Convention on Human Rights was passed, and it had teeth. It was the document any country had to sign and respect in order to join the European community. It still is. To enforce the Convention, a new European Court of Human Rights was created. In 1958 that court opened in Strasbourg, and Cassin was first vice-president (associate justice) and then in 1965 President (chief justice) of the European Court of Human Rights. On his retirement from that post in 1968 he was awarded the Nobel Peace Prize.

I have tried to emphasize the significance of exile politics during and after the Blitz in the emergence of a post-war human rights regime. In that effort, I have focused in particular on the work of René Cassin, partly because of its intrinsic interest, and partly because his path was shared by many others who suffered in one war, risked their lives in exile in a second, and who were determined to move from efforts to heal the victims of war to efforts to establish the new international order on a foundation of respect for human rights. The passage from war talk to rights talk under the Blitz and after is one that we should attend to, for it has had important ramifications for the construction of the world in which we live.

Notes

1   I borrow the phrase from M. A. Glendon, *Rights Talk: the Impoverishment of Political Discourse* (New York: Free Press, 1991). Thanks are due to Richard Overy for helpful suggestions.

2   The literature on veterans' movements is vast. For a start, see S. R. Ward (ed.), *War Generation: Veterans of the First World War* (Port Washington, N.Y.: Kennikat Press, 1975).

3   On this subject, the locus classicus is A. Prost, *Les Anciens combattants et la société française, 1914–1939*, 3 vols (Paris: Presses de la Fondation nationale de la science politique, 1977).

4   J.-J. Becker, *Le carnet B; les pouvoirs publics et l'antimilitarisme avant la guerre de 1914* (Paris, Klincksieck, 1973).

5   See Prost, 'Combattants et politiciens: Le discourse mythologique sur la politique entre les deux guerres', *Le Mouvement social*, n. 85, *Langage et idéologies: Le Discours comme objet de l'Histoire* (October–December, 1973), 117–54.

6   382AP/10, Cassin's report on the 'Commission de la Paix sur la CIAMAC'.

7   382AP/14 Cassin's report on the 'Commission de la Paix sur la CIAMAC', 1931.

8   League of Nations archives, Geneva, 'Protection of civilian populations against bombing from the air in case of war, Unanimous resolution of the League of Nations Assembly', September 30, 1938. Note the irony that this measure arrived precisely at the moment when Britain, France, Germany and Italy were drawing and quartering Czechslovakia in Munich.

9   382AP27, Diary, 1940.

10 *Trial of War Criminals before the Nuremberg Military Tribunal under Control Council Law No. 10*, vol. 15, *Procedure, Practice and Administration* (Washington, D.C.: Government Printing Office, 1946–49), 52.

11 *The Atlantic Charter; the Roosevelt-Churchill Declaration* (London: National Peace Council, 1941).

12 T. Jersak, 'Die Interaktion von Kriegsverlauf und Judenvernichtung', *Historische Zeitschrift*, 268, 1999, 311–49.

13 382AP/68, 24 September 1941, verbatim account.

14 382AP/63, Verbatim text of Cassin's speech to the Inter-Allied conference, 24 September 1941.

15 382AP/158, Cassin pocket diary, 1942, entries for January 1942.

16 'Allies In Conference', *The Times*, 14 January 1942, 5.

17 Kochavi, *Prelude to Nuremberg*, 28–32.

18 382AP/175, Fonds Cassin, 'Répression et prévention des crimes de guerres ennemis. Deuxième rapport du Professor René Cassin, Delegué de la France à la Commission d'Enquête des Nations Unies sur les Crimes de Guerre, 3 mai 1944', 1. Hereafter 'Crimes de guerre'.

19 'Crimes de guerre', 2.

20 Ibid., 4–5.

21 Ibid., 6.

22 Ibid., 7.

23 J. Cooper, *Rafael Lemkin and the Struggle for the Genocide Convention* (Basingstoke: Palgrave 2008), 24–47.

24 'Crimes de guerre', 13–15.

25 Ibid., 44.

26 Ibid., 45.

27 M. Mazower, *No Enchanted Palace: The End of Empire and the Ideological Origins of the United Nations* (Princeton: Princeton University Press, 2009).

Editors and Contributors

EDITORS

Claudia Baldoli is Senior Lecturer in Modern European History at Newcastle University. Her publications include *Exporting Fascism: Italian Fascists and Britain's Italians in the 1930s* (Berg, 2003) and *A History of Italy* (Palgrave, 2009). In 2004 she published a critical edition in Italian of the writings of Vera Brittain and Marie Louise Berneri on the bombing of civilians in the Second World War. She is currently working with Andrew Knapp on a comparative study of the Allied bombing of France and Italy.

Andrew Knapp is Professor of French Politics and Contemporary History at the University of Reading. His publications include (as author), *Parties and the Party System in France* (Palgrave, 2004) and *Le gaullisme après de Gaulle* (Seuil, 1996). and (as editor and contributor) *The Uncertain Foundation: France at the Liberation, 1944–47* (Palgrave, 2007).

His article on 'The destruction and liberation of Le Havre in modern memory', appeared in *War in History*, 14.4, November 2007, pp. 476–98, as well as in the *Cahiers du Centre d'Études d'Histoire de la Défense*, 37 (2009). He has also published, with Lindsey Dodd, ' "How Many Frenchmen did you Kill?" British Bombing Policy Towards France (1940–1945)' in *French History*, 22(4), December 2008, pp. 469–492. He is currently working with Claudia Baldoli on a comparative study of the Allied bombing of France and Italy.

Richard Overy is Professor of History at the University of Exeter and was the director of the AHRC project on 'Bombing, States and Peoples' from 2007–2010. He is the author of more than 25 books on the Second World War, the history of air power, and the Soviet and German dictatorships, including *The Air War 1939–1945, Bomber Command 1939–1945, Goering: the Iron Man*. His latest books are *The Morbid Age: Britain and the Crisis of Civilisation between the Wars* and *1939: Countdown to War*. He was the winner of the Wolfson Prize for History in 2004 and the James Doolittle Award in 2010 for a lifetime's contribution to aviation history. He is a Fellow of the British Academy.

CONTRIBUTORS

Vanessa Chambers was a Research Fellow on the project 'Bombing, States and Peoples in Western Europe, 1940–1945' in 2008–9. She completed her PhD at the Institute of Historical Research in London in 2007. Her thesis ' "Fighting Chance": War, Popular Belief and British Society' explored the impact of war on popular belief in British society and culture in the first half of the twentieth century. It will be published by Liverpool University Press in 2011. She has also published articles on popular belief and on the teaching of contemporary history. She is currently researching the material culture of magic as an Honorary Fellow at the University of Exeter and preparing an article on the history of newspaper horoscopes in the Second World War as part of the proceedings at a conference at the Sophia Centre for the Study of Cosmology and Culture, University of Wales, Lampeter.

Elena Cortesi achieved her Laurea at the University of Bologna and her doctorate at the University of Rome. She was director of the *Istituto di Storia della Resistenza e dell'Età contemporanea* at Forlì-Cesena for three years and is currently a researcher at the University of Bologna. She has worked and published on the material and psychological strategies for survival of both civilians and soldiers during the Second World War. In 2003 she published *L'Odissea degli Sfollati*, a case study of evacuation in the province of Forlì.

Lindsey Dodd is a doctoral candidate at the University of Reading and a member of the project team 'Bombing, States and Peoples in Western Europe'. Her thesis 'Children under the Allied Bombs in France, 1940–1945' uses oral history to explore the experience of being bombed as a child in wartime France. She published 'Are we defended? Conflicting representations of war in pre-war France' in *University of Sussex Journal of Contemporary History* in 2008 and was co-author with Andrew Knapp of ' "How many Frenchmen did you kill?" British Bombing Policy towards France (1940–1945)' in *French History*, 22(4), December 2008, pp. 469–492.

Olivier Dumoulin has taught at the Universities of Paris, Fribourg, Rouen and Lille, and at the *Institut d'Études Politiques* in Paris. He is currently Professor of Contemporary History at the University of Caen. Many of his publications focus on the practice of history, including *Le rôle social de l'historien* in 2003 and a biography of Marc Bloch, as well as numerous chapters and articles. More recently, he has begun a major research project on the 'cinema of reality' as a means of historical investigation.

Lara Feigel is Lecturer in English at King's College, London, and is the author of *Literature, Cinema, Politics 1930–1945: Reading between the Frames* (2010). She is also the editor (with Alexandra Harris) of *Modernism on Sea* (2009) and (with Natasha Spender and John Sutherland) of the forthcoming journals of

Stephen Spender. She is currently working on a book about British and German artistic responses to bombing and ruin during and after the Second World War.

Marco Fincardi is Lecturer in Contemporary History at the University of Venice, which he joined in 1998. He was educated in Paris (École des Hautes Études en Sciences Sociales) and Turin, where he achieved his doctorate. He is co-editor of *Memoria e ricerca: Rivista di storia contemporanea*, and has published widely on themes of social and cultural history in twentieth-century Italy. He is currently preparing a book for Laterza publishers on Allied propaganda and the reaction of civilians during the bombing of Italy in the Second World War.

Juliet Gardiner has been a Research Fellow at the Institute of Historical Research in London, the Institute of Advanced Studies in the Humanities at the University of Edinburgh and honorary Research Professor at Middlesex University. She was the editor of *History Today* in the 1980s, where she is still the review editor. After a period as an academic and publisher, she became a full time writer and broadcaster in 2001. Her most recent books include *The Penguin Dictionary of British History, Wartime: Britain 1939–1945, The Children's War* (in association with the Imperial War Museum) and *The Thirties: An Intimate History*. Her latest book *The Blitz: The British under Attack* was published in 2010. She is a frequent lecturer and broadcaster on radio and television and was the historical adviser for the film version of Ian McEwan's novel *Atonement*.

Stephan Glienke received his doctorate from the University of Hanover, Germany, in 2006. At present he has a post with the Historical Commission for Lower Saxony and Bremen. His research fields include German society and the air war in the Second World War, the crimes of the National Socialist regime, National Socialist justice, biographical research on former members of the Party and the German problem in 'overcoming the past' (*Vergangenheitspolitik*). He has published two books and a number of articles on this last theme and on the issues raised by the trials of former National Socialists.

Gabriella Gribaudi is Professor of Contemporary History at the University of Naples 'Federico II'. She is a member of the editorial board of the journal *Quaderni storici*. She has worked on the social history of southern Italy, on the Second World War and violence against civilians, using a mixture of written sources and oral history. Her book *Guerra totale: Fra bombe alleate e violenza nazista. Napoli e il fronte meridionale 1940–1944* was published by Bollati Boringhieri (Turin) in 2005.

Simon Kitson is Director of Research at the University of London Institute in Paris. He has written widely on France during the Second World War. His doctoral thesis was focused on the Marseille police between 1936 and 1945. Under the title *Vichy, Resistance, Liberation*, he co-edited a *festschrift* for his former doctoral supervisor, Rod Kedward. His monograph *Vichy et la Chasse aux Espions Nazis* (Paris: Autremont, 2005) was translated as *The Hunt for Nazi Spies* (Chicago UP, 2008). He is currently completing two books: *Experiencing Nazi Occupation: France, 1940–45* (forthcoming Manchester UP, 2011) and *Death and Liberation: The Allied Air Forces and Occupied France*, scheduled for 2013 with Chicago UP.

Marta Nezzo is Lecturer in Art History at the University of Padua. Her main research interests are in the protection of the historical-artistic heritage during the two World Wars. Among her publications is *Critica d'arte in Guerra: Ojetti 1914–1920* (2003). She also edited *Il miraggio della Concordia: Documenti sull'architettura e la decorazione del Bo e del Liviano, 1933–1943* (2008).

Michael Schmiedel is a doctoral candidate in social history at the Humboldt University, Berlin. He is working on the consequences for French society of Allied bombing during the Second World War. He studied at the RWTH Aachen, Université Reims Champagne-Ardenne and the Humboldt University.

Dietmar Süss teaches Contemporary History at the Friedrich-Schiller University at Jena. He produced a range of books and articles about German and British social and cultural history in the twentieth century. He is co-editor (with Winfried Süss) of *Das Dritte Reich – Eine Einführung* (Pantheon, 2008) and editor of *Deutschland im Luftkrieg – Geschichte und Erinnerung* (Oldenbourg, 2007). His new book about the air war and the politics of 'wartime morale' in Germany and Britain will be published in spring 2011.

Marc Wiggam is a doctoral student on the project 'Bombing, States and Peoples in Western Europe' at the University of Exeter. His thesis is a comparative study of the social, cultural and political impact of the blackout in Britain and Germany during the Second World War.

Jay Winter is the Charles J. Stille Professor of History at Yale University, where he has taught since 2001. He received his BA from Columbia and his PhD from Cambridge. From 1979 to 2001 he was Reader in Modern History and Fellow of Pembroke College, Cambridge. He holds the DLitt degree from Cambridge. He is the author of *Sites of Memory, Sites of Mourning: The Great War in European Cultural History* (1995).

Neville Wylie is Associate Professor of Politics at the University of Nottingham and head of the School of Politics, History and International Relations at Nottingham University's campus in Malaysia. His recent publications include *Barbed Wire Diplomacy: Britain, Germany and the Politics of Prisoners of War 1939-1945* (OUP, 2010) and 'Captured by the Nazis: reciprocity and national conservatism in German policy towards prisoners of war' in C-C. Szejnmann (ed.), *Rethinking History, Dictatorship and War: Essays in Honour of Richard Overy* (Continuum, 2009).

Bibliography

1 General Works

Baker, Nicholson, *Human Smoke: The Beginnings of World War II and the End of Civilization* (New York: Simon & Schuster, 2008).

Best, Geoffrey, *Humanity in Warfare: The Modern History of the International Law of Armed Conflicts* (London: Routledge, 1980).

Biddle, Tami, *Rhetoric and Reality in Air Warfare: The Evolution of British and American Ideas about Strategic Bombing* (Princeton: Princeton University Press, 2002).

Boog, Horst (ed.), *The Conduct of the Air War in the Second World War: An International Comparison* (Oxford: Berg, 1992).

Buckley, John, *Air Power in the Age of Total War* (London: UCL Press, 1999)

Budiansky, Stephen, *Air Power* (New York: Viking, 2004).

Cox, Sebastian (ed.), *The Strategic Air War Against Germany 1939–1945: The Official Report of the British Bombing Survey Unit* (London: Frank Cass, 1998).

Crane, Conrad C., *Bombs, Cities and Civilians: American Airpower Strategy in World War II* (Lawrence, Ka.: Kansas University Press, 1993).

Crane, Conrad C., 'Evolution of US Strategic Bombing of Urban Areas', *Historian*, 50, 1987, 14–39.

Craven, Wesley F. and Cate, James L., *The Army Air Forces in World War II*, 7 vols (Chicago: Chicago University Press, 1948–58).

Davis, Richard G., *Carl A. Spaatz and the Air War in Europe* (Washington DC: Office of Air Force History, 1993).

Ehlers, Robert S., *Targeting the Reich: Air Intelligence and the Allied Bombing Campaigns* (Lawrence, Ka.: Kansas University Press, 2009).

Garrett, Stephen A., *Ethics and Airpower in World War II: The British Bombing of German Cities* (New York: St Martin's Press, 1993).

Grayling, Anthony, *Among the Dead Cities: Was the Allied Bombing of Civilians in World War II a Necessity or a Crime?* (London: Bloomsbury, 2005).

Grebler, Leo, 'Continuity in the Rebuilding of Bombed Cities in Western Europe', *American Journal of Sociology*, 6, 1956, 463–69.

Groehler, Olaf, *Geschichte des Luftkriegs* (Berlin: Militärverlag der DDR, 1981).

Hall, R. Cargill (ed.), *Case Studies in Strategic Bombardment* (Washington DC: Office of Air Force History, 1998).

Harmon, Christopher C., ' "Are We Beasts?": Churchill and the moral question of World War II area bombing', *Newport Papers*, Naval War College, 1 (1991).

Harris, Arthur T., *Bomber Offensive* (London: Collins, 1947).

Hewitt, Kenneth, 'Place Annihilation: Area Bombing and the Fate of Urban Places', *Annals of the Association of American Geographers*, 73, 1983, 257–84.

Hewitt, Kenneth, 'The Social Space of Terror: Towards a Civil Interpretation of Total War', *Environment and Planning D: Society and Space*, 5, 1987, 445–74.

Hirschleifer, Jack, 'Some Thoughts on the Social Structure after a Bombing Disaster', *World Politics*, 8, 1955–6, 206–27.

Hopkins, G. E., 'Bombing and the American Conscience During World War II', *Historian*, 28, 1966, 451–73.

Iklé, Fred C., *The Social Impact of Bomb Destruction* (Norman: Oklahoma University Press, 1958).

Irons, Roy, *The Relentless Offensive: War and Bomber Command 1939–1945* (Barnsley: Pen and Sword, 2009).

Knell, Hermann, *To Destroy a City: Strategic Bombing and its Human Consequences in World War II* (Cambridge, Mass.: Da Capo Press, 2003).

Konvitz, Josef, 'Représentations urbaines et bombardements stratégiques, 1914–1945', *Annales*, 4, 1989, 823–47.

Lambourne, Nicola, *War Damage in Western Europe: The Destruction of Historic Monuments during the Second World War* (Edinburgh: Edinburgh University Press, 2001).

McFarland, Stephen L., *America's Pursuit of Precision Bombing, 1910–1945* (Washington DC: Smithsonian Institution Press, 1995).

Meilinger, Philip S. (ed.), *The Paths to Heaven: The Evolution of Airpower Theory* (Maxwell AFB, Alabama: Air University Press, 1997).

Middlebrook, Martin and Everitt, Chris, *The Bomber Command War Diaries* (London: Penguin, 1990).

Müller, Rolf-Dieter, *Der Bombenkrieg 1939–1945* (Berlin: Ch. Links Verlag, 2004).

Olsen, John (ed.), *A History of Air Warfare* (Washington DC: Potomac Books, 2010).

Overy, Richard, *The Air War 1939–1945*, 2nd edition (Washington DC: Potomac Books, 2006).

Overy, Richard, *Bomber Command 1939–1945* (London: Harper Collins, 1997).

Pape, Robert A., *Bombing to Win: Air Power and Coercion in War* (Ithaca, NY: Cornell University Press, 1996).

Parks, W. Hays, ' "Precision" and "Area" Bombing: Who Did Which, and When?', *Journal of Strategic Studies*, 18, 1995, 145–74.

Richards, Denis and Saunders, Hilary, *The Royal Air Force, 1939–45*, 3 vols (London: HMSO, 1974–5).

Schaffer, Ronald, 'American Military Ethics in World War II: The Bombing of German Civilians', *Journal of American History*, 67 (1980), 318–34.

Sebald, W. G., *On the Natural History of Destruction* (London: Hamish Hamilton, 2003).

Segrè, Claudio G., 'Giulio Douhet: Strategist, Theorist, Prophet?', *Journal of Strategic Studies*, 15, 1992, 351–66.

Sherry, Michael S., *The Rise of American Airpower: The Creation of Armageddon* (New Haven: Yale UP, 1987).

Smith, Melden E., 'The Strategic Bombing Debate: The Second World War and Vietnam', *Journal of Contemporary History*, 12, 1977, 175–91.

Stargardt, Nicholas, *Witnesses of War: Children's Lives under the Nazis* (London: Jonathan Cape, 2005).

Stephens, Alan (ed.), *The War in the Air, 1914–1945* (Fairbairn, Austr.: Air Power Studies Centre, 1994).

Tanaka, Yuki and Young, Marilyn (eds), *Bombing Civilians: A Twentieth-Century History* (New York: the New Press, 2009).

Terraine, John, *The Right of the Line: The Royal Air Force in the European War* (London: Hodder & Stoughton, 1985).

Verrier, Anthony, *The Bomber Offensive* (London: Batsford, 1968).

Voldman, Danièle, 'Les populations civiles, enjeux du bombardement des villes (1914–1945)' in Audoin-Rouzeau, Stéphane, Becker, Annette, Ingrao, Christian and Rousso, Henri (eds), *La Violence de Guerre 1914–1945* (Paris: Éditions Complexe, 2002).

Wakelam, Randall T., *The Science of Bombing: Operational Research in RAF Bomber Command* (Toronto: University of Toronto Press, 2009).

Watt, Donald C., 'Restraints on War in the Air before 1945' in Howard, Michael (ed.), *Restraints on War: Studies in the Limitation of Armed Conflict* (Oxford: Oxford University Press, 1979).

Webster, Charles and Frankland, Noble *The Strategic Air Offensive against Germany 1939–1945*, 4 vols (London: HMSO, 1961).

Wells, Mark (ed.), *Air Power: Promise and Reality* (Chicago: Imprint Publications, 2000).

Wilms, Wilfred and Rasch, William (eds), *'Bombs Away!' Representing the Air War Over Europe and Japan* (Amsterdam: Rodopi, 2006).

Zuckerman, Solly, *From Apes to Warlords: The Autobiography (1904–46) of Solly Zuckerman* (London: Hamish Hamilton, 1978).

2 France

Alary, Éric, Vergez-Chaignon, Bénédicte, and Gauvin, Gilles, *Les Français au quotidien, 1939–1949* (Paris: Perrin, 2006).

Aubery, Pierre, 'Le siège et la bataille navale du Havre – 1er au 12 septembre 1944', *Études Normandes*, 39, 1954, 889–900.

Barot, Sylvie, 'L'avant et l'après ... et si on en parlait?', in Gilles de la Porte (ed.), *Le Havre, Volonté et Modernité* (Le Havre, Éditions La Galerne, 1992).

Barthélémy, Général, 'Les bombardements alliés de la France pendant la deuxième guerre mondiale', *Azur et Or*, 72, December 1979, 11–16.

Battesti, Michèle, and Facon, Patrick (eds), *Les Bombardements Alliés sur la France durant la Seconde Guerre Mondiale: Stratégies, Bilans Matériaux et Humains'* (Paris: Ministère de la Défense (Cahiers du Centre d'Etudes d'Histoire de la Défense, 37, 2009).

Benamou, Jean-Pierre, and Robinard, François, *La Bataille aérienne de Normandie, 1944* (Caen: Éditions-Diffusion du Lys, 1994).

Bengtsson, Max, *Un été 44: de l'état de siège à la paix retrouvée* (2nd edition: Le Havre: Éditions-Imprimerie Grenet, 2004).

Besselièvre, Jean-Yves 'La défense passive en France 1930–1944: l'exemple de Brest', *Revue Historique des Armées*, 4, 1998, 97–103.

Besselièvre, Jean-Yves, 'Les bombardements de Brest (1940–1944)', *Revue Historique des Armées*, 211, June 1998, 97–108.

Bohn, Roland, *Raids aériens sur la Bretagne durant la seconde guerre mondiale*, 2 vols. (Bannalec: Imprimerie Régionale, 1997 and 1998).

Boiry, Philippe A., and de Salvatore, Gaëtan, *Paris sous les bombes: Auteuil, septembre 1943* (Paris: L'Harmattan, 2000).

Boivin, Michel, and Garnier, Bernard, *Les Victimes civiles de la Manche dans la bataille de Normandie, 1er avril–30 septembre 1944* (Caen: Éditions-Diffusion du Lys, 1994).

Boivin, Michel, Bourdin, Gérard, Garnier, Bernard, and Quellien, Jean, *Les victimes civiles de Basse-Normandie dans la Bataille de Normandie* (Caen: Éditions du Lys, 1996).

Boivin, Michel, Bourdin, Gérard, Quellien, Jean (eds), *Villes normandes sous les bombes (juin 1944)*, Caen, Presses Universitaires de Caen/Mémorial de Caen, 1994.

Boivin, Michel, *Les Manchois dans la tourmente de la seconde guerre mondiale, 1939–1945*, 6 vols (Marigny (Manche): Éditions Eurocibles, 2004).

Bourdin, Gérard, and Garnier, Bernard, *Les Victimes civiles de l'Orne dans la bataille de Normandie, 1er avril – 30 septembre 1944* (Caen: Éditions-Diffusion du Lys, 1994).

Caillaud, Paul, *Les Nantais sous les bombardements, 1941–1944* (Nantes: Aux Portes du Large, 1947).

Caillaud, Paul, *Nantes sous les bombardements: Mémorial à la Défense Passive* (Nantes: Éditions du Fleuve, 1946).

Castellano, Philippe, *Chronique d'un bombardement manqué aux conséquences tragiques: attaque de la gare de triage de Cannes-La Bocca fin de soirée du 11 novembre 1943* (Ollioules (Var, France): Éditions de la Nerthe, 2000).

Collomb, Olivier, and Bonfort, Christian, *Le Bombardement du 15 août 1944 et la reconstruction de Sisteron* (Lyon: Éditions Sup'Copy, 1994).

Courant, Pierre, *Au Havre pendant le Siège. Souvenirs du 1er au 12 septembre 1944* (Paris: Fayard, 1946).

Coutel, Marguerite, *Bruz sous les bombes: un village breton dans la guerre* (Rennes: Éditions La Part Commune, 2005).

Cumming, Michael, *The Starkey Sacrifice: the Allied Bombing of Le Portel, 1943* (Alan Sutton, 1996).

d'Abzac-Epezy, Claude, 'La Semaine sanglante: bombardements alliés sur la France, 26 mai–1er juin 1944', *Revue Historique des Armées*, 195, June 1994, 72–4.

d'Abzac-Epezy, Claude, 'Le Secrétariat général de la Défense aérienne (1943–1944), une 'armée nouvelle' dans la France occupée', *Revue Historique des Armées*, 188, September 1992, 79–89.

d'Abzac-Epezy, Claude, 'Les premiers bombardements alliés sur la France et leur utilisation politique', *Revue Historique des Armées*, 191, June 1993, 73–84.

Dandel, Michel., Duboc, Grégory, Kitts, Anthony, and Lapersonne, Éric, *Les victimes civiles des bombardements en Haute-Normandie, 1er janvier 1944 – 12 septembre 1944* (Caen: CRHQ-RED, La Mandragore, 1997).

Darlow, Steve, *Sledgehammers to Tintacks: Bomber Command Confronts the V-1 Menace, 1843–1944* (London: Grub Street, 2002).

Dodd, Lindsey and Knapp, Andrew '"How many Frenchmen did you kill?" British Bombing Policy Towards France, 1940–1945', *French History*, 22(4), 2008, 469–92.

Dodd, Lindsey, '"Partez partez"', again and again: the efficacy of evacuation as a means of protecting children from bombing in France, 1939–44', *Children in War*, 6.1, February 2009, 7–20.

Duboc, Grégory, Kitts, Anthony, and Lapersonne, Éric, *Les Victimes civiles des bombardements en Seine-Inférieure, 1er janvier–12 septembre 1944* (Université de Rouen, département d'Histoire: mémoire de maîtrise, 1994).

Duboscq, Jean-Paul, *Le Havre 1939–1944: Les abris sanitaires civils et allemands* (Le Havre: Editions Bertout, 1992).

Ducasse, André, 'Le bombardement du 27 mai 1944', *Marseille* (revue), 124, 1981, 74–9.

Ducasse, André, 'Marseille sous les bombes', *Les années 40*, 62, 1980, 1732–6.

Ducellier, Jean-Pierre, *La Guerre aérienne dans le Nord de la France: Les raids de l'aviation alliée sur le Nord, l'Artois, la Picardie, le Pays de Caux, la région parisienne, 27 mai 1944, 28 mai 1944* (Abbeville: F. Paillart, 1999).

Esdras-Gosse, Bernard, *Le Havre 1939–1944* (Le Havre: Association des Prisonniers de Guerre du Havre/Imprimerie Marcel Étaix, 1946).

Florentin, Eddy, *Quand les alliés bombardaient la France, 1940–45* (Paris: Perrin, 1997).

France, État-Major de l'Armée, *Les Bombardements aériens des chemins de fer français de janvier à août 1944* (Paris: Bureau Scientifique de l'Armée, 1945) (in Archives du Service Historique de l'Armée de l'Air, Vincennes).

Garnier, Bernard, and Pigenet, Michel, *Les victimes civiles des bombardements en Normandie* (Caen: La Mandragore, 1997).

Garnier, Bernard, Leleu, Jean-Luc, Passera, Françoise, and Quellien, Jean (eds), *Les Populations civiles face au débarquement et à la bataille de Normandie* (Caen, CRHQ, CNRS-Université de Caen and Mémorial pour la Paix, 2005).

Gaspérini, Alain, *Rouen 1940–1944: la guerre, l'occupation, la libération* (Rouen: Éditions Ouest-France, 1994).

Genet, Christian, and Ballannger, Bernard, *Royan sous les bombes, 5 janvier 1945* (Ligugé: Aubin Imprimeur, 1983).

Gildea, Robert, *Marianne in Chains: In Search of the German Occupation, 1940–1945* (Basingstoke: Palgrave Macmillan, 2002).

Gilonne, Georges, *Lyon de guerre: sous les bombes – pendant la Libération* (Lyon: Bascou Frères, 1945).

Godefroy, Georges, *Le Havre sous l'Occupation 1940–1944* (Le Havre: Imprimerie de la Presse, 1965).

Gondret, Louis, *Le livre d'or de la défense passive de Marseille* (Marseille: Leconte Imprimeur, 1956).

Gooderson, Ian, *Air Power at the Battlefront: Allied Close Air Support in Europe, 1943–45* (London: Frank Cass, 1998).

Guillemard, Jacques, *L'Enfer du Havre* (Paris: Éditions Medicis, 1948).

Hardy, Antoine, 'La défense passive à Rouen et dans son agglomération', mémoire de Master d'Histoire Contemporaine, préparé sous la direction de Jean-Claude Vimont et de Olivier Feiertag, Université de Rouen, Département d'Histoire, année 2005–6.

Hardy, Antoine, 'La défense passive à Rouen', *Études Normandes*, 57.1, 2008, 61–70.

Hitchcock, William I., *Liberation: the Bitter Road to Freedom, Europe 1944–1945* (London: Faber and Faber, 2008).

Huguen, Roger, *La Bretagne dans la bataille de l'Atlantique, 1940–1945. La stratégie du Bomber Command appliquée à la Bretagne* (Spezet (Finistère): Éditions Coop Breizh, 2003).

Jacquin, Frédéric, *Les bombardements de Brest, 1940–1944* (Brest: Éditions MEB, 1997).

Jame, Bernard, *Nantes Souffrance 1943: Témoignages* (Maulévrier: André Hubert Hérault, 2005).

Knapp, Andrew, 'The Destruction and Liberation of Le Havre in Modern Memory', *War in History*, vol 14, 4, 2007, 477–98.

Kulok, Jan S., 'Trait d'union: The history of the French relief organisation Secours National/Entr'aide francaise under the Third Republic, the Vichy regime and the early Fourth Republic 1939–1949', D. Phil. thesis, University of Oxford, 2003.

Laisnay Launay, Valérie, *L'Exode des populations bas-normandes au cours de l'été 1944* (Caen: Centre de Recherche d'Histoire Quantitative, 2005).

Lamboley, Christian, *40–45 – Strasbourg bombardé* (Strasbourg: Contades, 1988).

Lantier, Maurice, *Saint-Lô au bûcher* (Condé-sur-Vire: Imprimerie Corbrion, 1993).

Le Melledo, Paul, *Lorient sous les bombes. Itinéraire d'un Gavroche lorientais* (Le Faouet: Liv'éditions, 2003).

Le Roc'h Morgère, Louis, and Quellien, Jean (eds.), *L'Été 1944: les Normands dans la bataille* (3 volumes: Caen: Conseil Général du Calvados, Direction des Archives Départementales, 1998, 1999 and 2000).

Le Trévier, Paul, and Rose, Daniel, *19 avril 1944: Le Martyre de Sotteville, Rouen, et la Région* (Comever, 2004).

Le Trévier, Paul, *Objectif Rouen: 1er raid américain sur l'Europe*, St-Germain-en-Laye, Comever, 2005.

Lechat, François, *Nevers et la Nièvre sous les bombardements, 11 juin–14 août 1944* (Nevers: Centre Imprimerie Avenir, 1992).

Lecup, Albert, *Arras sous les bombardements de 1944* (Arras: Imprimerie Centrale de l'Artois, 1979).

Lefaivre, François (ed.), *J'ai vécu les bombardements à Condé-sur-Noireau* (Condé-sur-Noireau: Éditions Charles Corlet, 1994).

Legoy, Jean, *Le Havre 1939–1945: les Havrais dans la guerre* (Le Havre: Ville du Havre, 1994).

Legrand, Jacqueline, *Courageuse Abbeville, 3 septembre 1939 – 3 septembre 1944* (Abbeville: Imprimerie F. Paillart, 1990).

Martin, Georges, *Ambérieu, la rebelle*, Bourg-en-Bresse, Musnier-Gilbert Éditions, 2002.

Maurois, André, *Rouen dévastée*, Fontaine-le-Bourg, Le Pucheux, 2004 (1st edn Paris, Nagel, 1948).

Nières, Claude (ed.), *Histoire de Lorient* (Paris: Privat, 1988).

Nobécourt, R.G., *Rouen désolée, 1939–1944* (Paris: Éditions Médicis, 1949).

Pailhès, Gustave, *Rouen et sa région pendant la guerre 1939–1945* (Rouen, Henri Defontaine, 1948).

Pipet, Albert, *Mourir à Caen* (Paris: Presses de la Cité, 1974).

Polino, Marie-Noëlle (ed.), *Une Entreprise publique dans la guerre: la SNCF, 1939–1945* (Paris: Presses Universitaires de France, 2001).

Py, Évelyne, *Un été sous les bombes: Givors-Grigny-Chasse, 1944* (Saint-Cyr-sur-Loire: Éditions Alan Sutton, 2004).

Quellien, Jean, Garnier, Bernard, and Université Inter-Âges, *Les Victimes civiles du Calvados dans la bataille de Normandie, 1er mars 1944–31 décembre 1945* (Caen: Éditions-Diffusion du Lys, 1995).

Quellien, Jean, *La Normandie au cœur de la guerre* (Rennes: Éditions Ouest-France, 1992).

Queuille, Jean-Paul, *Bretagne: Lorient dans la guerre* (Montreuil-Bellay: Éditions CMD, 1998).

Ruby, Marcel, *Lyon et le département de la Rhône dans la guerre, 1939–1945* (Roanne: Éditions Horvath, 1990).

Sainclivier, Jacqueline, *La Bretagne dans la guerre, 1939–1945* (Rennes: Éditions Ouest-France/Mémorial de Caen, 1994).

Swanson, Marc, *Le bombardement de Saint-Étienne, pourquoi? 26 mai 1944* (Saint-Étienne: Actes Graphiques, 2004).

Verriez, André, *Cambrai sous les bombes, 27 avril au 2 septembre 1944* (Rumilly-en-Cambrésis: Clotilde Herbert, 1994).

Voldman, Danièle, 'La destruction de Caen en 1944', *Vingtième Siècle, Revue d'Histoire*, 39 (July-September 1993), 10–22.

Voldman, Danièle, *La Reconstruction des Villes Françaises de 1940 à 1954: Histoire d'une Politique* (Paris: L'Harmattan, 1997).

Zarifian, Christian, *Table Rase: 5 septembre 1944, Le Havre, ville assassinée* (Le Havre: Les Films Seine-Océan, 1988 (video)).

3 Great Britain

Addison, Paul and Crang, Jeremy (eds), *The Burning Blue: A New History of the Battle of Britain* (London: Pimlico, 2000).

Aldgate, Anthony and Richards, Jeffrey, *Britain Can Take It: British Cinema in the Second World War* (Edinburgh: Edinburgh UP, 1986).

Baldoli, Claudia (ed.), *Vera Brittain and Marie Louise Berneri. Il seme del caos: Scritti sui bombardamenti di massa (1939–1945)* (Santa Maria Capua Vetere: Edizioni Spartaco, 2004).

Barton, B., *The Blitz: Belfast in the War Years* (Belfast: Blackstaff, 1989).

Beaven, Brad and Griffiths, John, 'The Blitz, Civilian Morale and the City: Mass-Observation and working-class culture in Britain, 1940–41', *Urban History*, 26, 1999, 71–88.

Beaven, Brad and Thoms, David, 'The Blitz and Civilian Morale in Three Northern Cities, 1940–42', *Northern History*, 32, 1996, 195–203.

Bell, Amy H., 'Landscapes of Fear: Wartime London, 1939–1945' *Journal of British Studies*, 48, 2009, 153–75.

Bell, Amy H., *London Was Ours: Diaries and Memoirs of the London Blitz* (London: I. B. Tauris, 2008).

Bialer, Uri, 'The Humanization of Air Warfare in British Foreign Policy on the Eve of the Second World War', *Journal of Contemporary History*, 13, 1978, 79–96.

Bialer, Uri, *The Shadow of the Bomber: The Fear of Air Attack and British Bombing 1932–1939* (London: Royal Historical Society, 1980).

Biddle, Tami D., 'Bombing by the Square Yard: Sir Arthur Harris at War, 1942–1945', *International History Review*, 21, 1999, 626–64

Brittain, Vera, *England's Hour* (London: Continuum, 2005. First published 1941).

Brown, M., *Put that Light Out! Britain's Civil Defence Services at War 1939–1945* (Stroud: Sutton Publishing, 1999).

Bullock, Nicholas, *Building the Post-War World: Modern Architecture and Reconstruction in Britain* (New York: Routledge, 2001).

Calder, Angus, *The Myth of the Blitz* (London: Jonathan Cape, 1991).

Chandler, Andrew, 'The Church of England and the Obliteration Bombing of Germany in the Second World War', *English Historical Review*, 108, 1993, 920–46.

Chinn, Carl, *Brum Undaunted: Birmingham during the Blitz* (Studley: Brewin Books, 2005).

Collier, Basil, *The Defence of the United Kingdom* (London: HMSO, 1957).

Connelly, Mark, 'The British People, The Press, and the Strategic Air Campaign Against Germany, 1939–1945' *Contemporary British History*, 16, 2002, 39–58.

Connelly, Mark, *Reaching for the Stars: A New History of Bomber Command in World War II* (London: I. B. Tauris, 2001).

Connelly, Mark, *We Can Take It: Britain and the Memory of the Second World War* (Harlow: Longman, 2004).

Crosby, Travis, *The Impact of Civilian Evacuation in the Second World War* (London: Croom Helm, 1986).

Cull, Nicholas, *Selling War: The British Propaganda Campaign against American 'Neutrality' in World War II* (New York: OUP, 1995).

Essex, Stephen and Brayshaw, Mark, 'Boldness Diminished? The Post-War Battle to Replan a Bomb-Damaged Provincial City', *Urban History*, 35, 2008, 437–61.

Ewan, Shane, 'Preparing the British Fire Service for War: Local Government, Nationalisation and Evolutionary Reform, 1935–41', *Contemporary British History*, 20, 2006, 209–32.

Fitzgibbon, Constantine, *The Blitz* (London: Macdonald, 1970).

Freedman, Jean R. *Whistling in the Dark: Memory and Culture in Wartime London* (Lexington: Kentucky University Press, 1999).

Gardiner, Juliet, *The Blitz* (London: Harper Collins, 2010).

Gardiner, Juliet, *Wartime Britain 1939–1945* (London: Hodder & Stoughton, 2004)

Gaskin, Margaret, *Blitz: The Story of 29 December 1940* (London: Faber & Faber, 2005).

Gray, Todd, *Looting in Wartime Britain* (London: The Mint Press, 2009).

Graystone, Philip, *The Blitz on Hull* (Hull: Lampada Press, 1991).

Harrisson, Tom, *Living Through the Blitz* (London: Collins, 1976).

Hasegawa, J., *Replanning the Blitzed City Centre – A Comparative Study of Bristol, Coventry and Southampton 1941–1950* (Buckingham: Open University Press, 1992).

Hinton, James, *Nine Wartime Lives: Mass Observation and the Making of the Modern Self*, (Oxford: OUP, 2010).

Hylton, Samuel, *The Darkest Hour: The Hidden History of the Home Front* (Stroud: Sutton Publishing, 2001).

Inglis, Ruth, *The Children's War: Evacuation 1939-1945* (London: Collins, 1989).

Jones, Edgar, Woolven, Robin, Durodie, Bill, Wessely, Simon, 'Civilian Morale during the Second World War: Responses to Air Raids Re-Examined', *Social History of Medicine*, 17, 2004, 463-79.

Jones, Helen, *British civilians in the front line: air raids, productivity and wartime culture, 1939-1941* (Manchester: Manchester University Press, 2006).

Jones, Neville, *The Beginnings of Strategic Air Power: A History of the British Bomber Force 1923-1939* (London: Cass, 1987).

Lee, Gerald, ' 'I See Dead People': Air-raid phobia and Britain's behaviour in the Munich Crisis', *Security Studies*, 13, 2003/4, 230-72.

Mack, Joanna and Humphries, Stephen, *London at War* (London: Sidgwick & Jackson, 1985).

MacKay, Robert, *Half the Battle: Civilian Morale in Britain during the Second World War* (Manchester: Manchester University Press, 2002).

Macnicol, J. 'The Evacuation of Schoolchildren' in Smith, Harold (ed.), *War and Social Change: British Society in the Second World War* (Manchester: Manchester University Press, 1986).

Marvick, Peter, 'Print, Pictures and Sound: The Second World War and the British Experience', *Daedalus*, 114, 1982, 135-55.

McGrory, David, *Coventry at War* (Stroud: Sutton Publishing, 1997).

Meilinger, Philip, 'Trenchard and 'Morale Bombing': The Evolution of the Royal Air Force Doctrine before World War II', *Journal of Military History*, 60, 1996, 243-70.

Meisel, Joseph S., 'Air Raid Shelter Policy and its Critics in Britain before the Second World War', *Twentieth Century British History*, 5, 1994, 300-19.

Nicolas, Siân, *The Echo of War: Home Front Propaganda and the Wartime BBC, 1939-1945* (Manchester: Manchester University Press, 1996).

O'Brien, Terence H., *Civil Defence* (London: HMSO, 1955).

Oram, Alison, "Bombs Don't Discriminate!' Women's Political Activism in the Second World War', in Gledhill, Christine and Swanson, Gillian (eds), *Nationalising Femininity: Culture, sexuality and British cinema in the Second World War* (Manchester: Manchester University Press, 1996).

Overy, Richard, 'Apocalyptic Fears: Bombing and Popular Anxiety in Inter-War Britain', *S-nodi: pubblici e privati nella storia contemporanea*, 2, 2008, 7-30.

Overy, Richard, *The Battle of Britain*, 2nd ed. (London: Penguin, 2010).

Parker, Stephen, *Faith on the Home Front: Aspects of church life and popular religion in Birmingham, 1939-1945* (Oxford: OUP, 2005).

Patterson, Ian, *Guernica and Total War* (London: Profile Books, 2007).

Penny, John, *Bristol at War* (Derby: Bredon Books, 2002).

Phillips, Adam, 'Bombs Away!', *History Workshop Journal*, 45, 1998, 183-98.

Piette, Adam, *Imagination at War: British Fiction and Poetry 1939-1945* (London: Macmillan, 1995).

Postan, Michael, *British War Production* (London: HMSO, 1952).

Pugh, Michael, 'An International Police Force: Lord Davies and the British Debate in the 1930s', *International Relations*, 9, 1988, 335–51.

Ray, John, *The Night Blitz 1940–41* (London: Arms & Armour, 1996).

Reid, Helen, *Bristol under Siege: Surviving the Wartime Blitz* (Bristol: Redcliffe Press, 2005).

Rose Alexander, 'Radar and Air Defence in the 1930s', *Twentieth Century British History*, 9, 1998, 219–45.

Rose, Sonya, *Which People's War? National Identity and Citizenship in Wartime Britain 1939–1945* (Oxford: OUP, 2003).

Samson, William, *Westminster at War* (Oxford: OUP, 1947).

Saunders, Ann (ed.), *The London County Council Bomb Damage Maps, 1939–1945*, introduction by Robin Woolven (London: London Topographical Society, 2005).

Smith, Malcolm, *Britain and 1940: History, Myth and Popular Memory* (London: Routledge, 2000).

Smith, Malcolm, 'A Matter of Faith: British Strategic Air Doctrine before 1939', *Journal of Contemporary History*, 15, 1980, 423–42.

Stansky, Peter, *The First Day of the Blitz: September 7, 1940* (New Haven: Yale University Press, 2007).

Stansky, Peter, 'Henry Moore and the Blitz' in Bean, J. M. W. (ed.), *The Political Culture of Modern Britain: Studies in Memory of Stephen Koss* (London: Hamish Hamilton, 1987).

Stonebridge, Lyndsey, 'Anxiety at a Time of Crisis', *History Workshop Journal*, 45, 1998, 171–82.

Stonebridge, Lyndsey, *The Writing of Anxiety: Imagining Wartime in Mid-Century British Culture* (Basingstoke: Palgrave, 2007).

Thomas, Donald, *An Underworld at War: Spivs, Deserters, Racketeers and Civilians in the Second World War* (London: John Murray, 2003).

Thoms, David, *War, Industry and Society: The Midlands 1939–1945* (London: Routledge, 1989).

Tiratsoo, Nick, 'The Reconstruction of Blitzed British Cities, 1945–55: Myths and Realities', *Contemporary British History*, 14, 1999, 27–44.

Titmuss, Richard M., *Problems of Social Policy* (London: HMSO, 1950).

Venning, Norman, *Exeter: The Blitz and Rebirth of the City* (Exeter: Devon Books, 1988).

Wallington, Neil, *Firemen at War: The Work of London's Fire Fighters in the Second World War* (Newton Abbot: David and Charles, 1981).

Wasley, Gerald, *Plymouth, a Shattered City: The Story of Hitler's Attack on Plymouth and its People, 1939–45* (Exeter: Halsgrove, 2nd ed., 2004).

Welshman, John, *Churchill's Children: The Evacuee Experience in Wartime Britain* (Oxford: OUP, 2010).

Welshman, John, 'Evacuation and Social Policy', *Twentieth Century British History*, 9, 1998, 28–53.

Whiting, Charles, *Britain under Fire: The Bombing of Britain's Cities, 1940-1945*
√ (Barnsley: Leo Cooper, 1999).
Wicks, Ben, *Waiting for the All-Clear: True Stories from Survivors of the Blitz*
   (London: Bloomsbury, 1990).
Willis, Kirk, 'The Origins of British Nuclear Culture 1895-1939', *Journal of
   British Studies*, 34, 1995, 59-89.
Ziegler, Philip, *London at War, 1939-1945* (London: Pimlico, 2002).

4 Germany

Addison, Paul and Crang, Jeremy (eds), *Firestorm: The Bombing of Dresden,
   1945* (London: Pimlico, 2006).
Arnold, Jörg, Süss, Dietmar and Thiessen, Malte (eds), *Luftkrieg. Erinnerungen
   in Deutschland und Europa* (Göttingen: Wallstein Verlag, 2009).
Beck, Earl R., *Under the Bombs: The German Home Front, 1942-1945* (Lexington:
   Kentucky University Press, 1986).
Beer, Wilfried, *Kriegsalltag an der Heimatfront. Alliierte Luftkrieg und deutsche
   Gegenmassnahmen zur Abwehr und Schadensbegrenzung, dargestellt für den
   Raum Münster* (Bremen: Hausschild, 1990).
Bergander, Götz, *Dresden im Luftkrieg - Vorgeschichte, Zerstörung, Folgen*, 2nd
   edition (Weimar: Böhlau, 1994).
Beseler, Hartwig, Gutschow, Niels and Kretschmer, Frauke (eds), *Kriegsschicksale
   Deutscher Architektur: Verluste-Schäden - Wiederaufbau*, 2 vols (Neumünster:
   Karl Wachholtz, 1988).
Bessell, Richard, *Germany 1945: From War to Peace* (London: Harper Collins,
   2009).
Beyme, Klaus von, *Der Wiederaufbau. Architektur und Städtebaupolitik in
   beiden deutschen Staaten* (Munich: Piper Verlag, 1987).
Blank, Ralf (ed.), *Germany and the Second World War*, vol. IX/1, *German
   Wartime Society, 1939-1945* (Oxford: OUP, 2008).
Boberach, Heinz (ed.), *Meldungen aus dem Reich. Die geheimen Lageberichte
   des Sicherheitsdienstes der SS 1938-1945* (Herrsching: Pawlak Verlag,
   1984).
Boelcke, Wili A. (ed.), *Wollt Ihr den totalen Krieg? Die geheimen Goebbels-
   Konferenzen 1939-43* (Herrsching: Pawlak Verlag, 1989).
Borsdorf, Ulrich and Jamin, Mathilde (eds), *Über Leben im Krieg.
   Kriegserfahrungen in einer Industrieregion 1939-1945* (Reinbek bei Hamburg:
   Rowohlt, 1989).
Brunswig, Hans, *Feuersturm über Hamburg. Die Luftangriffe auf Hamburg im
   Zweiten Weltkrieg und ihre Folgen* (Stuttgart: Motorbuch Verlag, 1978).
Burgdorff, Stephan and Habbe, Christian, *Als Feuer von Himmel fiel: Der
   Bombenkrieg in Deutschland* (Munich: Deutscher Taschenbuch Verlag, 2005).
Busch, Dieter, *Der Luftkrieg im Raum Mainz während des Zweiten Weltkrieges*
   (Mainz: Hase & Koehler, 1988).

Childers, Thomas, '"Facilus descensus averni est": The Allied Bombing of Germany and the Issue of German Suffering', *Central European History*, 38, 2005, 75–105.

Clayton, Anthony and Russell, Alan (eds), *Dresden: A City Reborn* (Oxford: Berg, 1999).

Dettmer, Werner, *Die Zerstörung Kassels im Oktober 1943* (Fuldabrück: Hesse, 1983).

Diefendorf, Jeffry M., *In the Wake of War: The Reconstruction of German Cities after World War II* (New York: OUP, 1993).

Evans, Richard J., *The Third Reich at War* (London: Allen Lane, 2008).

Fischer-Pache, Wiltrud and Jochem, Gerhard, *Der Luftkrieg gegen Nürnberg: der Angriff am 2 Januar 1945 und die zerstörte Stadt* (Neustadt an der Aisch: Schmidt Verlag, 2005).

Feinendegen, Reinhard and Pützhofen, Dieter (eds), *22 Juni 1943, als Krefeld brannte: Augenzeugenberichte von der Bombennacht* (Krefeld: Verein für Heimatkunde, 1993).

Friedrich, Jörg, *Der Brand: Deutschland im Bombenkrieg 1940–1945* (Munich: Propyläen Verlag, 2002).

Fritzsche, Peter, *A Nation of Flyers: German Aviation and the Popular Imagination* (Cambridge, Mass.: Harvard University Press, 1992).

Gregor, Neil, *Haunted City: Nuremberg and the Nazi Past* (New Haven: Yale University Press, 2008).

Gregor, Neil, '"Is he still alive, or long since dead?": Loss, Absence and Remembrance in Nuremberg, 1945–1956', *German History*, 21, 2003, 183–203.

Gregor, Neil, 'A *Schicksalsgemeinschaft*? Allied Bombing, Civilian Morale, and Social Dissolution in Nuremberg, 1942–1945', *The Historical Journal*, 43, 2000, 1051–70.

Groehler, Olaf, *Bombenkrieg gegen Deustchland* (Berlin: Akademie Verlag, 1990).

Groehler, Olaf, 'Der strategische Luftkrieg und seine Auswirkungen auf die deutsche Zivilbevölkerung' in Boog, Horst (ed.), *Luftkriegsführung im Zweiten Weltkrieg: Ein internationaler Vergleich* (Bonn: Verlag E. S. Mittler, 1993).

Gutschow, Niels, 'Hamburg – the "Catastrophe" of July 1943' in Diefendorf, Jeffery (ed.), *Rebuilding Europe's Bombed Cities* (London: Macmillan, 1989).

Hage, Volker (ed.), *Hamburg 1943: literarische Zeugnisse zum Feuersturm* (Frankfurt am Main: Fischer Taschenbuch Verlag, 2003).

Hampe, Erich, *Der zivile Luftschutz im Zweiten Weltkrieg. Dokumentation und Erfahrungsberichte über Aufbau und Einsatz* (Frankfurt am Main: Bernard & Graefe Verlag, 1963).

Hanke, Marcus, *Luftkrieg und Zivilbevölkerung: Der kriegsvölkerrechtliche Schutz der Zivilbevölkerung gegen Luftbombardements von den Anfängen bis zum Ausbruch des Zweiten Weltkrieges* (Frankfurt am Main: Peter Lang, 1991).

Harlander, Tilman and Fehl, Gerhard (eds), *Hitlers sozialer Wohnungsbau 1940-1945. Wohnungspolitik, Baugestaltung und Siedlungsplanung* (Hamburg: Christians, 1986).

Hillmann, Jörg and Zimmermann, John (eds), *Kriegsende 1945 in Deutschland* (Munich: Oldenbourg, 2002).

Kershaw, Ian, *The 'Hitler Myth': Image and Reality in the Third Reich* (Oxford: OUP, 1987).

Kettenacker, Lothar (ed.), *Ein Volk von Opfern? Die neue Debatte um den Bombenkrieg, 1940-1945* (Berlin: Rowohlt, 2003).

Kirwin, G., 'Allied bombing and Nazi domestic propaganda', *European History Quarterly*, 15, 1985, 341-62.

Klee, Katja, *Im 'Luftschutzkeller des Reiches': Evakuierte in Bayern 1939-1953. Politik, soziale Lage, Erfahrungen* (Munich: Oldenbourg, 1998).

Krause, Michael, *Flucht vor dem Bombenkrieg: 'Umquartierung' im Zweiten Weltkrieg und die Wiedereingliederung der Evakuierten in Deutschland 1943-1963* (Düsseldorf: Droste Verlag, 1997).

Kucklick, Christoph, *Der Feuersturm – Bombenkrieg über Deutschland* (Hamburg: Ellert & Richter, 2003).

Lemke, Bernd, *Luftschutz in Grossbritannien und Deutschland 1923-1939* (Munich: Oldenbourg, 2005).

Lowe, Keith, *Inferno: The Devastation of Hamburg, 1943* (London: Viking, 2007).

Mierzejewski, Alfred C., *The Collapse of the German War Economy 1944-1945 Allied Air Power and the German National Railway* (Chapel Hill: North Carolina University Press, 1988).

Neumann, Thomas W., 'Der Bombenkrieg. Zur ungeschreibenen Geschichte einer kollektiven Verletzung' in Naumann, Klaus (ed.), *Nachkrieg in Deutschland* (Hamburg: Hamburger Edition, 2001).

Niven, Bill, 'The GDR and Memory of the Bombing of Dresden' in Niven, Bill (ed.), *Germans as Victims: Remembering the Past in Contemporary Germany* (Basingstoke: Palgrave, 2006).

Nolan, Mary, 'Germans as Victims during the Second World War', *Central European History*, 38, 2005, 7-40.

Nossack, Hans, *The End* (Chicago: University of Chicago Press, 2004).

Overy, Richard, 'Allied Bombing and the Destruction of German Cities' in Chickering, Roger, Förster, Stig, Greiner, Bernd (eds.), *A World at Total War: Global Conflict and the Politics of Destruction 1937-1945* (Cambridge: CUP, 2005).

Overy, Richard, 'From Uralbomber to Amerikabomber: The Luftwaffe and Strategic Bombing', *Journal of Strategic Studies*, 1, 1978, 154-78.

Permooser, Irmtraud, *Der Luftkrieg über München 1942-1945: Bomben auf die Hauptstadt der Bewegung* (Oberhachung: Aviatic Verlag, 1996).

Rieger, Susanne, *Brennende Erinnerung. Münchner Zeitzeugen berichten über den Luftkrieg* (Berlin: 2005).

Riegert, Willi (ed.), *Heimat unter Bomben. Der Luftkrieg im Raum Steinfurt und in Münster und Osnabrück 1939–1945* (Dülmen: 2003).

Rumpf, Hans, *The Bombing of Germany* (New York: Frederick Muller, 1962).

Rumpf, Hans, 'Der Irrweg des Bombenkrieges', *Wehrwissenschaftliche Rundschau*, 10, 1960, 548–54.

Sakmyster, Thomas, 'Nazi documentaries of intimindation: *Feldzug in Polen* (1940), *Feuertaufe* (1940) and *Sieg im Westen* (1941)', *Historical Journal of Film, Radio and Television*, 16, 2003, 495–514.

Schnatz, Helmut, *Der Luftkrieg im Raum Koblenz 1944–1945: Eine Darstellung seines Verlaufs, seiner Auswirkungen und Hintergründe* (Boppard am Rhein: Kommission des Landtages, 1981).

Speer, Albert, *Inside the Third Reich* (London: Weindefeld, 1970).

Spencer, Andy, 'The Fiftieth Anniversary of the Allied Air Raids on Dresden: A Half Century of Literature and History Writing' in Hüppauf, Bernd (ed.), *War, Violence and the Modern Condition* (Berlin: Walter de Gruyter, 1997).

Starke, Günther, *Das Inferno von Braunschweig und die Zeit danach*, 4th edition (Cremlingen: Elm-Verlag, 2002).

Steinert, Marlis, *Hitler's War and the Germans: Public Mood and Attitude during the Second World War* (Athens, Ohio: Ohio University Press, 1977).

Stephenson, Jill, *Hitler's Home Front: Württemberg under the Nazis* (London: Continuum, 2006).

Süss, Dietmar (ed.), *Deutschland im Luftkrieg: Geschichte und Erinnerung* (Munich: Oldenbourg Verlag, 2007).

Süss, Dietmar, 'Steuerung durch Information? Joseph Goebbels als 'Kommissar der Heimatfront' and die Reichsinspektion für den zivilen Luftschutz' in Hachtmann, Rüdiger and Süss, Winfried (eds), *Hitlers Kommissare: Sondergewalten in der nationalsozialistischen Diktatur* (Göttingen: Wallstein Verlag, 2006).

Süssmilch, Waltraud, *Im Bunker: Eine Überlebende berichtet vom Bombenkrieg in Berlin* (Berlin: Ullstein Verlag, 2004).

Thiessen, Malte, *Eingebrannt ins Gedächtnis: Hamburgs Gedenken an Luftkrieg und Kriegsende 1943 bis 2005* (Munich: Dölling & Galitz, 2007).

Turner, Ian (ed.), *Reconstruction in Post-War Germany: British Occupation Policy and the Western Zones* (Oxford: Berg, 1989).

Vees-Gulani, Susanne, *Trauma and Guilt: Literature of Wartime Bombing in Germany* (Berlin: Walter de Gruyter, 2003).

Vogt, Helmut, *Bonn im Bombenkrieg. Zeitgenössische Aufzeichnungen und Erinnerungsberichte von Augenzeugen* (Bonn: Bouvier Verlag, 1989).

Werner, Wolfgang F., *Bleib übrig! Deutsche Arbeiter in der nationalsozialistischen Kriegswirtschaft* (Düsseldorf: Schwann, 1983).

Wette, Wolfram, Bremer, Ricarda, and Vogel, Detlef (eds), *Das letzte halbe Jahr. Stimmungsberichte der Wehrmachtpropaganda 1944/45* (Essen: Klartext, 2001).

5 Italy

Abse, Tobias, 'Italy', in Noakes, Jeremy (ed.), *The Civilian in War: the Home Front in Europe, Japan and the USA in World War II* (Exeter: University of Exeter Press, 1992).

Aga-Rossi, Elena, *A Nation Collapses: the Italian Surrender of September 1943* (Cambridge: Cambridge University Press, 1999 – 1st Italian edition, Bologna: Il Mulino, 1993).

American Commission for the Protection and Salvage of Artistic and Historic Monuments in War Areas, *Report of the American Commission for the Protection and Salvage of Artistic and Historic Monuments in War Areas* (Washington DC: US Government Printing Office, 1946).

Baldoli, Claudia and Fincardi, Marco, 'Italian Society under Allied Bombs: Propaganda, Experience, and Legend, 1940-1945', *The Historical Journal*, 52, 4, 2009, 1017-38.

Baldoli, Claudia, 'I bombardamenti sull'Italia nella seconda Guerra Mondiale. Strategia anglo-americana e propaganda rivolta alla popolazione civile', *Deportate, Esuli, Profughe*, 13/14, 2010, 34-49.

Barberis, Walter (ed.), *Guerra e pace, Storia d'Italia. Annali*, vol. 18 (Turin: Einaudi, 2002).

Baris, Tommaso, *Tra due fuochi. Esperienza e memoria della guerra lungo la linea Gustav* (Rome-Bari: Laterza, 2004 – 1st ed. 2003).

Bermani, Cesare, *Spegni la luce che passa Pippo. Voci, leggende e miti della storia contemporanea* (Rome: Odradek, 1996).

Bersani, Cristina and Roncuzzi Roversi Monaco, Valeria (eds.), *Delenda Bononia. Immagini dei bombardamenti, 1943-1945* (Bologna: Biblioteca dell'Archiginnasio, 1995).

Boi, Maria Marta, *Guerra e beni culturali (1940-1945)* (Pisa: Giardini, 1986).

Bonacina, Giorgio, *Obiettivo: Italia. I bombardamenti aerei delle città italiane dal 1940 al 1945* (Milan: Mursia, 2005 – 1st ed. 1970).

Bravo, Anna, Foa, Anna and Scaraffia, Lucetta (eds), *Donne e uomini nelle guerre mondiali* (Rome-Bari: Laterza, 2002 – 1st ed. 1991).

British Committee on the Preservation and Restitution of Works of Art, *Works of Art in Italy: Losses and Survivals in the War*, 2 vols (London: HMSO, 1945).

Capaccioni, Andrea, Paoli, Andrea and Ranieri, Ruggero, *Le biblioteche e gli archivi durante la seconda guerra mondiale: il caso italiano* (Bologna: Pendragon, 2007).

Carli, Maddalena and Gentiloni Silveri, Umberto, *Bombardare Roma: gli alleati e la città aperta, 1940-1944* (Bologna: Il Mulino, 2007).

Caserta, Aldo, *Il clero di Napoli durante la guerra e la resistenza (1940-1943)* (Naples: Luciano Editore, 1995).

Cavallo, Pietro, *Italiani in guerra. Sentimenti e immagini dal 1940 al 1945* (Bologna: Il Mulino, 2000 – 1st ed. 1997).

Cavazzoli, Luigi, *La gente e la guerra. La vita quotidiana del fronte interno: Mantova, 1940-1945* (Milan: Angeli, 1989).

Chianese, Gloria, 'Quando uscimmo dai rifugi'. Il Mezzogiorno tra guerra e dopoguerra (1943–1946) (Rome: Carocci, 2004).

Ciancabilla, Luca (ed.), Bologna in guerra. La città, i monumenti, i rifugi, (Bologna: Minerva, 2010).

Coccoli, Carlotta, 'Repertorio dei fondi dell'Archivio Centrale dello Stato relativi alla tutela dei monumenti italiani dalle offese belliche nella Seconda Guerra Mondiale', Storia Urbana, 114–115, 2007.

Colarizi, Simona, L'opinione degli italiani sotto il regime, 1929–1943 (Rome-Bari: Laterza, 2009 – 1st ed. 1991).

Colarizi, Simona, La seconda guerra mondiale e la repubblica (Turin: UTET, 2003 – 1st ed. 1984).

Cortesi, Elena, L'odissea degli sfollati, 1940–1945. La provincia di Forlì in guerra: il forlivese, il riminese e il cesenate di fronte allo sfollamento di massa (Cesena: Il Ponte Vecchio, 2003).

Cortesi, Elena, Reti dentro la guerra. Corrispondenza postale e strategie di sopravvivenza, 1940–1945 (Rome: Carocci, 2008).

Della Volpe, Nicola, Esercito e propaganda tra le due guerre (Rome: Ufficio Storico Stato Maggiore dell'Esercito, 1992).

De Simone, Cesare, Venti angeli sopra Roma. I bombardamenti aerei sulla Città Eterna, 19 luglio e 13 agosto 1943 (Milan: Mursia, 1993).

Direzione Generale delle Antichità e Belle Arti (ed.), La Ricostruzione del Patrimonio artistico italiano (Rome: La Libreria dello Stato, 1950).

Ferrari, Paolo (ed.), L'aeronautica italiana: una storia del Novecento (Milan: Angeli, 2004).

Ferratini Tosi, Francesca, Grassi, Gaetano and Legnani, Massimo (eds), L'Italia nella Seconda Guerra Mondiale e nella Resistenza (Milan: Angeli, 1988).

Fondazione Luigi Micheletti, L'Italia in guerra, 1940–1943. Immagini e temi della propaganda fascista (Brescia: Fondazione Micheletti, 1989).

Franchi, Elena, Arte in assetto di guerra: protezione e distruzione del patrimonio artistico a Pisa durante la seconda guerra mondiale (Pisa: ETS, 2006).

Franzinelli, Mimmo, Il clero del duce, il duce del clero. Il consenso ecclesiastico nelle lettere a Mussolini (1922–1945) (Ragusa: La Fiaccola, 1998).

Franzinelli, Mimmo and Bottoni, Riccardo (eds.) Chiesa e guerra. Dalla benedizione delle armi alla 'Pacem in terris' (Bologna: Il Mulino, 2005)

Gallerano, Nicola (ed.), L'altro dopoguerra. Roma e il Sud, 1943–1945 (Milan: Angeli, 1985).

Gallerano, Nicola, 'L'arrivo degli alleati', in Mario Isnenghi (ed.), I luoghi della memoria. Strutture ed eventi dell'Italia unita (Rome-Bari: Laterza, 1997).

Gariglio, Bartolo and Marchis, Riccardo (eds), Cattolici, ebrei ed evangelici nella guerra. Vita religiosa e società, 1939–1945 (Milan: Angeli, 2007 – 1st ed. 1999)

Giannella, Salvatore and Mandelli, Pier Damiano, L'Arca dell'Arte (Milan: Editoriale Delfi, 1999).

Gioannini, Marco and Massobrio, Giulio, Bombardate l'Italia. Storia della guerra di distruzione aerea 1940–1945 (Milan: Rizzoli, 2007).

Gribaudi, Gabriella, *Guerra totale: tra bombe alleate e violenze naziste. Napoli e il fronte meridionale, 1940–1944* (Turin: Bollati Boringhieri, 2005).

Gribaudi, Gabriella (ed.), *Le guerre del Novecento* (Naples: L'ancora del Mediterraneo, 2007).

Harvey, Stephen, 'The Italian War Effort and the Strategic Bombing of Italy', *History*, 70, 1985, 32–45.

Isnenghi, Mario, *Le guerre degli italiani. Parole, immagini, ricordi, 1848–1945* (Bologna: Il Mulino, 2005 – 1st ed. Mondadori 1989).

Isola, Gianni, *Abbassa la tua radio per favore … Storia dell'ascolto radiofonico nell'Italia fascista* (Scandicci: La Nuova Italia, 1996 – 1st ed. 1990).

Lambourne, Nicola, *War Damage in Western Europe: the destruction of Historic Monuments during the Second World War* (Edinburgh: Edinburgh University Press, 2001).

Lehmann, Eric, *Le ali del potere. La propaganda aeronautica nell'Italia fascista* (Turin: UTET, 2010).

Lewis, Norman, *Naples '44* (London: Eland, 2002 – 1st ed. Collins 1978).

Lucioli, Roberto, 'Sfollamento, mobilità sociale e sfaldamento delle istituzioni nella provincia di Ancona', *Storia e problemi contemporanei*, 15, 1995.

Luzzatto, Sergio, *Padre Pio. Miracoli e politica nell'Italia del Novecento* (Turin: Einaudi, 2007).

Klinkhammer, Lutz, *L'occupazione tedesca in Italia, 1943–1945* (Turin: Bollati Boringhieri, 2007 – 1st ed. 1993).

Knox, MacGregor, *Hitler's Italian Allies: Royal Armed Forces, Fascist Regime, and the War of 1940–1943* (Cambridge: Cambridge University Press, 2009 – 1st ed. 2000).

Maida, Bruno (ed.), *Guerra e società nella provincia di Torino, 1940–1945* (Turin: Blu Edizioni, 2007).

Mangiameli, Rosario and Nicastro, Franco, *Arrivano … gli americani a Vittoria nell'estate del 1943* (Vittoria: Comune di Vittoria, 2003).

Maniscalco, Fabio (ed.), *La tutela del patrimonio culturale in caso di conflitto* (Naples: Massa, 2002).

Mercuri, Lamberto, *Guerra psicologica. La propaganda anglo-americana in Italia 1942–1946* (Rome: Archivio Trimestrale, 1983).

Mercuri, Lamberto, *La 'Quarta arma', 1942–1950: propaganda psicologica degli Alleati in Italia* (Milan: Mursia, 1998).

Morgan, Philip, *The Fall of Mussolini: Italy, the Italians, and the Second World War* (Oxford: Oxford University Press, 2007).

Morozzi, Luisa and Paris, Rita (eds.), *L'Opera da ritrovare. Repertorio del patrimonio artistico italiano disperso all'epoca della seconda guerra mondiale* (Rome: Istituto Poligrafico e Zecca dello Stato, 1995).

Nicholas, Lynn H., *The Rape of Europa* (New York: Vintage Books, 1994).

Ortoleva, Peppino and Ottaviano, Chiara (eds), *Guerra e mass media. Strumenti e modi della comunicazione in contesto bellico* (Naples: Liguori, 1994).

Paggi, Leonardo, *Stragi tedesche e bombardamenti alleati. L'esperienza della guerra e la nuova democrazia a San Miniato (Pisa). La memoria e la ricerca storica* (Rome: Carocci, 2005).

Paggi, Leonardo, *Il popolo dei morti. La repubblica italiana nata dalla guerra (1940–1946)* (Bologna: Il Mulino, 2009).

Palla, Marco, 'Il passaggio del fronte nell'Italia del 1943–45', *Storia e problemi contemporanei*, monographic issue on *Le guerre/La pace*, 1–2, 1988.

Panzera, Antonio Filippo, *La tutela internazionale dei beni culturali in tempo di guerra* (Turin: Giappichelli, 1993).

Paoli, Andrea (ed.), *'Salviamo la creatura'. Protezione e difesa delle biblioteche italiane nella seconda guerra mondiale* (Rome: Associazione Italiana Biblioteche, 2003).

Parolechiave, monographic issue on *Guerra*, 20–1, 1999.

Perry, Alan R., 'Pippo: an Italian folklore mystery of World War II', *Journal of Folklore Research*, 40, 2003, 115–48.

Pertocoli, Domenico (ed.), *Che c'è di nuovo? Niente, la guerra. Donne e uomini del milanese di fronte alle guerre, 1885–1945* (Milan: Mazzotta, 1997).

Piccialuti Caprioli, Maura, *Radio Londra 1939–1945* (Rome-Bari: Laterza, 1979).

Pivato, Stefano, *Sentimenti e quotidianità in una provincia in guerra. Rimini, 1940–1944* (Rimini: Maggioli, 1995).

Pizarroso Quintero, Alejandro, *Stampa, radio e propaganda . Gli Alleati in Italia, 1943–1946* (Milan: Angeli, 1989).

Provincia di Torino, *Gli ex voto della Consolata. Storie di grazia e devozione nel santuario torinese* (Turin: Provincia di Torino, 1982).

Rastelli, Achille, *Bombe sulla città. Gli attacchi aerei alleati: le vittime civili a Milano* (Milan: Mursia, 2000).

Rochat, Giorgio, *Le guerre italiane, 1935–1943. Dall'impero d'Etiopia alla disfatta* (Turin: Einaudi, 2005).

Rochat, Giorgio, Santarelli, Enzo and Sorcinelli, Paolo (eds), *Linea gotica 1944. Eserciti, popolazioni, partigiani* (Milan: Angeli, 1987 – 1st ed. 1986).

Vecchio, Giorgio, *Lombardia 1940–1945. Vescovi, preti e società alla prova della guerra* (Brescia: Morcelliana, 2005).

Villa, Andrea, *Guerra aerea sull'Italia (1943–1945)* (Milan: Guerini e Associati, 2010).

Index

Over the six years of the Second World War, most of urban Europe was subject to bomb attack, from the French Atlantic ports to the major cities of central Germany, from the Dutch and Belgian cities to the ports and towns of Sicily. Throughout the whole region perhaps as many as 700,000 were killed.

In this collection, an international panel of historians explores the immediate effects of that wartime disaster for both the urban communities that suffered it and for the surrounding society and political order that had to cope with evacuation, higher levels of crime or non-compliance and changing attitudes towards authority. Considering the cultural, social and political responses to bombing rather than the strategic and ethical dimensions which have formed the core of the discussion thus far, this collection makes it clear that the bombing had ripple effects far beyond the areas immediately targeted by the bombers.

Claudia Baldoli is Senior Lecturer in History at Newcastle University, UK.

Andrew Knapp is Professor of French Politics and Contemporary History at the University of Reading, UK.

Richard Overy is Professor of History at the University of Exeter, UK.

£19.99

continuum

Cover pictures: Marshal Pétain inspects bomb St-Étienne (France), June 1944. Courtesy of archives départementales de la Lo

9 781441 185686